EDMUND DELL

After war service, Edmund Dell became Lecturer in Modern History at The Queen's College, Oxford. Subsequently, he worked in industry before becoming a Labour MP, Cabinet Minister and European 'wise man'. On leaving politics in 1979 he was appointed founder chairman of Channel Four Television. His previous book, *The Chancellors*, was highly acclaimed. He died shortly after completing this book.

Political Responsibility and Industry
Report on European Institutions (with Barend Biesheuvel and Robert Marjolin)
The Politics of Economic Interdependence
A Hard Pounding: Politics and Economic Crisis, 1974–76
The Schuman Plan and the British Abdication of Leadership in Europe
The Chancellors: A History of the Chancellors of the Exchequer, 1945–90

A STRANGE EVENTFUL HISTORY

DEMOCRATIC SOCIALISM

IN BRITAIN

Edmund Dell

'Last scene of all that ends this strange eventful history is . . . mere oblivion'
William Shakespeare, *As You Like It*

HarperCollins*Publishers*

HarperCollins*Publishers*
77–85 Fulham Palace Road,
Hammersmith, London w6 8jb

www.**fire**and**water**.com
This paperback edition 2000

1 3 5 7 9 8 6 4 2

First published in Great Britain by
HarperCollins*Publishers* 1999

ISBN 0 00 653056 7

Set in Postscript Linotype Janson

Printed and bound in Great Britain by
Clays Ltd, St Ives plc

August 2004
All my love on your Birthday
Boobs xxxx
for Ben

FOR SUSI

ACKNOWLEDGMENTS

The material from the Public Record Office listed among the references is Crown copyright and is reproduced with the permission of the Controller of Her Majesty's Stationery Office. Material from House of Commons debates is subject to Parliamentary copyright and that from White Papers to Crown copyright. I am grateful to the Master and Fellows of University College Oxford for permission to quote copyright material from the papers of Lord Attlee held in deposit from University College in the Bodleian Library catalogued as MS Attlee.

CONTENTS

ILLUSTRATIONS

1. Keir Hardie. (© *Camera Press*)
2. Ramsay MacDonald. (© *Popperfoto*)
3. John Maynard Keynes. (© *Bassano/Camera Press*)
4. Harold Macmillan. (© *Popperfoto*)
5. Ernest Bevin. (© *Camera Press*)
6. Harold Laski. (© *Popperfoto*)
7. Evan Durbin. (© *Bassano. By courtesy of the National Portrait Gallery, London*)
8. C. R. Attlee. (© *Baron/Camera Press*)
9. Aneurin Bevan. (© *Kurt Hutton/Hulton Getty*)
10. Hugh Gaitskell. (© *Popperfoto*)
11. Harold Wilson. (© *Joe Bulaitis/Camera Press*)
12. James Callaghan. (© *Popperfoto*)
13. Michael Foot. (© *Lionel Cherruault/Camera Press*)
14. Roy Jenkins. (© *Trevor Humphries/Camera Press*)
15. Tony Crosland. (© *Tom Blau/Camera Press*)
16. Tony Benn. (© *Gavin Smith/Camera Pres*)
17. Denis Healey. (© *Camera Press*)
18. Jack Jones. (© *Hulton Getty*)
19. Roy Hattersley. (© *Chris Balcombe/Popperfoto*)
20. Neil Kinnock. (© *Richard Open/Camera Press*)
21. Margaret Thatcher. (© *Lionel Cherruault/Camera Press*)
22. Tony Blair. (© *Anthony Crickmay/Camera Press*)
23. Gordon Brown. (© *Paul Hackett/Popperfoto*)

PREFACE

The idea of writing this book came from memory of George Danger-field's classic *The Strange Death of Liberal England* which I read by way of preparation for my Finals at Oxford. I had thought of calling it *The Strange Death of Socialist Britain*. However, as I hope the book demonstrates, there was nothing strange in the death of British social-ism. Nevertheless the story told here does have many strange aspects which is the justification for the title I have given it, a title for which I am indebted to William Shakespeare.

As a Cabinet Minister under James Callaghan and a Minister for many years under Harold Wilson, I was a participant, though not a particularly influential one, in some of the events recounted here. Thus this book is informed by experience of government and by inside know-ledge and I hope that it is the better for it.

Where it seems appropriate, I have indicated my own role in a note. My lack of influence was not because I did not express views, rather because the views I expressed on political matters were not generally acceptable to my colleagues.

This book is in no sense a personal history but the reader is entitled to some enlightenment on my political trajectory. There should be no surprise that between adolescence and now, my eighth decade, my views have changed. There were events in my adolescence that impelled me sharply to the left, notably unemployment, fascism, and the Spanish Civil War. It is now over fifty years since I left the Communist party at Oxford and rejoined the Labour party of which I first became a member in 1936. This early excursion into Communist territory taught me to applaud Oliver Cromwell's adjuration to the elders of the Church of Scotland that they should think it possible that they might be mis-taken. I cannot date so exactly the lapse of time since I ceased to be a 'Clause Four' socialist. It was, perhaps, forty-five years ago, when I was employed as a manager by Imperial Chemical Industries. Working for I C I had for me the character of a university extension course. I travelled the world, living for a time abroad. I discovered how large multinational enterprises operated. I was not greatly impressed by ICI's efficiency but I certainly saw no reason to nationalize it. My experience of industrial management made me sceptical of the practicality of traditional socialism, and of economic planning. But I regarded the Labour party as the humane party and I did not feel that to remain a member I had to endorse Clause Four which, in any case, seemed no longer an expression of serious Labour intentions.

During the fifties I was for seven years a member of the Manchester City Council. It is a time to which I look back with pleasure. Manchester was an important local authority and it succeeded at that time in conducting its affairs without the intervention of much party dogma. The Labour group on the City Council considered that the use of the whip, except on rare occasions, would be an insult to its dignity because councillors were entitled to make up their own minds on the basis of the arguments presented. The Conservatives took the same view. This freedom, extraordinary by modern local government standards, was probably the result of a residual influence from Manchester's great days as a centre of liberalism. Serving on Manchester City Council was, therefore, an experience of a kind that Members of Parliament, marching to and fro under the instruction of whips, seldom enjoy.

In October 1964 I was elected Member of Parliament for Birkenhead. I came to the House of Commons rather late and without any national political reputation or connections with leading Labour figures. I was already well into my forties. I had ceased to be a socialist by any recognizable definition. And it was soon noticed. I never expected to be anything but a backbencher. To my surprise, hardly had I arrived when, in April 1966, Harold Wilson appointed me to his government. He had the idea, which he never abandoned, that my experience as a manager in industry might be of some use. The result was a series of Ministerial appointments in the 1960s largely concerned with industrial policy. Wilson records that he would have liked to put me in the Cabinet in 1969 but was unable to do so probably for reasons of political balance within the government.[1] During the later part of the period 1970–74, when Labour was in opposition, I served as Chairman of the Public Accounts Committee of the House of Commons. In 1973 the Committee, under my Chairmanship, recommended a special tax on North Sea oil, a recommendation which I was able to implement in 1975 when, as Paymaster General, I introduced Petroleum Revenue Tax. I entered the Cabinet in 1976 under James Callaghan as President of the Board of Trade.

In 1978 I decided to leave Parliament for a variety of reasons of which the most important was that my views on economic policy were increasingly at variance with those of the government, though of a kind that today would provoke a good deal less controversy within the Labour party. It was far from the first time I had thought seriously of leaving politics. Following that decision I was appointed by the European Council (heads of state and government of the European Community) a member of the Committee of 'Three Wise Men' responsible for preparing a report on the institutions of the European Community. We reported in October 1979. Some of our recommendations may have influenced the progress of European integration.

In the early 1980s, I saw friends in the Labour party being victimized for their support of British membership of the European Community and for their opposition to nonsensical policies. The Labour party had become totally unhinged from reality. I joined the Social Democratic party, though without any idea of returning to politics. In any case I was Chairman of the new TV Channel Four which barred political activity. In 1987, having retired from Channel Four, I led the small group of Social Democrats which negotiated the merger with the Liberal party. I soon thereafter decided that, in my late sixties, I had had enough of party politics. For more than ten years now, I have not been a member of any political party. So far, however, I have continued to cast my vote for the Labour party despite mounting disappointment that it seems to have lost the humane instincts which, in the past, had made membership tolerable for me even when I was in strong disagreement with its economic and industrial policies.

I am grateful to my then agent Jennifer Kavanagh, and to Michael Fishwick, Publishing Director at HarperCollins, for accepting from me the idea for this book, and to Diana Tyler at MBA Literary Agents who continued to give me the encouragement that I had always received from Jennifer before her retirement. I am grateful to Peter James whose perceptive editorial comments have greatly improved the book.

EDMUND DELL

A short history of British socialism

The high point of British socialism came in the years between the two great wars. It was the time of highest hopes, though paradoxically of least achievements. It was the time when two minority Labour governments, those of Ramsay MacDonald, failed. Yet socialists were at their most cogent about the validity, and even nobility, of their vision. It was the high point because it was the time of fewest doubts about a project that was in its nature extraordinary, the replacement of one order of society by another.

British socialism was special.[1] It was socialism but it was British. It spoke approvingly of internationalism but it was always highly nationalist. It comprised three predominant elements. The first was a utopian vision of a better society which would replace capitalism and which would be characterized by greater equality, common ownership, and production for use rather than for profit. The second was an intense belief in democracy and hence in the compromises and accommodations which alone allow democracy to operate successfully. The third was managerial and was inserted into British socialism largely by economists who, in a flush of overconfidence, believed that they knew how to eradicate the evils of capitalism and at the same time stimulate faster economic growth. It was the economists who transformed a utopian vision into a programme for government. The managerial element became highly centralizing because only by centralization could the prospective managers operate the control mechanisms necessary for the implementation of their plans. The prospective managers welcomed the idea of common ownership, a term which, though vague and interpreted differently by different socialist tendencies, came in practice to mean nationalization, ownership not so much by the nation as by the state. Nationalization would give the managers the necessary power over the economy. It would be found before long that these elements in British socialism did not sit easily together.

Democratic socialism excited the hopes, and attracted the devoted energies, of thousands. It even attracted some among the rich and powerful. The majority of its supporters, however, came from the ranks of the poor and powerless. The principal institution which emerged, and to which these energies were devoted, was the Labour party. The Labour party strove to achieve reforms in the political and social life of Britain many of which were direly needed and too long delayed. Many of the reforms which it advocated, or which were advocated by its members, were not party political, could find support in most parts of the political spectrum, but gained their principal impetus from the existence of the Labour party, which was a liberalizing influence in many sectors of domestic policy. But its principal objective was the realization of socialism by democratic means. In that it failed.

Between the wars, the idea of replacing capitalism by socialism gained great force because so much in daily existence was hard to bear and there seemed to many to be no other remedy. Democratic socialist writers of the inter-war years had proved, at least to their own satisfaction, that to attempt to humanize capitalism would be counterproductive. The compassion that should characterize human society demanded the replacement of capitalism because compassion was incompatible with capitalism. Capitalism could thrive only if it was accepted that the exploitation of the many was a tolerable price for the enrichment of the few. Either capitalists must be left unhindered to their rumbustious and competitive search for wealth, or the system would wither. Any attempt to protect the victims by taxing the few, however meritorious its motivation, would cause capitalism to vegetate and even shrivel. There would no longer even be crumbs off the table to share among those left behind in the competitive race. The answer was socialism because only socialism could reconcile compassion with economic progress.

This was wishful thinking. As a new form of society, socialism was never a practical project in Britain. Democratic socialism was a mirage, beautiful in the eyes of the beholder, but beyond reach. The hope that by democratic means one form of society, capitalism, could be replaced by another, socialism, proved to be nothing other than one of the more striking of human self-deceptions. Capitalism might evolve and, indeed, it did evolve until some of its critics claimed that it had evolved beyond recognition. But the evolution of a society, which takes place for many reasons other than political pressure, is a very different process from its replacement by a society entirely new. There was never a map defining a route along which the democratic socialist battalions could confidently advance and at the end of which was democratic socialism. Nor could there have been such a map because there was no such route. Some socialists believed that a map was unnecessary because they were on the bandwagon of history. They might not know where they were going, or how to get there, but history would know. History, alas, never seemed to know. It preserved an unpretentious silence. It moved, but it showed an ominous neutrality between different political philosophies. The insurmountable obstacle to democratic socialism was democracy, and democracy would have killed socialism's chances in Britain even unassisted by the ineptitude of successive Labour governments in managing the economy.

The history of socialism in Britain is one of advance followed by retreat. Each advance was shorter, each retreat longer and more painful. Retreat was covered by the redefinition of words. Even if socialism was being abandoned, there was still 'social democracy' and socialist 'values'. If there was no longer doctrine, at least there was pragmatism. Democratic socialists of a pragmatic turn of mind were always searching for a 'third way', a way that retained the essential qualities of socialism as they remembered it without the bother of an elaborate reconstruction of society as a whole. Each third way diverged by a greater and greater distance from socialism as the founders had described it. Each generation of democratic socialists would identify a new third way, leaving behind the previous generation of third-way socialists, and taking them further from socialism and nearer to, and eventually beyond, the acceptance of capitalism. This trend can be exemplified in the careers of individual leading members of the Labour party. Starting often from a far left, or even Marxist, orientation, they would move through a series of third ways from left to right, from radical intentions to an acceptance of capitalism modified only by a wish to root out its greater evils. In many cases even the wish to undertake serious reform disappeared.

C. R. Attlee, leader of the Labour party for twenty years from 1935, and its first post-war Prime Minister, was of the view, partly no doubt as the result of self-assessment, that leaders of the Labour party should emerge from the left of centre. Attlee's left of centre was the left of centre of the Labour party as he knew it. This probably meant someone who, having made his reputation by advocating policies a great deal further to the left, had not yet quite abandoned a utopian vision but was now prepared to be flexible. By the time Tony Blair became Prime Minister, and wrote approvingly of the left of centre, it had become the left of centre of the whole political spectrum, a location well to the right. Blair writes of a 'permanent revisionism'.[2] Over the years, socialism, repeatedly revised, was drained of its original meaning and converted into little more than an expression of good intentions. Democratic socialists committed themselves to do as much good for the victims of capitalism, and of the other numerous inequities and incongruities that disfigure society, as would be found compatible with economic progress. But economic progress was to be left in the hands of capitalists. The vague objective of greater equality proved to have a longer shelf life than the other objectives of democratic socialism. But equality was never defined and democratic socialists never made a serious attempt to achieve it. Socialism started a thrusting ideological career intended, as its climax, to supersede capitalism. It deteriorated into a plaster over the ineradicable ills of capitalism.

The tragedy for many raised in the inter-war years, who became committed to democratic socialism, was that they would find their lives consumed in the pursuit of a will-o'-the-wisp. For their leaders, it was different. They, at least, had the opportunity to find a more or less satisfying political career attempting, intermittently, to manage capitalism. The electorate, usually sceptical, occasionally optimistic, turned against socialism well before the Labour party had discovered that its declared purpose was unlikely to be practical and was probably not even desirable. The electorate sometimes appeared to want a reforming government of the left. Less and less did it want a socialist government. Ironically, the Labour party was to achieve its greatest majority in the House of Commons only when the electorate could feel confident that it had finally abandoned socialism. But that was nearly one hundred years after its foundation. The Labour party, mired in the ideology of democratic socialism, had always been a slow learner.

PART I

A VISION
TOO FAR

ONE

A new Jerusalem

DISCONTENT, RESENTMENT, ANGER, DISGUST AND EXASPERATION

In the years between the great wars, capitalism was under siege. It provoked discontent, resentment, anger, disgust and exasperation. The source of these emotions was the inequity and injustice of a system of society in which those at the bottom of the pile suffered extremes of poverty, unemployment, sickness, malnutrition, often premature death. Disgust was justified by the hardships imposed on great numbers as the price of affluence for a few. There were too many recessions. Unemployment represented an unforgivable waste of human life and human happiness. Exasperation was excited by the conviction that poverty, even if previously unavoidable, was so no longer. Technological advance should have rendered it merely a disturbing memory. That it was still a contemporary fact could be attributed only to capitalism. Disgust and exasperation, often combined with a sense of guilt, galvanized a few who, while they themselves might have enough, and even more than enough, were distressed that others had so little.

Discontent, resentment and anger flourished most powerfully among those who had not while others, so obviously, had. It was not simply that rewards were unequally distributed. Inequality would have been more supportable if there had been enough food in the house, the house had been sound and not overcrowded, and the rent could be paid. The victims of society, of whom there were great numbers, felt deprived, not just of the food and housing they needed for health, but of the hope that life would ever improve. The discontent, resentment and anger attached not simply to the society in which such things could happen but to those people and those institutions held responsible. Private enterprise, and the capitalists and managers who ran private enterprise, shared responsibility with governments that could be so careless of the welfare of their people.

Even worse were those who battened on the people without making the least contribution to society. The historian R. H. Tawney was one of the most eloquent if not most perceptive of socialist propagandists. In 1921, he published *The Acquisitive Society*, a book which strongly influenced generations of socialists. He derided the useless life of the property owner who lived on his rent but did nothing to enrich the community:

> The *rentier* and his ways, how familiar they were in England before the war! A public school and then club life in Oxford and Cambridge, and then another club in town; London in June, when London is pleasant, the moors in August, and pheasants in October, Cannes in December and hunting in February and March; and a whole world of rising bourgeoisie eager to imitate them, sedulous to make their expensive watches keep time with this preposterous calendar![1]

A TIME OF TROUBLES

The inter-war years were, for Britain, deeply unhappy. Many of the heroes of the 1914–18 war – and who was not a hero who had served in the front line? – returned to a life very different from the pledges they had received. The Lloyd George government had guaranteed what it knew not how to deliver. It had certainly not promised unemployment, and the fear of unemployment, as the reward for sacrifice. Unemployment meant, for the working class, desperate poverty. In addition, there were the humiliations. Some state support was provided for those in the direst need. But the family means test imposed on siblings a requirement to support one another, as the miner Aneurin Bevan discovered when he was unemployed in South Wales in the 1920s.[2] The vagaries of the capitalist system denied any hope of stability. Sometimes life was a little better and sometimes it was a lot worse. It was never free from dread of the future. Some organs of the press, and others ill qualified to speak, might attack the unemployed for lacking the will to work. It was false in respect of the great majority. Wilfred Fienburgh, a Labour MP after 1945, called it a 'monstrous niagara of misrepresentation'.[3] The unemployed were willing to work but the capitalist system first deprived them of the opportunity and then disclaimed responsibility for their fate. The recession of 1931 raised unemployment to three million, or over a quarter of the insured labour force, a far higher proportion than the figure of three million unemployed signified in the 1980s. It was a major crisis of the capitalist system. It might be the final crisis of the capitalist system.

Attlee wrote of the 'evils that Capitalism brings'. Like other socialists, he regarded what was happening in the 1930s as the pattern, capitalist recession followed by some recovery, the recession too deep and the recovery slow and deficient. It was natural, in the 1930s, to conclude that the evils of capitalism were irremediable. When he was writing in 1937, Attlee recognized that there had been some recovery from the depths of the 1931 depression, that capitalism had shown powers, to some unexpected, of recuperation. He could not rule out that there would be further improvements in standards of living. He insisted that, whatever had been achieved, there was still a great deal of room for improvement. He defines what he describes as a normal situation under capitalism, that is one not exceptionally disfigured as in the early 1930s by untypical levels of unemployment. A normal situation, Attlee writes, would mean, 'under Capitalism, that the unemployed are round about two million, and that the majority of the people are unable to obtain, with their purchasing power, enough food to keep them in full health, or enough house room for comfort, or a really adequate supply of the material bases of existence'.[4] This pessimism about a permanent level of two million unemployed was fully in line with what Ramsay MacDonald, former socialist, had told the House of Commons in 1932.[5] In fact unemployment continued to fall, in part because of the rearmament programme that preceded the second world war. Attlee, however, was unlikely to take a more optimistic view of capitalism than Ramsay Mac-Donald, the traitor Prime Minister of the National government. A figure of two million unemployed implied widespread misery. Were people really to be expected, without protest, to submit their lives, and their children's lives, to the haphazard, unplanned inanities of the market?

The waste of life represented by unemployment was compounded by the waste of commodities and of machinery. To excite indignation against the capitalist system, there was the deliberate destruction of coffee in Brazil designed to maintain or enhance the price. Anthony Crosland, theorist of democratic socialism, later commented that, in the 1930s, every Labour weekend speech contained its quota of references not merely to unemployment at home, but to coffee being burned in Brazil, to crops destroyed in the USA, to livestock slaughtered in the interests of restriction schemes.[6] John Strachey, Marxist publicist, wrote that, at the same time as millions of unemployed were lacking most of the necessaries of life, vast stocks of commodities, redundant harvests, rotting goods, rusting machines were gradually deteriorating all over the world.[7] Attlee concluded: 'the cause is the private ownership of the means of life; the remedy is public ownership'.[8] He assured his readers that under socialism there would be no question of the goods the workers produced being destroyed 'as surplus' simply because the economic system could not absorb them. Everything that was made would be used and would add to the country's wealth.[9]

The faults of capitalism as an economic system were not just evidenced in Britain. In the 1930s there was massive unemployment throughout the developed world and beyond. It was not as though other capitalist countries could teach lessons which Britain had neglected. Their people were suffering too. In those countries too, there was a search for answers. The capitalist system appeared to have become intellectually and morally indefensible and socialism offered a credible alternative, or at least an alternative in which great numbers were prepared to believe.

MONOPOLY AND WAR

Unreconstructed defenders of the capitalist system praised the stimulus it gave to competition and hence to efficiency. In fact capitalism was moving compulsively towards monopoly and restriction. If monopoly could not be achieved, the alternative was the cartel. Socialists characterized the trend to private monopoly as alarming and dangerous. Strachey, the Marxist, perceived an 'inherent tendency of individual producers to amalgamate, to form monopolistic enterprises, and subsequently for these monopolies to meet and pool their resources with those of national States'.[10] For emphasis, Strachey called on his classical education. '[M]onopoly is like Cerberus: strike off one of its heads and a new and yet more terrifying one grows instantly in its place.'[11] The trend was motivated by the lack of domestic demand. It was not confined within national borders and included price and market share agreements with foreign competitors. Monopoly gave the capitalist security from competition and enhanced his profit. The victim of private monopoly was the consumer. Prices were forced up. The power of the state was being used not to oppose or limit monopoly but to encourage it. Capitalists, desperate to prolong the life of the system of society that had given them so much, were no longer prepared to live by their own *laissez-faire* principles. Evocation of the competitive society might elicit applause at trade association dinners. But it was not real life. Karl Marx had foreseen the trend and this was one forecast on which he could not be faulted. And yet, socialists argued, monopoly was unavoidable. Small-scale industry was no longer consistent with the use of the most modern devices. If monopoly was at once unavoidable and dangerous, the only answer could be public ownership. Philip Snowden, later Labour's first Chancellor of the Exchequer, identified a process that would lead from competition, through monopoly, to socialism:

> [T]he Trust is a great step forward in economic advance. Like every advance it brings disadvantages ... But the Trust ... is doing a necessary work. Competition has served the purpose of weeding out the incompetent and ill-equipped capitalists. The Trust is concentrating industry and is evolving Capitalism to that state where the public ownership and control of the great industries will be possible. Competition, the Trust and then socialism.[12]

Thus socialists found the answer to monopoly not in policies to promote competition but in nationalization. They were hardly to be blamed because industrial managers never seemed to find much value in competition policy or indeed in competition. Only later, when it was seen that not everything could be nationalized at once was it perceived by some socialists that the enforcement of competition might provide, at least temporarily, some safeguard against monopoly.

Marxists warned that monopoly capitalism would lead to imperialist war. Capitalists, noting the limitations of the domestic market, were investing abroad and seeking markets abroad. They tried to monopolize the world market just as they attempted to monopolize the domestic market. To protect their overseas markets and investments they demanded that their own government should, wherever possible, use military force to seize political power and build an empire. With the advance of monopoly went the collapse of free trade. Great Britain, once the beacon of free trade, had turned brusquely to protectionism. Cobden and Bright had equated free trade with peace. But instead of free trade there was now the drive to monopoly and empire. Efforts were being made to isolate the British Empire from the current of world trade. What was the point of accumulating an empire and then allowing foreigners to share the benefits? But the capitalists of other nations had the same problems in their domestic markets and were similarly engaged. The result was conflict for territory, for markets, for profits. The inevitable outcome was war, imperialist war. As certain as the trajectory of the sun in the heavens was war under capitalism. J. A. Hobson, former Liberal, and Lenin, the Bolshevik, could be equally quoted in support of this thesis. Tawney was clear that the alternative to socialism was war.[13] The 1914–18 war had demonstrated the horrors of modern war. As the 1930s advanced the prospect of a war even more terrible than that of 1914–18 loomed again. The threat of war made the replacement of capitalism by socialism not merely desirable but urgent.

THE SOCIALIST PROSPECTUS: HUMANITY AND EFFICIENCY

The arguments for socialism were the more compelling, and the confidence of its advocates was the more irresistible, because the existing condition of society was indefensible. The verities of socialism were established not by its own successes but by the failures of capitalism. The socialist prospectus was persuasive and highly attractive. It dealt with two matters, humanity and efficiency. On both, capitalism was found wanting and socialism was offered as the solution. On the subject of humanity, socialism proposed to end poverty and the two greatest sources of poverty, exploitation and unemployment. Exploitation meant that the employer, anxious to maximize his profit, would resist paying his employees the full value of their work. Socialism would end exploitation. Unemployment provided an assurance to the employer that attempts by his work force to demand better pay could be smothered by the availability of alternative labour only too anxious to secure employment at whatever level of pay. Socialism would ensure full employment. If large differentials in income and property were objectionable, if they could be presented as the source of poverty, the most obvious way of removing the offence was to level the playing field of society. Socialism would level the playing field by ensuring much greater equality. Equality entered the socialist prospectus not just because it represented an ideal to which society should approximate but for a severely practical reason. It was believed that, without greater equality, poverty could not be eliminated. As Douglas Jay, economist, journalist and future Labour Cabinet Minister, put it in *The Socialist Case*, 'In most modern societies one of the chief reasons why the poor are very poor is that the rich are very rich . . . poverty cannot be removed without some mitigation of inequality.'[14] And if socialism had a single aim, it was the elimination of poverty.

The conviction that poverty was eradicable was quite understandable. If the unemployed were re-employed, more would be produced and everyone would be much better off. Moreover they would be better off without having to work harder. If the unemployed were re-employed, the problem would be one of redistribution rather than of wealth creation.[15] Thus, for socialists, it was not enough to claim that socialism would be a better, a juster, society than capitalism. They were convinced that it would also be a richer society. This was a message congenial to the Labour party. Having been founded by the trade unions to represent them in Parliament, it became infected with the belief that the economic problem was a distributional problem rather than a wealth-creation problem. Thence came the idea that the way to get a higher standard of living was to attack the employer and his profits rather than to co-operate in wealth creation.

It could hardly be gainsaid that the capitalist system was inefficient as well as inhumane. Whereas the inhumanity of capitalism invited disgust, its inefficiency prompted contempt. The profit motive was particularly excoriated. In 1937 Hugh Gaitskell, future leader of the Labour party, wrote, 'So long as production is left to the uncontrolled decisions of private individuals, conducted, guided and inspired by the motive of profit, so long will Poverty, Insecurity and Injustice continue.'[16] How could capitalism be efficient if it depended on competition? The optimal exploitation of modern technology obviously required co-operation, not competition. How could investment be efficiently planned in ignorance of competitors' planning? Competition implied that supply would be greater than demand and hence that there would be a waste of the resources required to produce the excess supply. It required the wasteful costs of marketing, an extravagant number of competing distribution points, and advertising. It did not discourage socialists that, on the wastefulness of competition, they found themselves in agreement with the monopolists. Under socialism the monopolies would be publicly owned and therefore differently motivated.

How could capitalism be efficient if it made technological progress dependent on the prospect of profit; or, to put the question the other way round, would not the wish to preserve profit discourage the introduction of new technologies which might threaten existing sources of profit? Science and technology had generated new products of value to mankind, it had created the opportunity for much higher productivity, and hence a much higher standard of living. But exploitation of the discoveries of science was inhibited by lack of demand and hence of the prospect of profit. Science, under capitalism, could be an embarrassment rather than a help. Opportunities for greater prosperity would be revealed only to be neglected. The profit motive was the enemy of technology. That was why socialism was essential to economic growth.

Socialism was the unique remedy for all the maladies of capitalist society. Socialism was rational, capitalism anarchic. Capitalism would be replaced by a rational, planned society. With the introduction of socialist planning, the poverty, the cruelty, the inefficiency, inseparable from capitalism, would disappear. Professor Harold Laski, political scientist, Marxist, but a leading member of the Labour party, wrote, 'We have the right to believe that increasing knowledge can, if we will, make for increasing wisdom in the rational disposition of human affairs.'[17] It was the belief that the knowledge was available that would make it possible to plan the economy that attracted many to socialism. On the one side they saw *laissez-faire*, the unplanned capitalist economy, society abandoned to the tender mercies of a market lacking any pretence to social responsibility. On the other, there would be the planned socialist economy responding to the dictates of human intelligence and human conscience. On the one side was the arbitrariness of unregulated economic forces. On the other, arbitrariness replaced by political decisions preferably taken through democratic processes. Socialist writers were obsessed by *laissez-faire*. To a socialist, *laissez-faire* was an insult to the power of reason. The irrationality of the market was a constant theme in socialist propaganda. The reference to its irrationality implied that the market was far from all-wise and all-seeing, or alternatively that it acted only in the interests of the rich. There remained the question how all-wise and all-seeing would be the governmental calculations with which the market was to be replaced. The rationality that was to govern society was the rationality of certain high priests – politicians, economists, civil servants. The explicit assumption was that they would know what was good for the congregation.

While obsessed by the demerits of *laissez-faire*, socialist writers devoted far less attention to the merits and practicality of economic planning. These, apparently, could be taken for granted. The planners would ensure that all labour was utilized, that it was paid the value of its work, and that no human life was wasted. As labour would be paid the value of its work, there would be a demand for everything that was produced. But, if labour was paid the full value of its work, there would be no profit. What private person would invest if there was to be no profit? The implication was that the means of production must be publicly owned. Investment would be undertaken by the public out of public resources, and the motivation would be utility not profit.

Accumulating the necessary public resources required that something out of the value produced by the worker would be diverted to the government, directly or indirectly. But that, apparently, was not objectionable because the money would not be going to private owners.[18] Common ownership would give the planners power to ensure that production and supply balanced so that, while there was always enough, there was no waste of resources in producing an unnecessary surplus. There was, in any case, something offensive about the making of private profit out of the needs of the community. What was necessary for supplying the needs of the community should be owned by the community.

For socialists, the control of the state was the great object of policy. Without control of the state, socialists felt helpless in a world in which their enemies had so much power. The battle seemed so unequal. They were opposed by capitalists who owned property and, with it, power. Their property and their power had long enabled them to control the state. Socialists had little property and therefore little power. The solution was to find a way to deprive the capitalists of control of the state, and win it for socialism, preferably by democratic political action. The state was the greatest depository of power and, under the control of socialists, that power could be utilized for socialist ends. Controlled by socialists, the state would plan. Reason and the public interest would prevail.

Socialism combined its therapeutic properties with many of the characteristics of religion. It was a creed that could be preached from the pulpit as well as from the platform. Many Christians found in socialism the earthly equivalent of their hope for salvation. Attlee asserts that 'In no other country has Christianity become converted to Socialism to such an extent as in Britain.'[19] It was one of the characteristics that made Britain special. He wrote of socialism that it was 'the key that will unlock the treasure house of a better world'.[20] It was intended to relieve suffering, to create a heaven even if only on earth. It was also an escape from the problems on earth. Because it was on earth, not everything could be guaranteed at once nor would every imperfection of current life disappear at a stroke. Attlee confessed that it would be some time before substantial economic equality was achieved. But 'ultimately it must be'.[21] That, for some, socialism was a religion is perhaps best illustrated by Tawney's *Acquisitive Society*. Having set out his socialist philosophy, Tawney explicitly says that it is of a kind that ought to be propagated by the Christian Churches – though, as he goes on to regret, it is a duty that they have long neglected.[22] His text frequently lapses into language appropriate to the pulpit, with a menacing content of hell as well as a promise of heaven. Thus *rentiers* may be rich but they are not happy. 'For they have abolished the principle which makes activity significant, and therefore estimable. They are, indeed, more truly pitiable than some of those who envy them. For like the spirits in the Inferno, they are punished by the attainment of their desires.'[23] Obviously the *rentiers* should feel nothing but gratitude to the socialists without benefit of whose earnest sermons they would never find salvation in a useful life. Tawney cries out against luxury. 'Is not *less* production of futilities as important as, indeed a condition of, *more* production of things of moment?'[24] Such thoughts would persist in socialist writings and speeches until the 1950s and beyond, until, indeed, it was found that contempt for luxury alienated many even of that part of the electorate for whom luxury was as yet beyond their means. There is a further analogy with religion. Not even the greatest faith, the finest works, can guarantee the right to heaven. It is a matter of trust. So it was with socialism. Would socialism, however defined, yield the benefits claimed for it? There was no evidence and therefore there could be no proof. The element of religious faith in socialism resulted for the Labour party in one great strength and one great weakness. The strength was the enormous amount of voluntary work that could be called upon by a party lacking much financial strength. The weakness was the ease with which the devotion of the faithful could be disappointed whenever Labour was in government.

Bernard Shaw, the Fabian socialist, insisted that, under socialism, incomes should be equal. 'Socialism', he wrote, 'means equality of income and nothing else . . .'[25] He conceded that, if incomes were equal, some encouragement or incentive would be needed to persuade people to undertake the less pleasant tasks. 'Give more leisure,' he suggested, 'earlier retirement into the superannuated class, more holidays, in the less agreeable employments, and they will be as much sought after as the more agreeable ones with less leisure.'[26] By the same logic, no doubt, those in the more agreeable employments would be allowed no leisure at all. Shaw presumably wrote to persuade, not just to amuse, but some at least of his readers may have been left with doubts about the practicality of his variety of socialism. Tawney, the professional historian, believed that, in the society which he envisaged, everyone would work to professional standards, irrespective of any special financial incentive, because there would be no question of a profit being made out of a worker's labours by a functionless capitalist.

No one has any business to expect to be paid 'what he is worth', for what he is worth is a matter between his own soul and God. What he has a right to demand, and what it concerns his fellow-men to see that he gets, is enough to enable him to perform his work ... If a man has important work, and enough leisure and income to enable him to do it properly, he is in possession of as much happiness as is good for any of the children of Adam.[27]

Though himself a professional, Tawney did not appear sensitive to the vested interests, and behaviour patterns, of professionals. The naivety of some socialist expectations is further exemplified by Tawney at his most idealistic.

The truth is that only workers can prevent the abuse of power by workers, because only workers are recognized as possessing any title to have their claims considered. And the first step to prevent the exploitation of the consumer by the producer is simple. It is to turn all men into producers, and thus to remove the temptation for particular groups of workers to force their claims at the expense of the public, by removing the excuse that such gains as they may get are taken from those who at present have no right to them because they are disproportionate to service or obtained for no service at all.[28]

In other words, once there are no more capitalists demanding unearned dividends or landowners demanding unearned rents, the interests of the workers as producers will be at one with their interests as consumers. Tawney's hypothesis may, of course, be true. We simply lack the evidence that would sustain it and it rather looks as though that will always be the case.

By their idiosyncratic attitudes, Shaw and Tawney gave some colour to the criticism that socialism made unrealistic demands on human nature. This was not a criticism that socialists generally could accept. Indeed many prided themselves on their knowledge of human nature and their understanding of the fact that human beings need incentives and expect reward in proportion to the value of their work. Though there would be incentives, and differences in reward, socialism would be in the interests of the great majority of the population.[29] Among socialist writers who took a less elevated view of human nature than Shaw and Tawney was J. A. Hobson. Hobson, former Liberal, self-described in his autobiography as an economic heretic, was seeking a practical form of socialism which would avoid capitalist crisis and be consistent with his more robust view of human nature. He recognized the importance of both the profit motive and individual incentives provided that they made a contribution to the sum of human welfare.[30]

The simple, socialist prospectus was, naturally, never uncontroversial. One would not expect the capitalists, or the hirelings of the capitalists, to welcome the socialist message. They, after all, would lose from socialism. The capitalists would lose their profits and the managers would lose the wages derived from the sin of serving the capitalists. On the other hand, the workers, the exploited, could be expected to welcome the message. They would be freed from dependence and exploitation. All that was required of them was to believe the message of hope they were receiving. That done, it would remain only to ensure that they or their representatives could find a way to implement socialism. But here there was reason to pause. Simple as was the message of socialism, persuasive as were its advocates, could they really be believed? Attracted as some might be by the vision of a Socialist Commonwealth, a sophisticated, if hard-pressed, electorate, might question whether this earth was in fact a possible site for a new heaven. Scepticism is the enemy of activity. Scepticism as to whether utopia was attainable could dampen the enthusiasm with which the expected beneficiaries might devote themselves to working for socialism.

The scepticism might simply derive from the conservatism of those who could not imagine a different society. Or it might derive from an uneasy, inarticulate, feeling that perhaps the world was not as susceptible of rearrangement in the collective interest as the socialist propagandists claimed or even from a sense that, if the collective interest requires everyone to be good, society would become stifling rather than stimulating. Or it might derive from the critical questions that were being put by those denounced as merely the hirelings of the capitalists. Those questions might imply worrying answers. Was the devil we knew, devilish as he might be, more trustworthy than the alternative offered which might bring a multiplicity of problems which the propagandists had not foreseen or which they were concealing in some private interest of their own? How could one be sure that socialism could be achieved without great damage to society? Supposing there to be a satisfactory answer to that question, where was the evidence that its benefits would outweigh its costs? If everything was to be planned, was everything to be dictated? Who were these wise men who could foretell the demand not merely for existing products but also for products yet to be born? Was competition all loss? Did not competition offer choice and quality? If the rich were deprived of their assets, who should own them? For most socialists, the state was the right repository of the compulsorily acquired assets.

They believed that the state belonged to the people or, in the Marxist version, could be made to belong to the people, and that therefore the people would all have a share in the new acquisitions. But would the state really belong to the people? Is a notional share in state property really ownership? Is it productive of the influence we, the people, feel we should have over the use of our other possessions? The state seems rather distant and rather too grand to submit to the influence of individual citizens. If the state was to own the means of production, distribution and exchange, would there be only one master, must everyone work for the state and must no one displease the state? If every source of employment was owned by the state, where would go the dissenter, the maverick, the individualist? Would he just starve? This was a question that had been raised many years before by the socialist William Morris.[31] It did not seem important in the inter-war years. Faced by a crisis of capitalism, and by unacceptable levels of unemployment, who would worry about theoretical problems of that kind? In the 1950s, in a happier economic climate, it would begin to be perceived, even by some socialists, that this was a real concern and that fragmentation of ownership was a better guarantee of personal liberty than monopoly state ownership.

The contrasts, injustices and miseries of life under capitalism might have provoked revolutionary sentiments among those who suffered the effects of deprivation. On the contrary, there were many, perhaps a majority, who felt that deprivation was part of the natural order and was unlikely to be corrected by political means. Much of the agitation against deprivation and inequality was left to academics, middle-class enthusiasts and some exceptional characters born in the working class who proved capable of rising above the limitations imposed by poverty and inadequate education. There was, at first, only a minority among the deprived who believed that a solution was to be found in political action. The Labour party and the trade unions might serve to defend the interests of the working class. But, in the view of many, perhaps most, of those they existed to serve, it was no part of their role to attempt also an assault on the capitalist system itself. This tendency to accept, however reluctantly, things as they are has been a handicap to socialism throughout its history. The electorate never invested too many hopes in socialist politicians and, when their performance fell below their ambitions, the disillusion was always greater among socialists than among the electorate generally.

TWO

The Labour party goes socialist

THE BEGINNINGS OF A LABOUR PARTY

The Labour party began life in 1900 under the name of Labour Representation Committee. It was constituted as a federation of three main elements. The first was the Independent Labour party, formed in 1893 under the leadership of Keir Hardie. The second was a socialist society, the Fabian Society, founded in 1884, and the third, sundry trade unions which were prepared to join in the enterprise of seeking direct labour representation in Parliament. The ILP was from the beginning socialist. Its objective was 'to secure the collective and communal ownership of all the means of production, distribution and exchange'.[1] But the trade unions which participated in the foundation were not yet socialist. Many trade union leaders were, in politics, inclined to Liberalism and their purpose was to strengthen labour representation in the House of Commons under Liberal party auspices. Hardie and the ILP nevertheless wished to secure the collaboration of trade unions. They were therefore prepared to accept that the LRC would not at the outset have socialism as its objective. The initial founding participants were soon joined by the great majority of the trade union movement, encouraged by the need to secure legislation to overturn the Taff Vale judgement of 1901 which had left unions liable for damages in industrial disputes. Repeatedly the trade unions would look to action by Labour in Parliament to secure redress of some grievance, whether it was the Taff Vale judgement, or the Osborne judgement of 1909 which declared all political action by trade unions to be *ultra vires*. In these two cases, the Labour party had already, before 1914, been successful. The LRC adopted the title 'Labour party' after its success in securing the election of twenty-nine MPs in the 1906 General Election. It was a success that had been achieved in electoral collaboration with the Liberal party.

It was its constitutional association with trade unions that gave the

British Labour party its distinctive character. The Party had the appearance, and much of the reality, of being the political wing of the trade union movement. Thereby the trade unions added a political instrument to the negotiating instruments available to them as trade unions. The association of the trade unions with political action through a political party was a defeat for the syndicalist tendencies within the trade union movement. It implied that it was not for the unions, at least directly, to govern. That was for Parliament and it was in Parliament that the workers must be represented.

As the trade unions had played such a major role in founding the Party, trade union leaders wanted a say in what it then did. Their money and their votes in Conference gave them a very powerful say. Their dominance was assured by the Labour party's 1918 Constitution, which bestowed upon them control of both the Conference and the National Executive Committee. The link to the Labour party enriched the life of trade union leaders with an additional interest that many of them came to cherish. Their involvement took them away from the day-to-day grind of wage negotiations and conditions of work into the more exciting fields of politics and international policy. Sometimes union involvement was an element of stability within the Labour party. At other times the responsible political leaders found themselves battling against union leaders who demanded influence proportional to their votes in Conference, and their funding, rather than to their insight and understanding. To preserve unity, policies had to be decided by compromise, an outcome not invariably acceptable to the politicians who might have to implement them.

The leading Fabians included George Bernard Shaw and Sidney and Beatrice Webb. The name of the Fabian Society was derived from that of Fabius Maximus Cunctator, a Roman general who fought against Hannibal, and of whom it was claimed that, though he delayed his blows, when he did strike he struck hard. In fact, neither Fabius nor the Fabian Society were given to delivering or advocating hard blows. Fabius retired from the war discredited and not victorious, and the Fabian Society devoted itself to the business of exerting pressure based on research. There were two elements in its strategy which gradually came into conflict. At first the Fabians tried to influence the dominant Liberal and Conservative parties in favour of measures of social amelioration. Although they had some success they found that they had exaggerated the persuasive force of their arguments. There were too many in positions of power whose interest it was not to be persuaded and who, perhaps, had even better reasons not to be persuaded than their interests. As it became clearer that influence on the 'bourgeois' parties would not be enough, the need for a Labour party was accepted within the Fabian Society and its members became active in its foundation, though, as the socialist historian, political theorist and economist G. D. H. Cole puts it, 'The Fabian leaders, intent on their policy of "permeation" and sceptical of the Labour Party's prospects, were hardly more than luke-warm supporters right up to 1914.'[2]

THE 1918 CONSTITUTION

The trade unions had continued reluctant to mingle their practical objectives, concerned primarily with wages and conditions of work, with the vision of socialism. The Labour party's only explicit objective had been 'To organise and maintain in Parliament and the country a political Labour party'.[3] But the approaching end of a great war seemed an appropriate occasion for raising sights beyond the short term. An agreed, if futuristic, prospectus would also help to reunite the Party, which had been badly divided by the war. The majority had supported co-operation with the government in pursuing victory. A minority, which nevertheless included some major Labour politicians, for example Ramsay Mac-Donald and Philip Snowden, was suspicious of the imperialist objectives of the Allied powers whatever it might think of German aggression. Labour's move to socialism commenced with its 1918 Constitution, adopted at a Conference in February 1918. Even then there was no specific mention of socialism. Nevertheless, the statement of objective inscribed in Clause Three (later Clause Four) of the 1918 Constitution became Labour's definition of socialism. The Clause defined the objective of the Labour party as:

> To secure for the producers by hand or by brain the full fruits of their industry, and the most equitable distribution thereof that may be possible, upon the basis of the common ownership of the means of production and the best obtainable system of popular administration and control of each industry and service.[4]

British socialism would now have a specific meaning, a meaning which the vast majority of Labour party members would come to accept and which would spread among the population generally as *the* definition of socialism. Socialism meant common ownership plus much greater equality. The new Constitution was accompanied by a policy statement, *Labour and the New Social Order*, drafted by the Fabian Sidney Webb, who was a member of the NEC. The title referred ambiguously to a new social order rather than to socialism. The statement itself presented the case for a minimum standard of life for all, for full employment, public ownership and greater equality. Cole describes *Labour and the New Social Order* as 'an historic document of the greatest significance' because 'it unequivocally committed the Labour party to Socialist objectives'.[5] Attlee remembered it as 'an uncompromisingly Socialist document'.[6] Nevertheless the hesitancy in brandishing the word 'socialism' suggests that careful drafting was still considered necessary if the agreement of the trade unions was to be secured. In June 1918, a further Conference adopted resolutions based on *Labour and the New Social Order*. In one of the resolutions, the Conference, greatly daring, called for 'the socialisation of industry in order to secure the elimination of every kind of inefficiency and waste'.[7] Thus did the Labour party adopt socialism, with caution and with a degree of imprecision necessary to comprehend a variety of different voices.

In particular, the meaning of 'common ownership' was imprecise. It was possible to envisage many forms of ownership, other than nationalization, that might be regarded as falling under that description and which could claim to be socialist in character. But, if all workers were really to enjoy the full fruits of their industry upon the basis of common ownership, the only conceivable way in which it could come about was through nationalization. No other system of common ownership could be other than marginal in its impact. It was thus that the Clause came to be interpreted, whatever the intention of those who drafted it, and that interpretation has never changed. The message of the new Clause sharpened the image of the Labour party. It was clearly directed against the capitalists, with whom the fault lay that so many lived poor and unemployed. It was a class message and could rally powerful emotions. The phraseology contented socialists within the Party while being acceptable to the unions. Trade unions had supported nationalization in particular instances and were therefore willing to accept the view of the Secretary of the Party, Arthur Henderson, and of intellectuals such as Sidney Webb, that support for extensive nationalization should be the criterion that separated the faithful from the heretics. Nationalization would create a whole new culture from which the objective of profit would be excluded. Production would be for use, not for profit. Britain would be freed from distasteful commercialism and exploitation.

There remained room for disagreement as to the purposes of nationalization. For Tawney, the purpose was simply to get rid of useless owners. Nationalization 'is a means to an end not an end in itself. Properly conceived, its object is not to establish the state management of industry, but to remove the dead hand of private ownership when the private owner has ceased to perform any positive function.'[8] Tawney wanted power dispersed. Socialist economists, on the other hand, wanted it centralized so that they could plan. There was always concern, expressed among others by the Guild Socialists, among whom Cole was at the time prominent, that socialism was being converted simply into an alternative system of economic management. In the process, much that had been understood by socialism might be lost. Guild Socialists, for whom Sidney Webb had little but contempt, believed in workers' control. Under nationalization, though they might be better off materially, the workers might gain no more power over their own lives, and over the character of the work they undertook, than they had had under capitalism. The Guild Socialists did not want workers to be the slaves of socialist bureaucracies any more than of capitalist entrepreneurs. They insisted that power over production must be decentralized into autonomous units controlled by their workers – though, to avert an obvious danger, ways were to be found of reconciling the interests of the guilds with the interests of consumers. The Guild Socialists were, however, more perceptive in their criticism of state socialism than in presenting a practical alternative to capitalism with its advancing technology and massive production units. Guild Socialism proved to be no more than a distraction from the main socialist argument, which became highly, and unapologetically, centralist.

Clause Four, as we will now call it and as it is remembered in history due to the various battles fought over it, would survive as the defining component of the Labour party Constitution for nearly eighty years. Those in the Labour party who wanted more public ownership were regarded as being on the 'left'. Those less demanding of extensive public ownership, or perhaps even of none at all, were regarded as being on the 'right'. In the eyes of many members of the Labour party, it was much better to be on the 'left', almost irrespective of the arguments for more public ownership. It became the shibboleth that divided the truly socialist from those who had succumbed to the temptations of capitalist society.[9]

Clause Four implied a social revolution. Socialism was not to be just a more humane form of capitalism. Society would be transmuted into something quite different from anything currently, or previously, experienced. It would be a form of society which could be spoken of in a kind of ecstatic language quite inappropriate to the materialistic capitalist system in which class was divided from class, the rich from the poor, *rentiers* from those who had to earn by the sweat of their brow, owners from workers. Clause Four provided the guidance, the Labour party the instrumentality. In *Let Us Face the Future*, the Labour party's manifesto for the 1945 election, it would state: 'The Labour party is a Socialist Party, and proud of it. Its ultimate purpose at home is the establishment of the Socialist Commonwealth of Great Britain.'

Once the Labour party had defined socialism, the influence of the definition was widespread. There were, however, some who, without questioning the key elements of common ownership and greater equality in the definition of socialism, would broaden its scope. In 1937, Attlee would quote Bertrand Russell, a lifelong member of the Labour party, on 'the essentials of Socialism':

> Socialism means the common ownership of land and capital together with a democratic form of government. It involves production for use not for profit, and distribution of the product either equally to all or, at any rate, with only such inequalities as are definitely in the public interest. It involves the abolition of all unearned wealth and of all private control over the means of livelihood of the workers. To be fully realised it must be international.[10]

Russell, with his misgivings about the Soviet Union, emphasized that there could be no socialism without democracy. That view was generally, but not universally, shared within the Labour party. Russell also noted that it must be international. That requirement would present the Labour party with unexpected difficulties.

Nearly seventy years after 1918, against a very different political background, Roy Hattersley, then deputy leader of the Labour party, wrote a book entitled *Choose Freedom*. He regretted that, following the drafting of Clause Four, 'the idea that socialism and public ownership are synonymous . . . slipped into the hearts and minds of Labour party members'.[11] For Hattersley the problem was that the idea, having 'slipped' in, proved very difficult to exorcize. But it was not surprising that the idea of nationalization adhered so obstinately to the minds of socialists. Apart from its class significance, nationalization was seen as yielding key benefits, security at work, distaste for materialism and competition, production for use not profit, the superiority of public service over private gain, and the possibility, if need be, of a socialist government subsidizing the pay of nationalized industry employees. Attlee was to make the essential socialist point. 'In a thousand and one ways [the worker] will feel the difference between working for a private Capitalist and working for the nation.'[12]

Later it would be argued, for example by Gaitskell and Crosland in the 1950s, that nationalization was a means, not an end. The end was greater equality, to which nationalization might, in certain circumstances, be a means. But this was certainly not the attitude in the 1930s. Nationalization was at the very core of Labour's ambitions. Combined with the other socialist objective of much greater equality, it was of the essence of socialism, and the views of Gaitskell and Crosland were highly controversial within the Labour party even in the 1950s. In 1918, Labour, flushed with its official conversion to socialism, was not yet seeking a third way. Hattersley was living in a different era in which the search for third ways had become a *sine qua non* of political survival. By then, it may indeed have seemed regrettable that such emphasis was placed on nationalization by Labour's founding fathers. But then it was always questionable whether Labour's adoption of socialism was an aid to the winning of power. While the Labour party had been converted to socialism, it is doubtful whether the majority of Labour voters ever were. The Labour party, in the course of its brief history as a socialist party, would be divided between those who considered socialism its greatest attraction and those who concluded that, whether or not it should be an attraction, it was in practice an encumbrance.

THE IMPATIENT PARTNERS

Though identifying itself as a socialist party Labour did not change its name to 'Socialist' or 'Social Democratic' party. It remained part of something called the 'Labour Movement', which consisted essentially of the trade unions and the Labour party. The balance of numbers and money was very much on the side of the unions and, sometimes overestimating their power, they could not always be relied on to act in ways conducive to the success of their partners in the Labour party. Their conversion to socialism could open to them to accusations of revolutionary intentions very much at odds with the Labour party's democratic professions. It was the defeat of the General Strike of 1926 that demonstrated the limitations of trade union power and any idea that there was a syndicalist reply to capitalism. Following the General

Strike, the trade unions suffered the constraints imposed by the Trade Disputes and Trade Union Act of 1927. These included some restrictions on the right to strike as well as threatening the Labour party's solvency.[13] Unions had exploited the inertia of their members to build up their political funds which helped to finance the Labour party. If members did not want to pay the levy in aid of union political funds, they could contract out. Under the Trade Disputes Act, it was required that they should contract in. It was unlikely that there would be as many volunteers as unwitting conscripts. Any hope of securing the repeal of an Act attributed by union leaders to political vindictiveness would depend on a Labour victory in a General Election. The trade unions were relearning the value of political action through the Party they had created. Ernest Bevin, General Secretary of the Transport and General Workers Union, and the Trades Union Congress understood the lesson to be gleaned from the General Strike. Bevin's became a voice for moderation in defining the Labour party's programme. Yet there remained those in the trade union movement for whom the capitulation of the TUC at the end of the General Strike was a betrayal, not a warning. Herbert Morrison, for many years Attlee's deputy, found it necessary, but sometimes unavailing, to stress that political strikes could only redound to the discredit of the Labour party and hence set back the struggle for socialism. The General Strike, he insisted, was a weapon to be used only in the gravest emergency, such as an attempt by a government to act unconstitutionally.[14]

The question that remained was whether the objectives of the trade unions would be consistent with the *socialist* aims of the Party. The fact that the trade unions had been prepared to accept the common ownership of the means of production, distribution and exchange as the objective of the Party they had helped to found did not mean that their members had suddenly become socialists or even supporters of the Labour party. Trade unionists were never anything like unanimous in their support either for socialism or for Labour at elections. There were members who valued the protection they received from their union but who never voted Labour. Large numbers would continue indefinitely to vote Conservative. However much the idea of socialism might attract their leaders, many trade unionists remained sceptical of long-range objectives that seemed to have little connection with the satisfaction of their immediate wage demands. If that were true of trade unionists, it was even more true of the wider working class that did not join trade unions. Moreover there was less solidarity within the trade union movement than socialist theory might suggest. It was far from monolithic in its constitution or its aims. The unions were divided by conflicting interests. For example the interests of the skilled could diverge from those of the unskilled worker. Differentials were important to those who earned them. It has always been easy for the expectant beneficiary to agree on the importance of redistribution. The problem arises with those required to contribute. For the Labour movement, redistribution was always something to be received, not subscribed. Yet, once the Labour party had adopted common ownership, the unions for their part inserted it in their rule books and constitutions. Their leaders coveted the panacea of socialism even if their members were understandably reluctant to make any sacrifices for it.

With the advent of socialism to their portfolio of objectives, the unions could hardly avoid becoming schizoid. Robert Taylor notes 'the real tensions that existed between a Socialist ideology glorifying in the collectivist power of the state to transform society and a pragmatic acceptance by trade unions of the market economy for resolving differences of opinion with capital through the practice of collective bargaining'.[15] On the one hand there was the socialist future, a future without class struggle and of prosperity for their members. On the other hand there was the immediate battle with the employers exploiting every opportunity to win better pay and conditions of work. Attlee was clear that the actions of trade unions were not invariably consistent with the interests of the community as a whole or, indeed, with those of the Labour party. Writing in 1937, he went so far as to suggest that some unions were tending to forget or ignore the ultimate aims of the movement. They had become so constitutional that they were in essence Conservative.[16] He insisted that the Labour party was not a mere political expression of trade unionism. It might even come to the conclusion that certain immediate demands of a trade union were in conflict with socialist policy.[17] This was more easily said than done. Labour's socialism, such as it was, was always striving to accommodate itself to the interests of the trade unions lest there be a breach which the Party could afford neither politically nor financially.

Attlee's concern was that trade unions, in pursuit of short-term advantages for their members, might sacrifice the long-term struggle for socialism. One expression of this concern was the fear of capitalist monopoly. Monopoly strengthened the power of the owners. Monopoly could be used by employers to seduce their employees away from the socialist faith. An attempt by trade unionists to exploit their power at the expense not of the capitalists but of other workers would not be compatible with socialism. Attlee wrote:

> Still more sinister are the approaches made from time to time to sections of the workers to join with the employers in using the position of a particular industry to extort concessions from the rest of the community regardless of the general interest. It would, for instance, be perfectly possible for a big monopoly, by conceding to its workers conditions above that of the general body of employees, to attempt to enlist them into its service so that they would become accessory to the exploitation of the community.[18]

There was nothing in their rule books that denied trade unions the right to exploit such opportunities as they might perceive for the benefit of their members. It was, after all, what they were in existence to do. They were not in the business of sacrificing the immediate interests of their members either to the interests of non-members or to some distant vision of the hereafter. The Mond–Turner talks of 1927–8, even though they had failed, had alerted Attlee to the dangers. Trade union leaders, including Ernest Bevin, had been invited by the Chairman of Imperial Chemical Industries and by other leading employers to discuss their mutual problems.[19] It was a gesture of conciliation after the General Strike. The participants in the talks were seeking a solution to conflict between large trade unions and major employers. But, if they were to find it, it was only too likely to be at the expense of the rest of the working population.

Herbert Morrison was also clear that there was a potential conflict between the short-termism of the trade unions and the long-term aims of the Labour party. He told Beatrice Webb that 'he feared an eventual split between the TUC organisation trying to make the best of capitalism and the Labour party attempting to supersede capitalism by socialism'.[20] Attlee and Morrison had to reconcile their recognition of a potential problem with the controlling influence that the unions could exert within the Labour party. They could be sure that, even if they tried to ignore the issue, they would soon be reminded of it both by the trade unions and by their political opponents. Attlee was confident that there was no insurmountable problem. The Party and the trade unions were both parts of the Labour Movement. Whatever differences might emerge between and within the political and trade union wings in the short term, there was no difference in the long term. Socialism would reconcile all divergences. This contention would be sorely tested over the years to come. The dilemma that was, in different forms, to confront all leaders of the Labour party, and all Labour governments, was that the short-term interests of the trade unions would often be found in conflict with the long-term interests of the community as a whole as interpreted by Labour governments. Just at the moment when the election of a Labour government would appear to bring promise of an advance towards socialism, the unions would find their own Party acting as spoilsport and telling them that, in the cause of socialism, they must hold back their wage demands. How should they choose? The unions could never forget their immediate obligations to their members whether or not Labour was in power. The dilemma for the unions would become even more acute when they discerned that the policies of Labour governments had little if anything to do with the pursuit of socialism and rather more to do with the management of capitalism. Socialism, it was found, was not and could not be delivered, but the unions were expected to behave as though it had been or, at least, would be. The failure of successive Labour governments to deliver socialism became not merely a bone of contention with the trade union movement. It enabled the unions to adopt a high moral tone in their dealings with Labour governments. The relationship deteriorated into one between impatient partners, impatient with each other even more than they were impatient for socialism. For the Labour party it was a perpetual quandary which would haunt it until the end of the century.

SOCIALISM AND THE LIBERAL PARTY

The adoption of socialism was a factor, but not necessarily the most important factor, separating the Labour party from the Liberal party, with which it had once been allied. If the Labour party had wished simply to be a subsidiary of the Liberal party, or had been content with the social policies of the Liberal party, it would hardly have been necessary to form it. Liberalism, according to George Dangerfield, was 'a profoundly conscience-stricken state of mind'.[21] The unions wanted more than lamentations about the condition of the workers. They demanded their own separate representation in Parliament because they believed that the interests of trade unionists required more vigorous advocacy than could be expected from the Liberal party. Once there was separate representation, there was likely eventually to be conflict between the two parties.

The Labour party's adoption of socialism helped to make the cleavage with the Liberals irreconcilable. But it had its own inevitability. If Britain was European in nothing else, it was European in the emergence of a party dedicated to democratic socialism. Socialism was an expression of discontent with the workings of capitalism, and that discontent was not to be placated simply by liberalizing and humanizing capitalism, which had become the policy of a dominant element in the Liberal party. Socialism was on offer as a new and better society, different from capitalism, which could be striven for not just by idealists but by men and women who, confronted in negotiation with capitalists, wished to deprive them of their power. Though, therefore, the centre-left of British politics was further divided by the Labour party's adoption of socialism, it is unlikely that anything else could have happened. The breach would be bridged only when the Labour party itself found from experience that its most practical objective was merely a humanized capitalism. Meanwhile the division on the left may not have been entirely without benefit. Considering its lack of achievement, the Labour party developed an extraordinary capacity for complacency. As the Liberal party moved to the left it became a source of pinpricks that helped to enliven Labour's somnolent conscience.

It would not be until eighty years after *Labour and the New Social Order* that a Labour leader would instruct his party Conference to regard the Liberals Lloyd George, Keynes and Beveridge as heroes alongside the socialists Attlee, Bevin and Bevan, and would claim, with questionable psephology, that it had been the divisions among the radicals that had made the twentieth century a Tory century. But it was the Labour party that had erected the impermeable wall by its obsession with class and by declaring itself socialist. Bevan, one of its heroes, later protested that, if Keynes was right, there was no need for socialism. His logic led him to conclude that, as there was an evident need for socialism, Keynes could not possibly be right. In the end it was discovered that Keynes was not more right than others of his profession but that there was still no possibility of democratic socialism.

MIDDLE-CLASS SOCIALISM

Many of the leading figures of the Labour party originated among the middle classes, often the upper-middle classes. Some were motivated by disgust at the conditions in which their fellow human beings had to live. For others, their Christianity found its expression in socialism.

Revelation in the late nineteenth century of the appalling conditions in which many in the working class were compelled to live had converted to socialism men and women of sensitive conscience whose gain from socialism would simply be that they would then be living in a society of which they need not be ashamed. There was already by the 1920s and 1930s a tradition of individual middle-class support for the Labour party. It was often channelled through the Fabian Society, to which many were brought by the intellectual attractions of socialism.

Entry of middle-class recruits into the Labour party was eased by the 1918 Constitution, which authorized individual membership, though members were required, if eligible, to join a trade union affiliated to the TUC. There was C. R. Attlee, a graduate from Oxford, trained as a barrister, so shocked by deprivation in London that he decided to devote his life to remedying it. Hugh Dalton was one of a number of prominent Labour Old Etonians.[22] The son of a canon of Windsor who had been a tutor to the Royal Family, he was converted at Cambridge by the intellectual force of Fabian socialism. He became an academic and was subsequently Labour's first post-war Chancellor of the Exchequer. Dalton became Labour's most active headhunter, drawing into Parliamentary politics many of its brightest post-war leaders. The leading figures he recruited or encouraged look back on Dalton with an affection which blinds them to his failings at the Treasury.

Stafford Cripps, who had made a great career outside Parliament before he ventured inside it, was a prominent example of Labour's success in headhunting. Wykehamist, distinguished barrister and devout Anglican, he was the son of Lord Parmoor, another distinguished lawyer, and, when elected to Parliament early in 1931, immediately took up the front-bench appointment of Solicitor General in the MacDonald government during its last few months. John Strachey, Old Etonian, son of the editor of the *Spectator*, once a follower of Oswald Mosley in his days as a Labour MP, became intellectually attracted by Marxism. While not a member, he moved close to the Communist party, though he had been a Labour MP and would later be a Labour MP again as well as a minister in the Attlee government. He was certain that the capitalists would never give up power voluntarily until Douglas Jay showed him an alternative, democratic path to socialism.[23] It was Strachey who, asked by dear old ladies why he had become a communist, replied, 'From chagrin, madam, at not getting into the Eton Cricket Eleven.'[24] There was Michael Foot, former Liberal converting to Labour, shocked by deprivation in Liverpool, who struggled to sustain something of the liberal tradition within the Labour party in its more totalitarian days. Other names which would appear in such a list include Hugh Gaitskell, Richard Crossman and Evan Durbin, all elected to Parliament in 1945, and Douglas Jay, elected in 1946 after serving as an aide to Attlee as Prime Minister. Gaitskell, Crossman, Durbin and Jay were all Oxford graduates, and Gaitskell, Crossman and Jay were Wykehamists. All those listed above came from the professional middle classes. Many were academics who, entranced by the idea of creating a new, and juster, form of society, employed much of their time during the 1930s debating how actually it could be accomplished by democratic means. Middle-class recruitment was encouraged by the break-up of the Liberal party between the Asquith and Lloyd George factions. The Liberal party was looking less and less like an effectual motor of social reform. Shaw was censorious in the manner of the sage who, having discovered religion early, is uncertain how much he really wants the heathen to be converted and inherit salvation. 'Careerists', he wrote, 'are deserting Liberalism for Labour because they think the Liberal ship is sinking.'[25] As the 1930s wore on, further recruitment from the middle classes was inspired by the rise of fascism.

Middle-class recruits were useful to the Labour party because, with the prospect of office, it needed in Parliament educated people able to discharge the responsibilities of office. Thus these middle-class recruits were helpful to Labour's early electoral prospects. Herbert Morrison always emphasized the importance of middle-class recruitment and middle-class support. In January 1945 he issued a statement saying,

> For many years, I have counselled the Socialist Party that if it is ever to secure an independent stable Parliamentary majority, it must gain and keep the support not only of the politically conscious organized workers, but also of large numbers of professional, technical and administrative workers ... the soundest socialist appeal is that which is most universal in its scope.[26]

At Oxford and Cambridge in the 1930s, many of the brightest undergraduates flocked to socialism, and even to communism. There were Anthony Crosland, Denis Healey, Roy Jenkins and, later, Anthony Wedgwood Benn, who was to fight a long and gallant battle to disclaim his father's hereditary peerage in order to stay in the Commons, and who, later still, transformed himself even further into the plebeian Tony Benn. Concern at the deprivations of the poor was in the longer term an unreliable source of recruits. Crosland noted in *The Future of Socialism*, published in 1956, that the sense of guilt among the middle classes had become less prevalent than in the 1930s, because of the improved standards of living among the working classes.[27] Middle-class recruitment to the Labour party continued, but more because of the continuing intellectual attractions of socialism, or even because of political ambition.

Dalton was hated by the Tories as a class traitor because they felt, possibly rightly in Professor Ben Pimlott's view, that he was less interested in helping the poor than in hurting the rich.[28] More generally, upper-middle-class recruits to the Labour party were accused of treason to their class. The accusation exposed the class nature of British society. The question was not one of merit. Was there, for example, any justice in the desperate battle of the miners in 1926 against a reduction in their wages following the misguided return to the Gold Standard, a battle that was to lead to the fruitless General Strike and much suffering by miners and their families beyond it? It was a question of class. This was true on both sides of the political divide and demonstrated to what an unhappy pass social relationships in Britain had descended.

Cripps had briefly managed an ordnance factory during the first world war. The experience may have helped to persuade him that he could run a peacetime economy as well as a wartime arms factory. None of these middle-class recruits, or their families, had more than the briefest experience of work in industry, finance or commerce. Their ability to theorize about industry was equalled only by their ignorance of everything concerning it. Writing in the 1960s, Bryan Magee pointed out how little the working classes knew of 'responsibility' because of the nature of their work.[29] But the ignorance of industry among the professional middle classes was quite as great. They proposed to reform industry without the least knowledge of industry. Douglas Jay records how, after getting a first in Greats at Oxford in 1929, he considered seeking employment in industry but 'nobody seemed able to advise me how to set about so eccentric a career'.[30]

One of the consequences was that there was never in the Labour leadership, and seldom even in a Labour Cabinet, anyone with whom industrialists could feel comfortable. Either they were trade unionists or they were middle-class intellectuals. Indeed, Labour's middle-class intellectuals were seldom comfortable even with the trade union leadership with whom they had to steer their impatient partnership.

THE GOVERNMENT OF RAMSAY MACDONALD

The persuasive force of socialist arguments was not supported by the electorate's experience of Labour governments. Labour, despite its middle-class recruitment, showed itself totally unprepared for the actual responsibilities of government, and its failures multiplied popular scepticism about the objective of socialism. After a brief tenure of office in 1924, Labour returned in 1929 with Ramsay MacDonald again as Prime Minister. It was the largest party in the House of Commons but lacked an overall majority. Its survival in office was dependent on Liberal support. Subsequently, the MacDonald government was subjected to severe criticism within the Labour party for its vacillating conduct even before the final catastrophe of August 1931. In retrospect, Attlee and Dalton outlined three possible courses of action. It could have refused office. It could have entered into an agreement with the Liberals for a joint programme. Or it could have followed the path that Attlee himself suggested he had favoured which was 'to accept office and invite defeat by putting forward a Socialist programme and putting the onus of rejecting it on to the Liberal Party'. In fact, Attlee complains, 'No one of these courses was followed.'[31] Or, as Dalton grandiloquently expresses it, 'The Parliamentary Labour Party of 1929–31 was a magnificent army which was never led into battle.'[32] It seems a little far-fetched to imagine that the MacDonald government could have gone into battle inviting defeat on a socialist programme for which the electorate had clearly not voted. The Liberals had no intention of becoming socialists overnight. To many such an approach by MacDonald would have seemed like capitulation, not heroism.

However, the subsequent disaster was not attributable to MacDonald's failure to make the choice Attlee favoured. It was due simply to the onset of the world economic crisis and its effects on Britain, which the government did not know how to handle. MacDonald, who understood little of these matters, found himself having to decide between incompatible approaches. The TUC, following John Maynard Keynes, had a programme which included protection and departure from the Gold Standard. Sir Oswald Mosley, Chancellor of the Duchy of Lancaster but outside the Cabinet, had been given some responsibility for the unemployment problem. He put forward ideas similar to those of the TUC though mixed together with a great deal about the radical reorganization of British industry. On the other hand, there was the Chancellor of the Exchequer, Philip Snowden, who believed in free trade and was sceptical of magical solutions depending on budgetary excesses. Snowden was Labour's authority on economic policy and, in the presence of authorities on economic policy, plain men quail. Other than by Mosley, Snowden's influence was barely questioned within the government. It was under the influence of Snowden that both the TUC and the Mosley proposals were rejected by the Labour Cabinet. Mac-Donald was left with a policy that has been condemned as representing nothing better than Treasury orthodoxy. It included a cut in unemployment pay which would hurt large numbers of Labour's supporters, although it was claimed that a cut was justified by a significant fall in the price level. It was on this cut that the Cabinet split. MacDonald had the support of a majority of the Cabinet, but there was a large minority which had no alternative policy but knew only that it did not wish to follow MacDonald's. In August 1931, MacDonald and his leading colleagues, unable to secure a collective decision from the Labour Cabinet, deserted the Party and formed a 'National' government in alliance with the Tories and Liberals. They then implemented the cut in unemployment pay. In Labour mythology, they were traitors who had gone over to the capitalist class.

David Marquand, the biographer of MacDonald, writes in a new introduction,

> Looked at from the vantage point of the 1990s, the Keynes of August 1931 looks less like a prophet of economic sanity than a pedlar of soft options. And one obvious implication of that heresy is that MacDonald was not only honourable and consistent, but also right, to do all he could to push the economy programme through the Labour Cabinet and to form a National government when it became clear that he had failed.

Snowden would be entitled to add that this was true not just from the perspective of the 1990s. Where, nevertheless, MacDonald and Snowden did go wrong was in following the Treasury beyond fiscal and monetary conservatism into the maintenance of an overvalued exchange rate. But then their critics in the Labour Cabinet also lacked the knowledge or the understanding to insist on departure from the Gold Standard. Ironically, it was Snowden who, as Chancellor in the new National government, abandoned the Gold Standard one month after he had opposed that course of action in the Labour Cabinet.

One effect of the events of August 1931 was to instil in Labour politicians a deep and abiding distrust of what was designated Treasury orthodoxy. Throughout the years of Labour governments to come, and the generations of Labour politicians, it would always be believed that more could be done to stimulate the economy and encourage economic growth than the Treasury recommended. All that was required was for Labour Chancellors of the Exchequer to reject Treasury orthodoxy. Labour Chancellors would be damned by their Cabinet colleagues if they were believed to have become slaves and purveyors of Treasury orthodoxy. For Labour politicians, Treasury orthodoxy was a state of mind which dragged the economy down below its true potential. The difficulty would be that, although Treasury orthodoxy did not invariably represent the summit of economic wisdom, ignoring it could destabilize the economy and destroy the reputation of Labour governments as economic managers. It was a lesson that Labour governments found it difficult to learn, even though its truth was repeatedly demonstrated in the years to come.

The General Election of October 1931 brought calamitous defeat to the Labour party. The events that led up to it had underlined a continuing doubt about Labour's competence. Here was a government which fell apart when faced by crisis. Labour blamed the deserters and the bankers when it should have blamed its own lack of preparedness for government. Bankers were always an easy target of abuse from the left. Their political prejudices were beyond question and naturally they would use their control over money to undermine any socialist government. But the abuse was counterproductive. Then, and in the future, it simply underlined the stupidity of electing a Labour government lacking the means to implement its policies. The judgement of the electorate on the Labour party was unequivocal. It gave an overwhelming endorsement to the successor 'National' government. Even at the subsequent General Election in 1935, despite the continuing depression and the continuing high level of unemployment, the electorate demonstrated again that it preferred competence to socialism. There was a further question, whether Labour was really fitted to guide Britain in a world in which, with the rise of fascism and Japanese aggression in the Far East, peace seemed increasingly at risk. Labour had recently been riven again by the resignation as leader of the pacifist George Lansbury, forced out by the oratorical hammer blows of Ernest Bevin at the 1935 Labour party Conference. Labour might claim that the National government had failed of its remit. It had not saved the pound, which it had been forced to devalue. It had abandoned free trade. By 1932 many of its policies had an uncomfortable similarity to those which the TUC had put to the Labour Cabinet. Such claims, however, cut no ice.

The National government might have had no alternative but to accept the realities from which Labour had turned away. But it had accepted them and was now comfortably in charge. Questions about competence would dog the Labour party's future steps. It had acquired a reputation which would be difficult to live down.

THE FRUSTRATIONS OF DEFEAT

Instead of the prestige that would have been won by a successful government, the Labour party had found nothing but humiliation. It never quite understood what had happened to its government in August 1931 and, because it was never quite understood, the reaction was instinctive and counterproductive. Its government had been hit suddenly and cata-strophically, in the midst of the summer holidays, by an external power that knew no mercy. The events of August 1931 became deeply etched in the collective memory of the Labour party. It was the great betrayal. For decades thereafter, the left of the Labour party would fear, especially at times of economic crisis, that the right would split away and enter into a coalition with the Tories. This obsession with treason inhibited both friendly relations and rational discussion of policy alternatives. As its immediate reaction, the Labour party went through the left-wing spasms which were to become a normal characteristic of its behaviour after defeat. It was the reaction of a frustrated child. The Party could not accept that the MacDonald government had been destroyed by its own incompetence rather than by the conspiracies of bankers, or the treason of its leaders. The question was raised whether socialism could ever be achieved in Britain by democratic means, whether the capitalist class would not always find ways of sabotaging a Labour government committed to Parliamentary processes. There were many within the Labour party who began to have thoughts bordering on the revolution-ary, and sometimes passing beyond that border, which were likely to be distasteful to an electorate profoundly constitutional in its instincts. Some sections of the Party felt that, if it could not win by the rules, it should tear them up. Others feared that if Labour did play by the rules and won, the other side would tear them up. Hugh Gaitskell recalled that this was the only time when he had questioned the practicability of democratic socialism. As late as 1936, he was seriously concerned whether a Labour election victory would prompt undemocratic forms of resistance.[33]

Prominent among those who began to suit the violence of their words to the violence of their resentments was Sir Stafford Cripps, formidable and prosperous lawyer, who had narrowly survived the electoral holocaust of October 1931. He never seemed able to find language strong enough for his condemnation of the ruling class except sometimes when reproaching his colleagues in the Labour party for their spineless inadequacy. Cripps, at the age of thirty-nine, was a late recruit to the Labour party but, when at last he arrived, he did not bring any doubts with him. His was a mind unadulterated by scepticism. He believed. As a Christian he believed devoutly in Christianity. As a socialist he believed devoutly in socialism. The Socialist League, of which he became the leading figure, had been established in the early 1930s as a ginger group within the Labour party, but it was not long before it seemed to be presenting itself as a more socialist alternative to the Labour party. In 1933, at a Socialist League meeting, Cripps proclaimed,

> Unless during the first 5 years [of a majority Labour government] so great a degree of change has been accomplished as to deprive Capitalism of its power, it is unlikely that a Socialist party will be able to maintain its position of control without adopting some exceptional means such as the prolongation of the life of Parliament for a further term without an election.[34]

Cripps, as a lawyer, presumably knew that the House of Commons could not, unilaterally extend its own life. It required the assent of the House of Lords, whose power, in this respect, had not been compromised by the 1911 Parliament Act. There was always the possibility of the creation of socialist peers, but the Crown could point to precedent for not assenting to a massive creation without a further election. Cripps, in short, was proposing a revolution.

On 6 January 1934, Cripps declared that when the Labour party came to power,

> [T]hey must act rapidly and it will be necessary to deal with the House of Lords and the influence of the City of London. There is no doubt that we shall have to overcome opposition from Buckingham Palace and other places as well. It is absolutely essential that it should be made perfectly clear to the people exactly what it is we ask for the power to do. There must not be time to allow the forces outside to gather and to exercise their influence upon the legislature before the key points of Capitalism have been transferred to the control of the State. I look upon these two points myself as being land and finance. If other people become revolutionary then the Socialist Government, like any other Government,

must take steps to stamp out the Revolution. The Socialist Government must not be mealy-mouthed about saying what they mean.[35]

Other Labour leaders were quite ready to engage in wild talk whatever effect that might have on the electorate whose support they were trying to reclaim. Their radicalism encompassed widespread nationalization, including of the Bank of England, and such equally traditional targets as the abolition of the House of Lords. In 1937, with restraint retrieved, Attlee wrote, 'The revulsion from MacDonaldism caused the Party to lean rather too far towards a catastrophic view of progress and to emphasise unduly the conditions of crisis which were being experienced, and to underestimate the recuperative powers of the Capitalist system.' There is sufficient evidence for this statement in Attlee's own conduct at the time. In a memorandum written after the collapse of the MacDonald government and just before the October 1931 election, Attlee, who had come to consider himself something of an authority on such matters, wrote that it was now beyond doubt that the position of London as the centre of world capitalism was incompatible with a socialist regime of even a 'moderate' Labour government. '"The City" in the middle of a socialist state is as anomalous as would be the Pope in Moscow.' He added a call for more drastic and complete nationalization of important industries straight away.[36] Party leaders occupied themselves intensively with the conundrum how to avoid a financial panic if Labour came to power once more. Finance was feared as a force of nature, both mighty and mysterious, which was the eternal enemy. Moreover it was an enemy whose blows could not be foreseen or deflected. The only thing to do was to seize it by the neck at the outset and strangle it. But, though the objective could be stated, the method was not obvious. In the aftermath of the 1931 defeat, Attlee supported the idea, adopted at the Party Conference in October 1932 over the objections of the Party's National Executive Committee, to make the nationalization of the joint-stock banks an immediate measure of an incoming Labour government. In January 1933, Attlee and Cripps submitted a memorandum to the Labour party's National Executive Committee entitled 'The Joint Stock Banks': It said,

> The moment to strike at capitalism is the moment of taking power when the Government is freshly elected and assured of its support. The blow struck must be a fatal one and not merely designed to wound and to turn a sullen and obstructive opponent into an active and deadly enemy. The difference, as we see it, between those who believe in immediate national-isation and those who do not is not really on the technical or economic

issue. It is much more upon the general issue of whether it is possible to persuade capitalism to hand over control to Socialism by gradual and restrained measures. We are convinced that to take such a course is to court disaster. So long as capitalism holds the power and the control, so long will it use every weapon to retain it.[37]

Another future Labour leader to support this idea at the time was Hugh Gaitskell, as did his close friend Evan Durbin.[38] The nationalization of the Bank of England would enable a Labour government to release credit. The nationalization of the joint-stock banks was necessary as a supplement so that the government could ensure that the credit flowed in the right directions. The Labour party wanted to establish a Banking Corporation in which the 'Big Five' joint-stock banks would be amalgamated. Dalton, in a more calculating mood, was less certain about the priority to be given to this idea. In his view it should depend on the behaviour of the joint-stock banks and their willingness to co-operate with the government and its agencies.[39] He considered the idea dangerous electorally and was seeking some intermediate, or third, way between the extremism of the Party Conference and electoral necessities. His manoeuvres eventually succeeded, though nationalization of the joint-stock banks was not finally buried until *Labour's Immediate Programme* in 1937.[40] Even then there were many in the Party who would persistently pray for its resurrection.

Dalton's moderation was only relative. He later recalled ironically that, in the early 1930s, he was constantly moving resolutions to nationalize the solar system only to face a Socialist League amendment to add the words 'and the Milky Way'.[41] Though he had his doubts about the Banking Corporation, Dalton was in favour of the next Labour government starting with 'a well-planned rush'.[42] To that end there would be an Emergency Powers Act that would enable the government to legislate quickly and effectively. The prime aim would be to overcome unemployment. The means would be nationalization and planning.[43] The concept of an Emergency Powers Act, or some kind of general enabling legislation, became a favourite recourse whenever, frustrated by defeat, Labour wished to demonstrate its anger and determination. Such an Act would eliminate Parliamentary delays, it would authorize Labour governments to move rapidly and decisively, for example in taking over companies in the private sector, and, above all, it would debar effective opposition from the Tories. The idea runs throughout the history of the Labour party as a socialist party. Its advocates, who came from all wings of the Party, seemed to forget that it would have to win an election first and that the electorate might not be happy with ideas that appeared to circumvent Parliament. There was something unreal about a Party with forty-six MPs, and a heavily reduced vote, entertaining itself with ideas of how, once more in power, it would achieve the rapid transformation of society. The forty-six members represented 6.65 million votes, or 30 per cent of the total votes cast, as against the 8.4 million, or 39 per cent, Labour had won in 1929. An optimist might consider that 6.65 million votes, won in such circumstances, constituted a potential revolutionary force. There were such optimists on the extremes of the Labour Movement. It needed time, and the further defeat in the 1935 General Election, to encourage more sober thoughts about the fundamental questions facing Labour.

ERNEST BEVIN

Relations between the TUC and the MacDonald government had been overshadowed by the gathering economic storm. The collapse of the MacDonald government, its failure to find the road out of capitalist crisis, underlined the dependence of the Labour party on the trade unions. When the Labour government and party split, the TUC stood steadfast with those who would not accept Snowden's proposed cut in unemployment pay.[44] That solidarity was a great source of strength at a time when the Party needed friends. The TUC was now a force for moderation. It was concentrating its influence on turning the Labour party from thoughts of revolution towards the practical questions involved in achieving the amelioration of working-class conditions. Labour now needed the comfort of the trade union embrace even more than before. That meant the embrace of Ernest Bevin. Bevin had been born in poverty. His education derived principally from what he later described to his Foreign Office officials as 'the hedgerows of experience'. He combined an impregnable base in the trade union movement with a powerful intellect and extraordinary personal force. He was a large man moved by massive, and incurable, resentments. His vanity exceeded even his enormous abilities. Later, as Foreign Secretary, his vanity would expand further even while his abilities were deteriorating. His regard for politicians generally fell well short of rapture. Ramsay MacDonald had seldom shown much sympathy for the trade union movement and Bevin, in reciprocity, had not been among Ramsay MacDonald's warmest admirers. He came to distrust many of the intellectuals with whom he was associated in the Labour Movement and he did not lack evidence for his suspicions. Intellectuals in his view had poor judgement and had reacted with absurd extremism to the events of August 1931. When he took aim at intellectuals, he frequently had in his sights the Marxist Harold Laski, eminent as a professor at the London School of Economics, a leading Labour publicist and an associate with Stafford Cripps in the Socialist League. But he was quite willing to add to the category anyone who displeased him, even if they would consider themselves ineligible for the distinction.[45]

Together with the General Secretary of the TUC, Walter Citrine, Bevin dominated the trade union movement and, through it, after 1933, the Labour party. His principal instrument was the National Joint Council of Labour, which was constituted of seven members of the TUC General Council, three from the Parliamentary Labour Party and three from the NEC. The General Council thus had a majority of the members. Bullock describes it as 'the most authoritative body in the Labour movement in formulating policy'.[46] After 1933, Bevin and the trade unions were forging a new Labour party. They could ensure that the trade union point of view prevailed at Labour party conferences. This gradually introduced some sobriety into Conference decisions after the spasms of the immediate post-1931 years.

THE WINNING OF CONSENT

Meanwhile, events were both strengthening and weakening the claims of socialism. They were strengthened by poverty and unemployment. They were weakened by the first experiences of Labour governments and by the divisions within the Labour party. But the inadequacies of Labour governments seemed in principle curable. The factors strengthening the claims of socialism appeared permanent.

There remained the problem, emphasized by the events of August 1931, of discovering the road to socialism. Despite 1931, Labour remained a democratic party. The social revolution implied by its policies was to be realized through the processes of democracy, not through an uprising against the state. The Labour party rejected the Marxist view that nothing was gained for socialism by taking over the existing state apparatus. It believed that much would be changed by its electoral victory and by subsequent acts of nationalization. It planned accordingly, and with all the enthusiasm that politicians seem capable of bringing to

a hopeless task. This confidence in the possibilities of democratic processes may seem the more remarkable given the result of the General
Election of 1931. But, on a sober view, there was really no other choice
than the constitutional choice.

To govern, Labour would have to win an election. Therefore, before
anything could be done, it was necessary to win the consent of the
electorate. There have always been within the Labour party two attitudes to the winning of consent. There have been those who believed
that consent would be most easily won by moderation in the presentation
of the socialist case. Their judgement as to what moderation actually
meant would differ from time to time as circumstances changed. Attlee's
moderation when, after the 1935 election, he became more moderate,
would have seemed intensely radical, and threatening to the whole basis
of society, in the 1960s and 1970s. The other attitude was of those who
knew in their hearts that the great majority of the electorate were
yearning for socialism and regarded any kind of compromise with capitalism as betrayal. The working classes voted Conservative only because
they were not being presented with a genuinely socialist alternative.
Those who held this attitude could hear the tramp of the marching
masses and could see the sun rising in the socialist dawn. Those in the
Labour party who dissented from them were not merely deaf and blind.
They might also be traitors. The relationship within the Labour Movement between the Labour party and the trade unions was not the only
example within it of an impatient partnership.

In retrospect, the Labour party owes a debt of gratitude to those
Labour leaders who, once their resentment over 1931 had cooled, turned
it away from extremism. One of the principal services of Attlee, and the
leadership of the Labour party, was to keep it as an opposition fit to
find a place in the wartime Churchill coalition, not a task to which the
extravagant extremism of Stafford Cripps made any contribution.

THREE

The unmapped road

In the inter-war years the urgency of despatching capitalism obscured among democratic socialists the problems of actually accomplishing it. It was not that the problems were not discussed. On the contrary they were intensively discussed. But the discussions left the participants too confident that the problems were soluble. A purpose so manifestly right must in the end prevail. Whatever the obstacles, a way would be found. In Britain there was encouragement in the fact that the political system had been democratized, against strong opposition but, so far, irreversibly. Democratization had, however, taken place over a much longer period than socialists would consider tolerable for the replacement of capitalism by socialism. Socialists wanted the prize in their lifetime. It was then found that democratic socialism had the frustrating quality of a mirage. However nearly one approached, it was always as far away. The illusion that there was a democratic road to socialism persisted even though it had not been found.

For socialists, there was an unresolved dilemma. It was a dilemma vigorously debated in the 1930s, especially following the experience and failures of the MacDonald government. Could socialism be achieved without revolution or, to put the question another way, supposing revolution in the UK to be inconceivable or, at the very least, highly improbable, could socialism be achieved through democratic processes? There was not necessarily an absolute answer. In Britain, with its long history of Parliamentary government, socialism through democratic processes might just be achievable. But, even in Britain, the events of 1931 raised questions whether democracy could win victory over capitalist self-interest. Would the capitalists who benefited so hugely from the existing economic system be prepared to relinquish their power simply because the Labour party won a majority in Parliament? Would they submit to what they would consider ignorance and ideology? Whatever the verdict of the electorate, the capitalists, it was feared, controlled the financial levers which would enable them to tip any socialist government into crisis and dissolution or, alternatively, force it to submit to their will. What was the point of being a socialist if socialism was a dream?

These questions needed a satisfactory answer if the electorate was ever to forgive Labour its incompetence in 1931. There were three main trends in the discussion of these questions in the 1930s. The first was Marxism, with its conviction that socialism was inevitable. If it could not come democratically it would nevertheless come, probably following civil war. The second can be conveniently associated with the name of the political scientist Harold Laski, who, while endorsing many Marxist assumptions, nevertheless concluded that the constitutional route should be tried first. The third was that of the non-Marxist socialists who reassured themselves with the idea that socialist measures, if taken with due caution by a Labour government, would prove irreversible, and that therefore socialism could be achieved incrementally over a period of more than one Parliament. This argument was most persuasively deployed by Evan Durbin in his book, published in 1940, *The Politics of Democratic Socialism*. Despite the force of Durbin's arguments, the conclusion of the discussion in this chapter will be that it was always highly unlikely that socialism, as defined by Clause Four, that is a society characterized by widespread public ownership and far greater equality, could be achieved in Britain by democratic means, or indeed by any other means.

MARXIST INEVITABILITY

Marx attempted to bring the comfort of science to the aid of socialism. Socialists wished to transform society. If society was to be transformed in a way which would command public assent, or even acquiescence, the transformation would have to be steered according to clear defensible principles. In the nineteenth century, science had acquired great prestige. It carried an aura of certainty. Socialist ideas were being advanced in an era of amazing scientific discoveries. Man's insatiable curiosity had penetrated the elements and had found yet smaller particles within them. It had elaborated a rational account of the origins of species. Could it not equally analyse the workings of the social system and discover its laws of motion? Out of his researches into the operations of capitalism in Britain in the nineteenth century, Marx spun a science of human development. His 'discovery' was baptized with the reassuring label of scientific socialism. His science established that the capitalist system would inevitably collapse and be replaced by socialism. Marx saw history as a story of class struggle. On the anvil of that struggle, socialism would, eventually, be forged. The fundamental idea that one form of society *could* be replaced by another was encouraged by the deceptive precedent of the emergence of capitalism out of the bowels of feudalism. At the next stage in historical evolution, socialism would emerge out of the contradictions of capitalism. It could then be assumed, despite the lack of evidence, that the metamorphosis would be to the benefit of the great majority of mankind.

Thus Marx had his answer to that debilitating disease, doubt about the feasibility and desirability of socialism. As socialism was inevitable, there was no room for scepticism. Irresistible historical forces were at work. Inevitability became not just a guarantee that socialism would arrive. It became a recruiting sergeant in the battle for socialism. Given inevitability, a seat on the bandwagon of history might be the safest point from which to observe the ride or, alternatively, to relax and enjoy oneself. There is discussion in the literature of socialism as to whether the idea of inevitability could lead to political passivity. It never seemed likely. Marxist political parties always insisted that history would need encouragement. The early Fabians, who had their own version of inevitability, were never examples of passivity. For those who believed in inevitability, the logical inference appeared to be participation in the struggle, not absence from it.

Marxism might foster the conviction that socialism was inevitable. But did it have anything to say as to whether it could be achieved democratically? Though Marx himself had held the view that Britain might prove to be different and that socialism might be reached by democratic processes, Marxist theory clearly led to the view that, even in Britain, it was only through civil war that the socialist victory could be won. Marxists distinguish between political revolutions which produce little if any changes in society, and certainly no benefit to the exploited, and political revolutions that are also social revolutions which radically change society and the distribution of wealth and power within it. Social revolutions, in the Marxist view, could be accomplished only by force. When, after its 1920 Conference, the I L P sent a delegation to Moscow to discover the implications of membership of the Communist International, they were informed that the victory of socialism in Britain could result only from civil war.[1] Britain's democratic history could, evidently, be discounted. One of the most eloquent popularizers of Marxism in Britain in the 1930s was John Strachey. Strachey did a great service to Marxism. He set out Marxist theory in a comprehensible, if uncritical and polemical, way. He assisted the British reader to grasp what it was all about without the strain of reading *Das Kapital* and the other writings of the founding fathers, Marx and Engels. It was, therefore, through Strachey that many in Britain obtained their introduction to Marxism. His writings were influential notably in British universities. Strachey wrote that 'a wise capitalist class will certainly not dispense with the serviceable mask of democracy, which has stood it in good stead, until no other course is open to it'. But, when no other course was open, and the capitalist class faced a real threat to its survival, it would sponsor fascist parties or turn the coercive weight of the state against the workers.[2] Thus democracy was a mask. Behind it lurked the coercive capitalist state. For the capitalists it was a useful mask. It softened the image of capitalist power. But in the end it was a dispensable mask. Strachey wrote of 'bourgeois democracy' thus:

> Capitalist democracies always turn out to be truly democratic so long as the workers vote for the capitalists, and not for one moment longer. For if the workers persist in voting for measures incompatible with the proper functioning of capitalism, the capitalists unhesitatingly scrap democracy and carry on their dictatorship without the assent of the workers.[3]

Strachey added that, even in Britain, this would happen because its existing imperfect democratic institutions were becoming more and more incompatible with capitalism.[4] It was certainly true that democracy in Britain was a protection for the propertied classes. It nurtured a civilized and free society that was at once too valuable to destroy and, for revolutionaries, too difficult to uproot. But, for democratic socialists, that was precisely the problem.

The arguments of those who foresaw civil war did not seem impossibly far fetched. Hugh Dalton, former Minister, was, by the standards of the time, far from being an extremist. He had been defeated in the rout of 1931 but was still a member of Labour's NEC. Dalton did not feel able to ignore the risk of resistance to a Labour victory.

> We are entitled to expect that . . . even vehement opponents of the Labour Party would, if defeated at the polls, behave with propriety and public spirit. If, however, this expectation is disappointed . . . it will be the duty of the new Government . . . to govern resolutely, and to take whatever steps are necessary to safeguard the national interests.[5]

Throughout Europe there were examples of democracy under challenge or actually destroyed by forces interpreted as having been created by capitalists to protect their property. There was fascism in Italy and Nazism in Germany. At the trial of those charged with starting the Reichstag fire, Georgi Dimitrov, a Bulgarian communist, had emerged as a hero for all those who cherished human freedom. He had insulted Göring to such good and public effect that in the end he was released. Hugh Gaitskell, during an academic year spent in Vienna in 1933–4, had been a helpless witness while the Austrian Chancellor Dolfuss employed armed force to destroy the socialist movement.[6] In 1939 in Spain, Franco, heavily assisted by Hitler and Mussolini, and by the 'non-intervention' of Britain and France, finally succeeded in suppressing the Spanish democratic republic after three years of civil war. There were serious threats to democracy in France. Everywhere democracy seemed to be in retreat.

Even in Britain there was the British Union of Fascists led by Sir Oswald Mosley, a renegade from both the Labour and the Conservative parties. It was of great advantage to the Marxists and communists that the destruction of democracy in civilized western European countries could be presented as examples of the way the ruling class protected its interests. Aneurin Bevan, who was not a stranger to oratorical extravagance, may nevertheless have believed what he was saying when he chivvied the Conservative benches in the House of Commons in April 1933:

> If we are allowed a large measure of liberty in this country, it is simply because we are not frightening [the capitalists] enough. When we frighten you sufficiently you will put us in gaol with exactly the same brutality [as the Nazis in Germany] ... Political toleration is a by-product of the complacency of the ruling class. When that complacency is disturbed there never was a more bloody-minded set of thugs than the British ruling class.[7]

The fighting of civil wars is less devastating contemplated from an armchair rather than on a battlefield. The Marxists did not seem too disturbed by the prospect and carefully presented the implications. To ensure that any civil war, once won, remained won, it would be necessary, they asserted, to establish a 'dictatorship of the proletariat' which would deny democracy to the defeated capitalists and to those who might be bemused by them into accepting capitalist arguments. Having won the war, only the proletariat would be permitted to enjoy the benefits of democracy. For them, indeed, it would be a higher form of democracy. They would be truly free whereas previously, under a façade of democracy, they were oppressed. Strachey offered a benign interpretation of the dictatorship of the proletariat:

we must face the fact that, for a period, the British ... workers will almost certainly be compelled to restrict the civil liberties of the dispossessed classes to an extent that these classes will consider outrageous. But even during that period the degree of liberty enjoyed by incomparably the greater part of the population will have been enormously extended. It will still be restricted and imperfect compared to the liberty which will be possible when a truly classless society will have emerged. But it will be incomparably fuller and richer than are those partial, if precious, liberties which we possess in Britain ... to-day.[8]

Thus socialism having inevitably arrived would be implacably defended. But the problem still remained. Democracy under socialism might be fuller and richer than under capitalism. But could socialism be achieved democratically?

The trouble with theories is that they can be undermined by events and by their own forecasts. Marxism, like other sciences, placed great emphasis on its power of prediction. Strachey refers confidently to the unique predictive power of Marxist economic theory.[9] What confidence could be reposed in predictions about the inevitability of socialism? Whereas its friends could point to Marxist predictions that had been borne out by events, its critics could point to others that had been falsified. The Marxist theory of the increasing immiseration, or pauperization, of the working class could be characterized as among the less fortunate forecasts in the history of science or even of economics. Between 1870 and 1938 real wages more than doubled.[10] It might not have seemed like it in the 1930s. It was, nevertheless, true. This was hardly pauperization. Economic imperialism, which, remarkably in view of his unique predictive power, Marx did not foresee, has been used as an excuse. It had delayed the pauperization of the masses in industrialized countries by enabling the capitalists to distribute crumbs from the table on which they counted their imperialist profits. Other predictions, falsified in the event, demonstrated that Marxism was no science. For example, it suffered from observation that, contrary to its central forecast, capitalism in Britain in the 1930s was recuperating, not dying. Unless the Soviet Union could be taken as an example, there was, apparently, no predestined march towards socialism powered either by the forces of history or by the contradictions and crises of capitalism. The fact that capitalism was not collapsing was a blow to the credibility of Marxism and hence to any theory of inevitability.

However persuasive Marxism might be as a theory, critics would look for better evidence of the inevitability of socialism. Before 1917 there was no example of a socialist society. Hence the interest in the writings and doings of Gerard Winstanley in the seventeenth century and of Robert Owen in the nineteenth. Whatever their failures, Winstanley and Owen had pointed the way. After 1917, evidence could be claimed. There was now the Soviet Union. Carrying the banner of Marxism, of scientific socialism, the Bolsheviks under Lenin won an historic success, the capture of the Tsarist state and empire. Did the October Revolution of 1917 provide support for Marxist theory? It happened in a backward country where even Marxists might have questioned whether the time was ripe for socialism. The victory of the Bolsheviks could more cogently be attributed not to inevitability but to Tsarist incompetence and the ravages of war.[11] Moreover the Bolshevik victory had certainly not been won democratically, rather in defiance of democracy. There was also reason to doubt whether what had developed after 1917 in the Soviet Union through victory in a civil war, and the imposition of a communist dictatorship, could legitimately be described as socialism. Particularly worrying was the entire absence of personal freedom. The interpretation of Soviet achievements became a source of controversy among socialists outside Russia who had retained, and cherished, freedom of speech and freedom of protest.

Supposedly, according to prescription, a dictatorship of the proletariat had been established in the Soviet Union. Some twenty years after the Russian revolution, the workers, therefore, should have been enjoying that enormously extended liberty that Strachey had claimed as their right. Unfortunately, that was not how it appeared to critical observers even among democratic socialists. There was no liberty of any kind. The communist rulers of the Soviet Union had established a dictatorship more efficient, and more terrible, than Tsarism had ever been. It was not the dictatorship of the proletariat but of the Soviet Communist party or even of a new Tsar, Joseph Stalin. By what definition was this socialism? Only, apparently, in that, having seized control of the state by force, the Bolsheviks had confiscated the assets of the rich, and even of the not so rich, without compensation. Industrial property was in the hands of the state. Agriculture was being forcibly collectivized. A series of Five Year Plans had been initiated to build the economic strength of the country.

Tyranny in the Soviet Union was the more readily condoned by western socialists because of their hatred for the preceding Tsarist tyranny. Some British socialists were prepared to allow the Soviet Union its claim to be a socialist society, and to make excuses for its abuse of human rights, perhaps for want of any other evidence that socialism was a practical objective. Their readiness to do so was supported by high authority in the form of Sidney and Beatrice Webb's *Soviet Communism: A New Civilization?* published in 1935. This authority became even more persuasive when, in a later edition, the question mark in the title was removed. There were others, more perceptive, who saw in the Soviet despotism such costs to personal liberty as to make it impossible to endorse its claim to be socialist. For them the Soviet Union proved nothing about the inevitability of socialism and nothing either about whether socialism could be won democratically.

Democratic socialists in Britain were warned but not disillusioned by observation of the Soviet Union. The Soviet Union could be regarded as a special case, the absence of civil rights attributable to Russian history. It was both an encouragement and a warning, an encouragement that socialism could be successful, because it was believed that at least economically it was successful, and a warning against totalitarianism. Socialism was still needed, but the example of the Soviet Union emphasized that it must be a democratic form of socialism. What was certain was that no guidance could be gathered from the Soviet experience as to the inevitability or even feasibility of socialism achieved through democratic processes in Britain. Could Marxism claim any other relevance to the British socialist dilemma?

Marxism was of importance in Britain, not because of the Communist party, but because of its influence on certain sections of the Labour party. That influence both reflected and reinforced doubts among some within the Labour party as to whether it was seriously intent on achieving socialism or whether its object was not merely a reformed capitalism. Strachey, in his Stalinist phase, described social democracy, in accordance with the doctrine then laid down from Moscow, as the servant of capitalism. He wrote that the future of social democracy would probably lie in opposition rather than in office. Nevertheless it still had a role, a despicable role, 'the role of the saviour of capitalism'.[12] The belief that there was too much truth in Strachey's attack grew stronger as the Labour party moved to the right after its unsatisfactory result in the 1935 General Election. Marxist influence was further fortified by Victor Gollancz's Left Book Club, established in 1936. The most prominent members of the Labour party who fell under Marxist influence were Sir Stafford Cripps, Aneurin Bevan and Harold Laski, though there was a Marxist flavour to much of Labour party argumentation stretching right across the Party. Doubts about the real commitment to socialism of the Labour party leadership led some to support the affiliation to the Labour party of the Communist party. The Communist party itself applied for affiliation. This was refused and its members were not allowed to become Labour party candidates. It was a sign of continuing doubts within the Labour party as to whether its advertised socialist faith could be taken at face value that it required a vigorous campaign by Herbert Morrison to ensure the exclusion.[13]

The British Communist party's main successes were in the trade unions, though its General Secretary, Harry Pollitt, exercised a rather wider influence due to the warmth of his personality and his considerable oratorical powers. On the left of the Labour party it was, despite the Moscow trials that began in July 1936, an added attraction, rather than a source of repulsion, that Pollitt could be regarded as speaking for the only socialist country, the socialist sixth of the world. The immense size of the Soviet Union seemed to elicit enthusiasm even when there were considerable doubts about what was going on within it. After 1936, the Franco revolt in Spain refuelled Pollitt's oratory with a subject which raised deeper feelings even than the regimes in Germany and Italy. Here was another democracy fighting desperately against fascism without the support to which it was entitled from democratic Britain or, for that matter, democratic France. The reaction of the Labour party leadership to the civil war in Spain seemed weak and unconvincing and reinforced doubts about its socialist virility.

Confronted by the rise of fascism, one consolation, at least for Marxists and those influenced by them, was that, in accordance with the theory of inevitability, they were convinced that fascism was the last stage of a dying capitalism. Gaitskell himself wrote in 1938 that fascism had become the last refuge of a crumbling economic system.[14] On the other hand, socialists, such as Gaitskell, while sharing a Marxist analysis of the nature of fascism, found in the tragedy of western Europe further confirmation of the value of British democracy and of the importance of defending it. They continued to believe that the existence in Britain of democratic institutions created the right environment for a peaceful transition to socialism.

DEMOCRATIC MARXISM

The view that democratic institutions were becoming incompatible with capitalism was held in this country not just by the Communist party, and not just by John Strachey, but by Harold Laski. He was certainly the most prolific, and among the most influential, socialist writers of the period. His influence extended into the USA, where his widely syndicated columns in the American press often embarrassed the Labour leadership. Laski struggled with the question whether there was a democratic route to socialism in Britain. He wanted there to be, but he was by no means sure that there could be. At times he was explicit that there was no such route.

> What looms before us is a battle for the possession of the state-power. What is now clear is the vital fact that the class-relations of our society have become incompatible with the maintenance of social peace ... in the choice between peaceful transformation, and the maintenance of privilege at the cost of conflict, the owners of property now, as in an earlier day, are prepared rather to fight for their legal privilege than to give way. That attitude is shown not merely by the barbaric overthrow of democratic institutions in Fascist countries. It is shown even more clearly by the resistance to social reform in the United States and Great Britain, and by the overt hostility of the Right to democracy in France.[15]

There were two ways in which this battle might be started. Either, as in Russia, the revolutionary proletariat would rise up against the capitalist system. Or, alternatively, the proletariat, through their political organizations, would win power in Parliament and then be challenged by a capitalist military uprising. Either way, battle loomed.

If democratic institutions were becoming incompatible with capitalism, socialism had become a prerequisite of the survival of democracy. There remained the question whether it was possible to progress to socialism along a democratic road when the prevailing social order was capitalist. Laski warns that 'The technical conditions under which modern government is carried on make it at least as possible that the outcome of war will be a reversion to barbarism as the victory of the working-class.'[16] The implication is that the achievement of socialism through civil war rather than through democratic processes is as likely to destroy as to preserve democracy. No one person more perfectly encapsulated the dilemmas of democratic socialism, seen from a Marxist standpoint, than Laski. In his book *The State in Theory and Practice*, published in 1935, he advances four propositions which seem consistent only on the basis that socialism, however desirable, is almost certainly beyond reach. The first of Laski's propositions is that capitalism is doomed by its own internal contradictions. 'I believe that we have reached a phase in the history of capitalism when this contradiction between class-structure and potential productivity is insoluble in terms of the present social order.'[17] The second is that capitalists, though doomed, will never relinquish power voluntarily.

> The conclusion that we have reached is the grave one that in a society where the instruments of production are privately owned the main fact of significance is the struggle for the possession of the state-power between the class which owns those instruments and that which is denied access to the benefits of that ownership. The conclusion implies that the state is always biased in the interest of the former; and those in whose interests the authority is exercised will not surrender their advantage unless they are compelled to do so.[18]

These first two propositions are well founded in Marxism. But then comes the discontinuity which takes Laski away from Marxism and towards democracy, and which makes it understandable that the unadulterated Marxist, Strachey, should have hurtfully characterized him as an 'English liberal'.[19] Laski's third proposition is that in Britain successful revolution is improbable. '[I]t seems to me clear that an unconstitutional conquest of the state by the workers, through insurrection, for instance, or by the use of such a weapon as the General Strike, is bound to fail so long as the army remains loyal to the state in being, and the normal machinery of government remains in effective operation.'[20] Which leaves us with his fourth proposition, that constitutional methods should be pressed as far as they will go. 'I believe that it is the duty of the citizen to exhaust the means placed at his disposal by the constitution of the state before resorting to revolution.'[21] Thus, to complete the circle, revolution is not ruled out even though its success is improbable. But democratic socialism is also improbable because the owners of the instruments of production will not relinquish power unless compelled to do so, presumably by revolution.

Not content with his pessimistic scenario, Laski introduces another worrying question, whether socialism could be achieved by slow stages. He was doubtful. 'If [a socialist government] goes slowly, it will suffer from all the difficulties which confront any government which tries, upon the basis of capitalist postulates, to effect their piecemeal transformation ... If it proceeds rapidly – and the case for rapid action is overwhelmingly strong – it is likely to meet with sabotage and resistance.'[22]

Whatever one thinks of Laski's analysis, history has certainly demonstrated how difficult it is to achieve socialism by slow stages. Desperately trying to navigate around the obstacles to progress which he has himself identified, Laski concedes that, to achieve the consent necessary for radical change without a reversion to barbarism, a price would have to be paid.

> This consists in guaranteeing to the class which owns the instruments of production the continuance of the privileges such ownership entails at least long enough to reconcile them to the new social order ... There is everything to be said, on grounds of expediency, against the kind of confiscation which would provoke a possessing class to conflict; it is amply worth while to pay a considerable price for their willing acceptance of a new social order.[23]

This was the direct opposite of Joseph Chamberlain's famous question, 'what ransom will property pay?' Socialism would need to pay the ransom of compensation. But why should capitalists, greedy for power as well as for money, accept the offer?

For good measure Laski adds, 'It is as foolish to ask the Labour Party to administer a capitalist society as to ask a Nonconformist to be Pontiff of the Roman Catholic Church.'[24] The cry that the Labour party had not come into existence to manage capitalism was common form at any Labour rally. It was a message that could be relied upon to gather in the cheers. Attlee himself wrote that 'The plain fact is that a Socialist Party cannot hope to make a success of administering the Capitalist system because it does not believe in it.'[25] Yet, if constitutional methods were to be pressed as far as they would go, there would be bound to be a period, probably a long one, during which a Labour government would be administering a capitalist society. The social revolution would have to be accomplished without a political revolution. Labour would have to realize, and would indeed eventually realize, that there was no sudden discontinuity between capitalism and socialism, no single action that would transform the one social system into the other, no single moment of time when it would be possible to say that capitalism had been left behind and socialism had been reached. Sidney Webb and the Fabians had spoken of 'the inevitability of gradualness'.[26] It was a warming concept. The only trouble with it was that Fabian inevitability could no more be guaranteed than Marxist inevitability. The inescapable paradox of gradualism was that the management of capitalism would be one of the prime responsibilities of a socialist party victorious in a general election, and that it could not afford to do it badly. Unless a Labour government could manage capitalism successfully, it would not sustain the confidence of the voters and thus would be unable to lead the country on to socialism. If, as Attlee suggested, that meant believing in capitalism, that would simply be another of the paradoxes of gradualism.

As revolution was both improbable and undesirable, as gradualism and conformity to constitutional processes was inevitable, Labour would have to learn to love capitalism. It would be many years, even decades, before any Labour leader would be prepared to hint at that message.[27] Meanwhile the left would disparage a succession of Labour governments for managing capitalism whereas the only justifiable criticism was that it was being managed badly.[28]

IRREVERSIBLE PROGRESS TO SOCIALISM

Democracy presented other difficulties to the ardent socialist. Winning one or two elections might not be enough. If the socialist programme of one government could be reversed by the Conservative programme of another, if each time Labour won it would have to start again from scratch, how could society ever be transformed unless, remarkably, a Labour government was more continuously popular than governments usually are? Even the planning apparatus might be wound up if the socialists lost an election, and would then have to be recreated. As Bryan Magee has put it, 'the consistent pursuit of long-term goals is made virtually impossible by the fact that the government itself can be changed, and its policies dropped or reversed, every few years'.[29] There was the simple-minded idea that because the working class was in a majority among the electorate, and socialism was obviously in its interest, Labour could be confident of winning election after election. Experience, notably the elections of 1931 and 1935, had proved this expectation to be invalid. The working class showed itself annoyingly resistant to socialist propaganda. There was the dispiriting example of the Liberal government of 1906. Lloyd George's radical programme, which had so offended the House of Lords, but which should have received an enthusiastic welcome from the working class, had not saved the Liberals from a serious setback at the elections of 1910. Partly because of economic recession, there was such a drop in Liberal support that Prime Minister Asquith had become dependent for his majority on the small group of Labour MPs and on Irish nationalists. The rich, apparently, were more ready to rally in defence of their privileges than the poor in insistence on their claims.

Hugh Dalton was, nevertheless, confident. He was undisturbed by the tergiversations of the Marxist Laski.

I believe that here [in Britain] it is possible to make a peaceful, orderly and smooth transition to a better social order; and that, with a working Labour majority in the House of Commons, five years of resolute Government could lay the foundations of that order. Thereafter, at the next election, the people would be free to choose whether or not the work of Socialist construction should continue.[30]

At any rate, it was clear that progress to socialism was far from inevitable. The electorate would decide at each stage whether they wanted the process to continue. The play of parties could lead, not to socialism but to the ding-dong society, socialistic in one Parliament, capitalist in the next. Dalton did not much fear this. He believed that, provided a Labour government acted judiciously, its legislation would not be repealed by a successor Conservative government and that, therefore, a subsequent Labour government would not have to start again from scratch.[31] Evan Durbin, economist and philosopher of democratic socialism, was later to write that 'the element of reversal or repeal is very limited in our political history'.[32] But attempts to create a socialist society were also rare. Past experience was hardly a guarantee of continuity if one form of society was being replaced by another.

There was thus little firm ground to support the theory that developed among democratic socialists, an implicit theory of socialist irreversibility under which each mile on the way to socialism represented an advance securely consolidated. The theory was based primarily on the pressures generated by democracy. The great majority of the relatively disadvantaged would demand reforms which would be impossible, for political reasons, to reverse. These reforms would irreparably damage the operations of *laissez-faire* capitalism. Socialism would be the cure. Socialist planners would, with the aid of nationalization, raise national prosperity, the mass of the population would benefit and there would be no desire to return to Conservative rule and, with it, the possible reversal of socialist measures. Evidence for the theory was found in the reforms that had taken place, discussed in the next chapter, and in the defensive reaction of capitalism which was producing monopoly, cartelization and even, among some leading industrialists, support for a measure of nationalization. As will be seen in the next chapter, there was widespread acceptance, far outside socialist circles, of nationalization as a preferred method of treatment for certain industrial ills and for a role for the state in managing the economy.

In fact, only limited comfort could be derived from these developments. There were two problems if they were to be relied on as evidence of the possibility of democratic progress to socialism. The first was that planning and nationalization might not produce the benefits expected and therefore might well be reversible. Economic planning had not been tried in peacetime and the benefits forecast were therefore speculative. Moreover, support from non-socialists for nationalization in certain sectors of the economy did not imply support for it over the wide stretch of the economy contemplated by socialists. There were certainly industries, particularly coal and the utilities, that could be nationalized without desperate opposition, sometimes even with business support, provided there was adequate compensation. But when, as required by the socialist programme, there would be an attempt to extend nationalization beyond coal and the utilities, the battle would wage more fiercely and the reversal of measures of nationalization became a distinct possibility. There was to be an example, after the second world war, in the successive nationalization, denationalization, renationalization and privatization of steel. This was not a process which increased the competitiveness of the British economy. Nor was it an example of democracy at its best. The country was saved from further excesses only by the moderation of both the main political parties, one tentative in its approach to socialism, the other tentative in its unwinding of socialism. The outcome was not a socialist society but an inflationary society, persistently in debt.

The second problem was that, although some reforms might, under democratic pressure, prove irreversible, that did not necessarily apply to all reform, particularly in a socialist direction. Even if there was, for the moment, a degree of consensus on the economy, that consensus certainly did not extend to an even more important feature of the socialist prospectus, equality. The ownership of private property bestowed power and wealth. If there was to be greater equality, there must be greater equality in the ownership of property. The capitalists must be deprived, if not of all their property, then at least of that property that enabled them to live conspicuously at levels far beyond those of the great majority of the population, and of that property, in industry, that enabled them to exercise power over their fellow citizens. The preferred method of achieving greater equality, when it was not nationalization, was through the taxation system. Douglas Jay would have been ready in principle to tax away all *rentier* income except income from savings earned during a working life.[33] Jay, indeed, believed that the abolition of *rentier* incomes, rather than nationalization, was the essence of socialism. 'Socialists have been mistaken in making ownership of the means of production instead of ownership of inherited property the test of socialization . . . It is not the ownership of the means of production as such, but ownership of large inherited incomes, which ought to be eliminated.'[34]

Even if Labour governments did not go as far as Jay would have wished, it was unlikely that equalizing taxation would pass the scrutiny of an incoming Conservative government without substantial amendment. Socialists always tended to overlook the risk to their plans inherent in capital taxes. Socialist governments can introduce them. But they are slow acting. Inheritance taxes, for example, operate only at death and large property owners may not time their deaths conveniently for socialist purposes. If, by the time the taxes bite, there is a Conservative government, they are likely to be repealed or so amended as to make avoidance easy. So capital taxes only work towards greater equality if socialist governments can ensure their own survival. It is understandable that Aneurin Bevan wanted twenty-five years of Labour governments to secure the creation of a socialist society.[35] Unlike Tony Blair, with his more modest ambitions, a second term would not be enough. It would be remarkable if an electorate, with a tendency to boredom and the accumulation of grievances, was that tolerant. Laski had once had his own answer to the problem. He had wanted from the Conservatives assurances of irreversibility. In *The Road to Serfdom*, Friedrich von Hayek made much of the fact that, in 1932, a year after the fall of the Mac-Donald Labour government, Laski had argued that, for the preservation of Parliamentary democracy, a Labour government would require guarantees from the Conservative party that it would not repeal Labour legislation should Labour be defeated at an ensuing election.[36] This was not, and could not be, the position of the Labour party. Yet it left open the question how a Labour government, using constitutional means, could keep itself in power for the long period required actually to achieve socialism.

THE DECAY OF CAPITALISM UNDER DEMOCRACY

There was a further, and apparently powerful, reason why socialist thinkers might believe that democratic socialism was a practical project in Britain. They were persuaded that capitalism was in irreversible decline. As socialism was the only available alternative, it was bound to be tried. Marxists believed that capitalism was in irreversible decline owing to its internal contradictions. Non-Marxist socialists attributed the decline to the pressures of democracy coupled with an inability on the part of the capitalists to see where their real interests lay. Democracy and myopia would combine to prohibit the necessary reforms to capitalism which might just save it. As usual with Harold Laski, he agreed both with the Marxists that the decline was irreversible and with the non-Marxist socialists that a combination of democracy, and settled ways of thinking, prohibited the capitalists from taking the measures that might just save them. There are conditions, he tells us, 'which, by their inherent nature, limit the power of reason to influence the minds of men'.[37] He adds that 'The inability of capitalists to accept postulates different from their own is born of the situation in which they find themselves.'[38] On this ground he ruled as politically impossible both the interventionist measures to save capitalism being developed by John Maynard Keynes and the retreat towards *laissez-faire* being advocated by economists such as Lionel Robbins. In the end it all worked to the same end. Whether it was democracy, or the ineluctable forces of the economy, or the inflexibility of the capitalist mind, capitalism was doomed. Socialism would get its chance because capitalism was in the process of burying itself beneath a mound of contradictions and incomprehension.

THE POLITICS OF DEMOCRATIC SOCIALISM

The most eloquent exponent of this case for democratic socialism was Evan Durbin. Durbin was a lecturer at the London School of Economics. Born in 1906, he became an adviser to Attlee during the war, in 1945 a Labour MP, Parliamentary Private Secretary to the Chancellor of the Exchequer Hugh Dalton, and then junior Minister. Regarded widely as being of the highest promise, a future Cabinet minister, Durbin was drowned in 1948 off the Cornish coast while saving the lives of a daughter and another child who had got into difficulties. Hugh Gaitskell was a close friend and his sense of loss at Durbin's tragic death remained with him for the rest of his life. Durbin's book, *The Politics of Democratic Socialism*, written in 1938-9, was published in 1940, after the outbreak of the second world war. Gaitskell and Tawney were among the dedicatees. Comparing Durbin with Gaitskell, Pimlott writes, 'Durbin was the better economist and philosopher, writing a series of important works that related political and economic thought to socialist objectives.'[39] Even in 1940, perhaps the most critical year in Britain's history, *The Politics of Democratic Socialism* made a great impression among those involved in socialist controversies. It was one of the foundation texts of British democratic socialism, exceeding in eloquence, conviction and depth of thought anything from any other contemporary British source. It encapsulates democratic socialism as it had developed after the further General Election defeat of 1935. It survived as an influence on Hugh Gaitskell well into the 1950s, in other words well after the experience of the 1945–51 Labour government.[40] When Malenkov, the former Soviet leader, visited Britain in March 1956, Gaitskell presented him with a copy, not a present the recipient was likely to appreciate.[41] *The Politics of Democratic Socialism* was not superseded by Anthony Crosland's *Future of Socialism*. Crosland's book was a reinterpretation of the meaning of socialism. Durbin had no wish to reinterpret socialism. He was an unrepentant centralizer and nationalizer. Durbin's object was to demonstrate that socialism could be achieved by democratic means through a series of cautiously calculated measures taken in more than one Parliament.

Durbin's argument for socialism was not founded in class hatred or jealousy. The problem, as he saw it, the reason that capitalism was in such trouble, was that it was no longer able to sustain the burdens placed upon it by democracy. It was democracy that had made socialism a practical necessity. In a democracy, the demand for greater equality and greater security was bound to force the hands of government. There had once been something which socialists called '*laissez-faire* capitalism'. Douglas Jay defined it as a system in which the exchange of goods and the accumulation, ownership and inheritance of property, including the means of production, are privately and not publicly controlled.[42] *Laissez-faire* was not an optional extra. It was an indispensable component of a successful capitalism. As Harold Laski put it, 'In a capitalist society, a rigorous policy of *laissez-faire* is the condition of economic well-being.'[43] For these socialists, *laissez-faire* had been the active ingredient of the great period of capitalism. Then it was brave, competitive and expanding. But it was also cruel. Under *laissez-faire* capitalism, property rights were absolute, carrying no obligations, and the capitalists could behave as they wished, relying on Adam Smith's invisible hand to reconcile their private interests with the interests of the community generally. Clearly, the invisible hand was not looking after the poor, the unemployed and the disadvantaged. Democracy was now compelling governments to take account of the human consequences of *laissez-faire* capitalism. Durbin wrote, 'Expansion is . . . the great virtue of capitalism; inequality and insecurity are its greatest vices.'[44] *Laissez-faire* capitalism was incompatible with the democratic demand for greater equality and greater security which was bound, in the end, to prevail. *Laissez-faire* capitalism was also incompatible with the planning necessary to prevent or mitigate the depressions typical of the capitalist trade cycle.

It had frequently been urged against greater equality that the wealth of the rich was necessary to fund future growth. It was an argument that Dalton had attacked and mocked. 'We must burn down the house of equality, in order to roast the pig of thrift.'[45] In any case, the facts demonstrated that thrift, such as it was, was producing little money for investment. Now Durbin turned the attack to argue that the democratic demand for greater equality, and the higher and differential taxation required to satisfy the demand, had implications for the success of the capitalist system. For what little had been accomplished, there was a heavy price to pay. As a result of meeting the demands of democracy, even inadequately, the savings from which the rich had earlier funded economic growth had diminished and even disappeared. Progressive taxation 'strikes heavily at the funds available for capital accumulation and economic progress.'[46] Property in private hands had lost its single justification.

> The institution [of property] is worse than indefensible – it is useless . . . And, with the withering away of the savings of the rich, the only rational justification for inequality in the distribution of property has finally disappeared. The propertied classes are now parasitic in the final sense that their income is purely a distributive share, and contributes nothing to the increase of production.[47]

This did not mean that capitalism would collapse as a result of its own internal contradictions, as the Marxists believed. Nor did it mean that growth would necessarily come to an end. The *rate* of growth must, though, be expected to diminish at a time when faster economic growth was required to meet the needs of the people for a higher standard of living and for greater equality. Democracy was undermining *laissez-faire* and with it was undermining capitalism. No longer could capitalism flourish as it had done under *laissez-faire*. *Laissez-faire* capitalism was failing as an engine of economic expansion. With the waning of *laissez-faire*, due to the pressures of democracy, the élan had gone out of capitalism. If fast expansion was to be resumed, capitalism must be replaced by socialism. There was a need for a new system of society the success of which was not dependent on *laissez-faire* and which could cope with demands for greater equality and greater security. Socialism had become an economic necessity, imposed by the consequences of the democracy. Socialism was to be a remedy as much for the problems thrown up by democracy as for the evils of capitalism. All this was argued despite the fact that, as Beveridge was to put it in his Report, 'the real wealth per head in a Britain of shrunken oversea investments and lost export markets, counting in all her unemployed, was materially higher in 1938 than in 1913'.[48]

Thus for Durbin, but also, as we will see, for Aneurin Bevan, the only answer to the conundrum how to reconcile democracy with the need for faster economic growth was the planned, centralized, socialist economy in which planning and, to an increasing degree, ownership of industry were in the hands of the state. As Durbin put it:

> We wish to use the power of the State to establish expansionist policies within the growing socialized sector of the economy; to restore and main-tain a high level of active accumulation; to moderate insecurity still further; to curb the cyclical oscillations of economic activity by a control of the income and investment position of the community; and to secure much greater equality in the distribution of the product of industry. It is only possible to do this by the supersession of private property as the seat of industrial control, as distinct from property as a form of personal reserve.[49]

The method by which the government would exercise direct control over production was nationalization.

Durbin believed that capitalism was being undermined not just by democracy but by the trade unions. He noted that there had been an ossification of the labour market under the influence of the increasingly powerful trade unions. He had little doubt that the increase in the average level of unemployment in Great Britain through all the phases of the trade cycle during the previous fifteen years was largely due to the rigidity of money wages.[50] This was a point which would have been entirely endorsed by Harold Macmillan, a Tory then seated on the government backbenches.[51] Here there was agreement between the Conservative, the democratic socialist and the Marxist. Strachey noted that powerful trade unions had to some extent succeeded in creating monopolies in certain types and categories of labour and so in obtaining monopoly prices for it.[52] Presumably Strachey, and indeed Durbin, thought that central planning would prevent the exploitation of the community by public sector trade unions. Durbin was always concerned that the self-interest of trade unions was in conflict with the interests of society generally. Socialism was to be a remedy for the power of trade unions as well as for the sickness of capitalism and the awkwardness of democracy. It was implicit in Durbin's argument that the battle for socialism could involve a battle with the unions. In that prospect lay the possibility of conflict between the trade union movement and a Labour government.

Could the trends in capitalism that Durbin identifies, and which were leading capitalism to its doom, be reversed? In his view, democracy would make that impossible. There is something in Durbin of the Marxist. Like the Marxists, he identifies historical trends which will neither change their direction nor abate their strength.[53] He criticizes such modern representatives of the classical school as Professors Mises, Hayek and Robbins for their wish to use the power of the state to free enterprise, to protect competition and so to restore to capitalism its earlier elasticity and power of spectacular expansion. He found it extremely difficult to see how such a policy was compatible with the maintenance of political democracy.[54] For example, could anyone imagine that the principle that the rich should be taxed more than proportionately could be reversed without overwhelming popular opposition?[55] He concludes that the restoration of a free-enterprise economy was inconsistent with the maintenance of responsible government. 'Freedom of enterprise seems incompatible with freedom.'[56] Socialists, in their writings at this time, appeared to believe in the inevitability of socialism even if it is not the mechanistic inevitability of Marxism. The appearance arises from their strong conviction that capitalism was in terminal decline and therefore must be replaced.

Durbin accepted that, under the impact of democracy, capitalism was in process of transformation. Capitalist governments were attempting to alleviate the condition of the people. Even under capitalism, government influence over the economy had increased, was increasing and was likely to grow still further.[57] 'In Great Britain and America ... the most fundamental description of the whole process of transformation is ... that it represents *a short-sighted adaptation of the institutions of laisser-faire capitalism to the needs of ordinary men and women.*'[58] Durbin assumed that what was being done to transform capitalism could not be enough. But it was too early to assume that capitalism had lost every recourse. The irony would be that the capitalist and Conservative mind would prove far more flexible than the Socialist mind. The former proved adaptable to challenges and ready to break from the philosophy of *laissez-faire* in defence of property. The latter, locked into a straitjacket of planning and nationalization, found change highly disagreeable despite much disillusioning experience.

Thus Durbin's argument was that democracy was creating demands which capitalism could not possibly meet. If this was in fact correct, and socialism was in truth the answer, its probability, if not its inevitability, did become stronger. The advance of civilization, of morality, of science, together with the advance of the masses and the selection of social priorities, would all propel society towards socialism whether it willed it consciously or not. Yet what Durbin had so far demonstrated, if he had demonstrated anything, was simply the inevitability of the decline of capitalism, not the inevitability of its supersession by socialism. Durbin was aware of the distinction. For Durbin, socialism is not inevitable. It is probable but only on certain conditions. First, to be socialism at all, it must be democratic. Secondly, it must be approached with the utmost caution, with the tolerance and restraint that alone make democracy workable.

In *The Politics of Democratic Socialism*, Durbin combined his advocacy of democratic socialism with a savage attack on dictatorship, whether fascist or communist. In his onslaught on Stalinist Russia, he was not to be put off by persiflage about the dictatorship of the proletariat. It was a dictatorship, cruel and repellent as all dictatorships must be. Some socialists were ambivalent about the Soviet Union, but not Durbin. Durbin knew no compromise. The Soviet Union was not socialist because it was not democratic. In Durbin's view, there was no socialism without democracy. Democracy was of the very essence of socialism.

> [T]he democratic method is not only essential for the achievement of socialism, but ... it is part of that achievement. In so far as we are democratic we are already, in some degree, socialist; and to betray democracy is to betray socialism ... It is not that democracy is the pleasantest, or most efficacious, or most certain method of achieving socialism, but that it is the only method ...[59]

Durbin would have agreed with Anthony Crosland that 'one of the errors the Marxists always made ... was absurdly to underrate the socio-economic consequences of continued political democracy'.[60] Durbin rejected the slur passed on British democracy by Marxists when they described it as 'bourgeois democracy', that is, by implication, democracy only for the rich. He was prepared, in defence of the democratic principle, to outlaw those parties which, if they achieved power, would deny the benefits of democracy to their opponents.[61] He denied to fascists and communists, as of right, the privileges of democratic society. Only those had the *right* to share in a democracy who were committed to the preservation of democracy. There had to be collective security among all democrats against the aggression of authoritarian minorities.[62] It was a view no doubt impressed upon him by the fate of the Weimar Republic in Germany.

Durbin was clear that, if socialism required the violent overthrow of the existing democratic system of government, the costs would be greater than any possible benefits. He knew that, if there was civil war, democracy would perish and the essence of socialism would perish with it. Even if the socialists won, socialism would have died with the war because, in all probability, democracy would have died with the war. Given the natural aggressiveness of man, democracy could only be a slow growth. Once established, it was a precious plant whose survival should in no way be endangered, certainly not by an over-hasty advance towards socialism. 'It is no wonder ... that democracy is difficult to establish. It requires toleration over the whole range of possible disagreement.'[63]

Laski had, at the end of his convolutions, chosen the democratic path because there was no realistic alternative. Durbin chose it as a matter of socialist principle. Nevertheless, Durbin employed arguments of realism as well as of principle. He insisted that revolution was neither practical nor in the interests of the working class. With the working class becoming richer, and with the stabilizing fact of a growing middle class, revolution was an impractical policy for a socialist party. The conclusion Durbin did not reach was that, if the only socialism is democratic socialism, there can be no such thing as socialism. That was a thought too far for a socialist in the 1930s.

The spectre of civil war

Durbin by no means rejected the possibility of civil war. He feared that it could occur even in Britain despite its centuries of civil peace, its long established Parliamentary system, and the readiness to compromise evidenced normally by the principal parties in the state. His study of the nature of man led him to fear its aggressiveness. He recalled the Irish Home Rule crisis before the first world war, which had almost led to civil war. It was an incident that shaped much of the political thinking of the time because it showed the fragility of Parliamentary democracy. If a reminder was needed it had been provided by the recent publication of George Dangerfield's *The Strange Death of Liberal England*, in which the Irish crisis plays a starring role. The Asquith government, under pressure from its Irish allies upon whom it depended for a majority in the House of Commons, had offered self-government to Ireland including Ulster, though Ulster was predominantly, though far from exclusively, Protestant. It was the inclusion of Ulster that threatened civil war. It was questionable whether the civil government could rely on the army to obey orders. Officers had been given the opportunity to resign their commissions so as to free themselves of the duty of obeying orders if they involved imposing the Asquith policy on Ulster. They took advantage of the offer in large numbers. The incident entered history as the Mutiny at the Curragh, an army barracks outside Dublin. Extensive gun running armed a force of Ulster Volunteers. All this was encouraged by the Tory opposition. The Conservative party seemed willing to contemplate civil war. As Dangerfield puts it, 'the Tory mind . . . did concoct nothing less than a rebellion in those years'.[64] The Asquith government retreated. To the disgust of Irish nationalists, who began to arm themselves, Asquith decided that Ulster would be excluded from the Irish self-government legislation. With the outbreak of the first world war, the Home Rule legislation was suspended in the interests of national unity. Dangerfield comments that 'but for the providential intervention of a world war, [England's Parliamentary structure] would certainly have collapsed'.[65]

This narrow escape dominated Durbin's mind. The country, he noted, had been taken to the brink. Perhaps the Conservatives had been exasperated beyond endurance by their defeats over Lloyd George's 1909 budget and the powers of the House of Lords. But Irish self-government, even including Ulster, presented no threat to the economic interests of the capitalist class. If, even without economic interests being menaced, relations between the political parties could break down to such an extent that civil war loomed, Durbin did not feel able to deny that the introduction of socialism over the opposition of the capitalist class might also lead to civil war. 'I do not think that there is any competent judge of the British political tradition, and of the distribution of power between classes, who doubts that a programme of action aiming at the rapid destruction of economic inequality – in, say, the lifetime of a single Parliament – would provoke civil war.'[66] Durbin's solution to the conundrum was to insist that socialism must be introduced only slowly and by stages. No single stage should so challenge the interests of the capitalist class that they would turn to war in an attempt to undo it. Never should a socialist government introduce any measures that might provoke armed resistance. He recognized that this condition, that the opposition should not be driven to armed resistance, set 'a limit upon the pace of change – beyond which the programme must not go'.[67]

It will never be known whether there was ever any real danger of civil war in Britain arising either from the existence of a socialist movement or from social discontent. That there was such a danger was not an obsession of Durbin's alone. The Labour party, in government, has never thought it wise to take such measures as might threaten armed resistance, either from native good sense, or following Durbin's advice, or out of a perception that the working people of Britain are not revolutionary by instinct and that they would, as Durbin indeed warned, desert any government that was so foolish as to provoke it.[68] Labour governments have wisely always rejected extreme measures, often thereby inciting dissatisfaction within their own ranks. It was, in any case, beyond the bounds of political possibility to nationalize in one Parliament all the country's major industries. It could not be done as a matter of Parliamentary time if democratic procedures were to be respected. Labour governments have also been cautious in the redistribution of income. High tax rates have been levied but always in ways that allowed escape routes to those well advised.

Moderation as a policy

Such moderation had another consequence. It followed from Durbin's analysis – as it had, unnoticed, from Laski's – that if socialism was to be introduced by stages, if the wilder resolutions of Labour party conferences were to be ignored, if nationalization in the first instance was to be limited to areas where there was in fact some cross-party consensus, a Labour government would face the task of managing capitalism. It would be inescapable.

Democracy, however, was not to be taken as an excuse for unnecessary delay. For all the reasons explained earlier, the road to socialism must be the democratic not the revolutionary road. That was the road ahead if the desires of the people were to be met. But, to be effective in the role that socialists allocated to it, government must be powerful. Democratic socialists were inclined to become impatient of democratic delay. It was an impatience stimulated in part by the desire to make the most of a Parliamentary majority in pressing forward with socialist legislation; in part by concern that democracy should be at least as efficient as the dictatorships on the continent. Hugh Dalton exclaimed, 'A slow and lumbering Parliamentary procedure, checking all rapid action, is not of the essence of democracy.' Nor should there be any change in the first-past-the-post system for Parliamentary elections, not even the Alternative Vote which the MacDonald government had tried to enact under Liberal pressure. The only changes should be to deprive certain voters, such as university graduates, of undemocratic privileges such as a second vote, and to abolish the House of Lords.[69] These were views entirely shared by Durbin. 'Any constitutional device that weakens Government – such as proportional representation, or the alternative vote, or uncompromising party programmes – must be sacrificed, by those who believe in the democratic method, to the overriding necessity of maintaining a powerful executive government.'[70] Durbin believed that governments must be democratically elected but that the democracy should then leave the responsibility to the government that had been elected. Government was too serious a matter, especially when reconnoitring the road to socialism, to permit the intervention of those not well informed technically about the complexities of government.

Durbin's concept of the leading role of Labour party experts in the management of the economy was unpleasantly close to the Communist party's view of its leading role in the Soviet Union. It followed the Webbs and their belief in expert administrators. We would not have found Durbin recommending a referendum as the answer to any problem of democratic consent. Nor did Durbin accept that a planned centralized economy managed, and increasingly owned, by the state involved any dangers to personal liberty. On the contrary, it would enhance personal liberty. As a result, he never examined the tensions that could exist between political democracy and the extensive programme of nationalization and planning that he had in mind. Yet a combination of central planning with massive nationalization is itself a kind of dictatorship. There was an implicit assumption that so bad were conditions under capitalism that, in order to be rid of it, people would willingly accept the extraordinary centralization of power that Durbin was advocating. It required heavy reliance on British traditions of Parliamentary government and personal freedom to believe that they could absorb, without loss, the consequences of Durbin's centralization.

The form of Parliamentary democracy existing in Britain was very attractive to socialists generally and not just to Durbin. The particular characteristic that appealed was the absence of a written constitution such as is found in 'less fortunate nations'.[71] Bevan obviously felt that the absence of a written constitution made it easier to introduce socialist measures. 'The British constitution, with its adult suffrage, exposes all rights and privileges, properties and powers, to the popular will. The only checks are those that arise from a sense of justice and social propriety.'[72] He showed no appreciation of the fact that this placed in the House of Commons a most terrifying power, highly dangerous to political liberty, and that it was not satisfactory that the only defence against the use of that power should be 'a sense of justice and social propriety'.

The Durbin programme

Durbin's own programme for a Labour government certainly met his own criterion that it should not risk provoking armed resistance. It had a great deal in common with the actual programme of the Attlee government after 1945. It concentrated above all on what he called 'socialization measures', measures, that is, that would strengthen the economic power of the state. He was looking for success through planning, and planning implied that the state must have power. Thus Durbin proposed the nationalization, with full compensation, of coal, electricity supply, transport, iron and steel. In addition, he wanted power to control the lending activities of the commercial banks.[73] The success of the Attlee government in avoiding civil disturbance confirms Durbin's judgement that nothing in the nationalization programme would incite rebellion, which was not to say that it would be universally popular. It was not too provocative a programme and those who might be provoked, principally the mine owners, were unlikely to have allies. The mine owners were probably the least popular element among the propertied classes, and no other members of the capitalist class were likely to rise in their support. Much that was to be nationalized was already in some form of public ownership, for example municipal ownership. There was to be full compensation. That was the price to be paid for social peace, but there were arguments for it other than that it was necessitated by a threat to social peace.

Durbin's programme differed, however, from that of the Attlee government in three significant respects. The first difference, and the most important, was that Durbin wished to avoid for the time being anything significant by way of additional social expenditure. He had, no doubt, noted the priority given to investment over consumption in the Soviet Union. For the Labour party too, the economy must, in his view, come first. He argued that the democratic socialist parties:

> should be willing to place further ameliorative measures in their order of priority after, and not before, the socialization of industry – or, to put the same point in a more extreme form, that they should be willing to reduce their social service proposals to the minimum consistent with the retention of political power in order to pursue more actively the transfer of industrial ownership.[74]

Durbin grossly exaggerated the benefits, if any, that would accrue from the socialization of industry. But, as an economist, he did not believe that the economy could yet be burdened with additional social expenditures without damage to economic growth. He recognized that this 'means abandoning the hope of rapid social betterment for some considerable time'. The electorate must be educated. '[T]he people at large must be made to think about, and care for, something less immediate than better housing and family allowances.'[75]

He understood that what he was bravely advocating would be extremely unpopular in a party, and among an electorate, that was looking to social improvements as an immediate dividend from the election of a Labour government. He also understood how important social expenditures could be to the re-election of a Labour government. Its unpopularity and the political risks that would be incurred did not, in his view, detract from the force of his argument. The Labour party, and the electorate, must learn to contain their appetites for social expenditure until the economy was in a better state to satisfy them. Certainly a government could tax in order to fund social amelioration. But taxes were already near the limit and the priority must be the state of the economy.

> It is not sensible, in the last resort, to tax property incomes to the limit and at the same time to leave the decisions about investment, employment, the rate of social accumulation and the volume of production in the hands of persons who look primarily to that source of revenue for their maintenance and guidance. It is not wise in the long run to live upon golden eggs and slowly to strangle the goose that lays them.[76]

Durbin was writing in 1938–9. Even at that time, he found himself, on this point, at odds with the leader of his Party. Attlee did not intend to brook any such deferment of benefit to those who so sorely needed it. 'While it is important that the basic problems of the ownership and control of industry and finance shall be tackled at the outset, Labour does not intend to delay the introduction of measures calculated to effect an immediate improvement of a far-reaching character in the social services.'[77] The Attlee government came to power in 1945 after a war that had devastated Britain's declining assets. If what Durbin recommended had been right for 1938–9, how much more right must it have been for 1945.

The second difference in the Durbin programme from that of the Attlee government was that he wished to defer egalitarian taxation until towards the end of a Labour government's first period in office. He wished the Labour government to be firmly established in office, with a record of successful economic management behind it, before the risk was taken of further outraging the capitalist class. Then would begin:

> a slow but systematic destruction of all large fortunes, a withering away of the institution and consequences of inheritance – to make a beginning for the equal distribution of the national income. But it would be disastrous, in my view, to start such purely egalitarian legislation until some substitute for the institution of property had been found – in the shape of the growth of State authority in the industrial sphere – to provide the saving, and secure the efficiency, that are both necessary for economic progress.[78]

Thus were mingled dramatic calls for greater equality with a typical Durbin warning to over-enthusiastic colleagues. In the socialist order of priority, the economy must come before equality.

While Durbin's caution in these two respects can be regarded as statesmanlike, it was also entirely unrealistic. No democratic socialist government could be expected to behave in the way he proposed. *Labour's Immediate Programme*, adopted in 1937, which provided the basis for the 1945 manifesto *Let Us Face the Future*, had included ameliorative measures together with measures of socialization. Durbin feared inflation but he had failed to observe that democratic socialism is inherently inflationary. It would be the object of a democratic socialist government to prove the superiority of its management of capitalism. That would give the electorate the necessary confidence to extend its support to the next stage in the march to socialism. It would attempt to stimulate growth by encouraging investment. That would be the purpose of planning and the objective of the planners. On the other hand, democratic socialist politicians would share the ambition of all politicians, which is to get re-elected. Indeed a democratic socialist politician has to place a particular premium on re-election. If his government is not re-elected then its first steps towards socialism are liable to be reversed by the successor Conservative government. The result of this combination of pressures would certainly be to encourage both consumption, in its various forms, and public sector investment to an extent beyond the capacity of the economy to bear. Inflation would be unavoidable. In theory the planners would neatly balance total demand against resources in order to avoid inflationary pressures. But it was questionable whether the planners would have understanding of economic processes and information accurate enough to make such calculations. Moreover it was certain that the politicians would judge their conclusions by political rather than economic criteria. There would, therefore, be inflation and, with inflation, the probability of economic crisis. Economic crisis would undermine confidence in Labour's management of capitalism and thereby block the road to socialism.

This is what happened not merely under the Attlee government but under all Labour governments up to 1979. When faced by economic crises, as Labour governments always were, they spoke of hard choices but always sought soft options. When a choice had to be made between cutting investment and cutting consumption, the cutting of investment always seemed to be the least embarrassing politically. Thus in practice the hallmark of Labour governments would be a concentration on economic development in words, on social amelioration in deeds. Durbin's statesmanlike recommendations merely indicated that he had not fully understood the real problems with democratic socialism. He knew that there were inflationary dangers. He did not see that they would in practice be unavoidable.

The third difference between Durbin's programme and that of the Attlee government was that Durbin intended to include agriculture in the nationalization programme. This was surprising in view of his fear of civil disturbance and his criticism of the forced collectivization under Stalin in the Soviet Union. Little as the intellectuals of the Labour party knew of industry, they had even less experience of agriculture. However, the inclusion of agriculture in his nationalization programme enabled Durbin to rebut anyone who might think that he had gone soft on the capitalists. He was proposing that one-third of the working population would be in government employment. He was aware that, just as he must avoid provoking the capitalists to armed insurrection, a Labour government must do enough to prevent disillusion spreading among its followers. Attlee, too, had had his eye on agriculture in 1937. '[T]he Labour Party stands for the national ownership of the land ... The Labour Government will, therefore, pass a measure giving power to purchase compulsorily whatever land it requires for whatever purpose.' Naturally, it would be with compensation.[79] The nationalization of land was, indeed, a longstanding element in socialist programmes. Its owner-ship by private individuals caused particular offence. Agriculture, Attlee wrote, presented 'A great opportunity for setting the unemployed to useful and necessary work . . .' He mentioned the possibility of public farming corporations, an idea perhaps too reminiscent of collective farms.[80] He believed that a great beginning could be made in planning the production and allocation of raw materials and foodstuffs, from which might be developed eventually global planning of economic resources.[81] In practice, under a combination of political and economic pressures, agriculture, still in private hands, became the petted darling of the Attlee government. Food production was needed to protect the balance of payments. When it came to the point, the Attlee government did not seem to believe that a nationalized agriculture would be more productive than private agriculture subsidized by the state. The nationalization of land was being narrowed down to the nationalization of *development* land, or even simply the control and taxation of devel-opment.

CONCLUSION

The Labour party selected the democratic route to socialism. It was a matter of principle as well as of political practicability. It would then find that the choice of objective confronted it with grave, even impossible, problems. A transition through revolution was in Britain so remote as to be inconceivable. But a transition through the processes of democracy would be extremely difficult, perhaps impossible, and, at best, very slow. The dilemma that would face any Labour government was that the transition from capitalism to socialism was urgent but that it could not be treated urgently. It was urgent in order to avoid the consequences of capitalist crisis, which included unemployment and, only too possibly, war. But it could not be treated urgently because of the risk of domestic resistance and of the destruction of democracy. On the horns of this dilemma, the Labour party was bound to choose the slow road to social-ism. It was, therefore, bound, did it ever return to government, to be faced with the task of managing capitalism for a more or less prolonged period. That would involve some co-operation with the capitalists and some consideration for their views. This, in turn, would inhibit the drive to socialism even if electoral considerations did not. As a result Labour governments regularly fell between two stools. They persisted with an objective of democratic socialism that was unlikely to be practical and their persistence always inhibited their ability to run a successful government within the capitalist system. Democratic socialism, as a third way between Marxism and capitalism, turned out to be a cul-de-sac. One can speculate whether there would have been any threat to democracy in Britain if socialists had realized that there was so little prospect of socialism being achieved by the democratic path. Whatever the outcome of such speculation, the misguided hopes placed in democratic socialism consolidated Labour's loyalty to the Parliamentary system.

FOUR

We are all socialists now

It was Sir William Harcourt, Liberal Chancellor of the Exchequer in the 1890s, who declared that we are all socialists now. But, to Attlee, such a sentiment was deeply offensive. Socialism would be a fundamentally new society, not just capitalism with the rough edges smoothed.

> There are those who will say ... that 'We are all Socialists now'; that there is no absolute Socialism or Capitalism; that it is all a matter of degree. I cannot accept this. Socialism to me is not just a piece of machinery or an economic system, but a living faith translated into action. I desire the classless society and the substitution of the motive of service for that of competition.[1]

Thus, for Attlee, there was not a small, bridgeable difference between socialism and capitalism. In this Attlee appeared at odds with his colleague Hugh Dalton, who did see socialism as a matter of degree.

> Socialism is a quantitative thing. It is a question, not of all or nothing, but of less or more. Doctrinaires on both sides of the controversy are apt to go wrong here. Broadly, we may measure the degree in which any particular community is Socialist by the relative extent of the 'socialised sector' and of the 'private sector', in its economic life ... But, relatively to many other countries, our socialised sector is narrow. Its rapid extension is one of the principal objects of the Labour Party.[2]

Attlee, evidently, was among the doctrinaires. In his book *Socialisation and Transport*, published in 1933, Herbert Morrison had set a test for measuring the success of a future Labour government. It was 'how much private capitalist property organised and conducted for profit has been transferred ... to the ownership of the community to be organised and directed for public service and for public ends'.[3] Thus Morrison, too, was setting a quantitative test. The disagreement between Attlee, on the one hand, and Morrison and Dalton, on the other, defines the frontier between the revolutionary and the democratic socialist. Here was delineated a division within the Labour party that would extend at

77

least into the 1980s. Was Labour a revolutionary socialist party, though acting within democratic norms, or was it an incrementalist, social reforming party? The activists usually wanted the first. The practical politicians became increasingly contented with the second. Attlee would soon adopt Dalton's stance. For him, too, socialism would become a quantitative matter, a matter of degree. Quantitative socialism would never satisfy the left. It would merely confirm its doubts as to whether the Labour party was, in any genuine sense, socialist at all.

Nevertheless, even the incremental socialism of Dalton was a world away from anything Sir William Harcourt had in mind when he ventured his apophthegm. When politicians such as Harcourt, followed by many others on the 'capitalist' side of the political divide, said 'we are all socialists now', they presumably meant that it was possible to treat serious social problems without seeking to replace capitalism. The statement was more than an oratorical flourish, but not much more. It was unacceptable to socialists, even of the incremental persuasion, precisely because they were visualizing a drastically remodelled society, not just the amendment of the old.

THE FINAL ABANDONMENT OF *LAISSEZ-FAIRE*

Yet when discussion moved down from these elevated spheres and considered the practical problems of managing an economy, socialist or capitalist, it began to appear that there might be something in Harcourt's dictum of which socialists should take note. Among socialists capable of a sober evaluation of August 1931, a need was perceived for a fundamental reappraisal of British economic policy. Within the Labour party, the crisis, plus the collapse of the MacDonald government, provided an incentive for socialist economists to develop their plans for the conduct of the next Labour government. Socialist ethics were uplifting and inspirational. But in government there was clearly need for something more. There is a mountain of evidence of the enchantment of the socialist idea for those seduced by it. But there is none more powerful than the willingness of numerous intellectuals, historians, economists and political scientists to spend hours of their time studying, discussing and writing about the problems thrown up by the socialist idea, and the MacDonald fiasco, at a time when a Labour victory lay beyond the limits of human foresight. Party policy could never have been formulated without the voluntary aid of such people. Among them, James Meade, future Nobel Laureate, Evan Durbin, Hugh Gaitskell and Douglas Jay were prominent. One effect was to alert them to the complexities of economic management in a socialist society. It would be no less challenging than in a capitalist society. And before they could even hope for a socialist society, they would, in government, face the inescapable necessity of managing capitalism.

The need for a reappraisal was perceived far beyond the borders of the Labour party. Evan Durbin had written to his brother economist Colin Clark in March 1931, 'Economics is in such a muddle that anyone can say what they think.'[4] The freedom of opinion to which Durbin referred has been a great comfort to economists, professional and amateur, throughout the ages. The old certainties that were already being challenged by Keynes and others were now being questioned across the political spectrum and across the economics profession. Was capitalism in its existing form still viable? Was free trade, to which Labour had been devoted as an expression of internationalism, really right for Britain? Should not the government take responsibility for planning the economy? What emerged from the discussions did not lack in ambition, though it may sometimes have lacked in practicality. Among those who detected a need for the radical overhaul of economic policy, very similar answers were emerging. There seemed to be a great deal on which socialist and non-socialist could agree. The agreement was to some extent superficial, based on differing and conflicting analyses. Yet, at the practical level, capitalist designs for preserving privilege seemed to have much in common with socialist designs for undermining it. The Labour party was now prepared, for whatever reason, to go slow on socialism and nationalization. This created an opportunity for a convergence between socialist ideas for social reformation and the non-socialist, but concerned, ideas of others whose objective was simply social stability.

It should not have been unexpected that capitalists and Conservatives would not be prepared to see the social system that conferred upon them so many advantages disappear under the impact of democracy's insistent demands. They, too, were conscious of the need to satisfy a democratic electorate. They accepted that the state might have a function in stimulating employment. No one, not even a capitalist, could be content with the level of unemployment in Britain. They were not deaf to the cries of the multitude, merely bewildered about what to do for the best. It is not even surprising that the capitalists were as blind to practicalities as were the socialists. The world was very confusing, and capitalists and socialists were both groping. Capitalists would struggle against socialism. They would not employ force or sabotage. Their weapon would be ideas, even, if necessary, ideas from the portfolio of their socialist critics. Capitalism was eclectically harvesting among the green fields of socialism. Analyses of the failures of *laissez-faire* capitalism being made in government and business with the object of preserving capitalism had much in common with those being made by socialists whose object was to destroy it. The two creeds were approximating to one another in the acceptance of planning and even of nationalization if properly confined. Socialists might complacently regard these concessions to socialist thinking as further evidence that capitalism was doomed. It should have been a warning that capitalism was by no means committed to suicide or to *laissez-faire* and that, to save itself, it had at its disposal more tricks than were thought of in the socialist philosophy. It was a mark of British insularity that it should have been imagined that the success of capitalism depended on *laissez-faire*. A glance at other capitalist countries would have been educational, but this was not a form of education which British socialists seemed able to absorb.

In *The Socialist Case*, Douglas Jay devotes chapter after chapter to a criticism of *laissez-faire*. It is easy to accept that a society left to the mercy of *laissez-faire* would fall far short of the most elementary provision of any kind of social justice. It would be more difficult to find any twentieth-century industrial society that still operated by the principles of *laissez-faire*. Britain certainly did not. There had already been, even in the nineteenth century, many departures from what Bevan was to call 'the gaunt austerity of *laissez-faire* principles'.[5] Incremental socialism could be regarded as an extrapolation from these departures. Thus originally there was no sewage system and the poor sickened and died. So the state intervened to build sewage systems. Incremental socialism was a generalization of the sewage-system principle. It was a process in which the Fabians played a notable part. As Denis Healey was to put it in *New Fabian Essays*, the Fabians 'found socialism wandering aimlessly in Cloud Cuckoo land and set it working on the gas and water problems of the nearest town or village. The modern Welfare State is their monument.'[6] The danger lay in the belief that because the state could deal with the sewage, more or less satisfactorily, it would have equal success in reorganizing society.

The National government of 1931, dominated by the Conservative party, found no difficulty in moving even further from *laissez-faire*. Hardly had the government taken up office when it devalued the pound, thus reversing the misjudgement of Churchill in restoring sterling to the Gold Standard in 1925 at $4.86, the pre-war parity. The effect of the return to the Gold Standard had been to make British exports uncompetitive, not just because of the overvalued exchange rate but because of the high interest rates required to sustain it. The world was retreating to protectionism, exemplified by the American Smoot–Hawley tariff, introduced in 1931, on which blame has been fastened for the consequent disruption of international trade and for allegedly deepening the depression of the 1930s. In 1932, the National government introduced a protective 10 per cent tariff. Tariff protection can, indeed, be regarded as one of the more effective forms of government intervention in industry, certainly more effective than many of the bureaucratic interventions in the economy which pass under the name of planning. The Ottawa conference of 1933 had aimed to establish a system of imperial preference. Under the Special Areas (Development and Improvement) Act of 1934, the government defined areas of high unemployment and sought to attract work to them. Kenneth Morgan writes that 'the special areas development was an ill-conceived, half-hearted palliative devised by Neville Chamberlain and other financially-orthodox ministers'.[7] That may well be the case but, for our purpose, it was a departure from *laissez-faire*. The flexibility of mind which Laski had denied to the capitalist class was being abundantly displayed by the National government. It is also equitable to observe that later, and more expensive, devices for the regeneration of development areas have been as notable for their costs as for their successes.

There had been a considerable advance in social services in the inter-war years under governments dominated by the Conservatives. Attlee recognized that there had been measures of social reform taken by non-Labour governments in the 1920s. They were not less measures of social reform because he regarded them as 'an insurance against revolution'.[8] Harold Macmillan was a Tory MP with views which, at the time, put him outside the mainstream of his party. He combined distress at the misfortunes of his constituents in Stockton-on-Tees with, as a publisher, easy access to the printing press. Macmillan, critic of things as they were, was ready to confess that 'A large proportion of our population is living in conditions of poverty.' But even he wrote in his book, *The Middle Way*, that 'The standard of life is generally higher, the system of social services is more humane and more efficient than in any other country or at any earlier time' – though he hastened to add, 'But there is a legitimate claim that standards which were endurable in an age of scarcity are unendurable when we have at our disposal a potential volume of production quite adequate to remove the old restrictions of scarcity.'[9] Years later, having grown to greater fame and influence, he would prove that we are, indeed, all socialists now. In Paul Addison's assessment, 'The social services in Britain, taken all in all, were the most advanced in the world in 1939, and the Social Democrats in Sweden, the Labour Party in New Zealand, and the New Deal Democrats in the United States, were trying to bring about many of the improvements which Conservatism took for granted.'[10] After all, it was precisely the readiness of British Conservatives to give way to democratic pressures that was, in Durbin's view, undermining capitalism.

So far, however, everything that had been done to provide for greater equality through, for example, higher and differential taxation had been outweighed by the greater inequality resulting, under capitalism, from the ever widening gap in the distribution of the national income. Douglas Jay calculated that:

> The plain truth is that the working classes themselves paid for virtually the whole of the social services; and the rich in turn having supplied themselves with the national debt interest, provided the workers with the blessings of an Army, Navy, Air Force, and police. There was scarcely any redistribution of income between classes under our [pre-1939 war] Budget system, except in so far as the working classes received for nothing their share in these services.[11]

It was certainly true that there was a great deal of room for redistribution of income. But Jay's resentment that the workers should be required to contribute to the costs of the nation's police and defence was somewhat myopic. Presumably the workers were part of a nation which had an interest in social order and the possibility of resistance to Hitler.

THE MIDDLE WAY

By the 1930s, there were many, in every part of the political spectrum, who were no longer prepared to live and die by the principles of *laissez-faire*, who had concluded that things could not be allowed to go on as they were, that there must be change, that the old wisdom that the poor are always with us must be challenged, that relief must be sought in one device or another, that the state must act. Harold Macmillan was an advocate of state intervention to cure unemployment. Like the socialists, Macmillan was seeking 'human emancipation' from 'uncontrolled economic forces'.[12] In 1936 he called for the creation of a centrist party, 'a fusion of all that is best in the Left and the Right', led by Herbert Morrison.[13] In the 1930s he wrote a number of books of which *The Middle Way*, published in 1938, became the most widely known. It was an attempt to combine the best features of capitalism with the best features of socialism.[14] Businessman as well as politician, Macmillan wrote that 'Capitalism has been changing of its own accord; it has, in fact, been searching out and reconciling with its own existence socialistic methods and principles where these have seemed more suitable for the performance of certain functions.'[15]

He asserted that a survey of 'the whole trend towards co-operative methods, both in the public services and in private industry', would show:

> that the doctrine of *laissez-faire* has been abandoned in practice, that the boundaries of 'public enterprise' have been very greatly extended; and that intervention by the Government in the economic life of the nation is increasing rapidly. It will show that in private industry the theory of free competition is also being largely abandoned in practice.[16]

His recommendations had much in common with the Mosley memorandum of 1930, which had also proposed dramatic interventions in the economic life of the country in order to cure unemployment. The Mosley memorandum had been supported at the time by left-wing Labour MPs such as Aneurin Bevan and John Strachey, but had been rejected by the Ramsay MacDonald Cabinet. Though Macmillan claimed to be mapping a middle way, his book turned out to be a better forecast of how Labour governments would actually behave when they got a chance than any book by socialist writers in the 1930s. The principal difference between Macmillan and the socialists lay in his belief that 'It is not necessary to reduce the incomes of one class in order to increase the incomes of another.'[17] Equality was not part of Macmillan's agenda.

Anthony Crosland was to argue later in *New Fabian Essays* that 'the fact that it was so fashionable to be politically left before the war is a sure sign that the educated class had lost its former faith'.[18] On this view, the loss of faith in the virtues of capitalism was evidenced by the final abandonment of *laissez-faire*, by the reversion to nationalism and protectionism, and by the drive to monopoly. There was, however, an alternative explanation. There had been no loss of morale; on the contrary there was a determination to fight. The capitalists were seeking an answer to the serious problems they were confronting. But they were not thereby capitulating to socialism. They were defying the premature forecasts of the death of capitalism.

NATIONALISM AND PROTECTION

Socialists always emphasized their internationalism. Socialism proclaimed that the interests of workers in different lands were consonant, not antagonistic. Marx and Engels in *The Communist Manifesto* of 1848 had called upon the workers of the world to unite. But was this the real nature of socialism or specifically British socialism? Socialist ideology always depended on the exclusion or control of imports, but not socialist ideology alone. The TUC believed that modern industrial communities must exercise control over trade.[19] The Labour party, in 1934, proposed the creation of import boards to ensure 'order' and to guarantee the position of the home producer.[20] Insistence on the exclusion or control of foreign competition was hardly a ringing endorsement of the proposition that all men are brothers. In 1934, when still a Liberal, Michael Foot, a future leader of the Labour party, made a very relevant criticism of socialism: 'Socialism with its ideal of the national control of consumption and production, its substitution of national barter for the processes of foreign trade, is by no means an international force ... It looks inwards rather than outwards and sets up a national economy, which every true protectionist should envy.'[21] Michael Foot's Liberal anxieties were justified. Socialists were endorsing a closed economy in which there need be no concern about foreign competition. But, after the war, ever freer international trade would undermine the prospects for socialism in one country.

The exclusion of profit from the objectives of a nationalized industry was inconsistent with international trade. This question would be particularly important if nationalization was to be widespread. Apparently either pay was to have no influence on prices in the mining industry or, if prices did reflect costs, the customer would simply have to pay. During his first year as MP for Ebbw Vale, Bevan insisted, 'We have a right to say that, if it means slightly dearer coal, then it is better to have slightly dearer coal than cheaper colliers.'[22] Attlee wrote that the Coal Board would get the best prices that it could, whether in competition or, preferably, by international agreement, but, whichever it was, there was no reason why it should affect the wages of the miner.[23] The optimal arrangement, apparently, was an international coal cartel. In any case, the coal industry was to have protection. There would be control of imported fuel, especially oil.[24] The thought that, if costs did not matter, there would be little effort to control them was not considered or, if considered, ignored.

It was understandable that Attlee should take this view given the history of coal mining since the first world war. As long previously as 1919, there had been a commission on the mining industry chaired by the Liberal peer Lord Sankey, who later became a Labour Cabinet minister. Webb and Tawney were members. It had, by a narrow majority, recommended nationalization. Nothing more than a narrow majority could have been expected given the presence on the Commission of mine owners. Less expected was that there was no agreement among the majority, which included representatives of the Miners' Federation, on questions of control and compensation. The Lloyd George government noted that there was no majority for any specific course of action and used this as an excuse to break its promise to nationalize the industry if Sankey so recommended. With the industry returned to the mine owners, employment and wages had been severely cut. The competitiveness of the mining (and other) industries was further prejudiced when, in 1925, Churchill returned sterling to the Gold Standard. There had been numerous strikes in which the miners had been defeated, including the great miners' strike of 1926 which led to the nine-day General Strike but continued for months beyond the end of the General Strike. Special regard for the interests of the miners was in the blood of the Labour party given the relationship between them and the Labour Movement. Protection would no doubt be attractive to miners who had struggled through the inter-war years to maintain a decent standard of living against the demands of the mine owners, who wished to depress pay in order to meet competition.

But the intention to protect went beyond mining. Douglas Jay wrote, *The general principle will . . . be to pay little heed to the price and cost calculus where it conflicts with clear human or social needs, but to take some account of it when it does not.*[25] Whether or not this principle would be sensible, its implementation would be possible only within a protected economy. Labour, in defending its ideological corner, would be forced towards protectionism in order to shelter its not-for-profit industries from foreign competition.

Later, similar questions would be raised about full employment. Could it be guaranteed in the open, free-trading society to which Labour had long been officially committed? The lack of interest repeatedly shown by socialist theorists in the competitiveness of the industries they proposed to nationalize can be explained only by their assumption that Britain would, under socialism, regulate imports and isolate itself from foreign competition. Difficult as physical planning must be in a closed economy, it becomes impossible in an open economy. Many of those keenest on planning thought in terms either of a protected home market or of a protected imperial market. As Dalton wrote, 'Free trade . . . is a denial of planning . . .'[26] He qualified this statement by referring to free trade in 'the old sense', which is, of course, the only sense. He argued that trade should be expanded but, using instruments such as quotas, on a planned, reciprocal, balanced and even bilateral basis.[27] The Labour party, despite its claims to be an internationalist party, was ready to follow fashion and adopt economic nationalism. The economic resources of the nation were to be mobilized as they had been in war. International trade, after all, was a form of war, of one nation against another, and the British nation must, like its enemies, muster its forces to fight the economic war and protect domestic employment and levels of pay. Thus there was much in Labour's developing programme that should not have been attractive to its idealist members who thought of socialism as benign, internationalist, anything but nationalist.

In all of this, socialists were accompanied by capitalists and it would be an act of supererogation to determine who was leading the way. As an era of protectionism, it was also an era of nationalism. It was an age of cartels and of tariffs, the cartels intended to protect profit from any competition, the tariffs intended to protect the home market from foreign competition. That was the significance of the introduction by the National government of the 10 per cent protective tariff. Macmillan, in *The Middle Way*, advocated protection. He felt that Britain's standard of living and Britain's industry were under siege. He wrote,

> I am by no means ready to accept the pure doctrine of free trade. The simple reason for this is that I am not prepared to wait until the standard of life of the most slave-driven industrial country has been raised before attempting to raise it in this country as a result of more intelligent methods of control. By following the cult of cheapness we should be conniving at a process which undermines the standards of the most advanced countries and rewarding, with a premium, the most ruthless exploitation of labour.[28]

Macmillan condemned the idea of allowing 'the pressure of competition to drive the least efficient units out of production . . .'[29] He then adds a wry comment that 'The odd thing is that the theory [of free trade] is supported by some of the intellectuals of the Labour movement – but only, I think, by the more remote. To them, of course, it is only a problem, on paper. They would do well to consult their Trade Union comrades regarding the human consequences of the process which they defend.'[30] So were the residual free traders within the Labour party reproved by the exponent of the middle way. In fact the difference between Macmillan and the socialist intellectuals he rebuked was not as he described it. Neither of them welcomed the human cost of *laissez-faire*. Both considered that competition was often wasteful. But, whereas Macmillan based his hopes for the survival of capitalism in a competitive world on what he called 'co-operation' but was actually monopoly, the socialist intellectuals claimed that industrial reorganization and cartelization, the favoured remedies of the time for inadequate international competitiveness, could only be a first step. The only ultimate rescue for the economy was to be found in socialism. In practice, though they approached the problem from different perspectives, there would prove to be a convergence as to action between the views of Macmillan and those of many socialists. Macmillan's middle way was the socialism of the early post-war years.

PLANNING

With nationalism, protection and monopoly went the idea of planning. That nationalization should be part of the socialist vision is easy to understand. It was equally possible to understand why socialists should think that there was something morally meritorious in insisting that production should be for use and not for profit. But planning was an accretion to socialist policy more difficult to explain. One of the problems in talking about planning is that, at least from the time of Keynes's *General Theory* onwards,[31] there were two types of activity to which the title 'planning' was ascribed. When the economist James Meade wrote of planning he was usually thinking of Keynesian demand management. It was indeed a kind of planning. But when most socialists wrote about planning they were thinking of physical planning, the determination of economic priorities, the distribution of resources, the location of industry and such matters. It could also include incomes policy on the ground that it was impossible to leave incomes subject only to free collective bargaining, or the discretion of employers, if everything else was to be planned. In this book the word planning is used to refer to physical planning of this kind. Keynesian demand management will be spoken of as Keynesian demand management.

There was nothing particularly socialist about planning. As Dalton put it, 'Planning is not the same thing as Socialism. Socialism is primarily a question of ownership, planning a question of control or direction.'[32] Yet planning became an inherent part of socialist policy. There were two influences. For some socialists, planning had a moral dimension which was attractive. It would enable the planners to make decisions on behalf of the people. No longer would they be deceived by advertising. No longer would their money be spent frivolously. Planners, with their access to the best information, and with their exceptional capacity for judgement, would make decisions which the ordinary consumer was incompetent to make. To such socialists, the idea of consumer sovereignty was an aberration which conflicted with the ends to which, they had decided, society should be directed.

The second influence derived from the conviction that planning would enable a faster rate of growth. It became a further justification for nationalization in the belief that a nationalized economy would be easier to plan. Among socialists of all varieties, it was taken as self-evident that planning would lead to faster growth. Any observer of the economy might conclude that it would grow faster if it was planned. It stood to reason that planning would do better than competition, that production for use would be more productive than production for profit. How could it be otherwise? It was obvious that if the mind of man, and particularly of the economist, was applied to the problems of economic growth instead of being left to the haphazard self-interest of the capitalist class, the result must be faster growth. As Douglas Jay put it in *The Socialist Case*, 'The case for socialism and planning in a free society is . . . nothing more than a plea for the application of reason and intelligence to the job of producing and distributing the good things of life.'[33] Concentrated human intelligence must serve better than blind market forces. Dalton was so confident of this proposition that he felt able to ignore contrary arguments except where he wished to make fun of them.

> Planning or drifting, looking ahead or living from hand to mouth, are two different styles of conduct . . . a good plan, well executed, is always better than no plan at all. Economic Planning is to be contrasted with *Laissez-faire*, Free Competition, Free Enterprise, the Free Play of Economic Forces, Service through Profit-seeking, Automatic Adjustments through the Price Mechanism. These are the soothing phrases, or some of them, which do duty in this controversy.[34]

But his principal evidence that planning would work came from the Soviet Union, 'where a planned economy has practically banished unemployment'.[35] Even socialist critics of the absence of liberty in the Soviet Union seldom went on to question its claims to outstanding

88

economic performance which was thought to arise from its combination of public ownership and economic planning. Dalton had visited the Soviet Union in 1932. He was impressed by the achievements of Soviet planning. He wrote, 'It is my firm conviction that, unless we in this country also adopt the principle of economic planning on Socialist lines, we shall find no solution to our economic troubles. And if the Russians can do it and can make much remarkable progress in so short a time how much more effectively could we in England do it!'[36]

The way to achieve a comparable result in Britain was by government expenditure and a large programme of public works.[37] Dalton had a particularly high regard for Lenin's slogan, 'Electrification plus Soviet Power equals Socialism', and for Soviet achievements in electrification.[38] Dalton was also briefly impressed by Mussolini and by economic planning in Italy.[39] The Soviet Union and fascist Italy provided him with hard evidence that central planning was feasible and could be successful. Attlee wrote, as late as 1937, of 'the great experiment in Socialist Russia'.[40] He appears to have been influenced by a visit he paid to the Soviet Union in 1936 at the invitation of the Soviet government.[41] Democratic socialists, however alienated they might be by the lack of freedom in the Soviet Union, were too often mesmerized by its claims to economic success. The truth, which for many decades escaped them, was very different. In the course of correcting the injustices of capitalism, others, far worse, were being imposed on the subject population. The communists claimed to bring justice to the poor. But it was justice as rationed by the communist dictators. The poor had no effective voice. And the Soviet Union lagged behind capitalist countries in the elimination of poverty. Centralized planning had destroyed freedom without the compensation of material benefits.

The idea of planning was not confined to socialists. Many who rejected socialism, and were not bewitched by supposed Soviet successes, did in fact conclude that, if the economy was planned, it would grow faster. Any capitalist could see that the nation must act as a nation if it was to repulse its economic enemies. The idea of planning, therefore, carried resonance in the thinking of businessmen. Businessmen too believed that *laissez-faire* was dead. Many, particularly those responsible for large firms, believed that competition was wasteful. They too wished to show, as Sir Basil Blackett put it, that 'planning was consistent with freedom and freedom with planning . . .'.[42] Blackett was a former Treasury official, a director of the Bank of England and author of a book, *Planned Money*. His name crops up wherever men of goodwill were gathering together to find ways of curing the current discontents. His views gave comfort to socialist leaders for, if a director of the Bank of England was advocating planning, and its consistency with freedom, could they be wrong?[43] Throughout its history as a party of government, Labour party leaders, lacking self-confidence and, usually, ignorant of industry, have been susceptible to the influence of successful businessmen offering help and advice, not always selflessly. The fact that senior businessmen had begun to talk about planning did not imply that they had thought the matter through and had any viable scheme ready at hand. They just saw that something must be done and they seized on the latest fashion.

Macmillan had also selected planning from the agenda of fashionable thoughts. 'The economic policy of a nation cannot be made up of a conglomeration of policies pursued by separate units of industry, commerce or finance operating in isolation from one another . . . The next step forward, therefore, in our social thinking is to move on from "piecemeal planning" to national planning . . .'[44] Dalton in his book *Practical Socialism*, published in 1935, had contemplated the establishment of a Supreme Economic Authority, consisting of a small permanent nucleus of Ministers together with an advisory National Economic Council bringing in the trade unions and representatives of both the public and private sectors.[45] It was an idea supported by Durbin.[46] Morrison had proposed a National Economic Council.[47] Bevan in his contribution to a Fabian pamphlet, *Plan for Britain*, published in 1943, called for a Supreme Economic Council.[48] Macmillan also was calling for a National Economic Council to co-ordinate the activities of a variety of planning authorities in the fields of finance, industry and foreign trade. Macmillan's National Economic Council foreshadows in its membership, if not quite in its powers, the National Economic Development Council established when he was Prime Minister over twenty years later. Robert Boothby, on the Tory backbenches, always an enemy of *laissez-faire*, a brilliant orator though perhaps over-excitable, became convinced in the early months of the 1939 war not merely that war would lead to planning but that it would lead to socialism. Nor did he seem afraid of the prospect. On 7 November 1939 he wrote to Lloyd George: 'Nothing is more certain than that this war will mark the transition from monopoly capitalism to socialism. By that I mean that the ultimate control of all basic monopolistic industries, the Central Bank, of money, of credit, will pass definitely and finally into the hands of the state.'[49] All this was the intellectual fashion of many of the brightest thinkers of that time.

Some central body must seize hold of the economy and give it impetus and direction. There would be no lack of able men with the qualities necessary to discharge this horrendous responsibility. After all, it was precisely what economists had been trained to do. For some socialists, one of the attractions of a supreme economic authority was that it could take economic management out of the hands of lay Ministers. Bevan, on the other hand, was insistent that the supreme authority was to be under Parliamentary control. It does not appear to have occurred to him that the possibility of practical Parliamentary control over such an authority was, at best, remote.

Above all, there was confidence that the planners could hardly do worse than unplanned capitalism. Dalton accepted that 'Planners will make mistakes, miscalculate the future, sometimes waste wealth and opportunities, often change direction. But they, at least, have their eyes fixed, not on abstractions, but on realities.'[50] Strachey also accepted that planners could make mistakes. But their mistakes could not be as serious as those from which the world was suffering in the present crisis. '[W]hen we look at the world in 1932, we are tempted to say that no planning authority, however foolish, myopic, or even corrupt, could achieve quite so grandiose a misdirection and waste of the world's productive capacity as is achieved by the present phase of capitalism.'[51] Here the Marxist was at one with the radical Conservative, Harold Macmillan. In Macmillan's view, 'Whatever errors we make in our attempt at planning, the consequences can hardly be worse than what we have already experienced.'[52]

The presumption in favour of planning had been reinforced by the experience of the first world war when essential industry had been brought under government control. Dalton wrote that the two outstanding examples of planning on a large scale in recent times were furnished by the world war and by the Soviet experiment.[53] If such control had been necessary in meeting the British nation's greatest crisis, could it be wrong in peacetime? The point was emphasized by Attlee in *The Labour Party in Perspective*. 'The war had seen a rapid extension of Government control over industry. Labour was anxious to retain the power of the community over those industries which were essential to the welfare of the nation.'[54] Attlee and other of his Ministers would derive a similar lesson from the second world war. Dalton, in working with Gaitskell, Jay and Durbin on the Labour party's plans for post-war Britain, was greatly influenced by his own experience as a minister in wartime. But the influence was to confirm his pre-war presumptions.

The experience of war did not create the idea of planning. The ideas on the role of planning in a socialist Britain had been developed before the war. What the experience of war did was to confirm in the minds of Dalton and his friends the practicability of planning. They had found, perhaps too readily, what they wanted to find. There could be no further doubt that planning would work provided, no doubt, that the planners enjoyed the kind of power over the community that the necessities of war had placed in their hands. Moreover, if Labour did, unexpectedly, win the election after the war, it would enjoy the bonus that the machinery of planning and control would already be in place. Whether the electorate would be happy in peacetime with an economic high command deciding priorities, investment policies, the location of new industrial developments, what consumers would be allowed to buy, was ignored. In so far as central planning involved controls, and even rationing, it could well be unpopular with many people who did not share the morality that preferred rationing to the price mechanism or, as Douglas Jay liked to call it, the price scramble. The necessity seemed so great, the achievement of full employment so important, that any effect on personal liberty, and even electoral prospects, was not worth a moment's thought.

The idea of planning as an instrument of economic growth is an example of economics rampant, promoted by economists rampant. It took economics far beyond its ability to deliver. There were vigorous disagreements between socialist economists as to the proper nature of planning, to say nothing of those between socialist economists and such non-socialists as also took to planning as a panacea. Planning in peacetime would be found to involve difficulties which Attlee's planning government after the second world war was incapable of surmounting. For its failure, it paid a high political price.

PLANNING IMPLIES PROTECTION

Planning was yet one more reason for protection. Competition could be avoided, and planning made effective, only if imports were excluded or, at least, controlled. Macmillan was fearful of instability in the British economy introduced through the channel of foreign trade. '[A] planned economy would be able to eliminate any serious intrusion of instability from the outside world through the channel of foreign trade . . .'[55] He refers to a memorandum signed by Keynes and Bevin dating from 1931 advocating 'restrictions on imports and aids to exports'.[56] He advocates a 'foreign trade authority' which would 'take decisions in the common national interest'. It would control imports so that 'they could be received without disturbing internal prices', and 'It would assist our export trades to exploit to the full the world market for those products in which we continued to enjoy a competitive advantage . . .' The foreign trade authority would discriminate between essential and inessential imports.[57] There would be bulk purchasing for some commodities.[58] These ideas went far beyond the protective tariff introduced by the National government in 1932 to the detailed regulation of trade on an industry-by-industry basis.

Macmillan's alternative strategy had a great deal in common with the 'alternative strategy' that was to be advocated by Tony Benn, advised by a long list of Cambridge economists headed by Nicholas Kaldor and Wynne Godley, in the 1970s. Imports must be controlled and exports subsidized. Protectionism, Macmillan wrote, quoting an earlier book, was not an end in itself but a preliminary defensive movement, 'an aid to planning the development of our national resources'. He continued:

> It is not necessary here to go into the arguments for and against Protection or Free Trade. Rightly or wrongly I am regarding that question as settled. We can continue to hope for an economic relationship between nations in which all would be producing the things they are best fitted to produce and exchanging these products to their mutual advantage. But if that relationship is to be established it will be, in my opinion, as the result of conscious and deliberate regulation.[59]

Durbin claimed that democracy was ending the reign of capitalism. Macmillan was clear that protection was ending the reign of *laissez-faire*. Divergent though these views might seem, they would converge on the same destination, protectionism. Free trade still had its advocates, notably Philip Snowden, Chancellor in the two MacDonald Labour governments, but they had been submerged by economic crisis and electoral inconsequence. Nineteenth-century *laissez-faire* had been abandoned under the influence of crisis, international competition and Joseph Chamberlain. Macmillan thought that the question of protection versus free trade had been for ever settled in favour of protection. But, in the post-war world, under American pressure, there would be a strong move towards more open markets. This was a contingency for which socialists, as well as Macmillan, were unprepared. Meanwhile Macmillan's planned economy was very similar to Labour's planned economy.

MONOPOLY, CARTEL AND NATIONALIZATION

The accepted wisdom in industry was now the merger and the cartel. One of the greatest enthusiasts for domestic mergers and international cartels was Lord McGowan, Chairman of Imperial Chemical Industries in the 1930s and beyond. McGowan was far from alone among industrial leaders. This was a form of wisdom which socialists could hardly overlook and from it they would draw confirmation for their socialist ambitions. Durbin wrote:

> Freedom of enterprise is not only withering spontaneously away, but it is also being deliberately, consciously and carefully destroyed amid popular acclamation. In its place is appearing an ever-thickening jungle of unco-ordinated government control, whose main purpose is restriction, and whose chief fruit is the substitution of monopoly for competition.[60]

As Attlee feared, businessmen were even prepared to contemplate extending their embrace to include trade union officials, for, on the face of it, their employees would benefit if allowed a share in the higher rate of profit and job opportunities that would follow the exclusion of foreign competition.

Even the *Economist*, longstanding defender of the *laissez-faire* faith, was prepared to accept government-sponsored industrial reorganization on conditions. In a comment on the cotton industry reorganization scheme on 23 October 1937 it wrote that:

> In one trade after another, the logic of events is compelling the abandonment of unrestricted free competition. But if *laissez-faire* is ruinous in one way, private monopoly is ruinous in another . . . the community has the right to insist, before its aid is sought, on two principles: that there shall be a limit to the enlargement of profits; and that the public shall be directly represented in the day-to-day management and control of the industry.[61]

If control, the socialist might ask, why not public ownership?

The politics of nationalization was made less confrontational by the widespread acceptance of the idea in circles well beyond the Labour party. The inefficiency of the energy industries caused particular distress to industrial leaders whose companies were dependent upon them for supplies. Their complaints led to inquiries which made a variety of recommendations for reorganization. In 1936, a committee under Lord McGowan recommended the nationalization of electricity supply.[62] The nationalization of gas supply was to be recommended in December 1945 by a committee presided over by Geoffrey Heyworth, the Chairman of the great Anglo-Dutch multinational, Unilever.[63] No industry provoked more complaints from industrial leaders than the coal industry, the nationalization of which had been recommended by the Sankey Commission in 1919. The uncertainties of coal supplies convinced many industrial leaders that nationalization was the only answer. Certainly the ideas of the Labour party for the nationalization of the energy industries were unlikely to provoke much distress among industrial leaders.

The nationalization of the Bank of England was another proposal which was considered on its merits far outside the Labour party. Many senior industrialists loathed the City of London and its financial institutions quite as much as any socialist. Industrialists had actual experience of the loss of profits due, as they found it convenient to believe, to the dominance of the Bank in the councils of government. The Bank had been a major influence in persuading Churchill, Chancellor of the Exchequer, to return sterling to the Gold Standard in 1925. When, after the war, Labour nationalized the Bank, Churchill was prepared to take a benign view. Nationalization, he said, would raise no great issue of principle.[64] For socialists, however, the nationalization of the Bank held a wider significance. It would be the key to planning. Even socialists as sophisticated as Dalton and Durbin imagined that, with control of the City of London and, in particular, of the Bank of England, money and credit could easily be directed where the planners dictated. Elizabeth Durbin writes of 'the party's appalling ignorance of the operation of banking and financial markets'.[65] It was an ignorance difficult to dispel in a party that despised the activities of the City. The nationalization of the Bank of England was at the forefront of their ambitions. Attlee, guided no doubt by Dalton, shared in the delusion, though at least he had abandoned the peremptory nationalization of the joint-stock banks:

> Through the Bank of England it will be possible to control the joint-stock banks and ensure that credit policy will be in line with the policy of the Government. When taking over control of the Bank of England provision will also be made for securing that credit shall be available and capital be directed into the channels of most advantage to the community by the creation of a National Investment Board. This will enable the Government to finance large schemes of national development such as Housing, Electrification, Transport etc., and the establishment of new industries.[66]

The idea of creating a National Investment Board was common form among Labour politicians. It had a long history in socialist and trade union thought.[67] There was much debate as to how best it should operate, but that it could stimulate investment and therefore economic growth was beyond serious doubt. Durbin at least realized that there was a limit to what could be done at once and that there were risks of inflation. Attlee showed no understanding at all of inflationary dangers. If the Bank was owned by the state, the credit would be available. Cole still thought that it would be necessary to nationalize the joint-stock banks as well as the Bank of England. Controlling the Bank of England would enable a Labour government to decide the amount of credit, but it was necessary also for the planners to decide the directions in which credit flowed. This formidable task would be eased if all the banks were nationalized.[68] The Labour party had rejected the nationalization of the joint-stock banks, but the fundamental idea in Cole's proposal, that the government should be able to control credit flows, was not discarded.

The compatibility of extensive nationalization with freedom was assumed rather than explored. Under Fabian influence, there was something highly prescriptive about socialist policy. Perhaps it arose also from longstanding trade union suspicion of 'free riders', those who benefited without contributing. Harold Macmillan was a relatively friendly critic even if a Conservative. Yet, in his book *The Middle Way*, published in 1935, he suggested that socialists had accepted 'economic totalitarianism'. He thought it might be effective in one sense but have deplorable consequences in another. 'Along this route [the socialist] might achieve a considerable elimination of poverty, but the further he goes the greater will become the danger of a surrender of individual liberty.' In addition it 'would sacrifice the beneficial dynamic element that private enterprise can give to society . . .'.[69] Macmillan's answer to the problem of reconciling personal liberty with the provision of basic human needs was 'private enterprise in the fields for which it is best suited', combined with 'a wide extension of social enterprise and control in the sphere of minimum human needs'.[70] This, perhaps, is where the Labour party arrived after the war and after much political and intellectual travail. At the time, socialists, despite strong democratic credentials, were not at all worried that a centralized state, with vast powers over the economy, might be prejudicial to freedom. Good men, socialist men, with great powers, would serve the community well.

THE MENACE OF NAZISM

International events were also serving to move Labour into the main-stream of British political debate. The 1930s brought increasing threats to peace exemplified by the Japanese invasion of Manchuria and the aggressive language and actions emanating from Germany after Hitler came to power in January 1933. Labour, nevertheless, opposed rearmament. It saw no reason to arm an imperialist British government whose use of weapons of war it could not control. It announced that it favoured total multilateral disarmament and the creation of an international police force. At least it did not propose unilateral disarmament as an example to others. Attlee, shortly to be leader of the Labour party, proposed in an article in the *Daily Herald* that 'all Air Forces should be handed over to international control, that all Air Lines with their personnel and fleets should be internationalised, and that all industrial establishments producing aircraft should be taken over by the League [of Nations]'.[71] As late as 1937 he was expressing his belief that the way to meet fascism was not by force of arms, but by showing that co-operation in the economic sphere would produce far better conditions than would be obtainable from pursuing a policy of aggression.[72] Policymaking of this character indicated little understanding of the real world. After 1935, Britain at last began to rearm, albeit in a dilatory way, as though the threat from Hitler could be deflected without harm to the British Empire. As the German menace increased, Labour's policy gradually changed to an acceptance of the dangers which Britain now faced. In March 1937, Bevin told the Executive Council of the TGWU that 'From the day Hitler came to power, I have felt that the democratic countries would have to face war ... I cannot see any way of stopping Hitler and the other dictators except by force.'[73] In July 1937, Dalton persuaded the Parliamentary Labour Party to abstain rather than to oppose increased expenditure on armaments. Though opposed to the left wing's campaign for a Popular Front of working-class and bourgeois parties against fascism, Labour leaders became prepared to enter into discussion with dissident Tories who were challenging Prime Minister Neville Chamberlain's appeasement policy. The dissident Tories were led by Winston Churchill with the support among others of Harold Macmillan. Despite the collapse of his Munich policy with the German occupation of the whole of Czechoslovakia in the spring of 1939, and despite the guarantee that he then gave to Poland, Chamberlain appeared undecided in a debate on 1 September following the German invasion of Poland. Arthur Greenwood, deputy leader of the Labour party, rising to reply in the absence of Attlee, who was sick, was adjured by the Tory imperialist Leo Amery to 'speak for England'. It was Labour that forced Chamberlain's resignation, after the military disasters of May 1940, by refusing to join a coalition government under his leadership. The irony was that the social reformer, Neville Chamberlain, was thus replaced by Winston Churchill, socialism's most dedicated enemy. But war dictates its own requirements.

These events were relevant to the future of socialism in Britain. First, socialism certainly had no future without the defeat of Hitler. Secondly, entry of its leaders into the Churchill coalition conferred on Labour a new credibility which it had sacrificed by the collapse of the MacDonald government and its subsequent divisions and extremism. Thirdly, the national consensus during the war fostered the illusion of an equivalent consensus after the war in support of the transformation of society. Fourthly, and probably deceptively, the coalition would give Labour Ministers experience of economic planning. Labour's participation in the Churchill coalition opened the road to its election victory in 1945.

CONCLUSION

Laski wrote, 'If it is said that, amid difficulties so profound, the part of the wise man should be scepticism, it is, I think, sufficient to reply that we cannot escape the need to decide what is right and what is wrong in politics.'[74] Politicians cannot escape the need to decide even if a decision will be counterproductive. The principle that, if one does not know what to do, it is better to do nothing is inconsistent with democratic practice. Democratic practice demands action, even blind action. It is also true that businessmen, particularly at times of crisis, will look to the government for activity rather than benign neglect. It has never been pretended, as a justification for democracy, that decisions will always be wise.

What might have been surprising to the innocent observer was the extent to which the socialist case and the capitalist case seemed to be converging. Planning and some nationalization were within the consensus. Progressive taxation as a means to greater equality could be acceptable if not taken to extremes. Support for such a programme could be found well to the right of the Labour party. The *Economist* wrote of Dalton's 'able and interesting' book *Practical Socialism for*

Britain that it contained hardly anything that would not be supported by progressive Liberals and Tories. The word 'Socialism' had become 'only a hindrance to the realignment of political parties in accordance with the real division of opinion in this country'.[75] The extent of the consensus would certainly simplify Labour's problems in the initial stages of the march to socialism if it ever did come back to office. Nevertheless, this was a gross underestimate of the significance of the differences that divided socialists on the one hand from Liberals and Tory reformers on the other. Consensus existed only in relation to the short term. There remained fundamental differences in the conclusions drawn by the two parties as to the optimal society. Labour remained a socialist party. It had its own vision of the good society but did not expect its vision to be so highly persuasive that it could capture the enthusiasm of all sections of society. It shared with Marxism the conviction that socialism would come as the fruit of the struggles of the workers against the capitalists. So far as the Labour party was concerned the struggle would be in the Parliamentary arena and through the processes of democracy, but it would, nevertheless, be a struggle between classes. Labour was at war with capitalism. The war was for the destruction of capitalism.

Moreover, Labour was a trade union party which gave priority to its perception of the interests of those of the working class organized in trade unions. In government, it would have to find some way of reconciling its allegiance to the trade unions with its allegiance to socialism. Many middle-class people joined it, but they were left in no doubt that they were joining a party which gave primacy to the interests of the workers represented by trade unions. They accepted the implications because they believed, if not in the class struggle in a Marxist sense, then at least that the interests of the working class did lie in extensive redistribution from the rich. A further difference lay in the matter of public ownership. For Labour nationalization was a matter of principle. It was not a pragmatic question, whether some industry might not serve the nation better under public ownership. Labour might start with a limited programme of nationalization. But the objective would be to extend it until there was real central control of the economy. The third difference was on the subject of greater equality to which nationalization was also expected to make its contribution. Others might see the arguments for reducing the wide differentials in income and in property. But Labour would intend, did it get the chance, to push much further than the reformers of any other major party would wish. That was how policy was developing, away from socialism as a religion, towards socialism as a system of management with all its bureaucratic and nationalistic implications. Next time, Labour should be far better prepared than it had been in 1929.

FIVE

The third way of
John Maynard Keynes

Even while socialists were dancing on the empty grave of capitalism, a variety of challenges to socialism were being prepared. The assumption behind these challenges was that obsequies for capitalism were premature but that its state of health required radical treatment.

Unemployment was the pre-eminent curse of the 1920s and 1930s. It was socialism's principal recruiting agent. For any socialist it was an unquestionable objective to achieve full employment, and it was a principal claim for socialist planning that, thereby, full employment could be assured. The problem for socialists would arise if full employment could be achieved within capitalism. That a way might be found had been threatened by the work of John Maynard Keynes, Liberal in politics but, at the time, autarchic in economics and anything but a devotee of *laissez-faire*. Whatever Laski might think about the inflexible minds of his political opponents, nothing could stop Keynes speculating about alternative methods of economic management which would ameliorate the ills of capitalist society. It was Keynes's view that the problems of the 1920s and 1930s were not inherent in the capitalist system. Rather they were the result of mismanagement, misunderstanding and muddle. It seemed that the 1931 recession, the source of so much unemployment, was as much due to government stupidity, and to the outmoded ideas of defunct economists, as to any innate tendencies in the capitalist system.

Keynes was not the only economist seeking a way out of capitalist crisis. Earlier, for example, there had been J. A. Hobson, whose work, probably uniquely, won praise both from Keynes himself and from Lenin.[1] Hobson, after starting life as a Liberal, joined the Labour party after the first world war, though he felt uncomfortable in the company of 'full-blown socialists'.[2] His under-consumptionist explanation of unemployment implied that there was a solution within capitalism or, at least, within a mixed economy, by means of the manipulation of 'effective demand'. Though Hobson gained a measure of approval from such dissimilar characters as Keynes and Lenin, he was not admired among orthodox economists, who regarded his prolific writings with the disdain reserved by professionals for mere journalists.

Keynes rejected the Marxist thesis about the inevitable decline of capitalism and would not have accepted the Durbin thesis that, while capitalism might survive, it could not solve the problems created for it by democracy. For Keynes, socialism was a clumsy, unsubtle, bureaucratic way of handling problems that should be treated with refinement and delicacy. In *The General Theory*, published in 1936, just before Strachey's *Theory and Practice of Socialism*, Keynes appeared to show that the problem of unemployment could be mitigated and that something which could reasonably be described as full employment was not beyond the reach of policy. But it would require intervention by government. He denied any self-regulating tendency within capitalism to return to a high level of employment. The instrument for achieving permanent full employment was to be found in the techniques of demand management. If investment fell because of lack of demand, if consumers saved too much instead of spending, unemployment would rise. But there was a remedy in fiscal policy. If demand was too low to sustain employment, governments could spend, or reduce taxation, thus incurring budget deficits or reduced surpluses. The spending could be in the form of public works or increased social benefits. By the same token, governments could reduce demand by means of budget surpluses if it was too high. In other words, governments could deflate or reflate according to the requirements of any particular economic conjuncture. If reflation was overdone, this might be inflationary, but that was an argument for caution not for rejecting a solution to the problem of high levels of unemployment.

Thus it was now to be the function of the government not just to watch the economy, and to suffer passively from capitalism's inevitable cycles, but to take a view of the economy and then, by fiscal action, to secure a suitable equilibrium. Within the ferment of ideas about how to deal with unemployment, Keynes's ideas were the most enticing, particularly to those who sought answers to economic problems in government intervention. Moreover they were advocated by an overpowering personality who, as we will later see, was capable of winning political support for far more unlikely propositions. It had not needed

Keynes to demonstrate that reflation could stimulate economic activity and reduce unemployment. That had been known for at least a century. But *The General Theory* gave such proposals a theoretical basis, and, in the context of the time, it was influential in changing attitudes. Keynesianism had the effect of arming the growing school of economists. They now had a cause that could win for them influence and esteem in public life. Keynesianism was not just a programme for government, it was a career prospect for economists.

The successful conduct of the war against Hitler would later be claimed as evidence for the Keynesian case. During the war there had been no difficulty in accepting that the government had a role in the economy and that *laissez-faire* was dead. The war provided evidence, if it was needed, that if the demand was there or was created, so would be the employment. Full employment had actually been achieved. Chancellor Kingsley Wood's 1941 budget was hailed as the first Keynesian budget. It was concerned with employing the total resources of a nation at war.

Keynes's thought had explosive implications for socialist ideas. The wartime success in achieving full employment had occurred within a capitalist system, admittedly a capitalist system subject to detailed government control, but still a capitalist system. At first sight, Keynesianism was an intellectual setback to socialists comparable with the political setback suffered in the destruction of the MacDonald government in August 1931. A book was published and, as its message permeated through the political establishment, decades of socialist thought became redundant. The effect was to question the whole purpose of socialism and of the Labour party. As unemployment was a prime source of poverty, as it was poverty that gave urgency to socialism, the apparent discovery that full employment could be achieved by methods of demand management within the capitalist system was a savage blow. It had been assumed that economic crisis and high unemployment were endemic, the outcome of capitalism's laws of motion, and beyond the power of government to cure. But if there was, within capitalism, a solution to economic crisis and high unemployment, it raised the question whether a transformation of society such as was required by socialism was really needed. If Keynes was right, an attempt to overthrow capitalism, and replace it by another system of society, did not represent the best hope of eradicating mass unemployment. For one thing, the attempt was likely to fail. No democratic socialist ever claimed that it could succeed except over a very long period. What were the unemployed to do in the meantime? Keynes's methodology was as open to a Labour government as to a Conservative government. He had, therefore, pointed a way of performing exactly the trick that Attlee and Laski among others had scorned, a socialist government administering a capitalist economy. Certainly, other socialist objectives such as nationalization, economic planning and equality were not satisfied by Keynesian literature. It could hardly be denied, however, that if unemployment was curable within capitalism it took the edge off socialist propaganda. There was no longer any need for haste, for the political excitement of ecstatic denunciation of capitalism from public platforms. Socialism might be a better society, but capitalism could be a tolerable society.

There was a paradoxical outcome to Keynes's ingenuity in saving capitalism. In the years to come when socialism had been drained of its original meaning, any economic policy that was Keynesian as against monetarist, that appeared to downgrade price stability in favour of the creation of employment, was excoriated by its critics as socialism or at least social democracy. Oskar Lafontaine, the first Finance Minister in a new German Social Democratic government, was, in the months before his resignation in March 1999, described as 'Red Oskar' because he was attempting to disinter Keynesian policies. Keynes presumably would not have been pleased that he had become the saviour of 'socialism', but, deprived of the rest of the socialist agenda, socialists could derive comfort from the fact that they still had at least one arrow in their quiver even if it had been placed there by a Liberal.

THE 1944 EMPLOYMENT POLICY WHITE PAPER

That there were ways of consigning high unemployment to history was endorsed by the 1944 Employment Policy White Paper. It was another early victory for Keynesianism. 'The Government accept as one of their primary aims and responsibilities the maintenance of a high and stable level of employment after the war.'[3] It was the Churchill coalition, and not merely the Labour party, that thereby committed itself to full employment. The Churchill government was not committing itself to socialism. The methods, apparently, were to be found within capitalism. As the economist John Jewkes later pointed out, 'There is nothing here of programmes for individual firms or industries, nothing of the establishment of social priorities which would bind the consumer or producer, nothing, in fact, of what is normally understood as comprehensive planning by the modern socialist.'[4] Rather the method contemplated was through the management of demand. 'The Government are prepared to accept in future the responsibility for taking action at the earliest possible stage to arrest a threatened slump.'[5] The Chancellor of the Exchequer would take account of the requirements of trade and employment in framing his budget. There would be no rigid policy of balancing the budget each year, regardless of the condition of trade, but equally there would be no departure from the principle that it must be balanced over a longer period. There was a commitment to a policy of cheap money. There were, however, warnings. First, employment in Britain was dependent on the condition of export markets and, by implication, on Britain's competitiveness. Secondly, there was a strong element of the experimental in what was proposed. In the words of the White Paper, 'the whole of the measures here proposed have never yet been systematically applied as part of the official policy of any Government. In this matter *we shall be pioneers*.'[6] Whatever the method, whatever its feasibility in all circumstances, whatever the cautionary words, the coalition, including Labour Ministers, had thereby given an assurance to the people of Britain that the sufferings of the pre-war years were never to be repeated.

During the discussion preceding publication of the Employment White Paper, the Treasury showed itself less confident than Ministers that a way had been found to ensure full employment. There was, naturally, the innate scepticism of the Treasury about any proposal that appeared to promise a miracle that had defeated previous governments. Treasury instincts have often been more reliable than Treasury economics. Sir Richard Hopkins, Permanent Secretary to the Treasury, was sceptical, as was the distinguished economist and critic of Keynes Sir Hubert Henderson, Economic Adviser to the Treasury, 1939–44.[7] Henderson could, however, be ignored. He had in the past been wrong, a fault which he shared with all other economists, not to mention humanity in general. Sir Wilfred Eady was another senior Treasury official who found it difficult to go along with the new economics. He commented on a paper written by Keynes that it was 'a voyage in the stratosphere for most of us'. He added, 'You will find your official colleagues obtuse, bat-eyed and obstinate on much of this.'[8] The Treasury, here with support from Keynes, was well aware how dangerous an instrument demand management could be in the hands of spendthrift Ministers. As a protection against profligacy, the White Paper insisted that full employment was not to be ensured by budget deficits. Among Ministers, Kingsley Wood, the Conservative Chancellor, was critical. Morrison and Dalton, from the Labour party, were supportive.[9] Treasury caution whittled down the promises that were to be made in the White Paper. They were in terms, not of full employment, but of high and stable employment. For the public, however, whatever the Treasury's hesitations, there was no difference and, with war-weary agnosticism, it looked to the politicians to deliver.

It had always been inevitable that the Labour party, if it came to power, would have to administer a capitalist economy. Even the Russian communists had had to pass through the era of the New Economic Policy before they arrived at their version of socialism. Labour's gradualist policies meant not merely that it would have to administer a capitalist economy but that it would have to do so for a long time. Now it had the guidance that it had needed. But was a mixed economy to be a milestone on the journey to socialism or was it to be the end of the road? In a 1944 letter to Laski, Attlee had written that, if there were a Labour government, 'it will be a mixed economy developing towards socialism'. He added that he would be arguing for 'the transfer to public ownership of certain major economic forces and the planned control in the public interest of many other economic activities'. Planning would be based on the objective of far greater economic equality.[10] Although all this could be represented as 'developing towards socialism', it was less clear that this was a route by which socialism could ever be reached. Attlee had, by this time, converted himself into an incremental socialist. But did Attlee's reference to the mixed economy imply that Keynes had successfully drained socialism, the new society, out of the Labour prospectus? If alleviating the condition of the disadvantaged in society was Labour's objective, only a dogmatist could rule out the possibility that Labour might now find that administering a capitalist economy would enable it to do all that it really wanted to do.

The Employment White Paper could have been an embarrassment for socialists. But calmer thought detected diverse ways of drawing consolation from the commitment to high and stable employment. First, if poverty could be relieved without revolution, it seemed an act of supererogation to demand revolution. If unemployment could be cured by fiscal manipulation, it would certainly drain any residual revolutionary inclinations from the British working class. The Labour party was thereby confirmed in its democratic predilections. It was enough to wean even such armchair revolutionaries as John Strachey from any revolutionary temptations. Strachey had once rewarded Keynes's earlier attempts to find a way out of capitalist crisis by describing him as a fascist.[11] Now Strachey was back on the democratic socialist path. His earlier conviction that capitalism would be destroyed by its own internal contradictions disappeared into a mélange of Marxism and Keynesianism with which he lived for the rest of his life.

Secondly, Keynesianism was attractive to the basic instincts of socialist economists. Keynesianism did not require detailed physical planning, but at least governments would have to intervene purposively and socialists are always attracted by recommendations for purposive government action. Keynesianism was not 'Treasury orthodoxy', which Labour politicians and advisers had come deeply to distrust. In due course the Treasury would allow itself to be converted by the Keynesian economists in the Economic Section of the Cabinet Office[12] and elsewhere. Meanwhile its scepticism would be no deterrent to all those who had witnessed the Treasury's frequent errors. Thirdly, socialists could find encouragement in the thought that, if Keynesianism was combined with detailed physical planning, the results would be superior even to those achieved by Keynesianism alone. There was nothing in Keynesianism, for example, which seemed to assure the higher rate of economic growth that socialists believed would follow from planning. Keynesianism might simply deliver full employment in a stagnant society. Elizabeth Durbin writes of her father, 'Durbin entertained lingering doubts about the suitability of the new Keynesian models to solve long-term problems of growth and stability in the socialist state.'[13] Durbin's doubts about the appropriateness of Keynesianism in the socialist state would certainly have applied as much to the capitalist state which Labour governments would be compelled to manage. There was, for example, the problem of inflation. In a letter to Keynes after the publication of *The General Theory*, Durbin, whose sensitivity to the dangers of inflation had been stirred by Friedrich von Hayek, wrote,

> you have given no reason for supposing that your 'cure' would not simply lead to an accelerated inflation, and ultimately rise in prices, and the continuous dilemma between allowing the movement to gain further impetus or checking it. And if the movement is checked the disappointment of expectations is the crisis and produces the depression ... I fail to see how you propose to stabilise the boom without allowing the expansion of money to go on after full employment has been reached.[14]

Durbin's doubts proved perceptive. That full employment had been taken as the objective of policy rather than price stability was to have profound consequences for every aspect of UK policy during the coming years. Keynes himself was aware of the dangers. Nevertheless nothing in *The General Theory* dissuaded Durbin from arguing in *The Politics of Democratic Socialism* that democracy represented a burden that capitalism could not bear.

PROVISOS

The meaning of full employment

In the years before the publication of the White Paper there was vigorous debate within the Treasury and the Economic Section of the Cabinet Office about the questions raised by the objective of full employment. They were questions that were to resound throughout the decades to come as Keynesian economics came to dominate policy. One question was as to the meaning of full employment. It was foreseen that in the immediate aftermath of the war there would be a shortage of labour before the armed forces were demobilized and the economy was refocused on peacetime needs. But what in the longer term? An innocent observer, unschooled in the language of economics, might have been enticed into believing that full employment meant full employment. But that was not the meaning. Full employment had no certain definition. Among economists, it certainly meant something different from a state of universal employment at all times. It was recognised that there had to be, as a minimum, transitional, or 'frictional', unemployment as workers moved from one employment to another. Without movement of people into new and developing industries, and out of old industries, the economy would become increasingly fossilized and uncompetitive. Movement from job to job, and hence transitional unemployment, provided the flexibility required in an economy competing with the rest of the world. Transitional, or frictional, unemployment was therefore required even if the objective was that everyone who wanted a job should be able to get one in reasonable time.

The definition, when it was offered, was in terms of the amount not of employment but of unemployment. That was logical politically because the human cost and the political hazard resulted from people being unemployed not from their being employed inefficiently or uneconomically. It was also logical economically because the level of unemployment might have a significant implication for inflation. It was always clear that full employment carried the danger of inflation. The danger had been signalled during the war by both Keynes and Beveridge. It was highlighted in the 1944 Employment White Paper, which said, 'Action by the Government to maintain expenditure will be fruitless unless wages and prices are kept reasonably stable.' The White Paper argument had been implicitly accepted by the TUC. Its 1944 interim reconstruction report said that:

> it is clear to us that no government can guarantee full employment unless they can be assured that the steps they are taking or propose to take, will not be rendered ineffective by the failure of the quite legitimate but powerful interests, including the trade union movement, to make their actions conform to the achievement of that objective.[15]

Not for the last time, the TUC was offering more than it was able, or was prepared, to deliver.

From the debate it was clear that participants were thinking of levels of unemployment much higher than 3 per cent. In some texts, the interpretation of full employment could permit as much as 7 per cent unemployment.[16] There was no clear guidance in *The General Theory* as to what Keynes meant by full employment. Robert Skidelsky comments that 'Keynes . . . seems to have thought of "normal" unemployment as that level of unemployment at which money-wages (and prices) are stable.'[17] In other words, Keynes did not want unemployment to fall so low that inflation would be stimulated. Keynes was fully conscious of the dangers of over-full employment. Though he could not be certain in advance what level of unemployment would be necessary, he was aware of the risks of reducing it even as far as 3 per cent. Beveridge's Report had assumed unemployment at a rate of 8.5 per cent after the war.[18] The Treasury thought it could be even higher. Keynes wrote to Beveridge, 'No harm in aiming at 3 per cent unemployment, but I shall be surprised if we succeed.'[19]

The external environment

Another question was whether the external environment would be favourable to full employment. James Meade of the Economic Section was a socialist economist who understood the likely impact of the external environment on domestic economic policy. This was because he was a 'market' socialist rather than a physical-planning socialist. He noted, in 1941, the difficulty the UK would encounter if it were alone in attempting to expand internal demand when other countries were 'wallowing' in economic depression. To counter the threat to the balance of payments, the UK might be obliged to restrict imports or to depreciate the exchange rate of sterling. It was, therefore, 'of the utmost importance to achieve international co-operation in the planning and timing of national monetary, budgetary and investment policies for the control of trade fluctuations'.[20] But would such co-operation be available? In April 1942, Meade emphasized the need to impose on countries with favourable balances as much of the strain of adjustment as fell on countries with unfavourable balances.[21] But would the countries with favourable balances accept their obligation? They would be under no compulsion, and goodwill might not extend that far. Other socialists went further than Meade and insisted that international trade would have to be regulated so as to ensure stability in the domestic market. This might not mean reducing trade. But it could well mean eliminating unwelcome trade. Socialists conceived of this happening by agreement between socialist countries all of which would be regulating their trade with each other in accordance with their own interests. But how many socialist countries on the British model would there be? Even on the most optimistic forecast, the USA would not be a socialist country. Yet it was bound to emerge from the war with a decisive influence on world affairs. The evidence was that it would insist on open markets. There could be no assurance that it would co-operate in the protectionist schemes of socialist countries. There was, of course, the exchange rate. Meade was always alive to the use of the exchange rate. The Economic Section, in a 1943 paper, mentioned the need 'either to lower money costs or the value of sterling' if falling demand for UK exports should threaten unemployment. Its main emphasis was on the need for any post-war international commercial or financial agreements to 'provide some latitude for adjustments of the rate of exchange and, as a temporary expedient, for the restriction of imports, when these are required to defend the balance of payments'.[22] But would such agreements be attainable? Analysing the lessons to be derived from the world crisis of the 1930s, countries might fear that their trading partners would engage in competitive devaluations. There appeared to be major problems about achieving full employment in one country in an unfavourable international economic environment.

Meanwhile Keynes was in negotiation with Harry Dexter White of the US Treasury for the creation of a multilateral post-war economic system. Keynes wanted the establishment of international institutions to ease the balance of payments problems which many countries, including the UK, would face after the war. He found that, contrary to his own more liberal ideas, the Americans would insist on ever harsher conditionality for the assistance that might be available from such institutions. It was agreed to establish an International Monetary Fund (IMF) and an International Bank for Reconstruction and Development (IBRD or World Bank). These were the two bodies which, after the White–Keynes plan had been agreed at Bretton Woods in 1944, would become known as the Bretton Woods institutions. Due to fear of competitive devaluations, the IMF was to have a role in supervising exchange rate movements. But the two institutions were allowed resources which fell far short of the needs that were likely to arise after the war. It was clear that the USA was not in a giving mood. It was intent on a multilateral world trading system but was not yet prepared to devote large US resources to ease any transitional balance of payments problems arising from its establishment. Given the disappointing mood in Washington, it was ever clearer that the world after the war would be one in which it would be difficult for the UK to live, let alone guarantee full employment. The Treasury had been converted to the White–Keynes scheme, but the Bank of England was critical. It was consumed by the idea of building up a wider sterling area in the post-war world, as independent as possible of the dollar, and was also reluctant to accept any international constraints on British exchange rate policy.[23]

The proviso about the external environment was never as prominent in the presentation of full employment as it should have been. Because, in the early years after the second world war, there was no return to the distressing experiences of the 1920s and 1930s, the public was allowed to believe that the problem of unemployment had been solved. Full employment was not, however, at the disposal of a British government. Its achievement depended on a level of international co-operation inconceivable without the participation of the USA, which had its own policy objectives, and not necessarily conceivable with it. Keynesianism could not guarantee the necessary level of international co-operation and therefore could not alone guarantee full employment. Keynes might justly reject socialism as a clumsy, unsubtle way of dealing with the problems of capitalist society, but his own ideas for international collaboration were equally susceptible of the criticism that they were unrealistic.

For the British government, particularly for a British Labour government anxious to secure full employment, these uncertainties about the external environment raised a variety of fundamental questions. They included whether the objective of British policy should be an open trading world and, by implication, sterling convertibility, and whether the exchange rate should be fixed or flexible, and at what level. The irony was that these questions were answered not, in reality, by the post-war Attlee government but by its servant Keynes, sent to negotiate a loan in Washington. It was thus a political Liberal, Keynes, rather than a socialist government who laid the foundations of Britain's post-war economic policy. The socialist government was so anxious for money from the USA that it accepted the views of the political Liberal, with unhappy results. It then defaulted on the commitments into which it had entered.

SOCIALIST DOUBTS

In his search for the power with which he could displace capitalism, Aneurin Bevan, miner extraordinary, had reached the House of Commons as early as 1929, and had therefore witnessed the collapse of the MacDonald government at close quarters. He was among socialists who hoisted storm warnings. He saw the Employment White Paper as a denial of the need for public ownership, for socialism and for the Labour party. If the panaceas implied by the White Paper worked, there was no reason for the existence of the Labour party. 'I will go so far as to say that, if the implications of the White Paper are sound, there is no longer any justification for this Party existing at all.'[24] For similar reasons, Bevan was privately critical of the Beveridge Report. Bevan felt in his bones that, whatever the White Paper might say, full employment under capitalism was not possible. To sustain his position he would insist on extreme definitions of full employment. The idea that full employment meant something other than full employment seemed to Bevan to justify his refusal to accept Keynesianism as an alternative to socialism. Writing after his experience of government, he denounced the concept of 'frictional unemployment'. He believed that planning could dispense with unemployment altogether, as supposedly in the Soviet Union. He argued for priorities rather than the price mechanism. 'A pool of unemployment is the necessary accompaniment of selection by the price mechanism.'[25] Planning could replace the price mechanism. Better, he thought, the heart-rending anxieties of difficult planning decisions than unemployment for any human being.[26] Bevan placed a high value on personal liberty. He does not appear to have asked himself whether the kind of planning that could guarantee full employment of the Soviet kind was consistent with the personal liberty that he treasured.

But there were socialist economists, such as G. D. H. Cole, who could deploy more sophisticated arguments for believing that, under capitalism, permanent full employment was not possible. The attempt would distort the operations of capitalism and undermine its efficiency. These criticisms had considerable force. But they were swept away in the general euphoria that an answer to high unemployment had been found, and that the leaders of the Labour party had felt able to commit themselves to it. It became unclear whether a Labour government would be committed to socialism as Aneurin Bevan and Harold Laski, or indeed Durbin, understood it. The Marxists had always claimed that the Labour party was not really socialist, that its real purpose was to protect capitalism, not to destroy it. Perhaps they had been right after all, at least in that. The truth of Bevan's perception that, if the assurances in the White Paper could be delivered, a socialist party was unnecessary took a long time to sink in. There were high institutional obstacles to his lesson striking home. The Labour party was, after all, a socialist party. There needed to be a case for socialism. As the Minister of War said when told that there was no evidence against Dreyfus, 'Let it be found.' The intellectual challenge, for those determined to preserve the case for socialism, and who yet accepted the implications of the White Paper, was to discover arguments that justified socialist policies even if they were no longer required to eliminate large-scale unemployment.

DOUGLAS JAY AND SOCIALISM AFTER KEYNES

The most notable attempt by a socialist writer to provide the justification for socialism even after Keynes was that by Douglas Jay, then City editor of the *Daily Herald*, in his *Socialist Case*, first published in 1937. It was a book that greatly influenced Strachey and helped to wean him back into the ranks of the Labour party. Paradoxically, Jay's adaptation of Keynesianism to his socialist purpose has a number of elements which, taken together, placed him well on the right wing of the Labour party, far away from Strachey's revised location. First was the acceptance of demand management. Jay brought forward the concept of 'total effective demand'. He had studied Keynes's *General Theory*. He tells us that he was careful to make his concept of total effective demand consistent with *The General Theory*, which had been published the previous year.[27]

If total effective demand was achieved, as Jay suggested, by intelligent monetary management, it would bring the unemployed back into work. This brings us to the second element in Jay's adaptation of socialism. The success of total effective demand hardly required massive, or indeed any, nationalization. Cole commented that 'there is little in [*The Socialist Case*] of what most people think of as socialism'. The reason for the comment was the low priority given in the book to nationalization.[28] In one sense Jay was an enthusiastic nationalizer. He recounts how, in 1945, he pressed for inclusion of what became the Attlee government's nationalization policy in *Let Us Face the Future*. As we have seen, a great deal of that programme was relatively uncontroversial. And to the part that was controversial, iron and steel, Jay was opposed.[29]

Jay did write, basing himself on wartime experience, that 'Government Departments, intelligently organized by minds capable of flexibility and constantly searching for results, could operate as quickly and efficiently as ICI at its best.'[30] Nevertheless, he was certainly far less of a nationalizer, and far less of a centralizer, than other socialists. He regretted that socialists had been 'mistaken in making ownership of the means of production instead of ownership of inherited property the test of socialization'. Beyond the utilities, he would have been content with state shareholdings in the private sector, ownership without control.[31] For this Keynesian socialist, nationalization was ceasing to be at the core of socialism.

Jay's downgrading of nationalization implies a third element in his adaptation of socialism which again made his views distinctive. Marxists, and most non-Marxist socialists, considered that there was no longer any long-term value to be derived from the private sector. The Marxist would take the earliest opportunity to eliminate it. The non-Marxist socialist would tolerate it for an interim period but would not expect any significant contribution from it to the progress of the economy. Indeed its continued existence was a nuisance. It was inconsistent with centralized planning, and was also an outrage because it was no longer rendering useful service to the community. Jay, on the other hand, did see value in the creativity of the entrepreneur.

> The entrepreneur of genius is worth an incalculable amount to the community. Without a certain number of men of this degree of enterprise and organizing power a modern economic system could not be maintained at all ... Great entrepreneurs of this kind are of a value so great that it would be impossible to overpay them. For their services must be obtained if the community is to live and nobody else can give them.[32]

Jay's is a kind of liberal socialism in which the private entrepreneur is valued and in which the real enemies are gross inequality and inherited incomes. However, even Jay saw an inevitable trend towards large scale and monopoly which would make the entrepreneur an endangered species.

Jay still sees a need for central planning, though of a very different kind from that of which Durbin was writing. He argues that market forces should be allowed the maximum scope consistent with social needs. Nevertheless, he claims that in any society a balance has to be struck between the multifarious needs of different human beings. It is unacceptable, in his view, to leave the striking of the balance to the *'blind, inhuman calculus of* laissez-faire',[33] as would happen if it was left to the market, even the market as adjusted by Keynesian techniques. Such decisions should be taken consciously through democratic institutions. It is, in his view, this consideration that is 'the essential justification of democracy; and the ultimate source of Socialist policy and Socialist thought'.[34] Thus, for Jay, the key element in socialism is the taking of social decisions through a collective and democratic process. '[I]t is impossible to be a socialist without being a democrat, or a sincere democrat without being a socialist.'[35] It was the kind of claim that was to win Jay, rather unfairly, a reputation for arrogance, forgetting his warning that *'one absolute limit must be set to the extension of planning in normal times; and that is the point at which it infringes on personal as opposed to economic freedom. Personal freedom means the right of the individual to do what he likes with himself, to work for whom, for what, when and where he chooses.'*[36] Jay's socialism made rather less arrogant claims for socialist planning than those of some of his contemporaries.

However, unlike Durbin, Jay does not seem at the time to have been alert to the inflationary implications of Keynesian economics. After the war, there was a constant search for means of containing inflation without prejudicing full employment. No satisfactory method was ever found. Throughout the Attlee government and in the 1950s, inflationary pressure was building up, was damaging British competitiveness and was a constant subject of anxious debate within and without governments. Nevertheless Jay tells us that:

> The main weakness in [*The Socialist Case*], not fully apparent to me till the 1970s, was my failure to see that, given vigorous collective bargaining on pay, the effort to manage demand without managing labour costs (pay rates) could generate cost-push inflation. But this facet of the problem did not become actual for nearly forty years because the collective bargaining power of labour grew only slowly.[37]

Jay was inclined to see the trade unions in a somewhat rosy light. He wrote, 'Trade unions have been called the most beneficial institutions in the world: and rightly, since they exert the maximum of social pressure at the point of maximum social need.'[38] Further experience seems slowly to have modified this enthusiasm. If the problem of wage inflation did not become critical until the late 1960s it was in considerable part due to the fall in commodity prices after 1952, a factor which was to be dramatically, if temporarily, reversed in 1973. Jay's failure to see the point before the 1970s shows that, like other socialists who had reached maturity during a period of high unemployment, his thought was concentrated on the domestic scene and on the priority of full employment, and that he never took adequate account of inflation or of the international dimension of policy. Any problems with inflation could be managed by appeals to the trade union movement or by incomes policies, and any balance of payments problems could always be mitigated by 'planning' and controls. In any case, as we shall see, Jay was not an inflation hawk.

A VISION TOO FAR – CONCLUSION

Despite the doubts about how far it was in the power of a British government alone to ensure it, full employment in a mixed economy became the policy of the Labour party. Socialism became increasingly irrelevant. Socialist measures might be introduced but they would have no effect, or even negative effects, on the fundamental questions facing the economy. Here was a theory of society developed over years by considerable minds and which gained mass support among the working classes and trade unions especially at times of capitalist crisis. It was intended to solve a manifest problem, the unemployment of millions of people. But socialism could not be tried in a democracy because in practice it alienated too many even of those it was intended to help. In so far as the problems of capitalism were solved, they were solved without socialism. Indeed socialism became an obstacle rather than an aid to their solution.

Yet socialism could not have been disproved by argument even when the arguments against it were presented with the force brought to the task by writers such as Hayek. It was inescapable that a working-class party should make the attempt to fashion a socialist economy, such was the crisis of capitalism in the 1930s. If the case for socialism was to be disproved, it could only be in the attempt to establish it. Keynes might have made its implementation less urgent and, in its more drastic forms, unnecessary. But he had not deflected its adherents from their ultimate end, a socialist society. The struggle for socialism had therefore to proceed. It had to be tested as a process and, if the end of the road were ever reached, as an objective. The process was, in fact, enough to test it to destruction. The history of the next fifty years can be seen as the slow eradication of socialist ideas from the body politic. The long decline of socialism can be interpreted as the slow education of socialists in truths they had bitterly resisted and even treated with contempt. Among the lessons were the diseconomies of state ownership, the impossibility of physical planning in a sophisticated modern economy, the value of profit and of incentives (including the incentive to work at all), and the limits to equality.

Here we come to a characteristic of democracy that Durbin, in his praise for it, overlooked. It is one of its most useful characteristics. The genius of democracy is that it allows a panacea to be tested to destruction without society itself being destroyed with it.

PART II

ATTLEE'S THIRD WAY

SIX

In the foothills of socialism

ILLUSION AND REALITY

Labour would not have won an election in 1939 or 1940. There was little public expectation that it would win the election in July 1945. It was to the hero, Churchill, that victory in the war was ascribed. Churchill, wildly turning his guns from Hitler to the Labour party, accused his recent allies of totalitarian tendencies. '[N]o Socialist system can be established without a political police . . . They [a socialist government] would have to fall back on some form of Gestapo . . .'[1] Whatever one thinks of the quality of Churchill's insight into the nature of British socialism, these were ill-advised words with which to attack opponents who had served with him in Cabinet until a few weeks before. Such intemperate language would, however, hardly deny him the reward earned by his courage in 1940, and by the inspiration he had imparted during the war. A vast swing against the Conservatives would be needed to bring Labour anywhere near victory. That was how the electoral prospects appeared to supposedly informed observers. In retrospect, Paul Addison has shown how sentiment in the country had moved against the Conservatives since the disasters of Dunkirk had demonstrated their guilt in leaving Britain inadequately defended.[2] The Labour party, which had hardly been in the forefront in demanding rearmament, escaped much blame because it had been in opposition.

The trend away from the Conservatives was not perceived among the leadership of the Labour party. Attlee, Bevin and Dalton would have been prepared to delay the election until victory over Japan had been added to victory in Europe and meanwhile to accept Churchill's offer of continuing in the coalition. They might even have been prepared to continue the coalition into the period of reconstruction after the war. They were in the best position to know how dire would be the tasks of any government that took office in the immediate aftermath of the war. Thomas Fraser MP, Dalton's Parliamentary Private Secretary in the last months of the coalition government, recalled: 'Dalton was totally at one with Churchill in believing that the national interest required the continuation of the Coalition under Churchill into the period of post-war reconstruction.' He added that Dalton 'believed that the electors would rally behind Churchill in the coming election and that the Labour Party would be cast into the wilderness for another generation'.[3] Morrison, on the other hand, had been unequivocal since mid-1944 that the coalition should not extend beyond the end of the war in Europe. This was not because he had great hopes of a Labour victory. He considered that too heavy an emphasis on Labour's socialist programme would be a vote loser rather than a vote winner. Ian Mikardo, at the December 1944 Party Conference, had succeeded in securing, without a division, the passage of a resolution demanding nationalization well beyond the leadership's intentions and including land and banking. Morrison warned him that he had thereby lost Labour the election.[4] It was comforting to have a scapegoat for defeat before battle had even commenced.

Yet 25 July 1945, the day the election results were announced, revealed that Labour had not merely won the election but had done so with a massive majority of 146 over all other parties in the House of Commons. As George Dangerfield writes in rather a different context. 'From that victory they never recovered.'[5] In this victory, Labour was helped by the electoral system. The massive majority was won with only 48 per cent of the votes cast. Deep in the instincts of the British people still lay their typical conservatism and scepticism of political promises. Yet this was a time when, if ever, scepticism could be discarded in favour of hope. The British people deceived themselves into imagining that the war had been fought, not to defeat Hitler, but for a better world. The sacrifices which they had made in the war became greater and greater as they contemplated them retrospectively. For what purpose had those sacrifices been made? There was never a better moment than this for the Labour party to exploit public longing for a secure and prosperous life. The electorate had turned to a party which, it believed, would protect it from the miseries of the 1920s and 1930s, and from a repetition of the disappointments that had followed victory in 1918. This time there would really be homes fit for heroes guaranteed by a Labour government that could be relied on not to default.

The Labour party, in its election manifesto *Let Us Face the Future*, had contributed to public expectations. It contained a raft of attractive but expensive promises. It would establish a National Health Service. It would proceed with a housing programme at 'the maximum possible speed until every family in this island has a good standard of accommodation'. Social insurance would be improved together with 'economic policies designed to reduce rainy days to a minimum'. There would be the expected programme of nationalization, including the fuel and power industries, inland transport, and iron and steel. The Bank of England would also be brought under public ownership and the operations of the other banks would be 'harmonised' with public needs. Above all, there would be full employment. The foreign policy section contained a list of admirable aspirations. What was missing was any analysis of the economic difficulties that Britain would face in the post-war world and which might make these promises difficult to fulfil. Yet Labour Ministers had served in the Churchill coalition and knew perfectly well that Britain would emerge from the war facing frightening economic problems. The programme of social reform had been prepared during the war years, and Labour Ministers had become psychologically committed to it, without thought for the ominous problems that any new government would inherit. The last wartime Government Economic Survey which appeared, with calculated coincidence, on 25 July 1945, warned that 'It is no exaggeration, but a sober statement of fact, to assert that our external economic problem after this war will be at least as considerable as that of Germany after the last war.'[6]

Britain, after the war, was in no position to pay for the imports it needed either to satisfy consumer demand or to reconstruct the economy. A long transition would be necessary before there was any hope of a British government being in a position, out of its own resources, to fulfil promises such as the Labour party had made during the election. None of this was any secret from those Cabinet Ministers who had served in the Churchill coalition. Yet the promises were made. Perhaps Labour felt more confident in making them in the expectation that victory would reward Churchill and that it would not fall on Labour to implement them. Indeed the promises may have been more lavish precisely because Labour feared an overwhelming Churchill victory. Or perhaps Labour really did believe in the efficacy of socialist planning. If so, it is surprising that it did nothing in the aftermath of its election victory to bring effective planning into operation. But, even on the happiest assumptions about socialist planning, it would take time to show results. No political party, not even the Conservatives, was prepared to say to the electorate that their sacrifices had not yet ended, that things might very well get worse before they could be expected to get any better. To issue such warnings at election time was not in the spirit of British democracy. Yet, after the election, the electorate would demand that Labour's contract with it should be fulfilled. Victorious Labour was entitled to be terrified by the consequences of its own irresponsibility. Nor would it be any excuse that the Conservatives had been quite as irresponsible and that, in a battle for votes, anything goes.

Britain, during the war, had been kept alive by American and Canadian assistance. These programmes had ensured that the British economy would remain viable, and hence its military capacity intact, when the reserves with which to buy food, raw materials and armaments had run low. The Canadians had been generous to their Commonwealth ally and had not enforced terms which would further weaken the British economy. But when the USA, before entering the war, offered assistance in the form of Lend–Lease, it extracted harsh conditions. Harsh as they might be, support from the USA was a *sine qua non* of the survival of an independent Britain. There was no alternative but to accept. The terms for Lend–Lease were finalized under the Mutual Aid Agreement of 23 February 1942. The conditions in no way recognized that Britain, for over a year standing alone with its Commonwealth allies against Hitler, was fighting a war on behalf of all democratic nations, on behalf of civilization as a whole. It was widely held in Britain that, in delaying their entrance into the war until attacked at Pearl Harbor, the Americans had done a great deal less than their duty to democracy and civilization, let alone their own interest in ensuring that Europe was not dominated by Nazi Germany. By that time Britain had been at war for over two years. While the USA hesitated and equivocated, Britain suffered. It must be doubtful whether, if it had not been attacked by Japan, the USA would ever have entered the war. Britain's cause was greatly assisted by Hitler's gratuitous declaration of war on the USA after Pearl Harbor. But for that gift to the Allied cause, the USA might well have given priority to the Pacific war rather than to victory in Europe.

Britain's crisis was regarded on the other side of the Atlantic as America's opportunity. Britain's empire seemed to be a target second only to Hitler's Germany. The USA appeared to have its commercial interests as much in mind as its duty to the future of democracy. Any concession of its commercial interests that could be squeezed from Britain in its moment of extreme peril would be squeezed. Britain had been compelled to devote itself entirely to the war effort and certainly not at all to competing with the USA in export markets. It had therefore been compelled to sacrifice to the demands of the war not merely overseas assets but overseas markets and the modernization of its export industries. The frequent expressions of gratitude by British leaders for American aid only partly concealed a great mountain of resentment. In public it was America's generosity to which tribute was paid. In the privacy of Whitehall, the vitriol of Ministers and civil servants was directed against the USA's crude and calculating self-interest. With the approaching end of the war, the Americans were already giving indications that they did not intend indefinitely to be a milch-cow for Britain and its Empire. It should have been a warning.

Just as it was not widely understood during the war how much Britain depended on Lend–Lease, so, after the war, it was little understood in Britain how much the UK continued to depend on American support. It was thought that the British were doing all these marvellous things, the war effort during the war and social reform after it, by themselves with their own money or, at least, with American money to which they were fully entitled as of right. The conviction that the Americans had done less than their duty implied that gratitude for any aid need not be deeply felt.

APPOINTING THE GOVERNMENT

The five leading figures in the Labour party in 1945 were Attlee, Bevin, Cripps, Dalton and Morrison. Despite a level of mutual intolerance surpassing even what is normal in the upper reaches of political parties, they were now bound to find ways of working together to implement *Let Us Face the Future*. The five would have survived in office, whatever their incapacity, moral, intellectual or physical, until the end, had not sickness forced the resignation of Cripps in October 1950 and death plucked Bevin in April 1951. Dalton was in retirement after he leaked his budget secrets in November 1947 but was brought back into the Cabinet after nine months. Conflicting ambitions are not a fatal flaw among members of a Cabinet provided they are agreed on what to do. Events would provide the test. The implementation of *Let Us Face the Future* would be a bond between them. In contrast, events, foreseeable and unforeseeable, might have a strongly divisive effect on their relationships. Whatever else could be said for socialism, it had not so far dethroned the ancient saw that there are no friends at the top.

At moments of crisis, of which there were many, the relationship between the five proved friable. Morrison, Dalton and Cripps felt disdain for Attlee, whose leadership of the Labour party they regarded as a matter of accident rather than merit. The accident was Morrison's temporary absence from the House due to his defeat in the 1931 election. He was therefore not available when, in 1935, an interim successor to George Lansbury had to be found among the forty-six members of the then Parliamentary Labour Party pending the 1935 General Election. The Labour party has never much liked changing its mind and, after that election, the interim leader, Attlee, was re-elected by the reinforced PLP and continued as leader for twenty years. Irritation with his inadequacies was never enough to persuade the PLP to bring upon itself the pain of replacing him. Attlee, in any case, enjoyed the inestimable support of Ernest Bevin. At first sight, this was difficult to understand. Attlee, in alliance with Cripps, had frequently found himself in conflict with Bevin in the early 1930s. He was not a charismatic leader and, in any case, charismatic leaders were out of favour after the defection of Ramsay MacDonald. But he did not strike his associates as being any kind of leader. There seemed to be two motives behind Bevin's enduring loyalty. The first was that Attlee had never done him any harm, at least since Attlee's revolutionary ardour had cooled. Nor, even more important, was he ever likely to. One of the many problems of the 1945 government was that Attlee would not have dared to do Bevin any harm. The second motive was that Attlee was not Morrison. There was a dreary history of clashes between the two men, Bevin and Morrison, the most powerful in the Labour Movement. Bevin's aversion to Morrison was longstanding. There could be many reasons. Morrison had supported the cut in unemployment pay which, in August 1931, destroyed the MacDonald government. He was suspected of actually having considered an invitation from Ramsay MacDonald to join the National government. He had opposed the idea of trade union representatives on boards of nationalized corporations. He was an independent force with his base not in the trade unions but in the London Labour party. To add to these crimes, he had been frequently spoken of in the 1930s as being prepared to enter a coalition with the Tories. But more significant than any specific disagreement was the fact that Morrison was the only possible challenger to Bevin's dominance of the Party. Bevin was a man to whom suspicion of the motives of others came easily. But his suspicions usually had a strong element of self-interest. He would not be the first man in a government of which Morrison was

Prime Minister. He regarded Attlee's leadership of the Party as the best protection against the emergence of Morrison as leader or indeed of those intellectuals, Cripps and Dalton, both of whom he distrusted. Cripps, in particular, he regarded, with inadequate respect for the recent facts, as too near to Moscow.[7] As for Attlee, he knew that his best guarantee of residence at No. 10 was the conflicting ambitions of his senior colleagues and the support of Bevin, who did not appear to want the top job for himself as long as he was the major influence in the Cabinet.

Morrison was sure that he ought to be Prime Minister. He insisted, in the aftermath of the 1945 General Election, that Attlee should not go to the Palace to kiss hands as Prime Minister before the new PLP had met to elect its leader. Perhaps he was not planning to replace Attlee himself, but merely trying to ensure that the PLP exercised its constitutional right to elect its leader. If it was an attempt on Attlee's leadership, it was counterproductive. Bevin told Attlee to ignore Morrison and to go to the Palace, an instruction which Attlee willingly obeyed. Attlee was more strongly entrenched in the position of leader than many thought possible for so inconsiderable a person or, for that matter, desirable. The result of Morrison's insistence on constitutional niceties was to add to his uneasy relationship with Bevin an uneasy relationship with Attlee, who, he felt, never paid sufficient attention to his advice.

Attlee's most interesting appointment was of Aneurin Bevan as Minister of Health responsible both for the government's housing programme and for the creation of a National Health Service. Bevan had acted as unofficial leader of the opposition during the war. Even during the war, when Churchill was the hero of the great majority of the nation, Bevan, already by 1939 an MP for ten years, exploited every military setback against the Prime Minister. Churchill's role in the General Strike remained for Bevan an offence that could never win absolution. His disrespect for Churchill was exceeded only by his contempt for the socialist members of the coalition, the sole exception being Cripps, with whom he had been expelled from the Party in January 1939. After all, everyone knew that Churchill was an enemy of the workers. His Labour colleagues were supposed to be their friends. Bevan's irreverence did him no harm in the Party in the country. In 1944 he was elected to the National Executive Committee, though this did not necessarily give him a claim on Cabinet office. There is disagreement between Attlee and Bevin as to who deserves the credit for Bevan's appointment. Bevin claims to have recommended Bevan, which, if true, would show that he could appreciate merit when it was not threatening to him personally. But Attlee denies Bevin's claim. He writes of Bevan that 'I felt he had it in him to do good service.'[8] At least both Attlee and Bevin seemed to think that credit was to be claimed. And it is questionable whether Attlee would have appointed one of Bevin's most persistent wartime critics without Bevin's approval. Nevertheless, there is no need to deny Attlee his rare good judgement because the decision in the end was his. In a Cabinet lacking sparkle in its junior ranks, Bevan was the exception, a man of eloquence, imagination and wit, though suffering from a disease common to many socialists, a reluctance to learn from experience.

A DEMAND FOR JUSTICE

Faced simultaneously by national bankruptcy and by its own election promises, the Attlee government's first hope lay in a continuation of Lend–Lease. Under the Act passed by the United States Congress, Lend–Lease could continue until the end of the war, and, at the time of the 1945 election, the war with Japan had not yet been won. The US administration had repeatedly stated that Lend–Lease would be provided only where necessary to ensure the effective prosecution of the war to final victory. It was not to be furnished for purposes of relief, rehabilitation or reconstruction in Europe or elsewhere. It had been thought that final victory might take a further eighteen months, during which a British government could continue to enjoy the benefits of American charity. The atomic bombs dropped on Hiroshima and Nagasaki early in August 1945 put an end to such dreams. Japan surrendered and with its surrender went Britain's hopes from Lend–Lease. It was perfectly well known in official circles in London that Lend–Lease could not survive the end of the war. The Act of Congress allowed President Truman no discretion.[9] Nevertheless, Truman's action, on 24 August, in cancelling Lend–Lease provoked cries of rage and frustration in London. Roosevelt, it was said, would have understood the justice of Britain's need for continuing assistance. It was the inexperience of Truman, it was claimed, that had led to this rebuff. The expressions of outrage emanating from the Attlee government could only have been synthetic, perhaps a preparation of the ground for explaining to the British people why the election promises could not be fulfilled. Writing years later, Aneurin Bevan was to describe the abrupt ending of Lend–

Lease to Britain as 'a grievous and unjust blow to the prospects of British recovery'.[10] The blow was certainly grievous for a government that had committed itself to *Let Us Face the Future* without the means to carry out the promises it contained. But perhaps the more significant adjective in the quotation is 'unjust'. Ministers came to believe that justice entitled them to preach to the USA about its proper line of conduct while at the same time cadging money from it.

Lend–Lease having been cancelled, the next best hope was for a new programme of aid from the USA. The British government had been lavish in its expressions of gratitude to the people and government of the USA for the benefaction of Lend–Lease. But there was no evidence that such disquisitions, even if appropriate, would lead to a more favourable consideration by the USA of pleas for further aid. That would depend on an assessment in Washington of US interests, not upon the warmth or frequency of expressions of gratitude by the beneficiary of past assistance. There had never been any commitment by the American government to sustain the British economy in peacetime. Congress had always had the gravest doubts about the wisdom even of Lend–Lease. It was absurd to expect that the US administration would regard it as any part of its post-war duty to sustain the British economy, certainly not unconditionally. Did not Britain claim to be a global power? Did it not have an empire? Had it not just put its trust in socialism? If further help was required it might be considered, but it would be on terms.

Despite the evidence of American reluctance, the Attlee government turned to the USA in expectation that the exceptional wartime services of impoverished Britain would be recognized, that its urgent necessities would be relieved, that the justice that could be so easily afforded by the USA would be done. Britain might be a decayed gentlewoman but she was entitled to look to her relatives for help despite the divorce that had occurred 160 years earlier. That the world should be made over in the interests of justice to all men was a profoundly socialist idea. The idea of socialism has always been particularly influential among those who hope to receive rather than among those who are expected to give. But Keynes, too, believed that the Americans should give Britain what was justly its due, thus perhaps showing that even he was not impermeable to socialist influences. This was not to be the only matter on which Keynes's judgement proved faulty. The Attlee government's hopes for unconditional aid from capitalist America, strange indeed in a socialist government, were to be disappointed. There was no sign in

Washington of any recognition of Britain's exceptional services, no readiness to accord the credit that Britain thought was its due. It was naive to expect it and deficient in imagination to suppose that Britain's role in the war would be perceived in the USA in the same light as in Britain. Americans also had died in the war. Americans had every right to feel that the USA had been compelled, for the second time in twenty-five years, to intervene in a European conflict, and to rescue Britain from the predicament in which this supposedly great power found itself. Resentment in America at the way that Europe's follies seemed to force sacrifices on the USA was at least as justified as British resentment that the USA did not see the war against Hitler through British eyes. The result of Britain's misconception was repeated humiliation when the USA either refused requests for help or ladled it out on terms which Britain felt to be the more humiliating in that pressing need dictated their acceptance.

Together with the sense that justice required the USA to assist the UK went another feeling. It was that Britain was a global power, though a fallen one. Its economic links spread throughout the world. It was therefore, according to this doctrine, in the interests of the world as a whole to help Britain and not to exact harsh conditions in return. This feeling was not limited to the Labour party but suffused political circles more widely. It persisted at least into the 1990s, by which time the world had lost most of the interest it might once have had in the fate of the British economy.

The sense of grievance that developed in Britain after the war was linked to the conviction that Britain was special and that its special nature was being ignored by all those around the world who should respect it. Thus the UK was not merely special in its wartime sacrifices. It had a special relationship with the USA. It was special in being the centre of a Commonwealth and of the sterling area. As a result, it was special in that, though located in Europe, it was not 'just' a European country. Its Parliament was special, ancient and sovereign. It had enjoyed a special economic revelation, the Keynesian revolution. Its democratic socialism, firmly based in the trade union movement, was special, distinct not just from the socialism of the Soviet Union but from that of western Europe. A few years later Churchill would conclude that his own special status as Britain's war leader would make him specially equipped to conciliate between the USA and the USSR. Later still, Bevan, as shadow Foreign Secretary, as equipped with illusions as Churchill had ever been, believed that as a spokesman of British democratic socialism he could fulfil a special role as intermediary between what he called the 'frustrated' powers, the USA and USSR. Being so special, Britain should not be required to fight for its living as did other less favoured nations such as France, Germany and Japan. On the contrary the rest of the world would be expected to accommodate its policies to UK needs. There was always deep disappointment, even a sense of betrayal, when major economic powers such as the USA, Germany and Japan insisted on putting their own interests, as they saw them, above those of the UK.

THE AMERICAN LOAN

With confidence in his own socialist cause, Attlee had written before the war, 'A Government should not require advice from experts as to what policy to pursue. What it needs is expert assistance to carry out its decisions. A Labour Government, having achieved power, will have no doubts as to the policy to be pursued.'[11] But now his government turned for advice to Keynes, the contemptuous critic of socialism, on what it should do to resolve the economic crisis facing it, and no one was more persuaded than Keynes that justice required the USA to give the UK massive and unconditional help.

The situation resulting in Britain, and for the Attlee government, from the cancellation of Lend–Lease was certainly serious. Lend-Lease from the USA, together with Mutual Aid from Canada and credits from the sterling area were, in 1945, allowing the UK to overspend its own income at the rate of about £2,100 million a year.[12] Of this £1,100 million was being provided by Lend–Lease. A further £250 million was being provided by Canadian Mutual Aid, which would also stop with the end of the war. The balance of £750 million consisted of credits from the sterling area. That also could also not be relied on in the longer term as sterling area countries became able to spend themselves what they had, during the war, been induced to lend to the UK.[13] On 14 August 1945, Keynes warned the Cabinet of the likelihood of a 'financial Dunkirk'. But then he softened the blow by holding out deceptive hopes. 'We have reason to believe that those members of the American Administration who are in touch with our financial position are already aware that we shall be in Queer Street without aid of somewhere between $3 and $5 billions and contemplate aid on this scale as not outside practical politics.' In fact he already knew from conversations with the American Assistant Secretary of State, Will Clayton, that aid from the USA was unlikely much to exceed $3 billion. The Cabinet also knew.

Keynes told the Cabinet:

> Washington will wish the assistance to be described as a *credit*. If this means payment of interest and stipulated terms of repayment, it is something we cannot undertake in addition to our existing obligations with any confidence that we can fulfil the obligations. It would be a repetition of what happened after the last war and a cause of further humiliation and Anglo-American friction, which we should firmly resist. If, however, the term *credit* is no more than camouflage for what would be in effect a grant-in-aid, that is another matter.

In fact Keynes already knew from Clayton, as indeed did Ministers, that any assistance would not merely be described as a credit but would in fact be a credit on terms requiring payment of interest and stipulated terms of repayment. These were terms which, in Keynes's view, 'we should firmly resist'.

Keynes further advised the Cabinet:

> The Americans will almost certainly insist upon our acceptance of a monetary and commercial foreign policy along the general lines on which they have set their hearts. But it is possible that they will exercise moderation and will not overlook the impropriety of using financial pressure on us to make us submit to what we believe is to our grave disadvantage. In fact the most persuasive argument we can use for obtaining the desired aid is that only by this means will it lie within our power to enter into international co-operation in the economic field on the general principle of non-discrimination. We should not seek to escape our obligations under Article VII of the Mutual Aid Agreement but should, rather, ask for the material basis without which it will not lie in our power to fulfil them. In my opinion we need not despair of obtaining an agreement which provides sufficient safeguards and will not seriously hamper the future development of our economy along lines freely determined by our own policies.

Keynes already knew, as did the Cabinet, that the Americans would insist on Britain meeting its obligations under Article VII of the Mutual Aid Agreement. He knew therefore that they would make assistance conditional on the early convertibility of current account sterling and British co-operation in creating a non-discriminatory trading world which would imply the end, over a period, of imperial preference. He thought that, if he could get from the Americans, whatever it was called, a grant of $5 or 6 billion, or even an interest-free loan of that dimension,

Britain would be able to afford compliance with these American demands. But he had already heard from the Americans the probable size of any loan and the terms on which it might be extended. There was no sign at all that the Americans would accept 'the impropriety of using financial pressure'.

Keynes also gave the Cabinet, on paper, this salutary warning.

> Nor must we build too much on the sympathy and knowledge of the members of the American Administration with whom we are in touch. It will be a tough proposition, perhaps an impossible one, to sell a sufficiently satisfactory plan to Congress and the American people who are unacquainted with, and are never likely to understand, the true force of our case, not only in our own interests but in the interests of the United States and the whole world. For the time being Ministers would do well to assume that no arrangement which we can properly accept is yet in sight; and that, until such an arrangement is in sight, we are, with the imminent cessation of Lend–Lease, virtually bankrupt, and the economic basis for the hopes of the public non-existent.

Despite this warning on paper, Keynes conveyed to Ministers a wholly unrealistic idea of what he could achieve if he was sent to Washington as negotiator on behalf of the UK government. After all he was proceeding to Washington to argue a case that, in his own view, was in the interests not just of the UK but of the USA and the whole world. The Attlee Cabinet was only too ready to imbibe his optimism, although quite aware of the warnings that Clayton had given. Later, Dalton would blame Keynes for his optimism, suggesting that Keynes had thereby deceived the Cabinet.[14] But the Cabinet was in reality deceiving itself about the prospects of a $5 billion grant or interest-free loan It would not otherwise have been prepared to deposit quite as much confidence in Keynes's powers of persuasion. What else could it do if it was not to default on its election promises? As Keynes warned, without US aid 'there would have to be an indefinite postponement of the realisation of the best hopes of the new Government'. The Cabinet was not likely to appreciate his further assurance that, even without help, 'It is probable that after five years the difficulties would have been largely overcome.' The Cabinet was not in the business of waiting five years before it could implement its promises to the electorate. It probably already had it in mind that, as Keynes himself conceded, 'In practice, of course, we shall in the end accept the best terms we can get. And that may be the beginning of later trouble and bitter feelings. That is why it is so

important to grasp the reality of our position and to mitigate its potenti-
alities by energy, ingenuity and foresight.'[15]

It was on this note of capitulation before the negotiations even began
that Keynes was sent to Washington as negotiator on behalf of the new
Labour government. The negotiations that ensued turned out as it was
always inevitable they would turn out. It was confirmed that the USA
did not see Britain's problems quite as Keynes and the Attlee government would have wished them to be seen. Keynes opened the negotiations on the basis that 'justice' was due to the UK. This idea was
speedily rebuffed by Washington officials. He proved not to possess the
energy, ingenuity and foresight to shift the Americans from the terms
on which they had already decided. A loan was conceded but of only
$3.75 billion, not the grant or interest-free loan of $5 or 6 billion that
Keynes had led the Cabinet to hope he might secure. It was some relief
that the Canadians made the total up to $5 billion by a loan of their
own. The conditions for the loans were exactly what the Americans had
always made clear they would extract for the assistance they would give
and which Keynes had described in advance as both unacceptable and
yet to be accepted. Britain would be compelled to make sterling earned
in current transactions convertible one year after Congress approved
the loan. It would also be compelled to join with the USA in creating
a multilateral, non-discriminatory trading world. Both conditions were
acceptable as long-term objectives. Neither was practical on the
timescale dictated from Washington. An additional condition required
Britain to ratify the unsatisfactory Bretton Woods settlement which
Keynes had negotiated with Harry Dexter White. That meant that any
idea of flexible exchange rates, discussed during the war as a support
for full employment, had to be abandoned.

Britain's exchange rate against the dollar was fixed at $4.03, the level
at the beginning of the war. Treasury official and former Fabian Richard
('Otto') Clarke protested that Britain could not live with such an
exchange rate, but Keynes brushed his criticism aside. Meade describes
Clarke as 'a man who temperamentally revolts against an idealist solution or a solution based on general principle'.[16] Clarke feared that
there would be, in the years immediately following the war, a serious
dollar shortage. There would be a great deal that its wartime allies
would wish to buy from the USA but little that they were in a position
to sell. Keynes brushed that fear aside as well. In fact the early post-war
years were to be dominated by an apparently insoluble dollar shortage.
As Clarke was to write later, 'it is rather remarkable in retrospect that

anyone should ever have thought that it was possible for the United Kingdom to emerge from [the] war . . . and still have the same exchange rate as on the day on which we went into the war'.[17] Keynes had been highly critical of Churchill's decision in 1925 to rejoin the Gold Standard at \$4.86, a level which made British goods uncompetitive. The return to the Gold Standard was held to be responsible for much of the subsequent ills of the British economy. Keynes's criticisms had helped to make his reputation as an economist equipped with unusual insight. Now he would be recommending the Attlee government to accept an equally uncompetitive fixed exchange rate within a system with unhappy resemblances to the Gold Standard. Dalton had shared Keynes's dislike of the Gold Standard. Labour had rejected in its propaganda any idea of associating Britain with anything like the Gold Standard. Now it was being recommended to accept a post-war settlement which had much in common with the Gold Standard and at a rate of exchange which would rapidly prove unsustainable.[18]

During the negotiations the Attlee government frequently blustered that conditions were being enforced that it could not be confident it could implement and which, therefore, it could not accept. Yet no Minister visited Washington with the purpose of persuading the Americans that the UK government could not agree terms on which it was likely to default. It needed the money and it knew that, in the end, no such scruples would be allowed to inhibit its acceptance. Attlee did visit Washington in November 1945 but his visit was not linked with the negotiations that were still in progress over the loan. However, he was to address the US Congress. The Ministry of Information wrote to No. 10 Downing Street on 5 November 1945 regarding topics the Prime Minister should address during his speech to Congress. The letter listed some points which Attlee's speech writers should bear in mind:

1. The American misconception of Britain's place in the world economy. Americans continue to be baffled by the concept of a great power which lives by foreign trade and which must export or die. Although this has been stressed by Lord Halifax and Lord Keynes at press conferences, the argument has not convinced Americans, many of whom suspect that we would prefer to retreat behind a protective wall to pursue our monopolistic, discriminatory and imperialist practices rather than to participate in a multilateral trading system.[19]

This perception in Washington, as interpreted by British officials, as to the kind of world in which Britain wished to live was not inaccurate.

Britain might be forced by its urgent needs to agree, in principle, to a multilateral non-discriminatory trading world. But could it be trusted? Would not this socialist government, at the earliest possible opportunity, retreat to monopolistic, discriminatory and imperialist trade practices rather than participate in a multilateral trading system? Was not this Labour government special in the reconciliation it had identified between socialism and imperialism? American officials could well have been aware that there was a longstanding Fabian tradition which authorized the British master race to found its world influence on the benevolent management of an empire. These were good questions and the USA did not have to wait long for answers.

Keynes then undertook the less burdensome task of persuading the Attlee government to accept the deal which the Americans had imposed over his objections. This was at last an assignment within his capacity. The Attlee government was compelled, as conditions of American largesse, to make promises on convertibility and non-discrimination that it would have preferred not to make and was dubious, to put it no higher, that it could fulfil on the timescale dictated by the agreement. Non-discrimination, apart from other considerations, was inconsistent with socialist economics because, once implemented, it would deny a socialist government the control over the economy which it craved. But this was not an argument which the Attlee government had felt able to advance in Washington. The Americans were not noticeably sympathetic to Britain's socialist ambitions. This new Labour government, with its massive Parliamentary majority, proved ready to accept whatever terms it could negotiate for whatever assistance it could get because otherwise it would have no hope of implementing its election programme. It lacked the courage to tell the electorate that, as the support from the USA was being offered only on unacceptable terms, it would not be accepted. The deal was done even though the Attlee government knew that it was highly unlikely that it would be able both to implement its election programme and to meet the conditions of the loan. Keynes did not warn, as he should have done, that, given the terms on which alone American assistance was available, the Labour government would not be able both to respect those terms and to implement their election programme. It was to be not merely socialism on credit but credit gained on terms on which the first British majority socialist government would default. Within the Cabinet, Aneurin Bevan, Minister of Health, opposed the loan agreement. He did not offer any alternative source of largesse which would have made possible his housing programme or the creation of a National Health Service of the kind he contemplated. He was, in fact, simply recording the anti-Americanism characteristic of the British left, though not of the left alone. Among those from the backbenches who opposed the loan was a future Prime Minister, James Callaghan, never a particularly left-wing or anti-American figure.

The acceptance of the loan robbed the Attlee government of any sense of urgency in tackling the country's serious economic problems, and the lack of urgency meant that the problems were never tackled. Britain, supported by American charity, did not need to change in any fundamental way. It could drift on. There was, of course, the programme of nationalization. But that was irrelevant to the country's economic problems. It was not just the government that was robbed of any sense of urgency. If the country's problems could be relieved by foreign charity there was no need for anyone, businessman or trade unionist, to worry about the perennial obstacles to growth, low productivity, restrictive practices in industry, low investment, that would slow economic progress in the UK during the post-war decades. The only problem was to discover a way of ensuring that foreign charity never dried up. The arrival of Marshall Aid two years later proved that the hope of continuing foreign charity was not unrealistic, for the moment at any rate. Thereafter the flow dwindled but it had already constituted a strong motive in Britain for leaving things as they were, however inefficient.

Labour governments in the years to come would borrow heavily from the international financial community. But it was always only with the greatest reluctance that they conceded that borrowing implies conditions that it is necessary to respect. As a result the terms of borrowing were always worse than they might have been. The spirit of these transactions was perfectly expressed many years later by Roy Hattersley who had been deputy leader of the Labour party. In an article criticizing the Blair government for its failures in relieving poverty, he wrote, 'In 1946, a National Insurance Act was implemented in full on the day when it came into force – although Lord Beveridge, its inspiration, advised a phased introduction. Attlee insisted that the demands of the poor take precedence over fiscal probity.'[20] Presumably Hattersley meant that Attlee, having borrowed a vast sum of money from the USA and Canada, then made the honourable decision to renege on the conditions. But no aspect of a government is examined with more hawk-eyed interest by its creditors than is its fiscal probity. Socialism in the UK was a borrowing socialism. The three post-war Labour governments of Attlee, Wilson and Wilson–Callaghan were all heavy borrowers. Labour governments and Labour Ministers never seemed to accept that fiscal probity is much more in demand among lenders than other forms of probity are among the electorate in general. There is therefore a question not just of honour but of self-interest, especially in the case of governments given to heavy borrowing. As we shall see, Hattersley was not the only Labour leader who imagined that fiscal probity could be rationed according to domestic political criteria.

THE WELFARE STATE

The Attlee government's enduring monument is the welfare state. It may be its only monument. It consisted principally of the National Health Service and the National Insurance Act. Proposals for both had been drawn up under the wartime coalition. But it fell to the successor government to implement them according to its own fashion. The Labour government's implementation ignored the cautionary advice given by Durbin in *The Politics of Democratic Socialism*, it was careless of the resource and public expenditure implications, and forgetful of the commitments it had entered into in return for the American loan. Alec Cairncross estimates that between 1936 and 1950 there was, in real terms, an increase of 80 to 90 per cent in social expenditures without counting food and housing subsidies. The largest single element in this increase was the NHS.[21] This occurred in a heavily indebted economy seriously weakened by war. Attlee informs us that 'Our policy was not a reformed capitalism but progress towards democratic socialism.'[22] It is perfectly true that what the government did was in the nature of democratic socialism. It was in the nature of democratic socialism that the Attlee government should bequeath to future governments inflationary pressures and expenditure burdens, both of which became politically inescapable given the limited political courage to be found among subsequent Conservative Ministers. There was little sense in the government that there had to be priorities, that not every expenditure could be borne without cost to the economy and its prospects of growth. If, as Bevan was to tell an astonished Labour Party Conference in 1949, 'the language of priorities is the religion of socialism', it was not a religion to which the Attlee government had yet been converted.[23] Thus the Beveridge Report had recommended the introduction 'for all citizens [of] adequate pensions without means test by stages over a transition period of twenty years, while providing immediate assistance pensions for persons requiring them'.[24] In fact, under the National Insurance Act, the contributory retirement pension was made payable from 1948. Universal benefits were to be provided even if they could not yet be afforded.[25] In the course of the Cabinet Committee debates on the Beveridge Report, during the life of the coalition government, Morrison, defending it against Treasury criticism, had written that 'finance is within very wide limits a handmaid of policy'.[26] In other words there is always enough money for whatever a government really wishes to do, the cry of the inflationist throughout the ages. On the other hand Bevin, as a man who had spent his life dealing with practical problems, had his doubts about the Beveridge Report.[27] The Exchequer was asked to bear not just expenditure on the welfare state but a global role far beyond the UK's post-war capabilities. Dalton records in his account of his time at the Treasury that Durbin, as his Parliamentary Private Secretary, was among those who warned him that his policies had 'dangerous inflationary possibilities'.[28]

Unfortunately Attlee, in a last-minute switch in intentions, had sent Bevin to the Foreign Office and Dalton to the Treasury. It was one of Attlee's most serious errors. He felt that the tension between Bevin and Morrison would prevent their working together on the home front. Therefore, contrary to his original intention of appointing Bevin to the Treasury and Dalton to the Foreign Office, he reversed the appointments. The result was that the strongest man in the Cabinet was at the Foreign Office spending money and resources on Britain's global pretensions instead of at the Treasury cutting them back. Bevin felt himself rightly positioned alongside the Foreign Ministers of the USA and the Soviet Union at summit meetings. His seat at the top table required that the speed of demobilization after the war should be slow and that British troops should be located at strategic points throughout the world. All this was at an insupportable cost to the British economy and to the British balance of payments. Bevin's ambivalence about the USA, shared elsewhere in Whitehall, ensured that he would demand the construction of a British atomic bomb. Dalton's feeble attempts to get the government to measure its commitments to its resources, supported by equally feeble threats of resignation, were brushed aside.

This extravagance with men, money and resources could not last. Gradually Britain did retreat from its global commitments, leaving them to the USA to pick up. But the burden while it lasted added significantly to the already grave economic problems with which Britain emerged from the war. The irresponsibility of these policies has been forgiven

because a welfare state was introduced, because historians have attributed little importance to the default on the American loan, and because
Marshall Aid came along to rescue the government from the worst
consequences of its follies. But, when the legislation establishing the
welfare state was introduced, there could be no confidence that the
USA would once more stand ready to provide aid.

Among the effects were inflationary pressures, present throughout
the life of the Attlee government; costs therefore in exports which the
country needed to balance its accounts not so much with the rest of the
world as with the USA, where the deficit in trade was enormous and
seemed unbridgeable; taxes higher than would otherwise have been
necessary, causing discontent among middle-class voters many of whom
would have voted Labour in 1945; price controls to prevent shortages
from resulting in a spiral of price increases; and rationing, even bread
rationing unheard of during the war, and other restrictions on consumption again lasting longer than might otherwise have been necessary.
After bread rationing came potato rationing. In August 1947, during
the convertibility crisis, the basic petrol ration was suspended. Rationing
was exploited by the so-called Housewives' League against the government. It was the case, as alleged by Labour MPs, that the leadership
of the Housewives' League was close to the Conservative party. It
remained true that the League could not have exploited the discontent
if it had not been there. There were those who considered rationing a
just and fair way of dealing with shortages or, alternatively, were prepared to give their government the benefit of the doubt. There were
those also who, expecting earlier relief from the shortages of wartime,
blamed them on the incompetence of the government.

NATIONALIZATION

The government carried through the programme of nationalization
anticipated in *Let Us Face the Future*. It was a limited programme and
certainly did not evoke the passions among the richer classes which it
had been the objective of writers such as Durbin to avoid. Little of it
indeed was seriously controversial except for iron and steel and road
transport. Notably uncontroversial was the nationalization of the Bank
of England, by which Labour planners had set so much store. Churchill,
who had had his own problems with the Governor of the Bank of
England when he was Chancellor of the Exchequer in the 1920s,

adopted a particularly benign attitude and Dalton had his work cut out to provoke the hostility on the Tory benches from which he always, as an Old Etonian, derived so much satisfaction. Care had to be exercised over how far the government could go in taking powers over the banking system because, at the time the Act was passing through Parliament, the American Congress was considering whether to ratify the American loan. Nothing must be done by Britain's sovereign Parliament to prejudice ratification. The Nationalization Act did not even give the Treasury powers to instruct the Bank to issue directives to the commercial banks, for example to limit lending.[29] Nationalization of the Bank yielded few, if any, benefits to Labour's ambitious economic plans. Indeed, it proved a damp squib. After nationalization it became a much repeated sick joke among economists, and left-wing critics of the government's economic management that it was time the Bank *was* nationalized. Given how much Labour party thinkers had expected from the nationalization of the Bank, it is ironical that when Mrs Thatcher embarked on her policy of privatization there was never any thought of privatizing the Bank.

Monetary policy now passed formally to the Treasury, where it had, informally, been located for many decades before. It was to remain in the Treasury for the subsequent fifty-one years, until the election of a very different kind of Labour government in 1997. Encouraged by Keynes, Labour Chancellors between 1945 and 1951 conducted a cheap money policy. Bank rate remained at 2 per cent throughout. Even when there was intense pressure against sterling, and Labour Chancellors were advised to raise bank rate, they refused to do so. The control of inflationary pressures did not provide, in their view, adequate reason. Adjustment of bank rate was, in their opinion, an antiquated device of the market economy inappropriate to a world of modern socialist planners. In any case, how could a Labour Chancellor plead with his colleagues to help him control public expenditure if he himself increased the cost of government debt by raising interest rates?

More important for the future of the British economy were the other nationalizations. Thereby 2.5 million workers were added to the public sector. These nationalized industries were, supposedly, the commanding heights of the British economy. The phrase was, in origin, Lenin's, and was adopted, cherished and popularized by Bevan.[30] There was an unvarying belief among British socialists, a belief that persisted well into the 1960s, that, whatever else was wrong about the Soviet Union, its economic management was a great success. In the Soviet Union there was concentration on the development of heavy industry. Consumption was considered a much lower priority. Similarly, in the UK, it was the heavy industries that, being the commanding heights, were nationalized – though, in democratic Britain, the government was forced to have some regard for consumption as well.

Ironically, the concept of commanding heights should have been a limiting factor on nationalization. The implication of the term was that key industries should be owned by the state but that other industries, not commanding heights, could be left in private ownership. That was not, however, how those most devoted to the commanding-heights concept, such as Bevan, saw the case. For them the nationalization of the commanding heights must lead on to more widespread nationalization, leaving at the end only a minuscule private sector. But that was not their only mistake. Their identification of the commanding heights, though understandable at the time, illustrated the dangers of economic forecasting. At the time a million people worked in the coal-mining industry. Who could foresee that by the 1990s that level of employment would have been reduced to under 50,000? Later it would be regretted that what had been brought into public ownership were the old, heavy industries, some of them unprofitable. The new, more flourishing industries, the industries of the future, had been left in private hands. Electrical generation was the only commanding height nationalized in the immediate post-war years that might still be listed under that heading. But to it have been added many industries, such as the electronic, which were only at the beginning of their rise to a commanding position.

It was immediately apparent that nationalization gave no help to economic planning. When the commanding heights were nationalized they planned their own independent courses without too much regard for any national interest or government ukase except when they needed public money to fund their deficits or their investment. A series of baronies was created which, while not immune from government influence, were quite difficult to influence against their own predilections. It was probably easier for the government to influence the conduct of the private sector than these great public monopolies. This was far from the central planning that had been part of the object of nationalization when it was advocated by writers such as Dalton and Durbin before the war. Durbin had emphasized the importance of a Supreme Economic Authority precisely because he feared that nationalized corporations would become too independent unless stringently controlled in the national interest.[31] Nationalization did not even help with the development of an incomes policy, although Emanuel Shinwell, the Minister of Fuel and Power, responsible for the nationalization of coal, gas and electricity, thought it should. He found himself opposed by Bevin and by the Minister of Labour, George Isaacs, both of whom disapproved of government intervention in wage bargaining.[32] Nationalized industries soon became a soft target for the trade unions. The ultimate employer, the government, had plenty of money if only it could be extracted, if necessary by inconveniencing citizens through the threat of strikes. The nationalization of coal had raised hopes of improved productivity which, as the country needed coal both for its own use and for export, would be important. Such hopes were disappointed, despite pleas from Bevin that more coal would ease his problems in conducting foreign policy. Things might, certainly, have been worse if the coal mines had not been nationalized. The practicalities of life were evidently submerging the socialist ambitions of the 1930s.

It was soon found that the nationalized industries had become a political albatross. Bernard Shaw's optimistic anticipation that a few uncontroversial nationalizations would 'make nationalization as normal a part of our social policy as old age pensions are now' proved to be another of his unfortunate forecasts.[33] Nationalization was never an advertisement for socialism, only a burden. Politically, it did not much matter whether it was a burden through the failings of the nationalized industries themselves or for reasons outside their control. They became an easy target for critics, including critics on the left, and they were making no obvious contribution to improved economic performance. To all who sought scapegoats, here they were. That they were publicly owned gave the public no sense of ownership. A further embarrassment for the Labour party, as it searched around for additional industries or companies to nationalize, was its discovery that many on the shop floor, as well as managers, were hostile. The poor reputation of nationalization was ascribed to the structure with independent boards of directors largely recruited from the private sector. It was a structure attributed to Morrison. Morrison's model was the London Passenger Transport Board. The directors were to be representatives of a national interest, and to be selected purely on grounds of their capacity to do the job. Morrison opposed the incorporation in the boards of special interests such as the trade union interest, though he had no objection to an able trade unionist, as an individual, being appointed to a board. This attitude had alienated Bevin and had certainly won Morrison no friends on the left. During the war, in 1944, Bevin had written to Attlee, 'I myself am being forced to the conclusion that a country run by a series of London Transport Boards would be almost intolerable.'[34]

Attlee, in the idealistic 1930s, had implied support for some form of industrial democracy. 'Socialism is not State Capitalism. The taking over of an industry by the State is not an end in itself – it is a means of attaining freedom. That implies a change in the status of the worker. He is in the future to be a citizen in his industrial as well as in his political capacity.'[35] It had always seemed that Bevin was favourable to an element of industrial democracy. Dalton had written:

> Socialism, as it is progressively achieved, will bring a great change in the social atmosphere. With the disappearance of private profit will go the power, often harsh and arbitrary, exercised by its recipients or their agents over their employees ... The workers will acquire a new status, both individually and collectively, no longer mere 'hands', but honourable partners in a true social activity, working no longer for capitalists, but for the community, to produce, not profits, but plenty.[36]

Experience of working in the nationalized industries never seemed to live up to Attlee's and Dalton's blissful vision. Any idea that nationalization should promote industrial democracy was abandoned. The Morrisonian structure did not provide for it. Nationalization as an instrument of planning did not require any element of industrial democracy. Indeed industrial democracy might have been an obstacle to planning rather than an aid to it. Durbin, the economist, had been adamant that the interests of the nation and, specifically, of the consumer must come before the interests of those who worked in the socialized sector. He insisted that industries must be controlled by, and operated in the interests of, the community, and not by and for the minority of workers employed in them.[37] He feared that the instincts of those who worked in an industry would be towards protection of their own interests even at the expense of those of the consumer.[38] By 1944 the TUC had concluded that *direct* representation of the employees on the boards of nationalized industries might compromise trade union independence.[39] In any case there was no conviction that workers could be found in sufficient numbers to shoulder the responsibilities of industrial democracy. Stafford Cripps, President of the Board of Trade, declared that 'From my experience there is not as yet a very large number of workers capable of taking over large enterprises.'[40] So the inadequacies of the workers combined with the requirements of planning to ban any form of industrial democracy in the nationalized industries. Certainly the new status was not evidenced by any development of industrial democracy nor by any other of the objectives of nationalization such as production for use rather than for profit, except in the sense that some of the nationalized industries were persistent loss-makers. Nationalization was a technocratic act, placing industries under the control of managers thought better capable of running them than their predecessors, though they were often the same persons. It was a technocratic act rather than a socialist act.

The left had always disliked the concept of unaccountable boards to run nationalized industries. It now regarded itself as vindicated. It thus had acquired a new stick with which to beat Morrison. He had failed to *socialize* the nationalized industries. The *method* of nationalization had damaged the whole nationalization project. The lesson learnt by the Labour party from the unpopularity of nationalization was not to stop nationalizing but to find other models of nationalization. Richard Crossman asked in *New Fabian Essays* in 1952: 'Is a centralised public corporation a more socialist method of running a public utility than municipal or co-operative ownership?'[41] But that was a debate extending far beyond Attlee's government.

One way proposed for dealing with the shortages characteristic of the post-war inflationary economy was competitive public enterprise, an idea which was given official blessing in *Labour Believes in Britain* presented at Labour's 1949 Conference, the last before the 1950 General Election.[42] Douglas Jay had advocated this possibility in *The Socialist Case*.

> [T]he Government should be ready to produce itself, in State factories such as the British Royal Ordnance Factories under direct public management, ordinary necessities on an ever-growing scale, where needed, in competition with private firms ... I believe this may be the most important single line of advance in British Socialist policy in the future, and that we must get away from the simple-minded idea that an industry must be either wholly nationalized or not all.[43]

Jay's 'most important single line of advance in British Socialist policy' seemed a doubtful prescription, hardly even a serious one. It had had, however, one possible application which had been neglected in the rush to nationalization. In principle it would have been possible to nationalize, not under the control of national boards, but in a way which encouraged competition between publicly owned companies. This could certainly have been done for the generation and distribution of electricity, in iron and steel, and in road transport. It could have been done in coal mining had there not been a determination to produce as much

British coal as possible whatever the cost, and thereby to defend both the incomes of miners and the balance of payments. The socialist ethos which demanded co-operation, not competition, which relied on economic planning and allowed excessive indulgence to calculations about optimum scales of production, was against any such adventurous innovation. And no doubt the miners would have been outraged at any proposal which suggested that one coal mine should compete against another. Thus a major opportunity to create competitive public enterprise, a favourite socialist panacea of later years, was neglected.

PLANNING

It might have been some consolation for the unpopularity of nationalization if it had added to the power to plan. Contrary to expectation, it had not. Nor was there much satisfaction to be derived from other attempts to plan. This was the more disappointing given the success of wartime planning. It is true that wartime planning would not have been enough if it had not been for Lend–Lease. Nevertheless, to wartime planning could be attributed the production of aircraft and tanks; the virtual elimination of unemployment; the increase in agricultural output; the improvement in the health of the people by ensuring that everyone had enough to eat. Attlee, like others, believed that 'our experience in the war had shown how much could be accomplished when public advantage was put before private vested interest'.[44] The success of planning, and the achievements of the economists and administrators who had manned the planning machinery, had created the right psychological atmosphere for the attempt to plan in peacetime. The popularity of the Soviet Union at the end of the war had helped to strengthen that psychology. The Soviet victory could be attributed in part to the heroism of the Soviet people, but also in great part to socialist planning. Could the Soviet Union, without benefit of the Five Year Plans, have withstood the German onslaught? Yet, even with the support of a highly favourable psychological atmosphere, the British attempt to plan faltered and fell.

So far as the Attlee government's favoured policy of planning was concerned, there was no sign even of urgency in bringing it into effective operation. If ever there was an opportunity to test whether there was a role for socialist economic planning, it was in the aftermath of a war which had robbed Britain of much of its means of livelihood. Above all it lacked the dollars that would be necessary to import the equipment and raw materials necessary for the refurbishment of British industry and for feeding the population. This was a challenge to socialist economic planning but not one which appeared to excite the Attlee government into making adequate arrangements for planning. If planning was to have the importance the Labour government claimed to attach to it, the constitution of the government was surprising. There were senior Labour Ministers who, during the war, had gained extensive experience of planning, Bevin at the Ministry of Labour, Cripps at the Ministry of Aircraft Production, and Dalton as President of the Board of Trade. Now, Bevin was moved to the Foreign Office, where his insistence on Britain's global role was a constant burden on those of his colleagues in the economic departments. Dalton was made Chancellor of the Exchequer with fiscal responsibilities which, according to the planning theology of the time, had little connection with the real meat of economic policy, which was physical planning. Thus two of the three senior Ministers who had experience of planning were dispersed from what was supposed to be the government's central responsibility, to improve the rate of growth through planning. That left Cripps as President of the Board of Trade. Two of the temporary civil servants, Oliver Franks and Edwin Plowden, who had contributed notably to the success of wartime planning, had been allowed to leave. It was not until the spring of 1947 that Plowden was brought back into the government machine as Chief Economic Planner and head of the Central Economic Planning Staff (CEPS). But Plowden, whose re-emergence as a planner was reluctant, believed in peacetime planning only as a transitional step to a free economy.

There was no planning department. There was no Supreme Economic Authority such as Dalton had proposed in his *Practical Socialism*.[45] There was no National Investment Board such as had been proposed both by Dalton and by some of his City friends and incorporated as a commitment in *Let Us Face the Future*. The responsibility for planning lay, not with a department, but with the so-called Lord President's Committee, chaired by Herbert Morrison. It included Dalton and Cripps, but committees are supervisory, rather than executive, bodies. Even if it was considered sufficient to leave planning to a co-ordinating committee, it was remarkable, if planning was seriously intended, that Morrison should have been put in charge. Even though he had a reputation as an administrator, he had not been a success as Minister of Supply during the war and had been rapidly moved to the Home Office. So the machinery of government was wrong and the Ministerial head was wrong. It was no wonder that Otto Clarke was so contemptuous of the government's attempts to plan. Given his pre-war work in the Fabian Society, it must have been a grave disappointment that Ministers, elected to plan, showed so little competence at it. This was hardly the central planning that Dalton and Durbin had envisaged before the war. Yet the failures were not just of personnel and machinery. Planning in peacetime yields a set of problems different from those in war. Those problems are the greater when the planners are confronted by consumers demanding variety, not the continuation of utility, and when, under the pressure of the United States, consideration had continually to be given to the opening of the British market to imports which the planners consider inessential.

Planning, as conducted by the Attlee government, consisted simply of the restriction of imports to what was considered essential and the allocation of scarce resources in order to encourage exports. As it was put by the Cambridge economist Robin Marris, who had served in the CEPS and had many criticisms of it, planning was 'mainly concerned with telling business men what they could not do; the raw materials they could not have, the investment they could not undertake, the export-type goods they could not sell in the home market, the foreign exchange they must not spend'.[46] This was a judgement confirmed by the man responsible for operating many of the controls, Harold Wilson, President of the Board of Trade 1947–51. 'Such controls were essentially negative. They can stop activity but they cannot promote it.'[47] This did not mean that the controls were without value. They were necessary because of the inflationary pressures in the economy which, without the controls, would have encouraged suppliers to concentrate even more on the domestic market at the expense of exports. The alternative of reducing the inflationary pressures in the economy was considered inconsistent with full employment. There was little to planning that was positive, though there was substantial state trading intended to secure low prices by offering long-term contracts. There was also a good deal of barter and increasing reliance on Commonwealth sources of supply as an alternative to dollar sources. The direction of policy was towards reducing dependence on dollar supplies even if this meant turning to more expensive sources of supply. State trading was not regarded as a temporary necessity at a time of shortage, rather as an expression of socialist planning. But it carried with it the potential for political embarrassment. For example, meat was bought from Argentina. If meat was short, it was the fault of the government. If the price was too high, it implied that the purchasers on behalf of the state were incompetent.

Yet things could have been worse if the economists had had their way. Another hangover from the war were the economists, not all of them of the quality of James Meade of the Economic Section, future Nobel Laureate. They were increasing in numbers and influence, slowly in numbers, more rapidly in influence. The ability of economists to deploy statistics, of however doubtful quality, was very persuasive. It was sometimes difficult to determine whether what was being done was the result of the enthusiasms of interventionist economists or because it was thought to be socialist. Socialism was becoming fashionable economics in action. Economists confidently claimed expertise in the business of running the country's economic life and cried out against the inflexibility and scepticism of the government machine. Some defence against the invasion was provided by the Treasury, which, Marris complains, appeared to believe, 'rightly or wrongly, that a First Class classic will be better at administering economic policy than a Second Class economist'.[48] It is not self-evident that this was an obtuse judgement. Marris wrote, 'there may have been Ministers who honestly believed that the modestly adapted machinery which eventually, rather belatedly, had evolved by the end of 1949, represented in fact an adequate solution to the general [planning] problem'.[49] Marris tells us that 'a Labour Government in Great Britain, pursuing a policy of "*Dirigisme*" or "The Mixed Economy" is in particular difficulty in the matter of economic planning and may require a more highly developed apparatus of central control than might the government of a completely socialist country.' And he adds: 'It is nearly impossible to discuss reform of the machinery of economic policy without ending up by arguing for a greater degree of centralism.'[50] One of the benefits of inherent civil service scepticism is that bad ideas are occasionally abandoned without the painful experience of actually implementing them.

It was only the experience of repeated failures in economic management that dimmed the hopes invested in planning. The government lacked the knowledge needed to plan. Marris writes of 'the manifest failure to provide the minimum statistics necessary for the construction and implementation of economic policy since the end of the war'.[51] It was Harold Macmillan who was later to speak of the inadequacy of last year's Bradshaw as a guide to action. It remains a problem for economic managers despite subsequent improvements in the quality of statistics. Democracy dictated that the planning must not be totalitarian but flexible, consistent with individual liberty, and perhaps, to use a French word, 'indicative'. Nobody could be compelled. Labour could not be directed.[52] But the indicative planning appeared merely as rationing and it was effective only as rationing. As such it was increasingly unpopular. Though it could be defended as being fair, to many it appeared unnecessary. Another reason why enthusiasm for planning faded was the experience of full employment. High unemployment had been a strong motive for finding better ways of running the economy. Planning had emerged, in part, as the answer. Planning was necessarily bureaucratic. The bureaucracy seemed far less justifiable when a principal object of planning had been achieved with, or without, the aid of Keynesian demand management.

THE NEGLECT OF INFLATION

The detailed allocation of resources, which went under the name of planning, would have been a great deal less necessary, and it could certainly have been phased out earlier, if the government had not been following an economic policy that was inflationary. James Meade, and some officials, saw themselves as advising Ministers how to run a market economy without excessive inflationary pressure. Meade advised the government that there was an inflationary gap, an excess of demand over supply. Ministers perceived themselves as socialist planners. Hence they thought in terms of various shortages, whether of manpower or materials. It was, in their view, the object of socialist planning to supply these shortages. In other words, inflation would be controlled by increasing supply rather than by restricting demand. Planning became an excuse for neglecting inflation. Meade wished to reduce demand towards supply. Ministers insisted that supply should be increased towards demand. It rapidly became clear which of these approaches was the most practical.

The differences in attitude between Ministers and officials produced repeated conflicts about policy options as well as murmuring by Ministers against their advisers. It also produced confused forecasts. For example, the 1947 Economic Survey as published was partly the work of Cripps, then President of the Board of Trade, and partly of Otto Clarke, a Treasury official. The outcome managed to combine a warning about increased inflationary pressure with a forecast of an improving balance of payments.[53] As interest rates were barred as a method of tackling inflationary pressures, the whole task fell on the budget. Meade argued the need for a budget surplus if excess demand was to be removed. He possessed what the historians of the Economic Section call an 'acute sense of the limitations of . . . controls that disposed him to advance constantly the alternative of using financial controls through the budget, monetary policy, and exchange rate adjustments'.[54] That view put the responsibility for fighting inflationary pressures on the Chancellor. But Dalton was himself an economist. He did not feel that he needed advice even from James Meade. To take the course which Meade seemed to be recommending, that is to reduce demand to eliminate the shortages, might have had a politically unacceptable effect on the level of unemployment. Dalton in his final budget of November 1947, formulated in the aftermath of the August convertibility crisis, raised taxes and thereby bequeathed to Cripps a large budget surplus. In other words Dalton was at last, *in extremis*, taking the path that Meade had mapped out for him.

Factors helping to ensure that inflation was not more serious during the life of the Attlee government included the resources made available to Britain by the American and Canadian loans and by Marshall Aid. Though there were a number of serious strikes particularly in the docks, the cause of relative price stability was also helped by the comparative restraint of the trade unions, attributable in descending measure to the fact that they had not yet appreciated their power in a full employment society, to the sense of national solidarity with which Britain emerged from the war, to regular consultation between the government and the TUC, and to the pleas of the great trade unionist Ernest Bevin and the austere Chancellor Sir Stafford Cripps. The most impressive gesture of voluntary co-operation by the TUC in the battle against inflation was the 1948 wage freeze, which was not in fact quite a wage freeze. Remarkably, it briefly survived the devaluation of September 1949. The trade unions, for the first time, found themselves not fighting for higher pay for their members but restraining their members from fighting for higher pay. It was against their nature and it could not last. Inflationary pressures became stronger. The outbreak of the Korean war in June 1950 sent commodity prices skyward. The end of Marshall Aid to Britain in 1950 did not help. At the same time, the patience of trade union members was found to have been exhausted. Bevin was now old and sick, Cripps had effectively retired from office by the summer of 1950 due to ill-health, and Gaitskell, his successor, lacked Cripps's moral authority. But, even if Bevin and Cripps had still been active, trade union leaders could no longer have bridled their members.

There had been some willingness among trade union members, and even more among trade union leaders, to regard the Labour government as 'their' government, which should be listened to and helped. Labour governments considered it natural, almost unquestionable, that the trade unions should be ready to help 'their' government in its difficulties, even though this might imply some sacrifice by their members. Many socialist politicians and academics were arguing for a permanent national wages policy. It seemed the natural response to the inflationary problems created by full employment. In his posthumously published *Problems of Economic Planning*, Durbin wrote, 'To the centralised control of a democratic community our livelihood and our security must be submitted.'[55] The concept was fatally flawed. There are limits to what can be done in a democracy even with the co-operation of trade union leaders. There was a limit to the amount of inflationary pressure that willingness to help, even at its highest, could contain. The relative success of the Attlee government in handling its relations with the trade unions until towards the end encouraged the overestimate among socialists and planners of the ease with which incomes policies could be negotiated. The seductive idea of an agreed division between workers and investors, and then among workers, of the annual increment in real wealth has seemed both rational and simple until it has had to be negotiated. Moreover, even successful incomes policies have their costs. They have political costs in their impact on personal liberty. They have economic costs in reducing the ability of employers to offer pay incentives to recruit more labour and respond to export opportunities. Incomes policies thus added to the rigidity of the economy. In wartime, it was possible to direct manpower, though this was not the first preference of the government. In peacetime, direction was unacceptable. Incomes policies were unlikely to work for long in Britain, and neither incomes policies nor voluntary collective bargaining were likely to contain inflation while unemployment was held at 2 per cent or below. That would be one of the lessons of the post-war era. Labour governments were particularly slow to learn, which was disruptive of relations between them and their friends in the trade union movement, and in the end undermined Labour's claim to govern.

THE IMPERIAL TRADITION IN INDUSTRIAL POLICY

In the problem of the inflationary gap there is to be found a stimulus to that favourite device of later Labour governments, the industrial strategy. As a direct confrontation with inflation might prejudice

Labour's relations with the trade unions, it was better to find another way around the inflationary gap. A successful industrial strategy would improve productivity and improved productivity would fill the inflationary gap. Industrial policy, throughout its history in the UK, was a diversion from confrontation with inflation. There would be no need to turn to fiscal and monetary policy and thereby threaten full employment. The problem would be solved without disturbing relations with the trade unions. It was a vain hope, doubly expensive because it deflected governments from taking effective measures against inflation while, at the same time, being exceedingly costly in public money.

In the first three decades after the second world war, there was within British industrial policy a tradition which I have elsewhere defined as the 'imperial' tradition.[56] 'If we were not to enjoy the prestige of empire, we would seek prestige through advanced technology, by becoming leaders in aerospace and nuclear energy. Only with lavish state aid could it be done. Military requirements encouraged its doing. It was expensive but it was consistent with our honourable desire for world leadership in some fields at least.'[57] The imperial tradition in industrial policy began its halting footsteps under Attlee. It was an aftermath of the war during which British nuclear scientists and engineers had contributed to the Manhattan Project which produced the atomic bomb, and during which British aircraft engineers had designed the aircraft which enabled the RAF to defend Britain against Hitler and to penetrate deeply into enemy territory. The imperial tradition proved as much a misfortune at home as overseas. The UK did not have the resources to compete alone against the USA in all these areas of advanced technology, and engineers who would have been better occupied modernizing the rest of British industry were diverted by the charisma of aerospace and nuclear energy into activities that would never yield a commensurate return. These public investments in advanced technologies started a trend in British industrial policy that would lead it expensively astray.

THE CONVERTIBILITY CRISIS

In February 1947, a shortage of coal caused widespread industrial dislocation and damaged the balance of payments. Unemployment rose briefly into the millions, and the reputation of the government was seriously impaired. It was the first in a series of events which raised questions about the competence of the Attlee government. The availability of borrowed American money had injected such complacency into the Attlee Cabinet that it remained inert month after month as the dollars disappeared. Dollar prices had risen substantially and much of the loans was being spent on imports of Virginia tobacco, important perhaps for the peace of mind of the electorate but not a contribution to Britain's economic recovery. It had been estimated, and hoped, that the American and Canadian loans would last for a period of five years. It became increasingly evident that they would be exhausted in less than half that period. The commitment to sterling convertibility by July 1947, one year after Congress approved the loan agreement, proved to be a humiliating disaster. Introduced, according to obligation on 15 July, it was reversed on 20 August. Once convertibility had been introduced, holders of sterling, lacking confidence in Britain's economic policies, rushed to escape into dollars. The dollars in the UK reserves were disappearing so fast that even the Americans accepted that there was no alternative to suspension. Those who had warned that the commitment could not be honoured were proved right. The convertibility crisis of July–August 1947 turned the British government and its advisers against convertibility and non-discrimination for the foreseeable future. But, with the loans virtually exhausted, Britain would have been compelled to cope with the constraint of dollar imports limited by its remaining reserves, its scarce dollar earnings plus anything that it could secure by way of commercial credits. Fortunately, in June 1947, at Harvard, Secretary of State General George Marshall had offered Europe a major programme of assistance. Confronted not just by the economic difficulties of western Europe but with the increasing intransigence of the Soviet Union, the Americans were showing their willingness further to assist European recovery. There was, in other words, a more realistic view in Washington of the needs of Europe than had been apparent at the time the American Loan had been negotiated. Once more the Americans would come to the rescue of British socialism.

THE EMERGENCE OF STAFFORD CRIPPS

Cripps, who would now emerge as the second man in the government after Bevin, had been expelled from the Party in January 1939 for advocating a Popular Front to include Labour, Liberals and dissident Tories, not to mention the communists. Having presented himself for much of the 1930s as a revolutionary socialist, he had been prepared, for the moment, to put socialism on ice due to the vital necessity of overthrowing the Chamberlain government. He had rejoined Labour only shortly before the 1945 General Election. Though, in the past, an almost invariable nuisance, he had earned sufficient credit in various posts during the war to command a senior appointment in the Attlee government. There were not many competent rivals for senior appointments. There are four consistent themes in Cripps's life, his devotion to the Christian religion, his fidelity to unorthodox medicine, his dedication to economic planning, and his impatience with his political colleagues. His impatience with his political colleagues led him to attempt in 1938 to substitute Morrison for Attlee in the leadership of the Labour party, to replace Churchill as Prime Minister during the war, and, once again, to conspire against Attlee during the Labour government. He was undoubtedly a man of exceptional talents. Morrison was prepared to concede that, in private discussion, Cripps was 'invincible'.[58] His dedication to economic planning was based on his own experience as a chemist during the first war and as a minister in the second. Unfortunately, his experience did not encompass any knowledge of the private sector or, at the time, of the management of an economy in peacetime. Throughout Cripps's political career he had shown exceptional confidence in his own abilities. He was convinced that he knew how to save the country, and the government, and was highly doubtful whether any of his colleagues did.

In the summer of 1947, overtaken by the convertibility crisis, there was a bitter sense of failure within the government itself. Within two years of its election, it was beset by crisis and internal controversy. The principal question now was the identification of scapegoats. Cripps and Dalton attempted to lay the blame on Attlee for poor leadership, and on Morrison for knowing nothing about planning. Morrison had failed as a planner. Attlee had failed in allowing Morrison to continue in a post which he had no capacity to discharge. Both criticisms were justified, though Dalton, who was as much to blame as anyone, was hardly the most appropriate Minister to launch them. In any case, the identification of scapegoats provided no answer to the problems inherent in the attempt to plan. Despite the experience to date, Cripps thought that he had the necessary skills. He thought it essential that he himself should be in charge of planning. He decided that it was necessary to reconstruct the government. Morrison, Dalton and Cripps were, jointly, to invite the Prime Minister to stand aside in favour of Bevin, an invitation which, coming from three such senior Ministers, Attlee could hardly refuse. Attlee was to be replaced by Bevin, and Morrison, so far as his planning duties were concerned, by Cripps. It does not say much for Cripps's political judgement that he imagined that Morrison would co-operate in a plot to replace Attlee by Bevin. Morrison demurred at the idea of Bevin, Dalton at accompanying Cripps on an expedition in which he wished him well but from which he expected little success. Cripps, alone, met Attlee. He instructed the Prime Minister to move next door, from No. 10 Downing Street to No. 11, from Prime Minister to Chancellor of the Exchequer, leaving No. 10 vacant for Bevin to occupy. If Attlee would not submit to the ultimatum, he could have Cripps's own resignation. At least Cripps had the courage of his convictions. He did not just conspire behind Attlee's back. He told Attlee to his face what he must do if the government was to retain the benefit of Cripps's services.

Cripps then found that political planning also has its problems. There were several flaws in this political plan. The most important was that Bevin was content at the Foreign Office and did not want to replace Attlee. He saw himself as dealing with great matters in his role as representative of a global power. He was, in any case, the first man in the government whatever his official function. His reported comment about Attlee, that the 'little man' had never done him any harm, was a measured combination of contempt and support.[59] Attlee, secure in the comfort of Bevin's patronage, had prepared for his meeting with Cripps and now offered him an alternative approach. Morrison was to lose his planning responsibilities, the larger part of his job as Lord President. Cripps was to become Minister for Economic Affairs, without departmental responsibilities but in charge of economic planning. Cripps succumbed to the temptation. It would give him the job he wanted and enable him to save the government and the country. In the course of his meeting at No. 10, he decided that he could allow Attlee to remain Prime Minister and to retain his own services in this new appointment. He was gazetted as Minister for Economic Affairs at the end of September 1947.

The suggestion that Attlee should become Chancellor of the Exchequer when replaced by Bevin illustrates Cripps's ignorance of the realities of economic management. He regarded the Treasury as a department which, whatever the importance of its responsibilities, had nothing to do with planning. Cripps was, in all innocence, offering Attlee the management of economic policy, the very job he wanted for himself. If Bevin had accepted the proffered crown, and Attlee had moved next door, the Treasury would still have been the governing economic department whatever planning duties, or Ministerial title, Cripps acquired in the new dispensation. It is perhaps true that Attlee would have been even less competent in charge of the Treasury than Dalton. But the incompetence of Chancellors is an annoyance rather than an inhibition to Treasury leadership on economic policy.

With Morrison and Dalton staggering under heavy loads of blame for the economic crisis, Cripps emerged, in the public eye, as the strong man of the government. Attlee survived, courtesy of Ernest Bevin, but it appeared to be on sufferance. Attlee would never make a strong Prime Minister, but the real weakness of Cripps's position would quickly have become apparent. He would have discovered that he had bought the traditional pig in a poke. He would rapidly have become disillusioned with his powerlessness in his non-departmental position. Fortunately for him, Dalton, already discredited by the convertibility crisis, leaked his November budget to a journalist and resigned. Cripps became Chancellor as well as Minister for Economic Affairs. In this capacity he discovered the powers of the Treasury and that his most effective planning instrument was the budget, not the bureaucracy. This view was not understood by Cripps's Cabinet colleagues precisely because it departed so far from the physical planning of socialist orthodoxy. The surplus from Dalton's deflationary last budget turned out much larger than Dalton had intended. It became Cripps's duty to defend that surplus against the predatory attacks of his Cabinet colleagues, who would always imagine that, if there was money in the kitty, they should spend it. This Cripps did with some success. His principal problems were with his old friend and admiring ally Aneurin Bevan. Cripps wanted to limit expenditure on the National Health Service and even to introduce charges. Bevan refused to contemplate such charges and Cripps regularly capitulated, leaving the inevitable confrontation to his successor at the Treasury, Hugh Gaitskell.

MARSHALL AID

Ironically, the most powerful stimulus to positive planning in Britain came from the Americans in 1948. They required a plan as a condition for issuing Marshall Aid and a *Long-Term Programme*[60] was produced. The Americans wanted evidence that Marshall Aid would do some good in Britain and decided that a 'programme' would provide the necessary reassurance. As usual with planning in Britain, the long-term programme was overtaken by events – though, happily, one of the events was the receipt of Marshall Aid.

Pimlott discovers in the arrival of Marshall Aid a defence for Dalton's failures in economic management. 'American intervention of some kind [e.g. through Marshall Aid] was always a reasonable expectation in view of the likely impact on the American economy of a British collapse. We may wonder, therefore, whether Dalton's sense of "personal humiliation" [at the convertibility crisis] was not excessive.'[61] In other words the USA was bound to come to Britain's rescue for the second time in three years because otherwise the UK would commit suicide on its doorstep. Such thinking is certainly in line with the British presumption throughout too many of the post-war years that the USA owed Britain support first because of its wartime sacrifices and secondly because the consequences of a British failure would be too unpleasant. As we will see, a similar situation would arise in 1964–5 over the devaluation of sterling. The alternative of finding policies that avoided a British collapse was, in the view of successive British governments and of historians such as Pimlott, politically unacceptable. In later times, economists would speak of moral hazard, the temptation to conduct profligate policies in the expectation that a beneficent patron would arrive with a rescue package just in time. It was a temptation to which Britain regularly succumbed. In fact, however, it was never at all clear, until General Marshall made his speech at Harvard on 5 June 1947, that such a gesture would be forthcoming from the USA. Much evidence, including the attitude of Congress, the abrupt cancellation of Lend–Lease, and the terms attached to the American loan, were against any such expectation.[62]

The offer of Marshall Aid was accompanied by further pressure for non-discrimination and for the end of imperial preference, and by an attempt to attach conditions which amounted to submitting UK economic policy to the approval of Washington. The most humiliating conditions were resisted, but there was a further condition that the UK could not withstand. The government was forced to accept that Marshall Aid would be channelled to Britain as part of a European recovery programme. William Clayton, American Under Secretary of State for Economic Affairs, was sent to Europe to explain Marshall's speech at Harvard. Bevin protested about the USA's new policy of providing aid to Britain only as part of a west European bloc. Britain, complained Bevin, would become 'just another European country'. But, if the US

Congress and administration insisted on channelling aid as part of a European programme, the UK had to like it or lump it.

In the summer of 1948, after three years in government with a stable majority and no effective opposition, having substantially implemented the policies on which it was elected, the Labour government was left with no alternative but to accept Marshall Aid despite its distaste for the conditions on which it was offered. That is a judgement both on the government's economic policies and on its pretence at economic planning. The Cabinet decided that, whatever its distaste, there was really no practical alternative but to accept Marshall Aid. The Treasury calculated that refusal would mean drastic import restrictions and one and a half million unemployed. Plowden comments that 'In February 1948 it was calculated that on existing policies the dollar drain would exhaust our reserves by the end of 1949.'[63] The CEPS had estimated what the basic food ration would have to be in the event of the reserves running out. 'The conclusions we reached were horrendous. The average daily calorific intake per person would, we estimated, have had to be reduced to something like 1,700–2,000, far less than in the war years.'[64] Cripps reported to Cabinet on 23 June 1948 on the readjustments that would be necessary if the Cabinet decided not to accept Marshall Aid:

> These readjustments to the balance of payments would administer a number of violent shocks to the home economy at a number of separate points. The results to the structure of output, exports, investment, consumption and employment are extremely difficult to assess. We should be faced with an abrupt transition from a partially suppressed inflation to something not unlike a slump.

Two days later, on 25 June 1948, Cabinet decided to sign the Marshall Aid agreement.

Bevin had hoped that Britain itself could take a lead in promoting the recovery of western Europe. For Britain to go into the programme and do nothing would involve the sacrifice of the 'little bit of dignity we have left'.[65] But, apart from the extension of sterling credits to fund the purchase of British exports, which might be interpreted as being as much in the interests of the UK as of the purchaser, the British government had no plan or, more important, resources with which it could assist European recovery. Neither had the Attlee government left itself with much dignity.

CONSOLIDATION

Halfway through the 1945 Parliament, the welfare state had been enacted, the Bank of England, coal and the major public utilities had been nationalized. The foothills of socialism had been reached. The next problem now was to organize the climb to the peaks. It was then found that the radical urge, such as it had ever been, had been expended.

Some Ministers, led by Morrison, had concluded that there should be at least a pause in the nationalization process while the existing nationalized industries found their feet and proved their success. He recommended 'consolidation'. He is alleged to have remarked that socialism is what a Labour government does. The remark cannot be authenticated but it sounds genuine. Some fun has been made of it, but it demonstrated both insight and caution. What he presumably meant is that socialism is what a Labour government is prepared to do. There were many things, implicit in socialism, that it should not be prepared to do. For example, Morrison wanted to delay steel nationalization. The steel workers' union was not enthusiastic for nationalization. The question was whether to go forward with the nationalization of iron and steel, or alternatively to seek some acceptable way of regulating it in agreement with the industry. This was a matter of controversy within Cabinet. The consolidators led by Morrison were in favour of finding some accommodation with the industry. Attlee encouraged Morrison to elaborate a scheme for iron and steel alternative to nationalization. But, when Morrison did as he had been invited, Attlee failed to support him in Cabinet 'because it was not my job to do so'. He also sacked John Wilmot, the Minister of Supply, who had supported a compromise.[66] Any idea of compromise was distasteful to the radicals, including Dalton, Bevan and Cripps. They insisted on going ahead. To Dalton, steel was the proof of Labour's socialist virility. He was right. That was not necessarily a sufficient reason for going ahead. But, under Attlee's weak leadership, the radicals won. The Cabinet overruled Morrison and decided to proceed with the nationalization of iron and steel. The controversy came to a head during the turmoil over the convertibility crisis, and there is no time when Labour governments are so determined to show their radical face as when they have run the country into economic crisis. The decision to proceed with the nationalization of iron and steel marked the end of the post-war consensus between the Labour government and industrial management. Now industrial management knew that Labour was its enemy, that is was really trying to be socialist, and that it would have to be fought and brought down. The Cabinet, while presumably understanding the political effect of its decision, did not seem to mind because it was so satisfied with the effects of its efforts thus far. Nevertheless, the controversy within the government about the nationalization of one of the defined commanding heights of the economy, and its inability to construct a rational programme of further nationalization beyond iron and steel, demonstrates the failing confidence in the nationalization project at the very heart of the Labour party.

There was little other evidence of a continuing radical impulse. Britain was not yet socialist, but there seemed a reluctance, curious in a socialist party, to proceed on the road to socialism. That would have involved a nationalization programme much more extensive than iron and steel. If, within a Labour Cabinet, there was to be a battle over steel, how much wider could the nationalization project be pressed as it came up against opposition not just from employers and employees but also from consolidators within the Labour government itself? And how much further would even the radicals wish to go? In his speech at the June 1949 Labour Party Conference, Bevan accepted that:

> the kind of society which we envisage and which we shall have to live in will be a mixed society, a mixed economy, in which all the essential instruments of planning are in the hands of the State, in which the characteristic form of employment will be by the Community in one form or another but where we shall have for a very long time the light cavalry of private, competitive industry.

He took for granted that, within the mixed economy, the public sector would predominate and that, therefore, most employment would be 'by the Community'. But the nearest he could get to any specific proposal was to add that 'We have to exercise our imaginations as to what we can do further. Indeed, we have to restate the relationship between the public and private sector.'[67] The idea of the 'light cavalry' was indicative. Perhaps Britain needed more light cavalry rather than less. Or was the light cavalry also to live under the permanent threat of take-over by the state? Interestingly, Bevan as Minister of Housing was against nationalizing the building industry. He said it would not build a single additional house. It was enough to require the industry to build for local authorities.[68]

Steel nationalization was delayed by the House of Lords using the reduced delaying powers left to it by the government. It had therefore hardly been nationalized when Attlee was defeated at the polls. Steel nationalization was then reversed. The reversal became a challenge to the Labour party. The reversal of Labour government legislation was inconsistent with the assumptions on which the idea of democratic socialism had been based. Whatever other policies a future Labour government might have, the renationalization of steel was bound to appear in its election programme. It remained the touchstone of socialist virility, even though there was no other obvious justification for thereby converting a major industry into a political pawn.

Morrison's policy of consolidation was certainly sensible. When there has been a great leap forward, it is not a bad idea to consolidate the ground won before the next leap forward. There might be much to learn from what had been done which would help to guide the next advance. The impression, however, was inescapable, that the object of consolidation was to stop, not to prepare the ground for further advance. A reason for stopping would be that Labour had lost confidence in the socialist ideas it had canvassed before the war, extensive nationalization and central planning. Though the radicals could not admit it, socialism was already under question. Future nationalization would require for its justification not the ideology of socialism but pragmatic arguments on the merits of the particular case. But pragmatism was not socialism. There were, of course, many things that a Labour government could do by way of ameliorating the condition of the people. But, though efforts might be made to redefine socialism in that sense, that was not socialism as it had been originally understood or as the left of the Labour Party understood it at the time. It would have been difficult enough at any time for the Labour party to convert itself into a Liberal party without splitting. There were too many socialists who were not yet disillusioned with their faith. There were others who were beginning to have doubts but who believed that there was still substance in socialism which could be brought forward as a substitute for the ideology of public ownership. Labour was entering a period characteristic of many aged institutions. Having lost its original purpose, it was seeking desperately for a new one which would justify its continued existence. Labour, however, had entered this transition period rather sooner after its birth than do most institutions. It then took rather longer to make the transition than was safe if it was to have serious prospects of survival.

SEVEN

Full employment in two worlds

CHOOSING THE TARGET

Kenneth Morgan tells us:

> Throughout all the vicissitudes of the 1947–51 period, the Labour government's most powerful claim to effective social engineering and to the unshakeable loyalty of its millions of trade-union supporters and their families, was that it was the Party of full employment ... Without this massive achievement, the welfare state would have been invalidated from the start.[1]

Whether full employment in the period 1947–51 was a 'massive achievement' will be discussed later. Labour Ministers certainly considered it a massive achievement. It had been feared that, after the second world war as after the first, there would be a period of deep deflation resulting in mass unemployment. When the contrary proved to be the case, the relief was palpable. Full employment was undoubtedly a blessed change from pre-war. There could equally be no doubt that it would be high on the list of Labour's claims to re-election. But, in order to preserve the prize of full employment, the government showed itself prepared to distort all other policies, in particular its attitude to price stability, to international trade, to the sterling area and to Europe. When, later, concerns grew about the poor competitiveness of the British economy, one of the causes would be found in the priority given to full employment above all other considerations.

DEFINING FULL EMPLOYMENT

The 1944 Employment White Paper had promised not full employment but a high and stable level of employment. What did that mean for the Attlee government? At what target should it aim? We have seen that Keynes considered it unlikely that unemployment could be sustained at as low a level as 3 per cent, or about 750,000. But, except during the fuel crisis in the winter of 1946–7, unemployment was at a much lower figure. This is how, in 1951, Gaitskell, when Chancellor of the Exchequer, expressed the full employment standard:

> [I]t is necessary to consider the possibility that factors arising outside the United Kingdom, such as a widespread fall in the demand for United Kingdom exports or a shortage of raw materials obtained from abroad, might make it impossible for a time to keep unemployment at the low levels of recent years. All possible counter measures would be set in train but they might take time to become effective. Furthermore, the danger of provoking inflation in such a situation would be more acute than in the case of unemployment caused by a decline in internal demand. The Government has therefore decided to make a small allowance for the factors mentioned . . . above and to express the full employment standard of the United Kingdom as a level of unemployment of 3 per cent at the seasonal peak. It must be stressed that the choice of this standard does not mean that the Government would allow unemployment to reach 3 per cent before taking vigorous counter action . . . In the event of severe difficulties arising in the sphere of foreign trade it is possible that even a level of 3 per cent unemployment might be exceeded for short periods . . .[2]

Thus 3 per cent was regarded by Gaitskell when Chancellor as a reluctant maximum, not, as Keynes would have had it, something that might, but was unlikely to be, achieved without destabilizing side-effects. The Attlee government was not prepared to sacrifice full employment, by its own definition, to external pressures. Should unemployment ever threaten to reach 3 per cent, there would be an imperative need of further measures. In practice, the Attlee government, and its successors, ran scared whenever unemployment threatened to reach 2 per cent and they were much more comfortable with unemployment at 1 per cent or even lower. The government thus committed itself to a level of unemployment that was, in the British context, too low not to have negative effects on inflation and international competitiveness. And because the Attlee government committed itself to it, so did its Conservative successors. Shortly after he had left government, Gaitskell privately warned Treasury officials that there would be 'a hell of a row' if unemployment was allowed to exceed 500,000.[3]

It was against the background of the Attlee government's full employment policy that Anthony Crosland declared final victory for Keynes over mass unemployment. In 1952, he wrote:

> The trend of employment is towards a high level, and a recurrence of chronic mass unemployment is most unlikely. The Keynesian techniques are now well understood ... The political pressure for full employment is stronger than ever before; the experience of the inter-war years bit so deeply into the political psychology of the nation that full employment, if threatened, would always constitute the dominant issue at any election, and no right-wing party could now survive a year in office if it permitted the figures of unemployment which were previously quite normal.[4]

Paradoxically, Ministers in the Attlee government, who had credited themselves publicly with this massive achievement, had not shared Crosland's supreme confidence in Keynesian techniques, and the time would soon come when he himself would fear that they were not enough. Crosland's predecessor as Fellow in Economics at Trinity College, Oxford, had been Robert Hall. In 1947, Hall became head of the Economic Section of the Cabinet Office. After he left government service in 1961, he wrote that, in the early years after the war, there had been deep fears that the problem of full employment had not been solved.

> Before 1951, it was a matter of constant concern to the Labour Government whether they could maintain full employment at all: and it was not generally recognized for several years after the Conservative Government came to power, that they would and could follow their predecessors in this respect ... In the event, full employment turned out to be much more easy to achieve than most people had expected ...[5]

There were two reasons for this constant concern. The first was the perception that full employment could stimulate inflation. As the government's economic advisers came to understand, an unemployment target of well under 3 per cent achieved by Keynesian demand management was virtually guaranteed to generate inflationary pressures. There was just too much pressure on resources and this created opportunities for inflationary wage claims which the trade unions could only too easily exploit. The second reason for concern was the unreliability of the external environment. The two reasons were connected in that domestic inflation could weaken the UK's balance of payments, thereby make it even more susceptible to external upsets, and thereby threaten full employment. It was this concern that would turn Ministers' minds to conceiving a structure for the world economy that would protect full employment despite domestic inflationary pressures and external turbulence.

The Attlee government itself was not unduly concerned at inflationary pressures provided they could be contained. Douglas Jay, Economic Secretary at the Treasury, considered that a modicum of inflation was acceptable in the interests of full employment. A rise of one or two points a year in the cost of living was probably 'a necessary implication of full employment and does no serious harm'. Indeed a general rise would relieve the dead weight of war debt and should not be regarded as proof of failure.[6] A borrowing socialism was always likely to have a deficient level of aversion to inflation. The Economic Section was not yet ready to treat the problem so lightly. One suggestion emanating from that source was to limit the guarantee of full employment by creating enough demand to allow full employment but only at constant prices. The note issue would be restricted to give effect to this policy.[7] But the government had no intention of employing monetary policy, and the threat of higher unemployment, or for that matter fiscal policy, as a discipline on the work force. Instead, it adopted the highly imperfect device of a prices and incomes policy supported by exhortation to the trade unions not to exploit to excess the power that full employment gave them. For decades to come, British governments were compelled to seek ways of fighting the inflationary pressures that they had unleashed in the interests of full employment without, however, ever summoning the courage actually to subdue them.

If the British economy was too open to foreign competition it would, apparently, be a problem. It might actually force Britain to control inflation, and achieve higher productivity, rather than sink back into stagnant complacency. As Robin Marris, previously of the CEPS, was to put it in 1954 when the economy was, in fact, far from open:

> [O]ne might well argue that were it not for the extreme 'openness' of our economy many of the matters we now consider so important on the internal front – control of inflation, growth of productivity, etc. – would not be so critical. If inflation were a little worse, the *rentier* would suffer a little more; if productivity rose a little slower, the standard of living would be a little lower; however, there would be no crisis.[8]

This was a recipe for autarchic stagnation in the interests of full employment.

THE USA

Politicians and economists recognized that pre-eminent among the external factors that might influence the security of full employment in Britain was the performance of the American economy. The American economy was by far the largest and most productive in the world. Commentators everywhere emphasized the dependence of world capitalism on American economic performance. It was a dependence full of risk. As British politicians and economists saw it, great power imposed consequential duties. The Americans must realize that the exceptional difficulties which Britain was facing required from its principal ally policies that would help to relieve the stresses of a return to a prosperous normality. It was the inescapable duty of the US administration not just to provide aid in satisfaction of the justice due to Britain's extraordinary sacrifices during the war but also to follow economic policies that would assist the world to recover from the war. The US administration must sustain a high level of domestic economic activity. Moreover it must be possible for British exporters to participate in satisfying American domestic demand. Thus American tariffs must be reduced and the multifaceted American system for protecting its domestic market must be dismantled. Washington should realize, in its own interests, that Britain did have an empire and that therefore there was a form of interdependence. The Americans must buy more from the sterling area and, as the sterling area could not export enough manufactured goods, the USA must buy sterling area raw materials.[9] Canada would have a comparable role.

The problem was to decide what reliance could be placed on the Americans seeing their duty in the same way after a war in which they had been the sole unquestioned victor. Keynes had been persuaded that a great deal of reliance could be placed on the Americans. First, they appeared as concerned to ensure full employment at home as were the British. They too had suffered an inter-war experience of depression and unemployment which no politician would wish to repeat. Only with the outbreak of war had American unemployment fallen to acceptable levels. Congress had enacted legislation that might contribute to the achievement of full employment in the USA. The American ambition to ensure full employment would justify the expectation that the administration and Congress would, whenever necessary, act to sustain demand within the USA. Full employment within the USA would contribute to the maintenance of full employment in Britain. All this was speculative, but it had appeared to Keynes a reasonable speculation. Confidence in American intentions as guarantors of full employment was strong enough to encourage Keynes and Keynesian economists to become, in the years immediately following the war, advocates of a 'one-world economy', an economy with external national trade barriers reduced to a minimum. This advocacy was modified to some extent by a desire to have one's cake and eat it. The one-world economy was not to interfere with imperial preference, which, within the one-world system, would grant British trade certain advantages within the Commonwealth and Empire. On imperial preference, there was to be a mercantilist bargain. If the Americans wanted to see an end to imperial preference, they must open their domestic market and stimulate their economy. After Keynes's death in 1946, and the convertibility crisis of July–August 1947, it was recognized that one world could not be achieved at once. The British economy was too weak and dollars were too short to permit non-discrimination in trade. But 'one world' was still accepted as the right objective, conditional only on American behaviour.

Despite Keynesian optimism, British Ministers suspected that the USA would never live up to its own professions of multilateralism and open its markets. On imperial preference, it would never offer the mercantilist bargain. It would simply find every way of exerting pressure on Britain for the unilateral abandonment of imperial preference. These misgivings were justified. It was the USA, not Britain, that in the end refused to ratify the Havana Charter which was to establish the multilateral non-discriminatory trading world. British fears were in no way relieved when General George Marshall made his speech at Harvard which was to lead to Marshall Aid. It at first appeared that the Americans would make the abandonment of imperial preference a condition of British eligibility for Marshall Aid. Britain successfully resisted the pressure, but it reinforced the apprehension that Washington could not be trusted to respect what Britain saw as both its right and its need to retain discrimination in trade as long as the dollar shortage remained. Even while resisting the more humiliating Marshall Aid conditions, Britain was preparing the ground for an international economic structure very different from the one-world vision which Keynes, far too optimistically, had taken to the grave. The Attlee government's priorities would be neither convertibility nor non-discrimination, but full employment. That implied a world economic framework consistent with its commitment to full employment.

In his autobiography, Attlee takes a sour view of American criticism of British imperialism. His asperity gives an insight into the real feelings in London about American pressures:

> Much of the criticism of British rule was very ill-founded but its strength could not be denied. Americans drew a sharp distinction between their own expansion from the Atlantic to the Pacific, in voting the Mexican War and the relegation to reserves of the original inhabitants, and British overseas expansion. The absorption of a continent seemed to be a natural process to them, but an empire containing numerous detached portions of land inhabited by various races at different stages of civilisation appeared an example of colonialism and rank imperialism.[10]

It was all very unjust. It was such a pity that Britain was forced to go cap in hand to a superpower so lacking in understanding, among other matters, of the benign nature of British imperialism.

THE 1948 RECESSION IN THE USA

The insupportable aspects of British economic dependence on the US economy were brought home by the American recession in 1948. It threatened full employment in the UK and was a major factor leading to the devaluation of sterling in September 1949. A draft paper for Cripps to the Economic Policy Committee of the Cabinet, dated 17 June 1949, had him saying, 'I believe that when [the Americans] appreciate the impact of their recession upon ourselves and upon the rest of the world, they will endeavour to do the right thing . . . they are committed up to the hilt to prevent their depressions from breaking up the world economy.'[11] But this was a hope. There was no evidence of a preparedness in Washington to abandon protection, stimulate the economy and open the US market.

During the crisis leading to the devaluation of sterling in September 1949, Sir Oliver Franks, then Ambassador to Washington, put the point thus:

> There is basic agreement between the two sides that the multilateral system of trade is the one to work towards. The necessity of bilateral agreements on the part of Britain for the time being is widely understood in the American Administration. Their worry is whether some of them are evidence of something else, the progressive inability of the United Kingdom to live in the same economic world as North America.[12]

Franks also pointed to a significant difference between US and UK attitudes to full employment. 'The difference between the Governments consists in the amount of unemployment thought tolerable. The American economy and American opinion can stand a rather larger proportion of unemployment than the British before the point is reached at which immediate and large-scale remedial action by the central government is taken.'[13]

TWO WORLDS

After the 1948 American recession, Labour Ministers came to oppose not just convertibility in the short term but convertibility as a long-term objective. Labour politicians, followed later by Keynesian economists, concluded, as Franks had suggested in his memorandum, that living in the same economic world with the USA was inconsistent with full employment and that it was time to distance the UK as far as possible from the influence of American policies and American recessions. In this switch in policy, Hugh Gaitskell and Douglas Jay were in the lead. Gaitskell was Minister of Fuel and Power. Jay was Economic Secretary to the Treasury. Gaitskell and Jay were two of the three young economists who were increasingly influential on Labour economic policy making. The third was Harold Wilson. When Cripps became Minister for Economic Affairs, Wilson, at the age of thirty-one, had been appointed President of the Board of Trade, the youngest Cabinet Minister this century. Their confidence in their own economic judgement surpassed by far their confidence in the advice they were receiving from their officials. The opposition expressed by Gaitskell and Jay to the concept of a one-world economy arose from their fear that Keynesian demand management might not be enough, within a one-world economy, to secure full employment. Thus Douglas Jay wrote to the Chancellor on 22 June 1949:

> The American recession might not go on but, on the assumption that the American recession is going on, the right policy for us – and this is the crux of the whole matter – both for the short-term and less short-term is to try to maintain in the sterling and non-dollar area a slump-proof world in which the highest possible level of trade goes on. We both should and can do this in OEEC, in the sterling area, and with countries such as Argentina. Our general principle must be that, if the United States fail to carry out their obligations under Bretton Woods and ITO to stop a major slump, we can at least see that this does not prevent other countries from trading between themselves. This is our prime duty to the world as a whole, and it can be done.[14]

Here we find an early statement of the two-worlds approach to economic policy accompanied by an expression of the deep concern for the world as a whole that was regularly advanced as justification for British self-interest. A delinquent USA was to be exiled from the community of well-intentioned nations so that they could safeguard full employment among themselves.

The existence of the sterling area made it possible to conceive of a two-world economic structure with a sterling world operating at arm's length from the dollar world. The government attempted to retreat not so much into a little England as into a little sterling area. The sterling bailiwick could, they hoped, be isolated from the world dominated by the dollar in which, it was feared, Britain could not compete. Ministers believed that the sterling area provided Britain with an alternative to co-operation with the USA in a one-world economic system. This alternative could possibly be extended to include western Europe, if western Europe would accept British conditions for what would amount to its incorporation into the sterling area. If it was possible to arrange, sterling, not gold or dollars, should be the medium of exchange within this second world as it was within the sterling area. Some Ministers regarded the sterling area only as a fallback if the Americans failed in their duty. Others, and these were the most influential economic Ministers, saw it as the better option both for its own sake and because it reduced British susceptibility to the consequences of American recessions. There would be some sacrifice of the benefits obtainable from free international trade but full employment would be more secure. Britain would even be prepared to pay higher prices in the sterling area if it thereby conserved dollars. In the balance between free international trade and full employment, full employment would weigh more heavily.

If, therefore, the Americans did not do their economic duty, the sterling area would represent a refuge for full employment. Even if US administrations tried to do their duty, so unreliable was Congress that it might be better from the start to seek refuge in the sterling area than accept the risks of free international trade. The two-world approach envisaged a hard currency area, principally the dollar area, and a soft currency area. Within the soft currency area, gold and dollars would be hoarded by the countries whose industries were skilled enough to earn them and they could then purchase from the USA those products which were essential and not obtainable elsewhere. It would remain a priority to encourage exports to the hard currency area. There was much that could only be bought there. The soft currency area would be a residual area for sales of goods that could not be sold to the hard currency area. The trick would be so far as possible to divert exports from the soft currency area to the hard currency area in order to earn dollars. But the dollars were not then to be used as a medium of exchange in trade outside the dollar area. Outside the dollar area, sterling must be the medium of exchange. The world would have been divided in two but at least full employment would be safer.

An inconsistency had emerged between full employment, as interpreted by the Attlee government, and the commitment that it had entered into at the time of the American loan to move towards non-discriminatory trade. The resulting friction with Washington did no good to Anglo-American relations, while the discriminatory trade policies adopted by the Attlee government to defend full employment did little good to British economic performance. British socialism was to become identified with sterling isolationism. By 1949 some 45 per cent of UK imports came from the Commonwealth as compared with 36 per cent in 1934–8. Fifty-one per cent of British exports went to the Commonwealth as compared with 43 per cent pre-war.[15] Later, British lack of competitiveness would be attributed, in part, to this concentration on Commonwealth trade. In defence of full employment, British socialism, which presented itself as internationalist, became narrow and inward-looking.

DEVALUATION – IN ONE WORLD OR TWO

The Americans had come to see the absurdity of the sterling exchange rate fixed at the time of the Bretton Woods Agreements. They perceived that with an uncompetitive exchange rate there was little hope of the UK participating in a one-world economic system. Much to the annoyance of Cripps, they began pressing for a sterling devaluation. When, in the wash of the American recession of 1948, a debate began in London whether sterling should be devalued, the Keynesian economic advisers to the government saw it as a step on the road to a one-world economy with convertibility and without discrimination. They had been among the earliest to see the need for the devaluation and did not resent American pressure. The existence of Marshall Aid, plus the pressure for devaluation, provided sufficient evidence of American co-operation to persuade them that they were justified in continuing to argue that convertibility and the abandonment of discrimination against dollar imports were the right objectives of policy even if not immediately possible for Britain. Treasury officials were not yet persuaded of the inevitability of devaluation but they fully shared the eventual objective of a one-world economy and were considering devaluation in the light of its contribution to that end.

A paper dated 25 June 1949 entitled 'The Rate of Exchange', written at a time when the Treasury had not yet quite made up its mind to recommend devaluation, set out the pros and cons. It concluded that there was a need to consider the issues involved 'on a much wider and deeper basis.' That basis was the role of devaluation in creating a one-world economy.

> Devaluation may play a part in such a context. What is in mind here is that fundamentally the economic and political future of the world as we know it is at stake. Either we find solutions to the fundamental problems or we slip back into a world much more divided and much more restricted than anything we in the United Kingdom have yet experienced.

Because devaluation was not just a matter for the UK, but part of a one-world strategy, there was a need for an Anglo-American understanding first of the issues involved and then of the measures that would have to be taken jointly.

> [T]he possibility or impossibility of convertibility is much more important than the issue of devaluation or no devaluation ... it will have to be realised that convertibility and non-discrimination can only be approached on the basis of Anglo-American agreed policy under which it would be an essential prerequisite that we should have taken the necessary internal steps and be willing to shoulder our part in the new external policy. Then together we should have to find means of dealing with such problems as our substantial dollar indebtedness, the dollar requirements of the rest of the sterling area, the building up of the sterling area reserves to whatever is the required level, and some form of direct or indirect American support for sterling.[16]

All this would need a great deal more preparation but, at the end of the line, there would be convertibility and non-discrimination. There was singular optimism in the idea that the US administration would provide further support for sterling. It was already pouring out Marshall Aid. How far would it be willing to become a milch-cow for British policies which, being socialist, were far from popular in Washington?

Officials assumed, wrongly, that Ministers endorsed the objective of a one-world economy. But Cripps, Gaitskell and Jay no longer accepted it even if they had ever done so. Whenever Ministers saw in Treasury documents advocacy of 'necessary internal steps', they interpreted it as a call for higher unemployment. But, if higher unemployment was the price of a one-world economy, Ministers were not prepared to pay. Because of their suspicion that devaluation was intended to lead to such 'liberal' policies as convertibility and a one-world economy, Ministers came late to the conviction that devaluation was inevitable. In his memorandum of 22 June 1949, Douglas Jay told the Chancellor he preferred devaluation to deflation, 'which is out of the question, and would reverse the whole policy of economic recovery by consent to which we are pledged.' Nevertheless:

2. I disagree, however, entirely with any proposal for devaluation at present, or in the immediately foreseeable future, which rests, I think, on a misreading of the present situation and would – as economic policy – be in present circumstances disastrous.

3. ... There is no evidence that our costs generally are too high for the soft currency and sterling markets. The real trouble is that we have failed in the selling, organising and administrative effort to steer our exports away from these markets to the dollar markets. It is not at all obvious that price is the main obstacle even in the dollar markets. Probably just as great is the failure so far of the great bulk of our small and medium firms to get into contact with North American consumers at all. This is a problem of organisation and not of costs and prices.

He suggested, as alternatives to devaluation, a search for non-dollar sources of supply (which would be in formal conflict with the conditions of the loan agreement), the further invigoration of the dollar export drive, for example by financial incentives, and long-term agreements and bulk-purchase contracts. In other words the competitiveness of the British economy could be dealt with by appropriate planning measures. Jay added: 'Generally speaking, devaluation is a weapon to use in a depression, when the danger is low prices rather than high, and not in a boom when it forces up prices and costs further. It was also the lesson of the 1930's that those who devalued first frequently started a run of depreciation against them, and had to devalue further at a later date.'[17] These views were shared by Cripps, who pledged himself against devaluation even after Treasury officials had, in early July, belatedly advised him that there was no escaping it and the necessary associated deflationary measures. Treatment of the problem by devaluation and deflation, that is by market economy measures, was out of the question and inconsistent with the government's full employment policy.

On 29 June 1949, Gaitskell wrote of the dilemma British policy faced:

we are at the parting of the ways. If we continue to aim at convertibility and multilateralism, I do not see how we can avoid deflation and devaluation now that the American slump is deepening. But if we do neither and go in for . . . trade discrimination in a big way against dollars and a great effort to replace dollar supplies with supplies from other areas, we risk the cutting off altogether of Marshall Aid.[18]

Gaitskell had a private conversation with Cripps in early July after the Treasury had recommended devaluation. Cripps told him that 'One of my difficulties is that my official advisers are all "liberals" and I cannot really rely on them to carry through a "socialist" (sic) policy . . .'[19] Gaitskell himself was very suspicious of officials. Economic liberalism, even when salted with Keynesianism, was clearly just one more expression of Treasury orthodoxy and therefore highly suspect. Gaitskell was acutely worried by those Treasury officials for whom convertibility was the main long-term objective, with devaluation and heavy deflation at home as the immediate steps.[20] A Ministerial meeting at Chequers criticized 'reactionary *laissez-faire* or liberal officials and economists'. It was decided that Ministers would have to supervise the preparation of policy more closely, and that they ought to recruit a sympathetic economist to help.[21]

Yet, only a week later, in the middle of July 1949, Gaitskell and Jay were both belatedly converted to devaluation. But it was not, as the Treasury thought, as a step to a one-world economy but simply on the ground of competitiveness. The evidence had become so overwhelming that even these dedicated socialist planners could no longer resist it. Jay had learnt from Commonwealth leaders that British goods *were* uncompetitive even within the sterling area and he had realized that the uncompetitiveness could not be cured in a short period even by socialist planning. Commonwealth leaders were more trusted on the question of British competitiveness than Jay's own economic advisers in London. The advisers were too liberal and their motives suspect. When Gaitskell joined Jay in favour of devaluation, his view also had nothing in common with the view of those Treasury officials who saw devaluation as the road to a one-world economy. For Gaitskell, too, these views were the unacceptable face of Treasury liberalism. Gaitskell, like Jay, had decided to advocate devaluation simply because the UK economy had become uncompetitive. But the fact that it was now necessary to restore competitiveness by devaluation did not mean acceptance of the one-world objective. For Gaitskell, the need to devalue served only to confirm the desirability of rejecting US pressure for convertibility and non-discrimination. He wrote to Attlee, Cripps and other leading Ministers in August 1949 while the UK government was still not fully committed to devaluation:

> 33. ... we should under no circumstances get committed to convertibility at any particular date – however distant or under any specific conditions. After all, convertibility with the dollar at fixed exchange rates does mean a return to the Gold Standard, to the 'automatic' system of achieving and maintaining equilibrium in international trade. It is almost certainly not compatible with the maintenance of our own full employment policy. It could be used to force deflation upon us and deprive us of certain instruments of economic planning, which even if they are not always to be used, should surely always be kept handy.
>
> 34. We must be wary of definite commitments not only on convertibility but also on specific steps towards multilateralism and non-discrimination. Progress here, for which there is no doubt much to be said, must come gradually as equilibrium is restored . . .
>
> 35. It cannot be too strongly emphasised that anything like a system of complete multilateral trade with free convertibility of currencies is quite out of the question until *after* the fundamental problem of disequilibrium between the dollar and the non-dollar world has been solved.[22]

So far as Gaitskell was concerned, that would not be until the Greek Calends. If Gaitskell's colleagues had bothered to read, and understand, his long memorandum, they would have been horrified. He was explaining to them what the government had done at the time of the American loan and which even Dalton, the economist, appeared not to have understood. By agreeing to convertibility at a fixed rate of exchange against the dollar, the government had in effect blindly committed the unforgivable crime of accepting a return to the Gold Standard. Now, in the interests of full employment, Britain must take the opportunity of devaluation to redeem its sovereignty and break away from any such ill-advised commitments.

Eventually, a distressed and disillusioned Cripps accepted that devaluation was inescapable. He and Bevin were sent by sea to Washington to inform the Americans and to attempt to secure some cover for the defeat of their policies in the form of some agreements that could be presented as a general settlement of economic issues between the USA and UK. They achieved some concessions such as permission to use Marshall Aid dollars to buy Canadian wheat, but most of what the Americans conceded was in the form of offers to think further once specific propositions were put to them. Meanwhile Gaitskell was worrying what these two old and sick Ministers might agree to in Washington under American and Treasury influence. 'Undoubtedly the danger is that these two most powerful Members of the Government on their own in Washington and advised by the Treasury, whose views are "liberal", will agree to long term ties which will be eventually ruinous to us for the sake of some short term gain. They may indeed be driven to this because of the state of the reserves by the autumn.'[23]

Thus was British economic policy being handled in the summer of 1949. Harold Wilson later described the devaluation as 'a realistic reappraisal of the value of the pound in the post-war world, in contrast to the excessive value placed upon it in 1945'.[24] But Cripps saw the devaluation as a defeat for the socialist policies in which he really believed. He was not the only Labour Chancellor to demonstrate by his failures the lesson that if one is to manage a market economy it is better to believe in a market economy. The idea that planning could solve economic problems was an inhibition to successful government in a market economy. To the end Cripps clung to his illusion that he, and probably he alone, knew how to plan what, despite the nationalizations, was still essentially a market economy. He resisted any advice which seemed to him to undervalue the possibilities of socialist planning and extol the value of the price mechanism and the market system. Distaste for 'market' mechanisms had led to delay in devaluation even when it had become inevitable. It then led to inadequate exploitation of the devaluation after it had occurred because the necessary accompanying 'cuts' in public expenditure were deflationary and therefore unacceptable to a socialist Cabinet. Cripps had lost the authority and, partly because he saw the devaluation as a defeat for socialist policies, he had lost even the will to insist on them in adequate measure. Moreover, having come from the left of the Party, he found it intolerable to be reclassified as a man of the right.

THE COMMONWEALTH AND EMPIRE

A two-world policy would have been inconceivable if Britain had not governed an empire and been the centre of the Commonwealth and the sterling area. The Labour party had come to office with a very idealistic attitude to the Commonwealth and Empire. Thus Attlee, in a broadcast in 1940, said of the Empire: 'We must abandon any claim to special rights . . . We must rid ourselves of any taint of imperialism.'[25] This was certainly an improvement on the view expressed by Bevin at the 1930 meeting of the TUC: 'You talk about the coal trade. Ought there not to be some control against the possible development of coal in Tanganyika and in East Africa, which might come into competition with your coal here at a time when the world does not want it?'[26] The idealism was rapidly to disappear under the burden of the UK's need to find a way in the world that guaranteed its full employment and prosperity. It had conceded independence to India and Pakistan, and thereby converted an empire into a commonwealth, but that recognition of inevitability was the end of its idealism. As *Socialist Commentary*, a journal of the Labour right, frankly put it, 'our development plans are partly inspired by our own needs'.[27]

David Fieldhouse, the historian of the British Empire, has shown that Britain exploited its overseas colonies between 1945 and 1951. First there was the treatment of the colonial members of the sterling area. Britain bought all the hard currency earned by the members of the area at the fixed rate of exchange and credited them with sterling balances. Colonial hard currency earnings fed the sterling area dollar pool. The effect on colonies which were net dollar earners, such as the Gold Coast and Malaya, was that they could not use the dollars they earned to buy the goods they wanted outside the sterling area. Yet Britain could not always supply what they wanted. 'The colonies were therefore compelled to run up large sterling balances representing not only the dollars they had been forced to exchange for sterling but also the surplus in their balance of payments within the sterling area. This meant compulsory lending to Britain at low rates of interest.' There was also the problem of the fixed exchange rates between colonial and metropolitan currencies.

> In short the sterling area was used after 1945 as a device for supporting the pound sterling against the dollar . . . At the same time the pound was kept strong against the colonial currencies to avoid an increase in the real burden of blocked sterling balances. In both ways the colonies were compelled to subsidize Britain's post-war standard of living.[28]

Trade with the colonies was also twisted to the UK's advantage. Britain controlled prices for colonial commodities below the world price level for the benefit of UK consumers. It also rationed the volume and type of goods exported to the colonies. 'Since Labour's order of priorities was first to earn dollars, then to satisfy the British consumer and manufacturer, the colonies came very low on its list of priorities.'[29]

Colonial development was also hindered. 'From 1945 the government strictly rationed all colonial borrowing from the city on the ground that the British economy had suffered most during the war and must be given priority . . .'[30] Fieldhouse calculates that 'one way or another, the colonies were lent or given some £40 million by Britain but were forced to lend or tie up in London about £250 million'.[31]

Similar conclusions are arrived at by the historian Scott Newton. It was the white Commonwealth that, in his view, benefited from the sterling area.

> The resources of the central [dollar] pool were . . . beneficial since they offset the dollar deficits of independent members against the dollar surplus of dependent members, and so provided them with more dollars than they would have been able to obtain outside the area. By running the sterling area as a discriminatory bloc, the British were therefore able to sustain multilateralism throughout the Commonwealth and Empire and insulate themselves against the deflationary pressures of the dollar shortage.[32]

Newton concludes, 'It is hard to deny that Asian and African peasants laboured to support . . . living standards throughout the white Commonwealth.'[33]

On 6 August 1947, in the midst of the convertibility crisis, Attlee spoke in the House in the course of the debate on the state of the nation. He paid tribute to the Commonwealth. He referred to the credit granted by Canada, and to the action by Australia and New Zealand in cancelling part of their sterling balances. There would, in fact, have been more reason to be grateful to Australia if it had refrained from drawing from the sterling area dollar pool more than it put in. Attlee continued, 'We are asking our Colonies to help us by restricting to essentials their claims on our foreign exchange resources which are of course also theirs.'[34] The colonies were not independent. They were not free to decide how to respond to such requests. And, Attlee added, 'The House has heard with approval the far reaching plans which the Colonial Secretary has initiated for making available to the world the potential wealth of our African colonies. These schemes will take time to mature.'[35] Thus the interests of the colonies were being sacrificed to those of Britain by a socialist government. The only excuse was that Britain had suffered during the war and that its sacrifices should be repaid even by people far poorer than British citizens.

ECONOMIC INTEGRATION WITH EUROPE

It was not only in the USA that delinquent conduct was to be found. It was present even in Europe. Labour Ministers feared that economic integration with Europe would endanger full employment by imposing deflation on the UK. One consequence of the commitment to full employment was therefore to downgrade economic relations with Europe. In a pamphlet *Western Europe – The Challenge of Unity*, Denis Healey, International Secretary of the Labour party, complained that continental countries could not plan, and could not deal with unemployment, even if they wanted to:

> The aim of state intervention in [Britain and Scandinavia] is to provide a decent economic standard of living for all citizens, to ensure that scarce goods are shared fairly, to guarantee full employment, and to balance trade with the outside world. In most of the other countries [of western Europe] the governments are either unwilling or unable to control the national economy . . . Thus classical methods of deflation and *laissez-faire* have been adopted instead . . . Unemployment is rife in Belgium, Germany and Italy . . . Moreover the French and Italian governments have failed to grapple seriously with their basic economic problems; their failure has been camouflaged only by large injections of American aid.[36]

In the summer of 1950, Gaitskell, employing arguments that would become common form for British Ministers over the next three decades, urged European countries to reflate along Keynesian lines to reduce unemployment and on no account to deflate, thereby imposing unemployment on their trading partners. His remarks were coolly received by his audience. British economic policy was already suspect as condoning inflation.

There was no enthusiasm in British government even for the liberalization of European trade. Liberalization would make British success in maintaining full employment uncomfortably dependent on the policies of European governments which had not shared in the Keynesian revelation. Strong pressure was coming from OEEC for liberalization of intra-OEEC trade. Douglas Jay thought it should be resisted. He criticized liberalization on inessentials as socially regressive. He recognized that it might be politically necessary to make proposals for liberalization. The American benefactors were demanding it as a condition of Marshall Aid. But it was not economically or socially right and would lead to lack of control.

Jay's views were not accepted by government economists. The effect of resisting liberalization would be to divide western Europe into a dozen high-cost markets but was unlikely to restrain total expenditure on inessentials. Jay remained impenitent. On 9 December 1949, he wrote to the Chancellor opposing any relaxation on imports within OEEC. There was, he argued, already too much sterling in the hands of foreigners. Relaxation on imports would add to it. 'The whole position of our reserves and dollar prospects is, in my view, far too precarious to take risks of this kind ... All the evidence is that the strain on our balance of payments is going to extend to non-dollar countries as well as dollar countries in 1950.' He then added two further arguments against relaxation. The first was that 'We are apparently asked to make [these relaxations] unilaterally, and lose foreign exchange on balance, although our controls are already more liberal than most others.' The second was that 'though the first step is clearly to relax vis-à-vis the soft currency countries, we know from experience that pressure is then brought to bear not to "discriminate" against e.g. Belgium and Switzerland or other hard countries'.[37]

In his pamphlet *Western Europe – The Challenge of Unity*, Healey endorsed Jay's view. Britain's problem was different:

> Britain's economic problem is fundamentally far greater than France's since France is much less dependent on foreign trade and imported raw materials. Moreover Britain has economic relations with her Commonwealth whose importance outweighs the potential benefits of economic co-operation with Europe. For example, by 1952 over half Britain's foreign trade will be with the Commonwealth as against 22 per cent with Europe. Also Britain's imports from the Commonwealth are mainly indispensable raw materials, whereas her imports from Europe are less essential.

In June 1950 in a statement on foreign policy entitled *European Unity*, the Labour party gave its opinion on the liberalization of trade with Europe:

> There has recently been much enthusiasm for an economic union based on dismantling all internal barriers to trade, such as customs, duty, exchange controls and quotas. Most supporters of this policy believe that the free play of economic forces within the continental market so created would produce a better distribution of manpower and resources. The Labour Party fundamentally rejects this theory ... Any further liberalization of intra-European trade will tend to offset the benefits of devaluation by making it easy to sell in Europe.

Thus the Labour party went so far as to believe that it was positively undesirable for European countries to reduce their barriers to imports from the UK because it would make it too easy for British producers to sell their products to Europe and thereby divert them from the main target, the dollar area.

It is fair to say that Labour's views on European trade were shared by many senior officials. They too suspected that the continental Europeans were engaged in a conspiracy against UK interests and imperial preference.[38] This led to scepticism whether there was any value at all in European trade. In a conversation between Sir James Helmore (Board of Trade) and Sir Edmund Hall-Patch (UK delegation to OEEC), Helmore said that:

> There was really no reason to pretend that in general an increase in the volume of intra-European trade would contribute to European recovery which depended not on Europeans selling more to one another but on their selling more for dollars. This was where competition and improved efficiency resulting from it came into the picture. Sir Edmund agreed . . . Indeed it was what Sir Edmund had been saying at OEEC.[39]

Moreover Europe was not to be allowed, by its deflationary policies, which did not respect the primacy of full employment, to suck gold and dollars out of the UK. Europe would have a part to play in British two-world ideas but only on certain clear conditions. First, it must eschew demands for gold and dollars in payment for any export surplus. Trade would have to be conducted in sterling. Secondly, it must grant extensive credit to its customers among other European countries and, in effect, become part of the sterling area. European countries would have nothing to do with such ideas. They refused to become honorary members of the sterling area.[40] Countries such as Germany and Belgium had much more concern about inflation than the UK, and they all wanted gold or dollars in payment for their surpluses, not sterling. They had much that they wished to buy from the USA and, if they earned dollars, there was no part of the world from which they could not buy. They could buy from the best and cheapest source whatever it happened to be. Sterling, on the other hand, was a doubtful store of value, was officially unconvertible and, though it could in practice be converted into dollars, only at a substantial discount. The UK condemned Belgium and Switzerland, which were conducting deflationary policies. Little Belgium achieved a particular hate status in British eyes even though it was a low-tariff country. On 17 November 1949, Jay minuted Cripps, attacking Belgium for running a restrictive economic policy which gave it an export surplus with Britain that would have to be paid for in gold.

Washington proposed that, to encourage trade within Europe at a time of dollar shortage, a European Payments Union (EPU) should be established. The Attlee government did not like the EPU, first because of the low priority allocated to European trade and then because there were to be gold points, that is points at which credit was exhausted and payment had to be made in gold or dollars. Unfortunately it was an illusion to imagine, as Gaitskell did, that it was possible to establish a European payments union which denied surplus countries the right to demand settlement in gold or dollars. Britain did in fact agree to enter the EPU in the summer of 1950 but its accession was the result of a great deal of American persuasion, some concessions on the credit that would be available within the system, and an injection of dollars intended to mitigate the deflationary effect of the scheme feared by the UK.

An additional reason for avoiding more than the minimum inevitable economic integration with Europe was Britain's confidence that it enjoyed a significant advantage in its access to Commonwealth raw materials. The fear that the price of raw materials was inevitably going to rise, and that the terms of trade would turn permanently against the developed world, was enhanced by the outbreak of the Korean war in June 1950. There then developed a serious shortage of raw materials, due mainly to American stockpiling. The resulting rise in raw material prices was a factor in the British balance of payments crisis in the second half of 1951. Who would want to sacrifice the advantage the UK had through its access to Commonwealth raw materials by joining with continental Europeans and letting them have a share? Continental Europeans were also worried by the shortage of raw materials and by the fear that it might get worse. They were by no means averse to discussing ways of involving the Commonwealth in their plans for European integration. The fact that there might be here a strong negotiating point for the UK in constructing the kind of Europe it wanted was ignored. Then it was too late. From 1952 the terms of trade turned in favour of the industrialized world and the UK then had nothing to offer. Raw materials became, in real terms, cheaper, not more expensive.

The Attlee government did want to be a leader in Europe, but it was on one condition – that leadership did not involve binding commitments inconsistent with what were seen as the UK's wider responsibilities. That criterion was interpreted as ruling out almost any commitment to the kinds of European economic integration sought by its continental allies. Specifically, it ruled out British participation in any purely European supranational institution. Ernest Bevin suspected that any form of supranationalism would give the Americans a further lever with which to influence or even control British policy. He was ambivalent about the Americans. He combined his public gratitude to the Americans with private suspicion of their intentions. He knew that they still wanted to get rid of the sterling area and imperial preference. He suspected that their method was to get Britain locked within a federal Europe. Then, by exercising their influence on the federal European government, they would control Britain.[41]

There were three treaties into which the UK did enter with its continental partners. There were the Treaty of Dunkirk (1947) and the Treaty of Brussels (1948). But those treaties were essentially about security and they were stepping stones to the North Atlantic Treaty (1949) and the creation of the North Atlantic Treaty Organization, which committed the USA to the defence of western Europe. NATO was, in a sense, supranational. But Britain insisted that European institutions which did not include the Americans must, if Britain's participation was expected, be intergovernmental, thus ensuring Britain a veto. Supranational institutions which just united European countries were ruled out because they were regarded as leading to a federal Europe, a destination unacceptable for Britain. The trouble was that the western Europeans did want to commence the construction of a new and peaceful Europe and their chosen method included the development of supranational European institutions.

THE SCHUMAN PLAN[42]

It was not surprising in the circumstances that Britain's response to the Schuman Plan demonstrated a lack both of insight into British interests and of elementary diplomatic skills. The Plan was announced in Paris by Robert Schuman, French Foreign Minister, on 9 May 1950. The French had at first tried, unsuccessfully, to persuade their wartime allies to separate the Ruhr from Germany, thereby reducing their enemy's capacity to wage aggressive war. They then decided that the next best option was to make friends with Germany on the basis proposed in the Schuman Plan, that is that all the coal and steel resources of Europe should be placed under the control of a supranational and 'sovereign' High Authority. The announcement of the Schuman Plan made an immediate, profound and favourable impression on international public opinion, notably in the USA. Only five years after the end of the war the French were striving for reconciliation with the Federal Republic of Germany, and the Federal Republic had at once agreed to co-operate. From the British point of view, there were problems with the French plan but nothing that could not have been corrected in negotiation. Britain, however, rejected the opportunity to participate in the negotiations. It was the crucial error whereby it excluded itself for a generation from any position of leadership in Europe and from European political and economic integration.

In British government circles there was immediate hostility to the Schuman Plan because of its supranational aspects. It was accepted that Franco-German reconciliation was a prime object of British policy and that the Schuman Plan was a major step in that direction. But supranationalism represented an insurmountable obstacle to British participation. Schuman had used the word 'federalism' in his announcement, and the sovereign High Authority was to have powers that would bind national governments. The thought of a High Authority that could bind governments evoked in London fantasies about what such an Authority might do. It could shut down steel plants and coal mines without the agreement of national governments. It could undermine the Attlee government's policy of bringing the commanding heights of the economy under government control. Attlee had not nationalized the coal industry, and was not proposing to nationalize the iron and steel industry, in order to surrender the power to plan them to a sovereign High Authority. Cripps disclosed to the French Ambassador in London his nightmare that the High Authority could even dictate to national governments their conduct of economic policy.

Repelled by its supranationalism, the government overlooked many positive aspects of the Schuman Plan. It was unique among proposals for European economic integration in that it did not impact in any significant way on Britain's perception of itself as a global power and as the centre of the Commonwealth. Whether that global role made sense for a Britain impoverished by war was a question insufficiently debated. But there was nothing inconsistent between participation in the Schuman Plan and a global role. Indeed it would help with Britain's global role. There would be fewer worries about quarrels in western Europe. Britain would not just be a global power and a Commonwealth power. In addition it would be a leader in Europe. There was nothing inconsistent between participation in the Schuman Plan and being the centre of the Commonwealth. Any minor inconsistencies between imperial preference and participation in the Schuman Plan could have been negotiated away. Britain was banker to the sterling area. There was nothing inconsistent between participation in the Schuman Plan and being banker to the sterling area. There was to be no bar on public ownership. The French did not abandon national planning because of the Schuman Plan. In any case, the British could not abandon national planning because they had not yet discovered how to do it. But, if the discovery was ever made, there would, in practice, be no inconsistency with the Schuman Plan.

To observe all this required thought and analysis. But there were several reasons why no serious thought was given to the Schuman Plan. First, there was the previously formulated policy of avoiding irreversible economic integration with Europe. Then there was no sense of solidarity with continental socialists, who were backing the Plan but wanted the reassurance of British participation. Continental socialists were not well regarded among British socialists, particularly but not exclusively, of the left wing. American Democrats were, among British socialists, preferred to European socialists. The only European socialists for whom much sympathy was felt were the Scandinavian, but Scandinavia had no part in the Schuman Plan. Cripps, the only senior Minister who, once he had got over his initial shock, was, even for a moment, prepared to think favourably of British participation, was sick and had already offered Attlee his resignation. Bevin was also ill and quite incapable of doing his job. He felt deep resentment at the lack of consultation by Schuman before the announcement – after all that the UK had, in his view, done for France. On 22 January 1948, Bevin had told the House of Commons:

> It is easy enough to draw up a blueprint for a united Western Europe and to construct neat looking plans on paper. While I do not wish to discourage the work done by voluntary political organisations in advocating ambitious schemes of European unity, I must say that it is a much slower and harder job to carry out a practical programme which takes into account the realities which face us, and I am afraid that it will have to be done a step at a time.[43]

The trouble was that, as the years passed, he never came up with any plan of his own which met his specification that it should be practical. Now the French had come up with a plan which might prove practical and had not even had the courtesy to consult him.

When to all this was added the fact that the continentals were not our kith and kin and that most of them were Catholics, the prospect of a British government noticing that, as the success of the Schuman Plan was a major British interest, the UK should help by participating was negligible. The case against Europe was summed up in the statement *European Unity* issued by the NEC of the Labour party a month after the announcement of the Schuman Plan:

> Britain is not just a small crowded island off the Western coast of Continental Europe. She is the nerve centre of a worldwide Commonwealth which extends into every continent. In every respect except distance we in Britain are closer to our kinsmen in Australia and New Zealand on the far side of the world than we are to Europe. We are closer in language and in origins, in social habits and institutions, in political outlook and in economic interest. The economies of the Commonwealth countries are complementary to that of Britain to a degree which those of western Europe could never equal. Furthermore Britain is also the banker of the sterling area.

It has been argued that the French did not really want British participation or, as an alternative, they did not want British participation in the negotiations but would have liked Britain to be a signatory of the Schuman Treaty, the Treaty of Paris, as eventually negotiated. Bevin himself told James Callaghan, a junior minister who thought the UK should participate, that 'they don't want us, Callaghan'. There may have been a certain ambivalence in Paris about British participation. But the probability nevertheless is that the French government did, on balance, want British participation. It had political problems in gaining popular assent to the Schuman Plan. The Plan envisaged reconciliation with the Germans when the memories of German occupation were still painful. There was uneasiness in Paris about being left tête-à-tête with the Germans. British participation would have eased the political problems of the French government.

Whatever the ambivalence in Paris, the British government had been invited to the negotiations by the French government. It could have accepted. Even the 'sovereign' High Authority was not really an obstacle. It was true that the French invitation was conditional on the acceptance of the principle of a supranational High Authority. Obviously the way in which it was to be established would be a subject for negotiation. Other countries invited to the talks had reservations, notably Belgium and the Netherlands. Belgium and the Netherlands were making it quite clear that, in the form proposed, the idea was unacceptable. They would not delegate to a purely nominated authority, consisting of nine unelected experts, powers of life and death over their coal and steel industries. It was unlikely that even the French government, which had proposed the idea under the influence of Jean Monnet, would be prepared to do it. It was easy enough to foresee that the High Authority would emerge from the negotiating conference as an institution very different from the original conception. The British Parliament would never have ratified a genuinely 'sovereign' High Authority. But nor, probably, would the parliaments of the other contracting powers. The negotiations in Paris resolved the problem. It was decided that there should be a Council of Ministers alongside the High Authority. The High Authority, when established, was aware that, in any matter of importance, it could not exercise its supranational powers without the assent of the Council of Ministers. There was no question of the High Authority shutting pits or steel mills without the consent of member countries.

The final British decision not to participate in the negotiations that were to take place in Paris occurred at a Cabinet meeting on 2 June. There had been an ultimatum from France demanding to know by the evening of 2 June whether or not Britain would participate. The French already had the agreement of the Germans to the commencement of the negotiations. That was the key to the success of their Plan. They also had the agreement of Italy and the three Benelux countries. Finally, they had the warm approval of Washington for the initiative they had taken. The time had come to make progress. Bevin was in hospital. Attlee and Cripps were on holiday, Cripps ironically enough in the country home of Maurice Petsche, the French Minister of Finance. Morrison, in charge of the government, had been told of the French ultimatum on the previous evening. He commented: 'It's no good. We cannot do it; the Durham miners won't wear it.' The Durham miners thereby acquired an unwitting place in the demonology of the Schuman Plan. But Morrison may have been mistaken. Sir William Lawther, President of the National Union of Miners, described by Roy Jenkins as being 'already more powerful than any six capitalists',[44] and who had previously been General Secretary of the Durham miners, was quoted as favouring participation in the negotiations.[45]

If the government had decided to participate in the Schuman Plan, it would have had problems with the unions, particularly the iron and steel union. But the problems would have yielded to political leadership just as far greater political problems yielded in France. The Cabinet of 2 June, instead of agreeing to participate, tried a diversionary manoeuvre in the hope of sabotaging the Schuman Plan without appearing to do so. It proposed a meeting of Ministers 'at which the question of the most effective and expeditious method of discussing the problems at issue could be examined and settled'.[46] The French at once rejected the British manoeuvre for what it was. Britain, after having been given a full opportunity to participate, had decided to exclude itself. Britain thereby lost its last best opportunity to become a leading partner in an integrated Europe. But there was no regret. For Labour, European integration was inconsistent with British socialism, full employment and Britain's global role. Ironically, the Conservatives, having appeared to favour European unity, also had no regrets. For them, too, British participation in European integration was inconsistent with Britain's global role.

'A MASSIVE ACHIEVEMENT'?

In the years before the 1944 White Paper on Employment, fears had been expressed that politicians were being too ambitious in giving assurances about a high and stable level of employment. But in what sense was full employment a 'massive achievement'? Throughout western Europe, it was not full employment that proved the great challenge of the post-war years but price stability. In the early years after the war there were enough influences making for full employment without the use of Keynesian techniques, and without the Attlee government's policy of isolating the UK in a second world. Governments were profiting politically from a happy combination of circumstances. There was the release of pent-up demand unsatisfied during the years of war enhanced by the need to repair the ravages of war. There was American aid, and private American capital exports. To some extent employment within Britain's national borders benefited from the continuing level of protection. These factors leading to full employment might one day be reversed. Full employment in Britain might be found vulnerable to an American recession. Protection might succumb to American pressure for open markets. Pent-up demand would eventually be satisfied, and retreat to more normal levels. The USA might become a net importer rather than exporter of capital. The truth was that governments did not really know how to guarantee full employment and there were those who suspected the truth. But that was not the problem during the life of the Attlee government. In Attlee's time the proof of policy was not full employment. It was price stability.

The Attlee government's decision to give priority to full employment rather than price stability had serious implications for the future performance of the British economy. The consequence can be seen by a comparison with Germany. The Germans, whose priority was price stability, achieved high and stable employment, though a little later than the British, combined with a strong balance of payments. The British, where priority was full employment, achieved it for many years but at the cost of continuing troubles with inflation and the balance of payments. Among the dangers of British policy was that the trade unions would assume that full employment was now guaranteed by government without benefit of any permanent contribution from wage earners to price stability and competitiveness. If full employment could be achieved by Keynesian tricks, the pressure for competitiveness, as an alternative route to high levels of employment, was reduced. The unions could continue with free collective bargaining without much thought for its effect on employment prospects. German unions had no such guarantee. The social consensus to which the objective of full employment contributed led to overmanning in industry, which also had its effects on competitiveness.

It was particularly the experience of the 1948 American recession that made the Attlee government nervous that what it deemed its major achievement, full employment, might fall victim to external circumstances. These fears encouraged it in policies which were inflationary and damaging to the UK's long-term economic and political prospects. Domestically, the Cabinet, and its advisers, showed an excessive tolerance of inflation as its contribution to the maintenance of full employment. It was only much later that Robert Hall, the government's Keynesian Economic Adviser 1947–61, came to accept that successive British governments had 'run the economy too full ever since I came to this job', adding, 'I feel that we ought to have put more weight than we did on the need for deflation from the beginning.'[47] Externally, the Attlee government sought to isolate Britain and the sterling area from the contamination of Europe and the dollar. But the pressures in the direction of convertibility and non-discrimination proved too strong and the successor Churchill government submitted to them progressively under a hail of criticism from Gaitskell and the other Labour economic experts.

As unemployment increased from the late 1960s through the 1970s, reaching peaks in the 1980s, it became apparent that the secret of full employment had by no means been found. There had been a period of success from which governments had derived the maximum political benefit. But the secret of full employment had not yet been disinterred. Capitalism could still play its unpleasant pranks and governments could remain mystified as to how to counter them. This discovery would have brought comfort to those who, all along, had protested that full employment required socialism, not just Keynesian fiscal tricks. Bevan had warned in *Tribune* on 3 February 1950: 'An insistence on the maintenance of full employment means constant intervention by government in the main agencies and streams of industrial and financial activity. Those who believe that the end can be achieved by injecting, or withdrawing, purchasing power from the financial system from time to time are pipe-dreaming . . .'[48] But this merely demonstrated that Bevan had learnt nothing, during his membership of the Attlee Cabinet, about the problems of economic planning.

In its attempt to defend its version of full employment, socialist Britain found itself at odds with the rest of the western world. The USA, despite Marshall Aid, was condemned in private thought, if not in public word, for its refusal to follow economic policies that would make life easier for Britain. Europe was felt to be merely a distraction from the serious business of restoring Britain's prosperity and, in the deflationary policies followed by individual countries, a danger to British solvency. Even the independent Commonwealth was unreliable, being insufficiently co-operative in solving Britain's problems. Perhaps only Canada passed the test. The colonies, of course, had no choice but to co-operate with British policies and suffered as a result. Politically, British socialism showed itself under Attlee nationalist, protectionist, inflationary and, in so far as it extended its embrace outside Britain at all, anglophone. The internationalists had become isolationist in anxious defence of socialism and full employment.

EIGHT

The climb interrupted

BEVAN AND GAITSKELL

At the General Election in February 1950, the Attlee government was returned to office with its majority reduced from 146 to 6. There had been a considerable defection of middle-class voters.[1] From that moment the Tory hyenas were prowling. In June that year, North Korean forces invaded South Korea. The Attlee government was confronted with yet one more crisis and one which demonstrated yet again the fissiparous tendencies of Labour governments under pressure. In the summer of 1950, the British rearmament programme was increased, at American insistence, from £2,300 million to £3,600 million over three years. In October, Cripps was at last allowed to resign and was succeeded by Gaitskell. Gaitskell had been Chancellor for two months when Attlee returned from Washington in December 1950 with a commitment to increase the rearmament programme yet further to £4,700 million over three years. Attlee had flown urgently to Washington to persuade President Truman not to use the atomic bomb in Korea. While there, he was told that, in the American view, there was imminent danger of a Soviet attack in the West. The British Chiefs of Staff were warning the Cabinet that there was a possibility of war in 1951, a probability in 1952. With whatever reservations such advice could be treated, a responsible government could not ignore it. Britain's lack of preparedness in 1939 would not be forgotten by Ministers who had played any part in the war. As recently as 1948 Czechoslovak independence had been crushed by the Soviet military. There had been the Berlin blockade as evidence that the Soviet government was not entirely friendly.

The Cabinet was, to all appearance, united on the rearmament programme. There were understandable expressions of concern about its economic impact. The burden was likely to become intolerable, especially given the rate of American stockbuilding and its effect on raw-material prices, and hence on the British balance of payments. A few growls from Bevan at this point were not merely understandable but appropriate. His concerns about the programme did not prevent him, in February, from defending it in the House. Harold Wilson shared, indeed stimulated, Bevan's anxieties. He claimed that, whatever the arguments for the rearmament programme, it could not be fulfilled. Gaitskell tended to discount Wilson's views because he was close to Bevan and had been considered an unreliable ally during the devaluation debates of 1949. Nevertheless, Gaitskell himself was perfectly aware of the economic problems that the programme would cause. He could hardly be unaware of it given that it was being increased from 8 per cent of Gross Domestic Product to 14 per cent. In January 1951, in Cabinet, Gaitskell warned of the problems that it would imply for the British economy. Attlee and Gaitskell, as well as Bevan, cautioned the House that it might be impossible to implement the programme. The claim that Bevan and Wilson displayed a very special insight into the problems rearmament would create for the British economy was not, therefore, justified. It was simply part of the propaganda war that broke out between contending sections of the Labour party. But both Attlee and Gaitskell realized that, if Britain wanted American protection in Europe at a time when Republicans in Congress were pressing for priority for Asia, it would have to make a major contribution to defence against communism.

It is arguable that Gaitskell, with what he knew of the state of the British economy, should have opposed the further increase in the rearmament programme that followed Attlee's visit to Washington, that his failure to do so undermined the successes of the Labour government and thereby ruined the prospects for socialism in Britain. But this is grossly to exaggerate what could have been expected from him at that time. However great his concerns, and even if he had agreed with the criticisms emanating from Bevan and Wilson, he was not in a position, as a new Chancellor, to oppose Attlee and Bevin.

Assistance for British rearmament had been vaguely promised by Washington. It rapidly became clear that it would be less than expected and long delayed. During a visit by Gaitskell to Washington, the concept of burden sharing was developed. Equity between allies required that the burden of security should be apportioned equitably. In London this was interpreted as meaning that the USA should carry some fair share of the UK's burdens in participating in the Korean war and in the rearmament programme that accompanied it. It was David Bensusan

Butt of the Economic Section who wrote of the danger of 'our equity ideas coming to be regarded as merely a queer Whitehall shibboleth, a quaint device for getting dollars without having to thank the donors, for reconciling a new and haughty independence with continued mendicancy . . .'[2] It was not widely understood in London that burden sharing, as seen from Congress, might mean the UK doing rather more and the USA rather less. Far more American lives and treasure were expended in Korea than British.

The rearmament programme presented Gaitskell with a difficult budgetary problem. How far should he dissipate the surplus which Cripps had diligently preserved in order to fund the rearmament programme? Dissipating the surplus would clearly be inflationary. As a small part of his answer, he decided to impose health service charges. This decision was the immediate cause of Bevan's resignation from the government in April 1951. Bevan was clearly not prepared to respect his language of priorities when it involved his NHS. Nevertheless, such charges were certainly justified and Bevan's principled opposition to them was obsessive. The cost of the NHS had mounted far beyond estimate and there was need for some control. But, in the context of the 1951 budget, the main function of which was to fund the rearmament programme, the income from the charges in the first year, a mere £13 million, was negligible. A stronger Prime Minister would have told Gaitskell that not everything could be done at once; that, after only months as Chancellor, he should not be impatient to demonstrate greater austerity even than Cripps, who had let the issue slip; that he could wait to exert his dominance over Bevan; and that Bevan should not be handed an excuse to resign which he was probably looking for in any case. Such counsel from the Prime Minister would have had to be associated with the promise of firm support in the future, the kind of promise Attlee was unlikely to give. One might have expected a Chancellor, even without such guidance from the Prime Minister, to understand the importance of keeping the government united with another election looming and not to be so anxious to force an issue that was hardly of immediate importance. Gaitskell, however, left to himself, unguided by the elders of the Party, became as passionate to impose health service charges as Bevan was to exclude them. The inescapable blame which attaches to Gaitskell derives from his exploitation of the issue to present Bevan with the unpleasant alternatives of humiliation or resignation.

Resignation is not a frequent attribute of Labour (or other) Cabinet

Ministers but the use of threats of resignation is. During the life of the Attlee government, particularly at moments of stress, threats of resignation flowed freely. Cabinet Ministers must have become inured to them. Threats were often more influential than the arguments advanced to justify them. Any Chancellor who questioned Bevin's infatuation with Britain's global role would be at once faced with a threat of resignation, a resignation which Attlee could not afford to accept. Nor was Bevan backward in threats of resignation, and their frequency sapped their credibility. Yet nobody actually resigned until the confrontation between Gaitskell and Bevan. To emphasize the force of their arguments, both Bevan and Gaitskell used threats of resignation in ways appropriate to their characters. Bevan's threat was trumpeted publicly in a way which was bound to infuriate his Cabinet colleagues. Gaitskell's was quiet, unpublicized, sweetened with the offer to retire humbly to the backbenches and not make trouble. It was some reinforcement to his courage in making the threat that the Prime Minister was unlikely to let his Chancellor go just before a budget. Unlike Bevin, Bevan was in the end expendable.

Harold Wilson resigned together with Bevan, in each case for a mixture of motives among which resentment and jealousy combined with genuine issues of policy. Though Wilson was a future Labour Prime Minister, his resignation was of little political significance and mainly demonstrated that, contrary to the criticisms of Gaitskell and Jay at the time of devaluation, he was capable of taking a risky decision and acting on it. The resignation that was important was that of Bevan. Bevan, undoubtedly, had a high opinion both of himself and of his contribution to the success of the Labour government. The high opinion may well have been deserved. But a more skilful politician, and a more modest man, would have kept it to himself. True, he was a great orator. But those who lack that capacity may become suspicious of it in others. MacDonald was a great orator but also, in the view of the Labour party, a great traitor. Critics may even regard oratory, as Froude did, as the harlot of the arts. The Welsh are particularly suspect. Such jealousy is not unknown in politics. Bevan was dismayed that he never seemed to win within the PLP the appreciation that he thought he deserved for the creation of the NHS. In the view of the PLP, the fact that he had carried out the policy of the Party at Health entitled him to no more credit than other Ministers who had also done their duty by Labour's election manifesto.

He had done more than his duty in only one respect, that is in defending the government in the House over a wide range of policies including, in February 1951, rearmament. That speech, made at his own request, was possibly a claim on the Foreign Office, which was clearly soon to become vacant due to Bevin's failing health. It was one of his greatest speeches. Nevertheless, Bevan's claim to the Foreign Office was overlooked and Morrison succeeded Bevin. Nothing had changed between Bevan's February speech and his resignation except the health service charges and the appointment of Morrison to the Foreign Office. Bevan felt he had already been passed over once when, the previous October, Gaitskell was chosen for the Treasury. Gaitskell's succession brought Bevan the additional mortification that it was on the recommendation of Bevan's old and admired friend, Cripps. Was his faithful service to secure no reward? In considering the ideological significance, if any, of Bevan's resignation, the contribution of pique cannot be ignored.

After his resignation, Bevan broadened the scope of his public attack on the government from the health service charges to the rearmament programme. He has won subsequent applause because he was 'right' about the rearmament programme. It did prove insupportable. One source of applause was Winston Churchill when he became Prime Minister and cut the programme back. Why should Churchill neglect any opportunity of exacerbating the split that was discomfiting the Labour party? There can be little doubt that, if the Attlee government had been returned in the October 1951 General Election, experience of the economic consequences of the rearmament programme would have led to just that reappraisal that the Churchill government then undertook. The programme would have been spread over a longer period and would thereby have become rather less of a burden.

A QUESTION OF SOCIALIST PRINCIPLE?

Did the conflict between Gaitskell and Bevan signify anything more than a battle for mastery between two highly ambitious men? Should one, for example, discern in the event a clash between, on the one hand, a prophet of socialism and, on the other, a technocrat, a desiccated calculating machine? Was it an engagement between divergent visions of socialism? The formation of the two men was certainly very different and it would not be surprising if, resulting from their personal histories, they saw the future of socialism differently. Gaitskell was born into an upper-middle-class family. He had passed through Winchester and Oxford to academic life as an economist at University College London. Discovered by Dalton, he had spent the war as a civil servant working for Dalton first at the Ministry of Economic Warfare and then at the Board of Trade. Bevan was a miner from the Welsh valleys. He had seen his family and friends suffer misery under the Tories in the 1920s and 1930s, an experience he would never forget and could not forgive. He was a class warrior whose suspicions of other classes extended even to those who, appalled by the sufferings of the working class during the depression, had joined the Labour party in its struggle for socialism.

Bevan was an explosive force whose instrument was oratory, an oratory enriched, as Gaitskell was prepared to concede, at least to his diary, by a fertile imagination and by striking phraseology.[3] As an orator he exercised an extraordinary domination over the House of Commons. He was, though strongly influenced by Marxism, a staunch Parliamentarian. But, despite these credentials, he was no match for Gaitskell in manipulating the levers of power. By resigning he had abandoned the field to Gaitskell. His sudden realization of the fact was perhaps responsible for the fury and hatred which disfigured his resignation statements in the House of Commons and the Parliamentary Labour Party. In two frenzied, and arrogant, speeches, Bevan succeeded in discrediting himself and his cause. He shocked even those colleagues most willing to sympathize with him. They were confessions of defeat and, for Bevan, nothing was more bitter than to be defeated by this sprig of the upper classes. His speeches were an attack not so much on the government as on Gaitskell. If the great issue was not the health service charges but the rearmament programme, the prime culprit was Attlee not Gaitskell. It was Attlee who brought back from Washington the demand for a further increase in the rearmament programme. Gaitskell merely tried to fund it. Yet Attlee suffered only sporadic criticism while most of the blame was laid at Gaitskell's door. One can only suspect that Bevan and the Bevanites made Gaitskell their target because he was the enemy, the man who had to be destroyed because he represented the younger generation standing in the way of Bevan's succession.

Gaitskell was no rebel. He knew the importance of keeping close to the leadership. In the early 1930s, when leaders such as Attlee were very radical, he was very radical. After 1935 he grew more moderate – with the leadership. In the war he was a skilled administrator. As Minister of Fuel and Power, he had had exceptional opportunities to establish friendly relations with important trade unions. It was a bonus, the value of which he fully understood. In the midst of the crisis with Bevan, Gaitskell was careful to pay attention to the trade union group of MPs and to make concessions to their views. Bevan, on the other hand, *was* a rebel, too often without sufficient cause. His streak of genius was mingled with inadequate self-discipline. Though a trade unionist, he could not command the loyalty of the trade unions. Though a former miner, he could not even command the loyalty of the NUM. As Gaitskell saw it he was 'a difficult team worker' and even 'a thoroughly unreliable and disloyal colleague'.[4] Because of his oratorical prowess, and because he was so often rumbling on the edge of rebellion, Bevan won adoration from the rank and file in the constituencies who loved him in a way in which Gaitskell would never be loved. Because of the indiscipline he won few friends within the leadership either of the Party or of the trade unions. In a conflict between the machine politician, Gaitskell, and the maverick, Bevan, there was little doubt who would win. As a politician, Bevan was his own worst enemy. Not even by Gaitskell could he be superseded in that role. Enormously gifted, he was also deeply flawed. Therein lies both his tragedy and his enduring attraction.

But did socialism, or distinct attitudes to socialism, play any part in these events? On policy, Bevan and Gaitskell had much in common outside foreign affairs. The health service charges, the original *casus belli*, could be regarded only by a fanatic as a serious blow to the NHS and had been intended to be temporary. During the subsequent years of opposition, Gaitskell would frequently emphasize that, whereas his charges had been intended to be temporary, the Tories were making them permanent.[5] Gaitskell who, as Minister of Fuel and Power, had been responsible for major nationalized industries, retained a strong belief in nationalization. He disliked competitive struggle. He maintained that in the private sector power was exercised without responsibility. He accepted that private sector power had been modified by government controls and the strength of the trade unions. But he was sure that it was still more decisive than it should be. He thought that nationalization would help to reduce inequality, insecurity and inefficiency.[6] There was a difference with Bevan in Gaitskell's support of the principle of the independent public board, whereas Bevan, for democratic reasons, advocated direct Ministerial control of the nationalized industries. But, even there, there was perhaps not so much of a difference because Gaitskell would have liked, as Minister, to be chairman of the board.[7] Bevan remained a bureaucratic socialist, rejecting any significant role for the market. Gaitskell, though sharing many of Bevan's views on policy, and also highly suspicious of the market, was more capable of growing out of bureaucratic socialism. But there was nothing that should have prevented the two men working together except resentment on one side and impatience on the other. There can be little doubt of Gaitskell's impatience with his elders, men too sick to do their jobs but apparently indispensable. Once he was Chancellor, he had a chance of seizing control. Having the chance, he would not be deflected. If, in the course of seizing it, Bevan, the great lion of the left, shot himself in the foot, it would occasion no serious regrets. Gaitskell claimed that his victory over Bevan was necessary in order to assure the electorate that Labour could provide responsible government. If, after six years in office, Labour had not persuaded the electorate of its responsibility, it was not Bevan alone, or principally, who was guilty.

In so far as there were serious differences on policy between the two men, they related to foreign affairs, an area where Britain's influence was diminishing, though the attempt to maintain it was extremely expensive. They differed on attitudes to the American alliance and the rearmament of Western Germany. Bevan had not strongly dissented from Bevin's foreign policy, though he did not approve of excessive dependence on the USA or of vilification of the Soviet Union.[8] He had even supported the manufacture of the British bomb.[9] He had lived with the American alliance for some years, without much complaint, despite his own anti-Americanism, in which sentiment he was far from alone in the Cabinet. Gaitskell, Attlee and most of the Cabinet wished to stand firmly with the American alliance, which, they believed, provided an essential guarantee of the freedom of western Europe. Bevan's objection to the rearmament of Western Germany was related to his anti-Americanism. Bevan and the left insisted on believing that the cold war was a struggle between a socialist country and the most powerful capitalist country in the world. Their sympathies, despite all the evidence, were with the socialist country. The rearmament of Western Germany evoked hostile feelings in part because memories of the war had by no means faded, but, above all, because Germany was being rearmed against a socialist country. Few in the Cabinet were more than reluctantly in favour of German rearmament. It was an issue on which British influence was bound to be limited, and differences on it should certainly not have prevented the two men working together.

Thus the differences in policy should have been containable. But the two men were divided by something more fundamental than policy. It was not just personal ambition. It was something that can perhaps best be described as colour. Gaitskell was grey, Bevan bright red. Gaitskell may have been a socialist but he could conjure nothing of the excitement of socialism. Bevan was all excitement, the excitement of a prophet who could lead his people out of bondage, a bondage from which he himself had suffered. Gaitskell could recognize something of the quality of Bevan. Bevan could recognize nothing of the quality of Gaitskell. Gaitskell was an upstart, a middle-class mole. To him, socialist tolerance need not be extended. He *was* nothing. It was Bevan who acted, both during the lifetime of the Attlee government and subsequently, as though he wanted to make co-operation impossible. The unforeseen cost of Gaitskell's victory was bitter division within the Party that lasted through most of the 1950s. Gaitskell carried throughout the remainder of his life a burden of hatred for having forced the resignation of the prophet, Bevan. It was a burden that he could not shed even during the period in the late 1950s of his reconciliation with Bevan. It was an offence so dire that, in the view of the left, not even its victim had the right to forgive.

It is arguable whether the conflict between Gaitskell and Bevan was a contribution to defeat in the 1951 election. From a public point of view, the resignation of Bevan was not necessarily all loss. He might be popular within the Labour party but it was he who had stimulated the Tories by casting at them the unforgotten reproach, vermin. The Korean war may, ungratefully, have redounded to Labour's advantage as the Conservatives were still led by the great warrior Churchill. The crisis which erupted in May 1951, involving the Anglo-Iranian Company's oil concessions in Iran, might have had the same effect. Peace was in peril and people may have thought that it was safer to have a Labour finger on the trigger. On the negative side, a Labour government had once more shown that it would split in a crisis, and that therefore Labour Ministers could not be relied on in times of trouble.

THE ECONOMIC LEGACY

In a speech at Walthamstow on 9 September 1950, Attlee said:

So let's take a look at [other European countries] under American aid and see how they are getting on. Let's look at countries which have followed the Tory policy of getting rid of essential controls. Do you remember what Churchill said about them last year – that recovery in all the European countries has been more rapid than it has in Britain. . . . [The Economic Commission for Europe has] just published a report telling how various European countries got on in 1949. British production, we read, has risen enormously and is one-third higher than before the war. Except for Norway and Denmark which have Labour governments anyway, this record is far better than any other western European country that took part in the war. Belgium, one of the Tory darlings and their model of free enterprise, is way down at the bottom of the list. Or have a look at unemployment. It's lower in Britain and Labour-governed Sweden than in any other country in western Europe, much lower than in the United States for that matter. . . . But full employment doesn't just happen. . . . This danger [of unemployment] can only be put down by continuing the very kind of planning that the Tories would like to get rid of. . . . Although real poverty has already been abolished, there are still far too many inequalities and injustices in our economic system.[10]

It was characteristic of Attlee that he appeared to believe that the Labour government's 'planning' had had something to do with the achievement of full employment. If he did believe it he would be gravely disillusioned after the 1951 election. Full employment as defined by the Attlee government was not the result of planning. The successor Churchill government dismantled the planning apparatus, such as it was, but full employment continued together with Britain's persistent balance of payments problems, the product of which was repeated economic crises. It was characteristic also that the Prime Minister of a government whose economic history had been marked by crisis after crisis should have been so complacent about its achievements. It was true that, in the early years after the war, Britain, which had not been invaded and occupied by the Nazis, appeared to be doing better economically than the rest of western Europe. Ten years on, the comparison would look very different. The economic performance of other western European countries, which the Keynesian message had not yet reached, was treated, without justification, with some contempt. This early success produced among British socialists a euphoria premature because the situation was changing. Germany, from the beginning, was seen to be a threat to British success once it recovered from the devastation of war, and the German industrial machine was, even then, moving into top gear. The evidence was that Germany would soon, once again, be a powerful competitor. It would then be found that Britain, through the inflationary policies of the Attlee government, had wasted the exceptional opportunity, given it by the temporary absence of Germany from world markets, to build up its own exports. British exports had expanded but by not nearly enough to justify Labour's self-satisfaction. The unemployed in western Europe would be drawn into employment producing for export, whereas from Britain exports were beginning to flag. The Attlee government had initiated the policies as a result of which Britain became the laggard of western Europe.

Much was made of the proud fact that Marshall Aid to Britain had been cancelled at the end of 1950, a year before the deadline. Yet, looking slightly further ahead, renewed problems were looming for the British economy. Gaitskell funded the greatly expanded rearmament programme following the outbreak of the Korean war mainly by dissipating Cripps's surplus. The result was to hand strong inflationary pressures to his successor at the Treasury, the Conservative R. A. Butler. Gaitskell, towards the end of his Chancellorship, confessed to his diary that he had taken quite inadequate action to deal with inflation.[11] The Attlee government would pass to its successors the most serious balance of payments crisis since the war. True, that could be attributed to the enormous rearmament programme inspired by the Korean war and to American stockbuilding. But, again and again between 1945 and 1951, external forces had blown the British economy off its planned course. It was not evidence of a strong or successful economy.

Although it claimed to be a planning government, planning, in reality, was more notable for its incoherence. This was not surprising as the government stumbled from one crisis to another on a two-year cycle, 1947, 1949 and 1951. The cycle could be explained and excused. Thus the 1947 convertibility crisis was attributable to the terms of the American loan, which should never have been accepted. The 1949 devaluation crisis was the inevitable outcome of the 1948 American recession and of the exchange rate fixed after the war. The 1951 crisis was due to the Korean war and the effect on commodity prices of American stockbuilding. Nevertheless the reputation of socialist planning was not enhanced by experience of this cycle. The reputation of the government for economic management would have been higher if the population had had the satisfaction of a more rapidly increasing standard of living even if starting from a lower base than that made possible by the American loan. The government's reaction to market pressures led to its becoming associated in the public mind with austerity. Cripps's identification as an 'iron chancellor', the epitome of austerity, may have done something to repair the reputation of the government in the market. But austerity, in any case inadequate, and necessitated by preceding inflationary policies, was unlikely to console an electorate which felt that it had been asked to suffer because of the failings of its government.

The identification of planning with rationing was a political burden greater than perhaps the government appreciated. Harold Wilson struck the right note with his 'bonfire of controls', but it was too little and too late to give the population the sensation of freedom after which it hankered. The bonfire might have seemed to endorse the principle that the main object of planning was to make planning unnecessary. This was certainly the attitude of Sir Edwin Plowden, appointed Chief Economic Planner in 1947. But it was emphatically not the attitude of Ministers nor of the Labour party. The claim of the Attlee government to be a government of socialist planners may have had its political benefits within the Labour party. But the Party was being force-fed with a diet of illusions. David Bensusan-Butt of the Economic Section wrote: 'Plans in the semi-socialist State seem to be much what Cathedrals are to the Church: they have an inspiring and soothing effect for the faithful in a wicked world.'[12] The planning machinery, such as it was, served one major purpose. When, by 1947, planning was seen so far to have failed, it provided economic Ministers with an excuse for failure which consisted of blaming Morrison rather than themselves.

There was, however, a missing element in the Attlee government's socialism. Its absence was no fault of the government except that the language in which the Labour party had promoted socialism had led to expectations that had not been fulfilled. Those expectations could not be satisfied by legislation, planning, nationalization, redistributive taxation, full employment, nor even by the creation of a welfare state. By implementing its manifesto, the Attlee government had doubly underlined the discovery that socialism, as advertised, was not to be created by such means alone or perhaps by such means at all. G. D. H. Cole was among those who felt bereft. He had abandoned Guild Socialism as impractical but he had not abandoned the hopes of a different quality of society that he had invested in Guild Socialism. Socialism was about feelings rather than systems, personal pride rather than centralized management. It required a dramatic change in the nature of the relationships between human beings. It should have revived the feelings of fraternity that had united classes when all were in danger during the wartime bombing, but which had since evaporated. There should have been exhilaration rather than the dull plod of everyday life. For socialists, the lack of the anticipated fruit of socialism was tangible. Until that gap was filled socialists would feel dissatisfied, but filling the gap was far beyond the capacity of governments. As a result, the sad truth was that socialists would always feel dissatisfied.

ATTLEE

Attlee has been accounted a great Prime Minister, but his principal achievement was to survive. His survival depended on Bevin, on Bevin's willingness to stay at the Foreign Office rather than move to No. 10, and on the rivalry between Bevin and Morrison. Most historians and publicists have given Attlee the benefit of the doubt. His character and his faults appeal to British public opinion. Here was this small, accidental figure, presiding over a Cabinet of alleged giants, while contentedly doodling away and letting his noisy and extrovert colleagues get on with it. And if there was to be any chance of introducing socialism into conservative Britain, it may well have been better to have, as guide, a reassuring figure like Attlee.

Why then should anyone criticize his inadequacies? After all, it was while he was Prime Minister that the welfare state was created, a great achievement even if his government had to borrow to do it. But an indictment is only too easy to draft. During the coalition government, he was an ineffective chairman of Cabinet committees. His natural position in charge of the home front had to be taken over by the former civil servant, Sir John Anderson, because of Attlee's inability to impress himself on powerful departments.[13] Contrary to his reputation, he was a poor Cabinet maker. He misplaced Dalton and Bevin at the outset and then proved unwilling to dispense with dead wood dating from the 1930s even though there was much young ability in the PLP from which he could have chosen. Younger people got their chances only when his hand was forced. He accepted without overt protest the terms for the American loan. He did not even raise the matter during his visit to Washington in November 1945. He played no part in economic policy before the summer of 1947, even though the country's economic plight was desperate. He gave Dalton no help in Cabinet when the Chancellor was pleading for savings on overseas and military expenditures in order to conserve the American loan. He dispensed with the ineffective and blustering Dalton only after the minor offence of his leak of his budget secrets, not because of the disaster of the convertibility crisis. Perhaps, like John Major after Black Wednesday in September 1992, Attlee realized that he shared responsibility with his Chancellor and that, therefore, it was a choice between them both staying or both going. He preferred that they should both stay.

After the convertibility crisis, Cripps, Dalton and Morrison all agreed that Attlee should go, the only disagreement arising from Morrison's conviction that he should succeed and Cripps's insistence that the successor should be Bevin. This conspiracy was in great part an attempt to exculpate themselves, but the plot would have been unthinkable if Attlee had not been so obviously inadequate. The plot collapsed only because Bevin did not want to move from his job as world statesman to the tedious tasks of regenerating the British economy. Even Bevin, Attlee's main prop, was prepared in private to criticize his Prime Minister for his weakness and the difficulty he had in making up his mind.[14] Attlee took six months after the fuel crisis of 1947 to eject from the Cabinet Emanuel Shinwell, who carried the main responsibility for it. Hardly had he rid himself of Dalton and Shinwell than he brought them back into the Cabinet. Apparently he could not bear to be for long without his old comrades of the 1930s, even when they had fallen down on their jobs. He continued senior Ministers in office even when their failing health left them incapable of discharging their responsibilities. During the devaluation crisis of the summer of 1949 he showed no initiative, depending entirely on the advice of the Treasury and his three Ministerial economists, Gaitskell, Wilson and Jay. He mishandled relations with western Europe and thereby earned the distrust of the Americans, by whom he very much wanted to be trusted. Cripps's resignation on health grounds, long after he should have been allowed to go, led him to appoint Gaitskell Chancellor. He then exercised no control over this inexperienced but ambitious newcomer to the Cabinet, but allowed him to force humiliation or resignation on Aneurin Bevan, thus dividing the Party, only months before he would call a general election. He lacked the imagination to appoint Bevan Foreign Secretary after the resignation of Bevin, although Bevan's services to the government had been extraordinary both as a departmental minister and as a spokesman in the House of Commons on a variety of issues outside his own departmental duties. He failed to avert Bevan's resignation – and blamed it on Morrison, acting in his own absence in hospital.

He was not good at one of a Prime Minister's principal responsibilities, selecting the dates of general elections. He allowed the suffering Cripps to dictate to him the date of the February 1950 General Election and saw the huge majority he had won in 1945 virtually wiped out. He rejected the advice of Morrison and Gaitskell on the date of the 1951 election, and seemed almost to welcome defeat and Churchill's return to office. None of his senior colleagues thought much of him. They saw him as a Prime Minister to be carried rather than to be followed. But, as Bevin had denied them the obvious choice, himself or Morrison, they were left with no alternative. Attlee then, after the 1951 defeat, continued as leader past his seventieth birthday, and through the 1955 General Election, with no other apparent purpose than to disappoint Herbert Morrison's ambition for the leadership. He was, he claimed, preventing a split in the Party between the right and the Bevanites, a split which he himself had failed to avoid in April 1951. He had spent so long keeping his head below the parapet that he no longer knew the way over the top. He had always demonstrated a certain capacity for political manoeuvre, but his survival was due first to Bevin and then, after the 1951 defeat, to the difficulty of getting rid of a leader, however inept, if he did not want to go. Attlee then showed that he had nothing to contribute by way of modernizing the Party and fitting it once more to hold office. He was a passenger rather than a leader and it was unlikely under his leadership that Labour would find the new role for which it was already seeking.

Attlee's legacy was a warring party which the trade unions were forced to dominate if their creation was ever again to have a chance of office. But though the trade unions, under such leaders as Arthur Deakin, Bevin's successor as General Secretary of the TGWU, might save Labour, their obvious control of the Party was bound to raise doubts in the electorate as to its eligibility for office. And the trade unions could not be relied upon always to support the 'responsible' right of the Party against the radical left. That was a discovery that would be made later.

DIMINUENDO

Already, at the February 1950 General Election, Attlee's huge majority was almost wiped out. Though many seats had been lost due to the redistribution of constituencies, this was not a cost which would have had to be paid by a more successful government. The electorate were offered sugar refining, cement manufacture and water supply as Labour's next candidates for nationalization and also the mutualization of industrial assurance. This programme, hardly consisting of any commanding heights, led nevertheless to much public controversy, not obviously helpful to Labour. Labour appeared to have no persuasive rejoinder to the sayings of the popular 'Mr Cube' invented by the sugar-refining industry as its response to Labour's haphazard choice of targets. Indeed the arguments for nationalizing Mr Cube were not compelling except on the dogmatic socialist ground that practically any industry of any size should be nationalized. The British people may have concluded that, if this was the best Labour could offer by way of policy, it had run out of ideas and hence of the right to govern. Even Crossman, who criticized Morrison in the columns of the *Sunday Pictorial* for attempting to appease the middle-class vote, admitted privately to him that these nationalization proposals certainly lost floating votes 'because they seemed to imply a vague threat of unlimited nationalisation'.[15]

Herbert Morrison's perception of the public mood was a good deal shrewder than that of most of his colleagues. In an analysis of the 1950 result he had written that 'the needs of the consumer and the problems of the housewife must be recognized as a real factor in politics, and Party policy and propaganda should take account of it'. He had suggested that the Party should not 'urge planning and control merely for the sake of it'. He thereby implied that the Party did appear to the electorate as urging planning and control for the sake of it. He was equally correct on the political consequences of nationalization. 'It is, I think, quite clear that the majority of the electorate are not disposed to accept nationalization for the sake of nationalization.' Labour supporters who had spoken to him had said that 'it was more important to pay attention to making effective and efficient the existing socialization rather than to proceed with a further nationalization programme *at the present time* . . .' He concluded with an appropriately contemptuous reference to the 1950 nationalization programme: 'We rather "invented" a further socialization programme of odds and ends . . .'[16]

All this amounted to a demand that the Party should change its centralizing image and, particularly, forget nationalization for the time being. Such a demand was unlikely to be popular with the left and Morrison was unable to suck vague threats of further nationalization out of the 1951 programme. Without naming particular victims, the threat of nationalization was left hanging over industries 'which fail the nation . . .'[17] Although Morrison had agreed this, it was worse even than the random list of victims in the 1950 manifesto, especially as Morrison himself, at the October 1950 Party Conference, emphasized that the previous proposals to nationalize sugar and cement had not been dropped.[18] The threat was now open ended. Any industry could be judged and found guilty on the haziest criteria by Ministers with no obvious qualifications as judges. There was also a proposal to create new enterprises wherever this would serve the national interest.[19] Without more detail of what was actually intended under this heading, this also would appear threatening to those who might fear that they would be forced to face subsidized competition.

So far as popular support was concerned, the significant election was that of February 1950. In 1950 Labour had been taught a lesson which by 1951 it had not yet learnt. The Attlee government faced its final election in October 1951 supported by the continuing and impressive loyalty of the trade unions and traditional Labour voters but facing the hostility of many of those who had enjoyed little improvement in their standard of living during the previous six years and who thought that the relaxation of controls and restrictions had been too long delayed. The government also found it had alienated many voters by its redistribution and welfare policies at a time of slow growth.

It is to the Attlee government that socialists have always looked back as the moment of triumph and success, after long years of waiting, because everything thereafter was disappointment. But the Attlee government also revealed the dilemmas of socialism – political and economic. There was a realization, within the Labour party as well as without, that, since 1949, with its programme enacted, the government had drifted aimlessly. It had conveyed no sense of where it next wished to lead the people of Britain. The inevitable suspicion was that it had no idea. It had become uncertain of the next steps to socialism and therefore could no longer convey any inspiration or sense of purpose. It was from socialism that the élan had disappeared rather than from capitalism. As a result, the Labour government's initial unity had fractured. There were divisions such as those between Bevan and Gaitskell and between those such as Morrison, who wished to 'consolidate', and those who believed that nationalization thus far should simply be the precursor of a further and faster drive to socialism. Its achievements had become overlaid by an impression of incompetence in handling the economy. The impression was confirmed by the haphazard selection of industries for nationalization combined with gathering economic crisis.

Nor was the government successful in retaining support among its own most fervent supporters in the Labour party. A consistent characteristic of the Party has been its willingness to injure and disparage those who in government take difficult jobs and then find themselves publicly censured for unpopular policies. Emanuel Shinwell, long a hero of the left, the man who had defeated the traitor MacDonald at Seaham Harbour in 1935, had taken the job of Minister of Defence and was therefore tarred with the defence programme. It was not his programme. It was the programme of the government. Nevertheless, at the Labour Party Conference in 1951, Shinwell was ousted in the election for the constituency section of the NEC. It was not enough for the delegates that he had nationalized the energy industries. No doubt if the constituency parties could have sacked the whole government, they would have done so and revelled in their achievement. In their view, the government had let them down and also the whole cause of socialism. Years later, Aneurin Bevan would learn that, for the left, one is only as good as one's last speech. Yet Labour was defeated not so much by the disillusion of its traditional supporters as by the discontent of the many voters, outside the ranks of its traditional supporters, who had thought it right in 1945 to give Labour a chance.

IF

There is an 'if' in this history that is just worth considering because it throws some light on the question whether it would have been possible to achieve socialism within a democratic system. Did Britain miss socialism only by the accident of Attlee's bad timing? The defeat of the Attlee government in October 1951 was so narrow that the possibility must exist that, with some slight alteration in circumstances, of which delaying the election for a few more months must be the most obvious possibility, it would have been re-elected. There could then have been ten or eleven continuous years of Labour government in which further substantial progress towards socialism could have taken place. It is conceivable that, after such an election victory, Attlee would have cleared out the dead wood in his Cabinet, which means about half of it, and brought in younger men with ideas and determination who would have pressed forward on the road to socialism. That this could have occurred cannot be denied. But before this possibility is embraced with too much enthusiasm, or too much regret, some cautionary words are indicated. First, the destruction of Attlee's vast majority occurred in 1950. This was before the Korean war and before any Cabinet resignations had divided the Party. Clearly, there had been a major loss of support in the country which suggests that, even if Attlee had won in 1951, the probability must be that the victory would again have been narrow and not one which would have encouraged radical departures. Then it is necessary to question whether there were any new ideas or any evidence of renewed determination. One interest in the *New Fabian Essays*, published in 1952, is that they suggest that the lack of will and purpose, which had infected the Attlee government from 1948 onwards, had penetrated the younger as well as the older members of the PLP. Dangerfield writes of the Liberals in 1910 that they 'had reached a point where they could no longer advance'.[20] Much the same could be written of Labour in 1948.

What then would Labour have done if it had snatched victory? It might well have attempted a few pointless acts of nationalization, each of them probably provoking opposition and resentment among the employees as well as the managers of the firms concerned. There could well have been a capital gains tax such as Gaitskell was contemplating for his second budget if he survived to open one, a beginning in comprehensive education, and another attempt at an incomes policy. There would have had to be restraints in public expenditure and this might have included wider health service charges, not the minor charges that Gaitskell had insisted on in his budget. This would not have been an exciting programme. The nature of society at the end of a further five years would have been imperceptibly nearer socialism than in 1951. Probably there would have been much dissension, which would have ended in defeat at the subsequent election, the reversal of the more equalizing measures of the departed government, and the denationalization of any industry nationalized except, probably, for energy and the utilities. The Labour party had lost its vision, and it is difficult to conceive that a narrow victory in 1951 would have recovered it. The divisions that had erupted in the Labour party were symptomatic of the fact that it had lost its way. Without a direction on which it could confidently embark, it descended into factionalism and strife. For the next forty years the Labour party would preach socialism without being socialist. It would preach it with intermittent but, on average, declining enthusiasm. Disraeli would have been tempted to call a Labour government an 'organized hypocrisy'. But the truth was not that simple. Without really knowing it, Labour was beginning the painful process of converting itself into an alternative, non-ideological party of government, but was being severely hampered in the task by its profession of socialism.

NINE

Pathfinders in defeat

MYSTERIOUSLY DRIVEN FROM OFFICE

On 26 October 1951, the Labour party, now out of office, looked upon what it had done and knew that it was good. The result of the election, the previous day, was, arguably, unfair. Labour had won more votes than the Tories. But, under the first-past-the-post electoral system to which both parties were wedded, it had won twenty-six fewer seats. But surely Labour, considering what it had accomplished, full employment, the welfare state, nationalization, should have won by a huge majority, not been defeated, even if only by a small margin. Throughout its life, the government had suffered the bitter criticism of the Conservative press under the control of owners such as Lords Beaverbrook and Rothermere. But its social achievements might have provided sufficient protection against the onslaught. Clearly they did not and there was a mystery as to why they did not which Labour took an appreciable time to unravel. Aneurin Bevan displayed a hubris which he shared with his former colleagues in the Labour Cabinet, a gross overestimate of what they had achieved and its significance for the rest of mankind. Britain, he claimed, had gained the moral leadership of the world. 'There is only one hope for "mankind" and that hope still remains in this little island.'[1] The paean of praise for Labour was sung with great fervour by John Strachey, who, though never a member of the Cabinet, had held responsible posts as Minister of Food and Minister for War. In his contribution to *New Fabian Essays*, published in 1952, Strachey wrote:

> It is in Britain that the democratic forces have really got a grip on the economy and begun to transform its nature. It is here that the democratic forces have been solidly united in one political party which has had the executive in its control for six consecutive years. It is here that the technique of contemporary central planning, either by means of physical controls or Keynesian fiscal means, is best understood. It is here that the

redistribution of the national income, and the turning of the economy to its true task of steadily raising the general standard of life, has been carried furthest.[2]

At times, indeed, Strachey becomes ecstatic. He invokes Pericles, who had said that Athens must make herself 'the education of Hellas'. It is clear that, in his view, the world had a great deal to learn from Britain. 'In the Labour Movement the British people have forged an unmatched instrument of continuing social change. It is our national task – our mission to the world – to develop, to sharpen and to use that instrument.'[3] It may be assumed that Strachey did not recall the words he had written in 1932 in criticism of those who were too easily persuaded that the ills of capitalism were curable. '[W]hat could be more comforting to men who have ceased to desire a socialist society, than to dream that capitalism will soon settle down, solve its difficulties, cease its struggles, and afford us all the stability of socialism without the necessity of fighting for it.'[4]

Seldom has a government left office with a greater sense of its own achievements. The self-satisfaction of former Ministers was compounded of two elements, disbelief that the Tories could long retain the power they had so narrowly won; and certainty that the record of the Attlee government was one of which all socialists should be proud. In six short years it had changed the nature of British society, and the Tories would not dare to reverse this historic achievement, at least in any fundamental respect. In its enthusiasm for its own achievements, Labour forgot two key political lessons. The first is particularly uncomfortable for socialists, and for all who seek to lighten the burdens of the poor. Right-wing Tories are often ready to blame the unemployed and disadvantaged as the authors of their own misfortunes. There are many Labour voters who feel exactly the same and resent the public money which they believe to be wasted on social welfare. The second lesson is that benefits provided by governments are rapidly discounted by the electorate. As the Marquis of Halifax put it three centuries ago, gratitude is a lively sense of favours yet to come. Governments cannot rely for re-election on the good they have done. The evil that governments do lives after them. The good is oft interred with their bones. Electorates have a lively sense of government incompetence. The Attlee government, hit by crisis after crisis, had proved to be a poor manager of the capitalist economy.

Self-satisfaction was not widespread among active members of constituency parties. Their expectations had been high and had not been met in six years of Labour government. There was a widening gap between the attitudes of the PLP and of Party activists in the country. The activists now took their revenge for their disappointment. The constituency parties elected seven members to the National Executive Committee of the Labour party. They took their first opportunity, at the Party Conference at Morecambe in the autumn of 1952, to dismiss Herbert Morrison and Hugh Dalton from the NEC. Morrison and Dalton thus followed Shinwell, who had been ejected from the NEC the year before. Six Bevanites, led by Bevan himself, won the constituency votes. It was no doubt, in the case of Morrison, gross ingratitude, but constituency parties were looking to the future, not to the past. They were looking for a new socialist lead and did not find it in Morrison's advocacy of consolidation. The ingratitude caused deep offence on the right and in the centre. Neither Dalton nor Shinwell deserved re-election to the NEC. But that was not the reason they were spurned. They had simply failed to accommodate themselves to the socialist priorities of the constituency parties. Having devoted their lives to socialism they were now the victims of a dissatisfied rank and file. In a speech at Stalybridge shortly after the Conference, Gaitskell attributed the defeat of Morrison and Dalton to frustrated journalists such no doubt as the Bevanites Crossman, Driberg and Foot, together with communist penetration of the constituency parties. Gaitskell had himself been unsuccessful in an attempt to get elected to the NEC in the constituency section. It had become virtually impossible for any right-wing figure, however distinguished his service, to gain a secure place on the NEC through the constituency section. Clearly the hunger for socialism in the constituencies had not been assuaged by the moderation at the outset of the Attlee government and the drifting thereafter.

However, former Ministers were equipped with a strong defence against threats of rebellion. They had the great bulk of the trade union leaders on their side. In 1950 the trade unions commanded five million votes at Conference as compared with under one million from the constituency Labour parties. Not merely did they dominate the Conference. They could also ensure a safe majority on the NEC, as eighteen of the twenty-seven members depended on trade union votes. As a result, the Party was secure from the assaults of Bevan and his friends, and those even further to the left. The feeling of security discouraged any serious reassessment of its actual record in office. It might have addressed its failures more urgently if it had felt itself at hazard. Former Ministers still controlled the PLP, which continued to tolerate Attlee.

Loyalty remained a marked characteristic of the majority of the PLP. It would have been difficult otherwise to understand how the ageing Attlee was allowed, without much complaint, to continue in the leadership up to and beyond the 1955 election. At first he had the cover of the even older Churchill, who was approaching eighty, but he comforted himself with the better excuse that he was keeping united a divided party. Gaitskell certainly would have liked to see the succession pass to Morrison, because Attlee showed only sporadic signs of activity against the Bevanites. But civil war was precisely what Attlee wished to avoid. Rather than detect any failure in himself, he preferred to attribute the loss of Bevan, and the disunity it had caused, to Morrison and Gaitskell. The PLP displayed similar complacency in refusing to enforce upon its old war-horses such as Chuter Ede, Emanuel Shinwell, Glenvill Hall and Hugh Dalton the honourable retirement for which they themselves failed to volunteer. Expecting an early renewal of their mandate, the elderly incumbents of the Attlee Cabinet put themselves up for election to Labour's shadow Cabinet and were, in fact, elected. As Lord Denning was reported to have said of himself at a later date, they showed every Christian virtue except resignation. By 1955, nine members of the shadow Cabinet were over sixty-five.[5] But why should they resign when the PLP still wanted them? Should they have sought an excuse, they could have found it in the fact that the young folk, though they might have brought more energy to the positions of leadership, showed little sign of bringing with them useful new ideas.

THE LESSONS OF OFFICE

Ministers left office in 1951 with certain firm convictions. First, they took the credit for full employment. They had no right to it. So far as government policy had affected employment, the methods used were inherently inflationary and therefore damaging to the economic prospects of the country and to its competitiveness. Secondly, arising out of their pride in achieving full employment, their attitudes were essentially protectionist, biased against exposing the British economy to international competition, and suspicious of such 'liberal' objectives as sterling convertibility and non-discrimination even in the long term. Instead they favoured strict exchange and import controls, not just in emergencies but as instruments of socialist policy. The price mechanism was still a particular object of suspicion. Though devaluation had worked for them after 1949, they regarded it as a defeat for planning. This thought would survive for many years and would find its echo in the decisions made in the immediate aftermath of Labour's return to office in 1964.

Thirdly, they still believed in physical planning even though any hopes from it, other than in the rationing of scarce resources, had been interrupted at two-year intervals by economic crises. Physical planning, they should have found, was in the longer term incompatible with inflationary fiscal and monetary policies precisely because they would lead to disruptive economic crisis at frequent intervals. Fourthly, they still believed in nationalization even though they were highly uncertain what should be nationalized next. They tended to make haphazard choices, as, for example, their plan to nationalize sugar refining which had been a heavy burden during the 1950 election. Their worry was whether the electorate would stand for more nationalization. But that was a question of tactics, not of principle. The 1953 policy statement *Challenge to Britain* contained proposals for public ownership in chemicals, machine tools and mining machinery. Gaitskell continued to believe that only through the state would it be possible to find the necessary resources for investment. Certainly the wealthy would not provide them.[6] He was to find, during the 1955 General Election, that Labour was on the defensive with workers in constituencies threatened by nationalization, for example employees of Imperial Chemical Industries at Middlesbrough and Cleveland.[7] Fifthly, they had never been persuaded that they had been wrong to think that the world owed Britain a living. They had repeatedly sought help from the USA and it had been lavishly provided. But Americans should never be allowed to imagine that they had discharged their duty to the UK. Much more remained that Washington could do. Despite their disappointments, the leadership clung to the Americans. This sentiment was not uniquely Labour. It had penetrated Conservative ranks, which were quite as willing to feel offended if the American President and Congress did not respond, or did not respond adequately, to British pleas.

TORY REPENTANCE

Ministers in office acquire an unwarranted sense of immortality. They may not be doing anything in particular but they are sure that they are the best people to be doing it. It struck home only slowly within the Labour party that the levers of power had inexplicably passed to other hands. Indeed, it may not have struck fully home until the further, and much worse, defeat in the 1955 General Election. If the Tories were now arriving in Ministerial cars at Ministerial offices, it must be only a temporary phenomenon, an unaccountable mistake by a forgetful electorate. The Tories were caretakers while the authentic Ministers rested after their heavy and successful labours. The Tories were caretakers, moreover, of Labour's welfare state and had better not damage it during their brief incumbency. No one was thinking of 'thirteen wasted years'.

There was, for the Labour party, a worrying consideration which, during the period of the 1951–5 Churchill government, was inadequately appreciated. To have let the Tories in spelt great danger. During their period in opposition after 1945, the Tories had recast, if not their policies, then at least the presentation of their policies. They too were committed to full employment or, at any rate, to do whatever was possible to prevent enforced idleness. They might not yet be socialists but they were accepting some of the fiercest socialist criticisms of capitalism. They were adding to the fashionable critique of capitalism as it had been and were looking for a middle or third way. The transformation was summarized in 1947 in the Conservatives' Industrial Charter prepared under the direction of R. A. Butler. The importance of the Charter lay not in its detail, most of which was eminently forgettable, but in the philosophy that inspired it. As Butler writes:

> Our first purpose was to counter the charge and the fear that we were the Party of industrial go-as-you-please and devil-take-the-hindmost, that full employment and the Welfare State were not safe in our hands ... The Charter was, therefore, first and foremost an assurance that, in the interests of efficiency, full employment and social security, modern Conservatism would maintain strong central guidance over the operation of the economy.[8]

Labour's only consolation was that the Conservatives faced a credibility gap which could not be bridged until the sweet words of the Industrial Charter were ratified by conduct in government. But that was precisely the ratification that the Conservatives, in government, could now earn.

In the General Elections of 1945, 1950 and 1951, Labour had been able to exploit the bitter memory of pre-war unemployment. In office, it had created a welfare state. It could warn that the Tories might ruin it. Ironically, given the political flavour of the Labour leadership, which had forced Bevan's resignation, one of Labour's strongest arguments for power was that it had created the NHS. Labour's greatest electoral asset would be lost if it was now found that the Tories had no intention of abolishing the welfare state and, like Labour, had been admitted to the secret of full employment. To the zealous mind of a dedicated socialist, it was a revelation that the Tories had no objection to prosperity, or to the working classes sharing in it. But it was accepted by the more perceptive minds within the Labour party that, whatever had been alleged in the heat of general election controversy, when truth is not invariably the guide, the Tories would have no intention of damning themselves for ever by substantiating their reputation as the Party of unemployment. The Tories had not been slow to learn the ingredients necessary to enable them to hang on to power once they had regained it. Keynesian techniques were as available to the Tories as they had been to Labour. They would do their best to sustain full employment and the welfare state. They would not dare to do anything else. Indeed they would regard the welfare state as part of the ransom they would have to pay for social peace and stability and for the enjoyment of their privileged status.

It was easier for the Tories to accept the welfare state because it had been built, so far as the Attlee government thought it could afford it, on a non-discriminatory principle. The welfare state was for all the people, not just for the poor. The Tory-voting middle classes had every reason to become addicted to it. They would still vote Tory. But they would be voting for a welfare state managed by the Tories. Experience confirmed that the NHS was no less safe in Tory hands than in Labour's. As Strachey confessed, with some suggestion of surprise at a startling discovery, 'British capitalism *has* been compelled, by the sheer pressure of the British people, acting through our effective democratic political institutions, to do what we used to say it would never, by definition, do.'[9] If, as a result of good luck or good management, or a modicum of both, life became easier for the great mass of the people, a major obstacle would have been set in the path of a party still claiming to be socialist and to speak for the disadvantaged. There was no worse nightmare for Labour than Tory penitence for their pre-war sins. If the penitence was sincere, all the Labour party would be left with would be socialism, and the bitter divisions within the Party as to what socialism now meant.

If, with greater prosperity, people acquired property, they would lose any enthusiasm for overturning society. It became the policy of the Tories to encourage home ownership. Economically this may not have been wise. Indeed it was thoroughly inflationary. But politically it was a stroke of genius. Home ownership would thin the ranks of the socialists. When, later, the Tories began to encourage the sale of council houses,

Labour was put on the rack. If it dissented, it would be unpopular with those who wished to buy their council house and become property owners. If it was supportive, Labour would be compelled to watch as Labour council tenants converted themselves into Tory home owners. The Tory slogan, a property-owning democracy, was a blow to Labour's hopes against which there was no defence except capitulation. But, if Labour capitulated, what would remain of socialism? Tory purposes were clear enough, prosperity for the people and exile for Labour.

Given the opportunities for political and economic manipulation open to any government, would it be so easy to regain power for a party that, under the ageing Attlee, had so clearly lost its drive, whose election campaigns in 1950 and 1951 had offered little except premature warnings about what the Tories would do if elected, and was itself bitterly divided? One comfort lay in the hope that the Tories could not act against their nature. John Strachey thought that if the Tory government was barred by democratic *force majeure* from indulging its instinctively regressive and *laissez-faire* instincts, 'it is unlikely that it will find any but the most temporary expedients with which to meet our national problems. In such a situation the prognosis for the Conservative administration can hardly be favourable.'[10] Richard Crossman, one of the brighter backbenchers whom Attlee had preferred not to employ, had different doubts. There was another factor that might rob the Tory government of longevity. '[I]t is self-deception to believe that the living standards and security enjoyed by the British people after 1945 were a *stable* achievement of socialism.'[11] But was Labour to depend on economic catastrophe to claw its way back to office?

There was in all this another lesson for Labour that its more subtle minds might have found rather worrying. Little that the Attlee government had done was explicitly reversed. True, during the subsequent decade the economy became more open, making the implementation of a socialist policy more difficult. Some nationalization was reversed, iron and steel and road transport. Direct taxation was cut, making the tax system less redistributive. Monetary policy, rejected as a counter-inflationary instrument by all three post-war Labour Chancellors, returned to favour. But none of this constituted the massive reversal of policy that might have been expected from a series of Conservative governments with increasingly large majorities following a socialist government. Yet, though there had been so little reversal of policy, no one would imagine that Britain under the Conservatives was very far along the road to socialism. The Attlee government had laboured for six years and, so far as socialism was concerned, had evidently produced a mouse. Almost everything that it had done could be comfortably encapsulated in the political world of Churchill and Macmillan.

BUTSKELL?

In 1954, the *Economist* manufactured the word 'Butskell' to suggest an identity of policy between R. A. Butler, the Conservative Chancellor, and Hugh Gaitskell, his Labour predecessor. It was true that they both wished to preserve full employment. But they differed fundamentally on the position of Britain in the world economy. Butler wanted to move towards a one-world economy and to open Britain's doors to the world. It was a slow process, inhibited by the fears of his Cabinet colleagues, but that was the direction of policy. Gaitskell wished to keep the doors tightly shut and opened only selectively and at discretion. Butler writes of his relationship with Gaitskell, 'Both of us, it is true, spoke the language of Keynesianism. But we spoke it with different accents and with a differing emphasis.'[12] It was a legitimate distinction. A thin line of liberalism runs through Conservative policy from Butler to Mrs Thatcher. It was the best possible antidote to socialism. The prospects for socialism in Britain were undermined by advance towards sterling convertibility in the 1950s and by the successive trade negotiations launched by the USA which opened markets and reduced tariff protection. Certainly sterling convertibility was nowhere on the socialist agenda. When Gaitskell heard, belatedly, that, in the Robot scheme of 1952, Butler and Churchill had toyed with the idea of sterling convertibility, he was at once horrified and regretful; horrified that such an idea should have been contemplated and regretful that it had not been implemented. Sterling convertibility was precisely the kind of Tory blunder that would have opened the way to the return of a Labour government.[13] As late as December 1958, when sterling employed in current transactions did become fully convertible, Gaitskell opposed it. There remained exchange control, which, for socialists, was a residual power over the economy that they regarded as essential to socialist management. Exchange control could, it was hoped, regulate flows of capital and would therefore be a defence against speculators whenever Labour regained office. Strachey wrote that 'the life and death of British social democracy depends' on exchange control.[14] Never did a life hang by a thinner thread. Conservative governments, themselves conducting inflationary policies, also cherished exchange control as a weapon against speculators. Exchange control therefore continued until 1979 but, with the world becoming more open, as an ever diminishing influence over capital movements, therefore as an ever weaker weapon against speculators, and as an ever more precarious defence for social democracy, whether of the Labour or Conservative variety.

THE FABIAN SOCIETY SEARCHES FOR THE NEXT STEPS

The Fabian Society had realized around 1950 that some thought was necessary on the question how to manage the next stage of socialism. There was no evidence that any new thought was coming from the Attlee government and, therefore, there was a gap to be filled. The attempt produced the *New Fabian Essays*, but not until 1952 after Labour had lost office. They were *new* Fabian essays in deference to the original Fabian essays, published in 1889, which had been a triumphant success. The original Fabian essays were written with supreme confidence in the socialist destination, though it would be necessary first to master all those human failings which induced one of the authors, William Clarke, to declare, 'The human race generally contrives to exhaust every device which stupidity can suggest before the right line of action is ultimately taken.'[15] The original Fabian essays sold many thousands of copies in many different countries. The *New Fabian Essays* were not to have a comparable success either in persuasion or in circulation. They failed on two counts. They lacked any analysis of why Labour had lost after such remarkable achievements. They failed of the original intention, which was to find a way forward for socialism. Despite the conviction that Labour had done well in government, and had advanced the cause of socialism, the *New Fabian Essays* show nothing of the confident certainties that had inspired socialist writers in the 1930s.

Attlee, who wrote a brief foreword, regretted that of the eight essayists only one, John Strachey, had had any experience of government. However, even if seven of the essayists lacked any past experience of government, four of them, Crosland, Crossman, Healey and Jenkins, were to become Cabinet Ministers in the 1960s and a fifth, Austen Albu, was briefly to hold Ministerial office in the Department of Economic Affairs.

Among the essayists, only Margaret Cole, writing with great vigour on education, was never an MP.

If, therefore, *New Fabian Essays* were disappointing it was not through any lack of calibre in the authors. In defining the next stage of socialism they were evidently, like the Attlee government in its last years, encountering great difficulties. A dense mist was obscuring the path to the socialist summit and there was neither map nor compass. The difficulties led, in the authors, to a surprising diffidence. Not merely were they lacking in new ideas. They seemed to think it was not for them to be too insistent in advocating such ideas as they did have. Even the left-winger Ian Mikardo, writing an eloquent and critical essay on the trade unions, ended by asserting that it was not for a single trade unionist such as himself, let alone in a Fabian essay, to instruct the great trade union movement. The sense of being lost was perhaps deepened by the debilitating discovery that socialism was not merely not inevitable but hardly even probable. Richard Crossman, the editor, wrote, 'To realise that the socialist society is not the norm, evolved by material conditions, but the exception, imposed on immoral society by human will and social conscience, is not to emasculate our socialism, but to set ourselves a challenge.'[16] Crosland added that 'There is . . . no reason in logic or history why the succession [to capitalism] should inevitably pass to socialism . . .'[17] This was perhaps the unexpected lesson of the Attlee government. History was not, after all, on the side of socialism. If widely appreciated, the effect on morale could be devastating.

If history was no longer on the side of socialism, the discovery imposed a heavy duty on the contributors to *New Fabian Essays*. If socialism was ever to be built they must find some way of evoking a crusading spirit among its supporters. But there can be found, in these essays, none of the crusading spirit that had made the original Fabian essays a major publishing success. The essayists' problem, and that of all socialists, was how to engender enthusiasm for socialism in a country dramatically changed from pre-war. Crosland emphasized the point. 'The worker can no longer be said to be exploited . . .'[18] Perhaps the crusade was over? Perhaps Jerusalem had already been captured without its being noticed? In politics and economics it is sometimes better not to formulate questions until one knows the answer. Here a question was being asked – what should be the next stage of socialism? – and there appeared to be no persuasive, and certainly no agreed, answer. There was nothing to set the pulse racing or the masses marching. Instead a series of tentative suggestions emerged without the support of any deep conviction.

That, at any rate, is how it appeared to many reviewers. A sample of the more critical reviews makes this point. The *Tablet* remarked that 'All the contributors . . . give the impression of having to blow on the embers of a moral indignation running perilously short of fresh fuel.'[19] Sebastian Haffner wrote in the *Observer* that:

> the problems under our noses today are not now (as in 1889) those of social injustice at home. They are those of our biennial balance-of-payments crises and the threat of a Third World War . . . These questions make hardly any appearance in the Essays . . . In thus ignoring our real problems and desperately searching for artificial issues in order to revive lost revolutionary ardour, the new Fabians provide the clearest demonstration of the danger now threatening the Labour Party.[20]

The *Economist* found that the new essayists had little to offer. 'The new Fabianism has no momentum because it has neither an engine nor a steering wheel.'[21] And the *Twentieth Century* concluded contemptuously that:

> There is no sign of the intellectual ruthlessness which made the Webbs a power in their days. The emphasis is on equality and the further democratization of society: an estimable programme inherited from the nineteenth century . . . To read these essays one might think that our only problem is how to divide the cake more equitably. This kind of pseudo-Socialism is useful only as a soporific. Taken in large doses it must be fatal to the organism.[22]

As there was no new idea, the essayists contented themselves with discussing old ideas and old problems. It is not in itself a criticism that the ideas were old. Socialism was already an old idea. Rather the criticism is that the essayists could not now muster much enthusiasm for the old ideas and yet still thought it necessary to repeat what they seemed unable to improve. Crossman gave his essay a title, 'Towards a Philosophy of Socialism', that encapsulates the tentativeness of the whole enterprise. Apparently, a century and a quarter after the birth of socialism, after the Attlee government, and after the experience provided by the Soviet Union, there was as yet no philosophy or, at least, whatever philosophy there had been had now to be rewritten, the old philosophy having been found wanting or having served whatever purpose it had had. Crossman admitted that Labour's reforms 'seemed to have exhausted the content of British socialism'.[23] He told his readers that 'We are certainly not in a position yet to map the new route to socialism . . .

The best we can hope to do is to ask the relevant questions, which must be answered before the second stage of socialism can be worked out.'[24]

Though he was still searching for a socialist philosophy and mapping the new route, Crossman remained certain that socialism was indispensable. In Australia and New Zealand, Labour parties had dispensed with socialism. Now there was a similar danger in the UK. Socialism might degenerate into labourism. If this happened, politics would become a matter of 'ins' and 'outs'. Soon there would be no deep difference between the two parties.[25] This deplorable outcome was clearly unacceptable. Even though the Labour party was not yet in a position to decide what its policies should be, they must be socialist, whatever that turned out now to mean, and they must be distinct from those of the Conservative party. There must be clear water between the parties, even if of uncertain colour. Crossman has been criticized for the bewildering frequency and rapidity with which he changed his mind. Yet Crossman was not just a politician but a political philosopher. By the 1950s, any political philosopher, confined by his political allegiances to a search for socialism, was bound to be bewildered. If anything is to be criticized it is not his inconstancy but his persistence in so fruitless a quest.

Others of the essayists, without actually doing much to identify the tasks ahead, were also consumed with the difficulties that socialists would face and the obstacles they would have to overcome. This was a pity if it was true that as Strachey, in a cataclysmic mood, adjured his readers, 'We must push on to socialism or, inevitably, in the end we shall be pushed back to unreformed, pre-war, capitalism.'[26] Crosland's conclusion in his own essay was so despondent that one wonders why he did not abandon politics and return to academic life:

> It still remains to create the new society of which socialists have always dreamed, a society which is not bedevilled by the consciousness of class. No one should think that this will be a short or an easy task. The easy and spectacular things have all been done, those that remain will need a prolonged and difficult effort of will. The pace will be limited, not only by the need to preserve the necessary minimum of social peace and cohesion, but also by the difficulty of engendering enthusiasm for further change in a population largely employed and enjoying rising standards every year.[27]

A guiding principle of the essays is that reform must not prejudice social peace.[28] Throughout the history of socialism in Britain, democratic society was protected by the unwillingness of Labour politicians, even when they had a secure majority in the House of Commons, to outrage democratic norms. Margaret Cole argued strongly in favour of what she calls the 'common school'. But the public schools and their clients did not need to worry too much.[29] Anyone who counted on the disappearance of Eton, Harrow and the other big foundations, other than over a very long period, 'is living in Cloud Cuckoo land'. Anyone counting on the disappearance of capitalism was clearly resident in the identical country.

INFLATION

One lesson from the Attlee government had struck home. Trade unions could exploit their power to extract inflationary wage settlements, thereby, paradoxically, stultifying the objective of Keynesian demand management, which was to increase employment. The essayists knew that Labour must solve the problem of inflation. It represented a danger to socialist achievements. It could defeat all their hopes. They perceived the problem but had no new thoughts about it. Crossman noted:

> Profits, wages and salaries are still determined not by any conditions of national interest or social justice, but by the traditional methods of *laisser-faire*. Under conditions of full employment, this must result in a continuous inflationary pressure, which undermines the real value of social security and small savings, as well as making our products less competitive in foreign markets and so jeopardising our capacity to maintain the standard of living.[30]

Strachey was also concerned about inflation but regarded it as just one more problem for a socialist government to take in its stride, as, he claimed, Cripps had done:

> I do not myself believe for a moment that the unmistakable fact that a full employment economy generates powerful inflationary forces is a fatal defect. It is a *bias* in the system which must be identified and vigorously counteracted . . . The habitual posture of the Chancellor of the Exchequer in a full employment economy will be that of a man pulling and hauling with might and main at the brake levers of the economy. It will not be a very popular or comfortable posture. But what of that? It is his job! . . . it is the imperishable service of Sir Stafford Cripps that he faced with superb political courage the inherent necessity for a Labour Chancellor to combat inflation . . .[31]

KᴇIʀ HᴀʀᴅIᴇ. Founder and unsullied hero.

Above RAMSAY MACDONALD. He bequeathed the Left its most valued inheritance, the evidence that it was only through treachery that Labour governments never achieved socialism.

Right JOHN MAYNARD KEYNES. The 'saviour' of capitalism who became socialism's last resort.

HAROLD MACMILLAN. His middle way became Labour's way.

Above ERNEST BEVIN. The man of Labour's century.

Right HAROLD LASKI. He sought a third way between Marxism and democracy.

Opposite EVAN DURBIN. The epitome of democratic socialism, he never quite appreciated that a democratic socialist government would be inherently inflationary.

Above C. R. ATTLEE. He had once believed that socialism was a fundamentally new form of society but lived to be content with a mixed economy.

Opposite above ANEURIN BEVAN. For his Party, the noblest socialist of them all; for his friends, constant frustration.

Opposite below HUGH GAITSKELL. He sought to unite the Party he had helped to divide but found it easier to divide than unite.

HAROLD WILSON. '. . . *omnium consensu capax imperii nisi imperasset.*'
('. . . had he never held the highest office, no one would have doubted
his ability to occupy it.' Tacitus on the Emperor Galba.)

One consolation for Strachey was that he felt able to doubt whether the Tories would be strong enough in combating inflation.[32] He was always ready to find comfort in some catastrophe or other. It is not clear whether he realized that, far from shortening their tenancy of Whitehall, the Tories' readiness to condone policies as inflationary as those of the Attlee government would defer Labour's return to office. Inflationary policies are not necessarily unpopular.

Essentially, however, the answer to inflation was the same as the answer to all other problems of society such as equality, education and economic growth. It was socialism. But, though socialism might be the eventual answer to inflation, it was an answer still beyond reach. The route to the next stage of socialism had yet to be found and, meanwhile, a Labour government would have to survive and manage in a mixed economy.

More prospectively, even though it was anathema to trade union leaders, there would have to be some form of incomes policy, which would have to be associated with other social reforms if it was to gain trade union consent. One problem was that, although the trade unions were founding fathers of the Labour party and regarded a Labour government as, in some sense, their own, they were not prepared to concede unconditional consent to its policies, the membership being perhaps more recalcitrant even than the leaders. Ian Mikardo argued that trade unions did not understand the new world after 1945 when their own government was in power.

> In those conditions, every strike was a blow not against an employer, but against their own Government and their own Party. High wages, which had formerly been the only means for giving the worker a bigger share of the wealth he created, were now represented as a threat to the success of budgetary action designed to achieve precisely that end. Increased productivity, which had formerly been the means of enriching employers and of putting fellow workers out of work, now became a means of helping their own Government and their own class. And the nationalised public corporations, their own brain-child, suddenly confronted them with the confusing spectacle of a boss who didn't belong to the boss class and a board which included a couple of their own members.[33]

This 'misunderstanding' within the trade unions was, therefore, an obstacle to be surmounted.

The idea of an incomes policy was consistent with the Labour party's presumption in favour of planning. How could other aspects of the economy be planned if incomes were not? The trouble with incomes policies was that the consent and co-operation of the trade unions was required to make them effective. The concessions made to the trade unions to win their support tended to recreate the inflationary problem that the incomes policy was intended to cure. Unfortunately, Labour was out of office. It could not try out its ideas. Nor would the Conservative government, indebted as it was to its Labour predecessor, provide a test-bed for the thoughts of Fabian essayists. The Churchill government was, at its outset, far more concerned not to alienate the workers and marginal voters than to enforce an incomes policy or any other method of dealing with inflation. It was not until the Macmillan government revived the idea of planning that it did begin to consider the possibility of an incomes policy.

THE END OF '*LAISSEZ-FAIRE* CAPITALISM'

The memories of each one of the essayists is dominated by something that they, and others such as Durbin before them, called '*laissez-faire* capitalism'. Under *laissez-faire* capitalism, the capitalists did as they pleased. But then the capitalists were brought under the control of the state in the interests of the working people. It was the intervention of the state that had rescued society from massive unemployment and bestowed the blessing of full employment. No government had done as much to bring capitalism under control as the Attlee government. Indeed it had done so much that, in Crosland's view, capitalism had evanesced. '[B]y 1951 Britain had, in all the essentials, ceased to be a capitalist country.'[34] Capitalism which was not *laissez-faire* capitalism was, apparently, not capitalism at all. Crosland was not the first to discover that capitalism no longer existed. Douglas Jay had come to that conclusion at least as early as November 1946. In the second edition of his book *The Socialist Case*, he wrote that neither 'capitalism', 'free enterprise' nor 'the market economy' really existed any more.[35] For Crosland, capitalism was changing into statism. Crosland confessed that statism was not a very elegant name but it was the best he could think of for the moment. Statism, Crosland emphasized, was not socialism. The final goal for socialists had not yet been reached. But the retreat from capitalism was inexorable. 'It is now quite clear that capitalism has not the strength to resist the process of metamorphosis into a qualitatively different kind of society.'[36] This was a very dialectical statement. The quantity of changes, those for example introduced by the Attlee government, would produce a qualitatively different society. There was, nevertheless, a great deal remaining to be done. But what? That was the question. Under statism the private sector does what it is told. That left uncertain what it should be told, but it established the principle.

Behind all this is the confident assumption, founded in the distressing experience of the 1930s, that no economic system can work satisfactorily without firm government direction. The private sector must do what it is told if full employment is to be secure. Moreover, in Crosland's view, the private sector would learn to love it. The business class liked making profits and government action was assisting. There was no evidence of an urge to suicide through an attack on government guidance.[37] Even if the business class did not learn to love it, it would have no choice. There is here a second confident assumption, that the socialist economist will know what instructions to give to speed the expansion of the economy. But, despite six years of the Attlee government, there was no evidence of it. One gets the impression of earnest people desperately striving to find credible arguments for interfering in one way or another with the private sector. The essayists tinker with such ideas as statutory dividend limitation and industrial democracy. But, while they are intently embroiled in a search for something convincing, their souls are not uplifted by any sense of discovery.

NATIONALIZATION

In an endeavour beset by so many uncertainties and hesitations, nationalization and equality provide bedrock. The existing form of nationalization may not have given satisfaction and it had left many problems unresolved. But that was not allowed to detract from the argument for nationalization so long as suitable candidates could be found. For any socialist it was desirable to find some diagnosis of the failures of nationalization that left the case for nationalization intact. Crosland warns that the further multiplication of public boards on the present model would not bring Britain rapidly nearer the socialist goal.[38] Nevertheless, those who advocated a vast extension of nationalization were right even if for the wrong reasons:

> Over the long run [a large-scale extension of nationalization] must certainly be part of the answer – not so much for traditional reasons (to facilitate planning, deal with monopolies, increase efficiency, etc.) – as in order gradually to substitute public rights for shareholders' rights, with

beneficial effects both on the distribution of income and the psychology of industrial relations. But it would be foolish to pretend that this can provide a rapid solution while so many unsolved problems remain in the existing nationalised industries.[39]

It was easy enough to deliver this fashionable attack on the Morrisonian structure of the nationalized industries. But those who wanted a large-scale extension of nationalization had not succeeded in persuading the Attlee government to try a different structure, nor did they prove capable in the future of demonstrating that any other structure, however democratic or decentralized, would yield efficient management or public satisfaction. If the Morrisonian structure was unacceptable, the best alternative to which critics might turn was to try competition, the option that had been neglected at the outset, starting with the dismantling of the existing nationalized industries. This, naturally, was not on the agenda of any part of the Labour party nor, for that matter, of the Conservative party cither.

Planning was no longer to be an argument for nationalization. There was a revulsion against centralization and planning which was reflected within *New Fabian Essays*. It erupted on both wings of the Labour party. Crossman wrote, 'After all, it is not the pursuit of happiness but the enlargement of freedom which is socialism's highest aim.'[40] He was concerned by 'the threat of the managerial society. The planned economy and the centralisation of power are no longer socialist objectives.'[41] He feared the managerial society because it raised questions about the consistency of socialism with liberty. 'The main task of socialism to-day is to prevent the concentration of power in the hands of either industrial management or the state bureaucracy – in brief, to distribute responsibility and so to enlarge freedom of choice.'[42] He added that 'the impression was given that socialism was an affair for the Cabinet, acting through the existing Civil Service'.[43] Roy Jenkins, who wanted more nationalization in the interests of equality, nevertheless tried to draw a line between planning and his own proposals.

> Transfers to public ownership in the future may in part be anti-monopoly measures, and may in part be efficiency measures, but they will be primarily egalitarian measures, and they will hardly be planning measures at all. It should consequently be possible to break away from the association of public ownership with a highly centralised organisation and to seek more intimate forms of ownership and control.[44]

Alas, intimacy was never to be a characteristic of public ownership in any of its relationships, least of all with its customers.

The attempt to distance socialism from planning was not universally applauded. Among the many elements of discord among socialist thinkers was the perennial battle between the centralizers and the libertarians. Companies which could not be nationalized could still be controlled and the residual planning instincts of the essayists could not be denied their outlet. Austen Albu, the industrial expert among the essayists, argued, with support from John Strachey, for legislation entitling the President of the Board of Trade to appoint directors to the boards of public companies where that was felt to be in the public interest. There were 12,000 public companies, so it was to be hoped that not all would need government-appointed directors. This extraordinary idea probably had its origin in a paper, 'The State and Private Industry', which Harold Wilson, as President of the Board of Trade, had presented to his Ministerial colleagues in May 1950 and which was later discussed by the Fabian Society. In the paper, Wilson advocated the appointment of government directors to the boards of 2,000–9,000 companies.[45] By this time he had had nearly five years in government and nearly three in the Cabinet. He had certainly not learned humility. It was not only Douglas Jay who had high confidence in the gentlemen in Whitehall.

EQUALITY

The inequalities in society were immense and could not be justified on grounds of morality or public benefit. These arguments had been deployed by Hugh Dalton long before in a book published in 1920 entitled *Some Aspects of the Inequality of Incomes in Modern Communities*. So there was not much new thinking required in presenting the ancient socialist objective of greater equality. Jenkins discussed whether equality is a danger to liberty. He dismissed the theory that the possession of great property is necessary to protect liberty. He described the theory as 'Whiggery'. It might have been true in the past but was no longer true. But protection for liberty, he insisted, was still necessary. '[I]t will be well to guard against the removal of its [Whiggery's] protection by ensuring that our new society of near equals is left confronting a state machine in which power, both economic and political, is as widely diffused as possible.'[46] There did not seem much hope for the diffusion of power with the President of the Board of Trade pulling on the apron strings of his 9,000 company directors.

The rather vague objective of 'equality' could mean more or less in accordance with the temperament of its advocate or, more dangerously, of a Labour government. It could mean the abolition of public schools and the extension of comprehensive education throughout the nation. It could offer opportunities for widespread intervention in the economic life of the country. For example it could suggest dividend limitation and a capital gains tax, even at 100 per cent, so that shareholders did not benefit from the appreciation of their shares. Any enhanced value that accumulated in the assets of the company would be abstracted by taxation and placed at the disposal of the government.[47] Socialists appeared to get much innocent pleasure from contemplating what they might do to society in the interests of equality if ever they won power; but, fortunately, when they did win power, they usually drew back part of the way, inhibited by what they were told would be the consequences for personal liberty or the workings of the economy. For many of them did place a high value on personal liberty and most of them, particularly when they took office at a time of crisis, were concerned to ensure that anything done in pursuit of equality, however desirable, did not damage the workings of the economy. Equality remained the proclaimed but neglected objective of Labour governments. Thus each generation of socialists, following each period of Labour government, was able legitimately to complain that not much progress had been made on the road to greater equality.

There was the question whether equality was among the arguments for nationalization. Roy Jenkins, who devoted his essay to equality, thought that it was. The time had obviously not yet come to consider him as a possible editor of the *Economist*.[48] 'A substantial extension of public ownership is . . . an essential prerequisite of greater equality of earned incomes and an inevitable concomitant of greater equality in the ownership of property. But the form of public ownership need not follow the existing patterns.'[49] On both counts, the old firm of Crosland and Jenkins were still agreed. The trouble was that nationalization was a protracted and expensive process. The compensation could be enormous. Even if nationalization was part of the answer to Jenkins's search for equality, it was not an answer which would yield fast results. He concluded that only a swift and devastating strike against the capitalists would bring equality rapidly. But was such a measure consistent with the Durbin principle that social peace must not be disturbed? Jenkins was not quite sure.

Great fortunes (and with them great unearned incomes) can only be ended, without provoking an avalanche of capital spending, by means of a sudden blow. Is such a blow compatible with progress within a framework of consent? It is not an easy question to answer ... The suggestion which offers itself is that of the state continuing to pay a part of the income from the surrendered property to its previous owner for either a lifetime or a fixed number of years.[50]

Thus we are back with the ransom socialism must pay. Jenkins, without apparently noticing it, had come across the fundamental dilemma of democratic socialism. A sudden blow is inconsistent with the framework of consent and hence could provoke resistance. If, on the other hand, a democratic socialist government operates within the framework of consent, it is unlikely that democratic socialism will ever be achieved.

Jenkins does see a problem with incentives. The economy has to be kept going and that depends on people who are susceptible to incentives. Is a progressive, expanding economy possible without incentives? Can equality be made consistent with monetary incentives? Would non-monetary incentives serve the purpose? But what could they be? Strachey, in his earlier incarnation, had pointed to the non-monetary incentives available in the Soviet Union, the Order of Lenin, the Order of the Red Banner of Toil, the Order of the Red Star. 'Nor is there any reason why a socialist society should not use those badges of public esteem, those medals and orders which, from their abuse, have become ridiculous in our societies ...'[51] Jenkins seems to agree but concludes that it is all very difficult. '[T]he evolution of stronger non-monetary incentives, while it is by no means an impossible task, is likely to be rather a slow one.'[52] The easier course, as Jenkins eventually came to perceive, was to downgrade the importance of equality in the Labour programme. It was a perception that was to divide him from Crosland.

THE RISKLESS ECONOMY

How was it that these essayists felt free to speculate in so cavalier a way about the different devices by which they might change society when, at the same time, they wished to achieve a strong rate of economic growth? The explanation is that they were thinking of a riskless economy isolated from the rest of the world. In other words, it was to be an economy beloved of socialist economists and politicians but unknown to anyone actually working in the market place. The logic was stark and, to them, entirely valid. Full employment guaranteed not merely security for the workers but expansion for the economy. As the capitalists had been given economic expansion by courtesy of the Attlee government, they had no right to complain if all manner of controls were imposed on their companies and they themselves were subjected to high, even confiscatory, levels of taxation. In any case there was no need to worry because the capitalists were no longer of either political or economic significance. The ownership of property and personal saving were no longer of economic significance. The state could do the saving. The world outside was not a consideration relevant to these speculations because, in so far as economic activity in the USA might affect the UK, there was always the contrivance of discrimination against the dollar and there was always the option of retreat into the Commonwealth and the sterling area. Too many socialist writers imagined that they could plan the future ignoring the outside world. In the Preface to his book *The Socialist Case*, Douglas Jay wrote: 'For purposes of clarity . . . the existence of international exchange is ignored, except where it is for some special reason relevant to the argument.'[53] Even for the purposes of clarity, that abstraction was not sensible. One might have expected that experience of the Attlee government would have given a more practical bent to these meandering thoughts. But the roseate hues in which the Attlee government was perceived blinded even writers as intelligent as these to what Tony Blair, many years later, was to baptize, rather belatedly, as the real world. As far as the essayists were concerned, the competitive society was dead, at least in the UK. According to Austen Albu:

> To suggest that any large part of our economy can return to the highly competitive conditions of the middle nineteenth century or can emulate the supposedly ruthless struggle of American capitalism, is both to misunderstand the nature of modern technical and productive processes and, without any justification, to admit defeat for the socialist conception of a society whose predominant force is human co-operation.[54]

'Crudely competitive instincts' might still be found among small businessmen but not among the directors of public companies.[55]

IN PLACE OF FEAR

The new Fabian essayists were intellectually bankrupt. They had nothing to offer socialism that was not there before they began writing. Was there any prospect of a salvage operation by Aneurin Bevan? Not if the hope lay in an injection of new ideas. Bevan's *In Place of Fear*, also published in 1952, is an unremitting regurgitation of old socialist ideas. It has the advantage, as compared with *New Fabian Essays*, of displaying something of Bevan's eloquence. It also demonstrates the dangers, for the author, of committing Welsh oratory to paper. The questionable generalizations and logical gaps that would be overlooked in a speech become only too visible in the printed word. There are flashes of insight rather than a considered and consistent thesis. The principal characteristic of the book is its total rejection of the market in favour of government decisions taken democratically. Much of the book could have been written before 1945. It suggests that Bevan had given little thought to his experiences as a member of the Attlee Cabinet, six years under economic siege, other than to accumulate grievances. His experiences had in no way dimmed his hopes of socialism or even alerted him to the fundamental problem whether a transition to socialism was feasible in a stable democratic, capitalist society. *In Place of Fear* constitutes Attlee's best defence for having denied Bevan any higher promotion within his government.

Bevan remained, he himself insisted, a convinced democrat. 'The only political system consistent with the needs of a modern industrial community is democracy. It is not possible to educate workers to perform the thousand and one activities necessary to modern industry, and still expect them to tolerate political subservience.'[56] He had, nevertheless, been strongly influenced by Marxism, and was always willing to bring comfort to the disparaged Marxists. 'Mountains of literature have been written to prove that Marx was wrong. If that be the case, then never was error more fertile in practice . . . A sympathetic understanding of what Marxists are trying to say to the world is a prerequisite to learning where the Marxist practitioners are liable to go wrong.'[57] Bevan was not prepared to deny himself the guidance of Marx even though he considered that 'classic Marxism consistently understated the role of a political democracy with a fully developed franchise'.[58] He shows no awareness that what he himself is proposing implies, not democracy, but a bureaucratic nightmare. Or, if he is aware of it, he finds justification in the supposed success of the bureaucratic nightmare that was the

Soviet Union. Bevan's fundamental misconception was that Soviet socialism was economically successful and certainly more efficient than capitalism. Stalinism no doubt disfigured the achievement. But he is quite prepared to argue that Stalinism was not of the nature of the USSR but had been imposed on it by the west, particularly by the attempt by his old enemy, Churchill, to suppress Soviet communism by force of arms after the first world war. Denied the opportunity of learning either at the Treasury or at the Foreign Office, Bevan's socialism is dogmatic and retrograde. It is easy, nevertheless, to understand the attraction of the book to a genuine socialist like Barbara Castle.

Bevan accepts the argument associated, for example, with Durbin that capitalism could not flourish under democratic government. 'It brooks no contradiction that if political democracy had existed at the time, the rate of capital accumulation would have been slower. I know the reply which will be made to this. I shall be told my argument proves that a rapid rate of economic progress is inconsistent with the existence of the universal franchise.'[59] The answer to the conundrum is socialism, the trick that reconciled economic progress with democracy. 'If confidence in political democracy is to be sustained, political freedom must arm itself with economic power. Private property in the main sources of production and distribution endangers political liberty, for it leaves Parliament with responsibility and property with power.'[60] It was a genuine dilemma for socialists. What was Parliament for if it could not manage the economy to the benefit of the working people and, if it did not own the major industries, how could it manage the economy? Bevan hated the market system and the price mechanism. They were an affront undermining the legitimate prerogative of democratic processes. Price movements, he argues, should respond to democratic decisions, not to the anarchy of the market. The price mechanism required the abolition of democratic institutions for its smooth operation.[61] Bevan's criticism might have put the matter rather high, but its spirit would have been widely endorsed within Labour ranks. Bevan demands that society curb and control 'economic adventurers'.[62] Though he understands that 'private economic adventure' had brought in modern industrial techniques, he wants an end to the uncertainties of life. It was the great mass of the people who were the victims.

> It is they who are stalked and waylaid, harried and tormented, their lives made a nightmare of uncertainty. To the extent that this is no longer so in Britain, and in some other advanced countries, it is because the economic adventurers have been curbed and controlled in one sphere of social

activity after another. Life has been made more tolerable by their defeat, not by their ascendancy.[63]

He believes in order and certainty to be imposed by the scientific planner supposedly under the control of Parliament. Anyone who thinks that private economic adventure is desirable is profoundly unscientific.[64] 'Science works for predictability; capitalist society is profoundly unscientific.'[65] Even Bevan needs to support his passionate convictions with the assurance that they are also scientific. But the science should not come from Keynes, an intellectual adventurer who had never accepted the need for a socialist society. Referring implicitly to Keynesianism, he writes:

> Private enterprise was still regarded, in that policy, as the dominant consideration, and the role of Parliamentary action was to provide a stimulant when it looked like flagging. This is wholly opposed to Socialism, for to the Socialist, Parliamentary power is to be used progressively until the main streams of economic activity are brought under public direction.[66]

Though himself not averse to the comforts of life, he is an enemy of consumerism. 'Soon, if we are not more prudent, millions of people will be watching each other starve to death through expensive television sets.'[67] He attacks a capitalist society in which 'Aesthetic values attend upon the caprice of the financially successful,' in which a Titian or a Renoir are bought 'more for their prospective appreciation in capital value than for their intrinsic merit'.[68] Among the priorities treasured by Bevan, consumer choice does not rank high. This might not be popular but, in Bevan's view, it is socialism. At the Labour party's 1959 Conference, Bevan gave classic expression to this abstemious view: 'The so-called affluent society is an ugly society still. It is a vulgar society. It is a meretricious society. It is a society in which priorities have gone all wrong.'[69] He was expressing the thoughts of rank-and-file members of the Labour party. But what they thought was not necessarily what the public thought. One can understand Bevan's resentment that voters were both acquiring television sets and repeatedly returning Conservative governments. But the way to return a Labour government was not, so overtly, to despise the consumerist ambitions of the working class.

Bevan shares the concern about inflation. 'The perils of inflation, ever threatening in conditions of full employment where most of the economy is privately owned, add further inflammable material to the political scene.'[70] The answer again is socialism and the strict controls which socialism would introduce and which would be acceptable under socialism in a way in which they were not under capitalism. He argues for a national wages policy. There must be sustained control of the investment programme by the state. The right to consume must be subject to an order of priority. Once that is accepted, 'bang goes at once a whole series of fetishes of the competitive society'.[71] In other words, the answer to inflation is nationalization plus planning, which means determining priorities. There is a conscious implication, which Bevan did not conceal, that among the 'economic adventurers' to be controlled are the trade unions. They too must accept the discipline of planning. It was a theme which would emerge fifteen years later when Bevan's follower, Barbara Castle, would attempt to enact her White Paper *In Place of Strife*. Bevan does not appear to notice that a whiff of totalitarianism is creeping into his planning proposals.

There a few old scores to be paid off. No doubt with his enemy Gaitskell in mind, he saw dangers in the accumulation of middle-class recruits. He had lost the Treasury to Gaitskell, who was certainly middle class. He had lost the Foreign Office to Morrison, who was trying to be middle class. He wrote that 'a political party which begins to pick its personnel from unrepresentative types is in for trouble'.[72] Yet, if Bevan thought that the Labour party was contaminated by recruits such as Gaitskell, he would have done well to remember that, without other middle-class recruits, he would often have felt even more lonely. Labour's middle classes had a penchant for radical poses.

RIGHT AND LEFT

None of the Fabian essayists was a typical right-winger though some, like Crosland, Jenkins and Albu, would have been regarded as being on the right of the Party. In foreign policy there were clear differences between Bevan and these right-wingers over matters such as the British rearmament programme, and German rearmament. Most of the right-wingers did not share Bevan's emphatic anti-Americanism. Bevan, once he had decided to resign, had concluded that it would have been inappropriate, and demeaning, for the British government to accept military aid from the Americans even if it had been forthcoming to the extent that the Labour Cabinet had thought itself entitled. He wrote that for the USA to make a direct contribution to help Britain finance its own defence was hurtful to national pride. It had the appearance, if not the effect, of making British soldiers mercenaries of the State Department. It would undermine Britain's independence in council.[73] At the same time, with that sense of superiority that he had imbibed from the English, he reflected more generally on the conduct of the American government. 'The United States is very strong, but is she sure she is as wise as she is strong?'[74] Bevan was hardly an impartial judge of the quantity and quality of American charity, and not even a wise one. His condemnation of assistance from the USA is odd coming from the man who decried the end of Lend–Lease as 'unjust'. But Bevan, in defensive mode, was no more committed to consistency than other politicians in pursuit of a grievance. Even John Strachey, while insisting that Britain must, in future, stand on its own feet, does find rare circumstances in which American help would be acceptable. 'Except possibly for the special case of rapid rearmament – which after all America herself is urging upon us – *we must not take any more American help*.'[75]

Policy differences between Gaitskellites and Bevan would always be exacerbated by personal resentments. But, anti-Americanism and German rearmament aside, there was much, in fact, that they all had in common. Jenkins and Crosland, as well as Bevan, appear to have been enemies of 'consolidation'.[76] They would have agreed when Bevan wrote, 'A sense of injustice does not derive solely from the existence of inequality. It arises from the belief that the inequality is capricious, unsanctioned by usage and, most important, senseless.'[77] His view of international trade seems to have had much in common with that, which we will see, Crosland argued in *Britain's Economic Problem*. He, like Crosland, feared a raw-material shortage. He advocated the need for some public agency of the UN to search for raw materials. Unless this was created, crippling physical limits would impose restrictions on what could be done to lift the standards of material comfort for the backward peoples.[78] The UK must use planning to enhance its negotiating power in world markets. Free trade in money and planned importing and exporting of goods were incompatible. He denied that he was suggesting autarchy, but rejecting it did not mean that Britain's economic life had to beat to the pulse of world commerce. Britain might not be able to insulate itself completely, but it could cushion the shocks. Britain's very dependence on world supplies could be made to work to advantage. The British market was too valuable to other countries for them to ignore the wishes of the British government. British buying power could and had been used to fit the UK's purchases with its overall needs.[79]

The Bevanites suddenly identified help to underdeveloped countries as an outstanding priority. Bevan had described it as the central issue of the 1951 election.[80] But although the Bevanites, and notably Harold Wilson, made much of the issue it was not a point of difference from the right. Strachey was worried about the future of democracy. He insisted that continued success for the democratic path depended on the USA. With help from the western European economies, it must fertilize the undeveloped world with capital. It must not be private capital because that was the path of imperialism. The old method of profit-seeking overseas investment on private account could never again fit the bill.[81] Only public capital, brought together by governments, would suffice. 'To the extent that this is not done all the old, morbid, fatal tendencies to glut, slump and crisis at home, and to aggressive imperialism abroad, will reappear. And to-day such imperialist tendencies could not fail to produce the third world war.'[82] This was not the only evidence that Strachey's mind, though converted, conditionally, to democracy, had not emptied itself of all Marxist and Leninist themes. In one sense this concern for the developing world was a welcome conversion. The Labour government had exploited the colonies in the interest of its own economic policies. The benefit of the conversion was, however, diminished by the sentimental belief within the Labour party that the problems of underdevelopment were susceptible of socialist remedies. Unfortunately, as experience was to show, underdeveloped countries practising socialist policies were even less successful in promoting economic growth than developed countries. The aid that they received simply encouraged them in policies which were counterproductive, except perhaps to those leaders with Swiss bank accounts.

There were differences but not wide differences on the subject of nationalization. Bevan, certainly, pushed the case for it harder and wider. '[A]s far as Britain is concerned State direction of our economy in one form or another has come to stay, and it might as well stay in a respectable fashion by a radical extension of public ownership.'[83] He even foresaw the day when the profits of nationalization could be employed in relief of other forms of taxation. A large part of public spending could be financed out of the surplus which now accrued to private owners. It would require only that a greater proportion of industry should be publicly owned. His reason for believing in this happy outcome was that compensation had been given in low-yielding gilt-edged, whereas the profit from industry would rise.[84] As an advocate of Parliamentary power, Bevan wanted direct Parliamentary control of the nationalized industries. He strongly disagreed with the Morrisonian structure.

The trouble with the Boards of the nationalised industries is that they are a constitutional outrage. It is not proper that a Member of Parliament should be expected to defer to a non-elected person. The Minister, by divesting himself of parliamentary responsibility, disfranchises the House of Commons and that means he disfranchises the electorate as well ... The present state of affairs reduces the Minister to the status of either a messenger or an apologist for the Boards.[85]

The young Gaitskellites would not have gone this far but they, too, asserted their discontent with the Morrisonian structure. They had not yet separated socialism from nationalization. It might not be electorally wise to push too much nationalization into an election programme. The reputation of nationalization was not being enhanced by the frequent industrial disputes in the public sector. But, wise or not, socialism still meant nationalization and they were socialists. Differences between right and left do remain, differences that would expand as Crosland moved even further towards a revisionist socialism. Bevan was still far more of a centralizer, a planner, than the others. Though there were differences between Bevan and those who were to become the revisionists, the differences were not serious enough to make it impossible for them all to work together if only they could get on the right personal terms. All of them considered themselves socialists and it was as socialists that they presented themselves to the electorate. Their problem was to find the path that led to socialism and then persuade the electorate.

THE CROSLAND TWO-WORLD THESIS

It will be remembered that the Attlee government, in its later years, was developing a two-world approach to the problems of the British economy, motivated primarily by the fear that full employment would otherwise be at risk. This fear had been accompanied by the conviction that the appropriate economic partner for industrial Britain was the Commonwealth, with its riches in raw materials, rather than Europe, from which came the threat of competition in manufactured products. The idea that a two-world system might be attainable persisted in Whitehall for some years, to be brought out and dusted down at times of balance of payments crisis. This concept of the economic future, and of the way to ensure full employment in Britain, found expression in a book by Anthony Crosland, published in 1953, grandly entitled *Britain's Economic Problem*. This was another old idea which had seized the imagination of this leading socialist intellectual. His argument was now shared by Keynesian economists in and out of the Economic Section with whom Crosland was in touch, and who had been aware ever since the discussions during the war about the Employment White Paper that Keynesian techniques would not be enough in themselves to ensure full employment. Crosland was one of the PLP's few serious economists but, like the others, he never really understood what was, and what was not, possible in the international economy. The policy which was being developed may not have been socialism in one country but it came near being socialism in one Commonwealth. As an old idea it had one advantage as compared with the other old socialist ideas. It was so rapidly proved to be nonsense that it disappeared from public view almost as soon as Crosland had given it public ventilation.

Crosland had discovered that the situation of the UK was exceptionally serious. Full employment was certainly at risk if an antidote to international economic instability could not be found. The British standard of living was to a quite exceptional degree dependent on external conditions outside the control of a British government and 'world economic trends are developing in a manner alarmingly adverse to British interests'.[86] The complacency and self-satisfaction of *New Fabian Essays* has entirely disappeared. There were three major problems, the world shortage of food and raw materials, the disequilibrium between the dollar and non-dollar worlds, and the instability of the American economy.[87] Britain was being worse hit than other countries by the dollar shortage. The central role of foreign trade made it unusually vulnerable to any adverse influence from abroad. Rearmament, following the outbreak of the Korean war in June 1950, had exacerbated the problems.[88] However, Britain's difficulties were of a much more fundamental nature than could be explained by the Korean war.[89]

Crosland examines whether the solution to Britain's problems is to be found in an expansion of exports to the USA. His answer is despondent. It would always be an uphill struggle to break into American manufacturing markets in view of the tendency for American industrial efficiency continuously to outstrip European. A further reduction in tariffs would make little difference. In any case the pressure in the USA was to increase tariffs not reduce them.[90] There might be something to be expected from defence aid and American foreign investment. But the prospects of a large expansion in American foreign investment were not great.[91] It would be absurd for the non-dollar world to seek a cure for the dollar gap in deflation.[92] Full employment must be preserved.

There was an additional danger in the possibility of an American recession. Crosland suggests that if, in the event of an American recession, tighter restrictions on dollar imports became necessary, the non-dollar world would have to employ every device of discrimination and bilateralism to maintain trade outside the US, and to concentrate the restrictions on dollar goods.[93] He discusses ways of avoiding unemployment in the UK as a secondary effect of an American recession.[94] He concludes that a determined government, by the use of fiscal policy, could reflate home demand. It could thereby confine the unemployment to only a half of what it would otherwise have been.[95] A government which adopted *laissez-faire* would soon see the unemployment figures surmount the million mark.[96] Still, domestic reflation was an imperfect answer which could only limit, not avoid, an increase in unemployment. What then could planning achieve?

In form, Crosland rejects the two-world thesis. But what he instead proposes amounts to the same idea in which the resurrection of multilateral settlements is deferred to the distant future. We now find Crosland doubling as the Labour party's Joseph Chamberlain. His proposals had much in common with those of some pre-war economists who had been trying to find, in the exploitation of empire, ways of avoiding repeated economic crises, such as that of 1931. They were also in the tradition of the United Empire Party of Lords Beaverbrook and Rothermere and of that oxymoron, 'Empire Free Trade'. British socialism, apparently, had much in common with British imperialism. Whereas, before the war, Marxists such as Strachey had urged that capitalism inevitably promotes nationalism in defence of its profits, after the war it was socialism that promoted nationalism in defence of full employment. There is thus a continuity between British imperialism and British socialism both having a common characteristic, to protect the British economy from foreign competition in a world which was not, and never would be, socialist.

Crosland's solution was based on the sterling area. He sought a way to the economic future that would ensure benefit not just to the UK but to the Commonwealth and the colonies. The countries of the independent Commonwealth could not be controlled. They had, therefore, to be enticed, by shared benefits, into seeing their interests in the way Crosland thought they should. Crosland had obviously forgotten, or was unaware of, Neville Chamberlain's experience at Ottawa in 1932 in attempting to negotiate a form of imperial preference that would be of benefit to British industry. The Ottawa agreements provided no help to British industry, though they did open the British doors to higher agricultural imports from the Empire.[97] The colonies, on the other hand, had, for the time being, no choice. They were under British control. That made it easier to ensure that they understood that their own interest lay in co-operating with Britain in the execution of Crosland's thesis for the world's economic future. An essential principle was discrimination against the scarce currency, the dollar.

Crosland's reconciliation of the interests of Britain with those of the Commonwealth and colonies was based on the Paley Commission report and, in consequence, on a misapprehension. The Paley Commission was appointed by the President of the United States to examine the threat of a shortage of those raw materials on which the American economy, like those of other developed countries, depended. It reported in June 1952 that the USA would in fact become increasingly reliant on imported raw materials as its own supplies were exhausted. It concluded that 'the consumption of almost all materials is expanding at compound rates and is thus pressing harder and harder against resources which, whatever else they may be doing, are not similarly expanding'.[98] The consequence must be that the prices of raw materials would rise and the terms of trade would turn against the developed world.

Crosland describes the report of the Paley Commission as 'the most diligent and elaborate study ever made in this field'.[99] Though acknowledging that the Commission might be wrong, he believed that it was right and he based his whole argument on the proposition that the terms of trade must be expected to turn against the developed world. '[T]he second half of the twentieth century seems likely to witness a reversion to the trend which frightened the nineteenth century from Malthus onwards, of a rate of demand for the earth's natural products which is always tending to outstrip their supply.'[100] He adopted for himself the conclusions of the Paley Commission. The terms of trade would move against the industrial nations, which would be able to adapt themselves only with difficulty to the changed world of dear food and scarce materials.[101] The Paley Commission's diagnosis was, at the time, supported by the fact that the terms of trade *had* been turning against the UK and the rest of the developed world. Crosland calculates what would have happened had it not been for this unfortunate state of affairs.

The burden imposed by this disturbing new factor in our affairs . . . easily exceeded that imposed by the wartime losses which had dominated the earlier discussions. It explains why the achievement of the 175 per cent export target did not suffice to guarantee solvency, and why imports had to be harshly restricted to very low levels. But for the worsened terms of trade, Britain would have been substantially in surplus from 1948 onwards, and the task of post-war recovery as such could be considered as completed in 1950 when exports finally reached the figure set for them.[102]

The implications of Paley were not entirely bleak. In the distant future there was hope of an end to the dollar shortage. As a result of declining raw-material supplies within the USA, it would become a major importer of raw materials. Hence, if the rest of the world would show a reasonable restraint in making dollar purchases, the present enormous surpluses on the US foreign account would give way to balance, if not actually to deficit, and the world's dollar problem would disappear.[103] But that would not happen for a long time and meanwhile the rest of the world, including Britain, had to live. The question was how survival could be managed until the worsening terms of trade reversed the present dollar shortage.

While the Paley Commission provided Crosland's context, planning provided his method. But it was planning on the scale of the sterling area, not just of the UK. 'Those who reject planning, and yet proclaim their devotion to full employment, have a difficult case to argue.' Crosland maintained that the choice lay between reinforcing disinflation with physical controls or abandoning full employment as an objective.[104] One victim of the future as described by the Paley Commission would be the liberalization of trade for which the USA had been pressing since the end of the war. Further liberalization of trade was out of the question for the time being. There would have to be strict quantitative restrictions into the indefinite future.[105] Full employment depended on it: 'The only other possible method would have been to abandon the full employment objective, and reduce home demand to the point where free consumers' choice itself dictated the lower level of imports. It is hard to imagine just what degree of unemployment this would have involved, but it must certainly have been very high.'[106]

On the constructive side, there would have to be a considerable expansion of domestic agriculture.[107] Crosland examines from what industries an increase in exports can be expected to earn the vital dollars and pay for other imports.[108] He detects potential in steel and coal. Both industries were performing badly and Crosland finds their poor performance to be an argument for the nationalization of steel even though, in his view, the nationalization of coal has left that industry performing badly.[109] 'It is not easy to estimate at all precisely the future demand for steel ... It is ... a virtual certainty that private steel industrialists will underestimate the need ... This affords a very strong argument for nationalization if the necessary expansion is to be assured.'[110] It would prove not at all easy for the state to estimate future demand either. It was not a good argument for nationalization unless the state was assumed to have money and to spare.

Limiting dollar imports implied that supplies must be obtained elsewhere, particularly in the sterling area. If the sterling area did not yet have the capacity to substitute for dollar imports, that capacity must be built up in the category in which the sterling area had a comparative advantage, raw materials. There was here, Crosland thought, a shared interest between Britain and the rest of the sterling area. Due to the expected rise in primary prices, governments of less developed countries concerned with acquiring the maximum foreign exchange incomes would be well advised to go slow on industrialization, and concentrate instead on expanding food and raw materials output.[111] '[O]n balance it is better for Britain that the less developed countries should not hasten on with industrial development too eagerly.'[112] He concludes:

> the main hope lies in the further development of alternative sources of supply in the Commonwealth, and the gradual switching of purchases to them: Rhodesian tobacco and copper, aluminium on the Volta River, bauxite in India. No amount of discouragement or political misrepresentation over the groundnuts scheme must be allowed to interfere with essential dollar-saving colonial investment; and British Governments will have to be adamant in preserving the right to discriminate, for as far ahead as one can see, in favour of new sterling sources of supply.[113]

His recommendations, Crosland believes, will be to the benefit of the colonies as well as of Britain.

> The colonies ought to be running their balances down, not building them up ... they should continue to earn dollars by selling their primary products to the Western Hemisphere, but not merely should their contribution to the dollar pool be balanced by a flow of goods from Britain, but there should be a further flow on top of this as part of a long-term plan of development.[114]

He insists that it must be in the interests of the primary-producing countries themselves to arrest the drift of resources into secondary industry, and to concentrate on raising their output of food and raw materials.[115] Indeed, if they would only see it, his proposals were in the interests of the sterling area as a whole, including the independent members that were producers of primary products.

Nobody wants to deprive the Australians of their all-Australian car, or the Indians of their brand new steel-mills. But if the cars and steel can be obtained from Britain, while American demand for Australian dairy produce may rise by 400 per cent and for Indian bauxite by 300 per cent, it hardly seems sensible to devote too large an investment to the former, and too little to the latter.[116]

If only it would bend to Crosland's thesis, the whole sterling area system would then become much more complementary, and it would be devoting its productive efforts to goods for which world demand was rising – Britain on engineering goods, the overseas area on food and raw materials.[117] Ideally the whole non-dollar world should co-operate in the Crosland plan. The essential condition of durable equilibrium was a large rise in world production outside the USA, properly distributed according to Crosland's assessment of comparative advantage, combined with an agreement among the non-dollar countries to buy each other's output in preference to dollar goods.[118]

Crosland's thesis was based on the forecast that the terms of trade would move against the developed countries and in favour of the developing countries. In fact, hardly had the Paley Commission reported when the prices of raw materials began to fall. The terms of trade began, and for many decades continued, to turn in favour of the developed world, not against it. This was enormously beneficial to the citizens of the UK, and to its Tory government, but it punctured Crosland's imperial project, the whole Crosland attempt to reconcile British economic interests with those of the rest of the sterling area in defence of full employment. Nevertheless the political attitudes behind Crosland's imperialism persisted. There was no longer a possibility of arguing that the interests of the UK coincided with those of the developing members of the Commonwealth. It could well be to the advantage of the Australians to produce their all-Australian car, or the Indians their brand new steel-mills. Yet the problem of maintaining full employment in a world subject to American recessions remained. There is a logical line of descent from the two-world speculations of Crosland in the early 1950s to the alternative strategy of Tony Benn in the 1970s. It helps to explain why, at the time of the IMF crisis in the autumn of 1976, there was so much in common between Benn and Crosland.

Despite the breakdown in the theory that Crosland had based on an incorrect forecast of future movements in the terms of trade, Labour leaders, for more than a decade thereafter, continued to look to the Commonwealth as the basis of British trade, unable to reconcile themselves to the differences in interest between Britain and the Commonwealth that were emerging. It was still thought that, for an industrial country like Britain, a complementary relationship with the raw-material suppliers of the Commonwealth, reinforced by imperial preference, was more advantageous than competition with other industrial countries within an integrated Europe. The attempt to continue a close economic engagement with the Commonwealth therefore deflected Britain during that decade from proper appreciation of the advantages of integration with western Europe. It was not until Labour returned to government in 1964 that the truth began to dawn. At last it became clear that if, due to differences of interest, the Commonwealth could not be constituted as a second protected world, as free as possible of the influence of American recessions, then the UK would have to look after itself. If the imperialist way of defending Britain and full employment from the world market would not work, another must be found. That might involve a belated attempt to join in the European project.

CONCLUSION

While all these non-events were occurring in the field of ideas, the Labour party was displaying its usual fissiparous tendencies in the field of real politics. The concentration of the left on foreign policy and on its opposition to nuclear weaponry during this period, and subsequently, was significant. It was attributable in part to anti-Americanism but also to a naive belief that the Soviet leadership would relax its tyrannical control over its empire if only it was treated kindly by the west. It was also due to the lack of any clear vision of the way forward at home and, therefore, to the difficulty of finding anything to say about domestic policy except more nationalization. But on that there was so much agreement between right and left that all the left could bring by way of criticism was that the right did not really mean what it said. Oddly, questions of foreign policy could be as divisive within the left as the Bevanites were within the Labour party. Bevan himself, though sharing the anti-Americanism and the optimistic expectation of the gradual democratization of the Soviet empire, was equally convinced that Britain should be as well equipped militarily as its economic strength made possible. The possession of nuclear weapons could save money on conventional armaments. And a British nuclear armament could be an expression of anti-Americanism.

Bevan's personality dominated all these issues, stimulating, on the left, dreams of socialist advance under his leadership and, on the right, nightmares of lost elections extending indefinitely into the future. Bevan's volcanic resentment of the Party's lack of appreciation of his eminent services would erupt at intervals which no seismic science could foretell. He would then behave atrociously, alienating not merely his critics but most of his friends. In April 1954 he resigned from the shadow Cabinet after repudiating Attlee in the House on a question of foreign policy and was then affronted when Harold Wilson, who had been runner-up in the elections the previous autumn, agreed to take his place. Gaitskell, always keeping close to the principal trade union leaders with large block votes at Conference, would swing erratically in his attitude to Bevan. Sometimes he seemed to understand that, however difficult his conduct, Bevan had in him something that appealed to the heart of the Labour Movement. At other times, due to a mixture of exasperation and the influence of the trade union leaders, he would seek Bevan's expulsion – for which Bevan provided frequent occasions. Attlee either gave no lead or, having appeared to give a lead against Bevan, then retreated into silence and equivocation when it came to action. He wanted to leave a united party to his successor and still thought that Bevan might be a worthy successor. In any case there was an election to come, and a Labour party united, if only with sticking plaster, might still just win and restore him to No. 10. He was therefore prepared to suffer the insults of the left and the contumely of the right. He was providing a precedent for the later behaviour of Harold Wilson. The Bevanites found a democratic principle in condemning the trade union block vote at Party conferences. The major trade union leaders cast their block vote in support of Morrison and Gaitskell against, as the Bevanites speculated, the wishes of their members. The Bevanites therefore protested as a matter of principle while hoping that a new generation of trade union leaders would switch the block vote in their direction. The Bevanites and Gaitskellites thought they were fighting over the personnel and policies of the next Labour government, whereas in fact their quarrels were burying Labour's prospects of office even deeper in the dust.

There is no need to follow these random occurrences in any detail. On neither side of the gulf that had opened up within the Labour party had there appeared any galvanizing new ideas that would stimulate the electorate. The Labour party was as much divided by its inability to find a path forward as by the Bevanite controversies. It was not until after the further defeat at the 1955 election that anything happened that could be regarded as a reappraisal of socialism in the light of its experience in government, and subsequent events. The bitter conflicts simply served to confirm the impression that Labour was unfit to govern and thereby ensured that socialism, of whatever variety, was a lost cause.

PART III

THE SECOND COMING

TEN

The Future of Socialism

REVISING DEMOCRATIC SOCIALISM

It was with the Labour party again repudiated at the polls in 1955, and badly divided, that Anthony Crosland, close friend of Hugh Gaitskell, turned to the task of reviving democratic socialism by revising it. The result was *The Future of Socialism*, first published in October 1956. *Britain's Economic Problem* had failed the test of realism. *The Future of Socialism* would fail by the same test. Democratic socialism, hardly out of its cradle, had already lost its fight for life.

The Future of Socialism was not just concerned with revising democratic socialism. There was the associated problem of making Labour electable. *The Future of Socialism* is addressed to a Labour party intent on ruining its own electoral prospects. The danger lay not just in its divisions but in its dismal reputation. It exhibited some very odd characteristics, for example a querulous attitude to affluence. Crosland warns that the Party would be ill advised to continue making a largely proletarian class appeal when a majority of the population was gradually attaining a middle-class standard of life.[1] The Party should recognize that its identification in the public mind with austerity, rationing and restrictive controls was highly damaging.[2] The world had changed. The old shibboleths must go or at least be reformulated and, if necessary, downgraded. '[C]onservative or indolent-minded people on the Left, finding the contemporary scene too puzzling and unable to mould it into the old categories, are inclined to seek refuge in the slogans and ideas of 50 years ago.'[3] It proved much more difficult than Crosland may have anticipated to disconnect the Labour party from ancient slogans and ideas. Yet, if the book failed in its purpose, it was at least an heroic failure. The book has its heroic aspects because it said many things that traditional socialists would find unpalatable. But it could equally be doubted how much it had to do with socialism.

The Future of Socialism expresses a deeply felt political philosophy. No one reading it could doubt the intellectual powers, and moral force, of its author. It was of much greater importance in Crosland's life than it ever was in the life of the Labour party. It gave him a frame of reference. It remained for him a statement of the socialism in which he believed and to which he would remain devoted for the rest of his life. His conduct of public affairs would be determined by the principles he had enunciated. Once Crosland had written *The Future of Socialism*, he forgot nothing to which, in it, he had committed himself, and became incapable of learning very much from the experience of the governments in which he subsequently served. The great revisionist ceased to revise.[4]

Crosland began by considering what socialism had meant in the century and a quarter since its original emergence as an idea of political significance. Past socialists had differed on the meaning of socialism. That, he felt, was justification for his differing from them and from his own contemporaries. He concluded that what was of value in the writings of his predecessors was largely their ethical drive, and that what had been overtaken was largely their economic content. He proposed to revise democratic socialism because, since the original socialists had written, fought and suffered for their cause, the world had changed economically beyond recognition. But he considered himself a socialist because he shared the ethical drive.

Thus it was as a socialist that Crosland undertook the task of revising democratic socialism. He was a revisionist but he still counted himself a socialist. The Labour party could not abandon socialism, and Crosland would not have wished that it should. The book did not spring forth fancy free from an uncluttered mind. Crosland carried with him a great deal of old socialist baggage. That baggage would strongly influence the argument of the book. Crosland, in the role of Moses, is discovered leading the Labour party (the people of Israel) out of Egypt, out of the slavery of traditional socialism. It was a role that fitted his personality and talents. On the other hand, Crosland's revisionism was bound to contain a great deal of traditional socialism. This Moses was in no position furiously to break the tablets of the law when, on descending from Sinai, he found his followers worshipping the golden bull. On the contrary he was compelled to write worship of the golden bull into his script. But this had its political advantages. As the apron strings were held tightly by the socialist past, the socialist future could not get out of touch. Crosland was certainly enough of a politician to understand that political leaders must not forget, or outrun, their followers. His book must persuade, provoke, but not outrage. If it outraged it would either be without influence or it would only serve further to divide. There must, therefore, be a balance. In the frenzied state of the Labour party at the time, in which, for many, new thought about socialism was in itself an outrage, it proved a balance impossible to maintain. Many traditional socialists were outraged. Yet, in hindsight, what impresses was how small were the steps taken by Crosland away from traditional socialism. He authenticated traditional socialism to a far greater extent than he revised it. Traditional socialists were uneasy at any challenge, however slight, especially from within the Labour party, particularly from a source so close to the new leader, Hugh Gaitskell, who had succeeded Attlee in December 1955. But their assault served one purpose probably not intended by Crosland. His reputation as a revisionist depends to a major extent on the outrage he provoked rather than on the extent of his revision.

The Attlee government had already acquired the lustre that has sustained its reputation through successive generations of socialists. Although Crosland wished to revise socialist theory, he by no means excluded everything that had been part of socialist tradition as implemented in the Attlee government with its commitment to welfare and full employment. In particular he had to find room in his argument for two socialist shibboleths, planning and nationalization. Without that, his chances of convincing Party members that socialism must be revised, or even that he was still himself a socialist, would disappear. Thus Crosland argues that the importance of nationalization as an element in socialism is overrated; but he accepts the need for more, unspecified nationalization. He wishes to relegate planning to a lower priority than it had enjoyed a decade earlier; but he still sees a need for planning and, indeed, places upon it a heavier burden than it could possibly bear. This then was the dilemma. The book could not reject nationalization and planning. But it must attempt to rescue socialism from the unpopularity of nationalization and planning. The electorate knew perfectly well what socialism meant. It meant nationalization and planning. The problem was how to persuade the electorate that socialism meant anything else but nationalization and planning. Crosland's resolution of this dilemma was twofold. First, he argued that nationalization and planning need not be abandoned but that their purposes and extent had to be rethought. Secondly, he sought to direct the public mind to other socialist objectives. *The Future of Socialism* is a conjuror's attempt to balance old-fashioned socialist notions with the more liberal fashions of contemporary thought.

The whole project of *revising* socialism suggested fundamental questions about its nature. In theory it would have been possible for Crosland and others to say that socialism as it had always been understood was dead. It had been tried under Attlee and it had failed. Despite the introduction of the National Health Service, despite the historic achievement of full employment, the Labour party had lost office. There was clearly something very unlikeable about socialism. It would have been possible, back in 1951, to argue, forgetting the real and indubitable nature of socialism, that the NHS and full employment were socialism or, at least, emanations of socialism. But, after the experience of some years of Conservative government, that argument was not open. Full employment and the NHS were now as much part of Conservatism as they had ever been of socialism. It was open to Crosland to assert that there remained to be accomplished a programme of reform that would justify the continued existence of the Labour party even if socialism was abandoned. Above all, there was greater equality. *The Future of Socialism* is principally remembered for its advocacy of greater equality. That too did not require for its accomplishment the apparatus of historic socialism. It was at least arguable that the case for greater equality had been damaged by being clothed in socialist apparel. But, working within the confines of the Labour party, Crosland had no choice other than to constitute his programme of reform within parameters that could be identified as those of socialism, flexibly defined. Crosland's vision had to be called socialist because the instrument of its policy prescriptions would be the Labour party, which described itself as a socialist party.

CAPITALISM METAMORPHOSED

Crosland's central insight was that capitalism had been transformed. It had changed in four fundamental respects. First, the old *laissez-faire* philosophy had been replaced by intervention by a state which, contrary to past experience, was no longer subservient to business. Crosland was convinced that the capitalist system had been tied down by the state and castrated so that it could no longer beget the evils, for example of unemployment, that had disfigured it in the past. The prime success had been that of Keynesianism in ensuring full employment. He finds support for state intervention in the business community. It too had lost much of its ideological attachment to *laissez-faire*.[5] Moreover the dangers indicated by Hayek could be forgotten. No one of any standing now believed that any interference with the market mechanism would propel the country down the slippery slope that led to totalitarianism.[6] There had been an explicit acceptance, by governments of both parties, of responsibility for full employment, the rate of growth, the balance of payments and the distribution of incomes.[7] Never again would a government dare to allow unemployment to rise to pre-war levels.[8] If it did, it would be ejected at the next election. Tory governments would be too scared of the political consequences deliberately to engineer unemployment in order to fight inflation. Full employment as a priority would always come ahead of price stability. There must be other ways of containing inflation than by allowing unemployment to rise. No one now supposed that a 1931-type slump was likely to recur, or that the trade cycle continued in its classical form.[9] One safeguard against slump was the level of public investment, which, being both large and dependable, would ensure a happy economic equilibrium.[10] The maintenance of full employment and of social welfare had required of post-war Tory governments the exercise of economic power on a scale and in a direction that would never have been countenanced by pre-war Conservative governments.[11] Society was no longer dependent on Adam Smith's invisible hand, which had attempted to turn individual selfishness into public good and had so manifestly failed in its task.[12] The state now stood in place of Smith's invisible hand as guarantor of public good.

The second of Crosland's fundamental changes was in the significance of ownership. Tawney had argued long before that property became objectionable when the link between it and its use was broken. An important example of the breach was the share in the capital of a company. The share was a new and strange form of property because it carried no obligation, only the right to receive an income. It was the managers who did the work and the shareholders who won the return. Other examples were the royalties accruing to mine owners and the rents accruing to landowners.[13] In capitalist theology, the shareholder is a risk taker.[14] But to the socialist he is a parasite on the work of others. Durbin had placed emphasis on the separation between ownership and management. It was the managers, not the owners, who now had the power and they were different people with different interests. This tradition in socialist thought which separates the manager from the shareholder continues as an element in Crosland's revisionism. It becomes an attempt to recruit the manager to the cause of Labour, an attempt which, however, only achieves significant success when socialism is entirely abandoned. For Crosland, it was unlikely that the pattern of ownership would uniquely determine anything.[15] It still had some influence but was of far less importance than in earlier times.[16] Major companies were now run not by their owners but by hired managers. The nominal owners had largely lost even the residue of control which they had retained before the war.[17] This was accompanied by a further change. The social attitude and behaviour of the business class had undergone a significant modification, which appeared to reflect a pronounced loss of strength and self-confidence.[18] The interests of the new class of managers now had much in common with those of society generally. Crosland even took a tolerant view of the salaries they paid themselves. Something might be done about it in the interest of greater equality but it was not a grievous problem and did not require urgent action.[19]

All this was very simplistic, recruiting fashionable arguments about the managerial revolution to the cause of socialism. It required a certain desperation in the search for arguments for the metamorphosis of capitalism to advance the managerial revolution as evidence of it. By way of excuse, it can be conceded that Crosland was conducting a battle against Marxists who emphasized class interests as being the dominant factor in history. He used the managerial revolution as an argument against the Marxists. He was not invariably discriminating in his advocacy. The battle against Marxism could be won without this particular contention, which ignored facts such as that it was the directors who were often the managers and that there was a greater mutuality of interest between owners, directors and managers (when not directors) than he allowed for. It was unlikely that the managers would be ready to accept the Crosland pattern for society. It is arguable that the separation of ownership from management had actually placed in the hands of executive directors, largely recruited from the richer classes, a nepotic power over resources immensely greater than they had ever controlled before the separation had taken place.[20]

The third fundamental change was that there had been a decisive movement of power within industry from management to labour.[21] So long as full employment was maintained then, whoever governed at Westminster, the organized workers would remain the effective power in industry.[22] Jenkins, in *New Fabian Essays*, had already given his readers such comfort as could be derived from the reminder that the President of the National Union of Mineworkers was more powerful than any six capitalists.[23] It was an argument which also appealed to Gaitskell.[24] It might be true but was that what socialists really wanted? Had they forgotten the fears of Attlee, Morrison and Durbin about trade union power? Or did they have to wait for Arthur Scargill to discover that this was not an ideal distribution of power? Though the shift in the balance of power between managers and trade union leaders might have attractions to a party so strongly linked to the trade unions, it had its dangers. It could draw in a Labour government, or a Labour Opposition, in support of the trade unions even in cases where their demands were inflationary and hostile to improvements in productivity. In any case, while employers controlled investment, the trade unions could not be more than a counterweight to the authority of employers. They could not run industry.

Despite this transfer in power, Crosland was a critic of industrial democracy. He was against worker directors in the private sector. He admitted the moral claim to worker representation, but there were a variety of practical obstacles. There was little desire for it, and it could not be guaranteed to produce any real benefit. The trade unions, he perceptively noted, feared the creation of a parallel hierarchy of workers' representatives. In other words, once trade union mastery was entrenched, the trade union leadership would not want it to be disturbed even by their members. There was, in any case, a shortage of potential worker directors of the right calibre. So elaborate a reform could not be justified if the result was to be no serious gain either in contentment or in social justice. Crosland was also opposed to government directors in the private sector.[25] So far as the management of nationalized industries was concerned, democracy would be exercised through the elected government. So the shift in the balance of power should not imply any move towards industrial democracy. Crosland's dismissive attitude to industrial democracy was not shared all the way across the Labour Movement or even, apparently, by Gaitskell, though Gaitskell did accept that there was a marked lack of enthusiasm for it among trade unions and that therefore it might be better to start with consultation.[26] G. D. H. Cole, on the other hand, was adamant. 'In any socialised enterprise, no matter what its form, socialisation requires that proper provision be made for the democratic participation of the workers in determining the conditions and allocation of work, both at the work place level and at the higher levels of management and control.'[27] Cole, the former Guild Socialist, was pointing, as ever, to an element in socialism which managerial socialists forgot or discounted.

The shift in the balance of power between capitalists and workers had been accompanied by Crosland's fourth fundamental change. Since 1939 there had been a considerable redistribution of personal income.

Most of the benefit had accrued to the workers. The losses had been suffered by the owners of property. The best evidence of the change, at least during the period of Labour government, was to be found in the intense antagonism of the better-off classes.[28] The Attlee government had implemented greater social changes than expected by the most sanguine of pre-war leftists.[29] It was 'rather absurd' to speak now of a capitalist ruling class.[30]

Crosland concluded that the economic system that now existed was no longer capitalism. He recognized that there were many social evils still to be attacked. What remained for socialists was to modify further the harsher, and unfairer, aspects of society. But capitalism had evanesced some time in mid-century. Providing a definition of capitalism which was typically insular but untypically vague, he wrote: '[T]he proper definition of the word capitalism is a society with the essential social, economic, and ideological characteristics of Great Britain from the 1830s to the 1930s; and this, assuredly, the Britain of 1956 is not. And so, to the question "Is this still Capitalism?", I would answer "No".'[31] In the *New Fabian Essays* he had baptized the new economic system 'statism'. But he had now concluded that 'statism' was not a good label. He would have liked to find a better label but, for the moment, it escaped him.[32] Crosland's declaration that capitalism had disappeared would hardly strengthen his influence with socialists to whom it was quite obvious that it remained an arrogant presence. They might even go so far as to regard his proposition as preposterous. If socialism could undergo the revisions which Crosland was about to prescribe and still be socialism, a similar flexibility could surely be permitted to capitalism. Capitalism could mutate and yet still be capitalism.

Crosland's attempt to find a word different from 'capitalism' has its own significance. How could a socialist writer proclaim that the evils of capitalism had diminished? If such an unlikely event had occurred, it could only be because it was no longer capitalism. Capitalism was, and remained, a hate word. Capitalism was a system in flux, changing in the ways Crosland had listed and in others, but socialists could not allow its reputation the benefit of the modifications it had undergone. It would always be evil. No reform could ever be enough. It must go. And if it could not be persuaded to go, a revisionist socialist must nevertheless justify his revisionism by alleging that, contrary to all appearances, it had gone. Even when Labour leaders became prepared to accept that what they would be doing in office was to manage capitalism, and claim to manage it better than the Tories, they shied away from allowing any credit to capitalism. They spoke rather of the market economy or the mixed economy.

His reappraisal of capitalism led Crosland on to an attempt to wean his readers from Marx. Marx's influence had been great even among those who had come to socialism from Methodism rather than from Marxism. It was time to recognize that Marx had been wrong. The state, equipped with pervasive economic power, was now acting in the interests of society as a whole rather than just to support the interests of the propertied classes. Contrary to Marx, capitalism had not pauperized its labourers. It had enriched them. Crosland informs us that 'traditional socialism' had been largely concerned with the evils of traditional capitalism, and with the need for its overthrow. But traditional capitalism had been reformed and modified out of existence, and it was with a quite different form of society that socialists had now to concern themselves.[33] The writings of Professor Harold Laski now sounded 'like an echo from another world'.[34] Other socialists found themselves unable to accept Crosland's optimistic assessment of the transformation in capitalism. It was a bad system even if it could be regulated to avoid high unemployment. Not all socialists were even of the view that full employment could be guaranteed indefinitely. Writing in the year after the publication of *The Future of Socialism*, G. D. H. Cole, the ageing Oxford socialist who had led many Oxford undergraduates to socialism, felt that another capitalist recession could not be ruled out. In any case, as Cole put it, capitalism 'encourages false values and forces its victims into ignoble ways of living . . .'.[35]

ASSUMING A HIGH RATE OF GROWTH

Among the characteristics of capitalism that socialists had never liked was its aggressive individualism. Crosland had an aesthetic distaste for aggressive individualism and this inspired his belief that it could no longer claim any social justification. 'There is no reason to believe that an acquisitive and individualistic pattern of behaviour is an essential condition of rapid growth, which on the contrary appears to be consistent with many different kinds of social relations and economic institutions.' He points out that rapid rates of growth were, at the time of writing, being achieved in countries such as Russia, Germany, Britain and America, with diverse institutions, motives, national characters, patterns of ownership and degrees of equality. Thus high growth could be obtained under a variety of circumstances.[36] There was now probably no country in the world where competition was less aggressive than in Britain, or individual exertion more suspect. To a large extent, security had replaced competition as the guiding rule of economic conduct.[37] Gaitskell believed that there was no longer 'the possibility of large fortunes being made by private individuals as a result of luck or shrewd judgement'.[38] As individual effort made little contribution to economic growth, it was only right that its fruits should be widely distributed without excessive regard for incentives. According to this philosophy, the economy needed managers rather than entrepreneurs, managers who were cogs rather than entrepreneurs who were initiators. Crosland warned that the antithesis of competition might be not co-operation, but economic stagnation.[39] Yet he expected that Britain would enjoy a high rate of growth in the absence of aggressive competition. He was in error in his belief that a high rate of growth was at the time being achieved by Britain and also, indeed, by Russia. It was true that Britain was enjoying a higher rate of growth than previously in its history. But it was lagging, not just in individual exertion but in rate of growth, behind continental western Europe.

Crosland assumed a high rate of growth. He assumed it even without socialism, a dramatic break from Durbin. It was a lazy assumption. His reasons for the assumption were far less substantial than he imagined. It was a matter of attitudes. The business community had accepted that prosperity was here to stay, not only because full employment would be maintained, but also because Britain had entered a period of rapid growth in personal incomes and consumption. 'This too little noticed revolution in business psychology is the most important economic event of our generation; and its implications for the rate of capital formation are too obvious to need underlining.' Business opinion had been joined by other opinion in assuming a high rate of growth. City opinion, weekly journals, economists and even less exalted publicists were all preaching to industry that it had a patriotic duty to invest, and praised it when it did so. It was a mistake to assume that a social consensus of this kind had no influence on economic decisions. Moreover there was no evidence yet to suggest that a mixed economy could not be run at a high level of employment and a healthy rate of growth, without a progressive enrichment of the shareholder at the expense of the rest of the community.[40] Growth without benefit to the shareholder was evidently superior to growth with benefit to the shareholder. But Crosland had no contribution of his own to make to the problem of growth. Growth was something that would just happen. It was in the system. It could be assumed. It was almost as though it did not require the intervention or activity of individuals. He concluded that, if one had to guess about the next decade, it seemed more likely that in a democratic, semi-egalitarian, full-employment economy of the post-war British type, investment would remain buoyant, while on the other side the tendency would be towards high consumption and inadequate savings.[41]

Crosland's social policy proposals depend explicitly on a high rate of growth. He lists the reasons for needing higher growth: more investment in underdeveloped countries; relief of hardship and distress at home; the backlog of social investment; higher personal consumption; the precarious situation of the balance of payments; and the need for 'a larger export surplus'. He concluded that a rapid rate of growth, at least for the next decade, so far from being inconsistent with socialist ideals, was a precondition of their attainment.[42] In other words the success of what everyone else except Crosland would continue to call capitalism is the precondition of socialism. But if capitalism, or whatever it was convenient to call it, was to be so successful, would the incentives to move on to socialism be strong enough to persuade a sceptical electorate? Crosland's arguments for a higher rate of growth were impeccable. Yet he assumed far too readily that his egalitarian policy proposals were consistent with it. What was to happen if it was not achieved? When he was forced to admit that he had been too optimistic about growth, he did not conclude that the whole basis of *The Future of Socialism* had been undermined.

The gyrations in Crosland's economic forecasts over the period 1950 to 1956 demonstrate the superficiality of his economic thinking. His *New Fabian* essay showed complacency in the wake of the success of the 1949 devaluation. *Britain's Economic Problem* reflected the balance of payments crisis following the rise in raw-material prices after the outbreak of the Korean war. All is gloom and the analysis leads to a most improbable imperial prospectus. By the time of *The Future of Socialism*, the terms of trade have turned generously in Britain's favour and we are back to complacency. Later, in *The Conservative Enemy*, Crosland had to admit that he had been too optimistic about Britain's rate of growth. Keynes declared that, when the facts changed, he changed his opinions. Crosland's conversions hither and thither were too rapid to convey any confidence in his understanding. His varying analyses provided too flimsy a basis for a successful revision of socialism or for an appreciation of capitalism.

EQUALITY

For Crosland, socialism is about equality. Underlying socialism must be a passionate belief in liberty and democracy.[43] But it is equality that is the distinguishing characteristic of socialism. For Crosland, the inequalities in society are an offence against social justice. Those privileged to have been born with talent or wealth have greater opportunities than the unprivileged and the poor. Crosland is preoccupied by the resentments in society due to the lack of equality. The path upwards from poverty may have been smoothed and widened over the past decades but justification for the resentments remained because there was not yet the degree of equality that there should be. The object of socialism, in the Crosland canon, is to reduce envy and the justification for envy. Envy is inimical to the quality of society. Again and again he recurs to what will cause envy, whether it be a better start in life, a better education, a better car or a better TV set. As the reduction of envy is the object, Crosland concentrates on those sources of envy that are visible. He knows he cannot eliminate envy, but envy is bad, and the way to reduce it is to reduce the visible provocations to it.[44] He is critical of the inheritance of great wealth. It is unjust because it does not derive from work, it is manifestly unequal, and it inspires envy. Nor did the wealthy have much to be said for them except that they were wealthy. 'Britain can perhaps claim in recent times to have had one of the most illiterate wealthy classes in history.'[45]

Inequalities in earned incomes could be unjust if qualification for them derived from access to an education, for example in public schools, not generally open because of cost.[46] They can be unjust if they seem to single out for huge reward the single quality of economic ability when there are so many other admirable human attributes.[47] 'It is the injustice of isolating, as a basis for extreme inequality, certain selected [traits] out of the multiple strands that go to make up the human personality, which constitutes the fundamental ethical case against any élite or aristocracy.'[48] Why, he demands, should society select for special reward intelligence rather than 'saintliness, generosity, compassion, humour, beauty, assiduity, continence or artistic ability'?[49] He then seems to shudder at his own impracticality. He recognizes that there are practical reasons for rewarding outstanding ability generously. It would be folly not to offer such rewards as would attract ability into the service of the community. But, with that admission made, he falls back on his socialist principles to insist that if large differential privileges create a distinct elite, privately educated and socially select, it is nothing other than an unpleasant concession to economic efficiency, and not intrinsically just.[50]

He leaves the reader uncertain whether, despite its injustice, he himself would be prepared to make this unpleasant concession. He has to find a balance between his new socialism and the economic needs of society. He demands greater equality. But he concedes the need for incentives because otherwise society will stagnate or, at least, the rate of growth will be insufficient. Thus he strives to balance the objective of equality against the need for incentives. Unfortunately it is very difficult to determine where this point of balance lies. There is no scientific method. It is a matter of political judgement. Crosland was rather optimistic in judging that the point lay far to the left where he, as a socialist, would have liked to find it. The intention of Labour policies was to benefit the poorer sections of society. If growth is encumbered by a serious attack on incentives, the poor would suffer along with everyone else. The conundrums of equality are numberless. In so far as Crosland is agitating for greater equality of opportunity open to ability irrespective of class origins, he is, as he is aware, seeking to set free the very qualities that may create a more unequal society through the successful aspirations of the able.[51] At one point he appears to consider a desperate appeal to patriotism. He expresses distaste for 'the greed of the richer classes, who claim they must have higher monetary rewards and reduced taxation as an incentive to greater effort, patriotism being evidently not enough'.[52] Patriotism may indeed help to persuade the investor to remain in the country of his birth and invest in the country of his birth. But it is probable that the patriotism will have to be topped up with tangible rewards.

He did not expect too much from redistribution of income. Its effects in increasing economic satisfaction would now be small. It would make little difference to the standard of living of the masses. To make the rich less rich would not make the poor significantly less poor. If all surtax incomes were distributed among the working class, the latter would gain by at most a few shillings a week per head. The main prop of traditional egalitarianism had been knocked away by its own success.[53] Nevertheless the case for redistribution could still rest firmly 'on certain value or ethical judgments of a non-economic character: on a belief that more equality, even though carrying few implications for the sum of economic satisfaction, would yet conduce to a "better" society'. This was for three reasons, relating respectively to the diminution of social antagonism, to social justice and to the avoidance of social waste.[54] But, if redistribution was now a weakened instrument, other routes should be found to greater equality. In order to achieve greater equality in old age, he proposed a universal compulsory superannuation scheme to be superimposed on the existing national insurance scheme.[55] A prime object of socialist policy would be conversion to a comprehensive system of education, the purpose of which was greater equality. Comprehensive education, he asserts, is much more important than the 'nationalisation of meat-procuring or even chemicals'.[56] Few socialists would wish to deny him his personal sense of priority. But the traditional socialist would demand *both* comprehensive education *and* the nationalization of meat-procuring and chemicals.

Crosland's book is full of good intentions towards the disadvantaged of society, but it is not at all clear why good intentions should be identified with socialism. He was criticized by traditional socialists because they saw perfectly well where his good intentions were leading, and they were right. They observed that even on the subject of equality, the key element in his reinvention of socialism, he was unable to define how much equality there should be. He was prepared only to say that large egalitarian changes were needed in the educational system, the distribution of property and the distribution of resources in times of need, and perhaps some, but certainly a smaller, change in respect of incomes from work. It was not sensible, he protested, to ask how much equality. 'We can describe the direction of advance, and even discern the immediate landscape ahead; but the ultimate objective lies wrapped in complete uncertainty.'[57]

Traditional socialists would feel that Crosland was attempting to cheat them of nationalization by emphasizing the greater importance of comprehensive education. They would be confirmed in this judgement when they found Crosland temporizing even about comprehensive education. Ideally, he notes, we would not start from here. He assures his readers that, if he had been presented with a *tabula rasa*, he would strongly favour a non-segregated, comprehensive system of schools, with other schools, not indeed abolished, but existing merely as an oblique appendage to the national system.[58] But the tablet is only too congested. He laments that many difficulties stand in the way, including the reluctance of local authorities to move aggressively. Even within the state sector there could be no question of suddenly closing down the grammar schools and converting the secondary moderns into comprehensive schools.[59] He therefore moderates his expectations. A Labour government should explicitly state a preference for the comprehensive principle, and then should actively encourage local authorities to be more audacious.[60] If that happens, 'Then, very slowly, Britain may cease to be the most class-ridden country in the world.'[61] As Secretary of State for Education, Crosland was, in 1965, to issue circular 10/65 requesting local authorities to draw up plans for comprehensive schools. The abolition of the state grammar schools became a Crosland crusade in the name of equality and, as a crusade, if not always educationally, it had considerable success not just under Crosland but under Margaret Thatcher as Secretary of State in the Heath government. Crosland, as Secretary of State, was less energetic in pursuing the public schools in the interests of equality.

Crosland frequently turns to the USA for examples of the kind of equality he is seeking. While he is far from adopting American society whole, or the policies of its government, he does find there considerable merit. Class distinctions are less pervasive and less hereditary, social attitudes less class conscious, the atmosphere more natural and unrestrained, the social ladder as a whole much shorter. There is less social envy and resentment, and social equality is greater.[62] Yet it had all been done in the most rabidly capitalist society in the world.

TESTING SOCIALIST METHODOLOGY

The primacy Crosland gave to equality was not in itself original. The originality lay in the implications that he drew from it. He tested the aspirations embodied in traditional socialism against the criterion of current relevance. He concluded that only two had current relevance, a concern for social welfare and the desire for an equal and classless society.[63] Therefore the traditional instruments of socialist policy must themselves be tested against the further criterion, what contribution did they make to the achievement of social welfare and greater equality. No aspect of socialist policy, including nationalization, must escape that test. That test would establish that the prime socialist instruments, the instruments available to achieve greater equality, were taxation and public expenditure, not nationalization and planning. Crosland's socialism required that much more use should be made of these prime socialist instruments. Taxation and social services were already redistributing income in the right direction. But, by socialist standards, much more needed to be done, on grounds of justice as well as of welfare, to raise the real incomes of the old, the sick and those with young families, relative to the rest of the population.[64]

PLANNING

We have seen that the two key requirements on anyone who wished to retain a claim to the title of socialist was that they should find room in their vision for planning and nationalization. For both, Crosland finds greater room that is generally remembered, though he presents them rather differently than would the traditional socialist. As a self-described revisionist, Crosland might differ from an old socialist like G.D.H. Cole, who, until the end, questioned whether Keynesianism without planning could provide a reliable guarantee of full employment and who took a somewhat totalitarian attitude to the market. But planning remains central to Crosland's socialism. He begins by relegating planning to a lower priority than it had been intended to enjoy under Attlee.[65] He goes so far as to draw attention to 'our limited knowledge of how the economic system works, and . . . the number and heterogeneity of the variables to be taken into account'.[66] He learns from experience under Attlee in identifying the inefficiencies of planning. He discovers that opinion on planning has changed due partly to the easing of the world economic conjuncture and partly to the discovery that the American economy had not justified the worst fears expressed about it after the war. But the main disincentive to confidence in planning is revealed as a general disillusionment with the whole notion of trying to control short-term production decisions from Whitehall through a detailed budget of production.[67]

However, from this point on, he begins to rebuild the case for planning. The failure of planning in the past had been essentially *political*. It had reflected the difficulty of planning in a democratic society. What was now wanted was 'political vigour and willpower, and a readiness to take unpopular decisions'.[68] He appears to support the argument of those who point to the price mechanism as the best way of allocating resources.[69] Nevertheless, he concludes, interference with the price mechanism is sometimes justified.[70] Few serious economists now believed that a free price mechanism would lead in practice to the maximization of economic welfare.[71] Thus the issue was not whether, but how much and for what purpose, to plan.[72]

Having engaged in a somewhat precarious balancing act, he now begins to pile on to planning responsibilities quite beyond its capacity to bear. He requires it to reconcile over-full employment with a sustainable foreign balance, with the defeat of inflation, and with progress to greater social equality.

The main objectives of planning ... are ... a steadily rising level of investment, and a sufficient volume of savings and risk-capital to match it; a volume of home demand which does not pre-empt goods away from export; a situation in the labour market which does not give rise to a wage-price spiral; and an increase in the proportion of the national income devoted to social expenditure – all these to be achieved against a background of growing social equality.[73]

Again:

it must be a government responsibility to ensure, where necessary by nationalisation, that the industrial base, characteristically composed of industries such as [steel], expands fast enough to support the expected rise in total output. But intervention need not be confined to the basic industries. The government should stand ready, by the use of subsidies, guarantees, bulk purchases, or any other method, to shoulder part or all of the risk in any case where it is clear that expansion is required but where private capital will not venture alone to undertake it.[74]

He points to industries where this has been done: aircraft, films, sulphur, hydraulic presses, titanium. Other examples where intervention would often be desirable are where private and social costs diverge and in managing the location of industry, economy in the use of coal, the balance of payments, and the avoidance of pollution.[75] He concludes that only if the planning role was performed successfully could Britain extricate itself from the intolerable situation in which the economy lurched from one inflationary crisis to another, each met by haphazard and damaging panic measures.[76] Planning, which appeared at one stage to be on the point of disappearing from Crosland's socialism, has re-emerged equipped with an arsenal of ambition but with no indication of how it is to achieve its great objectives. Willpower apparently is to do it all, despite limited knowledge of how the economic system works and the number and heterogeneity of the variables to be taken into account.

NATIONALIZATION

This brings Crosland to consider the role of nationalization. Crosland quotes John Strachey presenting the traditional argument for nationalization: 'We [nationalize] in order to extinguish the great *unearned incomes* which are to-day derived, not from anything that those who draw them do, but from what they own ... The real purpose of socialization is to secure the proper distribution of the net national product among those who create it.'[77] Crosland rejects this argument for nationalization.[78] He calculates the actual loss to previous owners of nationalized industries after taking account of compensation. It was certainly infinitesimal as compared with the effects of high taxation.[79] He concedes that it is certainly true that future nationalization of more profitable industries might have a greater redistributional effect. However, it would be possible to limit the net rewards to shareholders by methods other than nationalization.[80] He comments that the redistributional argument for nationalization implied that each Labour programme had to contain its quota of future state monopolies. But such a policy would be both wrong and impracticable. Impracticable because the electorate would be rather intolerant towards it; wrong because productive efficiency could well suffer.[81]

There are, in the Crosland canon, many better ways in which the ratio of new public to private savings could be increased: budget surpluses; heavy taxation of company profits; allowing nationalized industries to accumulate a surplus.[82] All these would be alternatives to nationalization, which was no longer the one and only large-scale method of redistributing the benefits of economic growth.[83] With a dismissiveness characteristic of his style but which did not make him much loved by his critics within the Labour party, he comments that socialism, whether viewed in social or ethical or economic terms, would not be brought much nearer by nationalizing the aircraft industry.[84] Moreover the Labour party's programme for further nationalization had hardly, in recent years, been coherent. He mocks the ambivalence of the Labour election programmes at the previous three elections. There had been one list of candidates in 1950, none at all, he says, in 1951, and a different list again in 1955.[85] His conclusion is that the ownership of the means of production has ceased to be the key factor which imparts to a society its essential character. Either collectivism or private ownership was consistent with 'widely varying degrees' of liberty, democracy, equality, exploitation, class-feeling, planning, workers' control and economic prosperity.[86]

Crosland concedes that there had been a host of unexpected problems with nationalization. There had been hopes that nationalization would rapidly and significantly improve labour relations.[87] This hope had been disappointed. There was the problem of control. He notes, wryly, that post-war experience demonstrates that whereas private industry can be subjected to a close degree of government control, nationalized industries sometimes behaved in a rather independent fashion, and proved not altogether easy to plan.[88] While control over the private sector had exceeded expectations, control over the public sector had fallen short of expectations.[89] This, however, was once again a question of political will. There was no insuperable *economic* difficulty about the government imposing its will, provided it had one, on either public or private industry.[90] However, Ministerial control of nationalized industries might be exercised for bad reasons. Nationalized industries could become subservient to Ministerial policy objectives irrelevant to their own future.[91] It could hardly be denied, he concludes, that Morrisonian nationalization, despite considerable achievements, no longer seemed the panacea that it once did. Experience certainly would not justify a further proliferation of state monopolies.[92]

There was also the problem that the highly competitive and export-oriented manufacturing industries, which might now be considered for nationalization, were very different in character, and in the problems they presented, from the industries nationalized under Attlee. Often they produced branded goods, and faced demand curves at once volatile and strictly indeterminate.[93] The implication was that nationalization might not work successfully in such industries. Crosland also begins to preach the virtues of competition. Monopoly, even when it was public, had drawbacks. Competition had greater advantages than pre-war socialists had realized.[94]

It might be thought after all this that nationalization would be stripped out of the future being painted by Crosland. In fact, hardly is it out than it is creeping back into the picture. In the end, Crosland finds justification for nationalization in two arguments, equality and efficiency. The ratio of public to private property needed to be increased in order to ensure that more of the gains from owning property accrued in public, and fewer in private, hands. Nationalization had not thus far even been permitted to fulfil the objective of adding to public savings relative to private savings. Quite a different pricing policy would have been required to achieve that objective. This again would require political will and encouragement to nationalized industries to make a profit.[95] When he comes to consider the forms of public ownership which would add to efficiency, his preference is for competitive public enterprise.[96] Economists and others were thrashing around for ways of improving the performance of the British economy and competitive public enterprise was one of the fashionable ideas that had skipped out of the bag. As we have seen, the best opportunity to create competitive public enterprise had been lost under Attlee. Crosland suggests various ways of creating competitive public enterprise in the future. There could, for example, be a government investment corporation. Nationalized industries could take the task upon themselves. So could the Co-operative Movement and local authorities. It might be undertaken even by the trade unions. Competitive public enterprise was to be envisaged 'at least as much in terms of . . . more variegated forms of social owner-ship, as of ownership by Whitehall'.[97]

He accepts that the competitive public enterprise must not be at an advantage as compared with the private sector. Competition between public and private firms should be, and should be seen to be, scrupu-lously fair. This meant that new capital should not be supplied on tap from the Treasury at gilt-edged rates, as it had been to some of the nationalized industries. Private firms must borrow from the market. The state concerns should borrow from a public finance body which charged full market rates, and applied normal commercial conditions.[98] Nevertheless, and rather worrying to competitors in the private sector, where a number of firms in the same industry might be taken over by the state to operate as a competitive public enterprise, there would be need for a 'public holding company . . . with strong powers of control . . .'.[99]

Was competitive public enterprise socialism? Not by the standards of the Crosland revised definition because it had nothing to do with equality, only with efficiency, which was desirable but not specifically socialist. It could not, for example, be imagined that competitive public enterprise would have any significant effect in increasing the ratio of public to private property. Not by the standards of the old faith because that was about co-operation, not competition. Competition was not socialist and was, by definition, wasteful. Parts of the industry into which the competitive public enterprise was injected would remain in private hands. The left were not interested in using the powers and resources of the state to make capitalism more efficient. They condemned such ideas as 'state capitalism', and regarded them as leading away from socialism rather than towards it. If competitive public enterprise was anything, it was a device for encouraging economic growth. Neverthe-less, though such ideas were rejected with contumely on the left, they would discover in the end that they represented all that was left of socialism. In the end, they were ready to be content because the competi-tive enterprises would be in public ownership, and therefore it was possible to feel that socialism would have touched them with its magic wand even if they were not inspired with the undiluted faith. In the retreat from socialism, a new habit developed encouraged by the scarcity of anything indubitably socialist. Because socialism involved state intervention, any state intervention came to be regarded as socialism. In the years to come, Labour governments would claim to be socialist because they believed in state intervention. But state intervention was no more socialism than was Crosland's competitive public enterprise.

Competitive public enterprise is not the only form of nationalization included in the Crosland manifesto. For example, he suggests that machine tools might be a candidate for nationalization as one industry.[100] Thus there could still be occasional examples where state monopoly would provide the right answer. The extent and complexity of Crosland's ideas for nationalization become clear as he proliferates suggestions as to the kind of institution that might be created. He suggests a new public corporation, responsible for all the state companies, bearing the same relation to Parliament as the existing public boards, but acting otherwise as a rather passive holding company with the bias always towards the maximum of independence, and the minimum of central interference.[101] He revives the hoary idea of general enabling legislation giving the government power to acquire existing or establish new industrial enterprises.[102] He concludes that the ideal approach would be to establish a state investment trust. It would be provided with public funds but would operate independently of the government, with instructions to make a profit by buying, establishing or selling productive concerns. This, according to Crosland, would avoid both the element of compulsion and the charge of non-commercial motives.[103] In the early 1970s, extravagant proposals were brought forward within the Labour party for a vast extension of public ownership by means of a state holding company. Crosland, who fought against them, was offended to be told that the inspiration for these proposals lay in *The Future of Socialism*.[104] Yet the reproof does not appear to lack foundation.[105]

And thus, finally, he brings to us a sketch of how the question of ownership fits into his vision of a socialist society.

> [T]he ideal (or at least my ideal) is a society in which ownership is thoroughly mixed-up – a society with a diverse, diffused, pluralist, and heterogeneous pattern of ownership, with the State, the nationalised industries, the Co-operatives, the Unions, Government financial institutions, pension funds, foundations, and millions of private families all participating. Since this is still a long way off, we need heavy taxation to limit profits and dividends ... We no doubt want more nationalisation

than we now have. But I at least do not want a steadily extending chain of State monopolies, believing this to be bad for liberty, and wholly irrelevant to socialism as defined in this book.[106]

What share the state would eventually have in this hodgepodge of distinct forms of ownership was left as undefined as the intended extent of equality.

Crosland was attempting to wrench the definition of socialism out of the hands of traditional socialists. Traditional socialists, of the right as well as of the left, were unlikely to be impressed by his arguments against nationalization. Without nationalization, where would be the radical reorganization of society which socialists had promised before the war? Where would be that socialism that was distinct from capitalism, not simply a humanization of it? Nationalization might or might not help to bring greater equality. What was certain was that private ownership of the means of production conferred great power on the owners or managers. It was power over employees and power over investment. Whether the owners exercised their power directly or through managers was, for the traditional socialist, a matter of indifference. Private power was unacceptable. For traditional socialists, socialism was a new form of social organization of which nationalization was a fundamental characteristic. Beyond that it was an expression of one of the most deeply felt of socialist objectives, that production must be for use, not for profit. The left would not accept that it was a sufficient reply that the power of the capitalists was these days limited in many ways and particularly by the ascendancy of the trade unions. The workers could not make take-over bids for the property of their employers. Therefore the state must do it for them. Nationalization was an instrument of class struggle.

Followers of Gaitskell and Crosland alleged that Clause Four, which appeared to commit the Party to wholesale nationalization, confused ends with means. Nationalization, they said, was a means, and not necessarily the most important means, to a socialist society. Contrary to Dalton, it was not in itself the criterion of a socialist society. But the argument depended on the definition of socialism. At the Labour Party Conference after the defeat in the 1955 General Election, and shortly before he was elected leader, Gaitskell made an emotional declaration as to why he was a socialist in which he had listed the ideals of socialism. He quoted Clause Four to distinguish the aim 'To secure for the workers ... the full fruits of their industry' from the means which was 'the common ownership of the means of production'. He then ended by saying, 'These to me are the Socialist ideals. Nationalisation . . . is a vital means but it is only one of the means by which we can achieve these objects.'[107] The assertion that nationalization was a means and not an end started the Labour party on a long process of rethinking that would extend beyond Gaitskell and beyond Crosland. From this position it moved on through a succession of revisions to the conclusion for which the electorate was clearly waiting. Nationalization, it eventually appeared, was not only not the most important means. It was hardly a means at all as the objectives could be reached quite otherwise. This movement away from nationalization was abhorrent to the left and worried even right-wingers who knew the unpopularity of nationalization but nevertheless were concerned that socialism was disappearing from the agenda.

THE END OF ECONOMIC POLICY?

Crosland was convinced that the economic problem, if not yet solved, would be solved in the course of the next decade or at most two. He wrote as though the age of abundance was almost upon us. If the present rate of economic growth continued, material want and poverty and deprivation would gradually cease to be a problem.[108] Yes, there was still a danger of inflation, there was still a balance of payments problem and, of course, there was the distribution of wealth and income to be corrected. But such problems could be solved by planning, given willpower on the part of a Labour government. They were problems for the moment, not for the longer term. A decade or so hence, we would be turning to other problems, a more cultured life, a better environment, and we could leave the economic problem, the importance of which would decline, to those whose unaccountable passions inclined them to economic controversy. This was a hope which Keynes in his time had shared, though perhaps his timescale was longer. But, contrary to their hopes, serious economic problems remain, there is still the problem of poverty and deprivation, and economists are no more successful than hitherto in solving them. Crosland's optimism was escapist. It was also a relief. It would have required much ingenuity to demonstrate that an economy suffering growing pains in the form of inflation and balance of payments deficits could carry also the burden of vastly greater equality.[109] It was easier to conclude that the economic problem would disappear within Crosland's own lifetime and was therefore not important enough to demand his attention. He succumbed to the temptation, common among politicians and political philosophers at times of apparent economic stability, to turn from the economic problem, with its distasteful vulgarity and intellectual complexity, to the far more attractive problems of how to reorganize society and redistribute its product. Quite a short period of stability can be enough to persuade that as things are, so they will always be. Crosland was exploiting the apparent opportunity created by a period of economic growth to find a third way between traditional socialism on the one hand and *laissez-faire* on the other. He was always unfortunate in his publication dates. *Britain's Economic Problem* was published just as the terms of trade turned in favour of the developed world. *The Future of Socialism* was published just as the easy hopes of a stable economic future were to be confounded.

There was something curiously anti-intellectual in Crosland's easy assumption that the capitalist system, whatever it should now be called, would yield the growth necessary for his social engineering. He assumed, in direct contradiction of Durbin, that the reforms which had taken place in capitalism were consistent with the rate of growth that he required for his redistributional policies. Keynes had become the all-provider and the ultimate guarantor. He had given full employment to socialists, and growth would follow as the answer to all the practical problems implicit in socialism of the Crosland school. It was always odd that Crosland should imagine that his egalitarian ambitions for society were consistent with fast economic growth. He was not a man who mixed with industrialists or entrepreneurs except perhaps those who had held posts in government service during the war. Perhaps he would have thought a little better of rapacity and aggression if he had found a more socialist description for these abominable characteristics. Keynes, who, whatever his other faults, knew both what made the world go round and how to obfuscate, wrote of animal spirits rather than of greed. Crosland, however, was none too fond even of animal spirits in the economic sphere. He was prepared confidently to deny the need either for greed and aggression or for animal spirits. He assumed that he could reap the benefits of growth for the purpose of moulding his version of socialism. But he did not consider it necessary to bother his head in order to make any policy contribution to the achievement of growth. He foresaw that inflation would be a problem, but he gravely underestimated how much of a problem it would be and how it would undermine the growth for which he hoped. These were not matters to which he found it necessary to give attention. He preferred to take economic growth for granted.

THE INTERNATIONAL DIMENSION

There remained a problem that *The Future of Socialism* did not even address. It ignored the international dimension. In this it was typical of British socialist writings. Free international trade and the free movement of capital were always inconsistent with socialism, even Crosland's revised socialism. Attlee wrote in his memoirs, 'We realised that the application of socialist principles in a country such as Britain with a peculiar economic structure based on international trade required great flexibility.'[110] Thus Attlee had learnt something from his experience of government which yet seemed to escape Crosland. There is in Attlee's comment some recognition that socialism and international trade do not mix and that socialism is a philosophy for a closed economy. But it was typical of British socialists that they should imagine that there was something 'peculiar' about an economic system based on international trade. In one sense, Crosland's failure to reconcile his socialism with the influences from the world outside is forgivable. The reconciliation would have been impossible to achieve. For a socialist it was another problem better forgotten. Communist countries dealt with the problem of international trade by regulating it through state machinery. Under the Attlee government there were many controls on international trade which continued into the early years of the Tory governments that followed. But international trade was getting freer. From January 1955, a year before the publication of *The Future of Socialism*, sterling had become virtually convertible. The trend towards the free movement of capital and freer international trade was accelerating. If the state leaves consumers free to make their own purchasing decisions, it cannot plan to any useful effect. If it permits the free movement of capital, egalitarianism of the Crosland variety faces formidable obstacles. If a country becomes part of a global economic community, it will acquire the colour of that global community with all those hateful characteristics of aggression and rapacity of which Crosland so strongly disapproved. It will acquire that colour or it will retreat once more into economic isolation with serious consequences for personal freedom and for growth.

ON THE MEANING OF SOCIALISM

Crosland claimed that what he proposed would amount to a considerable social revolution. He intended to be very radical and, indeed, his radicalism went far beyond anything that would in the end prove politically practicable for any future Labour government. Richard Crossman wrote to Crosland on 26 October 1956: 'Your proposals are in fact far more revolutionary in their effects than an electoral promise to nationalise ICI and most of engineering. If I was perverse, I would say that they are diabolically and cunningly left-wing and Nye [Bevan] should have been clever enough to think them up. But you put them forward as ways of ensuring a calm evolution towards higher living standards and more personal freedom.'[111] Crossman was too subtle. Crosland's radicalism would never reconcile those of his critics who felt deprived of their socialist agenda.

The concept of democratic socialism cannot be patented. There is no copyright in the word 'socialism'. Anyone can give the word whatever meaning he pleases. If Crosland was pleased to designate his views socialism, he could not be denied that right. Nevertheless, it is easy to see why traditionalists would insist that Crosland's argument missed the socialist point. He appeared to have no feeling for the motives that led to the demand for massive nationalization. His socialist critics would regard him as a lost soul and not one they were particularly concerned to mourn. John Strachey, by this time no longer a beacon of the left, reviewed *The Future of Socialism* in the *New Statesman* in October 1956. He argued that the 'social ownership of the decisive parts of the means of production is the only permanent basis for a Socialist, classless society'. He added that if socialists abandoned their commitment to public ownership, 'they will cease, in a very real sense, to be Socialists at all: they will subside into the role of well-intentioned, amiable, rootless, drifting social reformers'.[112] G. D. H. Cole emphasized the continuing importance, as a matter of principle not pragmatism, of the transfer of 'industrial ownership from private persons to the community . . . This will mean that all capitalist-owned business will tend to pass increasingly into public ownership . . .'[113] And in the dying cry of an old man who saw the youngsters he had taught choosing the wrong path, Cole expostulated, 'The need to allow conditions under which capitalist enterprise can be carried on successfully until it can be superseded by socialised enterprise must not be allowed to lessen Socialist zeal in the struggle to speed up the supersession of capitalism.'[114] But the zeal for socialism was visibly being sapped.

Crosland did not write *The Future of Socialism* with the object of proving that socialism had no future. But that may well have been his real achievement. In order to justify his claim that socialism had a future he was forced to give the word so general a definition that it became impossible to distinguish it from liberalism. It was equally open to others to decide that it was not socialism at all. To be a socialist under the Crosland definition simply meant having a kindly disposition to the rest of society, except perhaps the very rich. The state, rather than personal charity, was to be the principal instrument of the kindly disposition. When democratic socialism evaporated, there remained a package of good intentions which former socialists described as 'socialist values'. *The Future of Socialism* is an authoritative text on socialist values rather than on socialism. But it was an act of intellectual misappropriation. The socialist values cherished by Crosland were not the exclusive property of socialists except where they still incorporated ancient socialist prejudices such as a preference for the public sector over the private, for comprehensive education over grammar schools, and a readiness to make concessions to trade union pressures.

One influence of the book was to create a division on the right of the Labour party between pragmatists and ideologists. The pragmatic right-wingers were willing to adapt their politics to practical realities and the reactions of the electorate. They believed in politics rather than principle. Sometimes the pragmatic right had no defensible principles at all or at any rate none that had anything to do with socialism. Sometimes, as with Jenkins and his friends, it found new principles outside the Labour party, for example a devotion to European integration. The ideologists of the right were a small group among whom Crosland remained the leader and the inspiration. The group was far too small ever to carry Crosland near to the leadership of the Labour party. Its most notable other figure was Roy Hattersley, condemned to climax his political career as deputy leader rather than leader of the Labour party. The ideologists were even more inflexible and unrealistic than the left in their views. They were determined to prove their socialist credentials – by their own lights. But, while they still had political prospects of advancement, they always put loyalty to the Labour party ahead of any of their principles.

By 1956 it was perfectly clear that, if Labour ever came to power again, it would attempt to run a capitalist market economy. It might nationalize a bit for old time's sake or even to save a bankrupt industry from liquidation. But there would be nothing like the extensively nationalized, centrally controlled economy to which Durbin had looked forward in 1940. There would be attempts at socialist recidivism in the early 1970s and early 1980s, both vetoed by the electorate. But it proved impossible for the leaders of the Labour party to admit that socialism had flown, certainly not until the Policy Review of 1989 and, even then, the leaders found it necessary to continue using the language of socialism. In consequence, the Labour party's infidelity to its origins remained veiled from both the public and many of its members.

Crosland's attempt to change the accepted meaning of socialism was hopeless in the strict sense of the word. Socialism had long meant collective ownership and collective control. In attempting to rescue socialism from nationalization, except pragmatic nationalization, he was kicking at a door that would not open. To abandon principled nationalization was to abandon socialism.

TWENTIETH CENTURY SOCIALISM – A THIRD WAY

In 1956 there appeared a book by Socialist Union entitled *Twentieth Century Socialism*. This was not a minor publishing event. The book sold 32,000 copies. Socialist Union, which existed from 1951 to 1959, consisted of a group of well-meaning middle-class intellectuals whose socialism was essentially ethical and who had become close to Hugh Gaitskell. Among its members were many immigrants and, at first, Socialist Union opposed German rearmament. The two most prominent members were Rita Hinden, of South African origin, formerly of the Fabian Colonial Bureau, and Allen Flanders, an academic expert on industrial relations. Socialist Union produced a journal *Socialist Commentary*, edited by Rita Hinden, which often opened its columns to Gaitskell and his close associates, and which survived the disappearance of Socialist Union itself. Rita Hinden and Allen Flanders were the rapporteurs for *Twentieth Century Socialism* but it was the outcome of numerous discussions within the group. They define their task as finding a third way between the doctrinaires, who still believe that capitalism is on the point of collapse, and the empiricists, for whom socialism is nothing more than social engineering.[115] It was not indeed a book that was likely to summon the working masses to fight for their rights, although it does end with a peroration which would certainly have stirred the blood if uttered by Aneurin Bevan in a large hall.[116] The book was in many respects in line with *The Future of Socialism*. Equality was the core of socialism.

By this time 'ethical socialism' had become the recourse of those who had abandoned any hope of material benefits from socialism. For that purpose the material world had to be disparaged as compared with the world of the spirit. The book was not short of insights into the nature of socialism. The rapporteurs were quite clear that their ideal society would have to be isolated from the rest of the world by controls on trade and currency exchanges.[117] Even if in many respects unrealistic, the book was unequivocally honest. Yet, in at least one respect, Socialist Union went much further than *The Future of Socialism* in asserting the dangers of a Clause Four nationalization programme. A new, and important, anxiety was emerging in socialist quarters. Certainly 'We need more public expenditure, more public ownership, more public enterprise.'[118] Nevertheless, *Twentieth Century Socialism* bravely insisted that private ownership was essential to political liberty. The power of private owners could undoubtedly be abused. 'Yet, looking at the coin from the other side, private ownership can ... be seen as a condition of freedom.'[119] It was an argument that Crosland would later adopt in *The Conservative Enemy*. *Twentieth Century Socialism*, in fact, launched a far more fundamental attack on wholesale nationalization than did *The Future of Socialism*. 'The reason why a socialist economy requires a private sector is because socialists place a value on individual freedom.'[120] While advocating an extension of nationalization, they feared a nationalized economy. 'Experience has shown that the power of ownership, even in public hands, may still be dangerous. It is still open to abuse and the individual has still to assert his rights in face of it. Ways have to be found to control the powers of ownership, whether they are privately or publicly held.'[121] Public ownership could then only be defended in those few cases where there were arguments on grounds of efficiency, for which after Attlee there was not much evidence, or on the ground that having created a mixed economy (following Attlee's nationalizations), it was too much bother to undo it.

It was a book written with love, and with love of socialism as they understood it. The authors can hardly, therefore, have been delighted with the reaction of their friend Hugh Gaitskell. He found the book 'school-marmish in its flavour. It suggests the refeened middle-class lady holding her nose against the vulgarity that she sees around her.'

He disliked, for example, their insistence on elevating the quality of work rather than the quantity of its output. It seemed to him a priggish attack on affluence.[122] He felt constrained to write, 'People do want a higher standard of living, and I do not see why we should not accept this. Certainly if we fail to accept it there is precious little chance of getting ourselves accepted by the electorate.'[123] The ethical spirit of socialism was obviously unappealing to Gaitskell, even though its machinery – nationalization and planning – might still be useful.

What, perhaps above all, irritated Gaitskell was the book's fundamental pessimism. 'Because socialism has become identified exclusively with common ownership, loss of faith in common ownership as the great panacea often means loss of faith in socialism itself.'[124] As though that were not enough, the book advisedly declared that many lifelong socialists 'doubt whether the will for socialism still exists.'[125] If anyone was looking in *Twentieth Century Socialism* for inspiration, they would be disappointed. Yet combined with its 'school-marmish' idealism was a practical sense of the obstacles to socialism that should have conveyed a harsh warning to enthusiasts.

CONCLUSION

Crosland himself, though a professional economist, had priorities greater than the economic. He was as passionate about beauty, culture, architecture, personal freedom, fun, football, as about the redistribution of wealth. He could not claim his private passions to be particularly socialist but, for him, one reason for being a socialist was that Labour MPs were more likely to share them than Conservative MPs. The same preference for Labour over Conservative MPs was justified by his wish to abolish the death penalty.[126] In what is probably the best-known sentence in *The Future of Socialism*, he wrote, in an implicit attack on the now deceased Webbs: 'Total abstinence and a good filing-system are not now the right sign-posts to the socialist Utopia: or at least, if they are, some of us will fall by the wayside.'[127] The last sentence of *The Future of Socialism* reads: 'We do not want to enter the age of abundance, only to find that we have lost the values which might teach us how to enjoy it.'[128] In his mind, it was clearly a necessary, even urgent, warning. But the Webbs would have had their own doubts about Crosland's more cheerful socialism and, as socialists, they would have had some reason.

HUNGARY

In 1956, the Soviet army invaded Hungary. For many who had remained loyal to the British Communist party despite many provocations, this was the last straw. Many of the intellectuals among them, though abandoning Soviet communism, remained faithful to Marxism in one form or another. They were no more satisfied with capitalism than they had ever been. They gathered themselves together in groups, mainly academic, and they published prolifically. They were known as the new left. But this was not a political movement. Nor did it have political influence. Nor was it likely to survive other than as a forum for critics of capitalism who could find no other home. Capitalism remained their target and they had much to say about it of which it was as well to be reminded in an age when it was enjoying so total a triumph over socialism. Their criticisms could even be morally uplifting, but they did not point to any practical new course for mankind. They were critical of the values of modern society and they hoped for a transition to the democratic socialism in which they had always really believed. But they had no more idea how that transition was to be achieved than any other of those who had, in the past, striven for democratic socialism. Indeed the popular apathy that they condemned as one of the consequences of capitalism had become one of its most effective defences. Democratic socialism remained a mirage. But the congregation of the new left needed capitalism to give purpose to their lives. They were unlikely to be deprived. Capitalism might be a bad system but it was still undaunted, if only because it was better than any alternative system so far devised by the mind of man.

ELEVEN

Two leaders

A RARE CHOICE

Attlee resigned in December 1955, seven months after Labour's defeat in the General Election of May 1955. Labour thus had its first real opportunity for twenty years to select a new leader. The choice available did not give Attlee much satisfaction. There was no credible candidate from the centre-left. Morrison he had never liked and never thought suitable. He hoped that he would be considered too old. Morrison had never discovered how to avoid argument by silence, a skill in which Attlee excelled. That was also a problem with the younger generation. They had views, and views sparked controversy. Gaitskell was too right wing and might divide the Party. Attlee claimed that he had hoped that Bevan would follow him but he was forced to concede that Bevan had ruled himself out by his tumultuous behaviour. On the other hand, if Attlee had really wanted Bevan to succeed, he should have taken the risk in 1950 and appointed him Chancellor of the Exchequer. If he did not now much like the idea of Gaitskell, he would have to console himself with the thought that at least it was not Morrison. He could only hope that, if elected, Gaitskell would be as sensitive to the needs of Party unity as anyone coming from the left of centre.

Bevan could claim to be the natural successor. Dangerfield writes of another Welsh orator, David Lloyd George, that his words were 'filled with the instinctive music of his race' and 'lit up by the most alluring of imaginable smiles'.[1] So might it have been written of Aneurin Bevan. He alone among the leaders of the Party could lift socialism out of the rut of theological disputation and make it seem an attractive and realistic objective. As he stood on the platform, or at the dispatch box in the House, a captivating smile would suddenly suffuse his face and his expectant audience would wait entranced, knowing that they were about to be shocked, startled and amused by some extravagant imagery or compelling conceit. It was no wonder that, by those who saw him only from afar, he was adored. But, to those who saw him at close quarters, it was a perpetual source of dismay that such talents should be so grossly abused. He had disqualified himself not by his adherence to an old-fashioned socialism that was unlikely ever again to be acceptable to the British people but by behaviour inadmissible in any contender for the leadership of the Labour party. The only certainty about Bevan was that he regarded himself as a socialist by whose standards everyone else was to be judged, and that he was ambitious. Neither should have been an impediment, but his haphazard behaviour was. His resignation from the government in 1951, dividing the Party shortly before an inevitable general election, signalled unreliability. His conduct during the 1951 Parliament had caused deep offence. He had been publicly rude to the publicly revered Attlee. He ignored Party discipline as though it was not meant for men as great as he.

No doubt his behaviour was prompted by a deep sense of frustration at the inadequacy of his colleagues. A man so convinced of his own intellectual and moral superiority could hardly avoid feeling frustrated at the sight of lesser men, of one particular lesser man, challenging for the job that should clearly be his by right of ability, class and service to the great Labour Movement. Bevan acted as though he was already, by acclamation, the leader of the Labour party in the country and that the PLP, with whom the decision officially lay, had no option but to do its duty and endorse the country's choice. The PLP, however, did not see him in quite the light he saw himself. It decided that it would be too hazardous to put him in charge. For years, Bevan's remarkable gifts were squandered in dark resentment at the denial of what he knew was his due. Benn, later a tribune of the left, castigated Bevan in the privacy of his diary for his 'total failure . . . to offer constructive thought or generous personal leadership . . .'.[2] In 1968, the semi-detached Bevan-ite Richard Crossman delivered a harsh judgement. Bevan was, he wrote, 'unpredictable, irascible, brilliant and occasionally cowardly . . . I was not the only Bevanite who adored him as a boon companion but who secretly knew he should never be Leader of the Party.' Crossman refers also to Bevan's 'indolence', demonstrated perhaps by his inability to reassess his convictions in the light of experience.[3]

Morrison was no longer the natural candidate of the right. He had damaged himself during his brief, and much criticized, tenure at the Foreign Office in 1951. His speeches in the House had latterly given some evidence of failing powers. But his main problem in obtaining the leadership that he had long coveted, and which he was sure should always have been his, was that there was now an alternative candidate on the right, Hugh Gaitskell. Gaitskell had assumed, once Bevan had ruled himself out by his conduct, that Morrison would succeed Attlee. But while Bevan had ruled himself out by his conduct, Morrison was now ruled out by his age. He was sixty-nine. At the next election he would be well into his seventies. Gaitskell decided that the only way to ensure that Bevan did not win would be to stand himself. His elevation to the Treasury in 1950 had been attributable more to his supposed technical expertise than to any political standing. But his selection as Chancellor had marked him out. He did not seem to be a visionary leader, a charismatic leader, or even an amusing leader. But, *faute de mieux*, he was now the natural candidate not just of the right but of all those for whom Bevan was too unreliable and Morrison too old.

Lacking a wider choice, the PLP elected Gaitskell as leader by a very large majority, leaving Morrison humiliated and Bevan outraged. Among those who voted for Gaitskell was Harold Wilson, which demonstrates either insight into his own political interests, or disillusion with Bevan, or concern for the future of the Party, or perhaps all three. In retrospect it could be seen that Gaitskell had done everything right to achieve the leadership. He had been loyal, hard working, frequently outspoken in criticism of left-wing disruption, and he had cultivated his relations with right-wing trade union leaders who had no vote but who certainly had influence. At strategic moments in his career, Gaitskell would make speeches designed to convince Party members that he was not the desiccated calculating machine once excoriated by Bevan but, on the contrary, a dedicated socialist committed by his emotions as well as by his reason. At the Party Conference preceding the leadership election, he had won applause by expounding his devotion to socialism, though it was the socialism of a man who, while sympathetic to the hardship and injustice suffered by others, had never himself been touched by hardship or injustice. So, having been an MP for only ten years, having sat in Cabinet for only one year, he became leader.

Gaitskell was a socialist at a time when the interests of Labour as a party of government required that it be led away from socialism and converted into a party of social reform. This would have been difficult enough for any leader and certainly impossible for a new, young leader of upper-middle-class origins watched with hawk eyes by critics on the left. It was a task that would have been easier in government than in opposition. But, as he himself was a convinced socialist, it was not a task to which Gaitskell wished to address himself. His socialism had two sources. The first was distress at a society which he regarded as unequal and morally impoverished. The second was an assumption that he knew better than any rival, and certainly than any Tory, how to manage the economy. It was unlikely, however, that he would be a *good* manager of the British economy because he was unprepared to confront its most serious problem, inflation. Certainly he would seek ways of presenting socialism more attractively to the electorate, but that would have been beyond the powers even of a more inspirational leader. Moreover his attempts to find a more attractive presentation of socialism confirmed the doubts of those who accused him, quite unjustly, of not being a socialist. He was too much of a socialist for the good of the Labour party.

LEARNING TO LEAD

Gaitskell could have hoped for a better inheritance than a party he had helped to divide. It was not his fault alone. Socialists, like other theologians, are naturally disputatious. The Labour party has frequently described itself as a broad church. By this is meant that its walls confine bitter personal and ideological battles of remarkably little interest to those outside except perhaps as a source of entertainment. It was to peacemaking in this discouraging enclosure that Gaitskell now turned his hand. As Party leader, he placed a value on Party unity which he had not conceded as Chancellor of the Exchequer. He attempted to lead as though he came from the centre-left, the ideological source from which, in Attlee's view, Labour leaders should emerge. Gaitskell was ill rewarded for his good intentions. When he was not under fire from the left, it was simply because it was awaiting its next opportunity. The left would never forget that he had forced the resignation of Bevan in 1951, a crime compounded by his attempt to expel Bevan from the Party in 1955. He was not deterred. Criticism from the left strengthened him in the conviction that his great task was to bind the Party together, to find formulae which united rather than divided. He was to discover that Labour was a party easier to divide than to unite.

He was good at formulae. So good were his formulae that he attracted to his side his old enemy Aneurin Bevan, who yearned for a return to high office and came to accept that, in reconciliation with Gaitskell, lay his only hope. Bevan announced that he wanted office only in a truly socialist government. But he proved content in practice to seek office in a Gaitskell government. The rapprochement began with Suez. Gaitskell gained credit by his opposition to the Suez expedition. So crass was Eden's decision to invade Egypt in collusion with France and Israel that it was unlikely that any Labour leader could have taken a different stand. But the electorate looked for more than the always uneasy alliance between Gaitskell and Bevan. Gaitskell's conclusion that he had no realistic alternative but to seek compromise with the left, rather than confrontation with it, was itself a judgement on Labour's fitness for office. There were, however, three other anxieties that might lead the electorate to question Labour's fitness for office. They arose from the Party's relations with the trade unions, its persistence with the idea of nationalization and its attitude to defence. They were three separable issues but they merged into a single question, could Labour be trusted?

THE TRADE UNIONS

Gaitskell relied greatly on trade union leaders. They had helped him to the leadership. They then helped him to control the Annual Conference of the Labour party. Gaitskell's intimacy with the trade unions, of which his old friend Evan Durbin would certainly have disapproved, emphasized the subordination of the Party to the steadying influence of trade union leaders but also, inevitably, to their interests. This was probably inescapable given the radicalism of the constituency parties. But its longer-term effects were less happy. The Labour party was increasingly the hostage of the trade unions. Gaitskell's penchant for close relations with the trade unions led him into self-defeating commitments. As a Labour leader, he felt that he had to support official strikes, particularly those launched by the union with the largest number of votes at Conference, even if he thought them unjustified, and even indeed if much of the trade union movement was privately critical. Gaitskell supported the London bus strike of 1957, launched by the TGWU under its new leader Frank Cousins, though he knew it would cost him votes.[4] Eden's successor Macmillan dated the recovery of his government in popular estimation, after the catastrophe of Suez, from the defeat of the strike.

More worryingly for Gaitskell, the trade union leadership was becoming politically unreliable. The generation of trade union leaders among whom Arthur Deakin, Bevin's successor at the TGWU, and William Lawther, President of the NUM, were the most prominent passed from the scene. From the late 1950s onwards the trade unions increasingly lost patience waiting for what the Labour party, or even a Labour government, could do for them and their members. Trade union leaders never lost their preference for a Labour government over a Tory government. At moments of crisis they would still sometimes give help. But it was rapture modified by disenchantment. Gaitskell was sufficiently sensitive to the change in mood among trade unions to declare at the TUC before the 1959 election that, although the political and trade union movement were 'comrades,' they had different tasks to perform and must not attempt to dictate to each other.[5]

The change in spirit was signalled by the type of leaders the unions chose. The election in 1956 of Frank Cousins as General Secretary of the TGWU, the largest union, brought a dramatic transformation in the sentiments of trade unions as expressed at the TUC, at the Party's annual Conference and in its National Executive Committee. Frank Cousins was doing no more than representing the wishes of his members when, at his first TUC Conference as General Secretary, he said: 'We accept that in a period of freedom for all we are part of the all . . . What we are saying is that there is no such thing in this country as a place where you say "Wage levels stop here" and that we ought to be content, even if things remain equal.'[6] This constituted a challenge that a Labour government would have to meet without it being at all clear that it had the policy or the determination. Gaitskell was unwilling to take issue with the trade unions on the need to reconcile free collective bargaining, full employment and low inflation. It was a problem that could wait until Labour was in government. Meanwhile he did not wish to disturb his relationships with the trade unions.[7]

That there was a problem he knew. The Labour party's 1958 policy document *Plan for Progress* argued that future growth in money incomes should 'broadly keep in step with higher productivity'.[8] How this was to be achieved was unclear. It was easier to assume that it could be negotiated as a result of the goodwill between the trade unions and a Labour government than to go into details which might arouse criticism from those who saw no reason why any government should interfere with free collective bargaining. When launching his 1959 election campaign Gaitskell put the choice, as he saw it, before the trade unions. 'The Trade Union movement has a choice here between either cooperation with a government which is determined to carry out industrial expansion in a planned way, without inflation, or it will be driven back to an inactive role, kept quiet by a certain amount of unemploy-

ment, and not wielding any serious influence in the community. . . ."[9]
But had the trade unions a choice? What was the evidence that planning
would produce industrial expansion? Why should the trade unions surrender their independence to an incomes policy when there was no
convincing reason to believe a Labour government could deliver its part
of the bargain? Would a Labour government really be prepared to
allow unemployment to rise as a means of containing inflation? Or was
Gaitskell simply presenting himself to the electorate as a man of hard
choices when he knew perfectly well that there was one hard choice
that he would never voluntarily make?

Bevan has been criticized for failing to offer, during the 1950s, any
contribution to the development of socialist thought. But it would be
difficult to discern any contribution by Gaitskell either. It was not, to
socialists, a new thought that full employment threatened, and was
threatened by, inflation. For Labour it presented a difficult, even insoluble, problem, but it is surprising how little preparation there was,
during Gaitskell's first years as leader, to meet what would be his greatest
challenge if he became Prime Minister, a challenge far outweighing in
importance to the country questions about nationalization or nuclear
defence. Gaitskell's discretion in conducting the battle against inflation,
should he ever become Prime Minister, would be subject to two constraints. The first was the commitment to keep unemployment below
2 per cent. He was now in the ironic position of having to emulate the
Tories' record on unemployment. He would not be coming into office
as Her Majesty's First Minister in order to breach the consensus in
favour of 'full employment'.

The second constraint was the link with the unions. The question
was whether that constraint could be converted into an opportunity.
Labour hoped that the trade unions could be persuaded not to use their
power to push up pay faster than productivity. It was recognized that
this would require an incomes policy which would be fair and which
was associated with economic growth and an effective prices policy.
The ultimate judgement on fairness was bound to lie with those whose
co-operation was being sought, that is the trade unions. The trade
unions might not agree among themselves. There would always be the
question how far differentials were to be preserved within the incomes
policy or how far it could be used as an instrument of redistribution.
Skilled workers do not normally regard it as fair if their differentials
are eroded. Socialist principles might be taken as suggesting a reduction
in differentials. Trade union principles demanded their maintenance.

Socialism was only meaningful to most trade union members if it brought benefits, not if it exacted sacrifices. In conditions of crisis, the trade unions might find some temporary compromise over issues such as this. But it would be enforceable only for a short time if differentials were eroded. If trade union leaders did not then default on their promises to government, their members would do it for them. Others might not have exactly the same view of fairness but views, other than those of the trade unions, were far less important to the success of an incomes policy. The democracy may elect a government but, under conditions of over-full employment, the government has to have regard to the power brokers.

NATIONALIZATION

Gaitskell was ambivalent about how far he wanted to take nationalization either because of his own uncertainties or because of the political con-straints under which he worked. For electoral reasons he did not want to appear too enthusiastic about nationalization. But he was not prepared to knock it on the head partly because he did not want to damage Party unity but partly also because he believed that some, quite extensive, nationalization should be part of the policy of a future Labour govern-ment. Thus Gaitskell was known personally to favour the nationalization of chemicals, aircraft and machine tools.[10] Any party leader who wanted to nationalize chemicals was hanging a millstone round his neck but Gaitskell was willing to carry it. The chemical industry now qualified for nationalization, in whole or in part, as a 'commanding height'. He also favoured the nationalization of urban land, a vast project if ever undertaken.[11] Gaitskell's ambivalence is illustrated in his Fabian pam-phlet on nationalization. Most of it had been written in 1953. It was published only in 1956, the year of Crosland's *Future of Socialism*, when Gaitskell was already leader of the Labour party. But he would hardly have agreed to its publication if he had changed his views in any substan-tial way. He writes,

It still remains true that nationalisation of the means of production, distribution and exchange should assist the advance to greater equality, contribute to a full employment policy, associate with the power to make important economic decisions a far greater sense of national responsibil-ity, ease the development of industrial democracy, and diminish the bitter-ness and friction of economic relationships.

If Gaitskell really believed what he was writing, these were advantages substantial enough to justify a programme of extensive nationalization. Indeed he adds that there 'certainly are other important arguments in favour of nationalisation', arguments of efficiency and arguments concerning the protection of the public against private monopoly. But, after this moment of clarity, he switches horses and continues, 'Whether these advantages are sufficient to justify, from a Socialist angle, a rapid extension of the field of nationalisation depends partly on what other arguments there are in favour of this course, partly on what disadvantages may be expected to follow from it, and partly on whether the principal ideals of Socialism can be achieved in other ways.' So, having been marched up the hill, we have to follow General Gaitskell down again. Thus we come to the real nub of the matter. Whatever the arguments, and wherever the balance of advantage and disadvantage came down, it was all a matter of politics. '[W]e must remember that the British electorate will not be impressed with proposals to extend nationalisation into new and unknown fields unless there is a simple and clear-cut case for them.'[12] Evidently he felt he had not made that simple and clear-cut case in his Fabian pamphlet, and there was no sign that he wished to make another attempt. The simple and clear-cut case was to be allowed, so far as he was concerned, to go by default.

Traditional socialists, quite naturally, were critical of these tergiversations. Gaitskell seemed sometimes to think that it was a satisfactory compromise between the different trends of opinion within the Labour party to advocate nationalization as long as it was done without enthusiasm. Whatever the left's own occasional doubts about the political wisdom of more nationalization, his ambiguities were always useful as a weapon against Gaitskell whenever it wanted to challenge his leadership. He might say he wanted more nationalization but the absence of conviction suggested pragmatism at best, the abandonment of socialism at its worst. On the other hand, at times even Bevan showed a willingness to compromise as the prospect of office without downgrading nationalization became more remote.

Labour's 1957 statement *Industry and Society* was an attempt, in the end unsuccessful, to draft around all these ambiguities and hesitations. Naturally the renationalization of steel and road haulage appeared. That could be agreed as a matter of revenge for their denationalization even if there was no better reason. Then there was a generalized threat to whatever firms might be 'failing the nation'. There were proposals for the buying of shares and for state investment. *Industry and Society* has been regarded as killing off what was known as shopping-list nationalization. The obituary was premature. There was an implicit shopping list. Mikardo interpreted *Industry and Society* as implying, properly interpreted, the nationalization, through the buying of their equity, of 600 major companies.[13] Gaitskell wanted to do nothing of the sort but *Industry and Society*, by its vagueness, gave some colour to the accusation. And it has never been obvious to industries and companies that it was more acceptable to be nationalized as a matter of pragmatism rather than of principle. *Industry and Society* can be presented as Labour's acceptance of the 'mixed economy'. Labour was agreeing a capitalist element in the mixture. But what element? As the phrase does not define the mixture, it was a recipe for confusion and misunderstanding. Bevan had graciously written in his book *In Place of Fear* that he did not want everything nationalized. But in that book he had also written that public property should dominate. The lack of more specific nationalization commitments led Bevan privately to condemn *Industry and Society* as a 'lousy document', a view that *Tribune* expressed publicly.[14] The main effect of *Industry and Society* was to confirm that Labour was the Party of nationalization while leaving it open how far a Labour government would extend nationalization. A secondary effect was to give the left an opportunity to attack Gaitskell for abandoning socialism. Some on the left had participated in drafting *Industry and Society*. They did not find this an inhibition to distancing themselves from it once it began to attract criticism from colleagues even further left.

NUCLEAR DISARMAMENT

The left had not discovered how to build on the successes of the Attlee government a credible domestic policy that opened the road to socialism. It took refuge in insistence on simplicities, particularly two. The first insistence was on the vital necessity of extensive further nationalization. The second was on unilateral nuclear disarmament. There was a respectable argument that Britain itself should abandon its own nuclear weapons provided it continued as a member of NATO under the shield of the American nuclear armament. Hugh Gaitskell seems to have been prepared to take this line.[15] He asserted clearly that 'We are agreed that in the future Britain should not attempt to produce and provide her own effective nuclear weapons.'[16] But the idea that Britain should give a moral lead by renouncing nuclear weapons, both its own and the American shield, was an overestimate of Britain's special place in the world and an underestimate of the impact such negligence would have on public opinion.

Bevan, at the 1957 Labour Party Conference, correctly described the moral argument for renouncing nuclear weapons as an emotional spasm. For his pains he was considered to have betrayed both socialism and the left. His dismissive rejection of the left's moral high ground led even to a breach with his most faithful follower, Michael Foot. Foot, during the life of the Attlee government, had been prepared to accept Bevan's word on a whole range of foreign policy issues. He accepted the necessity of NATO and American action in Korea. He was prepared to support the idea of forcing a convoy along the Berlin autobahn to feed blockaded West Berlin. In the subsequent years he had followed the twists and turns of Bevan's political inspiration. But his hero's defence of the need for a British nuclear weapon was a step too far for his sensibilities.

GAITSKELL BECOMES A LEADER

Gaitskell's attempts at conciliation were rendered nugatory when, inconveniently close to the 1959 election, the left, feeling betrayed by Bevan's unwillingness to go naked into the conference chamber, resumed the battle for unilateral nuclear disarmament. The challenge irritated Gaitskell and aroused his qualities of leadership. Leadership did not come naturally to him. Exasperation with his followers was a necessary stimulant. He fought back but it was too late. In his anxiety to win the election, he made a blunder which strained the credulity of the electorate. He would improve social benefits, increase pensions and abolish health service charges but would not increase income tax. Shortly afterwards, Labour party headquarters made a pledge not to raise purchase tax. Apparently a Labour government would provide more but the electorate would not have to pay more. Despite what was otherwise accounted a professional campaign, it should have been no surprise when Labour was more heavily defeated in the 1959 General Election even than in 1955. It was the fourth successive election at which Labour had lost seats. Gaitskell, and those around him, began to think of desperate remedies.

Defeat weakens any political leader, even if the odds have, all the time, been strongly against him. Undoubtedly, as Philip Williams suggests in his biography of Gaitskell,[17] the left was preparing to blame Gaitskell for the 1959 defeat. But Gaitskell had eased its task by his eternal compromising, and by his failure to impress himself on his Party. He wasted the first four years of his tenure. It may be that Attlee had set a pattern from which no successor could at once diverge. Then, under the compulsion of yet one more defeat, Gaitskell seems to have decided that equivocation on great issues was a form of leadership which might unite the Labour party but which lost elections. He abandoned equivocation, and did his best to appear a strong leader who led from the front. He became the man who is today remembered – the man who wished to change Clause Four, who rejected unilateral nuclear disarmament, and who fought and fought again to save the Party he loved. He thereby discovered the full intensity of Labour's allergy to leadership, particularly leadership that could be represented as leading away from socialism, but he became the hero of the moderate wing of the Labour party and of public opinion more widely. Here was an honest man battling with the extremists in his own Party. The electorate is said to dislike divided parties but it certainly admires leaders battling with extremism. Yet, so far as Clause Four and nuclear disarmament were concerned, Gaitskell was also battling with his own past. He himself had always been a convinced nationalizer and, on nuclear disarmament, had, in the past, endorsed policies that could be held to compromise the security of the country.

During the General Election campaign of 1959, Labour had been accused of wishing to nationalize 600 separate companies which might be considered to be failing the nation. It was, after all, an interpretation which the Tories shared with Mikardo. After the defeat, Gaitskell wished to clarify the position by rewriting Clause Four. There was every possible Party reason against doing so. It would be divisive because so many members of the Party, who had no wish to nationalize 600 companies, felt that Clause Four spelt out their core socialist commitment. For them, it portrayed the ideal socialist society even if the time was not yet and might never be. Gaitskell's attack on Clause Four, delivered at the Party Conference shortly following the election, was an initiative particularly dangerous coming from a leader who knew he had to live with the disappointments of an articulate left wing. He did it though he knew he would be suspected of abandoning nationalization as a policy, he did it despite the dissuasion of his friends, he did it because he believed that it must be made clear to the public that Labour did not intend indiscriminate nationalization.

His initiative was the more surprising in that he was still a devout believer in nationalization and economic planning. He wished to convince the public that he was downgrading public ownership but he intended it still to have a major place in his Party's programme. He might say that he was advocating nationalization for pragmatic reasons whereas socialist fundamentalists did so for reasons of principle. In practice, this was a distinction without a difference. He thought more nationalization essential for the preservation of full employment, and for higher investment and productivity. In his speech to the Labour Party Conference in 1959 he insisted that there was no intention of abandoning public ownership and accepting for all time the present frontiers of the public sector. It was, therefore, not even clear that Gaitskell's proposal to rewrite Clause Four would have the electoral benefits he anticipated. So enthusiastic was he for further nationalization that a rewriting of Clause Four in accordance with his views would be unlikely to improve Labour's prospects with the electorate. It might easily injure them. A New Testament replacing the Old Testament could be a much more conspicuous target for Tory attack. But Gaitskell thought that the time had come for clarity about Labour's real aims.

Speakers at the Conference were overwhelmingly hostile to Gaitskell's proposal. Among his sternest critics were those in the trade union movement who had loyally supported him thus far. Many of them had a clause similar to Clause Four in their own constitutions or rule books. Gaitskell had emphasized that public ownership was *a* means, and not necessarily the only or most important means, to full employment, greater equality and higher productivity. On the contrary, for a socialist, it was *the* means, its implementation inhibited only by the blindness of the electorate. It had not made his attack on Clause Four more persuasive that it was so obviously motivated by electoral considerations. It was Labour's job to open the eyes of the electorate, not submit to its myopia. He was saved from total humiliation only by Aneurin Bevan making his last speech to a Labour Party Conference. Mustering his exceptional oratorical skills, Bevan succeeded, temporarily, in plastering over the rift that Gaitskell had opened up. He said that he had agreed with Gaitskell. He also was not in favour of a monolithic society. He also did not believe that public ownership should reach down into every piece of economic activity because that *would* create a monolithic society. But he added that the challenge was going to come from Russia because it was practising public ownership and economic planning.

The challenge is going to come from Russia. The challenge is not going to come from the United States. The challenge is not going to come from West Germany nor from France. The challenge is going to come from those nations who, however wrong they may be – and I think they are wrong in many fundamental respects – nevertheless are at long last being able to reap the material fruits of economic planning and of public ownership . . . Our main case is and must remain that in a modern complex society it is impossible to get rational order by leaving things to private economic adventure. Therefore I am a Socialist. I believe in public ownership.[18]

It was the message of *In Place of Fear*, unmodified by the preceding seven years of debate within the Labour party. Though Bevan might intervene to save Gaitskell's face, everyone knew that he did not agree that Clause Four should be rewritten. He had never regarded Gaitskell as a socialist. He had been prepared, in the hope of a Labour victory, to sink his differences in the years leading up to the 1959 General Election. Nothing could persuade him, however, that Gaitskell ought to be leader of the Labour party. His speech underlined the message to which Gaitskell was attempting to shut his ears, that socialism meant public ownership and planning and that, in those respects at least, the Soviet Union was the exemplar.

The eventual compromise was to leave Clause Four unmodified, indeed reaffirmed, but supplemented by a new statement of the principles of British democratic socialism. This new statement, accepted by the NEC and commended by it to the 1960 Labour Party Conference, illustrated all the dangers of an attempt to revise Clause Four. It was as bad as it could be. It emphasized that Labour's social and economic aims could be achieved only by an expansion of common ownership substantial enough to give the community power over the commanding heights of the economy. The phrase about the commanding heights of the economy was inserted at the insistence of the dying Bevan, who cherished it as his bequest to the Party he had never been allowed to lead. If these words meant anything, the commitment to an extension of public ownership had been strengthened rather than weakened. The Labour party, shocked at finding its fundamental convictions challenged by its leader, had insisted on restating them. The task now was to ensure that the new statement of principles was as deeply and thoroughly forgotten as Clause Four had been before Gaitskell raised its profile. It was indicative both of the real character of the Labour party, and of why the electorate refused to trust it, that it was so unwilling to follow

Gaitskell even on the principle of rewriting a text already forty years old.

Gaitskell has been criticized for making both tactical and strategic mistakes in raising the Clause Four issue, thereby re-emphasizing in the public mind Labour's commitment to widespread nationalization, showing insensitivity to his Party's honest socialist purpose, uniting against himself both right and left, weakening his own influence in the Party at a time when the nuclear defence issue was looming once again and, at the end of a year of controversy, accepting humiliation and defeat. This catalogue of errors can be extended endlessly. The quality of strategic thinking behind Gaitskell's assault on Clause Four had much in common with that behind the Charge of the Light Brigade. Like other generals, before and after, if he had foreseen the strength of the enemy he would never have ordered the attack.[19] It is a damning accusation. The charge can be rebutted only in words such as those of Philip Williams: 'we now know that the astute management which buys politicians temporary tranquillity, and the deviousness with which they approach desirable objectives, may prove costly later when illusions can no longer be preserved and confidence is finally shattered'.[20] Yet Gaitskell's greatest error was to exaggerate the differences between himself and his Party on the subject of nationalization and to do it for electoral reasons. So far as public ownership was concerned, Gaitskell's problem was not his differences from his Party but his agreement with it. If their shared views on public ownership were justified, as both he and his Party believed them to be, the course for a leader would have been to persuade the public. His Party would not have objected if he had emphasized the pragmatic reasons for public ownership. He obviously judged the task of popular education to be beyond his powers. If so, he was not mistaken.

Gaitskell's continued commitment to nationalization, as exemplified in *Signposts for the Sixties* in 1961 (and that of Crosland and Jenkins), becomes more comprehensible when it is remembered that it was now obvious that the UK was lagging economically behind its European neighbours. At about the same time as Gaitskell was raising the issue of Clause Four, the German Social Democrats were, at their Bad Godesburg Conference, abandoning Marxism. But then the German economy was the miracle of the western world. The performance of the British economy was far from miraculous. Gaitskell was convinced that the Attlee government, despite some setbacks, had got its economic policy about right and that, at that time, the UK had been doing better than the rest of Europe. He now perceived that Britain was in relative decline, that its rate of growth fell well behind that of western Europe and particularly Germany, and believed that it was the fault of Tory incompetence and complacency. Nationalization was certainly not seen as part of the problem, rather as part of the answer. His ideas on economic policy neglected the principal reason for the continuing pressure against sterling. This remained the lax fiscal and monetary policies of successive British governments. His partisan deployment of the superficial argument that the present British economic problems were due to Tory incompetence demonstrated his failure to notice that the domestic economic policies he was proposing were, in fact, very similar to those of the Macmillan government, particularly after the beginning of its 'planning' phase.

The Conservative governments after 1951 opened the economy to the world without at the same time abandoning the inflationary policies that they had inherited. Confronted by successive balance of payments crises, and increasingly conscious of the failure of its economic policies, the Macmillan government took refuge in planning. In 1961, the Tories set up the National Economic Development Council. Whenever the future of socialism was threatened by intellectual confusion or popular disdain, the Tories managed to provide life support. Macmillan did it with N E D C, whose creation provided justification for the socialist proposition that there was merit in planning. Edward Heath would do it with the Industry Act of 1972 embodying extraordinary, and potentially highly expensive, interventionist powers. N E D C was established in accordance with a theory that, if the wise men of industry, trade unions and government met together regularly, something of advantage to the economy must emerge. In fact, all that emerged was a growth target of 4 per cent which there was no hope of meeting but which encouraged Chancellor of the Exchequer Maudling in his inflationary excesses. Planning was no answer to the dilemmas caused by the opening of the economy. Macmillan's decision to revert to the policies of *The Middle Way* left him very near to Gaitskell in his views on economic policy. Macmillan offered planned expansion plus an incomes policy. Gaitskell offered planned expansion plus an incomes policy. He considered the N E D C 4 per cent growth target 'well within our grasp'.[21] There were differences. One lay in the optimistic supposition that an incomes policy designed by a Labour government, in co-operation with its friends in the trade unions, would be more effective because fairer than anything the Tories could do. Another lay in the role Labour intended for public ownership. A third lay in Macmillan's realization that the economy could not be indefinitely isolated from foreign competition and global market forces. But there was nothing in Gaitskell's economic policies that promised a faster rate of growth than that achieved under the Tories.

Gaitskell had accepted, and remained committed to, *British* nuclear disarmament, though with the essential qualification that Britain would remain in NATO and thus cower beneath the shield held by the USA, which would continue to target nuclear weapons.[22] Thus, if Bevan had become Foreign Secretary in a Labour government, and Labour in office had lived by its commitments, he would have been forced to go naked into the conference chamber. The clothes would have been worn only by the Americans.[23] An episode typical of the Labour party, but extraordinary by any other standard, was the attempt, before the 1960 Scarborough Conference which went unilateralist, to draft a compromise between Gaitskell and Cousins on nuclear weapons. Gaitskell agreed to the search for a compromise because it was his habit to seek the support of trade union leaders. Thus, even after the 1959 defeat, Gaitskell was still seeking compromises if he could find them. The reason compromise was sought was to be found not in the merits of the argument, but in the fact that Cousins could cast a large block vote at Conference. Compromise proved impossible. Gaitskell insisted that NATO, if not the UK, must retain nuclear weapons while the Soviet Union had them, Cousins that it should not. The failure of the attempt provided Gaitskell with a rather better launch pad for his reputation as a strong leader than his attack on Clause Four. When faced by defeat at Conference, he declared that he would fight, fight and fight again for the Party he loved. It is a tribute to his forbearance, or to his socialism, or to his habit of compromise with trade union leaders, that he should have continued to love his Party when it required him to seek agreement with Frank Cousins. A year later, he succeeded in reversing the decision of the 1960 Conference. Once victorious, he reconciled himself with Frank Cousins, which demanded a convenient tolerance of human error. It was of a kind which his successor, in his time, was also to display.

EUROPE

Labour, during the Attlee government, had come to distrust economic entanglements with Europe. It had refused participation in the Schuman Plan. Entanglements with Europe would imperil relationships with the Commonwealth and endanger full employment because European governments did not seem to have absorbed the Keynesian message. Their policies were deflationary and they were unwilling to grant sufficient credit to deficit countries such as the UK. Gaitskell, at the Treasury, had been the leading spokesmen of this insular point of view. He had submitted unwillingly to American pressure and had taken the UK into the EPU despite his doubts. He feared that membership would lead to deficits in trade with Europe and hence to loss of precious gold and dollars from the reserves. He had left government before these fears were justified by experience. Out of office, and without Ministerial responsibility, there had been no fresh experiences to widen his horizons. In 1962, with strong support from the majority of the Labour Party Conference, he denounced Macmillan's belated application for membership of the EEC, characterizing it as representing the end of a thousand years of history. In doing so he separated himself from some of his closest friends, such as Roy Jenkins, but not from Douglas Jay, whose repudiation of Europe was firmer, and even more consistent, than Gaitskell's. Jay had many arguments against joining the EEC. They included the fear that membership would inhibit planning.[24]

There were those, both in the Labour party and beyond, who were dismayed by Gaitskell's rejection of membership of the EEC. But the rejection was not surprising. Despite his claimed internationalism, and his friendships on the continent, his approach to economic policy had always been insular. His opposition to membership of the EEC, allegedly on the terms offered, resulted from his belief that poor British economic performance derived from the mismanagement of Tory governments, certainly not from failure to join the EEC. It would have been contrary to his nature to embrace the Community and it did him no harm to find one issue on which he was at one with the majority in his party and did not have to fight and fight again. Then, in January 1963, had come de Gaulle's veto on British membership. It was a few days after Gaitskell's death. For the moment, the veto took the question of British membership of the EEC off the British political agenda. But de Gaulle was not immortal either politically or physically. The time might come when the question would arise again. Clearly a Labour government, with the Party as at present minded, would not be seeking or seizing opportunities for membership.

Hugh Gaitskell's heroic status was ratified by his early death, when it had once more appeared possible that he would lead Labour to victory and become Prime Minister. His career demonstrates the burden which socialism had become for the Labour party. Ensnared by his own honourable convictions he was dilatory in assessing the full weight of the burden. When, at last, he was forced to recognize it, he found himself alone, politically friendless, in a party which, remembering Ramsay MacDonald, preferred accommodation of its prejudices to political calculation.

HAROLD WILSON

When, to succeed Gaitskell, the effective choice lay between Harold Wilson and George Brown, Gaitskell's deputy, a significant number of Gaitskellites voted for Wilson. But it was not with enthusiasm, rather with despair. George Brown was considered too unstable and too susceptible to alcohol. Thus the apostolic succession descended upon Wilson with support from all tendencies in the PLP. However, the descent claimed by Wilson was not from the departed leader, Hugh Gaitskell, admired perhaps but not much loved. It came from the deeply mourned hero of the left, Aneurin Bevan, forgiven in death, orator extraordinary, creator of the National Health Service. Wilson would devote a great deal of effort to demonstrating that he was in the tradition of Bevan rather than of Gaitskell. A tribute to Bevan was never out of place, particularly now that the deceased hero could no longer rise up to dismiss the careerism and opportunism of the man who had resigned with him in 1951 but had subsequently betrayed him. Wilson had regarded Gaitskell as a divisive leader with little feeling for the Party or understanding of its mythologies. In unifying the Labour party, he had one enormous advantage. He was not Gaitskell. It was not he who had forced the resignation of Bevan. On the contrary, he had resigned with Bevan. He might be even more right wing than Gaitskell, but he was not guilty of deicide.

Wilson's years in opposition had turned him into a first-class Parliamentary performer. He could hold the House in the palm of his hand. He could make it laugh with him at the expense of the exhausted volcanoes on the government front bench, overtly on his own backbenches, covertly on the benches opposite. He proved a brilliant leader of the opposition. He exploited the difficulties and embarrassments of Macmillan's last months better probably than Gaitskell could have done. He profited from the contrast between his own supposed economic expertise and the aristocratic illiteracy of the admirable but anachronistic Sir Alec Douglas-Home. Wilson might be a question awaiting an answer. But, in the circumstances, even a question awaiting an answer seemed marginally more attractive than an aristocrat with a matchbox. In a shadow Cabinet lacking many other stars, Wilson shone. Ten years later, revived by his unexpected victory in the 1974 election, Wilson, in high spirits, reminded the PLP of the role he had had to play, or claimed to have played, in the 1964 government. 'In the 1964 Government . . . I had to occupy every position on the field, goalkeeper, defence, attack – I had to take the corner-kicks and penalties, administer to the wounded and bring on the lemons at half-time.'[25]

Wilson had long been distrusted. The distrust was to be found on the left as well as the right of the Party. He came, reputedly, from the left, or at worst the centre-left, of the Party. As a young Cabinet Minister, he had resigned with Bevan, and thus had been touched by grace. But in 1954 he had, in the view of the further left, betrayed Bevan by filling the vacancy in the shadow Cabinet created by Bevan's ill-considered resignation. Wilson was not allowed the excuse that Bevan's resignation had been effected without consultation with any of his followers and on an issue not considered even by Bevanites to be of the first importance. Bevan seems to have imagined that Wilson's decision would cost him his seat in the constituency section of the NEC.[26] In fact Wilson continued to do well, which suggests that although the constituencies were left wing they still hoped for sufficient unity within the leadership of the Party to make victory in an election conceivable. On Bevan's death, Wilson had become the standard bearer of the left, though without showing much sign of actually sharing their convictions. His enthusiasm for nationalization fell well short of what the left would consider ideal.

On the right, the Gaitskellites saw the same facts from their own point of view. Just as Gaitskell's tenure of the leadership had been damaged by the hatred of the Bevanites, so would Wilson's by the contempt of the Gaitskellites. Wilson had been the only possible threat to Gaitskell's leadership. Gaitskellites despised Wilson because they admired Gaitskell. Only Gaitskell himself had been capable of taking a more sober view of Wilson, and that not always. Gaitskellites were as proud of their lamented leader's lately strict devotion to principle as they were disdainful of Wilson's flexibility. Gaitskell and Jay held contemptuous memories of the allegedly equivocal role played by Wilson at the time of the 1949 devaluation, the issue on which, by his forthright if belated stand, Gaitskell had gained the reputation which won him the Chancellorship. Jay, distraught at the loss of his old friend, never forgot. But Jay's memory may well have been at fault. He may have remembered more of Wilson's equivocation than actually occurred. The only certainty is that all three Ministers were very late in deciding to support devaluation. Thereafter, if Jay ever said anything favourable about Wilson, it was by inadvertence. The Gaitskellites had seen Wilson take Bevan's side over the dispute on health service charges at the time of Gaitskell's 1951 budget. Even if he had been proved correct in arguing that the Attlee government's rearmament programme was physically incapable of implementation, his resignation had simply proved him to be Bevan's poodle. He had then, in 1954, betrayed Bevan as, no doubt, he would betray any friend if the association became inconvenient. Wilson, in the view of the Gaitskellites, was always calculating, never sincere, always self-interested. He was always manoeuvring for personal advantage, never loyal, never taking a straightforward stand. In 1960, under pressure from the left, he had stood against Gaitskell for the leadership and had received a vote that, while less than half Gaitskell's, was certainly not derisory. He seemed ready to do anything to appease the left except genuinely to adopt their opinions.

Though Wilson shared the Oxford University background of many of Gaitskell's most intimate friends, his manner of life outside the House was incompatible with theirs. He was not clubbable. He did not look to political life for his intimate companions. If he had been that way inclined he might have drawn back after witnessing the way in which Gaitskell was damned by the left for the views of his friends even when he did not himself share them. Thus while Gaitskell had agreed with Douglas Jay on a great deal, including Europe, he did not agree with him after the 1959 defeat that the Labour party should change its name. Wilson's closest supporters, such as Richard Crossman, complained of his having no social life. 'It's a tremendous disadvantage that [Wilson] has no social life. Every time one meets him, it's a formal interview . . .'[27] But Wilson, like Gaitskell before him, never felt that taking the advice of Crossman was the summit of human wisdom. There were none of those sociable occasions which might have enabled the Gaitskellites to discover that Wilson was a likeable man despite political behaviour which, in their view, was unprincipled. Indeed social contact might have persuaded them that Wilson was no more unprincipled than those who spoke of him in such derogatory terms. After all, they all found it convenient to proclaim themselves as socialists, though it was questionable how many of them now were. That Wilson did have some principles was illustrated during his unpremeditated outburst, at the outset of the 1964 Parliament, against the racialist campaign conducted by the Tories at Smethwick which had deprived Patrick Gordon Walker of his seat in Parliament. For once Wilson allowed an emotion, in this case disgust, to escape the control of his judgement. He had equally sincere commitments to the Commonwealth and to overseas aid. He was always keen to protect overseas aid, which, indeed, became a token of the government's commitment to socialist internationalism. But he greatly overestimated both the commitment of the Commonwealth to British leadership and what he himself would be prepared to do by way of overseas aid in a Britain beset by its own crises.

NOT POLES APART

There was in fact more in common between Gaitskell and Wilson than Gaitskell's friends were ever prepared to admit. Crosland who, in this respect, was Gaitskell's licensed jester, used to annoy his leader by rebuking him for being insufficiently radical to be a Labour Prime Minister. He even expressed the doubt in his obituary broadcast. Wilson, though supposedly coming from the left, was certainly no more radical. Indeed, since the days of Ramsay MacDonald, the Labour party has had one conservative leader after another, though some had come to their conservatism from a radical position. Foot and Kinnock may be regarded as exceptions to this rule but both, once leader, moved strongly to the right, Kinnock after an interval during which he unravelled himself from his left-wing toils, Foot with the incoherence of a Cromwell who knew he would go furthest if he knew not where he was going. The conservatism of Labour leaders is not necessarily a criticism, but it had the effect of leaving economic radicalism to the Conservative party in some of its moods.

Wilson was cleverer than Gaitskell but not more flexible. Both were economists and technocrats, though perhaps Wilson was really a statistician marketing himself as an economist. Kenneth Morgan interestingly speculates that Gaitskell and Wilson, who both passed the war in the

UK in the civil service rather than overseas, saw 'post-war Britain less as an opportunity for social revolution than a laboratory for applied technocracy'.[28] Neither Gaitskell nor Wilson entirely understood their Party, a venial sin shared by hosts of other Labour party members. In June 1962, Wilson had apostrophized, 'The Labour Party is a moral crusade or it is nothing. We have to persuade the electors that we have the means and the men capable of transforming society into a Socialist society.'[29] He was sufficiently pleased with this evocation of a moral crusade to repeat the words three months later as chairman of the Annual Conference of the Labour party at Brighton in September 1962. 'This Party is a moral crusade or it is nothing.'[30] Those who heard them were, no doubt, inspired but hardly enlightened. But any correspondence between his actions and his oratory was inadvertent. Both Gaitskell and Wilson were compromisers, both put the unity of the Party high on their list of priorities, and both were reluctant fighters even against the damaging absurdities that seized the minds of their followers from time to time and endangered Labour's electability. Gaitskell fought against Bevan but was quite willing to make undesirable compromises with his trade union supporters. He made an ill-prepared attack on Clause Four and withdrew in disorder when he found that even right-wing trade union leaders were against him. He fought against unilateralism but really had no choice if Labour was ever to be elected to government again. Wilson, with his unprincipled reputation, nevertheless chose after 1964 to defend the exchange rate of sterling long after that policy became unsustainable. At the end of 1968, he began a battle for trade union reform, and was overwhelmed by the opposition this aroused within the Labour party. It was a battle in which Gaitskell, with his greater trade union dependence, was far less likely to have engaged.

Neither Gaitskell nor Wilson understood the full implications of the fact that their economic management, did they ever come to power, would take place in a more open economy than they had left in 1951. Although some control of sterling capital movements remained, sterling earned overseas in current transactions had been, since December 1958, freely convertible into dollars at the official exchange rate of $2.80. Most other controls, the basis of the Attlee government's claim to be a government of planners, had disappeared. Labour economic spokesmen were continually complaining that since the decision to support the transferable rate in 1955,[31] and the convertibility decision of December 1958, the UK had suffered one balance of payments crisis after another. That was true. But the answer could not lie in closing the economy. In

December 1958, Gaitskell denounced the move to convertibility: '[W]e shall increase the risk of and the scope for speculation against the £ in time of trouble ... while throwing away ... one possible weapon to be used against the speculation ... [so] we shall be told that our internal policies have to be adjusted ... that we must delay expansion ... because of what might be thought by speculators ... it will restore the power enjoyed by a minority of rich men in the past to vote with their bank balances.'[32] The polemic against the liberalization of the economy no doubt sounded attractive to Party members. But, if Gaitskell ever came to power, it would be a liberalized economy that he would have to manage.

Labour's fondness for controls derived from a belief in their utility in face of inflationary pressures which there was no wish to reduce because of the possible effect on full employment. As late as 1957, the only substance in Labour's economic thinking was a determination to find a way of discriminating between what it considered essential investment and what it considered inessential investment. It thought that a Labour government could undertake this vast planning exercise and that it would solve the problem of the excessive burden on resources. Thus, as Wilson wrote in a Fabian pamphlet in 1957, 'Under Labour policy, while monetary measures will play their full part, the ultimate decisions about investment would be taken by state servants under the direction of Ministers responsible to Parliament – not by bank managers burdened with an invidious task for which they have not been trained.'[33] He believed that, when retrenchment was required, it would still be possible by the use of such techniques to ensure that the essential as identified by Ministers would go forward while the inessential would be held back. There was extraordinary naivety in the idea that, whereas bank managers were incapable of making the discrimination between the essential and inessential because of lack of training, Ministers and state servants would be capable of doing so.[34] Other ideas were for a National Investment Board, by this time a hoary chestnut, and the use of the government's purchasing power to discriminate between companies that were serving the nation as they should and companies that were not.[35] It was because of ideas of this kind that Labour was unwilling to look at more market-friendly mechanisms for bringing the economy into some kind of balance, reducing inflationary pressures plus floating the exchange rate.

Wilson was believed to be knowledgeable on economic management not just because he was an economist but also because he had been President of the Board of Trade and, before becoming leader, had been shadow Chancellor. But the fact that he could demonstrate greater linguistic facility with economic prescription than the Prime Minister, Sir Alec Douglas-Home, proved nothing about his understanding of the needs of the moment. Wilson entirely shared Gaitskell's myopia in that he had not yet encapsulated within his thinking the changes that had occurred in the world, and in Britain's position in it, since 1951. He thought he would be a great manager of capitalism but his ideas on the subject derived from the Attlee stone age. Both Wilson and Gaitskell were backward looking, first in the sense that they greatly overestimated the economic achievements of the Attlee government and, secondly, in their belief that the complementary relationship with the Commonwealth as a supplier of raw materials to industrial Britain would be of greater value economically than integration in a highly competitive European common market. The world of 1964, the year in which Gaitskell and then Wilson could hope to become Prime Minister, was very different from that in which Labour had governed in the years 1945–51. By 1964 there was no possibility of reverting to the protected economy of the early post-war years other perhaps than as an emergency measure for meeting a major balance of payments crisis. Britain was now part of the world and could not hope to get off. It was also part of the European Free Trade Area, an association of seven European countries which had grown out of a failed attempt to persuade the EEC to agree free trade throughout western Europe. None of the three young economists of the Attlee government had sufficiently amended his ideas in order to make them relevant to the world in which they might inherit the government of the UK. Wilson would not have differed from Gaitskell in any of his expostulations against the way the world, ineluctably, was moving. He had no conception of what it meant to run an open economy. He was ideologically out of tune with the facts of life in the world with which the people of Britain were having to trade. But though the world was spinning in directions antipathetic to socialism there was nothing that, in government, either Gaitskell or Wilson would be able to do about it. Their policies were the same and totally inappropriate.

Another similarity between the two was a tendency, paradoxical in view of their criticism of Tory economic management, to overestimate the strength of the UK economy. Wilson, who, in 1951 attributed his resignation to a rearmament programme beyond the UK's capacity to bear, nevertheless wished to hang on to Britain's global responsibilities and keep forces east of Suez. Both thought, despite repeated disappointments, that, if British strength failed, they could safely look to the USA for support in time of trouble. Both seemed to think that they were drawing strength when, in Washington, they spoke to the American President or his officials. It never seemed to occur to them that they were, and in Washington were regarded as being, pawns of American policy. The French, once they had learnt the lessons of their hapless involvement in South-east Asia, were far more sophisticated. They benefited from the American shield without having to pay for it.

Despite his attack on Clause Four, Gaitskell was the more determined nationalizer. Wilson knew better how to lead the Labour party away from nationalization. He had always thought that the attempt to amend Clause Four was ill advised. He had dissented from Gaitskell's onslaught on Clause Four but it was for tactical reasons, not because he thought the Clause was currently relevant. It was better to ignore it than fight a theological battle about it, thereby stirring up the opposition of those who regarded it as defining an essential element in a socialist society. This did not mean that Wilson saw no role for public ownership. In an article in the *New Statesman* in March 1961, he threatened public ownership where a firm refused the demands put upon it in a national plan.[36] Iron and steel, which the Tories had denationalized, would be renationalized. For this there was a longstanding and apparently inescapable commitment. Politics demanded that it be done, however damaging to the industry such chopping and changing might be. He had shared Gaitskell's enthusiasm for the nationalization of all or part of the chemical industry. Nevertheless, Wilson was quite aware that harping on nationalization was not good politics, not if Labour sincerely wished to win. Once in power, Wilson showed no evidence of a desire to bring the great chemicals conglomerate, Imperial Chemical Industries, into the nationalized sector, even though it could be claimed that it had failed the nation in that its performance since the war had fallen far behind that of its German competitors.

Wilson, however, still strongly believed in the 'commanding heights of the economy' concept of economic management. It was not just a question of planning the economy. Nor was it because he was a socialist. As Philip Ziegler puts it, 'The advancement of socialist objectives was not a matter to which Wilson habitually devoted a great deal of thought.'[37] It was a question of preserving national independence. Technology had moved on. Were the heavy industries still the commanding heights? Wilson was now obsessed with computers and electronics. His attitude was brought out in his discussions with de Gaulle during his visit to Paris at the beginning of April 1965. De Gaulle took the opportunity of taunting Wilson with Britain's dependence on the USA. He 'was at pains to show that we were, and had been for years, satellites of the Americans and economically over-dependent on them'.[38] De Gaulle, who prized national independence at least as much as Wilson, was thinking primarily of the fact that Britain's nuclear deterrent was not independent but, on the contrary, was entirely reliant on American technology and supplies. Wilson could not deny it. He had indeed publicly argued that case and had made Sir Alec Douglas-Home's claim that it was independent the target of much polemic in the House of Commons. But Wilson had ready his rebuttal of de Gaulle's criticism. In response, he asserted his own approach to national independence:

> I rebutted this and instanced our Government's decision to establish a firmly-based computer industry, British-owned and controlled, in contrast to French experience, where the only sizeable French concern, Machine Bull, had been taken over by the Americans. In the world of the 1970s and 1980s, I said, where a country's strength would depend more and more on industrial technology, independence in computers and advanced electronics would matter more than a national independence in nuclear weapons.[39]

Wilson, not untypically, was claiming his new commanding height before he had scaled it. To perceive this, de Gaulle did not have to foresee that the life of the independent British computer industry would be short and not exactly virile. Wilson had little conception how difficult it would prove to establish British national independence in technology.

SCARBOROUGH – WILSON'S THIRD WAY

In the last year of opposition, a divide was already opening up between the activists and the new, supposedly Bevanite leader of the Labour party. Rather than contemplate yet one more defeat after those of 1951, 1955 and 1959, Wilson was concerned to win votes. He was less concerned to massage his Party's socialist prejudices. He had to recognize the decline in class consciousness which made the despoiling of capitalists less attractive to the great majority of the electorate than it might once have been. Policies needed a more persuasive justification than that they would hurt the ruling class.

In a speech at the annual Labour Party Conference at Scarborough on 1 October 1963, his first to the Conference as leader, Wilson provoked questions by filling socialism with a content intended to be less terrifying to the great mass of Labour and uncommitted voters. Logic might suggest that before filling socialism with a new content, it should be emptied of the old. But Wilson had no intention of opening wounds barely healed. He would add to socialism, not subtract from it. It would be found later that subtraction was the main object of the addition, but sufficient unto the day. It was a task that he could undertake more easily than a Gaitskellite leader precisely because he had, supposedly, come from the left. Technology now pointed the way to the socialist society. To the moral crusade had been added a technological crusade. Science and technology would create millions of new jobs, provided only that they were in alliance with economic planning. Science and technology had therefore made socialism more relevant even than it had been before. A new Britain would be forged in the white heat of this techno-logical revolution.[40] Apart from iron and steel, nationalization was not now to be a major element in the programme of the next Labour government. Wilson's redefinition of socialism to include the 'purpos-ive' use of science and technology was attractive to many scientists and technologists, led particularly by Professor Patrick Blackett, Nobel Laureate. It was attractive also to economists who still believed that they could dramatically improve the performance of the British economy through economic planning. It therefore carried not merely substantial intellectual support but intellectual support of unquestionable distinc-tion. Once more Labour was taking the fashionable intellectual high ground.

The speech was a clever patchwork designed to appeal to a wide variety of audiences. The eulogy of science and technology would entice the scientists and technologists. The insistence on economic planning would appeal to the economists and to many businessmen. His assurance that access to university education would be doubled would do him no harm with most academics. The electorate was being encouraged to believe that it was being offered the services of a visionary leader who would rapidly transform its economic prospects. And in case it might be alienated by the thought that it was being offered socialism concealed in sheep's clothing, Wilson was still at hand to lift the frown from its brow. In a later speech he explained: 'Socialism, as I understand it, means applying a sense of purpose to our national life: economic purpose, social purpose and moral purpose.'[41] Nothing could be less alarming.

The Scarborough speech was powerful in the sense that it gave to socialism a new twist which might make the electorate less hostile. In another sense it was anything but powerful. There was nothing in the speech by way of detailed substance. It seems to have been put together the night before its delivery, leaving time for the burnishing of oratory but none for the specification of detail. There was no indication of how the new Britain was to be born, what specific actions by government would mediate its birth. If Labour won its election, the detail would presumably have to be filled in, if at all, by civil servants. Certainly the new Prime Minister and his newly appointed Ministers would not have bothered themselves with such particulars. Wilson did not forget to weave the phrase 'the commanding heights of the economy' into his speech and thereby hoped to reassure Bevanites and the left. He derided the control of the commanding heights exercised 'by men whose only claim is their aristocratic connection or the power of inherited wealth or speculative finance . . .'. But there was nothing he could do to seize control unless indeed he did nationalize wide stretches of British industry, from which it was one purpose of the Scarborough speech to distance himself. In the event, technology would do more for the lives of the people than socialism. But it would be technology within capitalism, serving to raise the standard of living in ways which earlier socialists had ruled incompatible with capitalist mores. Capitalism could, apparently, be reconciled with progress in technology. It might, in certain sectors, require support from government to help it along, but that too was proving not incompatible with the new capitalism.

The argument of the speech depended to an unhealthy degree on a naive belief that what Wilson hoped to do in Britain under democratic planning had already been accomplished in the Soviet Union under communist planning. The Soviet Union represented the challenge which the new Britain would have to meet. Wilson, after talking to Khrushchev in Moscow in January 1956, wrote that 'in the next generation Russia's industrial challenge may well dominate the world economic scene'.[42] No senior figure in the Labour party knew the Soviet Union better than Wilson, due to his frequent visits, his conversations with Soviet leaders and the negotiations there that he had conducted as a minister. Yet Wilson's belief in the success of Soviet planning survived his visits, deceiving him as to the potentiality of planning. He had even been prepared to regard the Soviet invasion of Hungary as an aberration, 'a tragic reversal of policy' within a system that was irreversibly set on a liberalizing path.[43] Wilson's close political friend Richard Crossman wrote in the *Guardian* on 1 December 1961 that 'The last ten years have proved that the most backward totalitarian form of Socialism is superior to the decadent type of Capitalism we have in the Western World.'[44]

One question Wilson could not usefully ask himself. His government was to be a government of economic regeneration. But did he have the personnel to man a government of economic regeneration? With whom could he replace the aristocrats and the men of inherited wealth? He might have available in the PLP able people among whom to select a traditional government. But had they the knowledge and experience for the specific task of economic regeneration? It was of no use asking the question because Wilson would have to form his government from the resources at his disposal plus a few at Minister of State level who could be taken off the street and put in the House of Lords. It had to be assumed that the field from which he would make his choices comprised people who could make such a government effective even though there was little enough experience of commerce and industry. In his Scarborough speech Wilson had said, 'In the Cabinet room and the boardroom alike those charged with the control of our affairs must be ready to think and to speak in the language of our scientific age.' But there was no one in the shadow Cabinet who could speak the language of science and technology. There was no one even from the boardroom of a significant company. Callaghan was later to admit that the government had insufficient experience of industry to judge how effective its measures would be.[45] The government's prospects did not necessarily suffer from these deficiencies. There is no evidence that it would have done better had members of it been able to speak the language of science. Neither Vincent Bowden, a genuine scientist who was given a peerage and made a Minister of State at the Department of Education and Science, nor Charles Snow, novelist and scientist, also given a peerage and made Parliamentary Secretary at the Ministry of Technology, were notable successes in their junior roles. The embrace by government of science and technology as a panacea for British ills demonstrated a level of naivety excusable only because it was shared in the business community.

While the activists accepted for the moment Wilson's tactical reinterpretation of the meaning of socialism, they were sure that victory on a programme denuded of nationalization could not be more than a first step. They were not prepared to permit socialism to be redefined out of existence. It had always meant the public ownership of the means of production, distribution and exchange. That was what, for them, it still meant.

SOCIALISM

The vagueness which now encompassed the word 'socialism' was a gift to all those who wished to exhilarate their followers without being tied down to specifics. Socialism, whatever it meant, obviously described an ideal society and, as such, was an appropriate objective of political activity. Yet what Wilson had in mind at the outset of his 1964 government was not socialism but economic growth. His intentions were expansion through budgetary encouragement, through national planning and through technology. One of the ironies of the economic crisis inherited by Labour in October 1964 was that the government blamed the retiring Chancellor, Reginald Maudling, for bequeathing it an £800 million balance of payments deficit while, at the same time, most members of that same Labour government appeared to believe that 'expansion' and borrowing were the ways to escape, Houdini-like, from the constraints of the past on social expenditures. The new government argued that Maudling should have taken steps before the election to correct the deteriorating situation but on the other hand denied the need after the election, when the figures on the balance of payments had turned out even worse than expected, to take deflationary action. The truth is that Labour's ideas on economic expansion were essentially the same as Maudling's. Labour's criticisms during Maudling's tenure at the Treasury had not been that he was expanding too much but that he was expanding too little. Maudling had relished the advice of NEDC and had adopted at least the pretence of an incomes policy. Labour might place rather more emphasis on national planning and prices and incomes policy, and there was all the fuss about technology. But Labour's policies were, as Maudling's had been, to break through the constraints that they believed had limited British economic growth during the Tory years. Labour's policies could be presented as socialist, if at all, because they incorporated national planning. When Labour was elected it presented itself as a new departure. In fact it was the old policies under new, and less experienced, management. The immediate trouble was that Maudling bequeathed an £800 million balance of payments deficit, and funding it pretty well exhausted Britain's capacity for unconditional borrowing.

There were moderates in the Labour party leadership who also regarded themselves as radicals and as socialists. The ideological leader of this school was Anthony Crosland, faithful friend of Hugh Gaitskell and supercilious critic of Harold Wilson. They did not consider that, as a party and as socialists, they were merely offering alternative management of things as they were. Their agenda did not simply consist of Wilson's vision of an economy revitalized by technology. They had a vision of a more just society and they used the word 'socialism' to describe it. The argument of *The Future of Socialism* still held. Socialism was about equality. Crosland sought equality, partly through redistributive taxation and partly through the refashioning of secondary education into a 'comprehensive' system. The grammar schools had been considered entirely compatible with socialism when socialism had been about nationalization. Now, his new definition of socialism fashioned Crosland's strong disapproval not just of public schools, at one of which he had himself been educated, but of grammar schools, at which had been educated many members of the PLP. He also wanted people to enjoy themselves and part of his distaste for Harold Wilson may have arisen from the fact that there was no evidence that Wilson did enjoy himself in ways approved by Crosland. Followers of Crosland did not proscribe further nationalization. They simply recognized that advocacy of nationalization was an electoral handicap and they did not wish it to be placed in the forefront of their appeal to the people. They were confident that, even without dependence on nationalization, they could plan the economy more successfully than had the Tories. They had no doubt that they could achieve an even better record on unemployment. They could banish 'stop–go', that curse of the Tory years that had alternated recession with inadequate growth. By banishing stop–go they could raise the growth rate and thereby ensure that more resources would become available for social purposes. Improved social provision was the key element in their revised socialist agenda and, in their eyes, it had been starved both because Tory priorities had been wrong and because Tory governments had mishandled the economy. The Labour party was united at least in its conviction that it could manage capitalism better than the Tories and in its insistence on economic growth.

THIRTEEN WASTED YEARS

In the foreword to a book, *Twelve Wasted Years*, published in September 1963 by the Labour Party Research Department (LPRD), A. L. Williams, General Secretary of the Labour party, wrote, 'By the end of October 1963 the Tories will have been in office twelve long years; twelve wasted years.' By the time of the election in 1964, the twelve years had become thirteen. So it was as thirteen 'wasted' years that the Labour party, in its propaganda, attempted to stigmatize the Tory government in the minds of the public. It was a comprehensive indictment.

In what respects had the thirteen years been wasted? The LPRD had no doubt of the answer. Its indictment was eloquent and, as to the carefully selected facts, irrefutable. It recalled that the UK's growth target was the lowest among all the countries of the OECD.[46] It employed its undoubted arithmetical skills to calculate that 'Failure to achieve the "Neddy" 4% growth rate has cost us over £10,000 million in lost production since 1951.'[47] It described the Tory period as a time of crises attributable to economic mismanagement.[48] Economic crisis had brought with it unemployment. 'Unemployment in the one year 1962 cost the country in lost production more than *all* the strikes since the war.'[49] It warned that 'this is not the first time that the Tories have given us a grim reminder of the 1930s. During the six months October 1958 to April 1959 the numbers unemployed were consistently above half-a-million.'[50] Thus it was enough for unemployment to reach half a million (2 per cent approximately) to remind Labour of the millions unemployed in the 1930s. Labour had warned the electorate in 1951 that a return to the Tories might mean a repeat of the 1930s. Its prophecy of Tory misbehaviour had been so far unfulfilled. But it was always eager for any evidence that the danger remained. Then there was the declining trade position of the UK. 'In every single year of Conservative Government Britain's share of world export markets for manufactures has declined.'[51] The result had been repeated balance of payments crises.[52] The balance of payments problems had been occurring despite the windfall improvement in the terms of trade enjoyed by the country under the Tories.[53]

Twelve Wasted Years was equally critical of social provision under the Tories. 'Altogether it is estimated that over 8 million people (about one-sixth of the population) are living in poverty at or near the miserably low National Assistance level.'[54] It concluded that 'The combination of low earnings and inadequate social security benefits has meant poverty for some at a time when others have "never had it so good".'[55] Summarizing life under the Tories, *Twelve Wasted Years* again employed the undoubted arithmetical skills of the LPRD to calculate that:

> If in the whole period of Conservative government since 1951 production had gone up at the same rate as the rest of western Europe, the national income would now be a quarter greater and tax revenue would be £1,500

million greater without any increase in tax rates. This would be enough to more than double the level of expenditure in roads, houses, schools, hospitals and all other public investment combined.[56]

The implication was that, if Labour had been in power, growth would have equalled or surpassed that on the continent. The successes on the continent were not, of course, attributable to socialism. Capitalism seemed to have served the continental countries rather well.

Thereafter, there was a great deal more to be said about the effects of Tory policy on consumers, on industry, private and public, and on agriculture. The impeachment of Tory failure left only the question whether Labour could do any better. Could Labour raise the growth rate to that achieved in other western European countries? Could it double the level of expenditure on roads, houses, schools and hospitals? The Labour indictment seemed to assume that the Tory record in government had been so bad that Labour could hardly avoid doing better. Now, with Labour challenging for power, there might be a chance to prove its superior management in every department of government. The leaders of the Labour party were sure that they were cleverer than the Tories, had deeper insights into the mechanisms of economic growth, and certainly had far greater energy and resourcefulness than could be found in any possible Tory Cabinet. Britain, under Attlee, had recovered from the war faster than the continent. It was only afterwards that Britain had lagged. What Attlee had achieved, Wilson could certainly do. After all Attlee knew nothing about economics whereas Wilson was an acknowledged expert. The LPRD's catalogue of Tory sins would, only six years later, be converted into a catalogue of Labour failures. When Labour was approaching the 1970 General Election, the Labour party put out a new booklet, *Labour in Action*, which naturally concentrated on such successes as it could find in the record of the Wilson government. It recalled that, in February 1963, unemployment had been at the high level of 932,946. It ignored the fact that, in 1964, average unemployment had been just under 400,000. It drew no attention at all to the fact that average unemployment in 1970, the last year of Wilson's first government, had been over 600,000. The impartial presentation of statistics is not the most notable characteristic of Labour campaign books.

HOPES

Though distrust still existed on both sides of the Party, Wilson was now leader. With him lay the prospect of patronage, of Ministerial preferment, for the right of the Party as well as the left. Once elected as leader Wilson proved a unifying figure. The Gaitskellite Roy Jenkins, destined to be one of the stars of the Wilson administration, had considered giving up his seat in the House of Commons for the editor's desk at the *Economist*. Wilson encouraged Jenkins to stay by assuring him that, as leader, his intentions did not encompass revenge against the Gaitskellites. In all sections of the Party nothing would more rapidly dispel distrust of Wilson's personality, policy or intentions than victory in the coming Election followed by the offer of a Ministerial post. This is not to say that, once the post has been accepted, the distrust might not revive. Though aspirants for Ministerial office were prepared to feel grateful to Wilson if he gave them reason, an atmosphere of distrust survived and not merely among those who felt that they would certainly have been in a Gaitskell Cabinet but feared that their claims to promotion might be ignored by Wilson. The distrust was in due course to find its justification in Wilson's failures as Prime Minister. The trouble with Wilson was that, when he came to office in 1964, no one knew what he really believed, if he believed anything. There was little evidence that he believed in socialism, if he ever had. And yet he had no other great reforming project except perhaps the Open University and certain vague ideas about technology.

Wilson, in 1964, achieved, if only narrowly, what many in the Labour party had feared would never happen again. He won. Labour had lost three elections in succession. Each election had brought an ever larger Tory majority. It had begun to appear that a government in power could fix any election. All that was needed was a giveaway budget which would act as a timely spur to the economy. What Chancellors Butler and Heathcoat Amory had done in 1955 and 1959, Maudling appeared to have attempted in 1963. To ensure that Maudling's 1963 budget measures should have the maximum opportunity to create a feeling of goodwill towards the government, the election had been delayed until the last possible day. The Tories had shown great skill in ensuring a coincidence between the dates of elections and good times for enough of the electorate. Perhaps Tory government was foredoomed to extend indefinitely into a future. Even discounting Tory manipulations, the electoral effects of Labour divisions had been destructive of socialist ambitions, not to mention the personal ambitions of leading members of the Parliamentary Labour Party.

Wilson's success in the election brought intense relief within the Labour party, which had begun to think that victory might once more be snatched from it. The relief when the votes were counted was augmented by the narrowness of the victory. Labour had overturned a Tory majority of 100, a notable achievement. But, in doing so, it had lost votes as compared with 1959, even though the electorate was larger. The Liberals, on the other hand, had increased their vote by two million and the Tories had suffered from it. The curiosities of the electoral system had been enough to give Labour an overall majority of four. Wilson had broken the spell. If nothing more, his success would entitle him to a honeymoon with most sections of the Party. He acquired lustre not just by entering No. 10 Downing Street as Prime Minister but by proving that Labour, despite many doubts, could win again. Wilson was already speaking of Labour as the natural party of government.

The election of Labour in 1964 brought to the most active of its supporters the hope of a more just society. By a just society, they meant a socialist society. It was the second time in twenty years that such hopes had been aroused by a Labour election victory. They were the stronger in 1964 because of the perceived success of the Attlee government in advancing the socialist cause. The greater the expectation the more rapid would be the disillusion. As supporters begin to realize that their leaders have feet, if not of clay, then certainly no more capable of soaring flight than those of thousands of ordinary men and women, disillusion sets in. The intractability of the problems will have reduced the leaders to merely human proportions. Achievements on which these much diminished leaders place great weight will appear as nothing to their supporters. The disappointment of exaggerated expectations always redounded to the discredit more of the Labour party than of the Conservative party. The Labour party was the Party of hope, the Conservative party that of management. Usually the electorate preferred management to hope but when, inadvertently, it put its trust in the Party of hope there was a lazy expectation that it should deliver. The ability to deliver would be the test.

But, for the time being, the important fact was that Wilson had won. When, only a short time before, he had been elected leader he had merely been the reluctant choice from a flawed short list. Now it was different. Now he had proved his capacity to lead and his capacity to win. To paraphrase Tacitus on the Roman Emperor Galba, everyone would have considered Wilson capable of occupying the office of Prime Minister if only he had never held it.

TWELVE

Harold Wilson's hundred days

SOCIALISM AS A REMEDY FOR CAPITALIST CRISIS

A few days after its election, the Wilson government announced that, having 'opened the books', it expected for the year 1964 a deficit in the balance of payments of £800 million. This was its inheritance from the Maudling dash for growth, alternatively interpretable as the Maudling dash for re-election. The deficit was double Wilson's last best guess before coming into office. It was an enormous figure that took the market by surprise. It had been expecting a bad outturn for the year but not this bad. It had been the Treasury's longstanding ambition to accumulate a surplus in the balance of payments of about £400–500 million a year in order to cover both normal government expenditure overseas and private overseas investment. Only once, in 1958, had this been achieved. Indeed, since the virtual convertibility of sterling conceded in January 1955, the balance of payments had been a continuing worry and constraint. Now, instead of the surplus of £400–500 million considered necessary by the Treasury, there was an estimated deficit of £800 million. It was an ominous introduction to Harold Wilson's much vaunted first hundred days of dynamic action, an election idea which he had inherited from President Kennedy of the USA, a country with political lessons to teach but fewer, perhaps, than British Labour leaders sometimes imagine.[1]

It became common form for the Labour party to complain that it only won office at a time of capitalist crisis, that its periods in government were therefore dominated by a difficult inheritance and that, as a result, it had neither time, nor means, to pursue socialist objectives as far as it would have wished. But, from another point of view, Labour governments were only getting what they deserved. The Attlee government had launched the country on an inflationary path which the Tories, fearful of becoming once more associated with high unemployment, had followed. When, in anticipation of the 1964 election, the Tory

Chancellor, Reginald Maudling, launched a boom, the Labour Opposition told him that he had not done enough. If, therefore, Labour reaped a whirlwind in 1964, it could hardly deny that it had helped to sow the seeds.

The market's lack of confidence in sterling was justified by nearly twenty years' experience of post-war British governments. A variety of events or suspicions in the foreign exchange markets could give rise to pressure on sterling. Paradoxically it might arise from weakness of the dollar, which sterling tended to follow. It might arise from a revaluation of the Deutschmark or the expectation of it, or from a host of other causes not all of which were within the control of the British government. It could arise simply from the election of a Labour government. Labour was expected to be even more profligate than the Tories. It had been a Labour government that had devalued sterling in 1949. Labour governments were thought to have a preference for easy options. There was an expectation, deriving from the performance of the British economy over many years, that sterling would again be devalued. It would have taken harshly deflationary fiscal and monetary measures from the new government to eradicate the expectation. Certainly words from ministers would not be enough.

While the balance of payments might be an inhibition, though not a bar, to social expenditures of a type expected from Labour, it was a supposed merit of socialism that it was an answer to the problems of capitalist crisis. As long ago as 1937 Attlee had written of the possibility of Labour taking over government at a time of capitalist crisis that 'the seriousness of the economic condition may make it possible to increase the *tempo* of change because people will appreciate that drastic remedies are necessary'.[2] Therefore, if there had to be a capitalist crisis, the electorate had displayed inadvertent wisdom in putting its trust in Wilson. The doctor had arrived precisely upon the hour and in the nick of time. A Labour government could be expected, apparently, not just to mitigate the seriousness of the crisis but to build on it an earlier prospect of socialism which would extirpate capitalist crisis once and for all.

Wilson, writing in retrospect after the election defeat in June 1970, asserted that, during the lifetime of his 1964–70 government, he had been conducting socialist policies. Of the struggles of his government, he wrote:

> [The crisis] had meant the application of specifically Socialist measures, some of them newly-designed for the problems we were facing, to secure national policies in industry and a more purposive use of our national

resources for overcoming a national malady. It had meant, equally, through our social policies – including taxation and greater public expenditure – the creation of a fairer order of society, without which we could not appeal, with any hope of success, for the sacrifices, restraint and efforts which were necessary from a united people, and which alone made possible the achievement of a situation of national strength.[3]

Wilson thought that his socialist medicaments had been triumphantly successful. 'The sneers abroad about Britain's sickness had given place to admiration.'[4] He could venture this claim because he was prepared, as a propagandist, to narrow the focus of his government to one supreme achievement – success with the balance of payments. By 1970 there was a surplus in the balance of payments. Socialism was now not so much about equality as about the balance of payments. He was deceiving himself if he believed that 'socialist' measures had delivered success with the balance of payments. That was due to a combination of devaluation and deflation which he had bitterly resisted but which in the end he had been compelled to concede. He was deceiving himself also about the UK's new reputation. The last year of Wilson's government was dominated by rising inflation, and a discontented electorate would extract its revenge. But self-deception was seldom absent from Wilson's musings. Self-deception was the stimulant that kept him going.

The question in October 1964 was whether the residues of socialism that persisted in the thinking of Wilson and his new government would be of any assistance in solving the problems with which it found itself confronted. Unfortunately the socialist residues were a hindrance, not a help. Ministers would insist that they were engaged in a drive to reconstruct the government machine to fit it better to regulate and invigorate the economy. They did not seem to understand that, even if the measures proposed had had any merit, they could have yielded their fruit only in the long term. Though they had spoken of a hundred days of purposive action, they seemed unconcerned by their own lack of urgency. First, devaluation was rejected. No doubt there were strong political objections to devaluation in October 1964. There was the minuscule size of the majority which put the government at risk of a further election before the benefits of a devaluation came through. After Cripps's 1949 devaluation, Labour did not want to become tarred as the Party that always chose the 'easy' option of devaluation. Promises, certainly unwise, had been made to Washington that the sterling exchange rate would be supported. But, while these objections may have had a certain validity in October 1964, they had none in March 1966 after Labour had won a majority of ninety-seven. The continuing rejection of devaluation then arose from the government's confidence in its own 'socialist' policies. It had, it was believed, economic and industrial policies, policies of socialist intervention in the industrial and industrial relations fields, that would make devaluation unnecessary. In other words Labour's decisive argument against devaluation was not the political embarrassments of October 1964 but the conviction that a realistic alternative economic policy existed. It did not, but three years were wasted making the discovery.

Secondly, the inconsistency between the decision not to devalue and the social policies of the government was ignored. As a socialist government, and especially as a socialist government elected with a small majority, Labour wished, whatever the crisis it had inherited, to keep its promises to its supporters. Those promises were expensive at a time when it was entirely inappropriate to implement expensive commitments. The market, instead of being impressed by the courage of the new government in rejecting devaluation, could hardly believe that it could be so insouciant. There could not have been a wider gulf of incomprehension than that which existed between the market and the government, with only the Governor of the Bank of England, the suspect Tory Lord Cromer, to mediate between them. In the imagery of Labour Ministers, the market took on a disagreeable, subhuman form. It consisted of 'gnomes', and it seemed to be mainly located in Zurich, where the gnomes guarded their treasure and conspired to deny this socialist government the access to it to which they thought themselves entitled. Why, evidently being foreigners, they should also be accused, as they often were, of a lack of patriotism was unclear.

Thirdly, there was the National Plan, an exercise in make-believe, which fostered fantasies about the potential performance of the British economy. It encouraged expenditures that would not have been wise even if the planned growth rates had been achieved and which compounded the inflationary pressure and the problems with the balance of payments. Fourthly, there was the renationalization of steel, an action motivated by a grudge against the Tories, with no possible relationship to the urgent needs of the economy. Fifthly, there was the attempt to operate a permanent prices and incomes policy. On the one hand the government stimulated inflationary pressures. On the other it attempted to restrain them with its prices and incomes policy. The incomes policy became part of the government's solution to the balance of payments crisis without devaluation. At first the policy was voluntary. As the pressure on sterling increased, it was made statutory. Occasionally useful in an extreme emergency, the idea of a permanent prices and incomes policy could issue only out of the socialist almanac or Macmillan's middle way. The theory was that prices and incomes policy would lead to a planned growth of incomes without commensurately higher prices. The economic growth, of which Wilson had assured the trade unions in his plea for an incomes policy just before the election, did not materialize.[5] It followed that incomes growth would fail to meet the demands of trade union members. Co-operation crumbled. The trade unions, at first reluctantly compliant, became increasingly restless. Trade union leaders became less and less able to persuade their members to co-operate with the policy. Barbara Castle remembered the insistence of Aneurin Bevan that socialism necessitated an effective wages policy and that, if necessary to achieve it, the trade unions must be brought under control. The result was *In Place of Strife*, a White Paper proposing reform of trade union law, which the government then abandoned under trade union pressure. The capitulation to the trade unions was one more disaster to add to a record of disaster. Socialism had proved a snare, not to say a delusion. At every stage Wilson's 'specifically socialist measures' had made the situation worse, not better. In summary, this is the history of the Wilson government. Having drawn the charge sheet, it is now necessary to substantiate it by examining the record in rather greater detail.

A GOVERNMENT OF OUTSTANDING PEOPLE

Since the 1959 election, Labour had lost both Gaitskell and Bevan, the two mutually incompatible warriors whose eventual reconciliation had aroused hopes that Labour might win in 1959. Alfred Robens, Minister of Labour in 1951, had departed for the National Coal Board, no doubt despairing of Labour ever forming a government again. It was George Brown's view that, if Robens had remained, Harold Wilson would never have become Prime Minister.[6] Even earlier, Sir Hartley Shawcross, another Cabinet Minister of 1951 vintage, had decamped to more satisfying pastures. Thirteen years are a long time to put one's life on hold, awaiting opportunity. Despite these losses, Wilson was more fortunate than had been Attlee in 1945. There was an array of talent, some of it with years of service in Parliament. Wilson was bound to appoint to his Cabinet the members of the Parliamentary Committee, or shadow Cabinet, even though it contained many for whom he had not voted and many also who had not voted for him. There were some who had been elected for reasons of inertia, or sentiment, or political orientation, rather than potential. They would have to be given their chance. But they could be deployed where they could do least damage. This still left him free to recruit others to the Cabinet and he was able to include such close political associates as Richard Crossman and Barbara Castle, who thought themselves unlikely to secure appointment if Gaitskell had lived. But, Crossman reflected, 'as Harold Laski used to remind us, in British politics while there is death there is hope. Gaitskell died and Harold Wilson succeeded him. My prospects were transformed . . .'[7] Crossman may, however, have misdirected himself. Gaitskell, shortly before becoming leader, is reported to have said that 'the only Bevanites I would have in a Government would be Dick Crossman, Harold Wilson and Barbara Castle.'[8] Certainly much that this trio had done since 1955 had distressed Gaitskell but, in the aftermath of victory, and back to his search for unity within the Party, it is not at all unlikely that he would have included Crossman and Castle in his administration.

While traditional socialism may have had no further viability in the Britain of the 1960s, its apparent attraction had brought one very positive benefit to the Labour party and hence to the Wilson government. The hope among young people in the 1930s and 1940s that society could be reconstructed in a more humane way had attracted into the Party, and then into the House of Commons, numerous young men and women who combined idealism with outstanding ability. Many had been undergraduates at Oxford and some sported the most splendid academic honours. Richard Crossman, a former Oxford don, and Denis Healey were in the Cabinet from the start. Anthony Crosland, another former Oxford don, and his close friend Roy Jenkins soon joined them. By-elections in 1962 had brought into the Commons William Rodgers and Dick Taverne as well as a Member who would make his mark in the years to come in a way all his own, Tam Dalyell. The 1964 General Election saw the arrival of others whose names would later appear in the higher ranks of government. The best known at the time were David Ennals and Peter Shore from the Labour party's headquarters staff, and Shirley Williams, who, even at this early stage, was being singled out as a possible first female British Prime Minister.[9] Although very little of the talent had experience of government, there were enough men and women of calibre available for Ministerial appointment, even though it was to be a rather large government on the excuse that there was so much to do. These recruits to socialist politics may, by this time, have abandoned the more idealistic versions of socialism with which they grew up but they certainly had the potential to occupy high posts in government with distinction. The only doubt would be whether they would know what to do when appointed.

Barbara Castle notes that 'there was a clear right-wing majority in the [1964] Cabinet. The halcyon days of left-wing hopes were to be short-lived.'[10] It was, she writes, 'a Cabinet in which the Left was adequately represented, but not in the key economic or overseas posts'.[11] The problem, however, was not any wish by Wilson to under represent the left. He always wanted a Cabinet and a government carefully balanced between right and left, and with the trade unions and Scotland, Wales and the English regions properly represented. The problem was that, apart from Castle and Crossman, there was on the left only Ian Mikardo who could be assessed as of Cabinet calibre. Mikardo, one of the best brains on the left, and a businessman with interests in eastern Europe, was omitted not just from the Cabinet but from a government which Wilson was seeking, without much success, to fertilize with serious business experience. There was also the conundrum of Michael Foot. Foot, the hagiographic biographer of Aneurin Bevan, had inherited Bevan's seat at Ebbw Vale.[12] Wilson might have considered that Foot would be better in than out of the government. Instead, he was left to make trouble on the backbenches. That Foot was a future leader of the Labour party would have appeared at the time improbable to the point of fantasy. That it did, eventually, happen illustrates the dangerous tendency of the Labour party to descend into whimsy. These four apart, Cabinet calibre was more easily to be found on the right than on the left. The balancing of the government therefore had to be achieved in its lower ranks. The domination of the key economic posts by leading members of the right was to bring no comfort to the government because they, no more than the left, knew what to do.

Right or left, many of the members of the new government outshone their Conservative shadows. Healey was an outstanding Defence Secretary, though his tenure suffered from the weakness of the British economy. His intellectual command of defence strategy could not fill the gap left in Britain's defence capability by successive cuts in the defence budget. And he had much to learn. Musing on foreign and defence policy in opposition had left him ignorant of Britain's economic vulnerability and therefore prone to exaggerated ambitions for Britain's defence role. Barbara Castle was to show remarkable courage and determination as Minister of Transport and in her attempt to bring the trade unions within the law. Jenkins and Callaghan in their different ways gave distinguished service at the Home Office. Jenkins's liberalism was notable in many areas of policy, though not, perhaps, especially so in penal reform. Callaghan, though accused of illiberalism in the matter of immigration, was really doing what the majority of his Party, and perhaps the country, wanted. His handling of the renewed outbreak of violence in Northern Ireland won him particular praise. Moreover, though often compared to his disadvantage with his predecessor Jenkins, he did what he could for race relations and he does carry the credit, accidental perhaps in its timing, of having carried through the House the resolution that finally abolished capital punishment for murder in the UK. There was nothing exclusively socialist in the social reforms of this era. But much of it was more likely to be done under a Labour government than under a Conservative government. Crosland, loyal to his idiosyncratic socialist convictions, brought to the Education Department his egalitarian ideas, but that is not to say that he was ineffective in a difficult department where the ambitions of a minister so often exceed his reach.

If, then, the government failed, it was not through lack of able people. It was in economic management that Labour's grasp was seen at its weakest and that for a combination of political and ideological reasons. The socialist residues in its intellectual formation were an important cause of failure. Insensitivity to world financial opinion was combined with too much Keynesianism and too much of the detritus of socialism. A continuation of great power illusions prejudiced foreign, as well as economic, policy and specifically relations with the EEC.

THREE AGAINST DEVALUATION

The fateful decision to reject devaluation was taken by Wilson, Brown and Callaghan within hours of assuming office. Brown was now Deputy Prime Minister, First Secretary of State and Secretary of State for Economic Affairs. Callaghan was Chancellor of the Exchequer. They had yet, however, to acquire the wisdom that should accompany such impressive titles. Whether the political objections to devaluation were insurmountable is a matter of debate. Certainly, in public opinion, Wilson had a clear lead over any Tory leader as an economic manager. His endorsement of devaluation as a policy, had that been his view, and had he displayed the courage and leadership, should have carried weight with the public. There were strong arguments to hand, above all the unexpectedly large deficit. But it was not his view, and the question was never tested. The decision was taken without any strong input from the Treasury. The Treasury had been taken aback by the consequences for the balance of payments of Maudling's dash for growth. It had feebly watched the situation deteriorating during the summer of 1964 without making any strong representations either to Maudling or to the Prime Minister. Now it was frozen in immobility attributable partly to its conviction, particularly that of its Permanent Secretary, Sir William Armstrong, that no attempt must be made to dictate to Ministers new in office with an electoral mandate, however tenuous. Treasury orthodoxy was always more likely to incline against devaluation than for it, but for once, it lacked its normal clarion clarity.

What was true of the Treasury was true equally of the rest of the civil service. Its reaction to the election of a Labour government was passive. It submitted to the democratic will without conveying the strong advice which was its duty to provide. In his personal record of the 1964–70 Labour government, Wilson pays repeated tribute to the preparations made by the civil service in anticipation of the change of government. 'Whitehall', he writes, 'is always well prepared for a change of Government.'[13] It is certainly true that the civil service had informed itself of the policies of the incoming Labour government so far as this was possible. It had mastered the contents of Labour's manifesto, *Let Us Go with Labour*. It had read the speeches and articles of the leader of the opposition. It had thought about the proposed departmental reconstruction.[14] If, however, it found any of this worrying, it did not feel it part of its duty to make the fact known to the new Prime Minister. No one in the Treasury or the Cabinet Office advised Wilson that his reconstruction of government machinery had no relevance to the actual problems of October 1964. Its preparation for a change in government did not extend to the issues facing the new government in the economic sphere. Decisions were therefore left to three socialist Ministers who had been out of office for thirteen years while the world changed dramatically, and none of whom had any personal experience of economic management. Instead of devaluation, and the necessary associated deflationary measures, the three decided to introduce the emergency programme devised by Maudling against the possibility that his dash for growth might turn sour, a 15 per cent import surcharge and a small subsidy to exports. Douglas Jay, at the Board of Trade, warned that the surcharge was illegal under international trade rules and that import quotas should be introduced instead. But the Treasury considered that a surcharge would be less bureaucratic than quotas and Jay lost the argument. There would also be a voluntary prices and incomes policy. Although Labour was to remain in office for nearly six years, and to win a large majority at the General Election of March 1966, this early error determined the future of the government. If, as some have argued, the decision not to devalue was inevitable for political reasons then, for political reasons, the failure of the government was inevitable from the start. By the same token, any hope that the Wilson government would make progress on the road to socialism was frustrated at the start.

Wilson gives contradictory reasons in arguing that he was right not to devalue in October 1964. 'The financial world at home and abroad was aware that the postwar decision to devalue in 1949 had been taken by a Labour Government. There would have been many who would conclude that a Labour Government facing difficulties always took the easy way out by devaluing the pound.'[15] On the other hand he argues, rightly, that devaluation was not a soft option.

> I had always argued – and continued to argue for the next three years – that devaluation was not an easy way out; that, by its very nature in cheapening exports and making imports dearer, it would require a severe and rapid transfer of resources from home consumption, public and private, to meet the needs of overseas markets. This would mean brutal restraints in both public and private expenditure over and above what was required by the domestic situation we had inherited.[16]

These quotations reveal the incoherence of Wilson's thinking. A Labour government coming into office and adopting 'brutal restraints' in public and private expenditure would hardly be regarded by the market as having taken the easy way out. It was the absence of brutal restraints that, within weeks, undermined any confidence the market might have had in the intentions of the new government. Wilson did not seem, at the time, to realize that he would need restraints as brutal to avoid devaluation as he would to accompany it. There was no third way between devaluation and deflation. There was the way of devaluation plus deflation; and there was the way of deflation. Neither was taken. Instead the government loosened the reins on public spending, checked only by the increasing concerns of the market.

WILSON'S DILEMMA

The three paramount leaders had taken their decision and, indeed, other than Douglas Jay, it is difficult to think of anyone else in the Cabinet who could usefully have been brought into consultation. On devaluation, Jay shared their view. It was not a Cabinet equipped to take economic decisions. In so far as it had any understanding of economic questions, it shared Wilson's belief in planning and industrial policy. Wilson had that much justification for not taking the Cabinet fully into his confidence on economic policy. But it is difficult to understand how he could imagine that he could wage a successful war against devaluation without the full co-operation of a Cabinet which had come into office only too ready to spend money whatever the crisis. Wilson's dilemma was how to manage his Cabinet, his Parliamentary Party and public opinion, in the light of his three problems, a dire economic crisis, his election promises and the prospect of a further general election probably by the end of 1965 but possibly as early as the spring of that year. It was a dilemma to which he found no satisfactory answer.

The decision not to devalue placed on Wilson's limited powers of leadership a burden greater than they could bear. It was in the weeks after the decision, and thus very early in the life of the government, that Crossman began to be critical of Wilson's leadership, comparing his equivocations unfavourably with the directness of George Brown. Wilson had various options. One was to be frank with his colleagues and the public and tell them that much in the Labour manifesto, however desirable, would have to be deferred until the country was able to pay for it out of its own earnings. Frankness was the logical concomitant of the decision not to devalue. But frankness of this kind was not medicine that Wilson thought it advisable to prescribe. After so long out of office, the postponement of social benefits would have caused grave disappointment. Expectations in the Labour party were high. If he tried stern measures he might not be able to carry them through. Perhaps he thought that he could never persuade his Cabinet, new in office, and a PLP equally inexperienced, enthused with the prospect of socializing the UK, that unfortunately such dreams had to be deferred. The electorate might not have liked the message and might have turned against him. He was not a leader for that kind of risk. Wilson told his Cabinet what he, Brown and Callaghan had decided to do but he did not invite their comprehension or their collaboration. Crossman quotes George Brown saying at the first Cabinet meeting: 'Naturally you won't want to be told, for fear of the information leaking, how serious the situation is. You won't want to be told what methods we shall take but we shall take them.'[17]

It is only fair to add that Wilson's task of persuasion would have been more difficult because of the state of complacency about their economic performance into which the people of Britain had been duped by successive post-war governments. They had been taught by governments and by economists that Keynes had, once and for all, solved the problem of unemployment. They had been assured by Macmillan that they had never had it so good and they realized that they had never had it so good. A new government might talk excitedly about the balance of payments and accuse its predecessor of irresponsibility. But the balance of payments did not make the impact on the minds of the electorate, or even of the PLP, which would have been made by rising unemployment or runaway price increases. It would have been a shock to discover that there were still serious economic problems, the solution of which might demand sacrifices.

Wilson's other option was to bluff and to hope that the market would allow him to get away with his bluff. This was more in his character. He was a leader for the easy options and, if there were none available, for the options that deferred hard choices. The US administration and the Federal Reserve did not want sterling to be devalued. If it was devalued, the dollar would be exposed. With the support of the US administration it would be possible to borrow from the IMF and other central banks for the defence of sterling. If there was substantial borrowing, there would certainly be conditions. Given the attitude of the US administration, they might not be intolerable conditions. He would do the minimum he thought necessary to satisfy the Gnomes of Zurich and equally the minimum he could get away with in implementing the manifesto. He would also exhort his countrymen to do better and to meet the challenge, a recourse beloved of British Prime Ministers seeking to shuffle off their own failures on to the shoulders of the electorate. If he could do enough to satisfy his Cabinet and his Party, if, in addition, he did not inflict too much distress on those who had voted for his Party, and might do so again, he could hope to win the further, inevitable election. If the minimum he proposed to satisfy his Party proved too much for the Gnomes, he would make a tactical withdrawal to safer ground. In short, he would manoeuvre between the various pressures, political and financial, and hope that luck would be with him. Luck favours the brave and therefore Wilson would be brave.

Like Micawber, he was hoping that something might turn up. He had the comfort of a forecast that the balance of payments would improve in 1965. Faced by an economic crisis, by the narrow majority and by the prospect of a further election possibly within months, he would govern as though the government had a majority of a hundred and proceed to implement its election manifesto. He would talk as though his government did have a majority of a hundred. His panache would enable him to retain the loyalty of his backbenchers and make possible the winning of a further general election in due course.

In discussion with Crossman, Wilson used a military simile to describe the manoeuvres he had in mind. When, in November 1964, the pound was under pressure, he recalled the Duke of Wellington's campaign in the Peninsula. He told Crossman that he was retreating to his prepared lines at Torres Vedras. Wilson did not explain what this meant except to deny that it meant devaluation.[18] The probability must be that he did not have the least idea what he meant. Crossman was in fact being told not to bother his little head with matters he did not understand. Even Barbara Castle was 'meekly' content to be told to mind her own business and not to probe further. Writing many years later, she reports her own submissive acceptance of the decision to defend the parity, though clearly, in retrospect, she believes it was a terrible mistake and that there had been an escape from the constraints if only the government had shown sufficient courage.

> Like other members of the Cabinet I had meekly accepted the economic propositions which were put to us at our first Cabinet: defend the pound with the help of a 15 per cent surcharge on all imports except food, tobacco and basic raw materials; subsidize exports through a tax rebate scheme; enter into consultations with unions and employers on a prices and incomes policy and 'review' public expenditure. The latter exercise was not made easier by the fact that the Tory Government had announced during its last months a lavish five-year programme of public expenditure which its economic performance could not have sustained. It had also postponed a number of price increases in nationalized industries . . .[19]

She still clearly held that the economic performance of a Labour government should have been able to sustain higher expenditure, and that a more visionary economic policy would have made possible everything that Labour had promised in its election manifesto to do.

The Cabinet was thus left without any clear understanding of the government's economic policy or of the implications of the decision not to devalue. Consequently it acted as though there was no crisis. It had accepted without enthusiasm, or understanding, the decision not to devalue but had been consoled by Wilson's assurance that, despite the narrow majority, the government would pursue the Party's election promises. As a result, it was always ready to put on a display of annoyed surprise whenever it was told by Callaghan that there were limits on public expenditure imposed by the economic crisis. In the absence of discipline imposed by Wilson, it saw no reason to impose discipline on itself. Even those members of Cabinet who understood that there was an economic crisis, and who would have been ready to limit their departmental demands to ease the problems of the Chancellor of the Exchequer, were unwilling, in the prevailing rush for money, to deny their own departments access to the public purse. Nor was there any sense of priorities, the realization that perhaps certain things could be done but not others. None of this discouraged Ministers from strong statements about their determination to defend the parity.

Without any lead from Wilson, how could the Cabinet be expected to behave differently? Yet it was the Cabinet. It was the body that is supposed to enter into collective decisions about the future of the country. It was there to supervise Chancellors of the Exchequer and Prime Ministers with a tendency to obfuscation. Instead, it was content to be allowed to pursue its departmental objectives even though, presumably, it had not shut its ears or blinded its eyes to what everyone in the world had been told about the British economic predicament. If Wilson is to be allowed any excuse for not insisting in Cabinet that Labour's election policies were inconsistent with the decision not to devalue, it can only be that he would have confronted major problems in persuading his colleagues. He may have felt that he was manoeuvring at the limit of political possibilities. It may be that he shied away from the task of education because he believed it impossible. He made no effort to educate the Cabinet. Probably he feared that it would retort that there were specifically Labour policies which, if only Treasury orthodoxy would permit, would free them from boring constraints on public expenditure and even that the government *should* take the easy option of devaluation. In any case, he himself suffered from the illusion that, even if he acceded to the political pressures, his 'socialist' planning and industrial policies would nevertheless rescue him. Crossman summarized the position that had arisen. 'We can't persuade the Zurich bankers that we are sound because we won't carry out the genuine old-fashioned deflation, and we are not prepared to carry out that deflation because we won't face a retreat on the social services front . . .'[20]

Wilson's manipulative choreography was abetted by the absence of pressure from the Treasury. The Bank of England was, typically, more robust but even more suspect. Governor Cromer laboured to bring the reality home to Ministers, but he was a Tory and hence intensely distrusted in Downing Street and elsewhere in the Cabinet. But at least he was giving straight, though distasteful, advice. He had given equally straight, though distasteful, advice to Maudling and Sir Alec, but had been ignored. One problem was Wilson's evident belief that economically Britain was still an island in which governments could plot their course free of international pressures, especially under the protection of American benevolence. He would say that there had been an election and that the electorate, however narrowly, had chosen a Labour government with a Labour programme. If the British people had decided in their wisdom to elect a Labour government on a Labour programme, it was no business of the Gnomes of Zurich, or their spokesman Cromer, to say them nay. What the electorate had proposed, the market should not be allowed to dispose.

In November, the government issued a White Paper on the economic situation. It stated that, with some exceptions, there was no pressure on resources calling for action. This was code for a denial of any need for deflation. Apart from the fact that it was economic nonsense, it demonstrated political incompetence of a high order. It was now no longer possible to blame the Tories for the inheritance. From then on, all failures in economic management would be down to the new government. The Treasury must have been very much on the defensive to permit such language to be used because it was clear enough that there was pressure on resources calling for action and, if it was not clear to the Treasury, it was clear to the Bank of England, to other central banks and to the market.

It would require self-deception beyond the ordinary if Wilson did think that his policies were consistent with one another, particularly consistent with the intention to avoid devaluation. But from across the chamber of the House of Commons some comfort was being wafted. That expert in economic management, Reginald Maudling, the recently retired Chancellor of the Exchequer who had bequeathed Labour his vast deficit, was being supportive. It required even greater self-deception to imagine that Maudling was any kind of authority whose advice carried any weight or could convey any comfort. But he was soon being quoted in defence of Labour's short, but already disastrous, economic record. Maudling was prepared to return the favour Labour had done him in

1963 by accusing him of being too moderate in his plans for explosive growth. He told the House that the new government had been right to act directly on the balance of payments and not by stop–go or by deflation.[21] Indeed he appeared to be saying that the new government had inherited his analysis and his solutions. Maudling equally presented himself as an enthusiast for incomes policy, to the negotiation of which George Brown was now turning his hand. It had been the philosophy of the Macmillan and Alec Douglas-Home governments that, if there was an effective incomes policy, the economy could be run at full blast. Unfortunately neither Macmillan nor Maudling had discovered how to introduce an effective incomes policy and the idea had never been tested. But it was hoped that, with Labour's close relations with the trade unions, what had been impossible for the Tories would be possible for Labour. Wishful thinking was bemusing both the major parties in the British Parliament.

The Labour party's 1964 election manifesto, following Frank Cousins in 1963, spoke of 'a planned growth of incomes broadly related to the annual rate of production'.[22] No one, certainly, would be more effective in securing the co-operation necessary to achieve that end than George Brown, trade unionist and ball of fire. But, as a warning, Frank Cousins had said just before the election, 'It is [the trade unions'] purpose to sell our labour and use our skill in the open market to the best of our ability while we live under the present system.'[23] There was no question of any system other than the present system, as Cousins well knew. It was always a convenient riposte for the trade unions to proclaim that they would agree to an incomes policy if there was socialism but that as there was capitalism they would act like capitalists even if there was a Labour government. It was an argument stored in the trade union knapsack for unveiling as necessary. They often found it necessary. They may even have believed it. It was an alibi for impotence.

A continuing characteristic of Wilson was his annoyance that he had not won sufficient respect from the market simply by refusing to devalue and his inability to accept that there might be something in what the press, the City and the Gnomes of Zurich were saying about the incoherence of Britain's economic policies. He was unwilling, or unable, to tell the electorate the truth but insisted instead on blaming every difficulty on the political hostility of the market. Even if Wilson had been right in claiming that a great deal of the criticism was motivated by political hostility rather than by the actual economic dilemmas, he still had to take notice of it as long as he needed to borrow from those he came to regard as enemies. He was continually talking of those who 'sold Britain short' as though, in the interests of their political convictions, they were prepared to lose vast sums of money by speculating against a currency, sterling, which was much stronger than they alleged. Michael Foot, writing in *Tribune* on 4 December 1964, hit the nail on the head: 'It is not possible to build the society we want while the present desperate dependence on international finance continues.'[24] This was true. But Foot did not, and could not, explain how a government so dependent on foreign borrowing could escape from its desperate dependence on international finance. His perception of this part of the truth led him nowhere.

Wilson never gave sufficient credit to the market, by which, for this purpose, one must understand not just those whose profession it was to operate privately in the foreign currency exchanges but also the US administration and the Federal Reserve. The US administration and the Federal Reserve were regularly prepared to suspend disbelief in the hope that such action as the Wilson government did take under pressure would be enough to sustain sterling. Despite strong and continuing doubts on this score, they were prepared to extend financial assistance to Britain so that sterling might be saved. Britain's military and economic security had become dependent on the American bomb and American money. In one sense the market was being kind. It was giving the new British government its chance. Its restraint enabled Wilson to win a general election in 1966 with a large majority. It is a different question whether it was being kind to Britain. It would have been in the interests of Britain if the market had shown from the start its disbelief in the half-measures the Wilson government was taking and had swept it either into effective action or into history. To have acted thus would have been cruel but it would have been cruel to be kind. The Wilson government would probably have survived the experience. The members of the Cabinet, after all those years of opposition, were not in a resigning mood.

THE SOCIALIST REMEDIES — THE DEPARTMENT OF ECONOMIC AFFAIRS AND THE MINISTRY OF TECHNOLOGY

As Harold Wilson settled into No. 10 Downing Street he proposed not simply to form a new government but to equip it with new government departments. He believed that his new departments would be the instruments of his many 'socialist' departures in policy. All this creativity was perhaps influenced by the experience of war, when the creation of new Ministries, such as those of Food and Economic Warfare, had served some purpose. Wilson could remember those days as a wartime civil servant. There were now to be five new departments, the Department of Economic Affairs (DEA), the Ministry of Technology (Mintech), the Ministry of Overseas Development, the Welsh Department and the Ministry of Land and Natural Resources.[25] While the DEA and Mintech were undertaking the serious economic responsibilities of government, the Ministries of Overseas Development and of Land were to confirm that Labour was still a radical party. It would take overseas development, about which Wilson had written extensively in his Bevanite days, seriously, and would deprive landowners of uncovenanted profits made out of the initiative of developers. Crossman, later an enthusiastic devolutionist, refers to the Department for Wales as 'Another . . . idiotic creation . . . all the result of a silly election pledge'.[26] As Minister of Housing, Crossman had equally contemptuous thoughts about the Ministry of Land. These departments were not in fact exactly new. Their creation followed the precedent set by God. God deprived Adam of one of his ribs in order to furnish him with a companion in Eve. Wilson robbed existing departments in order to make his new departments. But, just as Eve succeeded in getting Adam expelled from Paradise, so would these new departments prove to be nothing but trouble to those that had been deprived.

The most important new departments were the two which were intended to spur economic growth in the UK. The DEA was to spur growth through planning and Mintech was to spur it through technology. These were two elements in Wilson's residual socialism. The DEA was intended to prove that it was Labour, the Party of planning, that really knew how to plan. Mintech was to be the departmental expression of Wilson's evocation at Scarborough of the white heat of technology. Mintech would be encouraging the adoption of the most modern practices in British industry as well as attempting to save the British computer industry. It would be striving to raise the status of engineers. In British industry, engineers, those qualified individuals now known as chartered engineers, were lowly paid and lowly regarded. Chartered engineers resented the fact that they shared their distinguished designation with undisciplined members of the Amalgamated Engineering Union. An accolade had been converted into a reproof. Now, under this new government, they were to be the midwives of the technological revolution. It might have been thought that chartered engineers could look after their own status. But no, this too fell to this interventionist government.

The preparedness of the civil service for the change in government was demonstrated by its ability to extract these new departments from the bodies of the old with the minimum of friction and disturbance. However, friction and disturbance could not be altogether avoided. Thus it proved impossible to draw a secure line between the responsibilities of the Treasury and the DEA. Wilson considered the 'fundamental distinction' to be between the monetary responsibilities of the Treasury and the DEA's co-ordinating responsibilities for industry and the mobilization of resources.[27] The DEA, in other words, was the department for promoting 'socialism', and the Treasury the department for managing capitalism. Managing capitalism in a fraught economic conjuncture was bound to drain any prospect of success from the DEA's socialism.

Wilson persuaded a somewhat reluctant Frank Cousins, General Secretary of the TGWU, to become Minister of Technology. This was not an original idea of Wilson's. Gaitskell also had sounded Cousins out.[28] His presence in the government would fulfil various, not entirely consistent, purposes. It would strengthen the left in the Cabinet, and Wilson always thought he could rely on the left in any battle for survival. Industry would see that in Cousins they would be dealing with a man whose substance did not just derive from his being a Minister of the Crown. Cousins's acceptance of a position in the government would seal the relations between government and trade unions at a time when difficult and sometimes unpopular measures would have to be taken. At Scarborough, Wilson had warned that the technological age would leave no room for restrictive practices. Cousins's appointment would encourage trade unions to co-operate in achieving higher productivity. In attaching the trade unions more closely to the government, Cousins would do for Wilson what Bevin had done for Attlee. But Cousins was not a man of comparable weight and was unlikely to exercise in Cabinet the dominant influence which Bevin could exert almost without noticing it. Cousins, moreover, did not have the personality to overcome the hostility of the House of Commons to any upstart whose career, however successful, had been made outside Parliament.

GEORGE BROWN

Wilson's principal problem in Cabinet-making was how to employ his deputy, George Brown. Brown evoked equal admiration and anxiety among his friends, and anxiety far exceeding admiration among his critics. Unlike so many leading Labour figures, Brown was of the working class at a time when it was rare, but not exceedingly rare, for a working-class child to achieve a university education. Of the three leaders of the Labour government in 1964, Wilson, Brown and Callaghan, only Wilson had had a university education. The other two sometimes seemed to worry about what they had missed through the lack of it. Because he was both working class and erratic, leading Labour figures who *had* been to university condescended to consider George Brown brilliant. He was even spoken of as the ablest of all the Labour Parliamentarians. His outstanding positive quality, however, was not brilliance but courage. His principal negative quality was demonic energy badly directed. He had proved his courage on numerous occasions. The most famous was his confrontation with Khrushchev during the latter's visit to London with Bulganin in April 1956. Another was when, at the 1962 Labour Party Conference, he had answered the debate on membership of the European Economic Community after Gaitskell had denounced the idea of Britain turning its back on a thousand years of history. Brown had demonstrated, in face of a conference that had enthusiastically applauded Gaitskell's speech, that there was within the Labour party a pro-Market stream as well as the dominant anti-Market stream.

He had been, in his role as deputy leader, the obvious candidate of the right for the succession after Gaitskell's death, and the right was in a majority in the PLP. But Callaghan had stood in the election, encouraged by a number of right-wing MPs who feared a George Brown leadership. Callaghan may thereby have deprived Brown. Brown was not the man to forgive such treachery. The support for Callaghan was an expression of distrust in Brown's judgement and, in particular, of his susceptibility to alcohol. He had made an unfortunate display of himself when, in November 1963, he delivered a televised obituary of President Kennedy when drunk. He was not a man who could conceal his feelings. He could be easily hurt, as he clearly showed when the despised Wilson was elected as Gaitskell's successor over his head. He had then retired, momentarily, to nurse his wounds. They never healed. There was no Parsifal to touch them with his spear. Even when Brown returned, he brought with him a festering resentment against Wilson for defeating him, and Callaghan for standing against him. His energy could rapidly turn into intolerance. Intolerance of colleagues does not make for harmonious relations in government. In government, it is the privilege of the Prime Minister alone not to suffer fools gladly. Brown's intolerance could rival that of Ernest Bevin. But whereas Bevin had been indispensable, at least in the early years of the Attlee government, Brown never was. Almost from the beginning his temperamental instability led to questioning whether the benefits of his presence in the government outweighed the costs. He was continually threatening resignation until, even among friends who had repeatedly striven to rescue him from the effects of his outbursts, the thought became irrepressible that perhaps it would be better if he went.

There were two questions in everyone's mind when George Brown became the second man in the Wilson government. The first was whether he could work with Wilson. The second was whether a constructive role in government would satisfy his nature or whether refuge in drink would be his response to the inevitable frustrations. Already by January 1965, it was becoming known within the government that it was proving difficult to get anyone to work for Brown as Principal Private Secretary.[29] Already by April 1965 it was being noticed that Brown's drinking was affecting his conduct and his performance. Wilson had had no choice but to appoint Brown to the most senior position in his government. He could then do little more than watch and wait as Brown alienated his friends and destroyed his own reputation. Yet, to the opposition press, Brown was in one sense indispensable in these early days. To praise Brown, a figure larger than life, displaying imagination and energy, was one way of criticizing Wilson. Later there would be others to serve exactly that purpose.

THE BATTLE FOR LEADERSHIP IN ECONOMIC POLICY

In 1963, George Brown was Chairman of the Home Policy Committee of the Labour party and was thinking of ways of restyling British government.

> We were all (at least, most of us who were concerned with Labour Party policy) expansionist at heart, and we thought that the economy was being held back, that unemployment was being kept high, that all sorts of barriers were being erected to keep down industrial activity, by reason of the orthodox financial policy of the Treasury. Out of this kind of

thinking grew the idea that it would be better to have an economic department, which (as I always saw it) would be superior to the Treasury in determining the country's economic priorities.[30]

If George Brown thought that, at any time since the war, the Treasury, under successive Chancellors, had been conducting an orthodox economic policy, he should have had a word with Lord Cromer, Governor of the Bank of England, who would have expressed a different view rather roughly. The thinking that led to the creation of the DEA did not in fact run particularly deep. There was to be a growth department, but no one had worked out how the new department was to stimulate growth. It seemed to be assumed that if there was a department there would be ways of stimulating growth, ways presumably offered to Ministers by civil servants on demand. Civil servants can reasonably be required to administer old policies. Yet, if new policies are to be introduced, they can equally reasonably expect Ministers to tell them how. If Ministers do not know how, it is unreasonable to expect civil servants to fill the gap. It is, however, one of the functions of the civil service to attempt to meet the unreasonable demands of its political masters. It is a function seldom adequately acknowledged.

The subsequent history of the DEA was to demonstrate a good deal of flurry and scurry. It was to intervene, too often destructively, in everyone else's business. Its Secretary of State was to show enormous energy. But no policy for growth emerged other than a so-called National Plan which made recommendations but which could certainly not be regarded as an engine of growth. Brown, not Callaghan, chaired the Cabinet's Economic Policy Committee and the National Economic Development Council. But in no other respect was the DEA made superior to the Treasury. This was fortunate. Even in the days of the DEA's honeymoon, when great things were expected of it, there was some restraint on George Brown's enthusiasms, even though the restraint was, too often, brushed aside. The fact that the Treasury still had a voice in the making of economic policy alarmed all those in the Party, including George Brown, who thought that the election of Labour should lead to an even faster expansion than that which had produced the £800 million deficit.

The corollary of making the DEA the superior department might have been paradoxical. It would have made George Brown, in his capacity as head of the DEA, in practice the effective Chancellor of the Exchequer even if that title had still been bestowed on James Callaghan. It would have changed the whole nature of the DEA, which would then have become responsible for fiscal and monetary affairs as well as its agreed remits of national economic planning and prices and incomes policy. It would have been the department for managing capitalism as well as the department for promoting socialism. The incompatible roles would have been far beyond George Brown's capacity and he would soon have been accused of selling out to Treasury mandarins. It is unlikely that Callaghan would have accepted such an arrangement. But, if it had happened, the Treasury, with George Brown as its instrument, would probably have regained control over the whole of economic policy even more rapidly than it did.

The DEA could have had as its purpose the encouragement of dissension between Callaghan and Brown. In retrospect George Brown reflected:

> I do think ... that [the Prime Minister] came to believe that a state of competitive existence between the DEA and the Treasury would keep everybody on their toes: in fact, all this internecine warring achieved was to make everyone work many times as hard and quarrel far more often than was necessary to secure an outcome that was practically no improvement on what had happened before.[31]

It was a sad admission that there had been no improvement on what had happened before. But nothing else, rather a deterioration, should have been expected. In the early years, the sheer irrationality of George Brown's approach to policy undermined the hopes for the DEA. At the Treasury, Callaghan had to be concerned with confidence. Maintaining confidence could imply raising interest rates and a deflationary budget. Brown was concerned with growth. As his concern was with growth in the short term, his instinct was to oppose increases in interest rates and deflationary budgets. Brown took time to learn that economic growth was a problem for the long term and that meanwhile there was a crisis in the balance of payments to surmount. Devoted to 'growth', he could not see the necessity of anything that, in the short term, was antipathetic to growth. Anything worse than a neutral budget, any increase in bank rate, any stiffening of hire purchase terms, all had to be opposed, whatever the arguments for them, because the DEA was the 'growth' department and he, George Brown, was charged with delivering growth. The management of capitalism was increasingly at odds with the promotion of socialism.

One of Brown's principal tasks was to establish an effective prices and incomes policy. Callaghan had to be concerned at inflationary wage increases. They could imply that he must reduce domestic demand so that exports should not be affected. Brown did not want the trade unions to be deterred from co-operation with his incomes policy.[32] In Brown's mind, an effective policy implied controlling the prices of nationalized industries. Callaghan, on the other hand, had to be concerned with the fiscal and demand effects of controls on the prices of nationalized industries. The whole Cabinet had to be worried about increases in nationalized industry prices when a general election was pending, quite independent of income policies or fiscal deficits. But the prospect of a general election was an argument on Brown's side rather than on Callaghan's. That there should be different points of view on major questions of policy was not surprising. If the DEA had not been separated from the Treasury, the differences would have been resolved within the Treasury. As it was they became battles in Cabinet, in cabinet Committees and even in the press between George Brown and James Callaghan.

Later, one of George Brown's complaints was that he had devoted too much time to prices and incomes policy at the expense of other measures that would have stimulated growth. He did not realize that the reason why he had spent so much time on prices and incomes policy, and on other interventions such as the salvation of shipbuilding on the Upper Clyde when it was threatening to collapse, was that he had nothing else of importance to do. Prices and incomes policy and his other miscellaneous interventions did represent opportunities for action by a man who was for ever demanding action. To discover the secret of growth, to implement policies which turned that secret into effective action, was beyond George Brown and his department for the simple reason that it would have been beyond any Minister and any department. An indication of the fragility of policy was the frequency with which Brown and Callaghan were threatening to resign. Brown's temperament is a partial but not wholly credible explanation. If he had felt he was achieving anything in his job at the DEA, he would not have been threatening resignation. Callaghan was a more stable character but his discomfort in his job, managing the economy on the edge of crisis and under constant criticism from Brown, also demonstrates a lack of confidence in the policy he was being compelled to follow.

It fell to Wilson to arbitrate between his two most senior colleagues. Arbitrate he did, not always wisely, often conciliating the clamours of Brown when the necessities pointed to the caution of Callaghan. Politics, and the imminence of another general election, too often pointed to growth and expenditure as the way forward, even if they were endangering his own commitment against devaluation. That apart, he became so tied up in overseas policy that, even if he had wanted to, he could not devote his mind to the urgent problems of the economy. From the beginning there was fear that the Treasury would win out in the end. George Brown, in retrospect, thought that if only he could have persuaded Sir William Armstrong, Permanent Secretary at the Treasury, to become Permanent Secretary at the DEA, he would thereby have ensured his victory over the Treasury.[33] On such little things, apparently, does the future of socialism depend. It is more likely that Armstrong would not have accepted the appointment knowing the difference between the Treasury, a central department powerful because of its control over fiscal and monetary policy, and the whimsical departmental extravagances of inexperienced Prime Ministers. Thomas Balogh, economic adviser to Harold Wilson, was so frightened that the Treasury would submerge the DEA that he warned Brown that he was making a mistake even in accommodating the DEA in the same building as the Treasury.[34] But it was not proximity to the Treasury that damned the DEA, simply the lack of any definable purpose other than as a vehicle for Brown's enthusiasms. The DEA was bound to fail because of the nature of its mission. The management of capitalism was bound to win precedence over the promotion of socialism. But it did not help that Brown, with all his weaknesses, was in charge. When faced by real problems, he was inclined to detect conspiracies. Two very different men, Wilson and Brown, had that at least in common. So, when Brown met difficulties and then defeat, he attributed it not to the existence of problems which he had not addressed, or not understood but to the malign intentions of opponents within the government.

The victor in the end was the Treasury, as Brown mournfully acknowledges.

> Once the heady first days had gone and the novelty had worn off, the Treasury began to reassert itself and with its absolutely superb mastery of the government machine gradually either filched things back or – more to the point – made it rather difficult for us to effect the grand design we had in mind so that a coherent and continuous economic policy could emerge.[35]

Brown never really understood the inevitability of the Treasury victory over his energetic but ill-directed efforts. There was no grand design. Brown did not provide it. Nor did it emerge from the officials of the

DEA, even though many of them were of the highest calibre and shared the hopes of the government that the new department provided the key to an escape from the miserable economic past.

Writing of his failure, Brown comments,

> So orthodox financial control won, and our basic social reformation failed ... Too many people had vested interests in our department *not* succeeding. Putting it in rather crude political terms, our success meant a tremendous threat to half a dozen old-established departments. Not only the Treasury, but also Labour, the Board of Trade, Local Government, and the Scottish and Welsh Departments felt themselves threatened. More serious still, this threat was also felt at No. 10. What came to be referred to as the 'strained relations' between the Prime Minister and myself was not due to any move on my part to oust him in any way. I fear that he has never quite believed this, but it is fact, true. I have never made any attempt to supplant him.[36]

Thus, even on the assumption that the DEA had some contribution to make to the regeneration of the British economy, the surrounding political circumstances were unfavourable. This was a government riven by personal distrust. In the early days the distrust divided the three leaders, Wilson, Brown and Callaghan, who should have been working together. Wilson, who was safe in his leadership but seemed obsessed by conspiracies, drew comfort from the fact that Brown and Callaghan were unlikely to unite against him. Later the emergence of Roy Jenkins and of the European issue would add to the divisions and the sources of distrust. Brown having exhausted his credibility, Wilson now had to draw comfort from the rivalries between Callaghan and Jenkins. Richard Marsh, who entered the Cabinet after the 1966 election, wrote that he had 'never worked among a group of people who disliked and distrusted each other quite as much as that band of brothers'.[37] But then Marsh had never been a member of the Attlee Cabinet.

THE GOVERNMENT UNDERMINES ITS RESIDUAL CREDIBILITY IN THE MARKET

In November 1967, Wilson was to concede that his biggest mistake had been to underrate the power of speculators against sterling.[38] That this was his settled opinion, or alternatively his settled excuse for failure, was demonstrated when he repeated this confession, in answer to a reporter, Chris Mullin, during the 1970 election. His biggest error, he then said, had been that he had 'underestimated the power of speculation to knock government policy aside'.[39] There was certainly evidence justifying this modest admission from the man whose chief claim to election was that he understood the economy. James Callaghan, when Labour's shadow Chancellor of the Exchequer, had always expected that the election of a Labour government would stimulate speculation against sterling. But it is quite clear that the Party as a whole was unprepared for it. Callaghan himself had not thought out how to deal with speculation against sterling. Now the risks to sterling had been compounded by the balance of payments deficit. Callaghan was left stranded, unable to enforce what he himself increasingly saw to be necessary. He was a second Dalton, expostulating ineffectively with his colleagues, seldom able to persuade. There was the question of pensions. Callaghan wanted to limit the increase to ten shillings (50p). Wilson probably would have preferred it if the Cabinet had accepted Callaghan's advice. But when the Cabinet indicated that it would not be satisfied with less than twelve shillings and sixpence (62.5p), Wilson went along with it. Crossman tells us that in the debate in Cabinet Wilson 'had remained cagily in the middle . . . until he could see which side was winning'.[40] Callaghan's 11 November budget was in form neutral. It authorized the higher pensions, abolished prescription charges and distributed other benefits to an expectant public, but also raised taxes. However, the neutral budget was received in the market with incredulity. How could a government announce an £800 million balance of payments deficit and then introduce such a budget? Even Crossman had been prepared to say in Cabinet that Callaghan's November budget was not tough enough.[41]

The Cabinet, dreaming its socialist dreams, and at last with an opportunity to implement them, did not believe that Labour's manifesto should lie hostage to the value of sterling. For them devaluation *would* have been a soft option. Castle reports that 'Labour MPs [in 1964] had become restless at the conventionality of the Government's economic policy. They were disappointed by the tone of Jim Callaghan's Budget statement in November when he had praised Victorian virtues of paying our way and not borrowing, rather than holding out any vision of an expansionist policy.'[42] Maudling had borrowed vastly. Why should not Labour be as imprudent as the Tories? Had not the Attlee government founded the welfare state on the basis of borrowed money? Should not the world provide the resources the Wilson government needed to fulfil its socialist ambitions? Ministers on the left such as Castle and Cousins would have been perfectly happy to defy the international bankers, and if, as a result, there was a forced devaluation, so much the better.[43] They saw no inconsistency between their desire to borrow and defiance of international bankers. For them protection of the pound's parity was the least of their worries and certainly should not be put ahead of the government's social programme. They believed devaluation would free them from all such problems. It would mysteriously create resources which could then be distributed to the proposed beneficiaries of the Labour party's election promises. They did not realize, or if they did would not accept, that devaluation itself would imply deflation or it could result in hyperinflation.

The November budget provoked a serious run on the pound. A suggestion by Lord Cromer, supported by Callaghan, that interest rates be raised by 1 per cent was rejected because Brown considered it inconsistent with his growth strategy. Inaction stimulated the run on the pound and forced an increase of 2 per cent two days later. It also led to a confrontation between Cromer and Wilson in which Wilson angrily proclaimed the sovereignty of the British Parliament and the British electorate over the machinations of the speculators. Cromer replied that if the government wished to borrow it had to show some respect for the views of the lenders. The idea that, as a large borrower, the government would have to inspire confidence in lenders was foreign to the Prime Minister. Wilson reacted by threatening to float sterling, which he never seriously intended because it would be contrary to his decision not to devalue and his assurances to President Johnson. Cromer responded that to float would cause an international financial crisis. Perhaps Cromer took Wilson's threat too seriously. Or perhaps he thought that the way the government was behaving would lead inevitably to devaluation or floating. He rescued the government for the moment by arranging a credit of $3 billion for three months from other central banks. This would have been impossible without American connivance. But Cromer could derive some satisfaction from the thought that, if the government wished the credit to be renewed on maturity, it would have to surrender some part of British sovereignty to the moneylenders. The credit did not at once stop the run on sterling but it did gain time. In February the credit was renewed, but it would expire in a further three months, that is in May. At that time the government would have to be very persuasive if it was to find anyone prepared to lend. Callaghan, in February if not before, had become clear that there was too much pressure on resources and that there was a need for a tough budget in April unless there was a quick election.[44] He was facing grave political as well as economic difficulties. He might think there was need for a tough budget but his Cabinet colleagues, especially Wilson and Brown, did not. Already by January 1965 Crossman had become concerned at the ill-preparedness of the government. '[I]t is clear once again that a socialist opposition in this country comes into office with very half-baked plans.'[45]

At the end of March, Wilson assured Barbara Castle that the budget would not be too bad. Only Professor Nicholas Kaldor, brought into the Treasury as an economic and tax adviser to Callaghan, was calling for more deflation. Thomas Balogh, Wilson's economic adviser at No. 10 Downing Street, who, in November, had thought the budget insufficiently deflationary, was now prepared to submit to the electoral pressures of the moment. Wilson quoted Balogh approvingly as saying that the trouble with Kaldor was that he was a theoretical economist.[46] In other words Kaldor did not understand politics, a proposition for which there was some evidence. Theoretical economist Kaldor might be, but he was one of the few advisers to the government who, from the beginning, had shown an accurate understanding of the predicament it faced, far more so than the lamentable Balogh, who understood political pressures only too well. With all this, Callaghan had to contend. The inevitable result was that his April budget did too little to regain the confidence of the market.

A SPECIAL RELATIONSHIP

Close relations with the USA were a cornerstone of Wilson's policy. He therefore sought, as soon as he had become Prime Minister, to arrange a meeting with President Lyndon Johnson in Washington. He had visited Johnson earlier in the year when he was still leader of the opposition. He optimistically took away from that meeting a sense of good feeling between the two leaders. On his election victory, there was a telephone call from the President offering his best wishes and congratulations. This was thought to portend well for relations between the two governments. However, when the December meeting was fixed, Johnson sent an adviser, Professor Richard Neustadt, to London to ensure that Wilson did not carry with him to Washington unrealistic expectations.

Derek Mitchell, Wilson's Principal Private Secretary, reported in a minute of 29 November 1964 on a conversation with Neustadt the day before:

Professor Neustadt repeated the warning already given by him to the Prime Minister and others that the Prime Minister should not bank on everything going his way when he got face to face with the President. Of course there was always in Washington a great fund of goodwill towards the UK and its representatives but the President was not looking forward to the talks with anything approaching the same eagerness as the Prime Minister . . . he looked forward to next weekend as more of a chore than a major act of policy. It was known that the Prime Minister had received a strong impression from his personal meeting with the President . . . when he was Leader of the opposition; and that he had been moved by the warmth of the message which was sent to him when he took up office. But the President himself had not the same recollection of the earlier meeting and the warm message of greeting was no more than the result of an instruction to officials to draft a warm message of greeting.

No one in Washington was quite sure what kind of treatment the President would offer. It might be the 'overwhelming friendliness' treatment, which would either be genuine or simulated. It might be the 'arm round the shoulder, talking eyeball to eyeball treatment' – and in this variant the President's gaze usually went through the other person's head. Or it might be the 'Gary Cooper treatment', in which the President sat in his rocking chair and listened with such gruelling patience that his opponent was eventually driven into the sands of silence.[47]

The meeting gave Johnson the opportunity of pressing upon Wilson the importance of the sterling parity. He expressed concern about the consistency between the Labour government's additions to social expenditure and its determination not to devalue. Wilson, who could hardly retreat on the measures he had so recently taken, gave Johnson such reassurance as words could supply. The two politicians understood each other quite well and Johnson, whatever he really thought of Wilson, welcomed any support from the UK for his foreign policy, particularly on Vietnam. Anything Britain could be persuaded to contribute would not fall on the US budget. Any forces that Britain could be persuaded to deploy in the war against communism meant a lighter load on American forces. Wilson resisted a British military commitment to Vietnam, though he did offer the use of the UK's jungle-training team in Malaya and also its teams for anti-subversive activities. The Americans knew enough about the British political situation not to hope that British forces would be deployed in Vietnam. Otherwise, everything went splendidly. The meeting proved to be a great success, at least for American policy. The Americans placed great emphasis on Britain's role East of Suez, which both Wilson and Defence Secretary Healey were determined to maintain. It would make the British economic situation even more difficult, but Johnson had Wilson's promise not to devalue. The Cabinet was told that Johnson, who had recently been re-elected, had shown himself deeply concerned about Britain's economic situation. He had in fact offered all aid short of advice to devalue. He had also expressed appreciation of the help which Britain had given him in the election and all that Harold Wilson's speeches had meant for him. 'They want us with them,' Wilson told the Cabinet by way of conclusion. 'They want our new constructive ideas after the epoch of sterility. We are now in a position to influence events more than ever before for the last ten years.' Crossman assures us that the humour was unconscious.[48] Wilson's intense desire to be loved in Washington was not the least of Britain's problems.

Wilson's confidential communications to Johnson appear to have created in Washington the sensation that American officials were in charge of British economic policy. It was not an unreasonable feeling given that sterling was highly dependent on American willingness to provide support. As the Americans felt that they had great influence over British economic policy, a debate began in Washington as to how the influence could be exploited. The State Department thought it could be used to extract British support for US policy in Vietnam even to the extent of sending troops. The US Treasury and the Federal Reserve realized that the weakness of sterling was a liability to the dollar and that therefore not much could be extracted from the UK in return for the support given to sterling. To press for too much by way of political and military support for US policies might be counterproductive. The principal US aim should be to discourage sterling devaluation, and for that purpose the UK government should be influenced to deflate to the limits of domestic political possibilities.[49] American policy was clearly being defined in terms of US interests. Britain's, under a Labour government, was still being influenced by its lost imperial past.

UK policy was a composite of unreconcilable elements. Only later, under economic pressure, would it be clearly formulated. First there was Wilson's determination to avoid devaluation. Second was the unwillingness to take the necessary accompanying deflationary steps which might just avoid a sterling devaluation. Third was his wish to retain the American relationship and US support for a British global role. The question that was not discussed in Cabinet in any depth was whether Britain could still afford its global role. Healey attempted to comfort the Cabinet with the information that, to the Americans, Britain's East of Suez role was far more important than its troops in

Germany.[50] But there was no realistic prospect of Britain withdrawing its troops from Germany, even though Callaghan, like Dalton before him, repeatedly complained about the cost. The European commitment was politically inescapable. What was done East of Suez was not an alternative but an addition. The problem was that Wilson's priorities were incompatible with one another. It was unlikely he could avoid devaluation. He certainly could not avoid it without deflation and while retaining a significant East of Suez role.

Wilson greatly exaggerated his rapport with President Johnson and the favourable impression he was making in Washington. He was not prepared to alienate Johnson and he rapidly found how easily Johnson could be alienated. On 11 February 1965, Wilson phoned Johnson in order to dissuade him from disproportionate action against the Vietcong, who had just launched a vigorous attack in the Saigon area. He suggested a visit to Washington so that he could give Johnson the benefit of his advice. He got a flea in his ear. 'I won't tell you how to run Malaysia and you don't tell us how to run Vietnam . . . if you want to help us some in Vietnam send us some men . . . Now if you don't feel like doing that, go on with your Malaysian problem.'[51] It is unlikely that Johnson would have spoken to President de Gaulle in this manner.

The cost of not devaluing in October 1964 included subservience to American policy, and a continuation of the UK's role East of Suez which was making UK economic problems even more difficult than they inevitably were. It included support for US policies on Vietnam, and the alienation of much of the PLP, not just on the left but including many of moderate and pro-European views. The question is often raised whether American support for sterling was explicitly conditional on UK support for its war in Vietnam and a British presence East of Suez.[52] Wilson feared that the US would *make* support for the pound conditional on support for US policy in Vietnam.[53] The real point was that the American priority was to avoid the devaluation of sterling. A US denial of assistance at key moments of pressure on the pound could have forced a devaluation. The UK therefore did have a kind of negotiating strength in its relations with Washington even if it was only the negotiating strength of a suicide threatening to cut his throat on his neighbour's doorstep. Yet Wilson never received any return for his decision, very much in the interests of the USA, not to devalue. The Americans won their undevalued pound free. Pimlott says of Wilson that his mode as a negotiator was 'cool, calm, high-profile statesmanship'.[54] Wilson was certainly very concerned with the impression he was making. It was always the short-term impression that mainly concerned him. But he would have been gratified to know that he was succeeding even with historians.

If the Cabinet had not been given a lead, the public had even less of an appreciation that the situation demanded measures that would be unpopular. What was true of the public was equally true of the ordinary members of the Labour party. At the delayed Party Conference in December, Wilson, in his Parliamentary report, gave little indication of how serious the economic situation was and of what steps the government would have to take as a result. Crossman comments on Wilson's speech. '[I]t was a grievous disappointment to me because it was just a Conference performance, a lightweight affair ... It didn't seem to me that he struck the right note and he certainly didn't steel our people for the difficulties ahead ... The fact is, deflation is really starting. That's what I feel in my bones. But it hasn't been said and Harold Wilson blithely denies it.'[55] Wilson left that disagreeable task to Brown. 'The morning ended with a magnificent speech by George Brown in which he did all the things which Harold Wilson should have done. George Brown DID talk about the difficulties, he did warn people, harden them, and the Conference ended up in pretty good form.'[56] As Tony Benn found when he went back to his constituency party executive after Christmas, they were complaining about bank rate, rising income tax, foreign policy 'and the lot'.[57] In Bristol they had as an additional reason for worry the future of the aircraft industry. Crossman and Benn thought that more must be done to inform the Party. But the only person with the authority to do it was the Prime Minister.

In January 1965, Gordon Walker, the Foreign Secretary, was defeated in a by-election at Leyton, the constituency to which he had retreated after his rejection in the General Election at Smethwick. Frank Cousins, the Minister of Technology, seeking membership of Parliament at Nuneaton, won but with a substantially reduced majority. The Leyton result gave the Cabinet an opportunity to reassess the political situation and its strategy for survival. Officials had been asked to retire. The discussion is reported by both Castle and Crossman. Frank Cousins took the line that 'we had been far too high-minded as a government and it was time that we became more political'. It was a view echoed by others.[58] What emerged was that the Cabinet did not know what its public position should be. Castle reports herself as saying: 'I suggested the trouble was that we had not been able to get a clear message across. Were we offering [the electorate] blood, sweat and tears? With hope of better things in, say, two years time? . . . Alternatively, were we merely saying that things were a bit difficult but it was on the whole business as usual?'[59]

Callaghan asserted that it was time to be honest with the electorate. He was in favour of blood, sweat and tears. He argued that the government must end illusions and tell the people honestly that expenditure was exceeding economic growth and that this could not go on. But, according to Crossman, 'George Brown replied that too much probity would destroy us. If we took Callaghan's advice we should be ruined . . . We must now have nothing but short-term tactics and prepare an offensive designed to put the blame back on the Tories.'[60] At least Brown noticed that the government had succeeded during the previous three months in freeing its predecessors of any responsibility for its economic inheritance. Crossman's diary comment was: 'I think that the defeat at Leyton shows that the Government has now lost one invaluable asset – the public belief that the Conservative Government was responsible for our present difficulties . . . quite quietly during these three months the responsibility for the evils created by the thirteen years has been transferred to us. Now we are the people responsible for high prices, for the cut in pensions, for the failure to keep mortgage rates down.'[61]

The conclusion drawn by Wilson and Brown from the Leyton and Nuneaton results was that they must be even less frank with the electorate. Brown, who had gained such warm approval from Crossman at the Party Conference in December, now understood the wisdom of Wilson's equivocations. The last thing to do was to be frank with the electorate. The government must be more political. It was fortunate, perhaps, that officials had been asked to retire. Though hardened by experience of previous governments, cynical about levels of political morality, they would nevertheless have been appalled by this discussion. It would not have added to their respect, already fairly low, for the politicians elected to lead them. But the time would come, through familiarity between Ministers and officials, and the assumption among Ministers that officials had come round to supporting their policies as well as implementing them, that such discussions would take place in the presence of officials.

In the first few weeks of the Wilson government, everything had been prepared, by lack of leadership, and incoherence in policy, for the eventual devaluation of November 1967. But Wilson had at least ensured, with the invaluable assistance of the Americans, that before the devaluation there would be a long-drawn-out period of misery leading to disillusion with the government and with socialism. Wilson had spoken of one hundred days of purposive action. What he had accomplished was one hundred days of equivocation.

THIRTEEN

The crusade aborted

Wilson's long account of the 1964–70 government devotes little space to domestic economic affairs. The book is dominated by Vietnam, Rhodesia and Europe. He had no choice but to deal with the unilateral Rhodesian declaration of independence. At meetings of Commonwealth heads of government, he had to justify his refusal to use force to restore legality. Beyond that there was Vietnam. Wilson was determined to avoid public criticism of American policy. The left wing of the PLP wanted nothing so much from its government as public criticism of American policy. It was much more interested in condemning President Johnson than in economic policy. Economic policy involved too much thought. Or, alternatively, it involved no thought at all, the simple answer to all questions being more nationalization. The answer being obvious, there was no need to argue it. The chamber of the House of Commons filled when there was an opportunity to condemn American policy in Vietnam. It emptied when economic policy was under discussion.

One way in which the left-wing members of the Cabinet could salve their consciences at a time when socialist policies were constrained by economic difficulties was to be critical of the Americans on Vietnam. Barbara Castle continually raised Vietnam in Cabinet. She eventually won a special Cabinet meeting on 30 March 1965 but nothing came of it. Crossman had concluded that foreign policy really had to be left to the experts. 'I must say that I felt this [Cabinet meeting] was the sheerest waste of time . . . My only conclusion was that a Cabinet consisting of busy departmental Ministers can't make much impact on how foreign policy is conducted.'[1] On Vietnam, Wilson could be of no help to the left. But in an attempt to keep it quiet he engaged in a frenzy of activity, trying to act as mediator in the Vietnam war, which led nowhere. He had too much sympathy with the American stance on Vietnam to be regarded as a valid mediator except in his role as co-chairman with the Soviet Union of the Geneva peace talks – if they could ever be revived.[2] The left would have been horrified if it had realized how much sympathy Wilson had with the Americans and that he was making that sympathy perfectly clear privately in writing to President Johnson.[3] He boasted to Johnson of the pressure he was resisting from his left wing. He thought of himself as amassing political capital in Washington against the day on which he might himself need a sympathetic ear. All this, together with sundry fruitless negotiations with Ian Smith, head of the illegal Rhodesian government, absorbed an immense proportion of Wilson's time and energy.

The main lesson for observers from all this activity was to confirm Wilson's penchant for self-deception. He gravely overestimated the influence he could have, given Britain's parlous economic condition and its dependence on the USA. He actually believed that he could find the answer to the Vietnam conflict, and his alleged economic expertise did not save him from a gross exaggeration of the effect of sanctions on Rhodesia. The Vietnam war was not settled, Rhodesia was not brought to heel, and his application for membership of the EEC was vetoed by President de Gaulle. Wilson, understandably, desired to draw attention to his heroic role overseas rather than to his inadequacies at home. Unfortunately his heroic role overseas led to no known triumphs. The time and effort expended upon his excursions into international diplomacy were more likely to make him a laughing stock than win him a reputation for statesmanship. When, as he frequently did, he informed the House of his latest conversation with President Johnson, his critics would wonder whether there had, in fact, been anyone listening at the other end of the telephone. There is no evidence, however, that the performance of his government would have been improved if domestic policy had enjoyed more of his attention. For one thing, the exchange rate of the pound had become an aspect of his foreign policy, the maintenance of the special relationship with the USA.

So far as domestic affairs are concerned, in the period up to devaluation in November 1967, more space is devoted in Wilson's account to such marginal matters as the absurd D-notice affair, 'one of my costliest mistakes',[4] and to the *Torrey Canyon* oil spill,[5] than to economic developments. After the initial months, any comment on economic developments is mainly devoted to self-congratulation on how well the economy was doing despite the difficult inheritance, and despite the malevolence of the City of London and the Gnomes of Zurich. On 24 July 1965,

Wilson spoke at Newtown, Montgomeryshire. He said that it was against the background of a rapidly improving balance of payments position that 'we have to set this flurry of loose and uninformed talk at home and abroad about our economic situation. It is not for me – at any rate here and now – to analyse the motives of those who at home and abroad want to sell Britain short. They have been wrong before . . .' He then went on to announce that, despite whatever improvements he had been able to detect, new economic measures would be taken 'in the next few days'.[6] There followed the deflationary measures of July 1965 taken under powerful external pressure. His audience at Newtown might well be ready to accept that their Labour government was gallantly fighting its way in a hostile world and that the hostility was motivated only by political prejudice. But Wilson, as a massive borrower, had to recognize that new economic measures were necessary. He might pretend in public, and even privately to himself, that the need for the measures lay only in political hostility. In the end he would be forced to accept that, whatever the motives of his lenders, he had to respect their views if he wanted their money.

The descent to devaluation was marked by repeated crises alternating with moments of euphoria when hope revived that all would, after all, come right. Throughout, British policy was under the careful supervision of the Americans, for, whatever sacrifices American policy imposed on Britain, the dollar must be safeguarded. The dollar had become an instrument not just of exchange but of the Vietnam war. American policy in Vietnam relied on the dollar being accepted internationally as a reliable store of value and it was vital that its standing should not be brought into question by the devaluation of sterling. The only trouble from the point of view of the Americans was that the policies of the Wilson government never inspired them with entire confidence that the devaluation of sterling would in the end be avoided. Wilson was perfectly well aware that the conduct of his government was being monitored in Washington. The deflationary July 1965 measures were widely thought, in Washington and elsewhere, to be inadequate. In August US Secretary of the Treasury Fowler was expressing doubts whether the voluntary prices and incomes policy put in place in December 1964 by George Brown was strong enough. Wilson himself tells us that he was apprehensive that if a further central bank rescue was required it would be difficult to mount if the UK had no better safeguard against inflation than the voluntary system. The brute force of Secretary Fowler's doubts was comprehensible even to Wilson and his government. They knew that they might well want to borrow again from central banks. It was necessary to take action that would persuade Washington to give the necessary lead to those central banks. It was in those circumstances that the government began first to think in terms of statutory powers. The decision to enact statutory powers was taken early in September 1965. In an attempt to soothe the concerns of Frank Cousins and the TUC, it was agreed that the powers, when enacted, were to be activated only by Order in Council requiring the assent of both Houses of Parliament. Wilson tells us that there was no question of Secretary Fowler attempting to give his government any orders. But there could be no clearer example of the government acting on what were in practice instructions from Washington.[7] Washington was in effect telling London that it was not doing its duty by the dollar, and London was only too ready to obey.

STEEL NATIONALIZATION

One way in which the government could show its socialist virility was by proceeding with steel nationalization. Fred Lee, the responsible Minister, wanted it deferred to the second session of the Parliament, but the Cabinet led by George Brown insisted that it had to be done at once.[8] At Cabinet, in March 1965, Brown declared that the government would have no dignity if steel nationalization was dropped.[9] Brown, leader of the right, was becoming a hero of the left, opposing deflation and, now, demanding steel nationalization. There was something to be said for his views on steel nationalization. As the government had committed itself to it in the Queen's Speech, it would look weak if it now postponed it. Whether it had to be done in the first session of the Parliament despite the narrow majority was another question. A greater question was whether steel nationalization had any relevance to the problems the country was facing. One hundred per cent steel nationalization was opposed by two Labour MPs, Woodrow Wyatt and Desmond Donnelly. There was therefore a serious question whether the House of Commons, with the narrow Labour majority, could be persuaded to enact it. Brown imperilled his heroic status with the left by assuring Wyatt in the course of a debate on steel nationalization that he was prepared to listen to the industry. Wilson had promised the PLP that no concession would be made. Brown's assurance outraged the left, which saw no reason for listening to the industry. The nationalization of iron and steel was part of the class struggle and one does not negotiate with the enemy from weakness. Wilson thought of briefing the press against Brown but was dissuaded by Crossman, who saw that a public repudiation would be extremely damaging both to Wilson and to the government. An emergency Cabinet meeting was held at which Brown was solemnly rebuked for giving this unauthorized assurance, though the Cabinet did not take the matter further by repudiating his statement.[10] Despite these skirmishes, the renationalization of steel had to wait until Labour had won a large majority in the 1966 General Election.

THE NATIONAL PLAN

The National Plan was a scissors-and-paste exercise. It was stuck together by the DEA, under the supervision of George Brown, from scraps of information produced by various segments of the economy. It proposed a rate of growth just short of the 4 per cent target which had been blessed by NEDC. It provided, however, no evidence that such a rate of growth, faster than any previous sustained rate, could have been attained even without the surrounding problems of the balance of payments and competitiveness. It was officially unveiled on 16 September 1965. However, it had been preceded by the first July crisis, that of 1965. The deflationary measures then taken undermined, in advance, any credibility that it might have had. Thus it was dead on delivery. In his memoirs, Jay tells us why, in his view, the National Plan collapsed. 'The Brown Plan of 1965 collapsed in face of reality because we had failed to re-introduce quotas on manufactured imports in 1964 and were forced by the illegality of the surcharge to withdraw the latter in 1966.'[11] Jay was living in a dream if he believed that, in the world of American pressure for freer trade, of the Kennedy Round and of EFTA, Britain could have long maintained import quotas on manufactured goods in order to sustain a National Plan. It was argued subsequently that the assumption upon which the National Plan had been drafted was the very devaluation which Wilson and Callaghan, supported by Brown, had been opposing. Wilson had thought of the National Plan as a way of avoiding devaluation, not as a reason for it. Indeed the only purpose of a National Plan would have been if it had helped to avoid devaluation. With devaluation, and the necessary associated measures, there would be no conceivable need for a National Plan. That this is so is demonstrated by events after the 1967 devaluation had taken place.

Although the government was dilatory in taking the necessary accompanying deflationary measures, and probably they were never adequately taken, it was the devaluation, without any aid from a National Plan, which led on to the single economic triumph of the Wilson era, the balance of payments surplus of 1970. The discovery that the National Plan was irrelevant to the economic performance of the country was a blow to serious socialist thinkers. They had placed great reliance on planning. They had been determined that it should be done much better than in the time of Attlee and Macmillan, and it had proved inoperative. Pimlott writes, truly enough, of Labour's abandonment of planning: 'A hole was created in Labour's *raison d'être* which, arguably, has never been filled.'[12]

The idea of planning did, however, leave behind it one dangerous residue. There was an atmosphere that the prospects for the economy should take a certain priority over personal freedom. Even in the absence of legal prescription or sanctions, people ought to behave in a disciplined way consistent with the government's economic ambitions. Trade unionists should not make claims that might undermine those ambitions. They should not strike except when they had gone through appropriate procedures and there was a justification which the government could understand. Unofficial strikes were, by definition, wicked. Employers, for their part, should invest to the government's satisfaction. The government having laid out its policies, employers and employees should co-operate in support whatever their private inclinations. If co-operation was absent, the guilty could not expect to avoid public rebuke. Above all, no one should behave in a way which annoyed Ministers, who must be assumed to know best, whatever the evidence to the contrary.

THE JULY 1966 MEASURES

The Government won its General Election in March 1966 with a majority of ninety-seven. It was a victory just in time. During the election campaign, Lord Cromer recommended an increase in bank rate as sterling was under pressure. Harold Wilson was very angry. He was afraid that an increase in bank rate might suggest that the economy was not as strong as he wished it to appear. Cromer's advice was supported by the Chancellor, James Callaghan, not normally regarded as a political innocent. He evidently thought that prudence was more important than political convenience. Wilson ignored the advice. He regarded it as an interference with the sovereign right of the electorate to choose a government without knowing the whole truth about the state of the economy. But as Callaghan's biographer, Kenneth Morgan, observes, 'Callaghan . . . had fundamentally the stronger case.'[13] Having won the election, Wilson launched, in a speech to the Amalgamated Engineering Union, on another crusade, not in this case a moral crusade nor even a technological crusade but a crusade against restrictive practices in industry and their inflationary effect. His Minister of Labour, Ray Gunter, spoke of 'our thriftless and dishonest way of living on foreign money'.[14] But strong words were still doing duty for action. Soon after the election, sterling was once more under severe pressure. The immediate cause was a seamen's strike. In government, the strike was interpreted as a communist-inspired attack on the incomes policy. The government therefore felt it had to show firmness of purpose in resisting the seamen's claims. But a seamen's strike would not have brought sterling under severe pressure had there not been widespread scepticism in the market about the economic policies of a government which was rejecting devaluation and yet not appearing serious in its battle against it. Even the settlement of the strike within the incomes policy did not protect sterling, and pressure continued.

By now economic Ministers were prepared to think in terms of devaluation. Brown had been converted to it. He now saw that his hopes of bettering the Tory economic record depended on it. Callaghan was hesitant, waiting to see whether his Prime Minister was ready to sanction a harsh deflationary package calculated to prolong the battle against devaluation. In the time won he could hope for release from the perpetual anxieties of economic management to some other less demanding responsibility. Wilson remained unshaken in his determination to avoid devaluation. If that meant deflation and the end, for the time being, of any prospect of economic growth, it was a price he was now prepared to pay. There followed the deflationary measures of July 1966. Adapting the naval vocabulary of his Chancellor of the Exchequer, Wilson proclaimed that the government had been blown off course. In the weeks before the July 1966 measures, it had been blown off course by the merchant navy strike led by politically motivated men. The electorate which, during the March election campaign, had been painted a glowing picture of the successes of Labour economic policy, was liable to feel deceived. But, for the moment, it could be ignored. It had awarded the government a handsome majority and it was in no position to withdraw the votes it had cast. As part of the deflationary measures of July 1966, the government enacted the statutory incomes policy decided upon the previous September, beginning with a six-month period of wages standstill to be followed by six months of 'severe restraint'. One benefit from this experience was a change in Wilson's language and analysis. At all previous moments of crisis, Wilson had excoriated the 'sell-Britain-short brigade' without any recognition that lenders have interests as well as borrowers. Now at last he denied 'the somewhat naive caricature that what has been going on is a machination of some bearded troglodytes deep below ground speculating in foreign currencies for private gain. Of course, there is a speculative element . . . But . . . one does not need to look for sinister interpretations.'[15] The Gnomes of Zurich were at last vindicated. They were, apparently, entitled to protect their interests. But the exculpation of the Gnomes was not to be taken as implying that Wilson considered his government at all to blame for its predicament.

Totally absent from these debates was any idea that 'socialism' had any part to play in managing the economy. Even Wilson would not have wished to include the deflationary action of July 1966 among his 'specifically Socialist measures'. Socialism had been finally ousted by the market. The measures contradicted everything that Wilson had argued in opposition about 'expansion' as the answer to the problems of the balance of payments, poor productivity and wage planning. They finally killed the National Plan and, as evidence of his disillusion, Brown moved from the DEA to the Foreign Office, announcing to the House as he departed that 'For almost two years we have tried to manage the economy in a way that no economy has been managed before.'[16] It was true but unfortunate and the House dissolved in laughter. The July 1966 measures were simply another attempt to avoid devaluation by the traditional deflationary means which Wilson and his supporters had hitherto condemned as counterproductive. If accompanied by devaluation, they might have served the purpose of rectifying the balance of payments. As it was, they failed to check the descent to devaluation, especially as Wilson was always looking for opportunities to relax the deflation, which was increasing unemployment, and return to the policy of expansion which he had advocated in opposition.

THE EMERGENCE OF BENN

One cost of the July 1966 crisis was the loss of Cousins. He was opposed to statutory incomes policies and, when the government resolved to ignore his settled opinions, he resigned, relieved to be once more a trade union general secretary able to impose collective responsibility on his union rather than submit to the collective responsibilities of Cabinet government. His departure encouraged backbench and trade union opposition to the statutory prices and incomes policy. There would have been opposition in any case, but Cousins's departure made it more bitter. His resignation did not appear too damaging given the large majority won at the General Election. Though the government had lost its quasi-Bevin, Cousins had not been an effective minister. He had never seemed the incarnation of a technological revolution. Moreover, in Anthony Wedgwood Benn, Wilson had an ideal substitute at the head of the Ministry of Technology.[17] Before the 1966 election, Wilson had considered replacing Cousins, if he resigned, with Foot. It would have been an appointment totally inappropriate on all grounds, except perhaps political. But Foot refused. On every issue on which Cousins disagreed with the government, Foot disagreed with the government.[18] Benn did not refuse when the offer came to him. Just as Wilson had once taken the place of Bevan on the shadow Cabinet, now Benn was willing to show his loyalty and enthusiasm by replacing Cousins in a real Cabinet. But then, at the time, Benn thought that the trade unions represented a major obstacle to the modernization of Britain. On 27 January 1965, he had noted in his diary, 'The control of the National Executive of the Labour Party by the trade union leaders with their built-in resistance to modern methods and financing is undoubtedly one of the sources of Conservative strength in Britain today.'[19]

Wilson had great faith in Benn, who was the very model of a modern technological Minister. Benn was to be in charge of the Scarborough programme. He combined the eloquence necessary to turn technology into a crusade with a naivety which led him to accept everything he was told by senior industrialists seeking subsidies. Of the use of technology in industry he knew nothing but believed everything. He did not yet understand that the Scarborough programme was political persiflage lacking economic substance. Though to some already a figure of fun, he was everything that could be desired by those sectors of industry that looked to a flow of public money as an answer to their problems of competitiveness. Benn announced that he was injecting the public interest into the private sector. As the injection took the form of subsidy, the private sector was a willing recipient. The distribution of subsidy was blessed with the title of 'industrial policy'. In fact it was a process whereby the private sector extracted money from the government without any sense that it ought to feel grateful. Only perfunctory thanks were necessary for, after all, government and industry were co-operating in what both knew to be a national crusade. That part of industry, the better part, that could do without the subsidies, despised the government's profligacy in throwing money at weaker brethren.

Later Benn would become imbued with resentment that he had been deceived and betrayed by industry. When Labour was expelled from office in June 1970, he at last perceived the emptiness of his crusade for technology. He decided to exploit the widespread sense of failure felt by the left by reverting to the advocacy of traditional socialism together with massive nationalization. The Labour party had not forgotten its commitment to nationalization, despite Wilson's evocation of technology. At the 1968 Party Conference a resolution had nearly been passed calling for the nationalization of the 300 monopolies, the private banks and the insurance companies. There was, therefore, a tide of opinion within the Labour party on which Benn might float if ever Labour lost office.

A LOVE AFFAIR WITH BIG BUSINESS

Dissatisfaction with the economic record of the thirteen wasted years was not confined to the Labour party. The managers of Britain's major industrial companies shared the dissatisfaction. They knew that the countries of western Europe were growing economically far faster than Britain. They had seen their counterparts in Germany overtaking them in earnings. They had been willing to co-operate with the NEDC experiment of the Macmillan government because it seemed to address itself to two problems that, they believed, required solutions if the British economy was to perform comparably with western Europe. First, there would have to be better planning of the national economy. Here the culprit they saw was the Treasury, with its continual chopping and changing of indirect taxation and its frequent deflationary interventions when the balance of payments fell into serious deficit. Secondly, there would have to be better industrial relations if British productivity was ever to be raised to that achieved on the continent, let alone the USA.

There could be no doubt that industrial management in Britain was a frustrating occupation. Manufacturing industry had become one of the sites on which the class war was fought.

Business was not enthusiastic about the election of a Labour government. Although Labour seemed to have abandoned nationalization on principle, there could be no certainty that it had finally and reliably purified itself of the impulse. Nevertheless, while there was a Labour government, it was better to coax it along the paths that seemed good to industry rather than to allow it, uninfluenced, to find more questionable directions. Moreover, it was observed, Labour shared many of the instincts of beleaguered British industry. Above all there was an innate protectionism carried over from the days of the Attlee government. This had, in part, motivated the government's decision, in reaction to the balance of payments crisis, to introduce an import surcharge rather than to devalue.

There were other indications of a willingness in the Labour government to absorb advice from industrial spokesmen. The new government had begun by taking over from its predecessors a Board of Trade Bill the purpose of which was the better regulation of monopolies and mergers. Big business could not be expected to welcome such legislation. Whatever, on public occasions, it might say about the merits of competition, it would never be enthusiastic about any tendency by government to preserve competition by preventing mergers. Apart from any more public-spirited considerations, a larger firm normally meant larger pay for the top managers. The new government seemed susceptible to the argument that what Britain needed was not fewer mergers but more mergers, and that the idea of an effective competition policy represented merely a hangover from the outdated philosophy of *laissez-faire* of which the Board of Trade was held to be the last citadel.

Harold Wilson had noticed a certain confluence of attitudes between New Labour and industry. He hoped that the prospects for planning and of his new departments, the DEA and Mintech, would be enhanced if industry could be persuaded to be sympathetic rather than hostile. He perceived that inducing industry to co-operate with a Labour government might be less difficult than originally supposed. Wilson was very proud of his creation of Mintech. Though he had first entered the Cabinet, under Attlee, as President of the Board of Trade, he was willing to be convinced that the Board's *laissez-faire* presumptions were an obstacle to economic growth rather than an encouragement to it. As a purposive Prime Minister he preferred the noisy activity of Mintech to the relative passivity of the Board of Trade. He showed so little faith in his former department that, over the years of his government, he stripped it of almost all its industrial sponsorship responsibilities, which were progressively transferred to Mintech. The argument that Britain needed more mergers was supported by the Nobel Laureate Patrick Blackett, who had become the government's most distinguished scientific adviser and was working at Mintech. He calculated the necessary size that a company must reach before it could fund the research necessary to keep it in the forefront internationally. He then found that many British companies engaged in international trade did not meet his minimum requirements. Unfortunately Blackett's insights into economics lacked the penetration of his insights into physics. It was known that Britain had many more large companies than Germany. But it was the success of Germany that was shaming British economic performance. The answer to any such criticism of the merger philosophy was that, while British firms might be large in comparison with Germany, that was certainly not the case in comparison with the USA and it was from the USA that, so far as the capitalist world was concerned, the principal challenge came. Moreover, in addition to the great companies of the USA, there were the massive nationalized industries of the Soviet Union. It was still believed in Labour circles that the Soviet Union represented an economic and not just an ideological and military challenge. The idea of an Industrial Reorganization Corporation was first mooted in Mintech. George Brown saw in the idea an opportunity for the DEA. As a former trade union official in the TGWU, Brown could claim a special role. Labour's ancient links with the trade unions combined with this welcome convergence of attitudes between Labour and industrial management would make for a successful tripartite relationship which would transform British economic performance. The DEA cruelly robbed Mintech of the role of marriage broker and took over the legislation which would establish the IRC with a remit to encourage private sector mergers. Less attractively, it was also given the remit, where requested by the government, to create competitive public enterprise, but, as in the past, this was not an area in which this Labour government proved to have any constructive ideas. As a sop to Mintech's pride and priority, a junior minister at Mintech was allowed to serve on the Standing Committee that considered the Bill after Second Reading.[20]

So far as business was concerned, Labour's conversion to marriage making in the private sector demonstrated that its heart was in the right place even if there were still some residual worries about government action to stimulate private sector marriages. Here was an activist government which showed itself determined to put public money where its mouth was. Industry would have preferred the government to abandon competition policy rather than intervene in the market. The private sector was always worried that Labour's use of state funds to promote capitalism might lead on to socialism. In the first place Labour's policy might simply be 'intervention' to assist the private sector, but in the second stage it could espouse nationalization. It was, however, at once clear in boardrooms that the most prospective reaction would be to control the IRC rather than attempt to dissuade the government from constituting it. Co-operation would be a better safeguard than condemnation. Whatever the private sector fears about government intervention in promoting mergers, there was at least the comfort that it would downgrade an even less desirable form of government intervention, competition policy. Unfortunately, because of the disfavour into which competition policy had fallen, there was insufficient attention, either in the IRC or in the government, to the fact that mergers can create as many problems as they solve. In retrospect, the merger activity of the IRC does not appear a notable success. Simple ideas do not always produce clear-cut results.

Few in the Labour government at the time probably were aware that in 1931, and again in 1938, Harold Macmillan had suggested an Industrial Reorganization Enabling Act. There was even to be an Industrial Reorganization Advisory Committee, corresponding perhaps to the IRC's board.[21] Macmillan proposed that, where action was undertaken under the Industrial Reorganization Enabling Act, 'it should automatically follow that the Trades Unions should be recognised for all purposes of negotiation, that facilities should be provided for the recruitment of all workers as members of their Trade Unions, and that appropriate conciliation machinery should be set up'.[22] J. A. Hobson, in the 1920s, had advocated an Industrial Reorganization Commission.[23] Lord Melchett, Chairman of Imperial Chemical Industries in the early 1930s, had introduced an Industrial Reorganization Enabling Bill into the House of Lords. Dalton, in 1935, without acknowledgement to Hobson, had proposed the idea of an Industrial Reorganization Commission as worthy of consideration.[24] The Labour government, evidently, had once more chosen the middle way. Or, inadvertently, it had demonstrated that in industrial policy there is nothing new under the sun.

The relations between government and industry seldom resemble those of a mutual admiration society. Each imagines the tasks of the other to be well within its own competence even though each may be making a hash of the tasks for which they are themselves actually responsible. There were various problems with the love affair between government and industrial management. The most important was that industry became increasingly disillusioned because its problems persisted. Industrial leaders felt none of the loyalty to the government that leaders of the trade unions, brought up in the Labour Movement, might be persuaded to feel. Industrial policy did not prove a miraculous cure. It left industry uncompetitive in world markets. The failure to devalue deprived business of the soft option which they were increasingly ready to embrace and which, indeed, in later years, became their favoured route to competitiveness. The love of soft options was not the perquisite of Labour alone. In the end industry would judge the government by the success of its economic policies, and its economic policies were obviously failing. A second problem for the government was that if there was to be a substitute for socialism, which was what Wilson's policies were intended to be, it must be successful. If it was not successful, socialists, and even stalwart trade union leaders, would begin to complain that they had sacrificed their convictions to no avail. The effect would be an unhappy PLP and an even more unhappy Party in the country.

Wilson's replacement of socialism by industrial policy may have been politically skilful but it brought no greater prospect of economic success than would a more clearly socialist policy. It could be argued against a more clearly socialist policy that it would have been even more expensive and that, like industrial policy, it would have yielded a nil return on the investment. It was understandable nevertheless that, after Wilson, socialists should have complained that their recipes had never been tried. They had reason for the complaint that all that happened under the beneficent gaze of Wilson and Benn was that public money had been given to private industry with nothing to show for it.

THE TRADE UNIONS

The close relationship between the trade unions and the Labour party raised false expectations. It encouraged the hope that a Labour government would be able to exercise influence against inflationary wage claims and in favour of restraint. Such a hope might have substance in the immediate aftermath of a Labour victory but not for long thereafter.

Indeed the election of a Labour government could have the effect of making the task of controlling inflation more difficult because for workers, particularly in the public sector, a Labour victory implied benefits in the form of cash on the table. Labour governments regularly overestimated what they could realistically seek from the TUC. The TUC was not an estate of the realm, though it was often treated like one.[25] It did not control the trade unions or their leaders; and the leaders could never be sure of controlling their members. Since Bevin there had been no Labour minister of comparable influence with the trade union movement. And even Bevin would not have been able to withstand the inflationary surge of 1951. Wilson was not personally close to trade union leaders other than, possibly, Frank Cousins. He was distrusted by many of them. So Wilson's personal pull on trade union leaders was weak, and even weaker on members of trade unions.

The wartime government's commitment in the 1944 White Paper on Employment to a high and stable level of employment, especially as interpreted by subsequent governments, gave the trade unions great power. They wanted a rising standard of living for their members. They thought that the way to ensure this was for governments to conduct expansionary economic policies. Keynes had left behind him the impression that economic success depended on governments. But if there were expansionary policies would the trade unions and their members show restraint in wage claims? If they pressed a claim it was probable that they would get a good part of what they demanded. But if, as was inevitable, the result was inflation and balance of payments crisis, the government would have no choice but to impose a stop on the economy and unemployment would rise. When Frank Cousins had spoken in 1963 of 'the planned growth of incomes', the phrase was held to imply that given sufficient growth, which would require planning by the government, trade unionists might accept the planning of their incomes. But no government could guarantee any particular level of economic growth. There was no evidence that the trade unions or their members would, except perhaps temporarily in an emergency, accept any planning of their incomes. Full employment gave them power and they would exercise it.

George Woodcock, the General Secretary of the TUC from 1961 to 1969, impressed upon trade union leaders the necessity of restraint if the 1944 Employment White Paper commitment was to be met.[26] Peter Jenkins observed that, for most of the members of the General Council of the TUC, Woodcock 'felt a disdain tempered only by charity'.[27] But Woodcock was the servant of the trade union leaders he disdained, not their master. Even if he had convinced them, it was highly uncertain whether the trade union leaders could for long convince their members. Moreover their members wanted money in their wage packets, not through social transfers. The concept, favoured in some left-wing circles, of a 'social wage' which should be regarded as part of the total wage, made no impact on their thinking. They would rejoice if the government of the day was so kind as to improve social benefits. But they should not be expected to pay for it by forgoing wage increases. To put the point another way, the members of trade unions were not interested in socialism if it required the planning of their pay. In practice their ideal appeared to be capitalism. Capitalism encouraged the exploitation of power in the promotion of private interests and justified it by the mysterious operations of the hidden hand, which would reconcile private interests with the public interest. The trade unions had become devotees of the hidden hand and had learnt to play the capitalist game. But, if that was their attitude, a Labour government, faced with the responsibility of managing capitalism, would have to seek ways of controlling their inflationary ambitions.

Socialists were divided in their reaction to this stance of the trade unions. Most claimed that nothing better could be expected from trade unionists in a capitalist society. Why should they hold back when the capitalists did not? On the other hand, some socialists were annoyed that trade unionists were so blind as to be unwilling to make present sacrifices for future socialism. Barbara Castle recalls how, after Labour's defeat in the 1959 General Election, Aneurin Bevan had commented: 'The trade unionist has voted at the polls against the consequences of his own anarchy.'[28] But in this respect at least the trade unionists were wise. They might talk about socialism. They might have in their minds some picture of an ideal society from which poverty and unemployment had been for ever banished. They might vote for leaders who could spark their imaginations with thoughts of greater equality. But, when it came to money, they were realists. As there was no early prospect of socialism they saw no reason to make present sacrifices. They demanded the supposed rewards of socialism without awaiting its coming. They took the waiting out of wanting.

In March 1967, Wilson put forward the idea of a 'National Dividend'. Every year, government and industry would sit together and work out, on the basis of figures of production, and the expected calls on that production, what should be the National Dividend for the year ahead.

The trade union movement would then ensure that the workers got their share 'on the basis of steadily rising incomes, and on a basis which ensures that the amount distributed does not run ahead of the amount we earn by our production'. But, comments Wilson, 'my words fell on stony ground'.[29] The idea that the national income could be shared on the basis of consensus between the government and industry as a whole was not attractive to those in the trade union movement who believed that the workers must fight for every penny they won and that that fight could not be suspended merely because there was a Labour government. In any case, how could a government guarantee a standard of living rising fast enough to satisfy trade union appetites fed by years of inflationary economic management? The close relationship between the Labour party and the trade unions was for this purpose counterproductive. There was too much support for trade union claims within Labour ranks. Michael Foot, speaking in the House of Commons on 10 July 1967, followed Bevan by declaring that he was not against an incomes policy. 'Indeed, we believe that such a policy is essential to socialism.' Then, employing the exaggerated language that was the hallmark of his oratory, he levelled his charge against the government: 'They have associated incomes policy with ferocious deflation, with their whole economic policy of stringency and the deliberate creation of unemployment.'[30] The deflation was not actually ferocious. But the real problem was that incomes policies were difficult to operate if the government was implementing deflationary policies, and impossible to operate if the government was itself implementing inflationary policies. Far from deliberately increasing unemployment, the government was doing everything it could to avoid it.

In a speech on 5 October 1967, Leslie O'Brien, Cromer's successor as Governor of the Bank of England, argued publicly for a larger pool of unemployment. On 7 November 1967, Callaghan, facing the personal humiliation of a now inevitable devaluation, himself argued for 'a somewhat larger margin of unused capacity than we used to try to keep'.[31] This could only be a plea for higher unemployment. In other words the socialist Chancellor and the Governor of the Bank were now at one in how to run a capitalist economy. Leslie O'Brien, a man of humble origins, was less provocative to socialists than Lord Cromer, scion of a great merchant banking family which had also provided the state with imperial proconsuls. Whatever his origins, O'Brien was teaching the same lessons that Cromer had endeavoured to teach but, under the impact of impending devaluation, was having greater success than

Cromer had ever had. Unfortunately these lessons never seemed to sink deeply into the minds even of those who had most intimately experienced the political and economic consequences of what Kenneth Morgan appropriately calls 'the drifting, rudderless character of British policy in economic [and other] matters . . .'.[32]

THE ALUMINIUM SMELTERS[33]

Desperate situations require desperate remedies. It was hardly possible to imagine a remedy for the British balance of payments more desperate than the aluminium smelter project. When the idea of the project first emerged, it was examined in government as a contribution to the avoidance of devaluation. After devaluation it remained, in the view of the government, an attractive import-saving exercise. In other words it might help to stave off further devaluations. By this time politics, both national and international, had become intimately entangled and any prospect of rational calculation as to the costs and benefits of the project had disappeared. Its political attractions included its presentation as an example of modern technology busily at work, stimulated by the government. Ironically, it fell under the auspices of the despised Board of Trade, not of the Ministry of Technology. The sponsorship of the small British aluminium smelting industry had been left in the hands of the Board of Trade as of no great importance. In fact the aluminium smelter project dwarfed all other technological extravagances of the Wilson government.

In 1966, the Atomic Energy Authority (AEA) informed the world how extraordinarily cheap would be electricity generated by an Advanced Gas-cooled Reactor (AGR), a nuclear power plant of its own design. At the time no full-scale AGR had been built. The cost of electricity from a full-scale AGR was, therefore, still speculative. The AEA had consulted its computers. It had, no doubt in all innocence and without the least intention to deceive, inserted the best information available and, unsurprisingly, the answer it wanted had issued. Aluminium smelting uses electricity intensively. It therefore normally took place where electricity was cheap, for example in the United States, Canada and Norway, where large quantities of hydroelectricity were available. British imports of aluminium came predominantly from Norway and Canada. Imports were large and mounting. Up to that time only about 36,000 tons of aluminium, or rather more than 10 per cent of the market, were being produced in Britain, at two plants in the Highlands, powered by hydroelectricity and owned by British Aluminium. Rio Tinto-Zinc, the great British resources company, owned a source of bauxite and alumina, the raw materials of aluminium. The electricity costs attributed to the new AGR attracted RTZ's attention. It calculated that, if it was allowed to build an AGR, and locate it in a development area where it would benefit from a 40 per cent investment grant then being introduced by the Labour government, it could smelt aluminium competitively in this country. Thereby it would acquire an outlet for its bauxite and alumina and capture for itself a market for aluminium that it had never owned before. Its AGR would produce far more electricity than would be required for the smelter. The surplus would be sold to the national grid.

One might expect that any businessman would understand that, if the AEA made a claim about the price of electricity from an AGR that had not yet been built, it was likely to be wrong by a large factor. RTZ believed what it was told and applied to the government for permission to build an AGR and smelter in Anglesey, in a development area. The government refused the application because it was regarded as impermissible for a private company to own a nuclear reactor and because it shrank from the immense cost to the Exchequer of a 40 per cent investment grant on a privately owned AGR. This rejection was, quite unintentionally, the best decision in the history of British industrial policy. If RTZ had been given permission to build an AGR, this great company would have been bankrupted. The government's refusal saved RTZ from suicide. Just as no one yet knew the real cost of electricity from a full-scale AGR, so no one knew how much a full-scale AGR would cost to build or how long it would take.

However, the government itself believed what the AEA had told it about the economics of an AGR and intended to build a few copies. It liked the RTZ idea even if it rejected the RTZ method. If some of the aluminium consumed in Britain could be smelted in Britain, there would be significant savings on the balance of trade. The government therefore sought an alternative method of achieving the same object. The method eventually proposed was described as a special electricity contract. It would allow certain aluminium smelters the benefit of the cheap electricity expected from an AGR while retaining the AGRs as the property of the nationalized generating authorities. The government proposed that one smelter should be in production by 1971 and another by 1974. Each smelter would be of 120,000 tons p.a. capacity (later reduced, in an attempt to conciliate the Norwegians, to 100,000 tons).

Harold Wilson was so delighted at finding that the white heat of technology might actually extrude a new British industry that, even before any contracts had been negotiated, he announced the project to the 1967 Labour Party Conference as a major example of the Labour government's use of public enterprise. It would demonstrate that public enterprise was possible without extending public ownership. It was in no way a matter for embarrassment that the original idea had come from the private sector not the public. It would be a project combining glamour with utility. The utility would be political as well as economic. Not merely would the balance of payments benefit from cutting imports of aluminium, the project would also dish the Welsh and Scottish Nationalists because one of the two smelters would be built in Anglesey in Wales and the other at Invergordon in Scotland. Actually there would, in the end, be three smelters. The Prime Minister, for political reasons, had assured Lord Robens, Chairman of the National Coal Board, that coal would be given the chance to compete. At the time there was deep resentment in the coal-mining industry about nuclear developments which could only be at the expense of coal. Wilson wished to take the sting out of an announcement at the Labour Party Conference that necessarily would concentrate on Britain's nuclear achievements.

So, at the Labour Party Conference of 1967, the announcement was made by the Prime Minister. The aluminium smelting project was launched, and public enterprise prepared to claim its greatest success. In the end offers were made to the government by three companies: RTZ itself now in association with BICC, British Aluminium and Alcan, then a major importer of aluminium into Britain. The offers of the three companies were submitted for assessment to the IRC. The IRC was to recommend which of the companies should be offered the opportunity to build the 1971 smelter and which the 1974 smelter. The board of the IRC was made up of some of the most respected businessmen in Britain. They were not at all sceptical of the AEA's claims about the cost of electricity from an AGR. Economists assured them that the vast subsidies that would be required were justified by the import savings. The board of the IRC believed that too. The IRC did a rapid review, placed the offers in order of merit from a balance of payments point of view, and proposed that instead of one contract for 1971, there should be two. They were convinced that the only idea better than building one aluminium smelter in this country in 1971 was building two. How could the government turn down the advice of some of the most respected businessmen in Britain? The government offered contracts for 1971 to both RTZ and British Aluminium. This was a major blow to Alcan. It therefore entered into heads of an agreement with the NCB. The NCB would supply cheap coal, from a pit at Lynemouth on the north-east coast of England, for a smelter with an initial capacity of 60,000 tons p.a. to be built above the mine. Thus England too would have its smelter. The total new capacity that would now be installed by about 1971 would be 300,000 tons, the whole of the market.

The outside world then broke into these very private British musings. The announcement of the project at the Labour Party Conference had produced an immediate outcry in Norway. The Norwegians at once took the matter to the Ministerial Council of the European Free Trade Area. They had always regarded investment grants as subsidies contrary to EFTA's rules of competition. Now they were being used to deprive Norway of a market in Britain for aluminium which a sensible division of labour within EFTA would have assured them. The Canadian government sent a delegation to protest that Canadian business was being deprived of a market contrary to the rules of international trade. The British government, supported by British public opinion as inter-preted by the press, its judgement reinforced by the senior businessmen of the IRC, could comfortably ride out the objections from Norway and Canada. But the critical gaze which these two countries were now directing at the details of the project meant that there could be no further subsidy beyond the investment grants. At a late stage in the development of the project it was discovered that, after all, the special electricity contracts would not alone, together with the investment grants, make the smelting of aluminium in Britain economic. There had been a misunderstanding between the government and the generating boards. No further overt subsidy was now possible due to the intense curiosity of the Norwegians and Canadians. Fortunately, given the pol-itical commitments already made, devaluation came to the rescue of the project. The increased price of imported aluminium covered the gap.

The smelters were built but the sceptics were proved right. The project was an economic disaster, even though blessed by some of Britain's most senior businessmen. Lord Plowden, Chairman of Tube Investments, and thus principal shareholder in British Aluminium, had been Chairman of the AEA. He had always thought that the idea of aluminium smelting in Britain was absurd. He took some pleasure in emphasizing that his past experience with the AEA justified his doubts about all its calculations. He questioned how far a commercial company, without the government behind it to bail it out, could accept the risk involved. He refused to enter into a contract to build a smelter unless given some reassurance by the government. As his smelter was to be in Scotland, his negotiating position was strong. Scotland could not be left without its smelter. Plowden proved to be entirely justified in his anxiety. The cost of building AGRs multiplied, the cost of electricity from AGRs multiplied. In 1974, on its return to office, the new Labour government was compelled to meet its extremely expensive moral liabilities under the reassurance it had provided. The story is told in a pamphlet written, just before his death, by Ron Utiger, who at the time of the inception of the aluminium smelter project was Managing Director of British Aluminium. His pamphlet is appropriately entitled *Never Trust an Expert*.

The aluminium smelter project emphasized a number of facets of the Wilson government. The first was its innocence in believing that wild technological extravagance could provide an answer to the country's balance of payments problems. The project was made possible only by the devaluation it was intended to help avoid. The smelters came on stream, in 1971, when the UK had already moved into substantial balance of payments surplus following the belated deflationary measures taken by Roy Jenkins at the Treasury. The second facet was the government's passion to intervene in order to demonstrate that it had a major contribution to make to the performance of British industry. The third was its protectionist bias. The Wilson government's approach to technology was always fundamentally protectionist. In its protectionism it was supported not just by the trade unions, whose instinct was always to protect jobs by limiting imports, but by leading businessmen gathered together on the board of the IRC who, apart from their own protectionism, were insufficiently sceptical about the AEA's claims. Labour's chief danger has never come from the enmity of businessmen engaged, as they should be, in making honest profits. Rather the danger arose from susceptibility to the advice of businessmen. Particular danger lay in the advice of individual businessmen who, for a mixture of motives, sought to befriend Labour Cabinet Ministers innocent of the least industrial experience. The most influential, at the time, was Frank Kearton, Chairman of the IRC, and also Chairman of the textile manufacturer Courtaulds. The textile industry had become one of the most protectionist of British industries and its leading figure took his philosophy into the IRC with him.

Protectionism and industrial policy could not provide an answer to the fundamental problem of the British economy, its uncompetitiveness and its tendency to levels of inflation higher than its major industrial competitors. The only solution was disinflation, plus devaluation when the pound had been allowed to become overvalued, or floating. But Wilson had always disliked such market-sensitive policies as floating, though he had sometimes threatened it as a way of defying the international moneylenders. It was an idle threat and, in any case, he believed that he had an alternative solution in planning and industrial policy. Too late, he found he was wrong. The consequence was that his government fell into disrepute and damaged the electoral prospects both of the Labour party and of any aspects of socialism that it was still interested in introducing. But no idea was more persistent in the minds of socialists, ex-socialists and *Middle Way* capitalists than the nagging conviction that it would transform British economic performance if only the British state could be persuaded to act in the same way as, allegedly, did other states such as France and Japan.

EUROPE

Like Gaitskell, Wilson had been opposed to British membership of the European Economic Community. It was a Labour tradition, dating back at least to Bevin, that Britain must not become irreversibly entangled with continental Europe. It was one of the few items on the American wish-list for Britain that Wilson was prepared to refuse. Now, his mind was changing. There were risks in such a change. The government was struggling and its prestige was low. It was not a good time to attempt to drag Labour away from an entrenched conviction that British socialism was incompatible with continental capitalism. Partly, perhaps, the change was due to experience of the responsibilities of government. There had been the obvious failure of the National Plan. If planning on a national scale was impotent, hopes from it should no longer be an obstacle to membership of the EEC. The Commonwealth was also proving a disappointment. Britain's trade with it was, proportionately, in decline. Its member countries persisted in putting their own interests first rather than seeing much mutual advantage in their relationship with Britain. Disillusion with the Commonwealth was also provoked by the attacks to which Wilson was being subjected by developing Commonwealth countries due to his failure to act effectively against the Smith regime in Rhodesia either by force or by sanctions. Probably the change of mind was even more due to Wilson's desire to find some historic novelty that would mark his occupation of No. 10 Downing

Street. The government needed a diversion, provided it was a successful diversion. Yet President de Gaulle still ruled in France and there was no reason to suppose that he was prepared to accept contamination of the Community by British Atlanticism. An application for membership might prove yet one more political humiliation. George Brown had, in August 1966, left the DEA in despair and disappointment to become Foreign Secretary. He had long been a 'European', so this could be a subject on which there would be concord between the Prime Minister and his deputy. Brown believed, and said, that de Gaulle no longer had the power to veto an application supported by all the other members of the Community. Indeed Brown had exaggerated ideas of what Britain could hope to achieve within the EEC. Willy Brandt, former German Chancellor and Chairman of the German Social Democratic Party, records that Brown said to him, 'Willy, you must get us in, so that we can take the lead.'[34]

There were many reasons why, on the left of politics, there was opposition to membership of the EEC. The oddest reason was that the EEC was a club of rich countries. Thus when, at the 1962 Party Conference, Wilson, as Chairman, had announced that Labour was a moral crusade or it was nothing, he had added that 'we are not going to join a rich man's club if it means turning our back on the rest of the world'.[35] That it should be thought undesirable to belong to a club of rich countries throws some light on the puritanical psychology of many socialists. More important, however, than that it was a club of rich countries was that it was a club of rich capitalist countries. This was unavoidable, as the only rich countries were capitalist countries. That Britain was still, by any definition other than that of Crosland, a capitalist country provided no excuse for linking its fate to those of other European capitalist countries. It was certainly an insufficient argument that European socialists appeared to want Britain's membership because, after all, they were not really socialists at all. Nor apparently was it an argument that rich countries were likely to be able to do more to help the developing world, an area of policy in which Britain's post-war record was not distinguished under either the Tories or Labour even though the Bevanites had identified the war on want as a prime mid-century theme. Moreover, the idea that Britain was special, special in its democratic socialism, special in its Commonwealth and its global responsibilities, retained its influence on Labour minds. Britain's special quality would be outraged by participation in the EEC.

There were, however, more serious arguments against British

membership of the EEC and their most powerful exponent was Douglas Jay, President of the Board of Trade. The Common Agricultural Policy would add to Britain's costs by raising the price of food, which could be obtained more cheaply on world markets. Membership would, therefore, make Britain less competitive. Moreover, for those who still hankered after planning, Europe was a danger. How could one plan if there was free entry of manufactured goods into Britain from the rest of the EEC? Jay had always believed that it was important to retain discretion over the import of manufactured goods. His view favoured free entry for raw materials which the UK did not produce but regulated entry for manufactured goods.[36] Moreover the ultimate destination of the EEC was very unclear. The idea of federalism, whatever that meant in a European context, had been broached. There was talk of monetary union. Membership of the EEC might, in the end, subvert Britain's independence and its ability to conduct its own economic, foreign and security policies.

Just as there were absurd, as well as serious, arguments against membership, so were there, on the other side, exaggerated claims made in favour of membership. The EEC had to its credit, supposedly, that there had been no war in Europe since 1945. France and Germany were now bound in friendship instead of divided in fear and hatred. Guaranteeing peace in Europe was a major interest for Britain which, twice in the twentieth century, had been dragged into European wars. The American presence in Europe was also a guarantee but not one that, in the ultimate, could be relied upon. The member countries of the EEC had, since 1950, grown much faster economically than Britain. Their higher rate of growth would, it was argued, extract from Britain a reciprocal performance. Competitiveness would be enhanced by competing directly against the highly competitive EEC economies. Certainly the Commonwealth could provide no equivalent challenge. Commonwealth countries, rejecting the unsolicited advice they had received from Crosland in *Britain's Economic Problem*, were excluding British goods in order to protect their own nascent industries. They were looking after their own interests, not those of Britain. In addition there were political arguments. Britain could hardly fail to be affected by the developments on the continent of Europe. It was more likely to have influence on those developments if it was a member rather than an outsider. Britain would have diminishing influence in the world if it remained outside the Community. Even though France had vetoed British membership in 1963, the other members seemed still to desire it. British membership would represent a further guarantee of European democracy, very much a British interest.

The balance of the serious arguments was difficult to determine. Probably the short-term economic arguments were against membership, the political arguments were in favour. Sensible and honourable people could take different views. It had been made clear to Wilson by none other than the Permanent Secretary to the Treasury, Sir William Armstrong, that membership was unthinkable unless preceded by the devaluation of sterling. The same view was expressed by European leaders and, when they said so in public, sterling trembled. Nevertheless, Wilson was not deflected from the intention he had now formed of seeking membership. He seemed to think that he had an ace with which he could trump French opposition. The ace was British technology. Britain's technological lead would fertilize European, not just British, industry. It would protect European industry against American domination. It would be an act of great British generosity to allow the rest of the EEC to benefit from British technological triumphs. Wilson began speaking about a European Technological Community. It was a concept which put Tony Benn, as Minister of Technology, in the forefront of Labour's claim for membership and unhinged him, temporarily, from his normal sources of ideological support, which remained opposed to membership. The French were not deceived. So far from Britain being a source of technological expertise and independence, it was a country with a weak economy pleading for entry into a community of strong economies. On 28 November 1967, de Gaulle 'gave the most resounding "*Non*" to any question of British entry into EEC'.[37] The British application was left 'lying on the table', but entry would have to wait until there was a new French President and, indeed, a new British government.

Nevertheless the fact that Britain, under a Labour government, had applied for membership was to have dramatic consequences for the Labour party. The Wilson government's application to join the European Community appeared to have reduced the policy differences between the two main parties almost to vanishing point. Appearances were deceptive. Once out of office, the Labour party would rebel against membership. The rebellion was part of Labour's reversion to socialist fundamentalism. But the fact that a Labour government had applied for membership would influence many members, who would consider it dishonourable for a party to repudiate in opposition the policies it had adopted in office.

THE DEVALUATION

In November 1967, sterling was finally devalued. The Treasury had at last discovered what it should have told Ministers three years previously that, on the policies the government was following, devaluation was inevitable. It now recommended devaluation as the only option. Wilson's fragile skiff had once more been blown off course and, this time, there was little argument that, whatever the Americans said or offered, devaluation could no longer be resisted. There was now no one to blame but the government itself. Crossman's private comment was that 'The Government has failed more abysmally than any Government since 1931.'[38] Callaghan resigned as Chancellor as a matter of honour and exchanged offices with Roy Jenkins. Although he would have liked to leave the Treasury in more pleasing circumstances, it was, for him, also a relief. He had long been tired of the uncertainties that beset economic management. No other office, even the Home Office, could be as bad. Moreover, after three years at the Treasury, he could claim to be an expert on Treasury matters, confident that he would never again have to be directly responsible for them. The fact that he had failed did not make him less of an expert. Like other experts on economic policy, he would, in retrospect, attempt to learn the lessons of his failure. Even if he never achieved understanding of the present, he would at least be excellently equipped to refight the battles of the past. Wilson made a broadcast and, in an attempt to be helpful to his countrymen who understood little of such matters, assured them that the pound in their pocket had not been devalued. It sounded like an attempt to conceal the defeat of his policies. The slip, at once exploited by the Tories, did nothing for Wilson's reputation for candour.

For Wilson, it was bad enough that he had been forced into devaluation. He knew that it must be accompanied by deflationary measures but showed no sense of urgency. Unfortunately his new Chancellor shared the lack of urgency. There was two months' delay before the main decisions were taken to cut public expenditure and a further two months' delay before the necessary deflationary budget. A highly symbolic action was the return of prescription charges, accompanied by a two-year deferment of the raising of the school-leaving age. The first was entirely defensible, though embarrassing. The second demonstrated that in its desperate fight for self-preservation the government had lost any sense of priorities whether of a socialist or any other kind. During this period of procrastination, sterling came near a further devaluation due to market scepticism as to whether the government had the will to take the necessary accompanying steps. George Brown, unaware perhaps that it is not done to kick a man when he is down, used a minor opportunity to launch a bitter attack on Wilson for the way he ran the government. Wilson and Jenkins had agreed, without consulting the Cabinet, to an American request for a temporary closure of the London gold market. It happened to be one of those occasions when Wilson's decision had been incontrovertible. But the timing of Brown's outburst was perhaps influenced by the imminent threat that the government was, once more, about to be blown off course. Brown, having made clear both to Wilson and to most of the Cabinet what he thought of the Prime Minister, then resigned, hoping to be summoned back. But Wilson had decided that he had had enough and offered no conciliation. The resignation became absolute and, on 15 March 1968, the George Brown phenomenon disappeared for ever from the precincts of Whitehall. The new sterling parity survived with further American help and at last Jenkins was ready with his first budget, which impressed the market even though the enormous increase in taxation it contained proved not in the end to be enough. There was then even further delay before domestic credit was brought under control. The delay prolonged the period of anxious waiting before the balance of payments turned because goods suitable for export were still being diverted to home consumption. At last, by 1969, with the help of yet further measures of restriction, the balance of payments was coming right. It was to be Labour's supreme achievement. Unfortunately inflation began to rise and the government proved incapable of finding the means to deal with it.

During the period leading up to devaluation and beyond, the British government acted as though it was entitled to special regard and assistance. If it did not receive it voluntarily it would issue threats. Unfortunately the threats signalled weakness rather than any negotiating strength. A favourite ploy was to threaten to withdraw British troops from Germany. Callaghan made the threat as Chancellor if Britain was not conceded sufficient by way of a German contribution to the cost of stationing British troops on German territory.[39] The threat was made while Britain was still maintaining commitments that it could ill afford East of Suez. There was no particular reason why Britain, having lost an empire, should continue to act like an imperial power. No doubt the British government was acting under the impression that the USA valued the British presence East of Suez more even than the commitment to NATO. It was a disappointment to Washington that, following the devaluation, Britain announced that it would be withdrawing from its commitments East of Suez. During the tense period after devaluation, when further devaluation was threatened, the British government pressed the Germans to revalue their currency. The Germans, always major competitors of British industry in overseas markets, had accumulated a vast balance of payments surplus. Everything pointed to the need for a revaluation of the Deutschmark. Despite pressure from other of the major industrialized countries, the Germans refused. They had an election in September 1969. International economic co-operation was not, for the moment, at the top of their agenda. This too led to threats by Wilson and Jenkins that British troops might be withdrawn from Germany. Opinion in Europe and the USA was unlikely to be impressed. Britain was strategically and geographically part of Europe even if not yet economically. It was in Britain's interests to help in the defence of the NATO boundaries. To reduce its commitment to NATO would not be just a confession of irretrievable economic weakness. It would also raise the question whether Britain was worth helping at all in its self-inflicted economic crises.

The devaluation provided a warning to others, far outside the Labour government, who had become concerned at Britain's poor economic performance. The Tories might have their own criticisms of the way in which the Wilson government had handled its inheritance. But there were some acute enough to realize that there might be something wrong more fundamental than was to be explained by Labour's incompetence. Was it perhaps the whole Keynesian system of economic management? Had successive governments in Britain given insufficient importance to the control of inflation? At the University of Chicago, Milton Friedman was advancing a monetary explanation for inflation. There was in Britain a 'new right' which was attempting to revive the economic liberalism which had been discarded thirty years before under the influence of the triumphant Keynesians. Sir Keith Joseph, shadowing the Board of Trade, was discovering the virtues of capitalism and turning those virtues into consistent criticism of the interventionist policies of the Labour government, except where, as with the aluminium smelters, there might be something to be lost politically by being too outspoken. Margaret Thatcher was developing similar qualms about the consensus economics of the post-war period. Both Joseph and Thatcher were in close contact with the Institute of Economic Affairs, which provided briefing and encouragement.[40] Joseph and Thatcher would appear to have forgotten their intellectual adventures in economic liberalism once they returned to office with Heath in 1970. Nevertheless questions had been raised in their minds and in those of others in the Conservative party and elsewhere. Peter Jay, economics editor of *The Times* and son of Douglas Jay, began to give warnings about the dangers of an explosion in the money supply.[41] Desmond Donnelly, Labour MP, who in the 1964 Parliament had opposed the renationalization of steel and had subsequently resigned the Labour whip, declared in a speech on 26 November 1968 that:

> the government's expenditure has continued to increase and it has not been matched by comparable expansion in industrial production. There is a simple equation. If we expand government expenditure by, for example, ten per cent per annum, and it is not matched by a comparable amount of goods, there are two alternatives; either that expansion has to be cut back or we have to print money.[42]

Thus the devaluation had helped to provoke a debate about the post-war economic consensus. A reappraisal had started which would have consequences during the even greater strains of the 1970s.

IN PLACE OF STRIFE

In 1969, the question of the relations between Labour and the trade union movement was raised in its most bitter, and perhaps unnecessary, form. The occasion was the White Paper *In Place of Strife*. The story begins towards the end of 1968. Devaluation had at last taken place but there were as yet few signs of the expected recovery. The balance of payments was still in serious deficit and there were fears of further, even more humiliating, devaluations. Disappointed expectations made the crisis appear even worse than that which had led up the devaluation of November 1967. If devaluation was not successful, what other hope was there for the economy or indeed for the government? There were a variety of reasons why the situation still seemed so desperate. For success, the devaluation had needed to be followed by substantial deflation. The government had reacted slowly and inadequately. The market's longstanding doubts about the courage and understanding of Labour governments seemed justified by the delays and irresolution.

But, in addition to these explanations for Britain's dangerously slow emergence from deficit, there was, in the view of an increasingly exasperated government, the British disease. The British disease was unruly industrial relations. It was a cause of low productivity. Its cost in exports lost was incalculable but probably significant. The British industrial relations scene, always liable to be disfigured by inexplicable disputes, had deteriorated even further following the devaluation. Members of trade unions found that their standard of living had suffered and fought to restore it. If they succeeded, they would add to the already strong inflationary pressures in the economy. They would undermine the economic policy of the government which required, through devaluation, a general fall in the standard of living in order to make industrial production more competitive both at home and in overseas markets.

The government, standing badly in the polls, desperate for some signs of recovery, exaggerated the impact on its prospects of the seemingly endless industrial disputes often on issues so minor as to suggest either total irresponsibility or political motivation on the part of those who initiated them. Sometimes the disputes were between unions fighting each other for members. Instead of waiting for the issue to be settled by arbitration or some other peaceful means, there would be immediate recourse to strike action supposedly against the employer, actually against fellow workers. Sometimes these disputes were unofficial, led by local leaders without authorization from their union headquarters. It had been discovered how a whole factory could be brought to a halt by just a few key workers. A small number would strike and thousands would be put out of work. Apart from the economic effects of these disputes, which may have been less than the government feared, they had a large political impact. This industrial mayhem was well publicized. A Labour government was supposed to possess a special capability in dealing with such matters through their links with the trade unions. As was now being notoriously demonstrated, it had no such capability, and its reputation with the electorate, already low, fell further. It fell even among trade union members, who themselves were often the prime victims of industrial indiscipline. Trade union leaders had little incentive to act effectively against unofficial industrial disputes. The union would not be liable in damages for breach of contract. The leaders themselves, sometimes subject to re-election, would simply make themselves unpopular with that small section of their membership that voted in union elections. Even if their position was secure, they would certainly be accused at union conferences of betraying the interests of their members. To sit on their hands and watch the world go by was an attractive alternative to any display of initiative. Or they could actually encourage the indiscipline. At the 1968 Party Conference Hugh Scan-

JAMES CALLAGHAN. His failure to call an election in the autumn of 1978 was followed by Labour's eighteen years in the wilderness – not a moment longer than the Party needed to rethink its policies.

Above MICHAEL FOOT.
A natural follower found
wandering uncertainly in
high places.

Left ROY JENKINS. Born
into Labour's aristocracy,
he found Europe a more
congenial objective than
socialism.

Above TONY CROSLAND.
The revisionist – who stopped
revising.

Left TONY BENN. Excited by
technology he became
convinced it could only yield its
potential if managed by genuine
socialists but found that there
was a problem of scarcity.

DENIS HEALEY. Labour's lost leader, a sacrifice to socialist folly or idealism

JACK JONES. His fear of treachery by the Right of the Labour party led him to co-operate with it in the battle against inflation.

Opposite ROY
HATTERSLEY.
The new revisionist
immured in the old.

Above NEIL KINNOCK.
The Welsh orator who
never persuaded the
English.

Right MARGARET
THATCHER. The
mother of New
Labour.

Left TONY BLAIR.
Modernizer in search of
a message.

Below GORDON BROWN.
With the highest aspirations
for the future, he scours the
past for a link between Old
and New Labour.

lon, President of the AEU, described the differences between the government and Conference as being concerned with 'a simple straightforward Socialist belief of ensuring that less of the national gross profit goes in rent, interest and profit and more goes in wages and salaries'.[43]

In April 1965, the government had appointed a Royal Commission under the chairmanship of a judge who had once been a Labour MP, Lord Donovan. After three years' study of the problems of industrial relations, it concluded that their solution was the responsibility of management and men. It proposed the creation of a Commission on Industrial Relations which might assist management and men to find solutions but saw no benefit in legal penalties. Politically, it was not an encouraging conclusion. It was because management and men had proved incapable of finding ways by which disruptive disputes could be avoided that the question had been referred to the Royal Commission. The Report was clearly not in tune with the public mood. If the government had hoped that it might obtain from the Donovan Commission some guidance as to what precisely should be done that might seem an effective antidote to industrial indiscipline, and to the inflationary pressures to which it supposedly gave rise, it was disappointed. To embarrass the government further, the Tory Opposition under Edward Heath had promised, if elected, to introduce an Industrial Relations Bill that would end the exceptional immunities of the trade unions, which placed them virtually beyond the law. If such legislation was enacted, trade unions would become liable for action for damages. It would be a revolution in British industrial relations.

It was in these circumstances that Harold Wilson invited Barbara Castle to make proposals for the reform of industrial relations. He had appointed her First Secretary of State and Secretary of State for Employment and Productivity partly for this purpose. Her new department, previously carrying the humbler title of Ministry of Labour, had won a reputation for complacency in face of the country's evident economic problems. The arguments so eloquently paraded in the Donovan Report had long persuaded successive Ministers of Labour. As a determined and effective minister, Barbara Castle would have the advantage that many of her officials were no longer content with those arguments and were eager to co-operate in finding a better answer to industrial indiscipline. Moreover she was a socialist, probably the most sincere socialist in a government of practical men. Unfortunately, whatever she proposed would be done from a position of weakness. She could not bring to the task the authority of a government that had surmounted its economic problems and was clearly on top of its job. On the contrary it was a government that had exhausted the patience of its followers and was now treated with weary tolerance at best. The proposals with which she came forward gave much to the trade unions by way of rights to recognition but were also intended to authorize intervention by the government in certain kinds of industrial dispute. There was, for example, a proposal for a twenty-eight-day conciliation pause and a suggestion that the government might take power to impose a settlement in inter-union disputes. Government intervention would be enforced by the threat of penalties in the form of fines. There was no intention that non-payment of the fines would lead to the imprisonment of workers or trade union officials. But this was a risk that could not entirely be discounted. It was intended to be a balanced package with new rights balanced against new obligations.

Moreover, it could be presented as a sound *socialist* bargain. The government would offer full employment and other benefits. The trade unions would offer discipline. If they did not, then pressure must be brought to bear on them to enforce discipline. As a socialist, Barbara Castle was convinced that it was impossible to plan the economy if pay was left unplanned. By the same token it would be impossible to make progress towards socialism if the industrial scene was disfigured by indiscipline. It had always been recognised that socialism required discipline. As a socialist in the tradition of Bevan, Castle believed in discipline. Workers must work just as planners must plan. If there was no self-discipline, the alternative must be the law. Barbara Castle could be naive. It was naive to believe that her vision of socialism was shared anywhere in the ranks of trade union leaders. For them, socialism meant money on the table, not government interference in their affairs. In theory they believed in socialism. In practice they believed in deploying their power.

That powerful institutions such as the trade unions should be brought within the law should have been uncontroversial. It was an anomaly that they had remained so long outside the law. Whether Barbara Castle's way of bringing them within the law, balancing increased rights against increased obligations, was the best way was another question. But the perfect occasion and the perfect wording would be unlikely to be found at the first attempt. If the trade unions were to be brought within the law, Barbara Castle's proposals would do for a start. Jenkins was, by now, questionably a socialist of any kind and certainly stood far apart from Barbara Castle in political orientation. But, whatever the ideological justification offered by Castle for her proposals, Jenkins became a willing recruit to a campaign designed essentially to save his economic policy. His economic policy required restraint in wage settlements. Incomes policy seemed increasingly ineffective. Castle's proposals would have to do as an alternative. The triumvirate of Wilson, Castle and Jenkins extracted from a reluctant Cabinet agreement to the publication, in January 1969, of a White Paper embodying the Castle ideas. The Cabinet was reluctant because, for the first time, the trade unions would be brought within the law and there were circumstances in which penalties might be extracted from them. Could this possibly be a task for the Labour party, the political offspring of the trade union movement? The title of the White Paper, *In Place of Strife*, paid blatant tribute to Aneurin Bevan's book *In Place of Fear*. A tribute to Bevan, if only in the title of the White Paper, might recall the already bellowing herds of the trade unions and PLP to their duty. If there was any such hope, it would be rapidly dashed.

The immediate reaction of the trade union leadership to the White Paper was hostile for the reasons foreseen in Cabinet. The unions felt that they were being unjustifiably blamed for the country's economic misfortunes. They were outraged that a Labour government which they had helped to bring to power should exploit popular hostility against them. In any case, as Donovan had shown, the Castle proposals would not work. That they had been brought forward demonstrated that neither Wilson nor Castle, nor indeed Jenkins, knew anything about industrial relations. As many members of the PLP were sponsored by trade unions, the hostility soon spread to a broad tranche of Labour MPs. But it hardly required sponsorship to produce hostility to the proposals on the Labour backbenches. Labour backbenchers had been brought up to believe in the indissoluble link between the trade unions and the Labour party. It was not for a Labour government to prejudice that link. There were those who questioned whether this was a fit subject for a Labour government. Surely, it was argued, such measures should be left to the next Tory government. What was a Labour government doing, however desperate its straits, attempting to reverse decades of legal immunity?

In fact, this should have been exactly a task for a Labour government. A Labour government should have been able to introduce a balanced package with support from the trade unions, who surely would prefer that legislation, inevitable at some stage, should be introduced by their friends rather than by their enemies. There was, however, little hope of extracting co-operation from the trade union movement in such an enterprise. It lacked the foresight to appreciate the value of doing a deal with the Labour government on a balanced package. It thought itself entitled indefinitely to retain the immunities it had long held. It did not accept that the grant of immunities when it was weak was no reason for continuing them when it was extremely strong. What made the prospects for co-operation even worse was that the Castle proposals were clearly in part a political manoeuvre, to outface Heath, and in part an excuse for the failure thus far of economic policy. The trade unions refused to become sacrificial victims of a political manoeuvre and the scapegoat for the government's failures in economic management. It remained true that the Labour government, their government, *was* in desperate straits, and it might have been expected that the wish of the trade union movement for the survival of their government would dictate co-operation. In fact co-operation was adamantly refused. Indeed, rather than submit to the proposed legislation, some trade union leaders would have preferred the removal of Harold Wilson as Prime Minister. The Chairman of the PLP was Douglas Houghton, a gerontocrat of no mean ability. He had no love for Harold Wilson, who had purged him from the Cabinet on the insufficient grounds of advanced age. He had also, in the distant past, been a trade union general secretary and had served on the General Council of the TUC. He was not sure that there was a majority in the PLP to change the leadership, a question in any case confused by the contending claims for the succession of James Callaghan and Roy Jenkins, but he was certain that Wilson and Castle must not be allowed to get away with *In Place of Strife*. Labour MPs also refused their co-operation. If the government brought its Bill forward, they would not vote for it. The Labour party was proving that it was not a socialist party, it was a trade union party. It was the Party not of a cause but of a vested interest. It was not a crusade. It was a lobby.

Wilson was not discouraged. Having launched this new departure, he was determined to have his way. Indeed he spoke of the proposals as essential to the survival of his government. At moments of drama Wilson always knew how to call for help from departed heroes of the left. In this case he called on the Gettysburg oration. If a Labour government could not enact proposals of this kind, if it was so far in thrall to the trade unions that it could not do what was required in the interests of the whole nation, the question would arise, suggested Wilson, whether this Labour government or any future Labour government could shoulder the burdens of government (or for that matter long endure).

There is a strong argument that the analysis behind *In Place of Strife*, even in so far as it was free from political motivation, was flawed. There were powerful reasons for bringing trade unions within the law, but the economic crisis was not one of them. The penal proposals would not work. They were the product of despair. None of the devices that had been tried by the Wilson government to tame inflation had really worked. Prices and incomes policies might enjoy a short period of success. But, even if statutory, their operation was subject to the consent of trade unions and their members. That consent had to be paid for at a high price in concessions to trade union influence. Trade union leaders had to feel influential. No price paid to the trade union leaders could guarantee, for long, the consent of their members. If the government was going to reject Callaghan's call for higher unemployment, there was no answer to industrial indiscipline, poor productivity and the inflationary pressures to which they gave rise. That was the history of post-war Britain, and the experience of the Heath government would confirm the message. *In Place of Strife* can be interpreted in different ways. Barbara Castle would regard it as part of a struggle between socialism and the atavistic activities of the trade unions. Or it could be regarded as a misconceived attempt to deal with inflation without imperilling full employment. But action which permitted a major growth in unemployment was not regarded as an option in 1968 or 1970 or 1974. On the contrary, though it was thought important to deal with inflation, it was thought even more important to maintain full employment.

In his April 1969 budget, Jenkins proposed that the statutory prices and incomes policy, which was under severe criticism from the TUC, should be allowed to expire at the end of the year but that, in exchange, a shortened Industrial Relations Bill should be enacted in the current session of Parliament. The shortened Bill would give the trade unions certain rights. But there would also be fines if government orders imposing settlements in inter-union disputes, or a twenty-eight-day conciliation pause, were not obeyed. The imminence of legislation further heightened the conflict between the government and the TUC. Wilson and Castle found themselves increasingly isolated not just in the PLP but in the Cabinet, where their most determined opponent was Callaghan. He, it was suspected, had mixed motives, the wish to revive his ravaged reputation supplementing his conscientious opposition to anything that threatened trade unions with penalties. In the end Jenkins defected and Wilson and Castle capitulated. Instead of legislation, they accepted a 'solemn and binding' undertaking by the TUC that it would strive to be helpful in securing an immediate return to work where it judged strikers to be in the wrong. Wilson's skill in presentation, not always in evidence in a crisis, was insufficient on this occasion to prevent his capitulation from being seen as a massive defeat for the government. He had stated that the proposed legislation was essential. He had questioned whether the government could continue if it did not secure its legislation. He was not getting his legislation and yet he was continuing in office. From this point inflation took off. The unions had discovered that the government was powerless against them. Why should they not exploit the weakness of the government to increase the incomes of their members? Though the unions might not, on certain economic theories, be responsible for inflation, their rejection of *In Place of Strife* – accompanied as it was by their humiliation of the government they were expected to support – sealed the fate of the first Wilson government.

CONCLUSION

During 1970 the balance of payments and the opinion polls began to look good for the government. The Cabinet which, a year earlier, could hardly have expected a renewal of its mandate at the next election, jumped at the chance. An election was called for 18 June 1970. The electorate was sceptical. It was more harassed by rising prices than impressed by the balance of payments surplus. It was now better acquainted with Wilson. Why was he calling an election nine months before it was due? The suspicion that there was some explanation which would do no credit to the government was reinforced when, in the midst of the election, one month's trade figures were in deficit due in part to the import of some large aircraft. Even the alleged triumph with the balance of payments appeared, momentarily, specious. Wilson found he had underestimated the electorate as well as the power of the trade unions.

The Wilson government failed. It hardly pretended to be a socialist government. But in the area where it did have pretensions, the management of the economy and the regeneration of British industry, it also failed. It was only as an efficient manager of capitalism that the electorate would trust the Labour party to resume the march to socialism. Yet it had lost the necessary trust. The Labour party felt the electoral judgement of June 1970 to be harsh. But it was deserved.

FOURTEEN

Interpretations of defeat

Labour's defeat in 1951 could be regarded as a merciful release, a blessing in disguise, though no doubt, as Churchill said on a comparable occasion, a blessing well disguised. The Attlee government looked exhausted and was exhausted. It was very different in June 1970. The defeat was an unexpected and devastating blow. The Wilson government had come through the fire and had emerged on the other side successful, at least by the criterion of the balance of payments. The electorate had, unfeelingly, discarded its bruised servants just at the very moment when, after so many travails, they could, at last, turn their hands to the lofty purposes that had brought them into politics, and which had had to await economic recovery and national solvency. The Ministers who had been defenestrated in 1970 did not then foresee that the return to office would come as soon as 1974 but that the future would be at least as disappointing as the past.

Labour's leading figures were all, by political standards, young. All felt that they had much yet to give to the government of their country even if what they had to give was questionably socialist. This was certainly not a group of men and women ready for retirement. Indeed, by every measure, of experience, energy and intellect, they shone as compared with their opposite numbers in the Conservative party, who seemed a dull lot, with Iain Macleod as their only undoubted star. For a group of capable and ambitious men and women to face once more the tedium of opposition was a setback very difficult to bear. After thirteen years of opposition they had savoured only six years of government. Labour Ministers left office on 19 June 1970 feeling empty rather than proud. Whereas in 1951 a return to office seemed probable and imminent, in 1970 there were many who doubted whether Labour, after a period in government empty of socialist achievement, would ever return to office. Not merely had Labour lost. It had lost with so many of its hopes unfulfilled. It had promised a great deal and delivered very little. Where was the new world which, as reputed socialists, they had aimed to create? Had they not merely added six more to the thirteen wasted years of which they had orated so eloquently in 1964? Of course defeat could be attributed to the ingratitude or ignorance of the electorate. Perhaps Wilson had been too obviously opportunistic in going to the country as soon as the poll figures turned favourable. Those bad trade figures, announced in the midst of the election, had seemed to undermine Labour's claim to have solved the balance of payments problem.

But whatever excuses might form on the lips of Labour Cabinet Ministers, a few days' thought recovering from the shock persuaded all but the blindest that the causes of defeat went deeper than this. After such a defeat there was bound to be a post-mortem and a reassessment. What should Labour learn from its experience of government? Could it now unite on its analysis and its remedies, on the causes of failure and the policies for the future? Could it bring back to the country at the next election a coherent socialist programme that carried the assent of the Party as a whole and was attractive to the electorate? The danger was that defeat and disappointment might encourage a reversion to socialist fundamentals which would seem irrelevant to most former Ministers and might imperil victory on the next occasion. After 1951 such a reversion had been prevented by the support given to the right-wing leadership by the trade unions. But now the unions had swung to the left. They had been alienated by *In Place of Strife*. Would a discredited leadership be able to avert an outbreak of extremism and maintain unity?

Some lessons suggested themselves without difficulty. There was an external world, one not enamoured of socialist projects but clamouring to be heard especially when it was required to bolster a sinking pound or fund an inflationary economic policy. There was the evident failure of industrial policy to yield any return on the public money invested in it. It hardly needed confirming that the leadership of British trade unions was either naturally stupid or had been left by membership pressures no alternative other than stupidity. The unregulated power of the trade unions had become an offence. If there was to be regulation, the trade union leadership might have perceived that it was better to have it enacted by a Labour government than by a Tory government. Thereby they would have had an influence on the legislation and also helped to revive the prestige of the Labour government as the Party of industrial peace. A Labour government, a government of *their* Party, might even have been re-elected in 1970. The evident stupidity, or helplessness, of the trade union leadership might have suggested to Labour politicians that, in designing an economic policy for a future return to office, the last group to be relied upon was the General Council of the TUC. There was, however, little evidence that any of these lessons had been learnt. Nor the important political lesson that, whatever Labour leaders might think of the skill and success they had brought to their government departments, that was not the way their record was perceived in the ranks of their Party.

The left had tolerated Wilson while he was successful but had grown more critical with every failure. He was its man *faute de mieux*, but it was *faute de mieux*. Whatever his faults, he might save it from Jenkins. But what had clearly been established between 1964 and 1970 was that he was not the omniscient leader who had enticed the support of the electorate in 1964 and 1966. The left would use him but it declined to be enthusiastic about him. Through almost the whole of his government there had been an incomes policy of some kind. Where was the effect on inflation which was to be the reward for accepting controls on wages? Labour had left office with inflation rising to unprecedented heights. With *In Place of Strife*, Wilson had even tried to blame the trade unions and bring them within the law contrary to the long traditions of the Labour Movement, not to mention the recommendations of the Donovan Report. He had largely abandoned nationalization, the left's remedy for most industrial and social ills, and had substituted technology. What had the apotheosis of technology achieved either for Britain or for the Labour party? Mintech, directed by Benn, had been lavish in its subsidies to private companies. But the only visible result was that large firms had grown larger, and therefore more powerful, but not obviously more efficient, and the returns to growth and to welfare had been negligible. Britain's economy, on the eve of Labour's defeat, was growing more slowly than in the last of those thirteen wasted years. Equally negligible had been any development in the accountability of the private sector to the public interest.

Benn himself now regarded the British ruling class as effete, conservative, unadventurous and unpatriotic. Even capitalism deserved better leadership than the British ruling class could provide. Labour had failed not because it had been too left wing but because it had been too right wing. Labour had been cosseting its enemies, the City and industry, at the expense of its friends, the working class and the trade unions. It had wasted the opportunity long awaited to build on the achievements of the Attlee government and enact a socialist society. The answer must be a return to nationalization. It might not be in the old Morrisonian form, large state monopolies. Other forms of public ownership could be considered. But certainly the programme of the next Labour government, if by good fortune there ever was another, must encompass a major advance in public ownership. Among the left there were consolations for Labour's loss of office. Those who had watched from outside, pleasurably expecting to be disappointed at the output of a government that had denied the true faith, had now regained total freedom to criticize without being accused of disloyalty. There are few greater satisfactions than proof that one has been right while others, wrapped in the panoply of office, have been so signally wrong.

THE ASPIRATIONS AND POLICIES OF TONY BENN

It was to the leadership of the left that Benn now moved. He started with untypical humility. His Fabian pamphlet of September 1970, *The New Politics: A Socialist Reconnaissance*, presented his first thoughts after the defeat of June 1970. In it he wrote, 'It is unwise today for any candidate to suggest in an election campaign, that if elected he, or his party, will be able to acquire through election sufficient authority to solve the major problems that confront the nation.' He added that political leaders 'will need to be much more modest in their claims for what they can do . . .'.[1] However, this self-critical phase passed rapidly. A refreshed, reformed and re-educated Benn sought to raise the Labour Movement against the leadership of the Parliamentary Labour Party and his former Cabinet colleagues. In his hand was the red banner of socialism, which he was never subsequently to let fall.

Barbara Castle had ruled herself out as a potential leader of the left by her advocacy of *In Place of Strife*. It would never be glad confident morning again. Time might patch what could never be healed. Meanwhile she did her best to emphasize her kinship with the left, and with the trade unions, by taking the lead, on Labour's front bench, in opposing the Tory government's Industrial Relations Bill. It was a role replete with irony. But it proved that Barbara Castle was not, after all, lacking in sense of humour and that Wilson, who had appointed her to that role, was not lacking in gratitude for the great sacrifices she had made in reputation by joining him in his failed attack on trade union irresponsibility. *In Place of Strife* now achieved its only victory. A penitent Labour party found itself tied even more intimately to the trade unions. The whipped PLP trudged through sleepless night after sleepless night voting hopelessly against clause after clause in the Industrial Relations Bill. It was offensive to many members of the PLP, and ludicrous in the eyes of the electorate, but evidently necessary to discharge the deep offence committed by *In Place of Strife*. The trade unions themselves were to prove much more effective in sabotaging the Industrial Relations Act than the PLP could possibly be in the night watches of the House of Commons. It was not even clear that the sleep fruitlessly lost by the PLP won it any credit at trade union headquarters.

For the leadership of the left, Benn's only possible rival was Michael Foot. And the love of Foot, especially within the left of the Party, was so intense that, at any moment when he felt like bestirring himself, he could stretch forth his hand and filch its leadership from Benn's grasp. He was already being encouraged to do so, was listening to voices that told him it was his duty to rescue the Party for socialism, and had secured election to the shadow Cabinet. Foot, unlike Benn, was entirely uncontaminated by the failures of the Wilson government. He had, indeed, been one of its severest critics. Now, he would adopt the role of prophet and call for forbearance for those who, in government, had strayed from the socialist path. He would bring the Labour party and the trade unions together once more and ensure that never again were they parted. Naturally peace would be sealed on the basis that the Labour government had been wrong and the trade unions right. By that admission of error, the cause of socialism, which had been defiled during the previous six years, might be cleansed. Above all Foot was deeply opposed to British membership of the EEC. It sometimes seemed that extracting Britain from entanglement with the EEC had become his predominant ambition, to which every other policy objective should, if necessary, be sacrificed. It made him impatient with anyone whose actions were imperilling Labour's return to office, and prominent among the culprits was the disruptive and unforgiving Benn with his new vision of a genuinely socialist Britain. To Michael Foot, Benn would have to defer, even though Foot's socialism had in it the rhetorical flavour of yesteryear while Benn could add a modern, bright, technological colour to old socialist themes. It seemed unlikely that Foot, a much older man, without experience of government, would ever claim the leadership of the Party itself, even if he had now found for himself a role other than as critic. Surely he would realize his own limitations.

Benn had acquired over the years, or perhaps had been born with, an exceptional presentational ability that could entice the Labour masses even if not his Cabinet colleagues. This ability was now turned to the presentation of old socialist truths in plain modern language, to distilling into socialist simplicities what he now discovered he had learnt about British industry when Minister of Technology. It was true that he would have to find some way of at once claiming the advantages of Ministerial experience while cleansing himself of the responsibility for failure that he shared as a member of the Wilson Cabinet. But that was not a task beyond Benn's eloquence. He too had been disappointed with the achievements of the Labour government and even of his own department, the Ministry of Technology. He entitled the third volume of his diaries (1968–72), *Office without Power*, three words that were both an excuse and a claim. The trouble, as he saw it, was that he had not had enough power because the public sector had been insufficiently expanded. In a paper of June 1971, *Towards a Socialist Industrial Policy*, he argued that a future Labour government should introduce a General Powers Act enabling it to buy shares, make loans, acquire assets and take whatever steps were necessary to run the businesses concerned under the Companies Acts. He wrote that:

> any money that the Government wishes to put in to help declining industries, finance advanced industries or cope with the consequences flowing from the economic collapse of vital industries could be injected in such a way as to expand the public sector and create a public portfolio and central management unit that would profoundly shift the balance of power in favour of the public sector.[2]

He had concluded that 'bribing, cajoling and merging industry' could not continue.[3] He would no doubt have been gratified to know that, over forty years before, Bernard Shaw had written, 'For every £100 granted to private enterprise the Government should demand a share certificate.'[4] After all, Benn was not looking for originality but for socialism. In September 1971, under the system of Buggins's turn among members of the NEC, he became Chairman of the Labour party.

One problem for Benn as a leader of the left was his support for entry into the EEC. He had made speeches in that sense as a minister and he still saw advantages in membership. Even when, as in his Fabian pamphlet of September 1970, he advanced the idea of a referendum on membership, it was not in a spirit of opposition but simply, he claimed, because such a major step, with deep constitutional implications, required explicit popular endorsement.[5] On 30 May 1971, he noted in his diary:

> I want to make it clear that I am in favour of Europe. All the arguments against it are short-term arguments, based on what it looks like now, and

omit the possibility that we might make changes when the time comes. But I can't get the Party to focus its mind on this and the possibility of a popular front in western Europe with the Italian and French Communist Parties cooperating with us on areas of policy where a European stance has to be taken.[6]

On 22 July 1971 Benn spoke for Labour during a House of Commons debate on entry into the EEC. In his diary he commented that 'The Tories did not like my case for the Market, which was to control multi-national companies, and of course they didn't like my case against going in without a referendum or an Election . . .'[7] Thus he did not want to be an anti-Marketeer. But the left did not agree and even Benn could not persuade them. In the end he concluded that, if he wanted to be a leader, he must learn to follow. In the idea of a referendum, he had found a means whereby he could gently slip into the camp of opposition and thereby reinforce his credibility with the left. By his treason, he qualified himself for the leadership of the left and, by his example, he encouraged others along the same convenient path.

Having abandoned Europe, Benn now possessed all the qualifications and qualities for the leadership of the left. He had charm, humour, extraordinary eloquence and a willingness to work which was certainly not emulated among the majority of his opponents in the Party. It was fashionable to say that he lacked judgement. Certainly his love of ideas was greater than his capacity for critical appraisal. At Mintech he had appeared naive or, as Ziegler describes him, 'guileless'.[8] To say that he lacked weight would be premature because weight could come, particularly if it was supplied by millions of trade union votes. Nor would it be fair to say of him that he was motivated primarily by thoughts of the leadership of the Party. He did know as early as 7 December 1970 that Wilson had set a term to his leadership of the Party.[9] It must always have been clear to him that he would never be elected leader if the choice was left to the PLP. The PLP could not be expected to be in love with him after he had started advocating that it should be easier for constituencies to rid themselves of their MPs. The increasingly populist, even revolutionary, tendency of Benn's orations on matters such as the collapse of Upper Clyde Shipbuilders added to his unpopularity with the great mass of the PLP, as did his tone on the occasion of the imprisonment in Pentonville of five militant dockers in July 1972 on charges under the Industrial Relations Act. He was even concluding 'that the time had come when the works of Karl Marx would have to be rehabilitated in the Labour Party because the Party without Karl

Marx really lacks a basic analytical core'.[10] This kind of thinking imperilled seats at general elections. The Labour party had long cherished the fact that it was a democratic socialist party which did not wish to be tainted with the suspicion of Marxism.

The distaste for Benn in the PLP was increased by his final speech as Party Chairman at the 1972 Conference. He referred to Dick Taverne's decision, having fallen out with his constituency Labour party, to stand at a by-election at Lincoln as a Democratic Labour candidate. Taverne was, in Benn's view, a candidate of the media, and the media deserved rebuke. He said: 'I wish the workers in the media would sometimes remember that they are members of the working class and have a sense of responsibility to see that what is said about us is true.'[11] He had said as much in his Fabian pamphlet, *The New Politics: A Socialist Reconnaissance*, when he called for 'greater industrial democracy in the mass media' which would force 'the owners of the existing outlets to share their power with those who work for their papers, or on their stations . . .'.[12] All this was making Benn increasingly unacceptable not just to the right of the PLP but to its broad central plains.[13] Healey's reference to him as a 'middle class Robespierre' was entirely appropriate.[14] In the elections for deputy leader of the Party in November 1971, he won only 46 votes against the 140 cast for Jenkins and the 96 for Foot. When, in April 1972, Jenkins resigned the deputy leadership, Benn prudently decided not to stand, leaving the field clear for Michael Foot as the candidate of the left. As he lamented in his diary entry of 25 April 1972: 'It is extremely difficult for anyone who has left-wing instincts ever to be elected to anything [by the PLP].'[15] Others might have lamented that it was extremely difficult for anyone with right-wing instincts ever to be elected in the constituency section of the NEC.

One lesson Benn had learnt as a member of the Wilson Cabinet. He had seen the policy of *In Place of Strife* subverted by the trade union movement. The trade union movement was obviously very powerful, powerful enough to dispel his earlier doubts whether Britain could ever be modernized against trade union opposition. Now he believed that 'it is this link with the workers . . . which offers the only serious chance of major social, political and industrial change'.[16] Clearly, the experience of *In Place of Strife* had demonstrated that Britain could be modernized only by methods which trade unionists supported. But where were such methods to be found? The two most prominent trade union leaders were now both men of the left, Jack Jones of the TGWU and Hugh Scanlon of the AEU. Benn persuaded himself that what trade unionists wanted was socialism, not the socialism of the revisionists, not the pink imitation of socialist policies employed by the Wilson government between 1964 and 1970, but real socialist policies. Benn, talking with his favourite trade unionists, would comfort himself with the thought that they were preparing 'not in any sense a revolution but for a transfer of power of an important kind'.[17] He decided that power had passed from Westminster to the workers and trade unions. For a member of the shadow Cabinet, speaking at Westminster was an inescapable duty. But it was in the country that the important audiences were to be found. He travelled widely, addressing meetings and absorbing their atmosphere. Like all orators he drew inspiration from his audience as well as conveying inspiration to it. Like some, he began to inhale the enthusiasm of his own words. Sober trade union leaders were suspicious of him. But, as they found him an advocate of their causes, they turned towards him – though without dropping their fundamental suspicion that his brilliance was of the kind that quickly tarnishes on exposure to light.

THE TRADE UNIONS

That trade union leaders were prepared to align themselves with Benn is a measure of the disappointment they felt with the record of the Wilson government. And the course they now took bespoke desperation at the failures of the government whose election they had hailed six years before. Now, because of that government's failures and its eventual defeat, they were being exposed to the enactment of an Industrial Relations Bill intended to manacle them into subservience to the employers. Where, then, should they turn? What had been lacking in the Wilson government's policies? They would certainly deny that any fault lay with them or their members. True, there may have been too many unofficial strikes, but what else was to be expected when 'their' government had failed to produce the regular annual increases in standard of living expected from it? The principal fault, they decided, had lain in their government's failure to control and regulate the private sector so as to compel it to invest and thereby increase productivity. In investment lay the secret of increased prosperity. They had no time for arguments that productivity failures and low investment were to any extent due to lack of co-operation between work force and management. They would no more accept that argument than they would adopt the premise that wage increases had anything to do with inflation. Wages were only one element in final prices. There were many other elements, and their government, while trying to control pay, had done, in their view, little enough to control prices.

As the trade unions had had no new thoughts about the economy, they would revert, like Benn, to old thoughts. There must be more nationalization. Over the residual private sector, there must be more control. Investment levels must not be left to the whims of private sector owners and managers who thought only of profit. If now, after the near breach in relations caused by *In Place of Strife*, the Labour party came to them beseeching their assistance, insisting that no economic policy would work successfully without an incomes policy, they would exact terms which would cover the whole field of government policy. The trade unions could not be expected to co-operate simply on the basis that an incomes policy was in the interest of their members. Elected governments must realize that the trade unions were important institutions in society. Whatever the electorate might decide in a general election, it must recognize where power really lay. There were limits to representative government placed by the power brokers of society. In 1969, Wilson had succumbed to the power of the trade unions and had abandoned *In Place of Strife*. If he now wanted to persuade the electorate that, though he had failed to regulate them, he still had influence with them, he would be able to do it only on the unions' terms.

A Liaison Committee was established between the Parliamentary Committee, the NEC and the TUC, which met for the first time early in 1972. It was constituted in an attempt to restore confidence between the TUC and the Parliamentary leadership after the breakdown in relations caused by *In Place of Strife*. Its existence would help Labour leaders to put a respectable face on submission to trade union power. In that submission would be found the key to full employment without inflation. Thereby emerged the disastrous Social Contract. It was embodied in a document agreed between the Labour party and the TUC entitled *Economic Policy and the Cost of Living* and was published on 23 February 1973. It promised the repeal of the Industrial Relations Act and was designed, in the optimistic view of Harold Wilson, to 'engender the strong feeling of mutual confidence which alone will make it possible to reach the wide-ranging agreement which is necessary to control inflation and achieve sustained growth in the standard of living'.[18] Despite Wilson, it is highly doubtful whether the trade union leaders who entered into the Social Contract saw it as interfering in any way with their right to pursue free collective bargaining. The Social Contract was not, of course, legally enforceable. After *In Place of Strife* there was no question of a Labour government introducing a statutory incomes policy. However conciliatory the government in its relations with the trade unions, any response would be a matter of goodwill. Whatever benefits the Social Contract brought to Wilson's campaign for re-election, he should have had little doubt that it would prove extremely damaging to his prospects of governing in the interests of the country as a whole. The commitments into which the Labour party entered regarding subsidies, the control of prices and the redistribution of income and wealth were bound to be inflationary, and so it proved. The Contract was negotiated before OPEC's fourfold increase in the price of oil later in the year. The oil-price hike made it calamitous.

The unions were now so powerful that they could dictate who should be Employment Secretary. After the February 1974 election, Jack Jones told Wilson that the unions would not stand for the somewhat right-wing Reg Prentice in that role. They agreed Michael Foot would be ideal.[19] Foot was appointed. It was an abdication of power by Wilson of a probably unprecedented kind. Never before had trade union leaders attempted to dictate to a Labour Prime Minister who should be the members of his Cabinet or in what role.

CROSLAND AND THE REVISIONISTS

Disappointment with the Wilson government was not confined to the left of the Labour party, or to the trade unions. Among the revisionists too there was a keen sense of failure. The disappointment was the greater in that the revisionists saw themselves as men of government. Who could say when, after such a failure, they could expect to be men of government again? The revisionists might not share the ideology of the left, but they regarded themselves as radicals. As radicals, they were prepared to march under the alternative banner which Crosland had raised, the banner on which it was written that socialism is about equality. Crosland's excavations into the socialist message made him the most prominent ideologist in the Labour party. He remained dedicated to the theory of socialism that he had designed nearly fifteen years before. He had given the best-known exposition of the new socialism and he now felt very possessive of his own creation. In a lecture to the

Fabian Society in November 1970, he restated 'the essence of social democracy in the 1970s'. There were four prime objectives, the relief of poverty, a more equal distribution of wealth, a wider ideal of social equality and strict social control of the environment. For him, these remained the essential socialist objectives. Whatever Labour might have achieved in its six years of office, it was not yet possible to move beyond them.[20]

In a book entitled *Socialism Now* written shortly before the 1974 election and published a month after, Crosland, ever systematic in his thinking, turned his mind to two questions.[21] The first question was what, if anything, had gone right with the Wilson government between 1964 and 1970. The second was whether, in the light of the Wilson experience, the revisionist thesis needed to be reconsidered. Was the left correct in its belief that what was now needed was a wholesale onslaught on the fortresses of capitalism, including the frank reinsertion of nationalization as the key element in a future Labour government's manifesto?

Crosland was not prepared to deny all merit to the government of which he had been a prominent member. He found that there had been 'solid progress' on a number of fronts such as public expenditure, income equality, standards of health, housing, education, regional policy and the quality of the environment. Indeed the government was to be congratulated for the fact that, 'pinioned though it was by constant economic difficulties', it had nevertheless raised total public expenditure from 41 per cent to 48 per cent of GNP. Moreover there were 'the many libertarian reforms helped on to the statute book by an enlightened Home Secretary...'[22] In addition, the distribution of income had become fairer.[23]

Yet, by the standards of what had been expected of a Labour government, all this was little enough. As Crosland acutely saw, in the very successes that could be claimed for the Wilson government lay the seeds of Labour's electoral failure. He had always argued that redistribution on the scale he wanted could be safely achieved only in a fast-growing economy. Those who were to suffer the higher taxes would accept the penalty only if, at the very least, their own net incomes were increasing, despite the higher rates of tax. Defeat in the General Election demonstrated that he had not been wrong to argue that redistribution had to be lubricated by economic growth. Moreover redistribution and additions to welfare would cause inflation if there was not adequate growth. He repeated the old story: 'Socialism and equality require a relative transfer of resources from private consumption to public expenditure; economic exigencies may demand a further transfer to higher exports or investment. But under conditions of slow growth, efforts to achieve these transfers inevitably provoke inflation.'[24] So Crosland's socialism still required a high rate of growth. He made himself unpopular with many environmentalists by insisting on the necessity of a high rate of growth. In fact, growth between 1964 and 1970 had been slower even than in the much criticized Tory years. It was not only the rich who had been squeezed but trade unionists too. Trade unionists had been assured that their standard of living would grow appreciably faster under a Labour government than under a Tory government. They had not found it so. As a result of Labour's successes as a party dedicated to equality and redistribution, 'the demands of public expenditure allied to those of the balance of payments left precious little for personal consumption, whose share in final expenditure indeed fell from 55 per cent to 51.8 per cent; and this had serious, perhaps decisive, consequences not only ... for wage inflation but also for the Government's electoral popularity'.[25]

Crosland's unsurprising conclusion was that it was not revisionism that had been at fault. He adhered to the views that he had expressed in *The Future of Socialism*, except that 'I was too complacent about growth ...'[26] His analysis of Labour's failure allotted only minor importance to too little nationalization or to the collapse of the National Plan. If socialism was about equality, the key question about nationalization was whether it helped towards greater equality. Crosland still did not think so. 'Developments in Britain during the last decade have been acutely disappointing to a democratic socialist, but the explanation does not appear to lie primarily in the British pattern of ownership.'[27] Nevertheless, he still thought nationalization might have a role in raising the efficiency of inefficient firms either by the acquisition of a public shareholding which could be as much as 100 per cent or by the instrument of competitive public enterprise. He therefore allocated a significant role to public ownership even if not the central role claimed for it by the left. David Lipsey comments that 'arguably as a minister [Crosland] did a bit too much of it ...'[28] But, although Crosland saw a role for nationalization, it seldom, in his view, helped much with the redistribution of wealth because fair compensation had to be paid. Generally, redistribution had to be achieved not by nationalization but by taxation. Labour, argued Crosland, 'needs a determination to "bash the rich", by a wealth tax, a gifts tax, the public ownership of land, and to communicate to the country a clear vision of a fairer and more equal Britain'.[29] Higher death duties would be another instrument in the same cause.

Crosland allowed exceptions to his rule that nationalization did not contribute to equality. The principal exception was the public ownership of development land, which he strongly advocated as a means of securing the redistribution of wealth. Other ways in which public ownership could foster equality included the creation of a National Superannuation Fund.[30] One way, derived from Denmark, was for the establishment of a National Workers' Fund to which companies would be compelled annually to contribute perhaps 1 per cent of their outstanding equity or the equivalent in cash. Workers in all industries would participate equally in the Fund through a growing annual entitlement.[31]

What had been at fault, then, was not the absence of major nationalization other than steel, nor the revisionist agenda, but inept macroeconomic management. Inept macroeconomic management had inhibited the economic growth essential to a successful policy of redistribution. 'The reason why the economy did not grow up to the limit of [its] higher productive potential was that the final *demand* was not there. This had nothing to do with too much or too little socialism; it was due to the deflationary policies which stemmed inexorably from the Labour Government's obsession with a particular parity for sterling.'[32] Crosland therefore demanded that next time there was a Labour government there should be what he called a 'flexible' exchange rate policy but also an effective incomes policy. Beyond this, it appeared that there was very little to be learnt from the experience of the Wilson years.

In this Crosland showed a complacency absent from the thinking of the left. The left was arguing that the experience of 1964-70 confirmed its suspicion of revisionism. It may have been coming forward with bad answers but at least it was asking some pertinent questions. But Crosland saw no need to change the revisionist agenda. All that was necessary was to reject an exaggerated loyalty to the exchange rate of the pound sterling whatever it might happen to be. By the time he wrote *Socialism Now*, there was a flexible exchange rate policy. Sterling and the other major currencies were floating. The Bretton Woods system of fixed but adjustable exchange rates had broken down. So Crosland had been given his first requisite of stronger economic growth.[33] Unfortunately, he was once more over-optimistic in his assumption that a flexible exchange rate necessarily meant higher growth. There was a difference between a flexible exchange rate in an era of fixed rates, when briefly a competitive advantage might be won, and in an era when currencies generally were floating. It was now much more difficult to steal a competitive advantage. In a world of floating exchange rates, a great deal more was needed to stimulate economic growth than 'flexible' exchange rates. Yet Crosland had no other prescription for achieving the higher rate of growth on which his whole theory of socialism had always depended. This most professional of Labour economists never seemed to appreciate the problem.

Equally the experience of 1964–70 had not led Crosland to question the need for an effective incomes policy, or the kind of Keynesian economic management that had led to a requirement for an effective incomes policy. An effective incomes policy remained key to the combination of full employment and low inflation for which he was appealing. This was for reasons of both principle and practice. The reason of principle was that an incomes policy was necessary for the purposes of equality. As some trade unionists were in the upper half of income earners, some sacrifice would be expected of them and not just from the seriously rich. Trade unionists must learn to behave in a way that respected the socialist revisionist concept of equality. The practical reason for an incomes policy was that, whatever the likely rate of growth, inflation would be unavoidable when massive resources were being transferred to welfare and for the purposes of redistribution. That was especially the case when a priority for all Labour governments would have to be the transfer of resources also into the balance of payments.

Thus an incomes policy was a key part of Crosland's socialism as it existed in 1974. The stark alternative was inflation followed by periodic bouts of deflation and unemployment.[34] The period 1964–70 was taken to demonstrate that *statutory* incomes policies do not work. The voluntary co-operation of the trade unions, and of their members, was required. But in that case there would be a *quid pro quo*. We have seen that Crosland's socialism required optimism about the rate of growth. It also required extraordinary optimism about the practicality of incomes policies. To a man less dedicated to his special theory of socialism, it should have been quite clear that an incomes policy, even more a *voluntary* incomes policy, could never fulfil the multifaceted role that Crosland allocated to it. His emphasis on incomes policy, which was shared by Jenkins, demonstrates a kind of desperation on the right of the Labour party. The right had to find some way of resisting the encroachments of the left and of defending its own record. Its efforts in managing a non-inflationary economy within a continuing Keynesian context had failed but it was not prepared to abandon the Keynesianism with which it had grown up. Nor was it prepared to abandon such socialist objectives as full employment and greater equality and it did not see how these objectives could have any future without an incomes policy. An incomes policy was part of a grand socialist strategy. The right glossed over the experience of 1964–70, which had demonstrated the impracticality of an incomes policy in Britain other than as an emergency measure in situations of extreme crisis. It was such thinking that betrayed the Labour party into the tragedy of the Social Contract. If this was the creative thought upon which the policies of the next Labour government were to be based, the outlook was poor.

There was a direct clash with the left on the subject of incomes policy, and the left certainly had the better of the argument. Crosland did not believe that it was possible to control prices, which the majority of the Labour Movement was happy to advocate, and yet let incomes go free. The left and the trade unions were against any attempt to control incomes, again for reasons of principle as well as practice. The reason of principle was that wage claims did not promote inflation. Wage claims were merely attempts to catch up with prices, and trade unionists could not be expected to see their standard of living depressed by escalating prices. For the proposition that wage claims were not a source of inflation, the left and the trade unions could have found sustenance in the views of the monetarists. However, there were some friends that it was better not to have and, for the trade unions, monetarists figured prominently in that list. The practical reason against incomes policy was that trade unions could not enforce them, it was not their job to enforce them and, even if there was momentary success, the policy would quickly break down.

THE ENDURING ATTRACTION OF PUBLIC OWNERSHIP

Not everyone in the Labour party supported either the extravagances of the left or Crosland's ineducable certainties. The majority of Labour's leaders were far from hostile to further nationalization. They felt themselves to be socialists and, for them, socialism really did mean public ownership. Crosland might argue that public ownership was not a necessary component of socialism, which was in truth about equality, but they knew in their bones that socialism was about public ownership.

They felt let down by the private sector both in the original battle against devaluation and in the subsequent struggle for solvency after devaluation. For them, too, it was time to remember their old socialist slogans. Labour leaders were not persuaded that public ownership was necessarily inefficient or even that it was less efficient than private enterprise. On the contrary, if public enterprise had been allowed to extend outside the narrow field of the utilities into the areas of industry which were modern, expanding and profitable, its value would soon have been established. Such deficiencies as existed were attributed to the inadequacy of the people who managed the nationalized industries, many of whom were thought actively to oppose the principle of nationalization. The economic achievements of the Soviet Union were still held in high regard. In the other democratic countries of western Europe there was evidence that public ownership worked very well. There were examples in Italy, France and even Germany. In 1971, the aero-engine company Rolls-Royce was threatened by bankruptcy. The Heath government decided to rescue it by taking it into public ownership. Rolls-Royce was one of Britain's major companies, a British industrial champion, a company believed to be at the forefront of technology. It had been heavily subsidized by Mintech in Benn's time without, it appeared, that degree of supervision which might have been expected from an interventionist minister. If a Conservative government could nationalize such a company there could be nothing wrong with nationalization by a Labour government of companies at the forefront of technology. It was impossible even for Labour right-wingers to renounce nationalization when a Conservative government had adopted it as an instrument of policy.

The trouble in Britain, as these Labour thinkers saw it, was that attitudes to public ownership were determined ideologically. To opponents ideologically motivated, nationalization just was bad and there was no argument that would persuade them. If only public ownership could be abstracted from the ideological debate, if it ceased to be the subject of partisan scrutiny, it would work very satisfactorily. But if this was the problem, it was the Labour party that had made it so. It could hardly be expected that nationalization could be abstracted from the ideological debate when the main argument for it seemed to be ideological, that is that it was a key component of a socialist society. In any case, such subtleties did not overcome the problem that nationalization had become profoundly unpopular outside the Labour party itself. The unpopularity of nationalization was reluctantly accepted by most Labour leaders. The threat or promise of widespread nationalization was not going to win votes in an election. If, therefore, they were cautious about any proposals for nationalization, it was not because they thought them wrong, or inappropriate, but because they feared they were electorally damaging.

One alternative to nationalization – long debated, never accomplished – was competitive public enterprise. It had the advantage that it did not always involve compensation. Benn reports Callaghan saying at a joint meeting of shadow Cabinet and NEC on 25 January 1973: 'Nationalisation poses problems of compensation and the banks and insurance companies have intangible assets, and therefore we must outflank them by setting up our own organisations, instead of trying to take them over.'[35] Labour leaders were not alone in contemplating new steps in public enterprise which would serve to improve the performance of the British economy. Policymakers in Whitehall had also been disappointed by the performance of the private sector. Everywhere there was a feeling that something needed to be done to shake the private sector out of its long sleep. Labour was offering more public intervention, which must imply public ownership. Edward Heath was supposed, originally, to be trying the alternative of disengagement from all public intervention, leaving the private sector to sink or swim. He abandoned disengagement prompted by rising unemployment, and a desire to use state power and public money to regenerate British industry. He had decided that the government could not afford politically to allow the private sector to sink, and the debate in Whitehall moved heavily in favour of more public intervention. In 1972 Heath enacted an Industry Act conveying to the government powers for intervention in industry that came near satisfying the most extravagant ambitions of Tony Benn for control over the private sector. The Act gave comfort to socialists, who were thereby confirmed in their belief that capitalism was on the brink of collapse. If, for its survival, capitalism needed Heath's Industry Act, and the large injections of public money into the private sector that it would authorize, why stop halfway on the road to socialism? It had happened on previous occasions that, just when socialism seemed to be off any practical agenda, a Conservative government would bring it back on.

Even the CBI had come to the view that, subject to safeguards, an agency capable of injecting public money into the private sector was necessary.[36] The cross-party Trade and Industry Select Committee of the House of Commons, chaired by William Rodgers, engaged in an examination of public assistance to industry. It concluded: 'The evidence we received from Industry and the City was on the whole rather more favourable to the idea of a para-governmental agency, or of particular attributes of an agency, than might have been expected.' It added: 'We believe that the advantages an agency may be able to bring of flexibility, initiative and industrial expertise should not be lightly written off, and deserve closer consideration.'[37] But however intervention was managed, and whether or not it should involve ownership, there was, after Heath's U-turn, little disagreement within the Labour party, the Heath government or Whitehall about the need for public money in the private sector. All this encouraged the Labour party in its belief that there remained a role for public ownership if only extensions in it could be made palatable to the electorate.

DECLINING CONFIDENCE IN KEYNESIAN DEMAND MANAGEMENT

Full employment was regarded as the major achievement of post-war governments, an achievement attributed to Keynes's teachings. In a speech in September 1971 entitled 'Government and Industry', Crosland restated his long-held view. 'The great service of Keynes to recent history is that we now know, in the way that governments did not know in the 1930s, how full employment can be maintained.'[38] But, despite Crosland, Keynesian techniques seemed to be losing their former potency. Labour had left unemployment higher than it had found it. Concern was growing that, even with Keynesian techniques, it was becoming much more difficult to guarantee full employment. As they watched Edward Heath struggling with unemployment, Labour leaders and advisers realized that there was a problem to which they must find an answer. Capitalism appeared to be facing another major crisis, not yet comparable with the 1930s, but serious enough. After a period of great anxiety as unemployment approached one million, the Heath government, in its 1972 budget, felt compelled to double the normal dose of Keynesian reflation. Having treated the principal disease, it would turn to the desperate remedy of incomes policy to control the inevitable inflationary consequences. The budget was introduced in the belief that the consequent adverse effect on the balance of payments would be self-rectifying once growth was fast enough. It was not too difficult to forecast that the combination of incompatible policies would prove hazardous at best, disastrous at worst.

What was emerging within the Labour party was a mélange of ideas with no particular coherence. At the base was Keynesianism, challenged but not dismissed. The question was what should be added to it to make it work more satisfactorily. The injection of greater demand into the economy as a whole would bring down the general level of unemployment. But to eliminate the exceptional levels in the development areas would involve injections of demand so great as to threaten both galloping inflation and large balance of payments deficits. Keynesian demand management had never been able to deal with the higher levels of unemployment experienced in the development areas. Differential subsidies, and the forced transfer of industrial investment, might have mitigated, but had certainly not solved, the problem. Declining confidence in Keynesian demand management persuaded leading members of the Labour party, far outside the Benn camp, to favour an extended role for public ownership. Part of the answer, it was hoped, could be found in a combination of Keynesian demand management with development agencies to promote employment in the regions. A variety of expedients were offered. There was nationalization, protection, planning, intervention, prices and incomes policy, floating exchange rates, regional policy, industrial democracy. Contending factions were prepared to fight to the death for their particular mixture of expedients. But none of the expedients offered, whether singly or in co-operation, seemed strong enough to carry much weight. Nowhere did there seem to be a reliable road to non-inflationary growth. Economic policy, in the Party of economists, the Party which devoted most attention to economists, and to which Keynesian economists directed most affection, had become a matter of wishful thinking. Here was the paradox that had, from the beginning, confronted socialist thinkers. If they could not show competence in dealing with the problems of capitalism, they would never persuade the electorate to vote for socialism. But, if they could find a way of dealing with the problems of capitalism, why bother with socialism?

EUROPE

Collective responsibility had concealed many differences within the Labour government. Above all, there was the question of Britain and the European Economic Community. Wilson had applied for membership and his application, though vetoed, still lay on the table. He had been able to silence the leading dissidents while in government, but could he exercise comparable discipline now that he no longer exercised the power and patronage of a Prime Minister? Would it now be possible to maintain even a semblance of unity?

Europe weakened the right of the Party by dividing it. There was a three-way split. There were the irreconcilable opponents of membership. These included Douglas Jay, ejected from the government supposedly on grounds of age in August 1967, and Peter Shore, who had, thus far, gone along with his master and creator, Harold Wilson, but whose antipathy to the Community was well known. Shore would now, through bitter opposition to British membership of the EEC, build for himself a stronger legitimacy than was constituted by Wilson's patronage. Shore, a fundamentally right-wing, even nationalist figure who had never been persuaded by Benn's wistful technological Europeanism, brought to his anti-Market arguments an intellectual passion which won him support in all wings of the Party. But Europe created divisions even among those on the right generally favourable to, or at least not dogmatically opposed to, membership of the Community. There were those for whom Europe was a desirable objective but second to the unity of the Party. Most important in this group was Crosland. For Crosland, membership of the EEC was desirable but not important because, for him, socialism in one country remained a practical objective. 'Membership of the Market would be on balance of advantage to Britain. But only on balance.' It was largely irrelevant to the key issues facing ordinary people, growth, inflation, housing, education. Susan Crosland accurately described his attitude: '[I]t would be an act of political folly to allow the Market to endanger the unity of the Labour Party . . . Europe remained lower on his priorities than the egalitarian policies which only a Labour Government would undertake.'[39] If membership had appeared to Crosland an obstacle to his concept of socialism, he would have opposed it. Europe was consigned to Crosland's ever extending list of unimportant questions. Further thought persuaded him that the economic case for joining the EEC was even weaker than he had previously calculated.[40]

Then there was the third group. They saw Europe both as an ideal and as a practical necessity for a country that had done poorly economically since the war and now could no longer look to the Commonwealth for sustenance and support. For them, Europe had become a substitute for the failed god of socialism. Membership of the EEC was possible. Democratic socialism was a mirage. Leading this group was Roy Jenkins. But Crosland was probably right in suspecting that in no recognizable interpretation of the word was Jenkins still a socialist. For Jenkins,

Europe had long overtaken socialism. Shirley Williams, clearly a member of this group, clung still to the hope that, whereas socialism in one country was no longer practical, in Europe it might be. On 10 April 1972, she wrote to Wilson that 'I continue to believe that the best opportunity we have to advance our socialist objectives lies in forging the closest possible links with our fellow socialists and trade unions across the Channel.'[41] It was a curious view because, given the political complexion of western Europe, socialism was not seriously on the agenda. For Shirley Williams, Europe had powerful attractions but her socialism would have made her hesitate if she had not been able to reconcile her two, actually contradictory, commitments, to Europe and to socialism. It would be socialism that, in the end, would lose out. There was little thought of it at the time but this third group, European but doubtfully socialist, had in it the potential to split the Labour party.

Europe became a defining point in the futures of three men with whom seemed to rest the future of the Labour party. Crosland, the socialist, contested the importance of Europe and abstained in the vote on 28 October 1971 when sixty-nine members, led by Jenkins, defied a Labour three-line whip and voted with the Heath government for the principle of membership on the terms negotiated with the Community.[42] Jenkins resigned as deputy leader on the curiously establishment ground that the Party was opting for a referendum on membership. A referendum, apparently, was alien to the British way of life. With him, he took many of those who would be expected to be the most effective Ministers if ever there were a new Labour government. He then devoted himself mainly to literature and to biography, both estimable pursuits but resented by Crosland at a time when the right in the Labour party had on its hands a battle with the left on the extent of public ownership. According to Crosland, Jenkins 'stood on the sidelines and wrote elegant biographical pieces for *The Times* for a fat fee'.[43] When Jenkins resigned the deputy leadership, Crosland offered himself as a candidate for the vacancy but the Jenkinsites threw their support behind Ted Short, who would be a *locum tenens*, not a rival. The last thing they wanted was for Crosland to inherit Jenkins's mantle. They need not have bothered with this manoeuvre. Jenkins's resignation had destroyed his chances of the leadership.

Healey, the third *papabile* figure, had always concentrated on international rather than domestic affairs. After the 1970 defeat he became shadow Foreign Secretary. In that role he travelled the world refreshing high-level contacts that might otherwise have grown stale following his loss of office as Defence Secretary. He might in some sense still be a socialist. But he took no part in the domestic wrangles of the Labour party until he was appointed shadow Chancellor after Roy Jenkins's resignation from that role. He had never been an enthusiast for membership of the E E C. His views on Europe had not much changed since he had been International Secretary of the Labour party and had opposed British participation in the Schuman Plan. After much apparent hesitation he decided to follow the Party line and voted against the principle of membership on 28 October 1971. Thereafter he was never really trusted by the Jenkinsites, who, in later years, might otherwise have seen him as a shield against the left.

Most of the left had never been enamoured of the decision to apply. They were perpetuating the tradition of their Party, which had always rejected the snare of Europe. It was Wilson who had changed, not they. Wilson might have abandoned the hopes he had once invested in insular planning but they had not. For them, planning had not failed, it had not been implemented or had been implemented badly. Entry into Europe would make socialist planning, as they understood it, impossible, and therefore they opposed entry into Europe. Now, out of government, they had the opportunity to make their views felt and drag the Party back to its traditional course. Not everyone on the left opposed membership. Where Tony Benn would be was not at first clear but there was not to be a long period of waiting. The left was not prepared to tolerate eclecticism. The centre would be likely to move with Wilson. Confronted by such a divisive issue, it was more comfortable to allow the leader to do the thinking. Where he would go would be decisive because, discredited as many felt him to be, he was still, as leader, irreplaceable for lack of agreement among the various pretenders. He might stand firm for the European views he had discovered in government, but there had never been, anywhere in the Party, great faith in the strength of Wilson's convictions or in his firmness of purpose under pressure.

Wilson, in a crunch, always felt more comfortable resting in the arms of his friends on the left. The reason, apart from old friendships, was that there was no conceivable challenge from the left. Nobody on the left would depose Wilson to make Jenkins king, nor Callaghan for that matter. Therefore, there was never much doubt where Wilson would find himself once the ancestral passions of the Party began again to reassert themselves. As early as 7 December 1970 Wilson indicated to Benn that he was planning to decide that the terms of entry into the Community were not right. At that stage, Wilson's knowledge of what the terms would be would have derived primarily from information he had received in government. Of course the terms were not right in the sense that Britain was suffering from its self-exclusion from the Treaty of Rome, and from the steps taken subsequently by the Six to protect their own interests. Britain, if it wished belatedly to enter, would pay a price. But Wilson had known the price and, in government, had decided that it was worth paying. In his diary, Benn commented that such a switch would destroy Wilson's credibility.[44] Benn was still claiming to be a pro-Marketeer in principle. But Wilson would soon be followed in his reappraisal of Europe by Benn, that other politically sensitive moth who was busily relocating himself not just on Europe but on all subjects where he now perceived that, as a minister, he had turned his eyes from the guiding light of socialism.

Confirming Wilson in his defection was fear of a challenge to his leadership. Wilson was always frightened by false fires, always more sensitive to attacks on his leadership than was justified by the actual strength of his position. Nevertheless he had certainly been weakened by his three serious defeats, over devaluation, over *In Place of Strife* and in the election. On the one side, he feared a challenge from Callaghan, whose every action since his humiliating exit from the Treasury in November 1967 had been designed to restore his own position in the Party. On the other side was Jenkins, hero of the economic recovery, steadfast in his European views, supported by a small army of proselytes, whose reputation in the media was both immaculate and a constant provocation to Wilson. A leader as anxious as Wilson about conspiracies was likely to have been worried when Callaghan renounced entry into the EEC. Callaghan had never been an enthusiast and the release from government was, for him too, an opportunity to rethink or at least to return to longstanding prejudices. On 25 May 1971, Callaghan made his attitude clear. He revived the memory of Gaitskell's last Conference speech on Europe. Membership would mean 'a complete rupture of our identity'.[45] With his ear ever tuned to the mood of his Party, and particularly of the trade unions, Callaghan had located himself on politically safe territory within boundaries acceptable to the growing anti-European majority within the Labour party and the trade union movement.

Wilson followed Callaghan away from Europe. At the Special Conference of the Labour party on Europe on 17 July 1971, he declared: 'I reject the assertions that the terms this Conservative Government have obtained are the terms the Labour Government asked for, would have asked for, would have been bound to accept.'[46] His reputation had already so suffered that few believed this declaration. It did not seem to be believed by his former Cabinet colleagues. Out of twenty-three Cabinet Ministers in the outgoing Wilson government, only nine voted against the principle of membership when it was put to the vote of the House on 28 October 1971.[47] Wilson, in reneging on his Market convictions, was not saving his leadership, he was devaluing it in the eyes of an important section of the public. He could have remained staunch in his convictions without imperilling his position. He could have fought, and fought again, for the Party he loved. As his defence, Wilson claimed that his manoeuvres were necessary to preserve the unity of a party that was seriously divided on Europe. The argument about the need to preserve unity had been influential, or convenient, since 1931. Even if unity was in fact in danger, the fact that such manoeuvres were necessary did the Party little good. It hardly improved the Party's reputation that it had turned against its position in office and had forced its leader to follow it. Wilson's shift may not have directly affected the opinions of many of Labour's supporters in the country. To them Europe was a distant issue which would not determine their votes at a general election. It did, however, affect the attitude of opinion formers in the media who had long ago lost sympathy with Wilson, and now saw a further set of his supposed convictions drowned in sophistry. Wilson's crucifixion in the press for his about-turn on Europe diminished even further his credibility as a leader and impaired the prospects of his Party at any subsequent general election.

One figleaf Wilson demanded. Labour's Opposition to membership of the EEC must be based on the terms. If it went as far as opposition on principle, his position, Wilson seemed to believe, would become untenable. There must be no question of the Party Conference demanding withdrawal on principle, whatever the terms on offer, once Britain had entered. He therefore besought his old friends not to shame him by resolving against the principle, only the terms. On 4 October 1972, the Labour Party Conference passed the critical resolution. It read:

> This Conference declares its opposition to entry to the Common Market on the terms negotiated by the Tories and calls on a future Labour Government to reverse any decision for Britain to join unless new terms have been negotiated including the abandonment of the Common Agricultural Policy and the Value Added Tax, no limitations on the freedom of a Labour Government to carry out economic plans, regional development,

extension of the public sector, control of capital movement, and the preservation of the power of the British Parliament over its legislation and taxation, and, meanwhile, to halt immediately the entry arrangements including all payments to the European Communities, and participation in their Institutions in particular the European Parliament until such terms have been negotiated and the assent of the British electorate has been given.[48]

Wilson found in the resolution justification for insisting that his criterion had been met and that therefore he could remain leader without apostasy. Others might have interpreted the resolution differently. The terms demanded in the resolution were not negotiable and therefore the resolution, despite its opening words, was in practice against membership in principle. But, in the end, the left did not wish to make Wilson's position, by his own flexible criterion, impossible. He was not denied his interpretation. An attempt to make withdrawal mandatory on an incoming Labour government was narrowly defeated in 1973 only by Wilson's threat of resignation.[49] He claims that he would have resigned if the Conference had bound him to withdrawal.[50]

In the end Tony Benn's idea of a referendum came to the rescue. It enabled Wilson, when he returned as Prime Minister in March 1974, to undertake a renegotiation of the terms, conclude that it had been successful, and then avoid resignations from his Cabinet by suspending collective responsibility and submitting the issue of Britain's continued membership to a referendum. When Benn first pioneered the idea, Callaghan, at the shadow Cabinet on 11 November 1970, commented: 'Tony may be launching a little rubber life-raft which we will all be glad of in a year's time.'[51] In the end, Callaghan's prophecy was found to be justified. Indeed it was difficult to argue that Britain should not have a referendum on membership when President Pompidou of France was asking the French people to vote on whether Britain should be admitted. The implicit compromise between the European and anti-European factions in the opposition was that there would be a renegotiation of the terms when Labour returned to office followed by a referendum to validate the result. The knowledge that these were the intentions, rather than a straight decision to take Britain out of Europe, made it possible for 'Europeans' to remain within the Party.

Edward Heath took Britain into the European Community on 1 January 1973. When Labour returned to office there was a 'renegotiation' of the terms which produced a minor amelioration from the point of view of the UK. The referendum on 5 June 1975 confirmed Britain's membership by a large majority. The outcome, disappointing to a high proportion of those who had demanded a referendum, was one of the few successes of Wilson's last government.

REDISCOVERING SOCIALISM

Labour's defeat in June 1970 opened a great debate within the Party about methods of achieving socialism, should Labour ever be so fortunate as to win an election again. It was another debate that would tear Labour asunder. In that debate, the left had great advantages. The fact that so many in the Labour leadership did not reject nationalization in their hearts but only in their calculating heads was a great advantage for the left. It was unsurprising that those who had watched with dismay the failures of the Labour government should now see a reversion to socialism, defined as the nationalization of the means of production, distribution and exchange, as the way forward. In office, Ministers had the means of resisting such pressure. They had, at their command, a civil service trained to ask questions about all policy proposals and to indicate to their Ministers when any answers they received were not really satisfactory. But now the former Ministers were bare of all such assistance. Faced by proposals from the left, they had to do the analysis and the questioning themselves. A stream of papers emerged from the Labour party's Research Department proposing ways to revive the socialist struggle. Academic enthusiasts added to the load of documents in circulation. Were the ex-Ministers to spend their time preparing replies to the effusions of inexperienced zealots? It was a great deal to ask and few were ready to undertake the task. One disincentive, deriving from a sense of failure, was the thought that the critics might have a point. Another was the uncertainty whether Labour would ever be in office again. It was easier to succumb to pressure, to grant a reluctant assent, to speak as though proposals for a major expansion in public ownership were being taken seriously, while relying on the common sense of Wilson, and the Parliamentary Committee of the PLP, to excise the nonsense when, in due course, an election programme had actually to be written.

Crosland did fight. In that he was almost unique among right-wing members of the Parliamentary Committee. It was in the Industrial Policy Committee that the addicts of more nationalization had gathered. Crosland was horrified by the proposals he saw emerging. The extent of the nationalization advocated as necessary to plug the gaps in Keynesian demand management shocked him. This was not his idea of socialism nor was it necessary for the creation of greater equality. Moreover there appeared to be a threat to all private economic freedoms in Britain. Crosland devoted himself to fighting the left at one committee meeting after another. He met little but hostility as one of the most prominent guilty men of the previous Labour government. Although he had some support[52] he was regularly outvoted, though not out-argued. As he saw it he was, like his friend Gaitskell before him, fighting to save the Party he loved from the extremists.

THREE INSTRUMENTS OF REVOLUTION

After Labour's defeat in 1970, what Wilson was later to describe as Labour's 'naturally self-destructive capacity'[53] was given its head. The plans that were developed in the NEC committees and subcommittees involved the virtually total conscription of the British economy through the use of three instruments. The first was to be a state holding company, baptized 'National Enterprise Board' (NEB). The second instrument was to be planning agreements with a hundred or so major industrial companies; and the third, an Industry Act giving the Secretary of State extraordinary powers over industry. The Industry Act was to enable the Secretary of State to extract information from companies, to provide support in return for an equity holding, to take companies over, to put in new management, to ensure control over the activities of multinational companies. It may seem surprising in view of the intention to enact such powers that planning agreements were seen as necessary. Planning agreements were intended to enable the government to prescribe a company's investment and employment policies as well as to ensure that it was not exploiting its customers by charging unreasonable prices. Thus Benn would be attempting to achieve by diktat what he had failed to achieve as Minister of Technology through incentives. His claim to dictate to industry derived from an unjustified confidence that he had the wisdom and experience to undertake so all-encompassing a role. It is difficult to choose between illusion and arrogance as the principal motivation for the implicit claim by the NEC on behalf of Benn, the intended Minister for Industry in any new Labour government, to an omniscience for which his previous history provided no evidence.

The key question regarding planning agreements was whether entry into them would be compulsory or voluntary. If planning agreements were to be voluntary the principal objection to what was proposed would be that it was pointless. What companies would volunteer to have a planning agreement with the government which might bind them in their future policies? There were only two sets of circumstances in which a company might enter into a planning agreement. The first might be if it thought that, with its greater knowledge of the industry in which it was operating, it could extract money from the government by blinding it with science. The second would be if a company was so desperate for an injection of public money that it would agree to anything if it enabled it to survive. It was perfectly clear to the left that a policy of planning agreements voluntarily entered into would be a fiasco. It therefore insisted that planning agreements should be compulsory.

The powers under the proposed Industry Act could have been designed to drive private investment out of the UK, unless it was enacted that they could be exercised only with the voluntary agreement of the company concerned. But, if the powers could be exercised only by agreement, it was difficult to see what was the point of legislation. It was clear to the more sober leaders of the Labour party that it would be a political millstone to ask of the electorate that it should grant a government such powers. They did not wish to oppose the idea of an Industry Act or of planning agreements. Both could be harmless in themselves. But they would fight to ensure that the use of the powers, whether to extract information, acquire equity or any other such power, should be subject to an uncoerced agreement with the company concerned, and that, similarly, the negotiation of planning agreements should be free of coercion of any kind.

Draconian as were the powers proposed by the left for the Industry Act and for planning agreements, it was the design of the NEB that provoked most controversy both within and without the Party. The idea was encouraged by the experience of the Italian Industrial Reconstruction Institute (IRI). Dalton, as we have seen, had been rather impressed by planning in Italy under Mussolini. The IRI had been created as a state holding company in the 1930s in order to save various companies which were in peril of collapse or even already insolvent. It had supposedly been highly successful in the subsequent management of these and other companies. The idea of an NEB was encouraged also by the growth of multinational companies. These were the new monsters in the capitalist zoo. They were indeed worse than any of the other animals in the zoo. They were not merely capitalist, they were not even necessarily, or normally, British. They might even be American. It was no consolation that some of them had been created with the assistance of Labour's IRC. They were out of control, depriving their host countries of command over their own economic destinies, avoiding tax, deploying their investments as the criterion of profit seemed to require, and with no regard for the welfare of their employees or for the country in which, earlier, they had begun their growth to multinational status. Unless, of course, they were American, in which case they were yet one more expression of the power of the greatest capitalist country on earth. Callaghan, introducing the statement *Building a Socialist Britain* at the Labour party's October 1970 Conference, had said: 'The growth of the industrial giants results in them taking private planning decisions of such magnitude . . . that they must seriously conflict with the economic policy of Government itself . . . it naturally follows that we must look, again, at the balance between the public and private sectors of the economy.'[54] The idea that major companies which had emerged in the private sector due to take-overs and mergers were now a threat to the economic powers of government was widely accepted in the Labour party, as was a perception that it was dangerous for too high a proportion of British manufacturing industry to be owned by foreigners.[55] The NEB would be an instrument in the battle against the power of the multinationals.

The idea of a state holding company for Britain had a long pedigree.[56] It had been mentioned in Labour's 1970 programme. At the 1971 Labour Party Conference, Harold Wilson informed delegates that 'We shall establish a State Holding Agency on the lines of the IRC – but written large this time, and with clearer power to ensure that where society invests in private industry, society will stake a claim in the profits.'[57] It was to promote joint ventures with private enterprise in the regions and thereby stimulate employment. Many on the right of the Labour party were sympathetic. The right was encouraged in this direction by the experience of the IRC, which had gained the support of distinguished industrial managers and, it was thought, had performed a useful role in promoting mergers. The state holding company was to have a somewhat wider remit, not being limited to the encouragement of mergers but being enabled to invest in private sector companies that wanted its support, to stimulate economic growth and to encourage industrial investment in the development areas, thus helping to reduce the high levels of unemployment to be found there. There had been much talk over the years of competitive public enterprise without any clear indication how it would be created. The state holding company could become the source of competitive public enterprise. It was an idea sufficiently modest for there to be a hope that support for it would be obtained from industrial management just as it had been with the IRC. Crosland supported the idea of a state holding company which, among other duties, would make investments which were too risky for the market, would take over inefficient firms in order to improve their management, and would launch competitive public enterprise to impose efficiency upon its competitors. The idea of a state holding company was endorsed by Roy Jenkins in a speech entitled 'Socialism and the Regions' on 5 May 1972. In the course of his speech, Jenkins praised the performance of the nationalized industries. He referred also to successful public enterprise in other European countries. He deposited his faith in a state holding company as the answer to the problem of unemployment in the development areas which had not been solved by Keynesian techniques. The state holding company could grow from existing public holdings in private companies together with selective nationalization.[58] Jenkins had come to the conclusion that demand management, as practised between 1964 and 1970, needed to be supplemented by direct intervention in the economy.[59] Keynesianism would be rescued by a state holding company.

The left was looking for a new model of public ownership and found it in the idea of a state holding company. However, it was not thinking of the tame animal being proposed by the right. It was looking to economic planning to restore the British economy. But this must not be planning by influence, indicative planning as it was called. That had been attempted at the time of the National Plan and had clearly failed. It must be planning by order. It would be a good deal nearer to the admired Soviet model of central planning than to the French model of indicative planning. In order to equip the NEB to perform its function in the planning system it needed, in the view of the left, to be a holding company on a massive scale. It would take over the public holdings in existing companies such as BP and Rolls Royce. It would acquire further public holdings of equity in return for any assistance that it gave to private sector companies. It would acquire companies which were both highly profitable and at the frontiers of technology. The NEB was not to be in the business of rescuing lame ducks. It was to build the future, not rescue the past. It was also to ensure that industry remained British and was protected from the expanding appetite of the multinational companies. Therefore, in addition to its other assets, it was to acquire, by the use of compulsory powers, twenty-five major industrial companies in the profitable private sector. For some of the advocates of this model, twenty-five was only the beginning. Progressively the NEB would nationalize the private sector and thus finally take the country to the socialist destination. The original twenty-five companies to be taken over were not named. It was thought that to name them might give rise to avoiding action. The nomination of the victims had, therefore, to be left at least to the day when a Labour government, once more in office, brought the legislation to establish the NEB before the House of Commons.

Thus the NEB was to be a monstrous industrial conglomerate supposedly subject to the planning control of the government. Yet the conglomerate would be so large that it would undoubtedly conflict with the economic powers of government. The NEB would be several times larger than the IRI, its supposed model. So far from being under the control of government, it was more likely to issue instructions to the government. Industrial democracy within such a body would be a farce. One Labour critic of this model of an NEB wrote that it should be rejected on democratic grounds if no other.[60] One of the lessons of post-war nationalization had been how difficult it was to control the nationalized industries. Yet the existing nationalized industries would be midgets as compared with the NEB as conceived on the left.

The purpose of all this political frenzy, according to Tony Benn, was to produce 'A fundamental and irreversible shift in the balance of power and wealth in favour of working people and their families'.[61] It was a fine slogan of which he became excessively proud. It could be set alongside Bevan's 'commanding heights'. It was better than Bevan's 'commanding heights' because Benn had not forgotten the working people. It sounded revolutionary. It aroused emotions without being intolerably specific. To some it would be a threat, but to those to whom Benn was more directly appealing it would be a promise. This phraseology also found its way into *Labour's Programme 1973*, where it was described as a basic socialist goal.[62] But this NEB, so far from adding to the power of working people and their families, would deprive even the government which they had elected of much of the power it had to influence their economic prospects. Benn's capacity for self-deception was never better evidenced than in his conviction that this kind of NEB was consistent with his repeated advocacy of democracy, industrial democracy and participation.

WILSON MOVES

Once the committees and subcommittees had prepared their reports, the battle moved to the NEC itself, of which Crosland was not a member. There, Wilson manoeuvred to prevent the Party being lumbered with the greater industrial absurdities and the heavier electoral millstones. He had come late to the fray because his first ambition on losing office was to produce a book embellishing the record of his defeated government. His return to active service was welcomed by those on the right who felt themselves unable to defend common sense without him. But the leader of the Party was just one member of the NEC and could be overruled. Members of the NEC showed no special regard for Harold Wilson. It was the failures of his government that were being explicitly criticized. Moreover Wilson was a highly unreliable resort for the right. Fearful of a challenge to his leadership, he was quite prepared to use words that gave comfort to the left. The experience of the 1964 government had not freed him of his illusions about the possibilities of industrial policy. Benn reports what he said at a joint meeting of the NEC and shadow Cabinet on 25 January 1973:

> He agreed with Michael [Foot] on the commanding heights of the economy, that the finance houses of the City and not just industry must be dealt with. He liked the idea of socialisation of investment with more interest in channelling funds into socially desirable purposes. We must use the pension funds for social purposes and stop Stock Exchange speculation.

If Wilson was to be regarded as the last resort for political sanity, his intervention could only be awaited with deep anxiety.

The hopes of those who condemned the excesses arising from the left next lay with the Parliamentary Committee of the PLP. The Parliamentary Committee now contained Michael Foot as well as Tony Benn, but the majority were regarded on the left as guilty men. If Labour was ever again to be in government, it was the members of the Parliamentary Committee who would occupy the Cabinet posts charged with implementing the schemes emerging from the NEC. It was not a responsibility most of them were prepared to accept. The problem for the Parliamentary Committee was that the ideas of the left came to it ready cooked. Already public, they had been acclaimed by the activist members of the Party. It was not at that stage very easy simply to reject out of hand ideas presented with the authority of the NEC, especially as they had already been endorsed by trade union leaders. Harold Wilson was by now deep into his 'saving of the Party' mode. The NEB in the form proposed proved more than even he was prepared to tolerate. At a joint meeting of the NEC and the shadow Cabinet on 16 May 1973 he made it clear that he and the Parliamentary Committee would veto its appearance in Labour's election manifesto. Healey commented: 'Do we really want to nationalise Marks & Spencer to make it as efficient as the Co-op.'[63] The remark is typical of Healey, whose capacity to make enemies in the Labour party was equalled only by Wilson's desperate search for anyone who would be his friend.[64]

Healey's sentiment was certainly shared by Wilson. In his decision to veto the extravagances that Benn and his supporters wished to impose upon the Labour party, he had some support from luminaries of the left who did perceive that a threat to nationalize twenty-five major companies might destroy any prospect of Labour's ever holding power again. Michael Foot, for example, was prepared to omit the figure, though he was not at all disturbed by the intention. At the shadow Cabinet on 20 June 1973, he virtually accused Benn of wanting to lose the coming election.[65] Ian Mikardo, one of the most determined nationalizers, was also prepared to omit the figure.[66] His hope was that the NEB would eventually nationalize virtually the whole economy. Mention of twenty-five major companies could therefore be omitted from the election manifesto without prejudicing Labour's long-term aims. Jack Jones, General Secretary of the largest union, the TGWU, and supposedly one of the most left wing of union leaders, was also against the mention of twenty-five companies in the manifesto.

Though Wilson's veto survived, there could be little certainty as to what protection it might in the end provide against the excesses advocated by the left. He had only too frequently given way under pressure. How would he act if he did achieve an overall majority in Parliament and was faced with demands for extensive nationalization from the left and the trade unions? It would have been optimistic to expect that one could deal satisfactorily with Benn by 'toning down' his wilder excesses. Wilson had a great deal of sympathy with the thinking behind the excesses. He had never abandoned his expectations from interventionist activism. Therefore no one on the right of the Labour party could feel confident that, in the end, Wilson's veto would stand. What the Party did say in its February 1974 manifesto was bad enough:

We shall ... take shipbuilding, shiprepairing and marine engineering, ports, the manufacture of airframes and aeroengines into public ownership and control. But we shall not confine the extension of the public sector to loss-making and subsidised industries. We shall also take over profitable sections of individual firms in those industries where a public holding is essential to enable the Government to control prices, stimulate investment, encourage exports, create employment, protect workers and consumers from the activities of irresponsible multi-national companies, and to plan the national economy in the national interest. We shall therefore include in this operation, sections of pharmaceuticals, road haulage, construction, machine tools, in addition to our proposals for North Sea and Celtic Sea oil and gas.

Moreover there are many ways of skinning a cat. In a press conference on *Labour's Programme for Britain*, in July 1972, James Callaghan, not notably on the left of the Party, had said, 'If the key control of prices means there are not sufficient funds available for investment, then we should expect the state to intervene with the necessary funds, perhaps in exchange for some holding – equity or otherwise, in the concern.'[67] In the ears of industrial managers, this sounded rather as though companies would be forced to the edge of bankruptcy by price control and then bailed out by the government, or by the NEB, in return for equity. There were too many other threats around for industrial management to feel complacent. For example *Labour's Programme 1973* offered a commitment 'To put in an Official Trustee to assume temporary control of any company which fails to meet its responsibilities to its workers, to its customers, or to the community as a whole'.[68] Who was to judge? Where would it all lead?

Public ownership had re-emerged as a major constituent in Labour's policies.

THE ELECTION OF 28 FEBRUARY 1974

Edward Heath had started with the Industrial Relations Act. But, having been forced to concede defeat in the miners' strike of 1972, and faced by growing unemployment, he reversed direction and sought agreement with the trade unions on an incomes policy even at the expense of the Industrial Relations Act. His U-turn encouraged the belief that the key to economic expansion lay in agreement with the trade unions. Agreement with the trade unions, he thought, would make it possible to combine an expansionary fiscal policy with an effective incomes policy.

His thinking had not moved on since Macmillan and Maudling. In Conservative ranks, the miners' strike had evidently been very educative. They, too, had now suffered from the power of the trade unions. Heath became more understanding of trade union requirements even than the Wilson government had been. Jack Jones wrote that no Prime Minister, either before or since, could compare with Ted Heath in the efforts he made to establish a spirit of camaraderie with trade union leaders. He added that Heath 'revealed a human face of Toryism ... Amazingly, he gained more personal respect from union leaders than they seemed to have for Harold Wilson or even Jim Callaghan.'[69] It might be truer to say that Heath, having denounced the unacceptable face of capitalism, was now revealing the frightened face of Toryism.

In the end, however, nothing Heath could do would win the overt co-operation of the trade unions. He was therefore compelled to introduce his statutory incomes policy without trade union agreement. Heath's experience with the unions confirmed to Labour leaders that they still had a strong selling point in claiming with the electorate a special qualification for government. Civil government was now, apparently, only possible with the sufferance of the trade unions. The popular impression that the Labour party was too close to the unions would be turned to advantage. Wilson, unlike Heath, would be able to humiliate himself sufficiently to make the necessary agreement with the trade unions. Heath's attempt to implement his incomes policy provoked a second miners' strike in late 1973. Its conduct seemed to bring into question the continuance of constitutional government in Britain. Heath had evidently not been frightened enough by the first miners' strike. He decided to withstand the demands of the miners in the interests of preserving his incomes policy and he then summoned the people to a general election to decide who should govern Britain. The cause, he told them, was the defence of constitutional government against the aggression of the miners. He found that Prime Ministers cannot impose a unique question on a general election. The people decided that, whoever should govern Britain, it should not be Heath. This would have been a shrewd judgement if there had been a more attractive alternative. Heath's conduct of government had been preposterous beyond the power of rational explanation. It had left the UK facing the oil-price hike of 1973 weaker economically, with a larger balance of payments deficit, and higher inflation, than any other major industrial country. It was hardly imaginable that a Labour government could have done worse, though it might well have done as badly. But to reject Heath because of his irrationality was not an easy option. The electorate might appear thereby to endorse the conduct of the NUM and give further encouragement to the impression that Britain could no longer be governed without the favour of the miners and other major trade unions. The unions, having seen Heath off, might become even more clamorous and irresponsible with their inflationary wage claims. Britain, with its long history of Parliamentary government, would seem to be abandoning constitutional rule to the dictatorship, if not of the proletariat, then at least of the unions.

Only twice during the February 1974 election did Wilson allow the word 'socialism' to pass his lips.[70] That was an increase of 100 per cent over his usage of the word during the 1970 campaign.[71] But British industry was saved from the embrace of Benn and his cohorts not so much by the Wilson veto, or by his abjuration of socialism, as by the fact that, when Labour did regain office, a few days after the election, it was without a majority and that, when it did achieve an overall majority in October 1974, it was so small as to make it inconceivable that revolutionary legislation would be passed by the House of Commons. The threats that had been held over industrial management were largely dropped, including the idea of an Official Trustee as the moral guardian of the public against the excesses of private industry. When, in 1975, the NEB was enacted, it was but a shadow of the left's intentions, and planning agreements were to be voluntary and, even if made, were not to be enforceable at law. As a result there was only a limited extension of public ownership under the 1974–6 Wilson government, and planning agreements were made only with companies so frantic for public money that they would accept any conditions even if they included the making of a planning agreement. The assault of the die-hard socialists was repelled by an electorate which was prepared to trust Labour marginally more than the Tories but not enough to equip it with the power to render the private sector the slave of a Labour government's illusions.

However, the plans that were frustrated by the electoral stalemate were not just those of the left. Those of the right were equally frustrated. The revisionists, like the left, were denied what would prove to be their last opportunity to remodel society under the banner of equality. Thus both versions of socialism suffered defeat. But, even without the recalcitrance of the electorate, other events such as the breakdown of the Bretton Woods system, the oil-price hike and the even deeper recession that followed were together creating a competitive international environment far less amenable to socialist experiments. The irony was that each time a Labour government faced a capitalist crisis, and it was becoming Labour's habitual inheritance, it judged it necessary, for political if not for economic reasons, to turn away from socialism towards the better management of capitalism. The management might not, in fact, be much better. But that was the direction in which Labour governments regularly turned. This might be cowardice. It might be lack of socialist conviction. It might be the merest common sense.

PART IV

THE RETREAT TO
NEW LABOUR

FIFTEEN

The age of reluctant enlightenment

The challenges facing the Wilson–Callaghan governments of 1974–9 were preparing the final crisis of British democratic socialism. For social-ists it was an age of discovery, leading, for some, to an age of enlighten-ment. The neo-Marxist socialism of Tony Benn and the Keynesian socialism of Tony Crosland were found to have much in common. Confronted by a demand from the rest of the world, conveyed through the International Monetary Fund, that Britain must at last put its own house in order, both socialist trends took refuge in threats of protection-ism. In the case of Crosland, this was combined with petty menaces directed against the UK's allies. Unless help was forthcoming on the terms dictated from London, Britain would withdraw its troops from Ger-many. The similarities that now emerged in the thinking of Benn and Crosland would have astonished anyone who had witnessed the bitter battles between them during the years of opposition, though not, perhaps, those better acquainted with Crosland's earlier intellectual peregrin-ations. The subject of controversy during the Heath years had been the nature and extent of nationalization to be undertaken by a future Labour government. Now, back in government, they were united in the demand that the rest of the world, having generously provided the necessary financial sustenance, should go away and leave Britain to its own devices.

If it was to reject Heath, the electorate had no practical option other than to return Wilson. This was done without enthusiasm, and without conferring the benediction of an overall majority. Labour had won 301 seats, the Conservatives 297 and others 37, including 14 Liberals. A large proportion of the electorate voted Liberal in despair at the choice facing them but not enough to overturn the cruel arithmetic of the first-past-the-post electoral system, which gives seats to the major par-ties out of proportion to their actual strength in the country. The lack of enthusiasm for Labour was attributable to the failures of the 1964–70 government and to the Labour party's subsequent behaviour. Whatever Wilson might claim in his book on the 1964–70 government, few others considered it a success and his damaged reputation fell even further due to his manoeuvrings on membership of the EEC.

The principal, though flawed, argument for voting Labour was that the Conservatives had run away from any attempt to control the unions in the interests of an incomes policy that rapidly proved counterproductive. In the course of running away they had inadvertently provoked a strike by the miners. Despite having a serviceable majority in the House, they had appealed to the country to settle the issue between them and the miners. It was a blatant flight from responsibility. If the unions were indeed to carry such influence in the future conduct of government in the UK then perhaps it would be better to have in power a political party which claimed a reciprocal influence on the trade unions. There was the Social Contract, which appeared to say that, if only Labour consulted the trade unions and took their advice seriously, there might be restraint in wage claims. Certainly the soft words of the Social Contract sounded different from, and perhaps more congenial than, the language of confrontation to which the Heath government had recourse once it had called the election. In fact Labour was to take the advice of the trade unions only too seriously. It conceded new powers to the unions, but there was, at first, no sign at all of restraint in wage claims as the rate of inflation rose towards 25 per cent and threatened to rise even higher.

THE WARRING SOCIALIST TWINS, MICHAEL FOOT AND TONY BENN

Wilson's government of the 1960s had, for most of the time, been remarkably cohesive considering the mutual dislikes and suspicions, and the different traditions represented in it, Bevanite and Gaitskellite. All its principal members could be regarded in the old phrase as 'men (and women) of business' in the sense that they were interested in exercising Ministerial office and were not obviously incompetent. They knew that they had to work together and, by and large, they did. Of the government that Wilson formed in March 1974 I later wrote, 'There is no comparable example of such intellectual and political incoherence in a party coming into office in the twentieth century history of the United Kingdom.'[1] The Cabinet was in an important respect different from those that Wilson had led during the 1960s. It contained Michael Foot. In other words it contained the man whose prestige in the Labour Movement was such that he could bring the government down, especially a government elected with so inadequate a franchise. Foot could decide the fate of the government but, if he resigned, he would also be deciding the fate of the Labour party. He was a man who had not learnt by experience the tensions and annoyances of working with colleagues. Would his tolerance extend sufficiently far? It would be a supreme test of his loyalty. It was a test which he passed with flying colours. He remained loyal through five difficult and disillusioning years. But there was a cost. His loyalty depended on his being persuaded, or at least on his being prepared to allow his colleagues the benefit of his very considerable doubts. Inevitably this made it the more difficult to fashion a policy suitable to the times. Michael Foot's translation from jester to minister and, later, to crown prince was to have dramatic effects on the Labour party.

No politician could ever be sure of his standing with the left of the Party. There was too much suspicion, too much calculation of the likelihood of betrayal. For the far left, even Foot was not beyond suspicion. But, in so far as any leading politician was trusted by the left, it was Michael Foot. During the Wilson government of the 1960s, Foot had been an eloquent, and amusing, critic of the government from a left-wing and trade union standpoint. He seemed to prefer the role of critic to participation in the work of government. Certainly it was a role which fitted him to perfection. He could defend the trade unions, he could oppose incomes policies, he could lacerate the government for submission to the IMF, above all he could decry its lack of socialist purpose. Together with Robert Sheldon and Enoch Powell, he had destroyed his own government's attempt to reform the House of Lords.

But he appeared to have no ambition himself to join in the tasks of socialist construction. Then, after the defeat of the Wilson government in 1970, he had been elected to the shadow Cabinet and now, with Labour's return to office, he was Secretary of State for Employment. He was there as spokesman for the trade unions and presiding spirit over the government's socialist convictions. Through him the trade unions were directly represented around the Cabinet table. One might say that they had been directly represented by Bevin under Attlee and by Cousins in the early years of Wilson's first government. But it did not feel the same. Bevin had been a national figure who had made his mark, not just as a trade union leader, but as a member of the Churchill War Cabinet. Cousins was ineffectual and, in any case, soon departed.

It was true that Labour Cabinet Ministers had often been sponsored by trade unions. But, paradoxically, trade unions, though they supplied money to the constituency parties of the MPs they sponsored, were, in most circumstances, far less demanding on 'their' members than was generally believed.[2] Certainly they did not attempt to dictate to Prime Ministers the constitution of their Cabinets. The arrival of Michael Foot did, therefore, imply a marked change. Foot was Secretary of State for Employment because the trade unions wanted him in that office and as evidence that the Labour party had decided that it could not govern without the co-operation of the trade unions. In any negotiation between a Labour government and the trade unions, the trade unions would now be sitting on both sides of the table.

Foot undertook, with relish, the repeal of the Heath government's Industrial Relations Act. The unions were no longer relying on their own strength to achieve their ends but conscripting the government to assist with legislation. New legislation was enacted which was intended to add to the ability of trade unions to recruit members, to enforce closed shops, to make it somewhat easier to secure recognition. Robert Taylor argues persuasively that none of this legislation made in practice much difference and that the unions' principal recruiting sergeant was high inflation and the need for defence against the consequences of inflation.[3] But, whatever the practical effect, there was no doubt about the intentions behind this legislation.

Foot was also anxious to provide speedy evidence of Labour's re-education on the subject of incomes policies. The Heath government's statutory incomes policy was brought to an end and the Pay Board established under it was abolished, though there were worries in the Treasury that there was as yet nothing effective with which to replace it. Yet, despite Foot's efforts and his record, the trade unions did not quite trust him. Unlike Bevin, he was not one of their own and, given his lack of administrative experience and application, there was always a risk that he would let matters pass that would be contrary to their interests. The TUC supervised him on a day-to-day basis and he was quite willing to be supervised.[4] But even Foot knew that entrenching trade union power was not the same thing as establishing socialism. His principal problem was that he was a member of a government which would have even less opportunity of implementing a socialist programme than that of the 1960s. For so dedicated a socialist, would it really bring any satisfaction to serve in a government which, by force of circumstances, was so unsocialist?

Unfortunately Foot's love of Parliamentary democracy in Britain did not extend to other countries. His friendship with Indira Gandhi led him to give support to her declaration of a dictatorship in India, to visit her as a minister during the period of dictatorship, and to make speeches which must have given her considerable comfort. British Parliamentary democracy was evidently special. He would not have approved of the suspension of Parliamentary democracy in Britain. Foot's biographer, Mervyn Jones, records how Mrs Gandhi was prepared calmly to explain to him the imprisonment of the socialist leader George Fernandes. Why should not Mrs Gandhi explain her policies to so undiscriminating a friend? Foot has, perhaps, the excuse that it had become customary for leading Labour party figures to give comfort to dictators in developing countries in the unfounded hope that their socialism would encourage development. He was therefore, he might claim, doing no more than had been done by others. Jennie Lee, wife of his hero Aneurin Bevan, was also supportive of Mrs Gandhi.[5]

The Wilson government of 1974 was also different in that it contained a reformed Tony Benn. He had concluded that everything he had done at the Ministry of Technology in the 1960s had been a waste of public money. Indeed much of it *had* been, though not in the sense Benn supposed. He loved technology but was now convinced that technology would work satisfactorily only if it was in the hands of genuinely socialist masters. He too enjoyed resonance with the left of the Labour party and the trade unions. But, finding himself in competition with Foot, he felt it necessary to behave very differently from Foot. Foot was sufficiently secure in the affections of his followers that he did not need to take up extravagant public poses. Benn was a recent convert from the centre of the Party. He had to prove his good faith and he discovered that the best way of proving it was to test collective Cabinet responsibility to the limits by presenting himself as a semi-detached critic as much as a member of the government. As a consequence he was, to Wilson, and to the Cabinet as a whole, even to Foot, a confounded nuisance. However, in a Cabinet in which there was seldom much to laugh about, Benn, sometimes intentionally, sometimes not, was a frequent source of light relief.

MEETING THE CRISIS

Wilson later wrote without exaggeration, 'Britain was facing an unparalleled economic crisis, the worse in that we were confronted by fourfold oil-price increases and by balance of payments problems unprecedented in our history.'[6] The balance of payments on current account had registered a deficit of £1,470 million for the year 1973.[7] It was now estimated that the increase in oil prices would add £2.5 billion to the UK's current account deficit. Another part of the inheritance, despite Heath's prices and incomes policies, was inflation, rapidly rising to levels again unprecedented in the history of the UK. Thus the economic situation when the Wilson government returned in 1974 was so serious that it might have been thought that the government, unlike in 1964, had no alternative but to be brave. Such a judgement would have been wrong. In 1974, Callaghan, the most prominent survivor from Wilson's original Cabinet, commented that 'we are a much more political government this time'.[8] Later his formulation of the problem was more brutal. He recalled in retrospect the 'tawdriness of the Wilson regime'.[9] Politicking became the order of the day. There was a second election to win and the economy was not to be allowed to be a hindrance to the necessary purchase of votes. Wilson adopted once again the heroic posture which had so impressed his Cabinet colleagues when Labour was returned with a narrow majority in 1964. He would govern as though he had a majority of one hundred. His target was not the recovery of solvency but triumph in the next election. The Exchequer was now at the disposal of the new government. Expensive improvements in social provision were implemented in accordance with the 1974 Labour party programme. Even Tony Benn was outraged at the cynicism of the government as it attempted to garner votes at the expense of the public purse.[10] One excuse the government had. Keynesian economists were arguing that the government *should* be spending money to offset the deflationary consequences of the oil-price hike and thereby sustain employment. In the short term, the advice was politically convenient to the government. In the longer term its inflationary consequences brought the government near collapse.

Attlee had preached years previously that capitalist crisis was exactly the time for rapid progress to socialism, not a reason to go slow on socialism.[11] This had remained part of the left-wing consensus. So it still appeared even to some members of the Wilson Cabinet. Benn assured the October 1973 Labour Party Conference that 'We shall use the crisis we shall inherit as an occasion for making the fundamental changes and not as an excuse for postponing them.'[12] His method of creating the right environment for the fundamental changes was the old British socialist way of shutting out the world. It was now known as the alternative economic strategy. Britain's trade would no longer be free but regulated. Such a policy had the additional advantage from the point of view of Benn and his advisers that it was inconsistent with membership of the EEC. Others, not on the extreme left, whether or not devotees of the alternative economic strategy, appeared to think that the government could follow domestic policies that ignored its need to borrow to fund the enormous balance of payments deficit. Extravagance was at first encouraged by the looming shadow of an inevitable repeat general election. But it continued beyond the second General Election of October 1974, at which a small overall majority of four was won, though on less than 40 per cent of the vote. The result was hesitation and confusion in the conduct of economic policy.

There was, in the desperate economic predicament, one source of comfort. Oil had been discovered in the British sector of the North Sea. In due course it would flow and would mitigate the effects on the balance of payments of the rise in oil-prices. Indeed, if the exceptional oil company profits made possible by the rise were taxed, it would bring substantial revenue to the government. Thus, when despair threatened, North Sea oil served to lighten the darkness. God, who had located the oil in the North Sea, was, evidently, not just an Englishman. He was a socialist. A Labour government plus North Sea oil would, it was hoped, equal socialism. But that would only be provided the government could survive in office. The full benefits of North Sea oil could not be cashed before it was on stream, much as it was talked about by all sections of the Party. Harold Wilson noted in his account of his final period of government. 'For years ... Government and Opposition had played a macabre game of musical chairs, in the hope of being in possession of the chair when the oil began to flow in quantity.'[13] In fact there was a gross overestimation of the value of North Sea oil to the UK. As a result, it detracted from the urgency with which the economic predicament was tackled. The developed countries that best managed the consequences of the oil-price hike were Germany and Japan. Neither had significant supplies of indigenous oil.

THE INDUSTRIAL STRATEGY

That Labour had discarded the nationalization of the unspecified twenty-five major companies did not imply that it was discarding an industrial strategy. Industrial strategy appeared as the socialist residual. While a Labour government insisted on intervening in industry it had some answer to all those who claimed that it had abandoned every nuance of socialism. The industrial strategy remained what it had always been, an excuse for avoiding a direct confrontation with inflation. It would deal with the inflationary gap by promoting higher productivity. As a device for avoiding a direct confrontation with inflation, it was no more likely to be successful in the 1970s than it had been in the 1960s. The intention now was to control the private sector through 'planning agreements'. These, as we have seen, would be agreements between the government and individual major firms on such matters as their investment programmes and their export prospects. To control the private sector might not be the same thing as to nationalize it, but it satisfied some psychological demands.

With nationalization unpopular and with the government hanging on by a thread to its majority in the House of Commons, planning agreements appeared, at least to the industrial strategists, to be the next best option. However, the government, under the duress of its weak position in the House of Commons, but also because of calming influences within the Cabinet, decided to meet the strenuous objections of industrial management to planning agreements. Benn, at the Department of Industry, produced a draft White Paper. Wilson described the draft as 'sloppy and half-baked', 'polemical, indeed menacing in tone'. He, evidently, had not felt strong enough in 1974 to appoint a less menacing minister to the Department of Industry. The redrafting by the Cabinet ensured that planning agreements would be voluntary. They were therefore unlikely to be negotiated except where a company fell into financial straits and came to the government for assistance. They certainly could not be used to control the private sector. The Cabinet's redraft also decreed that the National Enterprise Board was to act in co-operation with industry and not to have the 'marauding' role which Benn had sought for it.[14] Nevertheless, even in this restricted form, Wilson expected a great deal from the NEB. Indeed, in his speech to the Labour Party Conference in November 1974, he claimed to regard the idea of an NEB as 'the biggest leap forward in economic thinking as well as in economic policy since the war. For where private investment falls away, or even if it is not falling is on a scale far too small to ensure a high level of employment and modernization, when that is the position public investment is enlisted.'[15] Thus was Keynes stripped of his precedence by a Labour Prime Minister who may actually have believed what he was saying but was prepared to say it in any case. This was at best a gross overestimate of what any NEB, however well managed, could achieve. For one thing it never, fortunately, had enough money to fill such a role.

The White Paper, as redrafted, also put an absolute limit on the government's nationalization ambitions. The Parliament to be elected at the second 1974 election would confine itself to the community ownership of development land, the establishment of a British National Oil Corporation, the nationalization of the shipbuilding and aircraft industries and the extension of public ownership in road haulage and construction. There would also be schemes for bringing commercial ports and cargo handling under public ownership and control. The only 'commanding height' in the list was oil and there it was clear that the private sector, despite the creation of BNOC, would continue to play the major role. A further step away from interventionist policies was the removal of Benn from the Department of Industry, after the referendum on Europe, and his move to the Department of Energy.

THE CHRYSLER UK RESCUE[16]

On the principle behind the industrial strategy, the government declared itself firm. The industrial strategy would be directed to regenerating British industry and enhancing economic performance, not to rescuing lame ducks.

Late in 1975, the Chrysler Corporation of the USA (CC), which was itself in financial difficulties, announced that it was no longer prepared to suffer the losses which it had experienced ever since, shortly before the 1964 General Election, it had unwisely acquired 49 per cent of the shares of the British car manufacturer Rootes. Wilson had, at the time, bitterly attacked the deal as another example of the way that Conservative governments were permitting foreign, especially American, companies to buy into British manufacturing industry. Yet, in January 1967, CC had been permitted to complete its take-over of Rootes, which had been renamed Chrysler UK (CUK). Now, CUK faced imminent closure. CC could hardly be blamed except for the suddenness of its announcement and for its supine acceptance of labour relations so chaotic that hardly a day had passed without some industrial dispute. This was to be the supreme test of the industrial strategy, whether it was about the regeneration of British industry, as claimed, or about the salvation of lame ducks, which had always seemed probable whatever the denials of the government. Whether CC actually intended to close the firm so rapidly cannot now be known. Any loss of reputation arising from its apparent inability to exert discipline in its own plants would have been mitigated by the widespread awareness that, in all British car-manufacturing plants, industrial indiscipline was endemic. Nevertheless, it would have suffered considerable financial costs in closing its British subsidiary apart from the loss of export orders supplied from the UK, particularly to Iran, where it had a major contract.

The announcement of imminent closure having been made in Detroit, the Wilson government gathered to consider its reaction. The Department of Industry, and its Secretary of State Eric Varley, were opposed to any intervention to save CUK. It would be a waste of money as the future of the company was, in any case, bleak. It would also be contrary to its industrial strategy because it believed, with support from the Central Policy Review Staff, that there were too many car-assembly plants in the UK, most too small for economic production.[17] The disappearance of CUK would assist the recovery of the largest British-owned car-manufacturing company, British Leyland, which the government had felt itself compelled to nationalize, and BL was the Department of Industry's favourite son, so far as it was possible to regard any car manufacturer in the UK with favour. Under the influence of Sir Donald Ryder, an industrialist who was taking the chair at the NEB, enormous sums of public money were being expended on BL.[18] There was another argument that was thought rather than spoken. It would provide a valuable lesson if those responsible for the industrial disruption at CUK were not rescued from the consequences of their own follies. Such a demonstration of government courage in the face of industrial blackmail might help industrial relations at BL. The liquidation of CUK was therefore to be welcomed, not feared. The Treasury, which would have to provide any money that might be committed to the salvation of CUK, was equally opposed to any rescue. The NEB itself sensibly refused to use its funds to save CUK.

It seemed at first that the hands-off attitude of the Department of Industry and the Treasury was shared by the Prime Minister. He apparently had no option other than to brave the inevitable political storm and to allow the closure. CC having declared that it wanted to free itself of this encumbrance, the government would look exceedingly foolish if it sought to buy CUK or to nationalize it. Given the apparent absence of any alternative, the Prime Minister had decided, untypically, to be tough. Then, two events changed his mind. The first was that CC hinted that, in certain circumstances to be defined in negotiation, it might be prepared to withdraw from precipitate action. CC let it be known that this concession was being made, not out of concern for its own interests, but out of sympathy for the political dilemma it had created for the British government. CC was proving that it had a heart of gold even if it did not have much gold in its pocket. It was showing the acceptable, human face of capitalism. The second event arose from the fact that a significant part of the CUK operation was in Scotland. Closure would cause redundancy in Scotland. This was a time when Scottish nationalism was rampant, and when devolution of various powers to a Scottish Parliament was being planned as a way of containing the threat of Scottish independence. Once CC had suggested that there might be some alternative to closure, the Secretary of State for Scotland, William Ross, and his Minister of State, Bruce Millan, threatened resignation if CUK was allowed to disappear without a thorough investigation of alternatives. Scotland and Wales had long been the most socialist parts of the United Kingdom. It was Scotland and Wales that had provided Wilson with his majority, such as it was. Ever sensitive to political pressures, Wilson now had an alternative option. He no longer needed to be tough. He responded to their hint by proposing negotiations with CC. Once negotiation had been initiated, CC had the British government on the run. The Americans now knew that they could exploit the political weakness of the Wilson government to extract largesse. Wilson demanded of his Cabinet colleagues, some of whom at least were horrified, that they should 'think politically'. The deal was done. CUK won a further temporary lease of life. Most of those in the British government who had had anything to do with the issue felt ashamed.[19] But Scotland at least had been saved.

The industrial strategy was thereby utterly discredited. The episode proved that it was impossible for a Labour government to conduct an industrial strategy. It might claim that its motives were industrial regeneration and not the salvation of lame ducks. But let any politically significant lame duck limp into its presence and there would be a lavish outpouring of public money. It had been the same under Heath, whose policy of 'disengagement' had collapsed under the burden of comparable political pressures.

ECONOMIC MANAGEMENT

Heath, in a last desperate attempt to cool inflation, had inaugurated a statutory incomes policy. The third phase of the policy included a provision which, by means of 'thresholds', was intended to give the trade unions assurance against any suffering from unusual increases in the cost of living. In other words, under the statutory system, the unions were entitled to negotiate compensation for such unusual increases. Labour in opposition, while disagreeing with the statutory nature of the policy, accepted the threshold system. Unfortunately, in the autumn of 1973, there had occurred an unusual increase in the cost of living due to the oil-price rise. The result was that the threshold system became an inbuilt escalator for wage inflation. This inflation escalator was inherited by the new Labour government. Public sector unions insisted that their wage claims, however inflationary, were consistent with the Social Contract. Barbara Castle, Secretary of State for Health and Social Services, begged the trade unions to take account of the 'social wage', in other words the money and services they received as a result of the improved social benefits introduced by the government on coming into office. The unions, however, were no more inclined now to take lessons from Barbara Castle than they had been over *In Place of Strife*. Their members had paid for the social benefits by taking the trouble to vote Labour. Now they wanted cash on the table.

Wilson had spent so much time manoeuvring between the different wings of the Labour party that he had no time to educate it in current realities even if he had realized what they were. He took little interest in the conduct of economic policy by Chancellor Denis Healey until the credibility of that policy was almost exhausted. As usual, he was unwilling to tell the full unpleasant truth about the crisis the country faced. On 26 June 1974, the TUC General Council had agreed to provide 'guidelines' to unions making claims. It declared that 'Over the coming years negotiators generally should recognise that the scope for real increases in consumption are limited and a central negotiating objective in this period will be to ensure that real incomes are maintained.'[20] On 5 September 1974, Wilson responded. He warned the TUC that 'because of the crisis we face, including the oil surcharge, we cannot expect any significant increase in living standards over-all in the next year or two, indeed it will be a tremendous challenge to our statesmanship even to maintain average living standards'.[21] As Wilson knew, the truth was that, due to the severe deterioration in the UK's terms of trade following the oil-price hike, a *fall* in average living standards was inevitable. The trade unions might negotiate themselves out of that fall by imposing sacrifices on others. The effect would be seriously inflationary. Indeed, in the circumstances, wage settlements which simply kept pace with the cost of living would be inflationary. Thus the Social Contract, even if strictly applied, would be inflationary and it was not being strictly applied. It was exercising no influence on wage claims other than to provide the claimants with spurious justification. The problem for the government was what to do in a situation in which inflation was spiralling out of control. The unions were insisting on grossly inflationary settlements and quoting the Social Contract in their support. Rather than exert itself, the TUC preferred to remain oblivious of the deteriorating situation. For the TUC, any cut in the real income of its members was unacceptable even if the country had suffered a fall in its real national income imposed by the cost of raw material supplies, and even if those with less negotiating power suffered in consequence of inflationary settlements in which they could not share.

In his budget statement of 15 April 1975, Healey said: 'The general rate of pay increases has been well above the increase in the cost of living . . . As a result, by February, the retail price index stood 19.9 per cent over a year earlier, and the wage rate index was 28.9 per cent . . . Pay has been running about 8 per cent or 9 per cent ahead of prices. I do not believe that anyone would claim that the TUC guidelines were intended to permit this result'.[22] The government was faced with depressing options. It could abandon the battle against inflation, which could only lead to its own collapse. It could deflate in the hope that rising unemployment would send a signal to the trade union movement that it would understand. To some degree, the April budget was deflationary, thus alienating those in the trade union movement who perceived that such a departure from Keynesianism was implicitly an attack on their power. Or it could try to negotiate an effective agreement with the trade unions. The market was reading the implications of the high rate of inflation for the value of sterling. As sterling came under severe pressure, the need for action became apparent even to the Cabinet. Socialists might consider the market unreasonable but they were not risking their money on the exchange rate of sterling.

Wilson had banned any talk of a statutory incomes policy and, indeed, such a ban was necessary if Michael Foot was to stay in the government. But, faced with runaway inflation despite the Social Contract, he had to accept that something must be done. The trick was to negotiate an effective incomes policy to which the trade unions would voluntarily adhere. Fortunately, Jack Jones was willing to help, though for reasons of his own. He understood that, if nothing was done about wage claims, the government would fall. He feared that the right wing of the government might follow the path taken by Ramsay MacDonald and enter into coalition with the Tories.[23] The Labour party would then suffer a defeat comparable with that in 1931. The Labour party and socialism would be finished for another generation. Jones's motivation was in no way dishonourable and no one could say that he was misled by nightmares. The problem with Jack Jones was that, as General Secretary of a general workers' union, he wanted the incomes policy to become an instrument not just against inflation but for redistribution. In other words, though there must be sacrifices, *his* members must be protected. To get his support the government had to concede a flat-rate incomes policy which impaired differentials, was therefore disincentive in its effects and evoked hostility within much of the trade union movement, not to mention from earners outside the trade union movement. The eventual agreement between the TUC and the government was for a flat-rate £6 norm per week on wages and salaries up to £8,500 per annum.[24] In 1979, the Labour government was to pay a heavy political price for the contraction of differentials when large numbers of skilled workers demonstrated their resentment by voting Conservative. However, in the interests of its own survival, the government accepted the best it could get from the TUC. In addition, to persuade the market, ever sceptical of incomes policies, the policy included threats of statutory action in certain eventualities. So far as possible this was kept in the background to save Foot's face. In all honesty he indicated that, if there was any question of ever implementing the statutory provisions, he would not be the person to do it.

On 7 July 1975, Wilson made his appeal as Prime Minister to the trade union movement. The appeal was made in the course of a speech to the National Union of Mineworkers at Scarborough:

> It is now *Labour*'s Prime Minister, your Prime Minister, at a critical hour in the nation's history, enjoining this community, once again, to assert loyalty *for* the nation. It is not so much a question of whether that loyalty, that response, will be forthcoming in sufficient measure to save this Labour Government. The issue now is not whether this or any other democratic socialist government can survive and lead this nation to full employment and a greater measure of social justice. It is whether any government *so* constituted, *so* dedicated to the principles of consent and consensus within our democracy, can lead this nation.[25]

Wilson, as we have seen in Chapter 13, was never backward in turning for inspiration to the Gettysburg oration. This evocation lacks the clarity of President Lincoln, no doubt deliberately. It can hardly have been the intention of the Labour Prime Minister to set democratic socialism aside, but he does appear to be accepting that no government, taking as its objectives full employment and social justice, could survive without the permission of the trade union movement. It was not a happy thought for the population at large.

A White Paper, *The Attack on Inflation*, issued on 11 July 1975, announced the government's expectation that, following the agreement with the TUC, inflation would fall to single figures by the end of 1976. This was not achieved. The RPI rose by 15 per cent during 1976, compared with over 25 per cent in 1975. It was still rising at an annual rate of 15 per cent in the second half of 1976. A year after the agreement with the TUC, it was calculated that it had added 14 per cent to earnings even at a time of rising unemployment. Thus the agreement with the TUC may have brought some benefit but not nearly as much as the government had anticipated and not nearly enough to persuade the market that Britain was bringing inflation under control.

Despite the inflation, the exchange rate of sterling had been supported during the first two years of the government by an inflow of money from OPEC countries which had not yet seriously addressed the question where best to invest their surpluses. By long tradition they had placed a significant proportion of their resources in sterling. But it could only be a matter of time before the oil-rich countries realized the unwisdom of what they were doing, that their money would be at risk if they continued to invest it in sterling, and therefore began to diversify their holdings out of sterling. Already there had been threats that this would be done. An effective incomes policy was one step that might help to dissuade a catastrophic rush out of sterling. Another would be a cutback in public spending. Even Tony Crosland, now Secretary of State for the Environment, felt constrained to warn local authorities that the party was over. It was now urgent to devote some attention to the economy, especially in view of the dangers to sterling and the warnings of the Bank of England and the Treasury of what would happen if nothing was done. By the winter of 1975, Wilson had become persuaded that the government must, once more, engage in public expenditure cuts in order to satisfy the market that the economy was being responsibly managed. Resources had to be released into the balance of payments, still seriously in deficit. The Cabinet was reluctantly persuaded to consent to the operation. A saving on future expenditure was agreed significant enough to distress the Cabinet though not to reassure the market. A Public Expenditure White Paper was to be produced and presented to Parliament.

The Cabinet had consented, reluctantly. The PLP presented a more difficult problem. For many in the PLP there was no need at all for such cuts. They were unpersuaded, but then the Prime Minister had made no effort to persuade them. He had never been a great persuader of his dissident multitudes. He probably thought it an impossible task inconsistent with his ultimate ambition, which was to hold his Party together. Never should the Party be confronted with unpleasant realities. To hold it together, it must be allowed to dream its dreams. Now, known only to himself and a few others, he was in his last months as Prime Minister and the idea of attempting to educate his followers must have seemed an act of supererogation to a tired man awaiting the day of his release from the burdens of office. If he did think that an attempt at education was pointless, he certainly had reason. But his passivity left the White Paper exposed to defeat in the House of Commons if the left, or any significant part of it, abstained. On 10 March 1976, the left, by multiple abstentions, allowed the government, and the White Paper, to be defeated. They saw no reason why they should consent to a policy so clearly unsocialist as public expenditure cuts. The government immediately called a vote of confidence, and that was won. The desire to survive might inhibit dissident members of the PLP from actually voting a Labour government out of office. But a government which could not get its own Party to support its public expenditure plans did not have much credibility either in the country or in the world. Confirming the formal confidence of the House of Commons was one thing. Establishing any confidence in the market was quite another.

The Labour party, having been disillusioned by all Labour governments, frustrated in its search for socialism, was seeking desperately for anything that might delay acceptance of unpleasant reality. The ideology of the left, and not only of the left, was that the world owed Britain a living. Any other view was Treasury mystification. Large tranches of the PLP imagined that the market was a cash-cow from which indefinite sums could be milked. The easy answer to the scarcity of resources was to borrow. If the money was not available in the Exchequer, it could be borrowed. With borrowed money everything could be done. Public services could be maintained, inflationary wage claims could be met, the public sector greatly expanded, the Labour party's manifesto implemented. No thought was given to the possibility that borrowing would certainly be expensive and might even be impossible, so parlous was the state of the economy.

The argument that borrowing was a less dangerous or expensive route than had been alleged, had recently been put by, among others, Norman Atkinson. To this he added a demand supported, he said, 'by the great majority of the Labour party', that the public sector should be doubled over the following decade so that it would employ more than half the work force. 'I personally see the coming years as a desperate race for economic power between the public ownership of industry and the multinational corporations.'[26] Atkinson was a backbench MP but he was about to become a member of the NEC as Treasurer of the Labour party. He was an important and influential figure. His views were representative of much of the Party. Britain, apparently, had not yet borrowed enough. Whatever money Britain still needed for his purposes, the world should supply and, of course, without conditions. The more Britain borrowed, the more socialist it could be. After all, the money would come from bankers, foreign bankers at that. Bankers of any nationality were not held in high regard in the Labour party. They should learn to do what they were told.

Escapism such as this had come to dominate the minds of large sections of the PLP. For a socialist confronted by the necessity of deflation, the only comfort lay in escapism. It was not sufficiently appreciated that bankers might be restrained in their lending by the prospect of getting repaid. Nor was it understood that such borrowing capacity as Britain retained might be needed not to fund the welfare state but simply to prevent the collapse of the pound. A few days before the adverse vote on the Public Expenditure White Paper the Nigerians began to diversify out of sterling, sending a signal to others so ill advised as to put their trust in British economic policy.

A few days later, Wilson announced his resignation. He had been Prime Minister for about eight years in all. If the criterion of leadership is sparkling intelligence, resilience, victory in elections and flexibility, together with a willingness to fight one's own Party when one has little choice, then Wilson certainly has a claim to have been the best leader Labour ever had. But in Wilson the flexibility was too heavily prized and the willingness to fight too seldom in evidence. He totally failed in the role to which he himself made his principal claim, as a regenerator of the British economy. It was fortunate for the Labour party and the country that Wilson retired when he did. His time as Prime Minister had been a time of economic crisis. On the face of it he had been as well equipped as anyone could be to handle the frightening economic problems with which he had been confronted. Yet he had never given any evidence that he had thought deeply about the country's predicament. He had exhausted his credit with foreign governments and with central banks which might, in the near future, be requested to help suck the UK out of the bog into which it had fallen. He now lacked the strength, and the reputation, to handle yet one more economic crisis. Whatever he had achieved, he would not see a socialist Britain in his lifetime. But he would have been surprised if he had, not necessarily pleasantly. At least, in retirement, he had no reason to fear conspiracies by his Cabinet colleagues.

THE INHERITANCE OF JAMES CALLAGHAN

In the third and final ballot in the election for the leadership of the Party in succession to Wilson, Michael Foot received 137 votes against Callaghan's 176. The vote for Foot was a portent of what would happen nearly five years later when Foot *was* elected leader of the Labour party. Callaghan now became Prime Minister with Foot as his deputy. Callaghan had been Foreign Secretary for the previous two years and therefore had not been intimately involved with economic policy. Indeed the Foreign Office seems to have left him remarkably ignorant of the economic condition of the country. It was a surprise to him, when briefed by Healey, to be told how serious matters were. On entering No. 10 Downing Street in April 1976, Callaghan had discovered that, since early March, the world financial community had been selling sterling and that its value was depreciating daily. Any confidence it had had in the management of the British economy was exhausted. Inflation in the spring of 1976 was still very high, far higher than had been anticipated at the time of the 1975 incomes policy agreement. A further increase in inflation was threatened by the failing pound which would make imports even more expensive. In his spring budget of 1976, Healey offered income tax concessions conditional on an incomes policy based on 3 per cent. The trade unions insisted on, and won, 5 per cent but still were granted the income tax concessions. That would be the last time the trade unions would be prepared to concede anything to the government's anxieties about the continuing high level of inflation.

Wilson had left day-to-day economic management to Healey. Callaghan would have liked to leave it to Healey, and keep himself free to deploy his talents in the world of international diplomacy where a reputation for statesmanship might be won. But such neglect by the Prime Minister of the country's main problem could not continue. The political implications of the crisis were too worrying. His experience in the Treasury in the 1960s had not encouraged him to regard that source of advice as impeccable. Like so many other Chancellors, he had entered the Treasury with high expectations of the help he would be given in discharging his heavy responsibilities, and had felt himself let down. He was himself basically a Keynesian, as were nearly all Labour Ministers. He had not himself had direct experience of economic management after the breakdown of the Bretton Woods system in 1971 and the 1973 oil shock. He had not, therefore, shared the experience that, by 1975, had converted Healey from Keynesianism. Nor for that matter had that direct experience been shared by his friend Tony Crosland, the government's leading professional economist, or by his Policy Unit at No. 10. Both showered him with Keynesian advice in a situation in which it had become not merely inappropriate but dangerous.

A Parliamentary Party nearly half of which thought that Michael Foot was a suitable leader in the current crisis or, alternatively, was unaware that there was a crisis would not be easy to manage when difficult decisions had to be taken. It was such a Parliamentary Party that Callaghan now found himself leading in the most serious crisis that had faced Britain since the war. Yet there was some sign that Michael Foot himself was learning. He no longer believed Attlee's and Benn's thesis that capitalist crisis gave special opportunities to a socialist government.[27] At the 1975 Labour Party Conference, Foot had told the delegates that what socialists had so long believed was unworkable. Yes, there was a crisis of capitalism. But no, socialism was not the answer. Before proceeding to socialism, the Labour government must first solve the capitalist crisis within the parameters of capitalism.

> It is indeed ... a crisis of capitalism of a most formidable character, and we have to muster all our energies, all our skill, to deal with it ... It is of the first importance ... that this crisis should be faced and surmounted by a Labour government acting in the closest alliance and in good faith with the trade union movement ... People sometimes say: we will agree to some arrangement between the government and the trade unions about wages, but only when you have got the full panoply of socialist measures actually put into operation and in working order. I understand the argument, but I say it is unworkable.[28]

It would be too much to suggest that the speech convinced all socialists that socialism would have to wait. Nor did it seem to damage Michael Foot in the way his speech on unilateral nuclear disarmament had damaged Bevan. Perhaps the delegates did not notice what they were being told. There was evidence enough that Foot's Parliamentary colleagues were not listening. But it was significant that Foot himself had joined those who were struggling within the limits of capitalism to solve a capitalist crisis. There might still be differences between Foot and others such as Healey. But they were differences at the margin as compared with this great concession that Foot had made to realism.

While Callaghan and Foot might know that socialism was, for the moment, not an option, too many of their followers did not. Yet was the PLP really to be blamed? Healey and others were now attempting to educate it. But it was unwilling to be educated in what it considered Treasury orthodoxy. The education that was being offered violated every presumption of democratic socialism. If such education was to be absorbed it would take time, probably a very long time. It was not just the PLP that had no sense of any threat to its socialist ambitions. That also was the state of mind of many in the Cabinet. Socialist political patience was being exhausted by a Labour government's insistence that it must come to terms with bankers, moneylenders and foreign capitalist governments in the USA, the EEC and elsewhere. Socialist political conviction was reverting once more to its intellectual ancestry. Britain must isolate itself from the world by import controls. British socialism was not to mean internationalism but isolationism. The banks must be nationalized and thereby converted from dangerous enemies into humble servants of the socialist state. In July 1977 proposals were put forward at the Liaison Committee which included nationalization of insurance companies and joint-stock banks. It was evidence of the strong movement leftwards in the Party during Callaghan's brief years at the top.[29]

Callaghan headed a discordant Cabinet, a divided Parliamentary Party and a rebellious Party in the country. By autumn 1976, he had seen his minuscule majority in the House of Commons disappear. Yet, as a new Prime Minister, summoned unexpectedly to the highest post, his survival instinct would be very strong. It would need to be if his tenure of No. 10 was not to be poor, nasty, brutish and short. Callaghan had the valuable ability, inherited perhaps from his naval ancestry, to exude calm in a storm. Cabinet Ministers liked working for him because he gave reassurance without excessive interference in their departmental responsibilities. He had an unequalled command over the House of Commons and, with time, the sense that he was in command would extend to the British people as a whole. Unfortunately, beneath Callaghan's appearance of calm, there was a mind that was itself divided about the steps that now needed to be taken. He knew he could not afford to be diverted by socialist dreams. Yet he was a great deal less certain about how to manage the economic crisis that Wilson had so thoughtfully bequeathed. If he failed in resolving the crisis, the damage to the Labour party as a whole would be irreparable.

THE EMERGENCE OF ANTHONY CROSLAND

Crosland had been a candidate in the election for leader, had received a humiliatingly small vote and had been eliminated in the first ballot. Suddenly, with the arrival of Callaghan at No. 10 Downing Street, his prospects were transformed. Unlike Wilson, Callaghan was a friend. In November 1967, Wilson had overlooked Crosland's claims to the Treasury, despite Callaghan's recommendation, and had appointed Jenkins. In 1972, on Jenkins's resignation as shadow Chancellor, Wilson had again ignored Crosland and had appointed Healey. Now, Callaghan appointed Crosland Foreign Secretary, even though Jenkins clearly wanted the job. Combined with old friendship, Crosland's ambivalence on Europe decided the issue. It contrasted with Jenkins's commitment to Europe, unpopular in the Party despite the referendum result. Roy Jenkins then decided to take up the position of President of the European Commission. He had been deprived of his ambition to be at least Foreign Secretary and had concluded from his vote in the leadership election that he had no further prospect of the leadership of the Labour party. Thereby he had left the Jenkinsites, a group high in talent but insufficient in numbers, leaderless. Crosland had had many battles with the Jenkinsites, particularly over Europe, but relations had never been completely broken. In the referendum in 1975, Crosland had quelled his doubts sufficiently far as to support the campaign for continued British membership. The Jenkinsites might represent a potential base upon which Crosland himself might rise to the leadership on the retirement of the elderly Callaghan. Where else would the right of the Labour party find its candidate? The only alternative seemed to be Denis Healey, mired in unpopularity due to his thus far unsuccessful tenure of the Treasury. Crosland was, after all, the only right-wing figure who had attempted to give new meaning to socialism. This could attract to him not just the Jenkinsites, some of whom indeed would follow him in the months to come in his attack on Healey's economic policies, but others from the centre and the left who, with whatever misgivings, might prefer as leader a moderate who proclaimed himself a socialist even if of a rather unsatisfactory kind. If, in these circumstances, ambition revived in the heart of Anthony Crosland, it would not be surprising. This is not to suggest that, in his attack on Healey's economic policies, he was anything but sincere. The line which he took was, as ever, consistent with *The Future of Socialism*. But the knowledge that he was expressing opinions that would enhance his standing in the Party might lead him to pursue his argument with greater force and enthusiasm. In the months to come, Crosland's arguments would carry greater political significance than at any other time in his political career.

BRITISH SOCIALISM AND THE INTERNATIONAL MONETARY FUND

On 9 June 1976, with the exchange rate of the pound still falling almost daily, a standby credit of $5.3 billion was arranged with foreign central banks of which $2 billion was to come from the USA. The credit was not unconditional. The American administration insisted that, if there was any use of the standby, it must be repaid by 9 December 1976. If the UK government could not then make the repayment out of its reserves, which were already low, it must turn to the IMF. Getting support from the IMF would require submission to its dictates. Britain would lose its sovereign freedom to determine its own economic policy. The idea of assistance from the IMF was not, at first, offensive to the left. In Cabinet on 2 July, when another round of public expenditure cuts was under consideration, Benn suggested that the cuts could be avoided by an application to the IMF, which, he believed, would support British policies and be prepared to give aid unconditionally.[30] This merely demonstrated the total innocence that made Benn so enchanting an advocate. The IMF was not a sentimental institution and there was on its board a marked absence of friends prepared to agree special favours for Britain. Britain should be treated like any other supplicant.

Gradually the lesson penetrated that the IMF was unlikely to be accommodating to British sensitivities, that it would impose harsh conditions. It was then at last understood that, in requesting help from the IMF, Britain would be inviting a slight to its national sovereignty and an overt attack on its whole post-war policy of giving priority to the preservation of full employment over the containment of inflation. The humiliation of subservience to the IMF could perhaps be avoided, but only if the British government did voluntarily what the IMF would unquestionably demand from it. If that was done, it might just be that private sector funds would flow back into London, strengthening the reserves, stabilizing sterling and relieving the problem of repayment to the central banks which had provided the standby. But the government proved itself unwilling to act voluntarily. Repeatedly it had appeared to be willing to accept the verdict of the market and had endeavoured to cut public expenditure. Invariably its efforts had disappointed. It had made a succession of favourable forecasts about inflation and the balance of payments, all of which had been falsified by events. In July 1976 the Cabinet, conscious of the liability it would be under in December to repay the standby, once again cut public expenditure but again insufficiently to satisfy the market. The cuts questionably reached £1 billion when a minimum of £2 billion would have been required to restore confidence. The message issuing from Crosland, supported by most of the Jenkinsites, and from Benn supported by Foot and the left, was that greater cuts in public expenditure were unacceptable because inconsistent with the purposes of a socialist government and unnecessary, even counterproductive, in economic terms. There was, moreover, an offence to pride evidenced in a strong nationalistic emotion. A British government ought not to be ordered about by international financiers. Wilson had, in his time, made the point frequently enough. What were elections for if a government could not decide its own policies, free of external coercion? Its need to borrow large sums of money was not sufficient justification for the international financial community to impose its terms on the borrowing.

Callaghan, however, was beginning to teach a different and more realistic lesson. He made a speech to the 1976 Labour Party Conference, drafted in part by his son-in-law Peter Jay, which signalled that the government had no choice but to find its solution within the parameters of capitalism. It was bound to come to terms with the constraints imposed by the world economic crisis. His words were interpretable only as a direct attack on the economic policies of all post-war British governments, including those in which he had served in senior offices:

> For too long ... we postponed facing up to fundamental choices and fundamental changes in our society and in our economy ... The cosy world we were told would go on for ever, where full employment would

be guaranteed by a stroke of the Chancellor's pen ... We used to think that you could just spend your way out of a recession ... I tell you in all candour that that option no longer exists, and that in so far as it ever did exist, it only worked ... by injecting a bigger dose of inflation into the economy, followed by a higher level of unemployment ... That is the history of the last twenty years.[31]

It was very difficult indeed to reconcile these words with socialism or with any intention to make progress towards socialism. Callaghan was explaining his duty as Prime Minister, which was to manage a capitalist crisis aggravated by the previous policies of his own government. But to delegates at the Conference it was one more piece of evidence that the Labour government, so far from introducing socialism as a solution to capitalist crisis, was abandoning socialism.

At the end of September 1976, with the pound once more under pressure, Callaghan and Healey decided that they had no choice but to make an application to the IMF. They would not otherwise be able to repay the standby negotiated in June when it matured on 9 December 1976 without so reducing the reserves as to make sterling terminally vulnerable. British democratic socialism now found itself in a desperate struggle for survival against the forces of international finance represented by the IMF. For Healey, having to make the application was a blow because he believed that he had, at last, taken all necessary measures to restore the British economy. The trouble was that, although he might believe that, it was not believed in the market. Healey came to recognize that, however much had been done, for example by way of cutting public expenditure, more would need to be done to satisfy both the market and the IMF. It might well be overkill but it would be necessary if confidence in British economic management was to be restored. It has often been argued in retrospect that, if only the Treasury forecasts in the summer of 1976 had been more accurate, they would have demonstrated that, due to the measures already taken by the government, the British economy was emerging from the worst of the crisis. Private funds might then have flowed back into London, making an application to the IMF unnecessary. But, given the history, institutions with money to invest were unlikely to believe any forecast issuing from the British Treasury whatever it said and certainly if it said anything favourable. Too many Treasury forecasts had been falsified by events for anyone with money to lend to trust a Treasury forecast now. The task of restoring confidence becomes heavier the longer it is delayed, and it had been long delayed. Reluctantly Healey entered into a struggle with the Cabinet to persuade it to allow him to negotiate with the IMF the best terms he could get. That he needed to do so was, by implication, a criticism of his conduct of economic policy thus far. But if he and the government were to survive he had no choice. Among those still requiring to be convinced was the Prime Minister. Despite his gallant speech at the Labour Party Conference, Callaghan had been prepared at first to give credence to Crosland's claim that the problem arose simply from another bankers' ramp as in 1931.[32]

Callaghan thought that Britain, with its special claims, should be able to get unconditional aid from the IMF. From his period as Foreign Secretary, he had acquired influential friends, President Ford in Washington and Chancellor Helmut Schmidt in Bonn. Britain, after all, was Washington's principal, and certainly most reliable, ally, was it not? Schmidt headed a brother Social Democratic government which gloried in the possession of vast reserves available, surely, to relieve the poverty of mendicants such as the British. Both Ford and Schmidt ought to be ready to tell the IMF to desist from treating Britain as though it was any ordinary country. Callaghan never seemed to realize that it was as humiliating to pester Ford and Schmidt for help as to submit to the IMF's baleful mercies. Nor did the Labour party, which thought it quite normal that foreigners should be asked to bail Britain out of the consequences of its own folly. While Callaghan was awaiting the response from his friends, the Cabinet met repeatedly to thrash out a collective decision. Meeting after meeting came to no final conclusion. The near-fatal impression was being created that, once again, here was a Labour government which, confronted by a crisis, could not make up its mind and threatened to disintegrate.

Crosland was offended by the demands put upon Britain both in his capacity as a Keynesian economist and in his capacity as the author of *The Future of Socialism*. As a Keynesian economist he knew by instinct that there was already enough deflation in the system, together with a large enough depreciation of sterling to restore the balance of payments. As the author of *The Future of Socialism*, he found the further cuts in public expenditure demanded by the IMF an offence against the ideology which he had made his own. In both capacities he feared the inflationary effects of what was proposed. Despite experience, he retained deep confidence in the Social Contract. What would happen to inflation if the government capitulated to the IMF, thereby broke the Social Contract and lost its influence with the unions? It was not only Crosland who was deploying this argument. Both socialist left and

Jenkinsite right decried an agreement with the IMF which, by requiring public expenditure cuts, would kill the Social Contract. In November, Crosland told the Cabinet that 'Without the public sector unions the Social Contract . . . would collapse.'[33] He did not accept that the Social Contract, instead of helping to control inflation, had itself proved grossly inflationary. At the time of the July 1976 public expenditure cuts, Crosland, who opposed them on his usual ideological grounds, had noted in his commonplace book that the outstanding success of the last two years had been the involvement of the trade unions in national economic policy.[34] Clearly his contact with reality was fast disappearing. If this was success, it would be difficult to write the prescription of failure.

Another Crosland argument was the need to preserve the industrial strategy.[35] The industrial strategy was a great favourite with the trade unions because it offered the prospect of higher productivity and higher pay without disturbance to existing working practices, which would annoy their members. Crosland had never till now shown himself an enthusiast for the industrial strategy. It was ironic that he should dredge it up as an argument against agreement with the IMF. But now any contention which might move some section of the Cabinet was added to the pot. He gave no ground to the argument that all the industrial strategy had done was to allow Benn to waste public money supporting various unviable co-operatives and to fund the rescue of Chrysler UK.

In the debates in Cabinet Crosland sought to show that his ideas of high taxation and high public expenditure were still viable in a world in which Britain was an ever increasing debtor and in which growth was slow. He argued that so important to the world was Britain's survival that the IMF had no choice but to provide the money and forget its conditions. The very debility of the UK would, together with its centrality in the world economy, compel the IMF to unbend and offer help unconditionally. Benn reports Crosland climaxing his appeal to Cabinet with the cry: 'Our weakness is our strength, it is a test of nerve, and the IMF must give us the loan.'[36] Better than accept the IMF commands, and thereby undermine the Social Contract and the industrial strategy, was to defy the world, to threaten the IMF that Britain would go protectionist, and Britain's NATO allies with the withdrawal of troops from Germany. If British socialism could be defended only by isolation, Britain should accept isolation. These arguments had curious implications. Because Britain could threaten to withdraw troops from Germany and introduce protective tariffs, it could, supposedly, both extract money from the IMF and continue a policy of high taxation and high public expenditure. Britain could do it but no other country could do it if it lacked the ability to be comparably uncooperative. The arguments were a forlorn defence of Crosland's long-held philosophy of socialism. But to those who heard them they appeared desperate and unconvincing. The IMF was certainly not likely to capitulate to Britain's persistent infirmity. It had other basket cases with which to deal, for example Italy.

Controls on imports would almost certainly be in breach of Britain's commitments under the Treaty of Accession to the EEC. But Crosland had never allotted Europe a greater importance than the unity of the Labour party and the survival of his version of socialism. In advocating these desperate measures, he could not be suspected of taking his brief from the Foreign Office. It was all his own work. But, irrespective of the merits of Crosland's arguments, and their merit was highly question-able – the eventual agreement with the IMF did not prove to be deflationary – they implied default on 9 December on the UK's liabil-ities to the central banks that had provided the standby. Crosland's advocacy had one effect that he did not anticipate. He had begun his argument with the support of the Jenkinsite right around the Cabinet table. He found that, in the course of developing his case, he had alienated that support. Allies in Cabinet who had wished to oppose reductions in planned public expenditure fell away as they understood that Crosland's judgement was no longer to be trusted. They objected to the IMF and its excessive demands. But they were 'Europeans' and champions of NATO. Europe and NATO might not be important to Crosland. They were to them. If they were told that the only way of resisting the IMF was to betray convictions that they held at least as deeply as their socialism, they would switch their support to Healey. Crosland succeeded by his threats in sequestering himself from his natural political allies.

At the outset of the long debates in Cabinet, Crosland had com-manded attention at least in his role as a professional economist and the leading ideologist of the right. Benn had also to be allowed his say but there were few around the Cabinet table who expected any enlightenment from that source. Benn began by reminding his Cabinet colleagues of the dreadful events of 1931 when Labour had split. He then proceeded to advocate a course of action which could only lead to a further split. He had an advantage that Crosland did not have, and would not have wanted. He had advisers to do his thinking for him.[37] His advisers told him that now was the time to revert to the 'alternative economic strategy', protection plus subsidies to maintain employment. There was little new he could add to the alternative economic strategy except perhaps planning agreements. The alternative economic strategy had a long history and its origins were far from being exclusively socialist. Macmillan had advocated an alternative economic strategy in *The Middle Way*. The alternative economic strategy was a strategy for regulating international trade to the supposed benefit of all participants in it. The problem of the consequent additional inflationary pressure was ignored. Any suggestion that inflationary pressure should be managed by means of a statutory incomes policy, or any kind of effective incomes policy, would have put the alternative strategists at odds with the unions, and the unions were becoming a vital source of political strength for all such escapist ideas. Their present inspiration came from the University of Cambridge, where economists with more intelligence than judgement had extracted it from the refuse of history. The alternative economic strategy would free Britain from balance of payments deficits. Controls would be used not to reduce international trade but to balance it. Because there was no intention to reduce international trade, the idea would receive a global welcome. Britain had but to share the idea with its trading partners and they would all experience Pauline conversions. The real truth was that, if import controls had been introduced they would have been rapidly reversed because it would have proved impossible to sustain them under the enormous international pressure to which Britain would have been subjected. It would have been, for Britain, just one more humiliating defeat. As even Crosland had to admit, the alternative economic strategy would not even have eliminated the need for large cuts in public expenditure.[38] It was simply another example of the escapism in which the Labour left, and too many friendly but naive economists, was taking refuge. The alternative economic strategy had not the least chance of winning international approval and, if Britain had implemented it unilaterally, it would have been in disregard of its international commitments. For Benn and his followers it was no disadvantage that the alternative economic strategy would be in breach of the European treaty. It would reverse the result of the referendum on Europe. Nor was isolation a great terror to Benn and his friends.

Benn and Crosland had, between them, established something about socialism that would do the cause permanent damage. It required that Britain should default on all the obligations into which it had entered since the war and become a pariah among nations. But such was the outrage in the Cabinet at the treatment Britain was receiving from the

IMF that Healey was compelled to answer his critics. He had to tell them, for example, that no one outside the ranks of the British Labour party, and of unreconstructed Keynesian economists, and certainly not their brother Social Democrat Helmut Schmidt, regarded the IMF terms as deflationary, and that, in any case, they had no choice. At the same time, Healey was himself arguing a case which would leave moderates in the Labour party naked. If Keynesianism was to follow socialism into the limbo of discredited ideologies, what clothes did the Labour party have left?

At last Callaghan discovered that his 'friends', President Ford in Washington and Chancellor Helmut Schmidt in Bonn, would not or could not help him. They warned him that he must make an agreement with the IMF. When Callaghan found that, despite compassionate noises, he could get no help from his friends, he became resentful. He too began to seek ways of showing his resentment. He too appeared to be threatening the withdrawal of troops from Germany. He was advised that Britain could defend its sovereignty with the help of import controls. Fortunately, in the end, he realized that this was a time not for threats but for submission. Betrayed though he felt, Callaghan drew the inevitable lesson. It might be distasteful but it was better to eat humble pie and live than to make wild gestures and die. He knew that a large payment was due in December under the conditions of the June standby. If Britain did not make an agreement with the IMF, the money to make the payment would not be available and Britain would default.

Crosland, who had already suffered a severe loss of credibility among his Jenkinsite supporters, was warned by Callaghan in advance that he had made up his mind that the Cabinet must authorize Healey to negotiate with the IMF. He told Crosland to submit and, with bad grace, he did so. He claimed never to have been persuaded. He had merely accepted that the Prime Minister's decision must be final if the government was to survive. Healey then negotiated the December agreement with the IMF. The agreement was achieved on condition that socialist isolationism, whether of the Benn variety or that of Crosland, was abandoned. Expressed in a Letter of Intent from the government to the IMF, it promised substantial cuts in the Public Sector Borrowing Requirement and in Domestic Credit Expansion together with assurances about the increase in the money supply. From the moment the agreement was entered into, the economic prospects of the UK and the political prospects of the government improved. Kenneth Morgan, in his biography of Callaghan, writes of 'a lengthy period of economic success' following the accord with the IMF.[39] It was in fact a period of about twenty months. Jack Jones was once more helpful. He pressed the left to accept the inevitable and not, by multiple resignation, serve simply to bring down the Labour government. The left accepted Jack Jones's advice. But it added two names to its list of guilty men, betrayers of socialism, Callaghan and Healey.[40] They would never be forgiven. They had sold out to international capitalism.

Crosland died in February 1977, not living to see the disproof of all his doom-laden economic prophecies. He had never appreciated that an economy increasingly open to the world was inconsistent with the comfortable message of *The Future of Socialism*. The ideas that had provided the background to *The Future of Socialism*, that a high rate of growth could be relied on and that the problem of unemployment had been solved, were already at a discount. Contrary to *The Future of Socialism*, the economic problem had not been solved. The Keynesian techniques in which Crosland had deposited so much confidence had failed. It had proved impossible to reconcile full employment with stable prices. Under Heath unemployment had reached one million. When reversed by the expansionary 1972 Keynesian budget, it had left Britain with mounting inflation, a catastrophic balance of payments and more exposed to the consequences of the oil-price rise than any other major industrial country. In April 1975, Healey's budget had, for the first time since the war, given the battle against inflation priority over full employment. It was a turning point in Britain's post-war economic history.

The IMF agreement destroyed the last prospect of democratic socialism in Britain and also of Labour governments finding refuge from reality in little devices such as the Social Contract and the industrial strategy. Experience with the Social Contract had, at last, comprehensively disproved a trend in economic management dating from the time of Macmillan, the use of incomes policy as an emergency measure against the consequences of inflationary policies conducted by successive governments. Now the only recourse, and that implicitly chosen by the government, was to allow unemployment to rise. The industrial strategy, after the rescue of CUK, was simply a joke in bad taste. If Britain was being forced, at long last, to face economic realities, then socialism was certainly off the agenda. After the IMF crisis, Callaghan proved quite a good Prime Minister by the standards of the post-war consensus. But he saw nothing wrong in that consensus, felt no humiliation in the 1976 IMF crisis, felt that UK governments could go on nestling up to the unions as an ally in policy. He left it to a new brand of Conservatives to conclude that the UK just could not go on in the same old way which was becoming increasingly uncomfortable and increasingly humiliating. Among those who had been watching the government's safari into the land of wishful thinking, and its retreat therefrom, was the Opposition leader Mrs Thatcher. She, and at least some of her shadow Cabinet, learnt the lessons of the IMF agreement and from the course of policy that had led to it. The experience would convince her that Conservatism too must cleanse itself of socialistic presumptions, that what must be abandoned was not merely Labour's version of socialism but also that which had been implemented by Conservative governments since the war, including that of Edward Heath, in whose Cabinet she had herself served and whose inflationary policies had precipitated political and economic calamity. How completely the break was made is a matter for separate discussion. But, in the race to be 'new', the Conservative party beat the Labour party by almost two decades.

INDUSTRIAL DEMOCRACY

There was a longstanding debate within the Labour party as to whether democracy was something only for the political arena or whether it should extend in some form into the place of work. The idea of extending democracy into the work place became known as industrial democracy. Industrial democracy could take a variety of forms. A moderate form would be a system of consultation between management and work force which, while not binding on the management, gave employees influence and might gain their co-operation by taking account of their concerns. A more developed form would be to allow the work force to elect board directors, and it was this form that the strongest advocates of industrial democracy had in mind. In the 1930s, as we have seen, there were those such as Durbin who considered that industrial democracy was inconsistent with central planning; others, who included Attlee and Bevin, who thought that a democracy was incomplete if the work force had no influence over the policies of its employers; and those again who regarded any form of industrial democracy as an example of class collaboration and hence of class betrayal. We have seen that, in *The Future of Socialism*, Crosland accepted that the workers had a moral right to industrial democracy but argued that as they did not seem to want it, and as there was little chance of such a major reform gaining for them any real benefits, the idea should be abandoned. *In Place of Strife*, on the other hand, smiled on the idea of experiments in worker representation on boards of directors. As, by the 1970s, any idea of central planning had evaporated, the continuing controversy within the Labour Movement was limited to two conflicting tendencies: industrial democracy as an extension of democracy into the work place, and hence appropriate in any country claiming to be democratic; and industrial democracy as class collaboration and class betrayal. The principal exponents of these two tendencies within the trade union movement were Jack Jones of the TGWU, who, following in the footsteps of his great predecessor Ernest Bevin, was an advocate of industrial democracy, and Hugh Scanlon of the AEU, who regarded it as a form of class collaboration. By the 1970s Jack Jones had won a half-hearted majority within the TUC for his point of view, which meant workers on the board.

An idea that had long been the subject only of debate and controversy within the Labour Movement threatened therefore to become a reality in the 1970s. At a time of economic crisis, industrial democracy had one advantage as compared with most other Labour commitments. So far as the Exchequer was concerned, it was costless, at any rate in the short term. Its introduction would demonstrate Labour's socialist purpose without imperilling the public finances. There were even directors of major public companies who, disheartened by the state into which the British economy had fallen, and the incessant industrial disputes, believed that there was merit in some form of industrial democracy, even one which included worker directors on the board. Trade union power suggested the need for co-operation not conflict. These industrialists had come to the conclusion that as the representatives of the workers could not be ignored they had better be co-opted. They hoped that industrial democracy would help to bind the trade unions and their members to their company and to anti-inflationary economic policies. Industrial democracy was reputed to have had that effect in Germany. A system of industrial democracy had been introduced in Germany after the war involving worker representatives on the supervisory boards of German companies. To that system was attributed the philosophy of 'concerted action' between the federal government and both sides of industry, which had maintained industrial peace and hence contributed significantly to the success of the German economy. Helmut Schmidt was an eloquent exponent of the merits of German industrial democracy and he had considerable influence with Callaghan and with the Labour government. If industrial democracy brought such benefits in Germany, why not in the United Kingdom?

The question as to what the Labour government should do about industrial democracy was first considered while Wilson was still Prime Minister. Labour's precarious position in the House of Commons would have created difficulties even if there were no other problems to be solved in introducing industrial democracy. Two such problems were immediately obvious. In Germany there was a two-tier system of company boards. In the German system of industrial democracy, the worker representatives sat on the supervisory board, not on the management board. In Britain there was only one board, which combined the functions of management and of the supervision of management. A second problem was whether the representation of the work force should be through trade union machinery. In Germany, and indeed in other European systems of industrial democracy, workers were allowed to vote in the election of their representatives whether or not they were members of trade unions. But one of the fears of the TUC was that, if a vote were conceded to non-unionists, it would undermine the claim of the unions to be the single authoritative representatives of the workers in any company. The TUC insisted, therefore, that any system of industrial democracy should embody what was known as the 'single channel'. Democracy in other words would be extended to trade unionists within the work force but not to those who were not members of unions. Non-unionists were not to be allowed to be 'free riders', accepting the benefits of union negotiating power without contributing to it. This proposed disfranchisement of non-unionists gave rather a curious slant to industrial 'democracy', but it was a condition of TUC co-operation in anything the government might decide to enact. A further question was what proportion of the board should consist of worker representatives. In Germany the proportion had for many years been a third of the supervisory board, but the success of the system there had encouraged an increase towards 50 per cent.

The Wilson government decided, in face of these many problems, to establish a committee including trade unionists and employers under the chairmanship of the historian Lord Bullock, biographer of Ernest Bevin and a Labour peer. The Committee reported in January 1977. The majority of the Committee came down in favour of the TUC position. Representation was to be through the single channel on the unitary board. The number of worker directors was to be equal to the employer representatives, with one or more independents holding the balance. The employer representatives on the Bullock Committee dissented. The furthest they were prepared to go was to accept, after a preparatory period, one-third of worker directors on the supervisory boards of holding companies. Company law would have to be changed to authorize the two-tier board structure.

The report caused inevitable difficulties within the government. Those on the right who were involved in considering the Bullock Report rejected its findings. They opposed the single channel as a matter of principle, and they opposed also the idea of equal representation on a unitary board as a matter of common sense.[41] They found themselves in conflict with the TUC, which, from the beginning, had made clear that it would not co-operate in any other system than the single channel. By this time the Callaghan government had lost its majority in the House of Commons. It was dependent on support from the Liberals and there could be no expectation that the Liberals would vote for the single channel. The question was therefore returned to the deep freeze via a tentative White Paper. The right was left uncommitted to the extravagances of the Bullock Report. The TUC believed that the door was still left open for its interpretation of industrial democracy. Industrial democracy thus became unfinished business to be left over until there was a Labour government capable of taking decisions on so sensitive a matter. Meanwhile those of the public interested in this abstruse subject would perceive that Labour was still so dominated by the trade unions that it could not rule out *ab initio*, and as a matter of simple principle, a system of alleged 'democracy' which began by disfranchising a significant proportion of the industrial electorate.

THE END OF ANOTHER LABOUR GOVERNMENT

By 1977, the trade union leadership, representing the increasing impatience of its members, had become uncooperative. Trade unionists were repudiating their collaborationist leaders, of whom the most prominent was Jack Jones. Failing to achieve agreement with the TUC, the government, in the summer of 1977, laid down a 10 per cent guideline for pay settlements. It was now facing the old problem of securing exit from an incomes policy without a wage explosion. But 'responsibility' in pay claims had become the victim of the earlier successes. 'Free collective bargaining' was once more the rule. Once more increases in pay levels were grossly exceeding increases in prices. Failing in a further attempt at agreement with the TUC, Callaghan, in the summer of 1978, persuaded the Cabinet to endorse a 5 per cent pay policy. The argument for the policy was that 5 per cent was the maximum which, allowing for drift, contained any hope of reducing inflation. By rejecting the 5 per cent, union leaders demonstrated that, while they might give verbal support to the reduction in inflation, it was not an objective in which they could any longer collaborate. A Prime Minister who had begun political life as a trade union official, whose rise to power had been greatly assisted by his loyalty to union interests during the battle over *In Place of Strife*, who prided himself on his negotiating abilities, found himself unable to persuade his erstwhile allies and was deserted by them. At the 1978 Party Conference, Terry Duffy, shortly to be President of the AEU, moved a resolution, which was overwhelmingly passed, that rejected wage guidelines 'until prices, profits and investment are planned within the framework of a socialist economy'.[42] A socialist economy was, as the AEU well knew, far below the horizon. The Party was rejecting wage guidelines in any foreseeable circumstances.

As there was no agreement with the TUC, it was left to the government to enforce the policy in the public sector and to employ such sanctions as it could muster in the private sector. By the same token only a government with renewed authority, derived from victory in a general election, could hope for any success in either the public or the private sectors. There was, however, no election in the autumn of 1978. By that autumn, it had even appeared that Labour might win another election. Callaghan's decision not to take the risk was a miscalculation contrary to the interests of his country, which needed a re-elected government, and of his Party, which was entering a period of turmoil in industrial relations which would acquire the title of the winter of discontent. Callaghan assured the British people that nothing would be gained by having an election a year before the statutory limit of the Parliament. In November 1978, with Labour once more ahead in the polls, Callaghan became confident both of his wisdom in not calling an election the previous month and of victory when the election did come. He discussed with colleagues how long he should stay on as Prime Minister after his coming victory.[43] The intervention of the winter of discontent of 1978–9 disrupted any such premature optimism. The government was left powerless in face of an upsurge of wage claims, and strikes to enforce them.

After the failure, due to opposition among Labour backbenchers, of an attempt to apply sanctions against the Ford Motor Company, which wished to settle a strike of its workers at 16.5 per cent; after oil-tanker drivers had been bought off with an increase averaging 20 per cent; and after striking road-haulage workers settled at about 21 per cent, the government in effect abandoned its struggle to enforce its policy in the private sector. Subsequent strikes by public sector unions led to massive disruption of public services. The unions were proving that they could destroy not just a Conservative government but a Labour government also. They did not foresee that the effect of their actions was to ensure that the next government would, almost inevitably, be Conservative and that it would have no choice but to regard the trade union movement as its enemy and to bring it under control not just by legal regulation but by abandoning Keynesian economic policies. The so-called winter of discontent was a severe blow to the remaining authority of the Callaghan government. It deprived Labour of its best claim to office – that it knew how to deal with those powerful trade unions that appeared so ready to disrupt society. Callaghan lost much of his prestige by capitulating on his incomes policy, more of it because of his inability to preserve public services, and yet more because of the obvious breach in the relations between the Labour government and its supposed friends and allies, the trade union movement. But, equally, the unions finally lost their negotiating status as an 'estate of the realm'. They had prejudiced it by their attitude to *In Place of Strife*, they had undermined it by their exploitation of the Social Contract, and now they threw the remnants away. But then their negotiating status as an 'estate of the realm' had always been invalid, and a comfortable excuse for successive governments to escape the painful responsibilities of anti-inflationary economic management.

The government had not yet had time to recover from the winter of discontent when it was forced into an election by the loss of a vote of confidence on 28 March 1979. At the subsequent General Election, Labour obtained its lowest share of the vote since the 1930s. About one-third of trade unionists appear to have voted Conservative.[44] But the Conservatives did not do so well either. Evidently, while the electorate was tired of an ineffective Labour government, it was by no means enamoured of the alternative. At least the Conservatives had the consolation of victory even if not a victory proportionate to the demerits of their predecessors. The election of Mrs Thatcher as leader of the Conservative party had been a great reinforcement to Labour's prospects. It was not her fault, rather her luck, that Labour threw away the opportunity of an election in the autumn of 1978. Callaghan's diminished prestige still stood higher than that of the Opposition leader. But although, despite all the evidence of his failure, there might still be confidence in Callaghan, there was now little enough in his government. His government, like the Wilson government of the 1960s, had utterly failed. It had failed as a socialist government. It had failed in managing the economy. It had failed in controlling the trade unions. It did not deserve to survive.

Bernard Donoughue records that, during the campaign leading to the May 1979 election, he drew attention to improving public opinion polls in an attempt to give Callaghan some comfort. Callaghan's depressed response has become more influential on historical opinion than it deserves: 'You know there are times, perhaps once every thirty years, when there is a sea-change in politics. It then does not matter what you say or what you do. There is a shift in what the public wants and what it approves of. I suspect there is now such a sea-change – and it is for Mrs Thatcher.'[45] Thirty years before 1979 takes us back to the last days of Attlee. Callaghan would remember those days. In 1951 a tired Prime Minister virtually abandoned office to his opponents because he no longer had the spirit to carry on. Now, twenty-eight years later, another tired Labour Prime Minister was abandoning hope of victory. He claimed that there had been a sea-change. But, the previous November, Labour had been ahead in the polls. Labour's performance in the 1979 election confirmed what many had thought at the time, that if Callaghan had had the courage to go to the country in the autumn of 1978 he might well, undeservedly, have won. Instead, his reluctance to face the electorate was followed by eighteen years out of power. By the time it was re-elected on 1 May 1997, it was the Labour party that had undergone the sea-change. But it might have changed more rapidly had it remained in office.

THE RECORD

The Attlee government is remembered for the NHS and the welfare state. The first Wilson government is remembered for the Open University and liberalizing legislation, particularly the abolition of the death penalty for murder. Under the Wilson–Callaghan governments of the 1970s there was only one measure of permanent value that might be regarded as having about it the tinge of socialism, Barbara Castle's

Social Security Act, but that claim was somewhat dimmed by the fact that it was passed with the support of the Tories. After the failures of Crossman and Keith Joseph in the field of pension reform, it was the third, and at last successful, attempt to find some way of improving pensions in old age. Wilson, with typical hyperbole, regarded the measure as representing 'an economic and financial revolution perhaps greater than all the post-war nationalization measures put together'.[46] This was more an assessment of the value of the nationalization acts than of the Social Security Act, creditable as that was. The Treasury was aware at the time that the Act could involve costs which in the longer run would be unacceptable. But, accurate as that forecast might be, this non-partisan measure has served for a quarter of century and is still being vigorously defended by Barbara Castle.[47] Legislation was enacted creating a devolved parliament in Scotland and an assembly in Wales. But a referendum in Wales voted strongly against implementation and, in Scotland, the positive vote did not reach the 40 per cent of the electorate required by the legislation. A Capital Transfer Tax was introduced but, before it could have any impact, it was repealed by the Tories. A Wealth Tax was considered but discarded as too complicated and of questionable additional effect to the Capital Transfer Tax which had already been enacted. In any case, if it had been enacted in a way which had a significant equalizing impact, it too would have been repealed by the successor Tory government. The irony is that, if economic management by Labour governments had been more competent, if they had not always been beset by an atmosphere of self-induced crisis, if, as a result, they had been re-elected, certain desirable, not exclusively socialist, objectives of policy might have been achieved and become accepted. Perhaps the most important of these lost objectives would have been the restoration to the community of a fair share of increases in land values. Attempts at this were made, including during the 1974–9 Labour government, but were always repealed by the successor Conservative government.

Wilson's other major achievement was to keep Britain in Europe largely, if not entirely, on the terms that Heath had negotiated. But then it was Wilson who had thought of taking Britain out. Terms which were unacceptable while Wilson was in opposition, and his main concern was to keep the leadership and the Party united, became acceptable when he was back in Downing Street. He was, no doubt, aware that the 'Europeans' in his Party would not follow him if he decided to take Britain out of Europe. Wilson, together with his Foreign Secretary,

James Callaghan, began the renegotiation they had pledged. Slight modifications of the terms were obtained, though nothing that should have made the difference between British membership and British withdrawal. The Cabinet, by a majority, then decided to recommend acceptance of the renegotiated terms in the referendum. On 5 June 1975, public assent to staying in membership on the renegotiated terms was obtained by a majority of about 2:1. The vote in the referendum was supposed to end the debate on British membership. That was much too optimistic. The left and the planners remained totally hostile to the European project. They regarded it as an obstacle in the way of socialism surmountable only by withdrawal. They would never accept membership until, at least, they had better reason to do so than the vote of the British people. That better reason was eventually found, eighteen frustrating years out of office.

JAMES CALLAGHAN'S GREATEST SERVICE

The loss of the 1979 election was perhaps James Callaghan's greatest service to the British people. Callaghan might have gone to the country in the autumn of 1978 and won another term of office. He might have survived the vote of confidence that brought him down in March 1979. If he had survived until the autumn of 1979, enough of the electorate might have forgotten the winter of discontent to return Labour to office. But, while the return of Thatcher was not inevitable, it seems unlikely that Callaghan would have known what to do with victory if he had won it, whereas a Conservative party that had cleansed itself of Heath and Macmillan was more likely to respond to the imperatives of the early 1980s. A new Labour government would no doubt have turned to unfinished business. After a time it might have revived the idea of devolution for Scotland and Wales about which Scotland had shown itself half-hearted and Wales strongly opposed. The 1979 manifesto had proposed the nationalization of the commercial ports and cargo handling. This might have been implemented depending on the majority.[48] The government might, despite the winter of discontent, have returned to its ideas on industrial democracy and the danger would have been that, in an attempt to buy off the trade unions, it would have enacted a form of industrial democracy based on the Bullock Committee's idea of the single channel. There would certainly have been continued fruitless dabbling in industrial policy. Even Mrs Thatcher's government was prepared to subsidize British Leyland and attempt to rescue de Lorean, the motorcar-manufacturing company which Labour had helped to establish in Northern Ireland and which, despite further aid, rapidly descended into liquidation. Certain measures taken by the Thatcher government would not have been taken by a Labour government or at least would not have been taken without considerable delay. Exchange control would not have been abolished in the autumn of 1979 thus further opening the British economy to the hated forces of international capitalism. There would have been no trade union legislation unless both the government and the rest of the union movement had been intolerably provoked by the irresponsibility of the National Union of Miners under the leadership of Arthur Scargill. Although it must be questionable how effective the legislation of the Thatcher era was in containing industrial unrest, there can be no doubt that it was long overdue that the trade unions should be brought within the law. There would have been no privatization at least until budgetary constraints forced the hands even of a Labour government.

But the real problem for Labour would have been inflation. It must be highly questionable how a new Labour government would have met the inflationary pressures that were once more developing, stimulated by its own policies and reinforced by the further doubling of the price of oil in 1979. The winter of discontent was indeed symptomatic of those pressures and proved, once and for all, both that the trade unions' patience with wage restriction under Labour was at an end and that Labour could no longer rely on its relationship with the unions as a weapon against inflation. Even if forced eventually to adopt quasi-monetarist policies, there would certainly have been a period of uncertainty, disruption and hesitant leadership. It would probably have led to the kind of crisis that provoked a split in the Labour party in 1931, the danger to which Tony Benn had pointed in 1976. Such a split could have occurred from either side. The right might have demanded the adoption of the quasi-monetarist policies followed by the Thatcher government in its early years. That would have meant accepting that there was little that could be done about rising unemployment. If that course had been rejected, if it had seen the government complacently accepting ever higher inflation, the right might have concluded that it had no choice but to leave the government, in which case the kind of coalition, fear of which had motivated Jack Jones's helpful interventions in 1975 and 1976, might have emerged.

Another possibility would have been that the left would have at last put its actions where its mouth had long been and would have withdrawn its support, thus bringing the government down. It would once more have offered the alternative strategy as its solution. Such a policy would have led to exclusion from the European Community and to hyperinflation. It would have been rejected by the right and could have led to the departure of the left. This dramatic outcome would probably have been avoided by some conciliatory gestures by the Prime Minister. He would not have had to pay too much because the left had nowhere else to go. Just as it had swallowed hard in 1976 it would probably have swallowed hard again and found reasons why it should remain in the government. The trade union leaders at least might have brought pressure on the left to accept quasi-monetarist policies on the ground that anything was better than Thatcher, and a split might thereby have been avoided. We have not had many heroes among our political leaders since the war. They have regularly doffed their caps to what they claimed to be political necessities. We can be grateful that, in 1940, Churchill showed himself the ultimate political innocent and fought on when Britain was facing defeat. But the record does not suggest that much heroism could have been expected from James Callaghan. Though, in the end, he might have been forced into the necessary anti-inflationary paths, it would have been after much debate, many sighs and wriggles, innumerable meetings of the Cabinet, and with such evident regret as to deprive the electorate of any confidence that he knew what he was doing. It is in this sense that he was probably serving the country better than he knew when he failed to call an election at the moment when there was the best hope of a Labour victory, in the autumn of 1978.

NEGLECTING THE LESSONS

Labour, out of office, repudiated the lessons of 1974–9 that socialism is incompatible with an open economy and that, in economic management, price stability must take a higher priority than an exaggerated interpretation of full employment. It proved itself once more ineducable unless by long periods of opposition. It was a typical Labour reaction to confrontation with unpleasant facts. Better to ignore them than to recognize them. The principal reason for the repudiation is probably the Party's culture of betrayal, a culture inherited from the desertion of Ramsay MacDonald in 1931. Ministers, clearly, were corruptible. It could never be assumed that they were honestly seeking solutions to the problems they faced, and had not simply become the slaves of Treasury orthodoxy. They must be traitors to socialism. As they were traitors, there was no point in examining their arguments. To extract from the Party a willingness seriously to examine their arguments would be difficult enough in any case, given that those arguments had so little in common with traditional socialism. But the suspicion of treachery made it impossible. When Jack Jones came to the government's rescue over incomes policy in 1975 and the IMF crisis in 1976, it was consciously because he feared that it might be the only way to avoid a betrayal by the right that would make the Labour party irrelevant for another generation. But there was another reason why the lessons were not learnt. In the IMF debates, Crosland had conceded defeat but not to the arguments, merely to the authority of the Prime Minister. In his view there had been another way, a better way consistent with his interpretation of socialism. Crosland's rejection of the agreement with the IMF could only confirm in their suspicions all those in the Labour party, and they were a majority, who did not wish to learn the lessons of the IMF crisis. If Crosland refused to learn, or was unable to learn, why should others in the Party, less eminent, less authoritative on economic policy, absorb lessons that they did not wish to absorb? Better to turn to the simple explanation of what had gone wrong. Callaghan and Healey were slaves to Treasury orthodoxy. They had deserted socialism. Thereby, though his views had remained entirely consistent with *The Future of Socialism*, Crosland committed a grave disservice to the Party that he, like his friend Gaitskell before him, loved.

SIXTEEN

The holy anger of the left

THE LEFT'S DILEMMA

Great as was the blow to Labour represented by the winter of discontent, and by the election defeat of May 1979, worse was to follow. The left could legitimately claim that, once more, a Labour government had broken its election pledges. Once again a Labour government had failed to implement a socialist programme. Certainly there were excuses. Labour had inherited an economy in crisis. But it knew the situation and had made the pledges. The disillusion was not just that of the left. It was shared throughout the Labour Movement. Almost nowhere in the ranks of the Party, or of the trade unions, could be found anyone who considered that the Wilson–Callaghan governments had done well. From a socialist point of view it was as though they had never been, except that they had committed treason against socialism. Defeat demanded a post-mortem. But, for the left of the Labour party, there was no need of a post-mortem. It already knew the reasons for defeat. It had been here before. After 1970 the left had preached the necessity of socialism and Wilson had successfully deflected its efforts. The 1974–9 government had been, if that were possible, more of a disaster for socialism even than the 1964–70 government.

The idea, traditional in the Labour party, that capitalist crisis reinforced the need for socialist measures had been abandoned even by Michael Foot. Certainly it was not the way that the Labour government had acted, had ever intended to act or, indeed, could have acted. But the breach of faith went beyond the death of an empty slogan. Labour leaders had failed to tell the truth either to their own members or to the electorate at large. The electorate had rejected them. Now they were left face to face with their own members. It was easy to argue that the membership should have appreciated the difficulties faced by Labour Ministers and should have trusted them. But Ministers had not trusted their members. They had forsaken socialism but had been unwilling to reveal their dirty secret. The result had been an ever widening gap between leaders and followers. The left would have wanted its leaders to be socialists in the old sense. But, from the way they had acted, they had not appeared to be socialists even in the Crosland sense. Benn wrote in an introduction to his published diaries that Labour 'was rejected by its own supporters because it had abandoned almost all pretence to radicalism, and those who had given it earlier majorities felt disappointed at Labour's inability in office to pursue the policies on which it had been elected'.[1] It is unlikely that it was the abandonment of any pretence of radicalism that had led Labour's supporters to desert it at the election. But, on its own assumptions, the left certainly had grounds for arguing that the Wilson and Callaghan governments had done nothing to advance the socialist cause, and that Labour should dispense with leaders who had betrayed the faith they claimed to hold.

At the 1979 Party Conference, Ron Hayward, General Secretary, asserted with all the virtue of innocence, 'In my forty-six years of membership of this party I've never yet seen it try Socialism in any sense.'[2] This, though an exaggeration, was a pardonable exaggeration, however uncomfortable for Party leaders, and in particular for the former Prime Minister James Callaghan. The Labour party had become an organized hypocrisy and now the leaders, who were guilty of the deception, had finally been found out. When the left asked itself why leaders who were professed socialists never achieved what they promised, its simple answer was that its leaders had betrayed it. There was some truth in this accusation because the leaders were no longer socialists. But it was far from the whole truth or even the most important truth. The most important truth was that democratic socialism was a mirage and had been perceived as such by most Labour leaders. The second truth was that Labour governments were elected to manage capitalism, not to introduce socialism. But neither of these truths had been recognized on the left or admitted on the right. The left was very angry. It felt deprived of all that it had worked for, all that it believed in, all that the leaders of the Labour party had assured it that they too believed. This must be the last betrayal. The left, therefore, had this excuse for its attempt to cleanse the Party of its opponents. Socialism needed socialists, not craven supplicants genuflecting before the idols of international finance. The left now had the power to commence its act of political cleansing. Such was the disillusion in the Party that the left had acquired widespread support, including in the unions It had the Party at its mercy.

The left proceeded to use its momentary power, built on widespread disillusionment, to refashion the Labour party. It did not attempt to enfranchise the silent majority of Labour party members. It preferred the ancient revolutionary method of the putsch. It had always believed that a genuinely socialist programme would win elections. It now had the opportunity to forge a genuinely socialist programme and impose it on the Party. But, with the opportunity, went a serious risk. If it purged the Party, imposed its programme, and still lost elections, the left, and its theories, would be as discredited as those it had expelled. So it happened. After the devastating General Election defeat in 1983, far worse than in 1979, it never recovered. It might have taken a different course, a democratic course. It might have decided that its first duty was to persuade the majority of Labour members to be socialists, which they clearly were not, as a preliminary to persuading a majority of the electorate. It might have argued that the evidence of the past demonstrated that an electoral victory was worthless if it was not a socialist victory. The left's hero, Aneurin Bevan, had said as much even if, towards the end, he had appeared ready to strive for office on the basis of a mere electoral plurality. It might take a very long time. But, it might have felt, the creation of a genuinely socialist society would be worth the waiting and the effort.

The left probably suspected that it was an impossible task. It would not convince the electorate, and the Party would tire of waiting for victory on the left's terms. Rather than invest the time and effort in what might prove a hopeless endeavour, it preferred to seize the day and to implement its putsch. It almost succeeded in capturing the Party. But, in its moment of triumph, it lost the electorate. In retrospect it must be apparent even to socialists that neither course was likely to bring the success for which the left yearned. The method of the putsch would bring electoral defeat. The democratic way would never persuade the majority of Labour party members, let alone of the electorate. Either way the left was lost. It was because democracy is, for the extreme left, so unsatisfactory, so lethargic, that, in 1917, Lenin chose the putsch and established a dictatorship. But seizing the Labour party was not like seizing the state. In their book, *The End of Parliamentary Socialism*, Leo Panitch and Colin Leys tell us that the intentions of the left were, in fact, highly democratic. They say that 'the special importance of the Labour new left is that it envisaged a much more far-reaching, active and inclusive kind of democracy than anything currently known to the British state or the British Labour Party . . .'[3] When one reads such words, one hears the sound of the tumbrels advancing in defence of 'democracy'.

DEFECTION

Labour has always boasted a leavening of moderates who could reassure and attract the electorate. Some were simply pragmatists. Some were prepared to accept Crosland as their patron saint, though never as leader. The same man is not always ideal in both roles. Now the moderates were to be presented with unpleasant alternatives, either accept the policies and the leadership of the left or leave the Party. The moderates have always been at their strongest in government. When there was a Labour government, they constituted the majority in the Cabinet. In government they had the prestige, the authority, the information. Above all they could always use the argument against their critics that they surely would not want to bring in the Conservatives. But now the Conservatives were in office and the moderates were out. Their morale was low through a sense of failure, even by their own standards, and they were defenceless. In 1970 the feeling of failure had been less and the sense of achievement, oddly, had been greater. Now there was nothing. After 1970 some of the moderates, notably Crosland, had been ready to fight. Now there was little spirit remaining with which to fight. In 1970 the moderates still controlled the PLP, though their control was soon to be weakened by divisions over Europe. In 1979 their control of the PLP was tenuous. In 1970 the Labour party had still been their Party, the vehicle of their hopes for society, and of their personal ambitions. Now some of them at least were prepared to abandon the Party to its unelectable left wing. They knew they had failed. It was unlikely that they would ever again hold office in a Labour government. For what should they fight? Were they to turn themselves into a camouflage for the left, adopting its policies in which they did not believe while deceiving the electorate by remaining in the Party?

The left had two fetishes by which it seemed to define socialism. One was withdrawal from the EEC. The other was unilateral nuclear disarmament. Most of those who would, a little later, defect to form the Social Democratic party were 'Europeans' and multilateralists. These were battles that, in the past, they had fought and won. They did not want to have to fight them again. They engaged in a few symbolic skirmishes at Labour party conferences and elsewhere but were met with a reception that did little credit to Labour party tolerance. They felt that they had little support from Callaghan, who held on as leader although clearly his time had passed, or from Denis Healey, regarded as Callaghan's most likely successor. Indeed they felt that Callaghan and Healey, so far from trying to bar the tide which was sweeping the left into control of the Party, were allowing themselves to be swept along by it. The idea of leaving the Labour party, and forming a Social Democratic party, at first unthinkable, became increasingly attractive. How could they be expected to vote for unilateral nuclear rearmament and withdrawal from Europe? When, in November 1980, in succession to Callaghan, the PLP elected Michael Foot, rather than Denis Healey, as leader of the Labour party, they defected. Loyalty to the Labour party permitted some MPs who regarded themselves as 'Europeans' and multilateralists to remain in the Party. But, in March 1981, David Owen, William Rodgers and Shirley Williams, now joined by Roy Jenkins returning from Brussels, led a group of about twelve Labour MPs out of the Party. The leaders were dubbed the 'Gang of Four' but, fortunately, were not to suffer the duress of their Chinese proto-types. The Social Democratic party of the Gang of Four could not have had less than it did in common with, say, the Marxist Social Democratic Federation of H. M. Hyndman founded in 1881, let alone with the Russian Social Democratic party (Bolsheviks), which, under Lenin, had made the 1917 October revolution. The selection of the name Social Democratic party nevertheless suggested that the Gang of Four and their followers were still socialists, and perhaps some of them were. But their inevitable electoral alliance with the Liberal party cast doubt on how serious their socialist intentions now were. For the left, their depar-ture was good riddance. The Labour party might thereby have become a narrower church but it was at least a more socialist church. The defection did not, however, improve Labour's chances of winning a general election. The 1983 General Election manifesto, described by Gerald Kaufman as the longest suicide note in history, committed a Labour government to take the UK out of the European Community without even the benefit of another referendum. It was not as popular a cry as the blinkered left imagined.

The Social Democrats were clear what they were fighting against. They were less clear what they were fighting for, unless it was to ensure that there would be a credible alternative party of government. It was a respectable ambition at a time when the Labour party was making itself unelectable. The early popularity of the SDP was attributable to the hope that there was an alternative to Thatcher and Thatcherism which was not the Labour party. The Social Democratic party, when it was formed, did not seem to require new ideas. For the time being at least, it was content to make do with old ones. It seemed to be fighting for a kind of revived Keynesianism to set against the Thatcher government's monetarism. In some elderly recesses within the Social Democratic party, Keynesianism lived on. The party also seemed still to treasure the moderate interventionist industrial policy on which the Wilson–Callaghan governments had settled after the struggle against Benn. Under the leadership of its Prime Minister candidate, Roy Jenkins, the 1983 election programme of the Liberal–SDP Alliance, with its inflationary bias, would not have disgraced old Labour. It aimed to reduce unemployment over two years to one million from the three million it had reached under Mrs Thatcher. This was supposedly to be achieved without any increase in inflation by means of substantially increased government borrowing.[4] The hope, perhaps, was that the European Community, an object to be cherished rather than repulsed, might agree a common Keynesian course. But the inauguration of the European Monetary System in March 1979 had confirmed that such a possibility was becoming more, not less, distant. Ironically, the Alliance programme was grossly at odds with British membership of the Exchange Rate Mechanism of the European Monetary System, which Jenkins himself strongly favoured, of which, indeed, he regarded himself as a progenitor. The quality of its economic thinking was not the SDP's proudest achievement between 1981 and 1983. The defectors did not seem at first to realize that it was not simply socialism that was dead. So was social democratic Keynesianism in one country, in devotion to which they had lived their political lives. Owen, who had been something of a Croslandite during the hard days of 1976, was the first of the Gang of Four to find new principles in market economics – to a degree which alienated some of those who had joined with him in the attempt to 'break the mould' of British politics.

THE LEFT'S THREE PYRRHIC VICTORIES

The left enjoyed three great victories, each one of them in the end counterproductive from its own point of view. The first was to threaten Labour MPs with 'mandatory reselection'. The PLP had always been a major obstacle to the ambitions of the left. Moreover, when in government, it was from the PLP that were selected the Ministers who had betrayed socialism. Now the PLP would be terrorized into submission. There would be mandatory reselection before every General Election. This was adopted by the Party Conference as early as 1979. Non-believing MPs who did not behave could be reported to the activist members of their constituency parties and their services could be dispensed with at the next election. It was a powerful threat to MPs who had no private means and were very reliant on their membership of Parliament. There could be no objection in principle to MPs having to submit themselves to reselection. There is no entitlement to a life tenure in safe seats, though that is the way it had sometimes appeared. MPs should be leaseholders, not freeholders. But the narrow left-wing caucuses dominating many constituency Labour parties were hardly representative even of Labour party members, let alone Labour voters. The democratic principle of reselection was being exploited for the benefit of a small minority of putschists.

The left must have found the outcome educative. At first its terror succeeded with too many Labour MPs. But, in the slightly longer term, the acquisition of new power by constituency parties led to a determination on the part of their members that small activist minorities should not make key decisions. What the left did not appreciate was that most dormant Labour party members, and certainly the great majority of Labour voters, were to the right of even the most right-wing Labour MPs. Once the silent majority in the Labour party was activated, it would be the end of the left.

The right and centre of the Party had been greatly at fault in not themselves insisting long before on mandatory reselection. This was partly inertia, partly fear that the immediate effects would be adverse because it would put them at the mercy of the activists in their constituency parties, partly the risk it would open up for penurious Labour MPs who depended on the House of Commons for their bread and butter, partly the fact that it would put upon MPs the boring obligation of organizing and persuading their own quiescent supporters. The left, realizing that it was totally unrepresentative both of the Party as a whole and, even more, of Labour voters, did, to some extent, grasp that there was a danger what it was doing. It talked of the need to 'educate' the members of constituency parties. It feared that it had not sufficiently 'structured' public opinion.[5] It was a hopeless task. Democracy would work in ways that the left might uneasily dread, could nevertheless hardly believe given the obvious righteousness of its cause, and would for ever regret. The left had relied on unleashing the vote of the constituency parties against right-wing MPs. It did not foresee that it would, in the end, be deserted even by the constituency parties. The subsequent introduction of mandatory 'one member one vote' selection of candidates (OMOV), with votes cast by post, sealed the fate of the left in the constituency parties. It drove some of the most extreme Labour MPs so far to the right that they would find themselves sitting comfortably in a Blair Cabinet. Among those enfranchised were new recruits who would never have thought of seeking membership in the days when the Party seemed subservient to Foot, Benn and miscellaneous trade union leaders.

The left can hold it to its credit that the Labour party is today further to the right, less socialist, less radical, than at any other time in its century-long history. This, however, has not led to complacency on the part of the Labour party's leadership. Having exploited the advantages of democracy against the left, it now finds itself confronted with its uncertainties. Philip Gould, adviser to Tony Blair, records how he told his master that 'Labour has to become a genuinely one member, one vote party. That is the only ultimate future for Labour.'[6] The trouble is that a democratic, OMOV electorate cannot, in all circumstances, be trusted to select candidates acceptable to the leadership. A Labour government is bound to face criticism from within the ranks of its own Party. Attractive but unreliable candidates may stand for election with real prospects of success. They may cause trouble, not least in the devolved assemblies that Labour has created in Scotland and Wales. The Labour party leadership has been discovered summoning back the trade union block vote. It seems to be prepared to forgive the irresponsibilities of the past provided it can find sufficiently staunch support among union leaders. Any lifeboat will do in a storm. The question will be whether there is a price.

The left's second triumph was to elect Michael Foot as leader of the Labour party on Callaghan's retirement in October 1980. Foot was the darling of the left but was also respected across the Party for his loyalty to Wilson and Callaghan. As we have seen, he too had rejected socialism as a way out of capitalist crisis. Thus there was now much about Foot than the left had to forget and forgive. It did not seem to matter, even on the left, that Foot's socialist oratory had descended into meaningless rhetoric. The most important consideration for the left was that Foot was their only candidate who could hope to win the leadership. At the time of Foot's elevation, the election of leader still lay with the PLP alone. Given an effective choice between Foot and Healey, the PLP, some of them influenced by the dangers of reselection if they did not vote the right way, opted narrowly for Foot on the final ballot by 139 to 129. Callaghan had always intended to stand down as leader during the course of the Parliament even if he had won the election. Foot's succession shows how well advised the electorate had been to turn to the Tories. It is, of course, possible that, if the Party had still been in government, it would have chosen Healey. But inflation would have compelled a new Labour government to follow 'right-wing' policies. The government would certainly have been unpopular with its followers in the PLP and the trade unions. Recalling the vote that Foot had obtained in the leadership election in 1976, there would have been a high probability that Foot would have been elected leader even if Labour had been in government. The country would have been faced with life under Prime Minister Michael Foot.

The majority of the PLP may have feared that to elect Healey, the Chancellor of the Exchequer who had forged the detested agreement with the IMF, would create an unbridgeable breach between it and the Party Conference, which was, at that time, developing a system for electing the leader which took the decision out of the sole hands of the PLP. The Party Conference did not love those who had wrestled with the economic crisis Labour had inherited in 1974. If these fears of a split were justified, it demonstrates to what a pass the Labour party had come that it had, for that reason, to deny itself its most capable and respected leader. In fact it was the election of Foot that made a split inevitable. Some of those who then left for the SDP would have paused to see how Healey performed before leaving the Party. It was rumoured that Foot won the votes of some Labour MPs who had already decided to desert the Party and form the SDP, whatever the outcome of the leadership election.[7] If they had to form a new party, Foot was exactly the Labour leader they would most like to leave behind them, at least if they could not have Benn. Foot's leadership would be an encouragement to other Labour MPs and to other Labour party members to join them. If this story is true, it showed a shrewd judgement. Foot's unsuitability rapidly became apparent even to many on the left who had voted for him.

The left's triumph in electing Foot turned to dust. Foot's great achievement was to revive in the Labour party the idea that the object in an election is victory and that, to achieve it, it must approximate its ideas to public opinion at least to some extent. Foot was seized by honourable ambition. He wanted to be Prime Minister. There could have been little joy in being leader of a party that was condemning itself to defeat and possibly even obliteration by the emergent Alliance of the Liberals and Social Democrats. There had long been little love lost between Foot and Benn. The Bennite left found that, in Foot, they had elected not a friend but a most dangerous enemy, difficult to attack because of a reputation that could comfortably withstand any criticism from their camp. As the Foot tenure progressed, they suffered defeats. They lost their majority on the NEC. In 1982, those two great stalwarts of the left, Tony Benn and Eric Heffer, were removed from their influential positions as Chairmen of the Home Policy Committee and Organization Committee of the NEC. Benn, even earlier, had decided not to stand for election to the shadow Cabinet and instead devoted his time to making wild speeches, sometimes without the least consultation, demanding that, on the election of a Labour government, the whole of industry should be at once brought under government control, the joint-stock banks should be nationalized, and the House of Lords abolished with the help of the prerogative creation of a thousand peers.[8] It sounded like Stafford Cripps at his worst. Benn, in his contempt for the capitalists whom he had once garlanded with public money, was now jettisoning the idea that had motivated Labour party policy since the 1930s that consent, or at least tolerance, was an essential element in the reform of the British economy and society. He was clamouring for his 'fundamental and irreversible shift' with all its revolutionary intonations.[9]

With such speeches, Benn might win ever more dedicated support from an ever reducing fraction of the Labour party. He was making it ever more difficult for Labour to win an election. At the 1983 General Election, Labour only narrowly exceeded the votes obtained by the new Social Democrat–Liberal Alliance. Labour won many more seats than the Alliance because its vote was concentrated. But many MPs who had voted for Foot as leader must have gone down to defeat. There had been informal consideration, before the election, of Foot's replacement by Healey, who had become deputy leader. But Foot showed no inclination to stand down and Healey would not move against him. Foot's tragedy was to take the blame for a humiliating defeat that was inescapable given the character of the Party he had chosen to lead. One can, however, moderate one's sympathy in consideration of the long history during which he had been the unacceptable face of socialism, condemning without recourse the strivings of his Party colleagues to make something of such opportunities for government as the electorate allowed. After Labour's disastrous defeat, Foot rapidly withdrew to his literary pursuits and was replaced by Neil Kinnock, who had moved over the years from the extreme left to that desirable location, centre-left, from which Labour leaders have sometimes been selected.

The left's third triumph was to deprive MPs of the sole right to elect the leader of the Labour party. At a special Labour Party Conference in February 1981 it was decided that in future the election of leader should lie with an electoral college in which 40 per cent of the votes were allocated to the trade unions and 30 per cent each to MPs and the constituency parties. There was certainly an argument for the proposition that it was wrong that a small body of MPs should have the sole right to elect the leader of the whole Party. It was what had happened from the beginning, but tradition was not in itself a good enough reason to validate it for ever. The trouble was that, despite Foot's best efforts, the alternative system selected gave a predominant voice to the unions. Instead of appearing more democratic, it emphasized the power which the unions held over the Labour party. As time passed, the system introduced for the election of its leader would compel the Labour party to think very seriously about its own internal democracy as well as that of the trade unions. The reconsideration led to a demand for each member, whether of the Party or of the trade unions, to have a vote and for the Party to distance itself from union influence by reducing the share of the total vote cast by trade unions at Labour Party Conferences. The process of democratizing the unions was assisted, perhaps inadvertently, by the 1984 Trade Union Act, which was described as returning the control of the unions to their members, and required ballots before strikes and regular confirmation of the maintenance of political funds. OMOV, though not yet fully achieved in the trade unions, would be the death of left-wing extremism in the election of the leader as it had been in the constituency parties.

The left almost won a fourth triumph, the election of Tony Benn as deputy leader in place of Denis Healey. Benn had once more succeeded in disentangling his reputation from that of the governments in which he had served. His lustre might have been tarnished by his refusal to resign but his eloquence was undimmed and was equal to any challenge, even the challenge of polishing his own image. For Foot, winning the coming election was important. He wanted to occupy No. 10 as Prime Minister. Experience warned him that he could not expect Benn to be a helpful collaborator in that enterprise. Foot was sufficiently perspicacious to see that a Foot–Healey partnership would be more attractive, electorally, than a Foot–Benn partnership. The public was entertained to the spectacle of Michael Foot, socialist, unilateralist, beloved of the left, defending Healey, questionably socialist, certainly multilateralist, despised and hated by the left, from the attacks of Benn's numerous, and sometimes rowdy, supporters. Healey scraped to victory by the narrowest of margins at Labour's Annual Conference in September 1981. It was one of those moments, few in those days, which demonstrated that the Labour party did want to survive.

THE LEFT'S HISTORIC ACHIEVEMENT

The historic achievement of the Labour left was to ensure, by dividing the opposition, that Thatcherism had its chance, and to allow a new and different Tory government to try another road to economic regeneration. In this it found itself in unintentional alliance with the Social Democrats. Crosland had written that no government would ever again dare to subject the British people to the levels of unemployment reached during the early Thatcher years. But, with a divided opposition, Mrs Thatcher could accumulate satisfactory majorities in the House of Commons with well under 50 per cent of the vote. She, and her Chancellor Geoffrey Howe, gave the battle against rising inflation absolute priority over the rising unemployment, even though it was to reach three million. The post-war commitment of governments to full employment was renounced. This historic change was confirmed in 1985 in the Thatcher government's White Paper, *Employment: The Challenge for the Nation*. Mrs Thatcher became deeply unpopular. It seemed to do her no harm. She was greatly assisted by the atavistic activities of the left of the Labour party, which made it all but impossible to conceive that a Labour government would be returned whatever unpopularity her government was prepared to incur. Thatcherism was challenged from within the Thatcher government. It was challenged by the remarkable, but temporary, rise of the Alliance. It was not challenged, at least not effectively, by the official Labour Opposition. Labour was too busy converting itself back into a socialist, anti-European, unilateralist, union-dominated party to provide an effective Opposition. Hence, despite levels of unemployment unheard of in the post-war years, and with considerable help from victory in the Falklands war, the first Thatcher government was enabled to pursue a firmly anti-inflationary economic policy dramatically epitomized in its 1981 budget, which was furiously condemned by 364 economists as lacking any basis in economic theory.[10]

The Thatcherite project started with the abolition of exchange control in the autumn of 1979. By 1979, exchange control was already a feeble weapon with little influence over events. The second oil shock of 1979 made its abolition urgent rather than courageous. Like so many dramatic and long-awaited moments, when exchange control finally went there was little sense of drama, rather of inevitability somehow long delayed. Douglas Jay, remembering no doubt the struggles of the governments of Attlee and Wilson, pronounced on the 'folly' of the move.[11] That revisionist socialist, Hugh Gaitskell, would never have countenanced it. The Thatcher government then proceeded to initiate a policy of privatization, deregulation and reform of the laws governing the trade unions. A hundred years of British public ownership was largely dismantled. It was a notable departure from British tradition to bring the trade unions within the law and to keep them there. The Labour party, aghast, could only watch and suffer. The trade unions, declared the Thatcher government, were to be taken away from the trade union bosses and returned to their members. Heath had tried to do it but had retreated when he began his search for an incomes policy. Socialism, if it had ever been tried, would have required the trade unions to be dragged within the law, as Barbara Castle had perceived. But there were other and better reasons, for example democratic accountability.

Mrs Thatcher has the reputation of having killed socialism. The truth is that there had never been, in Britain, any socialism to kill, only half-hearted, unconvincing and usually counterproductive measures of 'intervention' which were as characteristic of Conservative governments as of Labour. Nevertheless, it would be unjust to deny Mrs Thatcher her credit, even if, in the eye of history, it seems less than it appeared to partisan thinking at the time. By her privatization and her trade union legislation, she made it more difficult for any future Labour government to regress. By abolishing exchange control, she and Geoffrey Howe removed the last obstacle, such as it was, to the free flow of capital into and out of the British economy. Socialism was not made for open economies. Liberalization was always its greatest enemy. The result of Mrs Thatcher's measures, taken together, was not to kill the socialist idea but to buttress the defences against its resurrection as an effective force in British politics.

But those defences were already extremely strong. The principal contribution to the dismissal of socialism, even as an idea, was that of the 1974–9 Wilson–Callaghan governments. Michael Foot had announced that the management of capitalism must take priority over progress to socialism. Under irresistible pressure from market forces, Healey's 1975 budget, deflationary at a time of rising unemployment, signalled the government's acceptance that inflation must take priority over full employment. The 1976 IMF crisis reinforced the message. That was the turning point. If a British government could no longer freely decide its own policies, if the global market was the decisive influence, socialism was off the agenda of practical politics in any sense that had any relationship to its past meaning. It was appropriate that the *coup de grâce* should have been delivered by a Labour government. Indeed it may be that only a Labour government could have delivered the *coup de grâce*. Any attempt to do so by a Conservative government could never be more than half successful. It would always be open to argue that what a Conservative government could do, a Labour government could undo. But, if a Labour government demonstrated that there was no avoiding respect for market forces, that would be the nail in the coffin that would be most difficult to extract.

That it had become possible to overturn so much that had become accepted in the life and institutions of the British people can be attributed to one needling perception. The country was being repeatedly humiliated by its poor economic performance, its repeated economic crises, its rate of inflation and its seeming inability to take care of itself without pleading for outside help. Following thirty years of consensus government, a country which had once presented itself as a model was now a model only of how government should not be conducted. That perception was clearly not so widely dispersed throughout the electorate as to give Mrs Thatcher a large majority in the 1979 election. It was not even unanimously perceived within the victorious Tory party, many of whose leading members thought it quite possible to go on in the old traditional way. Moreover the initiation of actions intended to improve the economic performance, and restore the reputation, of the United Kingdom rapidly ran into trouble with the electorate which had only narrowly returned the Thatcher government.

All governments, even the most secure, become frightened as an election approaches. In 1982, the Thatcher government submitted to a challenge from the National Union of Miners, just as had the Heath government ten years earlier. It was searching for votes and was not averse to the traditional practice of purchasing them with the contents of the Exchequer. Even the disarray in Labour ranks did not prevent considerable loosening in the government's public expenditure controls as the election approached. Suddenly Thatcher was no longer Thatcherite, at least in the run-up to the 1983 election. There was, after all, the Social Democrat–Liberal Alliance and no one could say how well its third way might fare in a general election. The Alliance had shown itself as opposed to Thatcherite economic policy with its initial strong disinflationary bias, as was the Labour party. Mrs Thatcher need not have equivocated. Her government was re-elected with a greatly increased majority, even if with approximately the same share of the national vote. The time had become ripe for the full flood of Thatcherite legislation and for the final battle against the NUM led by its President, Arthur Scargill, whose revolutionary rhetoric had gone to his head and whose members were to suffer heavy casualties during the year-long miners' strike of 1984.

SEVENTEEN

The flexibility of the soft left

NEIL KINNOCK

Its crushing defeat in the 1983 election left the Labour party with a conundrum. Foot resigned at once. Who should now lead it? Healey, presumably, was too old. By the time of the next election he would be at least seventy and Britain was not China. Britain had not yet appreciated the benefits of gerontocracy.

The answer to the conundrum proved to be Neil Kinnock. He won the leadership with an overwhelming 71 per cent of the vote in the electoral college. In the absence of any compelling alternative from the previous Labour Cabinet, he emerged as the choice of the trade unions, which now had a decisive voice in the election of the leader. His election was a gamble, but there was some desperation. It was the first time since Ramsay MacDonald that Labour had chosen a leader who had never held government office. Among Kinnock's attractions to the Party was that he was a man of the left. He bore no responsibility for the past, having refused office under Callaghan. As recently as 1979 he had described capitalism as 'senile and selfish', and had condemned it as a 'system of economic gambling, commercial whim, speculative profiteering and profligate waste of the earth's resources...'. He had declared that the central socialist purpose was 'to fundamentally transform the structure of power and system of ownership in Britain...'. His eloquence had been littered with references to Aneurin Bevan, and had conjured up once more the commanding heights of the economy.[1] High and rising unemployment under Mrs Thatcher had confirmed him in these fundamentalist views.

But by the time of his election as leader he had become a softer and more flexible left-winger. He had made his first breach with the far left in 1981 when he refused to support Benn in the deputy leadership election. That he was a man of discriminating taste was demonstrated by his vote in that election for John Silkin on the first ballot, effectively an abstention. He then abstained in the final ballot between Benn and Healey. Presumably he thought it preferable that Labour should have no deputy leader than either of these candidates, or that it was a choice so unimportant that he did not need to participate. His defence is that, having a strongly Bennite constituency party, he displayed political courage in not voting for Benn. Other MPs voted for Healey despite having strongly Bennite constituency parties. Later he would express regret that he had not voted for Healey.[2] In the House of Commons, in the 1970s, he had shown himself a capable, even eloquent speaker, best evidenced by his determined opposition to Welsh devolution, a subject which he understood and about which he held strong views. But, lacking Bevan's intellect and imagination, his Welsh oratory could degenerate into verbosity. A wide range of critics, stretching from Benn on the left to many on the right, found his oratory empty of content. Unlike Bevan, he could not dominate the House of Commons, where it is often easier to get away with nonsense than with emptiness. As leader he was often disappointing in the House, a major example being in the debate on the Westland helicopter controversy in January 1986, when two Cabinet Ministers had resigned and when he had been found incapable of mobilizing the case against the prime target of his censure, Mrs Thatcher. Kinnock had to preside over a Parliamentary committee dominated by members of the previous Labour government. He had leapt over their heads. He appeared to deserve it neither by service nor by intellect. It was not surprising that the loyalty Kinnock expected from his senior colleagues was not always freely given. In this respect Blair would have things much easier. He presided over a Parliamentary committee as inexperienced as himself yet even more desperate for office.

Despite Kinnock's inadequacies, the Labour party was, perhaps unwittingly, shrewd to reject the other plausible prospect, Roy Hattersley. With the departure of the Gang of Four to the SDP, Hattersley emerged as the candidate of the right wing. As a recently elevated member of the Cabinet, Hattersley, during the IMF crisis of the autumn of 1976, had supported Crosland against Healey. During those Cabinet debates, he had been Crosland's most loyal confidant, never abandoning him even when other right-wing support fell away. His support was, perhaps, compensation for the fact that he had voted not for Crosland but for Callaghan during the leadership election earlier that year. In ideology, he was a follower of Crosland. He believed socialism was about equality. Crosland, shortly before his death, had awarded Hattersley the ultimate accolade in his idiosyncratic portfolio of honours. Hattersley was, said Crosland, 'a genuine egalitarian'.[3] Later, after Crosland's death, Hattersley was to admit that Healey had been right after all at the time of the IMF crisis. Later still, he refused to defect with his erstwhile friends to the SDP. His loyalty to the Party was too great, though he assured his constituency that he remained a 'European' and an opponent of unilateral nuclear disarmament.

It may be that it was because of his history that Hattersley's candidature was not greeted with enthusiasm, though his peregrinations were not more egocentric than those of other party leaders. Or it may be that, with unusual foresight, the Party perceived that Hattersley did not have the qualities required to lead his troops to victory. Labour needed to change, and to change far beyond Crosland. A man so insistent on the doctrines of Crosland would find it difficult to change. Crosland, in his lifetime, had demonstrated that doctrinal right-wingers find it very difficult to transform themselves into pragmatists. Many coming from the further left are more flexible. As a socialist in the Crosland tradition, Hattersley could be expected to be less ideologically malleable than Kinnock, who was demonstrating his own flexibility by moving from the extreme left to the centre-left at a velocity carefully calculated in accordance with the exigencies of the moment. And as, among the changes, had to be a transformation in the Party's economic approach, it was a drawback that Hattersley knew little of economics, and yet had strong Keynesian views on economic policy. The Labour party now needed in its leader a malleability beyond Hattersley's intellectual or moral capacity. At best it needed malleability combined with principle, a combination rather difficult to find. But, if it could not find the combination, it would have to be content with malleability. Kinnock was clearly ideal. Meanwhile Hattersley made his contribution to what was described as a dream ticket by accepting the deputy's position under Kinnock. It was a dream ticket because, supposedly, it balanced Kinnock, man of the left, with Hattersley, man of the right. The dream underestimated Kinnock's volatility. The day would come when Hattersley, who had been docketed as on the right under Wilson, Callaghan and Foot, would find himself assigned to the left under Blair. Truly, he insisted, it was not he that had changed.

At first Kinnock was a disappointment. Once leader, he trod with excessive delicacy, avoiding uproar and upset among Labour's numerous ideological clans. It is debatable how far he initiated the revisionist

developments in Labour party policy and how far he followed the growing sentiment in the Party that, between 1979 and 1983, Labour had
gone mad and now must return to sanity if ever it was to be re-elected.
Kinnock himself was later to write,

> In the years between our defeat in 1979 and our defeat in 1983 Labour
> was increasingly seen to be a party slipping towards impossibilism, suc-
> cumbing to fads, riven by vicious divisions, speaking the language of
> sloganised dogma – usually voicing it in the accents of menace. It was
> almost as if sections of the party measured the purity of their socialism
> by the distance which they could put between it and the minds of the
> British people.[4]

This summary of the period 1979–83 is accurate even though, understandably, it does not dwell on Kinnock's own contribution to the vicious
divisions of 1979–83. There was a time, not so far distant, when Kinnock
himself would have preferred the purity of his socialism to any compromise with the minds of the British people. Now that he had perceived
his own earlier unwisdom, he had to prepare to discard policies which
he himself had long advocated. Party leaders are denied the right cherished by other citizens to change their minds in private. As it has to be
in public, there is a calculation to be made whether apostasy is better
committed at a stroke or in measured steps. Kinnock chose a measured
apostasy. After all, the hard left, though weakened by the overwhelming
election defeat in 1983, was still entrenched in the Party's institutions.
So, if he tried to reverse too much too soon, he would face tough
opposition embittered by his own apostasy. And it would seem insincere
if the Party suddenly denounced the policies it had itself advocated up
to 1983. As Harold Wilson, not the most notable exemplar of political
consistency, had said after the 1959 election defeat when many alter-
ations to the Party's policies and organization were in the air, 'I would
not be able to feel – and I am sure the electorate would not be able to
feel – any confidence in a party which decides a few days after an
election, or indeed at any other time, that policies it had believed to be
right and appropriate should be thrown over because they were thought
to be electorally unpopular.'[5]

The Party had expended so much credit in the early 1980s that its
rehabilitation could, at best, be accomplished slowly. Kinnock has
excused his own sloth in beginning the process of reform by referring to
the very strong forces and institutions against him, and to the year-long
miners' strike. '[W]ithin five months [of my election] the emotions and
politics of the Labour Movement were totally absorbed, not to say

obsessively distracted, by the beginning of the year-long Miners' Strike.'[6] Scargill was plucking Labour heartstrings. The miners have always touched the emotions of the Labour Movement. Kinnock's attitude to the miners' strike had much in common with Gaitskell's to the London bus strike of 1958. Gaitskell had found it necessary to support the London busmen. Now Kinnock found it impossible to dissociate Labour from the strike, let alone to denounce the miners' leader, Arthur Scargill. Such perfidy was beyond him, even in the circumstances of 1984 when the NUM's own constitutional arrangements were being violated by calling a strike without a national ballot, when the strike was splitting the NUM and certainly appeared to be an attack on constitutional government. It was not a good start for a leader whose design was to make the Labour party electable. It displayed the links between Labour and the trade unions at their worst. It confirmed all the fears stirred in the electorate by the rejection of *In Place of Strife*, by the great inflation of the 1970s and by the winter of discontent.

At its 1984 Congress, the TUC gave its formal blessing, but the strike had little support in the trade union movement generally. Scargill demanded a guarantee that no coal mine should be closed simply because it was uneconomic. He did not understand that the world had changed and that his own leadership of the NUM was squandering the normal sympathies of the public for the miners. But Kinnock should have known how the world, and the attitudes of the public, had altered. Once more the Labour Movement seemed to believe that the coal industry could be isolated from the forces of international competition and that it was reasonable for British industry, which Labour said it wished to strengthen, to pay more for energy in order to protect the mining industry. The miners eventually returned to work on 5 March 1985 without any agreement with the NCB, but by that time the strike was crumbling and many miners had already drifted back. This final defeat of the NUM was due not so much to legislation, or even to loss of public sympathy, as to international trade, and to the availability on the market of alternative and cheaper sources of fuel. Never again would the NUM bring down a government. It had exhausted, even within the Labour party, much of the sympathy that in the past had given its product preference. Later Kinnock would express regret that he had not said clearly and publicly that there should have been a ballot before the strike.[7]

Thus a combination of considerations dictated Kinnock's measured approach to apostasy. The regrettable need for Kinnock to unwind himself slowly exasperated some young members of the PLP, who felt even less commitment to socialism. But it became ever clearer to Kinnock that apostasy it must be if he was ever to occupy the tied cottage at No. 10 Downing Street. Leaders of parties have a particular incentive to change policy when they see it necessary to win an election. If they do not win, the doors of No. 10 will open to them only as guests of other Prime Ministers. There is nothing necessarily discreditable about a political party's desire to win power. Democracy requires the possibility of alternative government. Those who had earlier been at the receiving end of Kinnock's left-wing eloquence might regard his transformation with a wry humour, but they would understand the imperatives of the moment and try to avoid bearing a grudge. Yet a whole Parliament was wasted before there was a serious attempt at reform. While accepting continued British membership of NATO, the Party was demanding the removal of American nuclear weapons from British soil. It took Kinnock too long to disconnect himself from his commitments to nationalization and unilateral nuclear disarmament.

As late as the 1986 Party Conference, Kinnock underlined the Party's commitment to unilateral nuclear disarmament by his histrionic declaration: 'I would fight and die for my country, but I tell you I would not let my country die for me.'[8] He then faced the problem of how to resile from this thoughtless soundbite. It was a problem exacerbated by the influence of trade union leaders, particularly Ron Todd, General Secretary of the TGWU, who were content, without much by way of consultation with their members, to leave Labour unelectable in pursuit of their personal political obsessions. It was not until three years later that Kinnock finally decided that he must accept Britain's nuclear armament and therefore, presumably, the possibility that his country might die for him. In May 1989 he told the NEC that, on visiting Washington, Moscow and Paris, he had found political leaders uncomprehending as to why a British political party should wish to give up its nuclear weapons without obtaining anything in return. In future, he too would insist on getting something in return.[9] If this was to be the reason for dumping the unilateralist case, it was a thought that might have occurred before. Indeed he could have secured the same advice from the same sources at any time over the previous six years had he found it politically convenient. The collapse of the Soviet Union brought one important benefit to the electoral prospects of the Labour party. The Labour Party Conference, in 1990, against the advice of the leadership, was demanding heavy cuts in defence expenditure. With the end of the cold war, doubts about Labour's commitment to the defence of the UK would be less

495

of a distraction from any positive domestic elements in a Labour election programme.

The high point in Kinnock's early period of leadership was his denunciation of Liverpool councillors associated with the *Militant* newspaper at the 1985 Party Conference. The councillors had announced that they would be making Liverpool council employees redundant as, having been rate-capped, they did not have the money to pay them. They hired taxis to take individual redundancy notices to each employee's home. This gave Kinnock an opportunity to dissociate himself and the Labour party from a far-left trend not merely lacking any electoral appeal but positively repugnant to the great majority of Labour voters.

> You start with far fetched resolutions. They are then pickled into rigid dogma, a code, and you go through years sticking to that, outdated, misplaced, irrelevant to the real needs, and you end in the grotesque chaos of a Labour council – a *Labour* council – hiring taxis to scuttle around a city handing out redundancy notices to its own workers. I'm telling you, no matter how entertaining, how fulfilling to short term egos, you can't play politics with people's jobs and with people's services or with people's lives.[10]

This has been accounted a speech of great courage. Rather it shows how far the Labour party had departed from reality that it should be thought to have required great courage to make such a speech. There was no choice unless the Labour party was to make itself finally unelectable by condoning what its members were doing in Liverpool. Denis Healey was quoted as saying that Kinnock, by this speech, 'had shifted the centre of gravity not just of the Labour Party but of the Labour movement as a whole, decisively'.[11] No doubt the speech was a great relief to the great mass of the Party. But the centre of gravity would not be shifted far towards centre ground, or even left of centre ground, by an attack on the extremist fringe of Militant councillors or even by their expulsion, which, in many cases, then followed.

One of the problems of the apostate is how to treat one's former friends. Kinnock extended no indulgence to those less wise or less pliable than himself. He was ditching socialism. Yet he continued to talk and write as though he was still a socialist. That was necessary to ensure the unity of the Party, which still believed itself to be a socialist party. But Kinnock's socialism, such as it still was, had been made subservient to electoral convenience. Socialism, by its very nature, cannot be subservient to electoral convenience. A democratic socialist party must wait until it has persuaded the electorate, even if that takes many a long and tedious year. It was embarrassing, and a nuisance to any leader of the Labour party, that there should be noisy elements within it which were refusing to relinquish socialism. It was obvious that continued adherence to socialism put a distance between anyone so attached and the British electorate. That was why any Labour politician who wanted to be elected to government wanted to put a distance between himself and socialism. But it was unkind for Kinnock to blame old comrades who were less malleable than himself, or who regarded electoral victory as empty if it was simply the victory of the Labour party and not also the victory of socialism. At least he shared out his contempt equally between left and right. He despised those that he, in an earlier but quite recent phase of his gathering political maturity, had helped to drive out of the Party. His disdain for the Social Democrats seemed to increase the more he approximated to their views. In his 1986 book *Making our Way*, he tried to present himself as a thinker, but he was not in the Crosland class. The best he could do was pick eclectically among the revisionist refuse while denying that he had succumbed to the temptations of social democracy.

Right-wing leaders of the Labour party have frequently attempted to move the hearts of the left with a plea which they consider to be invested with high persuasive force. It is that the left should not pursue its divisiveness too far because division would prevent the election of a Labour government and hence deprive of the benefits of a Labour victory all those who were yearning for it. The implication has been that its dissidents must compromise in a greater cause, so that Labour could return to office and help the disadvantaged. Evidently socialists were being selfish in sticking to their socialism, thereby inhibiting a Labour victory and thereby causing untold harm to millions awaiting salvation. The beneficiaries of a Labour victory were to be found world-wide and not just in the UK. Thus, before the 1959 election, Callaghan, then shadow Colonial Secretary, pleaded with Frank Cousins not to allow the debates on unilateralism to prevent the election of a Labour government for which the people of black Africa were said to be craving.[12] At the Labour Party Conference just after the 1959 election, Denis Healey asked 'who are the people who suffer if we lose elections. In Britain it is the unemployed and old-age pensioners; and outside Britain there are thousands and millions of people in Asia and Africa who desperately need a Labour Government in this country to help them.'[13] This plea has echoed through the decades of Labour in opposition. It was an approach that Kinnock adopted with mounting frustration towards those who persisted in demanding socialist policies when, in Britain, the poor, the sick, the old and the unemployed were, supposedly, waiting for the Labour victory that would relieve their sufferings. It was a plea that possessed less persuasive power than exasperated Labour leaders imagined. Much of the left saw no particular reason for rewarding its leaders with office if they were no longer socialists. It was socialism, not the renunciation of socialism, that would make it possible to assuage the sufferings of the poor. If the object was simply office, they should have found some other party to lead, not a professedly socialist party. There was no clarity that Labour, even when it did succeed in getting itself elected, would actually know what it should do to satisfy the demands of the expectant millions in Britain, let alone around the world. Evidence from recent Labour governments did not suggest it.

GLOBALIZATION

When, after four years of internal turmoil, Labour, under Neil Kinnock, turned its attention to ascertaining what was going on in the world outside, it found that much had changed. The discovery presented Labour with grave political and philosophical difficulties. There had been many intimations of change during the Wilson–Callaghan government of the 1970s. But the failures of that government had been attributed to lack of socialist purpose and to a most distressing willingness to submit to the dictates of the IMF and other funders of Britain's persistent current account deficits. It had not therefore been noticed, in the ranks of the Labour party, that the world had become less tolerant of the exigencies of lagging economies such as that of Britain. There was no young Crosland ready and able to write another *Future of Socialism* and to provide a redefinition of socialism appropriate to the 1980s. There were no great thinkers left in the socialist camp, even thinkers of the stature of Durbin and Crosland. Of course, Durbin and Crosland had had it easy. When Durbin was writing, socialism was the wave of the future. Even though, by the time Crosland was putting pen to paper, socialism had lost its varnish and was looking rather tattered, there could still be a market for a new definition. Now the philosophical challenges were far greater. It was no longer sensible to think of Britain as an island isolated from global economic forces and fashioning its own destiny independent of them. The philosophical debate took Labour in a variety of directions. Some put a toe back in the waters of Marxism, but it was too discredited by the excesses of the Soviet Union, and then by the collapse of the Soviet Union, not to mention its own failed prophecies, to command much support.

In 1984, Roy Hattersley, Kinnock's deputy, told what he describes as 'a sceptical Labour Conference' that arguments about exchange control were futile since, whatever its theoretical merits, 'exchange control could not be enforced in a global economy.' Thus he was, by his own standards, contributing to the process of modernizing the Labour party.[14] This was five years after exchange control had been abolished. Labour was catching up, making its accustomed painful and dilatory adjustment to changing circumstances. Its accommodation to the market economy would be equally slow and equally painful. Hattersley's courage at the 1984 Conference shows that at least some Labour leaders were now standing out against the entrenched prejudices of their own Party. Its instincts had always been protectionist. It was beginning to realize that the UK was part of the world and that, even under a Labour government, it could not get off. The question that remained was how its residual socialism could be made consistent with the global economy about which Hattersley, belatedly, had been preaching to the still unconverted.

Mrs Thatcher informed the world that there was no alternative to the economic policies of her government. She may well have been right that there was no alternative to privatization, to strict control of public expenditure and borrowing or to the free market. Or if there were alternatives they were bad alternatives. It was proudly claimed on Mrs Thatcher's behalf that her wisdom was being endorsed by the governments of many other countries that were following a Thatcherite path. The examples included socialist governments in Australia and New Zealand. Moreover socialist governments in France and Spain, though part of the social market tradition, were taking steps in a similar direction. Something of the same kind appeared to be happening in Sweden, long the model of social democracy most admired in the British Labour party. It was observed also that many less developed countries were adopting market-oriented policies having discovered that neither socialism nor foreign aid had in any way relieved the poverty of their citizens. Throughout the world, another phenomenon was becoming apparent. When left-wing governments replaced governments that had followed market-oriented policies, the left-wing government had said, yes, we will have more regard for social justice but we will not change the market-oriented policies.

None of these countries was following Mrs Thatcher. They had merely discovered, as she had done, that there was no good alternative. There had been a big bang in international economic relations with vast and abrupt capital flows, enabled by technological developments, far exceeding trade flows. The capital flows could not be stopped. They could be exceedingly destabilizing. Governments found themselves at the mercy of events they could not control. The only defence was to be found in confidence-building measures such as fiscal and monetary conservatism, and even that might not always be enough. The trend towards fiscal and monetary conservatism was reinforced in Europe when, as part of the Maastricht Treaty of 1992, qualification for monetary union in the European Community required strict discipline on borrowing as well as convergence on inflation at a low level. There had been a coincidence of judgement on what economic policies were suitable in a global economy characterized by these enormous capital flows as well as by increasingly free trade. With all the hesitations and delays of a party still clinging to its socialist past, Labour in Britain was about to commence the task of bringing its thinking into line with a global environment which it did not like but with which it would be forced to live should it ever again find itself in government. Yet a global market is not, by its nature, a caring market and Labour still wanted to be a caring party.

ACCEPTING THATCHERISM

The Labour party was unlikely at first to submit to the lure of Thatcherism. It could hardly go wrong in criticizing a government under which unemployment had reached three million. It thought Thatcherism special to Britain, and to a particularly unsympathetic Conservative leader. It did not notice that comparable policies were being followed elsewhere even by supposedly socialist governments. Then, at a stately march, it came to terms with Thatcherism, hoping to add a human face though unclear how. Once Labour began to think outside the narrow boundaries of its sectarian preoccupations, it was compelled to re-evaluate its gut reactions to what it had accounted Thatcherite atrocities. Democratic socialism lacked attraction. It had fallen into disrepute owing to the failures of nationalization, the record of Labour governments and the excesses of the 1980s. Labour was forced to consider which of its traditional commitments it should retain and which could be interred as the detritus of history. As it went through the list, more and more of the traditional commitments were buried. Commitments that survived the first round of reappraisal would fall at the second. The Labour party was passing through a distressing experience, watching its traditional policies being hollowed out in a manner rather more ruthless and far-reaching even than under previous Labour governments. Every step taken made the felonies of past Labour governments appear as less like betrayal, more as a hesitant and insufficient accommodation to irresistible pressures. In the end, almost nothing of traditional policies that could be reasonably called socialist was left except for full employment. Full employment could remain because as Bryan Gould, Labour's Campaign Co-ordinator in the 1987 election, put it, and as Crosland had believed before him, 'There is no particular difficulty in bringing it about.'[15] In the end, even that conviction would have to be renounced.

Municipal housing

In the 1970s there was much evidence of a desire by many council tenants to buy the house which they were occupying. Bernard Donoughue, head of the No. 10 Downing Street Policy Unit under Wilson and Callaghan, recommended a policy which would have gone some way to satisfying this desire. He records that it was strongly supported by Harold Wilson until his resignation in April 1976 but that the reactions of Anthony Crosland, Secretary of State for the Environment, though not of his officials, were 'particularly disappointing'. This negative Ministerial reaction to the Policy Unit's ideas was repeated when Peter Shore took over as Secretary of State for the Environment. The Labour party showed too great a loyalty to Bevan's fixation on municipal housing. Many members of the PLP had been local councillors and were proud of their own record in building and managing subsidized municipal housing. The left of the Labour party was bitterly hostile to council house sales and there was not much enthusiasm anywhere in the Party. Sales would reduce the public stock which it was Labour's purpose to increase. They would also reduce possibilities of patronage. It had been noticed that people who owned their own houses were more likely to vote Conservative. Donoughue legitimately comments that the Labour government was 'trapped in . . . out-dated prejudices'.[16] A popular issue was thus handed to the Conservative party, which, on the election of Mrs Thatcher in 1979, decided to allow tenants of municipal houses to buy them at a discount to their market value. It took too much time before Labour would accept the sale of council houses, and more private building. Kinnock himself comments that the policy of refusing to allow council tenants to buy their houses was 'perverse'. The perversity was not officially recanted until May 1985.[17] But, as usual in such matters, it took a long time before many in the public realized that there had been an adjustment in Labour policy. Philip Gould, an adviser to the Labour party, believes that Labour's reputation as being opposed to the sale of municipal housing to tenants was still affecting it adversely as late as the 1987 and 1992 elections.[18]

Privatization

Nothing could be more offensive to the deepest instinct of the Labour party than privatization, unless it should be trade union reform. Privatization, which was becoming a major theme of the Thatcher government, was contrary to every instinct of a party brought up on an equivalence between socialism and nationalization, which now saw that even the nationalizations of the Attlee government were being reversed. Helplessly, it watched socialism, such as it was, being dismantled before its eyes. The 'mixed economy', always vaguely defined but lately cherished by socialists of all brands because it was the best they could ever hope to achieve, no longer existed. There was nothing now that seemed irreversible. Labour's first reaction was that privatized industries would be renationalized under a future Labour government. Ancient prejudices provided the basis of opposition. Threats were made against investors who were so bold as to buy shares in a privatized industry. Renationalization might even take place without compensation. To make matters worse, the industries were being privatized too cheaply. Somewhat inconsistently, it was also argued that the industries were being privatized more with an eye to the needs of the Exchequer than to the consumer's need for greater competition. After further thought, the most worrying threats were withdrawn. There would certainly be renationalization but, equally certainly, *with* compensation.

For Labour the embarrassment was that privatization did not seem to evoke more than minimal protest from the electorate. The population at large seemed quite happy to be deprived, uncompensated, of their nominal ownership of these industries. The absence of protest appeared to suggest that the population did not consider that it had been well served by the nationalized industries. Under privatization, service might improve. It was less likely to get worse. If Labour was to stand against these sentiments it would be adding a further millstone to the number it already carried. Privatization had won numerous adherents whose loyalty was encouraged by the possession of shares. Some workers, either covetous or classless, were prepared to acquire a few shares in the well-founded hope that, having been sold cheap, they would appreciate in value. The record was sullied by some failures and particularly by the greed of many of the directors released from the constraints of the public sector. But there were few in the electorate for whom the failures or the greed provided sufficient rationale to propose renationalization. There was no longer the energy in the body politic to reverse privatization. Political parties just could not go on treating great industries as political pawns, nationalizing and privatizing as governments changed. Ironically, the only nationalization measure dating from Attlee that seemed sacrosanct to Thatcher was the nationalization of the Bank of England.

Labour's policy of nationalization could not, of course, be scrapped at a stroke. There had to be a carefully designed path consistent with the unity of the Labour party. The first step was to denounce Morrisonian nationalization. That had, in any case, been unpopular within the Labour party for decades. The next step was to revive ideas from the 1940s and 1950s such as co-operative ownership, ownership by regional public bodies, and competitive public ownership. As late as 1989, *Meet the Challenge, Make the Change*, the Labour statement announcing the outcome of the policy review initiated after the 1987 defeat, demonstrated that Labour still had its eye on the utilities that had been privatized. Bryan Gould was recommending that a Labour government should regain control by means of majority holdings and by extinguishing, possibly with compensation, the voting rights of privately held shares.[19] None of this seemed any more persuasive in the 1980s than it had in the 1950s. What was it all for, other than to salve the consciences of discredited socialists? The final position was to accept privatization as a *fait accompli* while not ruling out the possibility of further public ownership in remote circumstances which could not be precisely defined in advance. This concession to realism was not too difficult except for the far left. Labour, disembarrassed of the millstone of nationalization, might even be more electable. Mrs Thatcher was being helpful to Labour's electoral prospects. In his 1998 Fabian pamphlet on *The Third Way*, Blair conceded that 'Some of the [Thatcher government's] reforms were, in retrospect, necessary acts of modernisation, particularly the exposure of much of the state industrial sector to reform and competition.'[20] This reads like a curiously worded endorsement of privatization. But the endorsement is given 'in retrospect'. Once more Labour, imprisoned by ideology, had clung to the past longer than was wise.

The trade unions

The reform of trade union law, however reasonable in itself given the disruption to which society had been subjected in the past, could hardly be acceptable to a party that was so dependent on the trade unions and had failed in the task itself, abandoning its only attempt. Nevertheless the Labour party's bitter opposition to the Thatcher laws was due not just to its dependence on trade union votes and trade union money but to a hidebound frame of mind which limited its capacity for fresh thought. Once more the Labour party was showing itself to be the party of a vested interest incapable of taking a national view until forced by public opinion. This is not to say that there were not many in the Labour party who had long been disillusioned with the trade unions, which were thought to have let Labour down. Beginning with the end of the 1948–50 wage freeze, there was increasing discontent with the irresponsibility, as it was thought, of the unions and its effect on British economic performance. Ideas sprouted, derived frequently from foreign examples. The trade union movement should be restructured on the basis of industrial unionism as in Germany. The TUC should be given greater power to enforce change. But Donovan and *In Place of Strife* killed any urge to reform. The vested interests of the trade unions had always been resistant to change and what change had taken place had been largely the result of union mergers. Dissatisfaction with the inability of the unions to reform themselves led, eventually, to Heath's Industrial Relations Act. That failed due to trade union resistance and to Heath's desire for an incomes policy in co-operation with the very trade unions that he had alienated. Thus the first thirty years after the war were wasted in the preparation of misguided recommendations from a variety of experienced sources and by ineffective legislation. While whingeing about the trade unions, governments were not prepared to take the action which was actually within their power, that is to give price stability priority over full employment. Nor did those commentators whose criticism of the trade unions assumed full employment recommend a change in priorities. Tentatively in Healey's budget of 1975, and then more dramatically in Howe's budget of 1981, that priority was given. In dealing with the 'trade union question' this was far more effective than the legislation of the Thatcher epoch, justified though that legislation was, as Labour eventually came to accept.

The distancing of Labour from the trade unions, a slow process still far from complete, had to move *pari passu* with realization in the trade union movement that a promise to restore the old immunities under the law, of which the Thatcher legislation had deprived them, could make their political party unelectable. The first Labour reaction to the trade union legislation of the Thatcher era was that it would be reversed. Trade union rights to consultation and representation would be extended, though balloting before strikes would normally still be required.[21] Later the reform laws were to be amended to eliminate the most opprobrious elements. In 1989, Bryan Gould brought forward socialist principle as justification for going at least part of the way with Mrs Thatcher. 'It was clearly a serious political mistake, and a denial of socialist principle, to allow others to espouse the cause of democratising the trade unions.'[22] It was true but, as usual, rather late. Once more a divergence had emerged between socialist principle as understood by some leading members of the Labour party and by the trade unions. The Labour party was changing but at its usual deliberate pace. Finally came virtually total acceptance by Labour of the Thatcher legislation.

The Thatcher legislation brought a not unimportant gain to the trade unions as well as to the Labour party. It was a long time since the trade unions had been popular. The Tories could always revive memories of the winter of discontent. But the unions which, for so long, had exhibited nothing but contempt for public opinion now felt able to appeal to its sense of fair play. Trade unions regained popularity as their membership dwindled and their power diminished. There were even those who began to think the unions were hard done by. When, in 1992, there were threats of closure of more of the dwindling number of mines in the UK, there was cross-party opposition supported by a large demonstration in London. Scargill became, temporarily, a popular hero, though the outburst of opposition delayed rather than prevented the closures. The Tory attacks on trade unions began to attract widespread scepticism. This was a trend in popular sentiment which Labour did not want to reverse. It seemed that the Tories would threaten the unions with additional burdensome legislation whenever, in desperation, they wanted to recapture lost popularity. They did not notice that popular hostility to unions was no longer there to be milked. Once Labour had relinquished any thought of more than limited amendment of the

Thatcherite legislation, it could breathe another sigh of relief. Another millstone, the unpopularity of its union brothers, was no longer hanging round the party's neck. Mrs Thatcher, once again, seemed intent on making life easier for Labour. It also helped that, under Kinnock, the size of the block vote at party conferences was reduced to 70 per cent and the unions' weight in the local electoral colleges which selected Parliamentary candidates was reduced to 40 per cent.[23]

Accepting capitalism

The final apostasy, and the final capitulation to Thatcherism, was the acceptance of capitalism. That which Crosland had sent to a nameless grave, Kinnock resurrected. In his 1986 book *Making our Way*, Kinnock was still declaring himself in favour of 'the control of the forces of production, distribution and exchange and communication by . . . society through a variety of democratic means'.[24] The words echoed Aneurin Bevan's *In Place of Fear*. Indeed they echoed Clause Four of the Labour party constitution. But it was a dying echo.

After Labour's defeat in the 1987 General Election, Kinnock decided that the time was not ripe to persuade the Party to rewrite Clause Four. In 1988 he easily defeated a challenge from Tony Benn for the leadership of the Labour party. But he still seemed to fear that there was strong support in the Party for the principle of Clause Four socialism, and that a direct assault on the sacred text would be divisive. The tone and policy of the Party could, Kinnock thought, be changed without treading recklessly on too many ideological toes. Like Gaitskell when he had lost the battle over Clause Four, he decided instead to draft his own statement of aims with the help of Hattersley. When Kinnock and Hattersley presented a *Statement of Aims and Views* to the shadow Cabinet, it was criticized by John Smith, Bryan Gould and Robin Cook as being too enthusiastic about the market as a means of distributing most goods.[25] Bryan Gould, of the moderate left, was still describing Clause Four as 'the best and most widely accepted definition of Labour's aims'.[26] However, at the 1988 Party Conference, Kinnock insisted that 'the fact is that the kind of economy that we will be faced with when we win the election will be a market economy. That is what we will have to deal with and we will have to make it work better than the Tories do.'[27] Thus, by 1988, the stage had been reached in which a socialist blessing could be given to the market. It was to be a market economy with a difference, a market economy in a social context. It must be a market system from which the masses benefited, not just the few. Naturally the market was not perfect. It had to be regulated and supervised. Moreover there were services such as education and health which must remain outside the market. Above all, Labour must not show an excess of enthusiasm for the market. Nevertheless, at long last, a Labour leader had proclaimed publicly that democratic socialism consisted of making the market work better than could the Tories, not actually a demanding requirement but one that Labour had not previously achieved. The message did not penetrate very deep below the tranquil surface of traditional party philosophy. The 1988 *Statement of Aims and Views* suffered the same fate as Gaitskell's attempt at authorship thirty years before. Though approved at Conference, it then disappeared without trace. There was nothing in it that would give it a shelf life of even a few years. The electorate seemed to want rather stronger evidence of a real transformation in Labour than a statement of the meandering thoughts of a passing leader.

At the 1989 Party Conference, Kinnock declared 'that while the market is an adequate system for deciding the price and availability of many goods and services, the market has not been, and never will be, an adequate mechanism for deciding upon the supply or the quality of health care and education and so much that is fundamental to a decent life'.[28] Kinnock's use of the word 'never' in relation to the ability of the market adequately to supply health care and education was, perhaps, dangerous in a politician who had come so far in so short a time. But it was, no doubt, comforting to Labour party members who wanted to believe that there were some things that capitalism could not do adequately. Why else should they be socialists? Yet many capitalists would have agreed that the market needed supervision and regulation and that there were services which would be better provided by the state.

The 1989 Party Conference passed *Meet the Challenge, Make the Change*. After a two-year Policy Review, the Party abandoned nationalization, high taxation and nuclear unilateralism.[29] The journalist Peter Kellner commented that the Policy Review represented the 'wholesale abandonment of what we used to call socialism, when the word was synonymous with state ownership of industry'.[30] Socialism had departed, though the Labour party had no great new idea of its own to put in its place. Socialists used to say that it was not their job to manage capitalism better but to change the economic and social system. But, by the time of Crosland's revisionism, socialists of his kind were incorporating capitalism into the socialist project. They were claiming that they could run capitalism better. The management of capitalism was becoming a department of the socialist project, even though Crosland refused to call it capitalism. By 1992 Kinnock had joined the ranks of the capitalist socialists. There did, however, survive in Kinnock a belief that Labour had secrets of economic management unknown to the Tories and that the Conservative party remained a conspiracy against the multitude. In other words, while cleansing himself of socialism, Kinnock retained a class approach to politics. The truths of economics evidently lay somewhere hidden among the workers, and were available only to Labour, while the Tories were predestined by their class origins to be irredeemably monetarist and evil.

The acceptance of capitalism was as significant as the disappearance of socialism. The acceptance of capitalism had to be made consistent with a declaration of continuing loyalty to democratic socialist values. The best that could be done was to emphasize the enduring relevance of democratic socialist 'values'. Values are less controversial than policies. Values can be shared whereas policies divide. The word 'capitalism' was still not used with approval. The word favoured was not capitalism but 'market'. *Meet the Challenge, Make the Change* was still Keynesian in tone, but that aspect was already coming under challenge from the shadow Chancellor, John Smith, who, supported by Kinnock, wished to signify Labour's final break with fiscal irresponsibility by supporting membership of the Exchange Rate Mechanism of the European Monetary System. Among other matters, that implied that Labour would attempt to free itself of the accusation of being a party which taxed and spent beyond the capacity of the economy to bear. In other words, not merely would it shed the socialism of Aneurin Bevan. It would also shed the socialism of Anthony Crosland. In moving beyond Crosland, Kinnock was thereby starting a process which would leave Hattersley far behind.

To the outside observer, the most striking revelation was of Kinnock's ability to make declarations on economic policy as though he was giving voice to original ideas. He had made the astonishing discovery that, for some purposes, the market worked quite well. But the discovery had been made only as a result of the intensive study that had been conducted through the Labour party's Policy Review after the 1987 election. A great deal of time might have been saved if he had read a few elementary textbooks which had been in print for many years. But then the tasks of political leadership are sometimes comparable to those of the one-eyed man in the kingdom of the blind.

Suddenly Labour began to perceive the advantages of Europe. Kinnock, evidently, was privately of the view that the commitment in the 1983 election manifesto to withdraw from the European Community was absurd and would never be implemented.[31] No doubt, later, he regretted not having made this view public at the time. There had always been, within the Labour party, Europeans like Roy Hattersley and John Smith who had not abandoned their convictions at the behest of Tony Benn and his cohorts. They had told their own constituents at the 1983 election that they did not agree with the policy of taking Britain out of the European Community. But, by their candidacies, they were trying to achieve for Labour a victory in an election when the effect, if promises were not broken, would have been withdrawal. They were fortunate never to be faced with the dilemma of what they would do if Labour had won. Now they enjoyed the pleasure and relief of discovering that the Party was changing in their direction. The European Community could not be wholly bad if Mrs Thatcher despised it so much. Some in the Labour party were discovering global market forces, so-called globalization, and were turning it to advantage in their European advocacy. They were alarmed that the control exercised by governments of single nations over the forces of the market was evaporating. If governments could not regulate the international economic environment, if their efforts significantly to influence relative economic performance had failed, if their power to tax was limited by the refusal of electorates and by the readiness of those with capital and skills to go elsewhere, if their capacity to borrow was constrained by market scepticism, the outlook for caring policies of the kind envisaged by socialists was meagre. For some the answer seemed to lie in Europe. What one nation could not do alone, a club of nations might do together. The great issue for defenders of the post-war inheritance of the social market is how to defend the social gains from the assault of global capitalism. Many defences are in place and others are being constructed. David Marquand tells us[32] that the creation of the single currency is motivated in part by a desire to defend Europe's social market model. Evidently that model needs defences, old and new. Whether, despite the size of the European economy, Europe is a reliable refuge for residual socialist values has yet to be established. Market forces lap even against the shores of Europe. Thinking in the Labour party became infused with a new European fantasy. The Keynesian policies that seemed no longer practical on a national scale might still be within the capability of Europe acting together. Europe, which had been condemned as the enemy of planning, was suddenly lauded as the saviour of Keynes. When first advanced, these ideas ignored the deep antipathy in Germany to economic adventurism of this kind. Still, British politicians abroad have never lacked confidence in the power of their advocacy, despite much frustrating experience. The election in Germany in 1998 of a left-of-centre government refreshed hopes for co-ordinated Keynesianism at a time when a Labour government in Britain was displaying some scepticism as to the validity of this ancient wisdom. However, the early resignation of Oskar Lafontaine as German Finance Minister suggested that British scepticism was not an isolated phenomenon.

Labour's move back to Europe was encouraged by the then President of the European Commission, Jacques Delors, who had served under President Mitterrand as Finance Minister in a socialist government. In September 1988, Delors addressed the Trade Union Congress and was given an ecstatic welcome. If Labour could not win an election in Britain, and as defeat followed defeat it began to appear that Labour might never win again, there was comfort for the British trade unions to find in Europe. Even Europe's more conservative leaders, whether Christian Democrat in Germany or Gaullist in France, thought in terms of a social market, not a free market. In continental Europe, Christian Democratic values were preserved. They rejected the uncontrolled impact of market forces on the labour force. Trade unions, according to this theology, were social partners, not enemies of the people. As the years passed, there would be more and more members in the trade unions and the Labour party for whom Europe was the cause, not socialism. Socialism had become for them an empty carcass. Europe was the real challenge to their idealism and even to their internationalism. Some of them found in Europe, and in the 'social market', forms of social solidarity foreign to Britain but intensely attractive. Christian Democracy was becoming a refuge for lapsed socialists. It might not be socialism but it provided for the citizen a warm reassuring embrace absent from Anglo-American individualism. If the trade unions were becoming European, could the Labour party be far behind? A European socialist, if that is what Delors was, found himself being taken seriously in the Labour party. It was not too long before Labour was the European party confronting a government party dominated by Eurosceptics. After doing its best to ignore the question of Europe during the 1987 General Election, the Labour party presented itself as the more European party during the elections in 1989 to the European Parliament. Labour was encouraged by its good showing in those elections, though it had the help of an unusually large vote for the Green party.

There is a tradition in British politics that Europe is always a subject of party controversy. There is another tradition that parties that come into power European leave it Eurosceptic, and, indeed, vice versa. These are not laws. There have been exceptional periods of brief harmony between Britain and the European Union in its various manifestations. But inspection of post-war history will provide much evidence for these traditions. Elsewhere in Europe there is the contrary tradition that, whatever political parties may disagree about, they agree about Europe. While Labour became the European party, caution dictated that it should not become overly enthusiastic for Europe. At a time when the Tories were becoming increasingly hostile to entanglement with Europe, it would not do for Labour, desperate to win an election, to outrage nationalist feeling in the UK, by proposing to throw away all defences against European incursions. There was therefore much emphasis on the 'veto', the preservation of which would remain sacrosanct for any Labour government. In the light of this politically calculated caution, it was reasonable to ask whether, in accordance with this British tradition, Labour, should it manage to win an election, would reverse course. It could not be ruled out. It could even be likely as Labour, having accepted so much else of Thatcherism, had also accepted its flexible labour market philosophy. Labour's commitment to the adoption of the Social Chapter of the Maastricht Treaty, a feeble device designed to protect European workers from the ravages of global market forces, was a residue of the period when John Smith was leader and Delors President of the European Commission. Tony Blair, when his time came, did not seek to revoke the commitment, but he certainly hoped to limit its impact on the UK. Labour's embrace of the continental social market philosophy would be cautious and sceptical.

FOREIGN INFLUENCES

The failure of socialism in France in the early years of President Mitterrand, and the subsequent retreat from it, had been influential in demonstrating that, even in a relatively protected economy, international pressures could disrupt socialist policies backed even with French political will. Dragging his party behind him from the vantage point of the

Elysée Palace, Mitterrand abandoned nationalization and turned instead to the policy of the *franc fort*, with a view eventually to European Economic and Monetary Union. Before the British General Election in 1992 the further discovery had been made that Soviet-style socialism had not worked at all well. Soviet communism took a long time failing. By the late 1980s it was seen to have failed even by its own leaders. They were left with the dilemma whether to intensify their socialist methods or to relinquish them. As there was no answer to the dilemma, they swerved one way and then another. The result was chaos, and their downfall, leaving behind them as successor Boris Yeltsin, whose populism had led them to exclude him from the leadership. The Soviet Union collapsed, and the newly independent countries that had extracted themselves from the former Soviet empire were busy returning to capitalism. The economic challenge from the Soviet Union which Dalton, Bevan and Wilson had feared as Britons, and welcomed as socialists, had turned out to be no challenge after all. Three generations of Soviet citizens had seen their liberty purloined for the sake of socialist achievement, and yet there was no achievement. If the economy of the Tsarist empire had been allowed to develop freely over the seventy years since 1917, the probability was that the people of the empire would have been better off than they had become under Soviet dictatorship. The Soviet collapse made a major impact on the thinking of socialists. Certainly, what had failed was not democratic socialism but Soviet socialism. As a distinction it made no difference to the popular understanding of what had happened. If ever there had been any chance that the British people, or the people of any western European country, might be persuaded to adopt socialism, that chance had now disappeared. Never had a system of government and of thought been more comprehensively disproved. The renunciation of socialism had become the *sine qua non* of the election of nominally socialist parties.

CONCLUSION

Were the changes that took place in Labour policies during the Kinnock era a matter of conviction or of political necessity? The answer matters because there was a fear that, if Labour was elected, it would revert to its socialist origins. It is a question to which, nevertheless, no convincing answer could be given. Only experience would tell. Clearly there were some in the Labour party whose socialist beliefs remained unshaken.

There was a growing number, especially among the leadership, who recognized political necessity but equally recognized that, in a changing world, the political attitudes with which they had started out on life needed also to change. To that extent the conversion could be trusted, even though it proved harder to acquire the trust even than to achieve the conversion.

Gradually during the Kinnock era, Labour was regaining support at the expense mainly of the Alliance and then the Liberal Democrats. The Labour party had taken a long time to perceive that socialism had failed. But it did, in the end, abandon it, with striking benefits to its electoral prospects. By 1989, it was taking the lead, sometimes a substantial lead, in public opinion polls. The fact that, despite its history, it was Labour rather than the Liberal Democrats that was benefiting from the increasing unpopularity and arrogance of the Thatcher government certainly says something about the class structure of the British electorate and the problems of 'breaking the mould' of British politics. But Labour's recovery was a slow process, even after the widespread public outrage caused by the introduction by the Thatcher government of the community charge or poll tax. The credibility lost by Labour in the 1970s and 1980s was proving difficult to recoup and the Kinnock leadership, though successful in moving the Party away from its most unpopular policies, did not seem to carry sufficient conviction with the electorate. His flexibility might win him credit with some part of the electorate, but there was a cost. It did not help that he had so manifestly changed the policies which he had supported when elected leader. Whatever his success at Labour party rallies, his failures in the House of Commons left doubts whether he had the intellectual weight to occupy the position of Prime Minister. He did not appear equipped to hold his own in an assembly of European or world leaders. And there was one blow to his prospects that the Tories could inflict which he could not control. They might change their leader. In November 1990, Mrs Thatcher, by now desperately unpopular, was replaced as Prime Minister by John Major. The Conservatives now had a new, and more conciliatory, leader. The electorate might think that the country had a new government which should be given a chance. It was a savage blow to Kinnock's hopes of residence in No. 10 Downing Street.

The word 'socialism' was not mentioned in Labour's 1992 General Election manifesto.[33] In the election, the Tories under John Major defeated Labour for the fourth successive time, gaining an overall majority of twenty. Despite thirteen years of Tory rule and the growing desire for a change, Kinnock's efforts had been inadequate to win power. Labour had not been able to win even at a time of recession. The electorate had been offered the enticement of a return to public control of the National Electricity Grid and of water supply, the privatization of which was believed to have been unpopular; and, despite its absence from the manifesto, Kinnock had flourished the word 'socialism' in his speeches with an abandon which would have horrified Harold Wilson. To some extent this disappointing outcome may have been due to the concerns raised by the redistributive 'budget' presented by John Smith, as shadow Chancellor. In his 1988 budget Chancellor Nigel Lawson had reduced the highest rate of income tax to 40 per cent. Just before the 1992 election, Smith had proposed a 50p tax rate on incomes over £40,000. The proposal may have reignited fears that Labour was still the Party of tax and spend, that Labour's election promises implied much higher taxes than Smith had threatened. Perhaps, in addition, the electorate distrusted Labour's claim to be able to secure a higher rate of economic growth from which to fund its election promises, which included better pensions and child benefits. When, after his departure from the leadership, Kinnock in an interview was challenged on this point he replied, with the innocence of inexperience, that 'a lot of our programme could be financed from the improved growth record we would have secured'.[34] Though Labour had never yet succeeded in procuring a better growth record than the Tories, it still claimed special insights into the problems of economic growth. But there were clearly other reasons for the continuing rejection, including possibly the leadership of Neil Kinnock, which had never been as compelling among the electorate as it had become within the Labour party and which came under sustained attack from the Tory tabloid press, notably Rupert Murdoch's *Sun* newspaper. For Kinnock the disappointing truth was that, whatever he had achieved in reforming the Labour party, it was not yet enough.

EIGHTEEN

Alternative medicine for the market economy

Crosland's *The Future of Socialism* was notably complacent about the future of the British economy, a complacency which had partly evaporated by the time of his *The Conservative Enemy* in 1962. Thereafter socialist and radical thinkers elaborated plans to improve the performance of the British economy. The Macmillan government had already shown its sensitivity to the problem by establishing the NEDC in 1962. But tripartism was not a new idea, rather a very old idea that had already failed but was to be given the opportunity to fail again. No governments could have been more anxious to improve the performance of the British economy than those of Wilson, Heath and Wilson–Callaghan. Success eluded them and the disappointment led, by the 1980s, to Thatcherism. Socialists came to admire Mrs Thatcher because she appeared to have a philosophy and threatened to implement it without any tincture of compromise. There was to be no suggestion of consensus or consent, the fatal flaws in democratic socialism. Thatcherism had its attraction for socialists because it was, or was presented as being, an idea. Socialists wanted to discover an idea, as well as a leader with comparable political force. Socialists dealt in ideas and it was with envy that they saw an idea so successful, even one that was, in other respects, abhorrent to them. If Thatcherism had caught the ear of the right, it was necessary to find an equivalent theory with which to recapture the ear of the left.

Throughout the 1980s, Labour was hunting for an idea which would have a power comparable to the power it detected in Thatcherism. If experience was to be the guide, the problems of finding one would be immense. Labour had been searching for an idea ever since the Attlee government ran out of steam in 1948. It had scoured the past and found nothing satisfactory. Now it was looking overseas. To the search were recruited think tanks and thinkers. The input always appeared greater than the output. It is not easy to find powerful political ideas. They do not litter the landscape waiting to be picked up either by the scholar in his study or by some adventurous new leader. Mrs Thatcher had been lucky. For her idea she could go back to Adam Smith. That Thatcherism was not the invention of the lady, and was very old, did not inhibit these searchers after the truth from seeking something new with which to match Thatcherism. The attempts to reinvent socialism merely confirmed that, as a practical policy, or as a compelling theory, democratic socialism no longer existed, if it ever had. From their researches, it began to appear that all that was left for the modern age was Thatcherism, modified perhaps by a little more humanity. It has been of no small aid to Blair in remoulding the Labour party that persuasive ideologies alternative to traditional socialism, but still presentable as socialist, have not been forthcoming.

Panitch and Leys put fairly the policy problem facing socialists and indeed all those concerned by the likely effects of global capitalism on civil society. 'Outside the ranks of the market fundamentalists there was a growing unease in face of the growing social costs of "market society", and a dawning realisation that defining a new social order in which the market would be re-subordinated to society, and finding a political route to it, was the new millennium's greatest challenge.'[1] The trouble was that, by the 1990s, the number of people even in the Labour party who considered that this policy dilemma could be solved by socialism, or any variant of it, was rapidly in decline. If Labour was to retain any links with its past it had to find a way of presenting itself as a party that still had something to offer the poor and disadvantaged and had some regard for the principle of equality. It must show that it was still a party that cared and that, in moving to the middle ground which had, in any case, moved to the right, it had not abandoned everything for which it had once stood. The Labour party would have to demonstrate that it could mix policies directed to better economic performance, which by now implied accepting the market to some extent at least, with more regard for humanity than was allowed by a free market.

Much of the literature that flowed from socialist or erstwhile socialist pens in the 1980s and 1990s was concerned with finding something for the state to do. For how could they be socialists if they retired the state? The things that they found for the state to do would hardly have been controversial among many Tories and certainly did not warrant the name of socialism. They were largely concerned with stimulating economic growth, where Britain was laggard. Faster economic growth, desirable on its own account, would provide more resources for humanizing the market. Many of those who took part in the Labour party's debates would have regarded themselves as socialists, but their offerings bore less and less resemblance to socialism on any previous definition. But if socialism was, in practice, out of the door, other old preconceptions remained. There was the idea of social partnership, or community, not an idea which will move many obstacles to economic growth. There was the notion that the nature of British society could be changed to match societies more successful economically, such as Germany and Japan. There was an inclination to protectionism, though now in forms more subtle than the direct control of imports. There was the misconception that if only politicians who knew nothing about industry instructed civil servants who knew nothing about industry to intervene in the affairs of industry, intervention lubricated naturally with public money, something good was bound to emerge.

As there was now a Social Democratic party, writers who wished to have influence in the Labour party had to draw distinctions between democratic socialism, which was good, and social democracy, which was the pale pink imitation of socialism still favoured by certain of the deserters, and was clearly bad.

UNEMPLOYMENT

One great worry was the problem of unemployment. The problem that had been solved suddenly appeared insoluble. There had been a steep rise in unemployment under Mrs Thatcher. It now appeared that governments which had claimed to have the solution had deceived themselves and their public. The restoration of full employment became an objective of first-class importance. The Tories could be blamed for the level of unemployment, but it could hardly escape observation that unemployment had risen in other developed countries, that it was much higher than it had been in the first twenty-five years after the end of the war, that, indeed, it had risen under the previous Labour government and under socialist governments elsewhere. The solution might be found in international co-operation. But the record of international co-operation since the death of the Bretton Woods system had not been encouraging. Labour might, nevertheless, try again and hope to do better in mustering international co-operation against the curse of unemployment, but it was difficult to base too much hope on such a success. There was still, among some, not only on the left, an attachment to Keynesianism combined with a desire to resurrect economic planning together with some extension of public ownership. The combination was still seen as the only system of economic management that could ensure full employment. But Keynesianism now required, it was believed by some, an injection of a further element, an element in which Keynes himself had once believed, protection.

Overt protection, as advocated in the alternative economic strategy, was prohibited by membership of the European Community, now gaining favour, not to mention a stack of other treaty commitments. But another technique was now attractive to some Keynesian thinkers in the Labour party. During the early years of Mrs Thatcher, British manufacturing industry had been seriously damaged by the rise in the exchange rate provoked both by the second oil-price hike of 1979 and by the monetarist policies of her government designed to repulse inflation. The object now was to make Britain more competitive by devaluation. As Bryan Gould, perhaps its most prominent advocate, has put it:

> The notion that we might actually use the exchange rate positively in the interests of promoting and maintaining the competitiveness of our industry and extending its productive capacity – something successful economies do as a matter of course – is totally foreign to us. As a consequence, we have no experience of what it might be like to be truly competitive and of what it might mean to plan aggressively to extend market share in the markets that really matter – the international markets for mass-produced goods.[2]

This was a naive idea supported by members of a Labour party increasingly remote from government and totally inexperienced in economic management. It took no account of the difference between the fixed-rate system of the Bretton Woods era when devaluation might be accepted by trading partners as a way of correcting a fundamental disequilibrium in the balance of payments, and the floating-rate system that had operated since the early 1970s. It took no account of the fact that devaluation could only work in combination with a profound deflation. It took no account of the unwillingness of Britain's Community partners to become victims of such elementary British tricks. They had heard of competitive devaluation before and would not tolerate the practice if adopted by Britain as a deliberate policy. They had a power of reaction against any such devices. Many of the advocates of such tricks had long been opponents of British membership of the Community. But, after 1983, the time was past when policies that depended on Britain's leaving the Community had any political viability.

In any case, the question remained how to reconcile full employment with stable prices, especially if devaluation had become the instrument of choice. The failure of past incomes policies did not seem to discourage a reversion to this technique. Too many within the Labour party, even among those who had never been noticeably tinged with the wilder fantasies of Bennery, were finding it difficult to reassess their ideas in the light of experience. Even while they struggled to be free and original, they were still the slaves of defunct socialist economists. None of these ideas carried any conviction outside the Labour party and, even within the Labour party, their attraction was fading. On the contrary, the Labour party in accordance with current fashion became fixated on membership of the Exchange Rate Mechanism. Advocacy of membership would be a sign that New Labour had abandoned old Labour soft options and had become financially respectable. Membership would provide stability, and stability had become the great objective of the more influential Labour thinkers such as Gordon Brown.

Meanwhile it was being noticed that the country that seemed to be doing best in dealing with unemployment was the USA, with its flexible labour market. This, stripped of its economists' language, utilized to conceal rather than to enlighten, meant presenting the labour force with alternatives, either to sell one's labour at the best price one could get for it or rapidly to run out of social security. It did not mean the more comfortable social market economy of the European Community which, by providing high levels of social security, delayed the return to work of people made redundant. Was there an answer to be found in the USA rather than in Europe? Could Labour be tough with social security, more tough even than the Tories were now becoming, with a view to forcing the able bodied, and even the disabled, back to work? A socialist party, or at least some of its members, was allowing itself to think the unthinkable.

CHOOSE FREEDOM

Roy Hattersley addressed himself to the Labour party's dilemmas in the book *Choose Freedom*, which he published early in 1987, the year of Labour's third successive General Election defeat. This was a time when the Labour party, as it was coming to realize, desperately needed either to set aside its confidence in the old ideology, adherence to which was Hattersley's distinguishing characteristic, seek a new one by which it could hope to live, if such a thing existed, or submerge itself up to its neck in the murky waters of pragmatism. Hattersley's book is an expression of a 'socialist' ideology of a kind. Hattersley would not seek comparison with Anthony Crosland's flawed masterpiece, *The Future of Socialism*, and in that he would be right. His is a book from which any fundamental rethinking in the light of experience is totally absent. That is one characteristic which it shares with the later writings of Crosland. It is an argument for socialism, presented with vigour but insufficient to inspire Lazarus to rise. Essentially, the book sought its solutions in the past.

Hattersley has a chapter entitled 'In Praise of Ideology', that is, of course, socialist ideology, not the ideologies of its critics. He parades his philosophical heroes and villains, the latter decorated with pejorative adjectives. Thus, for example, 'the philosophical edifice built around F. A. Hayek . . . is a ramshackle construction, derelict behind its elegant facade'.[3] One might respond that Hattersley's book is an extended Aunt Sally. The 'neo liberals of the far right'[4] whom he delights to excoriate are straw men who may fill academic textbooks but have exercised far less influence on the actions or thinking of Conservative politicians than he would like to pretend. Hattersley gives no recognition to the fact that the re-emergence of neo-liberal influence, such as it was, followed the repeated failures of interventionist governments of both the left and the right. Understandably, this led to widespread questioning of previous policies and gave the neo-liberals their opportunity. One target of neo-liberal criticism has been meddling by the state. In that it was perfectly right, as a glance at some of the activities of governments of which Hattersley was a member would demonstrate.[5] But no serious right-wing politician was advocating the repudiation of the state, simply that it should retreat rather than advance. In any case, globalization, which has had a greater effect on governments even than past experience, is the effect not of neo-liberal political philosophy but of market forces operating with a power multiplied by information technology.

Hattersley's inheritance from Crosland includes the conviction that socialism is about equality. An important expression of his search for equality is his defence of comprehensive education. 'Had the proponents of the "comprehensive experiment" not won the argument we would, today, be a less well educated society.'[6] Others would argue, and indeed have always argued, that the destruction of the grammar schools was a crime, an invasion of freedom that denied many of the poorer in the community an education worthy of their ability.[7]

The campaign for equality has, in Hattersley's view, its own justification needing no economic buttress. Nevertheless he seeks an economic buttress. He asserts that 'Had Britain been a more equal society, there is little doubt that our recent decline would, at least, have been less rapid. Further, greater equality would certainly improve our future economic performance.'[8] Whatever the evidence for this proposition, and evidence for it is strikingly lacking in Hattersley's book, it can hardly be claimed to be certain. One might expect that, in a book written in the tradition of Crosland, an attempt would be made to eschew claims to certainty where it is absent and to support assertions with evidence. Hattersley's mind is so fixed in the Croslandite past that he probably does not notice when he is claiming certainty for controversial statements. He ignores the limitations which even Crosland recognized were necessary in the pursuit of equality. He writes that 'The theory [that too much equality holds back economic advance] is dependent on the view that the enthusiasm of the talented few is more important to the material well-being of society than is the full involvement of the whole of that society's members.'[9] First, the theory is not dependent on the extreme proposition with which Hattersley attempts to kill it. Secondly, even Crosland recognized the importance of incentives, which suggests that he realized that the contribution of the talented few to material well-being was greater than the contribution of others and that, therefore, too much equality would be economically damaging.

Hattersley looks back sadly on the policies of the governments of which he was a member. The sadness is justified but it is inappropriately directed. Thus he wants a permanent incomes policy but not of the kind that Labour governments attempted to implement. He argues that the next Labour government needs:

> to begin with a firm statement of why some income planning is necessary and the clear and categorical assertion that the system which socialists devise should not be an incomes policy of the old model, with its norms, ceilings and acceptable exceptions. Such a system will not work and does not deserve to work, for it can only be introduced, and would only be temporarily accepted, as a desperate expedient . . . A national view of the overall level and general distribution of wages must become a permanent part of both our economic and social strategy, advocated and accepted on its own merits.[10]

With such an expression of pious intention, the next Labour government is to solve the ancient dilemma presented by inflation under conditions of full employment.

Hattersley is still persuaded by industrial policies of the most primitive kind. Thus he lists practical arguments for the national organization and ownership of the basic utilities. These include:

> 4. It is necessary for a socialist government to plan both the level of demand and the location of industry. Ownership of a number of major enterprises enables it to determine employment levels, prices and investment over a wide area of the economy. A government which owns the coal mines could subsidise coking coal and thus hold down the price of steel, and encourage employment in the steel-using industries.[11]

Governments can influence, rather than 'plan', the level of demand. They can, with the necessary agreement from the European Community, influence the location of industry. What they cannot do, within the rules of the European Community, is employ discriminatory subsidies to achieve the other purposes which Hattersley has in mind. Britain has advisedly attacked the discriminatory subsidies used to assist continental steel industries and that is a better course than duplicating such nonsense in the UK. If Hattersley had, momentarily, forgotten about British membership of the European Community, that is perhaps understandable in view of the Labour party's programme at the 1983 election, which envisaged British departure from that association.

He damns old Labour for allowing 'nationalization' to be hung round its neck when it should have been arguing for 'social ownership'. It is in 'social ownership' that Hattersley sees the future. His arguments show the persistence in his mind of dreams emanating from the 1950s and even before. He presents his argument in a chapter entitled 'The case for Clause IV'. Thus does the Gaitskellite turn from his master.

> The narrow obsession with extending public ownership by Acts of Parliament, which specify complete state acquisition of whole industries and their management by government nominees, has limited the extent of public ownership in Britain. Acceptance of a wider definition would have produced a larger socially owned sector and set free forces which would have generated social ownership without every extension becoming an act of political controversy and which would have almost certainly gone on generating co-operatives, employee buy-outs, employee share-option plans and municipal enterprises – even during periods of Conservative government. The Labour Party now needs to develop and encourage diversity within the public sector – different patterns of ownership, influence and control which complement and overlap each other. The pluralistic economy should not be divided by rigid lines which determine where public ownership begins and private ownership ends. It should be made

up of companies with a variety of owners, neither wholly public nor wholly private.[12]

The book is notably reticent on how all this is to be done. There are, of course, many employee buy-outs and employee share-option schemes, but they are not usually associated with socialism, rather the opposite. As for the other forms of social ownership suggested, the most one can say is that they would not be likely to get very far, that they might well need the support of discriminatory government finance, and that their contribution either to a socialist society or to economic progress would be insignificant. Hattersley states a categorical principle: '*Public ownership, in the form of state corporations centrally owned, planned and administered, is essential for the public utilities.*'[13] Since he wrote, it has been shown that public ownership is not essential for the public utilities, though of course the privatized utilities are far from perfect, like the rest of the public and private sectors.

The book was evidently intended to recapture the banner of freedom for the Labour party. Its claim to that banner had been badly marred by what Hattersley unerringly calls its 'damagingly authoritarian reputation'.[14] He insists that 'the immediate intention of socialist policies is the creation of a more equal society within which power and wealth are more evenly distributed. But socialism's fundamental purpose – indeed the purpose of the equality which we seek – is the extension of liberty.'[15] It was a claim that was unlikely to make much impression on the electorate, which was, at the time, less concerned with Labour as an enemy of freedom than as an enemy of sanity. It would be wrong to deny Hattersley his devotion to freedom, although he himself is happy to refuse his opponents either honesty or understanding.[16] He writes defensively, 'Socialists, believing in freedom as well as equality, do not support the rigid bureaucratic imposition of equality that impairs liberty as well as efficiency.'[17] He adds that 'It is not surprising that British socialists are thought to undervalue liberty; they do not talk about it sufficiently to give a credible impression of concern.'[18] Ironically, it was devotion to freedom that was among the obstacles that made socialism, even in the heavily diluted form adopted by revisionists such as Crosland and Hattersley, impossible of achievement. Socialists lacked the determination to enforce the redistribution and equalization that they thought was necessary, partly at least because they realized that to do so lay beyond the boundaries of democratic consent.

THE DEVELOPMENTAL STATE

Since socialism had shed such aberrations as Guild Socialism, the state had been at the centre of socialist thinking. If it was now necessary to abandon nationalization and economic planning, the road from socialism would be made less embarrassing for former socialists if they could find something for the state to do. Hence arose the concept of the enabling state. Kinnock, in the course of his farewell from socialism, adopted the enabling state.[19] In his 1998 Fabian pamphlet *The Third Way*, Tony Blair writes of one of his policy objectives as being 'A dynamic knowledge-based economy founded on individual empowerment and opportunity where governments enable, not command, and the power of the market is harnessed to serve the public interest'.[20] It is unclear how the market will be harnessed to serve the public interest if the method is to enable, not to command. However, it is clear that the new task of the state, according to a range of ex-socialists, is to enable rather than to act. Or, in addition to itself acting in some limited fields, it would enable. 'Enabling' became a catchword of many socialists who wanted the state to do something but could not think quite what. It litters the literature of the time. It was a fuzzy idea, expensive to implement. The costs would arise as those who felt they should be enabled with public money made their claims. The concept may have brought some comfort to former socialists. But it was only too obvious to their left-wing critics that capitalist states had themselves, for long past, done their fair share of enabling and that an enabling state was not a socialist state. States would no doubt go on enabling in one way or another. A high proportion of the enabling would probably be, as in the past, a waste of money, but there might be a role for it. It would be optimistic to imagine that the enabling would make much difference to economic performance or that, however much there was of it, the outcome would be anything that could be presented as either socialism or socially significant.

An idea more suggestive of constructive possibilities is the developmental state. It arises from a theory of British economic failure associated with the names, among others, of Bryan Gould, who departed from British politics after an abortive attempt to become leader of the Labour party, but particularly perhaps with the name of David Marquand, who argued it in his books *The Unprincipled Society* and *The New Reckoning*. The authors of this idea had noted that at crucial stages in the industrial development of the United States, Germany and Japan they had been protectionist. They had opened their markets to international competition, so far as they ever did, only when they were strong and could contemplate international competition complacently. These thinkers noted that, in contrast, the theories of Adam Smith and David Ricardo had exerted a strong influence over British policy, notably in the nineteenth century when Britain was losing its industrial lead. They discovered in the culture of countries such as France, Germany and Japan a willingness to find consensus among the different economic actors, and also with the state, in the promotion of economic development. Following the writings of Michel Albert, they noted a distinction between the 'Rhenish', or consensus, capitalism practised on the continent of Europe, and the Anglo-Saxon, or individualistic, capitalism practised in Britain and the United States. Rhenish capitalism, they found, was a great success. Anglo-Saxon capitalism was, comparatively, a failure. Even the United States, that mighty exemplar of individualistic capitalism, had, relatively, fallen back. A number of these judgements proved to be premature but, as can be repeatedly observed, economic theories can long survive the evidence.

The trouble with Britain, according to Marquand, is that, unlike France, Germany and Japan, it never matured into a developmental state.[21] A developmental state, he emphasizes, is not a socialist state, but it does give a leading role to the state. A developmental state is one which, by means of state intervention, encourages new industrial development and the adjustment of the existing economy to competitive pressures. In the course of this argument Marquand rejects both the 'neo-liberal' and 'neo-socialist' approaches to economic development. While both of them can offer relevant criticisms of existing society, neither of them can help in the construction of a developmental state because they are class based, whereas development requires collaboration between the state and all engaged citizens both across classes and across industries. Despite its inappropriateness to the UK situation, the neo-liberal tradition has, in Marquand's view, imbued the British state, which has thereby been rendered passive in face of the country's considerable developmental needs. Moreover, according to this thesis, Britain lacks 'common-interest organizations' such as trade unions and trade associations which are sufficiently encompassing to make agreements with the state and ensure that they are respected.[22]

Other inhibitions to the emergence of a British developmental state are the Westminster Parliamentary model, with its illusion of absolute Parliamentary sovereignty, and the nature of the British civil service. The Westminster Parliamentary model means that 'a jealous political class' refuses to devolve public responsibilities and powers among economic agents.[23] The civil service is bad at the exercise of the discretion necessary to make a developmental state successful.[24] It rejects attempts to make it favour prospective beneficial developments and lacks the experience to do it successfully. Unlike in other countries, the civil service is characterized by 'neutrality and passivity'.[25] Will Hutton, in *The State We're In*, makes the same point.

> The Civil Service tradition that officials should not engage in private sector activity remained strong and, unlike France or Germany, Britain had made no systematic attempt to train a class of officials competent in commerce and finance. The accent was still placed on administration rather than intervention; on high policy rather than commercial strategy. So the state had no apparatus for making British industrial policies work . . .[26]

When the British state does get involved the result is 'negotiated inertia rather than negotiated adjustment'.[27] To compound the problem there are other faults such as 'an élite which is at best ambivalent about, and at worst positively hostile to, the process of wealth creation'.[28] What, apparently, is needed is a drastic change in the assumptions and conduct of political life in the course of which the state will learn how to effect positive discrimination on behalf of constructive economic activities, and economic actors will learn how to respond to the state's offer of discrimination. Thus the Marquand message, while not being socialist, is frankly collectivist and corporatist. Although not socialist, it is of a kind that will appeal to those who have abandoned socialism but are still seeking an interventionist role for the state. It is a theory with obvious attractions to three groups of anxious enquirers: socialists seeking a substitute for socialism; ex-socialists who have discovered that socialism is not superior to capitalism but search nevertheless for some explanation of Britain's relative economic failure; and to capitalists of the middle way.

There has long been a danger that the Labour party, in modernizing itself, would itself find the middle way attractive. Marquand's theory appears to ignore the evidence that, among Britain's problems, is the fact that, so far from not having been a developmental state, it has been too much of a developmental state. Wilson's aluminium smelters are a case where government intervention procured the development of a substantially new and large British industry. There are other examples of which the most prominent are civil nuclear energy and aerospace, both of which were lavishly supported under the Wilson government.

There is the particular example of Concorde, an aircraft created in co-operation with the French developmental state and of which it was said, with pardonable exaggeration, that however much had been spent on its development, there was always as much more to spend. The IRC intervened vigorously to establish mergers on the theory that size would aid competitiveness, but few were notable successes. There have been numerous examples of uncompetitive firms being rescued expensively by the British developmental state. These rescues have been encouraged by an interventionist psychology which claims that, with state aid, lame ducks can be converted into swans. Marquand tells us that 'The economies that have succeeded most spectacularly have been those fostered by developmental states, where public power, acting in concert with private interest, has induced market forces to flow in the desired direction.'[29]

There is no doubt that in recent British industrial history there are only too many cases where market forces, attracted by public money, have flowed in the direction that the state desired. In all these cases the British state has invested vast resources, one might say on an imperial scale. In each case it must be almost certain that the resources and skills which the state invested would have been better employed elsewhere. The development of these industries was in no way inhibited by the Westminster Parliamentary model. On the contrary, if anything it encouraged the waste. In all these cases, and others, civil servants have been required to exercise discretion. They may have done so reluctantly. They may have been ill equipped to exercise it wisely. But they have done so. The more they have done so, the more they have become reconciled to doing so. Indeed they have constituted a vested interest in the public service insistent that the state, and public money, have an important role in economic regeneration. In many of these cases Ministers and civil servants have had the advantage of advice from senior industrialists who spend their lives exercising discretion. The major mistakes, however, have resulted not from the inadequacy of the civil servants, their 'neutrality and passivity', but from the decisions of Ministers acting from a mixture of motives from which political advantage has seldom been absent.

We are left with the fact that the British economy, despite all these interventions, has lagged and, although it is impossible to be certain of the reasons, it does not appear to have lain in the neo-liberal tradition of the British state, a tradition far more respected in the neglect than the observance. In Britain, we have had a developmental state and it has wasted a great deal of money. Marquand concedes that 'efficiency can best be promoted by devolving responsibility to private owners', and that the state has been found to lack 'the knowledge and capacity to control the undertakings it owns'. Despite these concessions to 'neo-liberalism', he thinks it necessary that the developmental state should retain 'the regulatory powers to ensure strategic oversight'.[30] In other words, the state cannot run its own undertakings but it is equipped to give strategic direction to the private sector. It seems unlikely. The aluminium smelters, nuclear energy and aerospace all testify to what can happen if the state gives strategic direction.

The search for explanations of poor British economic performance is fascinating and endless. Even before the appearance of theories about the developmental state, it was argued that industrial policies have worked overseas and that therefore there cannot be any reason of principle why they should not work in the UK. Unfortunately those who seek examples of success from overseas are unlikely to know the full story. This is not surprising because the full story is difficult enough to unravel if one looks at one's own country. The most one can say is that industrial policy has clearly not worked in the UK, that the availability of industrial policy instruments has led to expensive interventions which have often had a political rather than an economic motivation, that the cost has clearly exceeded any benefit, and that, though this does not establish an absolute case against industrial policy, the presumption must be against it. Moreover, even if the overseas lessons teach what is claimed, the problem of transferring foreign systems and cultures to Britain remains unsolved. This is not an argument against learning from overseas. It is an argument against learning from a misunderstanding of what happens overseas. In any case the attractions of the Japanese model are, at the time of writing, less obvious than they once were and, even when Japan was outperforming the world, it seemed to owe much more to the entrepreneurial genius of Japanese industry than to the supervisory activities of the Japanese Ministry of International Trade and Industry. The Japanese example also illustrates one of the risks in developmental states, that the injection of public money into private enterprise can become a source of corrupt actions and influences. Lacking any more compelling analysis of the British predicament, it would have been better to stop wasting resources on industrial policy.

These theories, whatever their merits might be, did not seem particularly exciting to those seeking a grand vision with which to win back popular opinion and to appeal to the idealism of youth. Something more captivating was needed, especially as the idealism of youth was being deflected from party politics to single-issue groups concerned by a variety of really important issues, notably the environment. Soon there were more people engaged in single-issue groups than the total membership of British political parties.

Whereas there is nothing particularly attractive to idealism in David Marquand's arguments, he does identify a threat. In his book *The New Reckoning*, Marquand concluded that 'Globally and nationally, we shall sooner or later have to choose between the free market and the free society.'[31] Although the statement lacks the specificity required to convert it into a policy, one can surmise that Marquand believes that the market as it stands, with the degrees of freedom which it enjoys as the new century begins, is inconsistent with the continuance of a free society because of the pressures it exerts on social harmony, and that therefore governments should endeavour to impose severe restrictions on the market which would be additional to those already in force. This is a depressing judgement for at least two reasons. First, it is unclear how the choice between Marquand's alternatives can be made. The choice of whether there will be a free market, or of the restrictions to be placed on its freedom, is not for one country alone or even for one conglomeration of countries such as the European Union. It can hardly depend on the actions of a single government, such as that of the UK, unless the UK wishes to opt out of the World Trade Organization system, which seems at this stage unlikely. There is no suggestion that the Blair government wishes to revisit the isolation contemplated by earlier Labour governments. There is no international consortium of states that is likely to make such a choice. How then will it be made? If there were a serious recession in the industrialized world, as after 1931, there is certainly the risk that there might be a general reversion to protectionism. But, and this is the second reason why Marquand's judgement is depressing, protectionism is a limitation on the free society. The free market represents an important dimension of freedom. Society will be less free if there is no free market. No doubt the free market can damage individuals. But impediments on the free market can also damage individuals. The challenge therefore is not to make a choice between the free market and the free society but to ensure a balance that enables humanity to enjoy both the free market and the free society. There is no evidence yet that this cannot be done. Certainly the Blair government shows no sign that it is considering the choice that Marquand wishes to impose upon it.

WHAT A STATE WE'RE IN

In the search for a new idea, some looked to something called 'stakehold-ing'. There would be no more public ownership but everyone would have a stake in the community and would feel that they had a stake. The idea of stakeholding conveys a warm glow at a time when the fire of socialism is burning low. Stakeholding may not be socialism but at any rate it is co-operation and commitment and, as such, an enemy of *laissez-faire* at a time when Thatcherism had created space for enemies of *laissez-faire*. Stakeholding had some unfortunate links to the rather dictatorial system of government in Singapore, but its main problem was that it lacked resonance and, for the modernizers in the Labour party, seemed to worry some of the businessmen whom they were seek-ing to win as allies.

The principal thesis published on stakeholding is that of Will Hutton in his book *The State We're In*. The success of Hutton's book demon-strates that there is still a large audience for panaceas. If scapegoats for this country's poor economic performance can be identified, that will be an additional marketing advantage. In this case the scapegoat is the Conservative establishment, which, embedded in this country's financial institutions, is judged responsible for the short-termism which, in the view of Hutton and many others, has so seriously damaged this country's manufacturing industry. 'The story of British capitalism is at heart the peculiar history of the destructive relationship between British finance and industry. Our financial institutions and the ideology of perfect com-petition and free markets have deep and interlinked roots.'[32] This thesis is by no means original but here it is argued not merely with journalistic skill but with an enthusiasm sustained by the author's evident conviction that he has discovered new truths. Hutton's desire is to rid this country of short-termism and to substitute co-operation and commitment in all walks of life. In particular, the UK's financial institutions are to be reconstructed on a federal basis. Regional and local banks are to demon-strate commitment to regional and local manufacturing industry by investing long term. They are to be supported by financial institutions created specifically for the purpose of attracting long-term money. 'Britain should copy other industrialised countries and create a public agency that will act as a financial intermediary collecting longer term deposits and channelling them to lending institutions.'[33] There is much in common between Hutton and the socialism of the 1930s. In the 1930s, socialists wished to replace capitalism by socialism. Hutton wishes to replace one form of capitalism by a different form of capitalism. There is no reason to think that the task would be any less difficult. For the socialists 'the City' was a major part of the problem. For Hutton 'the City' is a major part of the problem. Socialists proposed to deal with the City in part by nationalization but also by the creation of a National Investment Board which would recruit resources for investment. Hutton makes clear that he is not a socialist, but his NIB is his 'financial intermediary'.

The model is to be Germany, which, with its federal system of government, its industrial democracy and its banks' long-term investments in German industry, has been an example to the rest of Europe and even to the world. Japan and East Asia also come in for praise for their successful post-war economic development. 'Economic success', Hutton tells us, 'has been elusive, except in East Asia . . .'[34] On the other hand in the USA, the epitome of *laissez-faire* capitalism, industry has been 'hollowed out' by the short-termism of US financial institutions. 'The US is increasingly unable to finance its deficits; open up the vast Asian market; or control its capital outflows. Further US decline, and an ever weaker dollar, now seem unavoidable.'[35] The UK appears at the bottom of the class because, together with the short-termism of its financial institutions, and the neo-liberalism of twenty years of Conservative government, it lacks even those elements of federalist commitment which, to some small degree, have rescued the USA from the worst effects of *laissez-faire*. Britain's financial institutions may be doing well but it is at the expense of British manufacturing industry. 'With European levels of unemployment and American levels of working poor, Britain has unleashed the processes that have hollowed out American industry without any compensating dynamism.'[36]

One problem with Hutton is that, as an economist and economic journalist, he takes economics too seriously. His simplicities illustrate the dangers of inhaling economics – of any school. He launches a slash-and-burn attack not merely on Britain's financial institutions with their short-termist practices but on 'neo-liberalism'. He is out to prove that Mrs Thatcher's alleged neo-liberalism has brought Britain few if any benefits. It has left Britain in the economic doldrums. And this assertion, for which there is much evidence, is supported by an attempt to resurrect Keynes. No artifices of the human intellect are more easily susceptible of destructive criticism than economic theories. It is a game in which economists possess a comparative advantage. They know more about what their colleagues believe, and what they themselves once believed, than any unprofessional observer. But the fact that economists have a comparative advantage will not prevent outsiders playing the game. Governments have no choice but to play the game because they have to conduct economic policy. Government, in its attitude to economics, is necessarily eclectic. All economics is an attempt to understand market processes, which, unlike natural and physical processes, are not capable of being reduced to a science, and while most economics of whatever school provides some insights into some parts of the processes, none provides a secure basis for understanding the whole. Circumstances vary and, with circumstances, the recommendations at least of those economists who are not slaves to some defunct prophet. That is why, in the end, economic management is a matter of fallible human judgement rather than science.

Hutton seems to think that economics is a science. Life would be so much easier if it were. When a government, such as that of Mrs Thatcher, moves in what Hutton sees as a neo-liberal direction, it is not because neo-liberal theory has been swallowed whole or has escaped the scepticism which even conviction politicians bring to the business of government. It happens because governments conclude that, of late, the state has been too interventionist and in directions which have brought costs rather than benefits, and that therefore it is reasonable to move to some degree in a contrary direction. Yet the distance moved by Mrs Thatcher was certainly not vast, as is demonstrated by her failure to meet her original goals of reducing public expenditure. There was never any question of Mrs Thatcher disestablishing the state in the interests of neo-liberal economics. Indeed, as Hutton admits, she was a great centralizer. Mrs Thatcher's Britain could be considered neo-liberal only by contrast with Benn's alternative economic strategy or Hutton's dirigisme. Hutton's attack on neo-liberalism effectively destroys an Aunt Sally but has no real relevance to any actual British economic problem. That seems to be the view of the Blair government.

A similar criticism can be brought against Hutton's resurrection of Keynes and Keynesians. He tells us that:

> Over the last decade a new generation of Keynesians, American almost to a man and woman, have been mounting a vigorous fight-back resurrecting and updating Keynes' ideas – and devastating the free-market position as effectively as Keynes ever did . . . And their policy proposals . . . are more subtle than the diet of never-ending pump-priming through public spending increases and tax cuts, which governments in the UK followed after 1945.[37]

Most governments, in post-war Britain, imagined that they were following the latest Keynesian wisdom with their 'never-ending pump-priming', even though they thereby did as much as they could to establish Britain as an inflationary society. If their members were still alive, they would be distressed to discover a Keynesian rebuking them for their unsubtle Keynesian pump-priming. There were those who thought so at the time, and others who became critical of this unsubtle Keynesianism on the basis of experience of how it worked in practice. It is even argued that Keynesianism, particularly this unsubtle Keynesianism, is an incorrect interpretation of Keynes. This is the trouble with economic theory. It develops and changes and it is a matter of chance whether its latest manifestations approximate more to the truth than its earlier manifestations. Economic theory is to be treated with care. It can damage one's economy.

Hutton believes that the current disrepute of Keynes can be attributed to a combination of intellectual confusion and class prejudice. He writes:

> The conclusion for Britain and its institutions is very uncomfortable. Here is an economy and society predicated upon the perfectibility of the market mechanism and whose élite consider any restraint on their freedom by the state an intrusion on liberty. The class system is founded upon the merits of individual choice which permit the scions of the upper class to send their children to privileged schools and to network amongst themselves in the pursuit of power and privilege. Free market economics is a powerful comfort, for it appears to legitimise such arrangements as natural and unimprovable. Keynes proves that they are not – and invites the state to make good the shortcomings. Small wonder he is held in such disdain.[38]

One can bring a variety of justifiable criticisms of the British class system but no one in authority, or outside academe and economic journalism, believes in the 'perfectibility of the market system'. They may believe that no one has yet discovered a better system, which is rather different. Elsewhere Hutton attributes to neo-liberals the more nuanced conviction that the market is 'unimprovable'. It must be doubtful whether anyone outside academia believes that the market system is unimprovable. What we do know is that many of the attempts to improve it have been counterproductive and have involved colossal waste. No one is saying that there should be no government. There has simply been too much government of the wrong sort. Few would suggest that the use of so-called 'Keynesian' methods is never appropriate. But the use of such methods at times of economic recession long predates Keynes.

And neo-liberals certainly believe that the market system needs to be supported by laws and regulations enacted by the state and which are necessary restraints, though they may be criticized as intruding on liberty. Hutton also seems to ignore the historical fact that, for well over a generation, Keynes was not held in disdain by the privileged classes. On the contrary, he was the reputed saviour of British capitalism.

The space that Hutton devotes to remedies is relatively brief but not less than dramatic. The recommendations consist in great part of a hotchpotch of constitutional reforms which have been widely advocated by a variety of authorities though normally on simple democratic grounds and without any idea that they would do much for economic performance. No one can accuse Hutton of presenting simple solutions to the UK's undoubted *economic* problems. As he confesses, what he proposes by way of remedy amounts to a revolution. 'The urgent necessity is to construct an interdependent institutional structure in Britain that will permit commitment and co-operation in the context of a competitive market. And that . . . implies nothing less than a British revolution.'[39] Such a revolution will be difficult to achieve because reconstructing society must always be problematic and those with power are always reluctant to abandon it. Indeed the practical politician might be tempted to ask whether it would be right to undertake a revolution on the slender basis of Hutton's analysis of the UK's dilemmas. He may think that it would be ill advised, on so slim an hypothesis, to hobble one part of the British economy, the financial, that is doing well, in order to promote another part, the industrial, that is doing badly. He will need better reasons for decentralizing power and creating in Britain a federal structure than the hope that, on Hutton's analysis, this will do something for the lamentably performing British economy.

Hutton's remedies, so far as they fall in the economic category, are essentially a cry for a world that has gone. He tells us that:

> Private interests have too easily slipped the national leash and have used the ungoverned world beyond national frontiers to undermine what they regard as tiresome, inefficient and bureaucratic efforts to assert the moral and social dimension in human affairs. This escape from responsibility cannot and should not be allowed to become permanent.[40]

But his answer to the problem, in which he himself seems to lack much confidence, lies in forms of international economic co-operation. He wants a new Bretton Woods. 'The world's financial markets need to be brought to heel.'[41] Nostalgia for Bretton Woods is widely shared. It has led to frequent attempts at co-operation. Arrangements have been made between the great economic powers and have repeatedly failed, except sometimes in the short term. The interests of participants have been at odds, as is demonstrated by the rapidity with which such agreements have broken down. It is not clear that such arrangements have always been in Britain's interests. Britain's enthusiasm for international co-operation often seems motivated as much by fear of being left out as by any expectation of benefit, and its declining influence means that it cannot always get what it wants even if it is represented. There may be a change in the possibilities for co-operation now there is a Euro to look the dollar in the face, but it would be premature to rely on it, and certainly premature to be certain that what would emerge would be acceptable to Britain.

Hutton's remedies are also very 'British' in the sense that they are intended to make Britain a champion. Economic horizons now have to be much wider than the creation of national champions, even if the championship is now to be won, not by an industry as in the past, but by a whole nation. Economics has become international just as capitalism has become even more international. The effect is likely to be liberalizing rather than socializing. The essence of Britain will be preserved in its character and its culture. It may be also that the performance of the British economy will improve because Britain, due to its own domestic experience and attitudes, is better prepared for a liberalized world than some other countries. It may be that, precisely because we do not have the collaborative capitalism of Europe, the UK will survive better than the rest of Europe in a world of intense global competition. But that is to verge on optimism, not a sensible emotion where the British economy is concerned. No one knows. We will have to see.

It might seem unfair to Hutton to suggest that his message is principally directed to those who have not yet reconciled themselves to the death of socialism. He emphasizes throughout that what he is looking for is a successful capitalism. Nevertheless it is in the part of the political spectrum that still yearns for socialism that his thoughts will be found most attractive. Precisely because it is interventionist and radical, his book will bring some comfort to socialists who are uneasily aware that their philosophy has been 'hollowed out'. But what should be ruled out is a revolution that takes the UK backwards. In practice this prohibition has not proved difficult to enforce. Hutton's publishing success is unlikely to be paralleled by influence. The Blair government, which, in opposition, was looking for radical policies for economic revival, and momentarily seemed influenced by Hutton's ideas, now seems to have retreated from stakeholding of the Hutton variety. Hutton tells us that, with the election of Tony Blair to the Labour leadership in 1994, Labour had become 'explicitly committed to developing a British social democracy'.[42] But, now in government, it does not appear committed to Hutton's version of social democracy.

Such a retreat may have been provoked by scepticism encouraged by recent experience. Hutton's book was published in 1995. He lists 'successful' British firms which have refused 'to abandon co-operative relationships and instead enjoy the benefits of worker and financial commitment'. His list includes Sainsbury, GEC and Rover.[43] It is questionable whether, only a few years later, these firms were accounted among the more successful in Britain. His hero countries now seem less healthy economically than when he wrote. Japan and East Asia have been giving the rest of the world some cause for alarm because of the possible effect of their distresses on global economic health. German unemployment is a tragedy which, as yet, the ideals of co-operation and commitment embodied in its financial and industrial structures have failed to remedy. Indeed, as the twentieth century ended, its problems appeared to be getting worse rather than better. Within six months of election in 1998, the new Social Democratic government had lost its first, and Keynesian, Finance Minister, Oskar Lafontaine. Early signs suggested that the new Social Democratic government in Germany did not intend to rely on the traditional German ideals of co-operation and commitment as its answer to unemployment. Contrariwise, the performance of the *laissez-faire* US economy has become, for the moment, a beacon to the rest of the world. No doubt books are currently being written about the state Germany and Japan are in. It would be too much to expect that they will be pointing to the UK as an exemplar, but the 'hollowed out' US economy should give better opportunities. Of course economies, like clothes, go in and out of fashion even if at longer intervals. The torch of economic leadership passes hither and thither for reasons not entirely understood. Defenders of the Hutton thesis would certainly be able to suggest explanations for the unfavourable turn of events in Germany. Germany has not yet emerged from the trauma of unification. One needs to look at the whole economic cycle not just at a brief period of years. But the suspicion among practical men, not slaves of defunct or living economists, will be that there is more to be understood about the performance of economies than Hutton, or indeed anyone else, has fathomed and that it would be risky to engage in revolutions on the basis of so rickety an analysis. Whatever the merits of the Hutton economic recommendations, and to this author they seem few, the test would lie in their likely effect on economic performance. Fortunately, or otherwise, we are unlikely to be supplied the evidence because the scepticism of government will deny them implementation.

THE BLAIR REVOLUTION

In the years leading up to the 1997 General Election, the most detailed and authoritative exposition of the ideas associated with what was becoming known as New Labour appeared in *The Blair Revolution: Can New Labour Deliver?* by Peter Mandelson and Roger Liddle, published in 1996. Mandelson was so close to Blair, and evidently so influential, that the book probably gave a more reliable indication of what Blair, before the General Election, was prepared to reveal as the contents of his mind than any manifesto.[44] The object seems to have been to lower expectations, admirable for a political party that had still to win office. Blair would only make promises that he was sure could be implemented. It was an unprecedented act of self-denial.

Outside the field of constitutional reform, *The Blair Revolution* offered a revolution only in the sense that its revolutionaries seemed set on persuading the electorate how little can be done by governments in the modern world. Because of the modesty of its claims, the book was severely reviewed by representatives of old Labour. It was certainly attempting to re-educate the surviving adherents of old Labour ideology. Markets, we are told, are more sovereign than Ministers.[45] The authors try to mitigate the dreadful implications of such assertions with banalities like 'The more secure, more cohesive and, as a result, more equal our society, the better our chances of economic success.'[46] Hattersley had asserted much the same in his time, but these authors are as unsuccessful in providing evidence for this contention as Hattersley had been. The book protests that 'There is no single idea, no clever policy wheeze which is going to transform Britain's prospects overnight, but small step-by-step changes in a consistent direction will produce gradually more impressive long-term results.'[47] The problem is at once manifest. Consistent directions are difficult to find. To guarantee that, if found, they will yield long-term results is beyond the bounds of human foresight. Yet, because the results of the Blair revolution would only emerge long term, it would not be enough to win one election. To implement the cautious proposals of this New Labour government, there must be two full terms of office. Indeed Blair was arguing for a second term before he had done anything in his first.

With expectations lowered as far as politically possible, the programme set out was still too ambitious. The authors ask themselves a number of strategic questions. Each is reminiscent of the thinking of every past Labour government and of most Conservative governments. No previous government had found the answers. 'How can we take the outstanding record of the best British companies and use it to raise the mediocre performance of the rest? How can we take the industrial sectors where we are strong and deploy government support – for example in research and development – to build out from them?'[48] Nowhere in the book is there any answer to these questions. The suggestion of 'government support' is at once counterbalanced by an admirable warning against the use of public money for venture capital. There would be 'too great a temptation for political log-rolling and attempts to pick winners'.[49] That danger exists with any form of government support for industry. Indeed it is not clear that, in all cases, the temptation for political log-rolling is being resisted by the Blair government.

Much hope is invested in education and training, the recourse of frustrated politicians throughout the ages. As long ago as the *New Fabian Essays*, Crossman had described education as the most glaring gap in the programmes of 1945, 1950 and 1951.[50] But then comes the wise admission that improved education and training will take a long time to have any discernible impact.[51] Those impressed by Blair's allocation of absolute priority to education, education, education, should be alerted both by this warning from Mandelson and Liddle and also, perhaps, by Andrew Adonis and Stephen Pollard who, in their book *A Class Act*, tell us that 'there are no quick fixes, no blueprints; and if there are plenty of radical ideological experiments waiting to be tried, the experience of the 20th century may, perhaps, teach the 21st to be a little cautious and sceptical'.[52] As Mandelson and Liddle have already warned us, we live in a world without quick fixes. But in that realization might lie hope, hope that the era of exaggerated claims and promises from parties contesting elections has come to an end.

Despite the caution of *The Blair Revolution*, the Blair government, on election, initiated a search for something entitled, in advance of its discovery, the 'third way'. Blair was, evidently, dissatisfied with the mindset with which he had come to power. He felt something to be lacking, a philosophy which would make the adaptations of the previous eighteen years coherent, and would give guidance for the future. But if a Prime Minister comes into office lacking a philosophy, he is unlikely to find it on the hoof. He will probably be left with pragmatism, and the pragmatism is not likely to be more successful because it is called the third way.

NINETEEN

Obsequies for socialism

MAKING LABOUR NEW

Following his defeat at the 1992 General Election, Kinnock at once resigned and, for two years, John Smith led the party. There was some ground for optimism. It was, in seats, a narrower defeat than any of the previous three, leaving the Tories with an overall majority of only 21, well down from just over 100 at the 1987 election. Indeed the result was so narrow that Smith, not by nature a radical, saw little argument for much further radicalism. As no new idea had surfaced which would confer any novelty on a party that had mislaid its original ideological motivation, the old idea of rewriting Clause Four re-emerged. When Jack Straw raised the question, he was severely rebuked by Smith. The electorate had never shown itself worried about Clause Four, only about Labour election programmes and Labour competence. An assault on Clause Four would be divisive. It would cause more trouble than it was worth. Like Kinnock before him, Smith preferred to proceed by means of a personal statement of values. But the project was pre-empted by Smith's death in May 1994 from a heart attack. In addition to other objections to an assault on the Labour party's historic covenant with itself, Smith thought that it would be a diversion from his more important battle against the union block vote, and in favour of OMOV in the election of the Party leader which, by a hair's breadth, he won at the 1993 Party Conference. The outcome left the unions with a reduced but still over-mighty status within the Party. Smith's success demonstrates that, already before Blair, some unions were willing to help Labour, even at some sacrifice of their own influence, and would not repudiate the Labour leader. They had probably made a calculation. Less influence within a party that might win an election was worth more than more influence within a party that could never hope to govern.

Some younger modernizers, notably Tony Blair and Gordon Brown, found Smith's limited radicalism exasperating. They knew that the 1992 score in seats won was deceptive. Labour had still been 7.6 per cent behind the Conservatives in its share of the popular vote. It had less popular support even than in the 1979 General Election. Labour had scored as well as it did in seats only because of the distribution of votes in the country and the disproportionate operations of the first-past-the-post electoral system. The Conservatives were in the unfortunate position of having to do substantially better than Labour in the popular vote even to achieve a hung Parliament, let alone a majority in the House of Commons. Blair and Brown were sure that a great deal more needed to be done to make Labour electable. Labour had not yet transformed itself enough either to win an election or to confront a world which had changed almost beyond recognition since Labour was last in government. A thorough reassessment of the Party's policies and constitution was necessary. Labour could not afford to lose again. At the next election, the electorate must be left in no doubt that Labour had jettisoned for ever the unattractive features that had, for so long, repelled support. It was not realized how much the Tories under John Major would do to help by their incompetence, by their bitter personal divisions and by the conduct of a few Tory MPs.

Just as Mrs Thatcher's resignation in 1990 had been a severe blow to Labour, so now John Smith's death was a severe blow to the Conservative party. There was in him much of old Labour. Though highly respected, and a skilled performer in the House of Commons, he reminded the electorate of what Labour had been rather than conveying any message as to what Labour could become. There was little that he could have brought to a new Labour government except perhaps experience of the failed attempt at devolution in the 1970s. He was the leader who, in the complacent way of the Labour party, had had to be allowed his turn at the helm. He had been briefly a Cabinet minister and Secretary of State for Trade before Labour's defeat in 1979. But there was no evidence that he was equipped to deal with the political and economic circumstances of the late 1990s. Like Roy Hattersley he was tied honourably to a socialist past which he was unwilling entirely to repudiate. During his campaign for the leadership he said, 'If radical change involves the Labour Party subverting its principles and aborting its mission, then I'm conservative in that very narrow sense.'[1] The young modernizers would not, of course, admit that their recommendations involved subverting the principles and aborting the mission of the Labour party, but that was clearly the interpretation that Smith himself put upon their purposes. In other words victory had not yet become for him the prime objective. It must be victory consistent with his residual socialist principles. For that reason, he could only be an obstacle to the modernization of the Labour party, if modernization was taken to imply the sacrifice of everything that stood in the way of a Labour victory. In retrospect, it appears that he would have won the 1997 General Election. It would probably have been with a smaller majority but also without immolating so many old 'socialist values'.

With Smith's disappearance, the opportunity was opened for a new generation headed by Tony Blair and Gordon Brown. The next stage of Labour's transformation from a party of socialism to a party in power could now begin. There are those who doubt whether Blair would have gained the leadership of the Labour party after Smith's death without the changes to its electoral system the year before.[2] In fact so desperate were the Party and the unions that Blair's emergence could be regarded as preordained. He won with 57 per cent of the votes cast, with John Prescott trailing with 24 per cent and Margaret Beckett, Smith's deputy, even further behind at 19 per cent. For the Tories, Blair had long been the most threatening figure on the Labour front bench. How could they attack a man whose convictions seemed to run so closely with their own? And if the Tories felt threatened, Labour could begin cautiously to hope. Old Labour could only swallow its fears and trust that there was, in Blair, more of a socialist than appeared on the surface and that he did not really mean to abandon Labour's historic mission. Whatever Blair had been when he became an MP in 1983, or in 1986 when he was still a member of the Campaign for Nuclear Disarmament, by 1994 there did not seem much sign of socialist convictions. Philip Gould tells us, following much discussion with focus groups, that Blair 'connects to a rich vein of empirical common sense that has always been central to the British people'.[3] This flattering appraisal of Blair and the British people is confirmed at least by their joint rejection of socialism.

With Blair and Gordon Brown came a group of Scottish MPs who were ready to follow their lead. The Party was increasingly dominated by Scotsmen. It was, and could only be, through ability. As disillusion with the practicalities of socialism grew, fewer young English people of high ability were to be found among the successive generations of recruits to the PLP. Not until it had been borne home that the Labour party was no longer socialist, that it was a political party not a crusade, that it was perhaps once more a party of government but of pragmatic government, and that therefore it offered the latent politician a career of interest, did many able young people from England invest their futures once more in the Party. The 1997 recruitment of Labour MPs was to include some such people. Scotland was different. There, socialist illusions, and therefore socialist convictions, persisted for longer than in England. They had survived the disappointments of the 1960s and 1970s. In Scotland, unlike England, socialism was not yet a dogma without friends. Scotland still provided an environment which encouraged talented young Scots to enter left-wing politics. They joined the Scottish Labour party intent on changing the world for the better. They were still socialists and had grown from socialist soil. It is questionable how long their socialism outlived experience of the world at Westminster and successive defeats in elections. By most of them, socialism was shed as they watched and waited. But they were there when the opportunity for office at last arrived. Even Blair himself, though sitting for an English constituency, attended a school in Scotland. When victory came, Blair would form a Cabinet many of whom could have constituted, without much competition, the Cabinet of an independent Scotland. But, though they demanded devolution for Scotland, they did not intend to limit their own scope by severing Scotland from England. Their dominance in the Blair government has become one of the stronger ties linking Scotland to England.

CLAUSE FOUR

During his campaign for the succession, Blair gave no hint that rewriting Clause Four was on his agenda.[4] Yet, with a decisive victory in the leadership election behind him, he set out to achieve the reform that had defeated Gaitskell. Blair saw that, even though a new clause might say nothing illuminating, a change would be symbolic of the fact that Labour itself had changed. Old Labour would have become New Labour. He announced his intention at the 1994 Blackpool Party Conference, his first as leader. To confront Clause Four had dramatic potential. The left would whinge and whine. Some trade union leaders would confirm by their conduct that their minds were no less insulated from the external world than those of their predecessors in the late 1950s, and might not even consult their members. Indeed, the opposition proved sufficiently large to demonstrate how deeply entrenched socialist convictions, or at least the addiction to socialist shibboleths, still were among members of the Labour party. Perhaps the principal lesson of the war against Clause Four was the vocal, if not voting, strength of the opposition. But the more the left and the unions protested, the more likely that the public would be persuaded that Labour really was a new party. The risk of failure was acceptably small. Gaitskell had launched his attack on Clause Four after an election which he had recently lost, and when it required both courage and imprudence to do so. Blair assaulted Clause Four when, as a new leader, he could not be humiliated as Gaitskell had been humiliated if there was to be any hope of victory in the coming General Election, and when the left was punch drunk by defeat after defeat inflicted both by the people in general elections and by Kinnock in changing the whole direction of party policy. Victory at the polls had become so dear to old and New Labour alike that most would accept in silence anything that Blair thought necessary to secure it. To defeat the Tories came now above any other consideration, including any consideration of loyalty to the socialist past. Blair was benefiting from a strong tide of opinion against the Tories which made their dismissal from government no longer an idle dream.

The Party had long abandoned Clause Four in practice. Clause Four, its critics argued, might have been apt in 1918 and 1945 but it was clearly not appropriate for 1994. Nevertheless, a survey of opinion among Labour MPs taken before the 1997 election found that 68 per cent of those polled regarded 'public ownership [as] . . . crucial to the achievement of social justice'.[5] After the 1997 election, only 48 per cent of the much larger, and younger, PLP were dedicated to the principle of state ownership of major public services.[6] It was still a large percentage in a party that had begun to describe itself as New Labour. It demonstrated the extent to which New Labour was a camouflage for deep-seated instincts that Blair had not yet charmed away. It remained unclear whether Blair himself would have conceded in 1995 that Clause Four had been apt at any time, even in 1918 and 1945.

In his battle against Clause Four, Blair recruited the support of John Prescott, seen as the malleable face of old Labour – in the then view of Robin Cook, the moderate left's most articulate spokesman, the too malleable face of old Labour.[7] Prescott had, in 1993, come to the aid of John Smith facing defeat at Conference on the subject of OMOV. Now he was deputy leader constituting with Blair the new dream ticket of right and left. It was a dream ticket without any destination except victory and from which socialism had been firmly deleted. On 25 January 1995, Robin Cook capitulated and announced a change of mind. He too was prepared to be malleable in the service of the Party. In the past he had opposed Scottish devolution. Now he allowed no quarter to any opponent of devolution. Abandoning old Labour, he was now in favour of rewriting Clause Four. '[A]s the debate has progressed I have come to recognise that it would be possible to replace Clause Four with a statement of aims that would be more radical in its values and more exciting as a political programme.' No other European social democratic party would recognize a definition of socialism that was confined to the single issue of public ownership.[8]

The revised Clause Four is said to have been conjured up by Blair himself, possibly assisted by John Prescott, a combination unlikely to produce uplifting prose. A Fabian socialist text was replaced by a politically convenient text. There was little in it of the ancient socialist creed but a great deal of mood music. The danger was, as in Gaitskell's time, that a new clause might be more damaging to Labour's electoral prospects than the old. It might remind the electorate that Labour was a socialist party. In the redraft, this danger was mitigated by the absence of any commitments to socialism in any sense that Bevan, Gaitskell or Crosland would have recognized. Blair had moved far beyond Crosland. There was no definition of socialism, merely vague words about 'common endeavour' and about 'power, wealth and opportunity' being in 'the hands of the many not the few'. As in the long past days of the Labour party as a socialist party, ambiguity was everything. The new Clause began by affirming that 'The Labour Party is a democratic socialist party.' Such an assertion was risky but inescapable. The Labour party has shown during its history that the word 'socialism' could be distorted to mean anything that it, its members or its leaders wanted it to mean. But even this flexibility had not been enough to reconcile the electorate to socialism. Blair could probably rely on the assertion not being taken seriously outside the Labour party. How far it was intended to be taken seriously in the new Labour party which Blair was in the course of inventing lay deep in his breast. At the 1993 TUC Conference, when he was seeking trade union support for OMOV, John Smith had recommitted the Party to full employment. Gordon Brown, the shadow Chancellor, had been dismayed. Experience since the early 1970s had suggested that it might be impossible to return to full employment as it had been defined by governments in the 1940s, 1950s and 1960s. To make such a commitment in the revised Clause Four would undermine its credibility. Nevertheless, some union leaders wanted an explicit reference to full employment in the new draft.[9] The final version endorsed 'the opportunity for all to work and prosper'. No doubt some read this as a confirmation of the traditional objective of full employment. Others could mourn or welcome, according to their economic tastes, the departure of full employment from the Labour party's portfolio of objectives together with wholesale nationalization.[10] The new draft showed the Clause Four exercise to have been intended not to write any new commitments but to abandon the old. Robin Cook should have been disappointed when he saw the new draft. There was nothing radical and nothing exciting. Although it has the special honour of a place in the Labour party constitution, the new Clause Four has suffered the fate of previous statements of aims and values. It displays none of the confidence in collective action, no doubt misplaced, which shone through the 1918 draft, nor has it the power to move. It was instantly forgettable and today, only a few years later, it must be doubtful whether anyone can recall it unassisted.

The new Clause was presented for approval to a special conference on 29 April 1995. With the trade unions casting 70 per cent of the vote, Blair won with a majority of 65 per cent, which included overwhelming support from constituency parties. A small majority even of the union vote was cast for the new text. It was a vote of confidence in the new leader which would certainly have been even more impressive if more unions had consulted their members. Socialism of a kind which the public had long regarded as a threat rather than as a promise was now officially extinct within the Labour party. It had been replaced by 'socialist values' to which anyone, not on the far right, could respond positively if they considered it worth while thinking about them. Blair had slain a dead sheep. But the successful battle helped to establish him in the public eye as a new and different leader. As the 1997 election approached, the question became what Labour might privatize rather than what Labour might nationalize. Labour had spent the first eighteen years of the century acquiring socialism and the subsequent eight decades disembarrassing itself of it. There was one criticism that could no longer be made of the Labour party, that it was not interested in power. All that could now be safely contended was that no one would know under Blair, any more than under Wilson or Callaghan, how that power was likely to be used.

A by-product of the Clause Four battle was the further distancing of the Labour party from the trade unions. The behaviour of major unions in not consulting their membership, but nevertheless casting their vote against the new Clause, was damaging to their reputation. Moreover Blair was benefiting from the severe weakening of the unions during the 1980s. Since 1979, when Labour was last in office, membership of unions had fallen from thirteen million to eight million. This was due to a variety of causes. Employment in manufacturing industry had fallen from seven million to about four million. Employment in coal mines had fallen from about 235,000 to under 18,000 and in steelworks from 150,000 to 36,500. The 36,500 were nevertheless producing 80 per cent of the previous output. On the other hand employment in the service industries, in which representation by unions was less common, had risen from 58 per cent of all employees to more than three-quarters. Other causes for the decline in the power of the unions were higher unemployment, privatization and the increase in part-time working.[11] Just as the unions had once asked themselves whether they really needed the Labour party, so now the Labour party could ask itself whether it really needed the unions. Leaks from sources close to Blair reported that he would be quite happy to see the link with the unions broken altogether, deterred only by the consequences for Labour party finances. There was, however, another deterrent to a final break. Blair, who had evidently studied Labour history, would be aware that there had been a time when the unions supported the leadership against the left. It was not inconceivable that such a time might recur and the support of the union block vote might prove a comfort when the exigencies of government demanded policies unpopular with Labour activists. It was with some relief that the unions discovered that this Labour leader cherished Party unity enough, or feared Party dissension sufficiently, to confirm Labour's commitments to a minimum wage (though at a level to be determined), to be prepared to ease the path to union recognition in recalcitrant companies and to adopt the Social Chapter of the European Union. Blair would, nevertheless, test the ancient saw that the Labour party needed a firm base in the trade union movement in the same way that Antaeus needed to have his feet on the earth. It had been agreed at the 1993 conference that if individual Party membership rose to 300,000, the trade union proportion of the vote at Party conferences, once 90 per cent, would fall from 70 per cent to 50 per cent. The figure would still leave the unions with unwarranted, if further reduced, influence within the Labour party. A membership figure of 300,000 was easily reached. By the end of 1996, membership was 400,000, and the change was implemented.[12]

In 1995, Blair gave a lecture to the Fabian Society. He celebrated his successes in renovating the Labour party. He paid various tributes. He spoke 'of the courage of one man. We would not be here, proud, and confident today, but for that man, Neil Kinnock. It grew under the wisdom of John Smith who guided us through the revolution in our Party democracy. We have transformed our party. Our Constitution is re-written. Our relations with the trade unions changed. Our Party organisation improved.'[13] He did not add that, so far as he was concerned, socialism was now defunct. There was always great care in selecting the wording with which to express the new leadership's revolutionary ideas. Thus, in a series of speeches on economic policy made by shadow Chancellor Gordon Brown in 1995, it was not nationalization that was abandoned but 'wholesale nationalization'. Or as Tony Blair put it on 13 March 1995, 'I don't think that anyone now believes that vast chunks of industry should be taken over by a Labour government.'[14] Some in the Labour party did still believe it, but the most they could hope for under a Blair government was small chunks, and doubtfully even that. Nevertheless, the left must still be able to feel at home in this new Labour party. It must not be provoked to become too obstreperous, at least until it was too late.

It would probably be wrong to suggest that Blair, in sacrificing socialism, had any regrets. Socialism, he clearly thought, was confronted by two irresistible forces. One was global capitalism. The other was the scepticism of the electorate about anything that smacked of socialism. This was perhaps unjust, because socialism had never really been tried in Britain. But the whiff of it to which the electorate had been subjected had evidently been enough. Blair's healthy respect for global economic forces, and for the opinions of the electorate, ensured that he would show only that minimum regard for traditional socialist values that he found politic. In his Mais lecture of 22 May 1995 he said:

> The growing integration of the world economy – in which capital, and to a lesser extent labour, moves freely – means that it is not possible for Britain to sustain budget deficits or a tax regime that are wildly out of line with other major industrial countries. One of the requirements of our tax structure is to attract enterprise into the UK from overseas.

Within the scepticism about socialism Blair detected hostility among the public to funding an unreformed welfare state. It was a sentiment that had been creeping slowly into Kinnock's mindset in his time. On 14 May 1997, in the debate on the Queen's Speech, Blair, now Prime Minister, said:

> Let us be clear: we have reached the limits of the public's willingness simply to fund an unreformed welfare system through ever higher taxes

and spending ... The blunt truth is that the world of 1997 bears little resemblance in work patterns, in industrial production and in social or family life to the world of 1947. Change is inevitable; but that change must be right and fair.[15]

In *The Middle Way*, his Conservative predecessor Harold Macmillan had written:

> While I think that ... there is room for some improvement in the social services financed [by taxation], I feel that it has become quite clear that in any circumstances which are conceivable under the existing conditions of economic life, *the limit of taxable capacity would be reached long before a satisfactory minimum standard of comfort and security could be guaranteed by this method alone.*[16]

Sixty years on, Blair had decided that the room for improvement in social services financed by taxation had now been exhausted. Fairness had replaced socialism as the criterion. But the forces of global integration, of which Blair had spoken in his Mais lecture, were not notable for their concern with fairness. And in any case the criteria for measuring fairness are more debatable even than those for measuring equality. The remaining question was whether he would stick to this hard choice under the countervailing pressures of government and of his Cabinet colleagues, some of whom did still cherish socialist values.

Tony Wright MP, one of the intellectuals of New Labour, tells us that 'Socialism is not defined by the size of the state's welfare bill any more than it is defined by the extent of public ownership.'[17] It is sad that New Labour seeks to justify itself by such facile juxtapositions. Public ownership was a shibboleth of old socialism. It is dispensable. Any civilized state, whatever the ideology of its governing party, will wish to ensure to the best of its ability a sufficient quality of life for those disadvantaged by birth, health, unemployment or other cause. A welfare bill is not dispensable.

WELFARE TO WORK

A programme, sometimes described as a 'New Deal', was to be developed to attack youth unemployment. The objective was to provide work or training for 250,000 young unemployed during the first New Labour Parliament. The programme was to be funded by a windfall tax on the excess profits of the privatized utilities. The policy was apparently announced without previous discussion in the shadow Cabinet. There was concern that the policy might involve a degree of coercion. There was suspicion that the idea was derived from the American workfare system. Gordon Brown was dismissive of any such fears. He asserted that 'This is not a lurch to the right. It is the Labour party stating values of decent hard-working people in this country – that in a modern society rights are matched by responsibilities.'[18] Thus the hard-working people of this country were set against those whose unemployment could be attributed to lack of effort. Whatever its prospects of reducing youth unemployment, such a programme had manifest political attractions, if not among old Labour then at least among the electorate generally. It would kill a flock of birds with one single stone. It would demonstrate that Labour would be tough on welfare, often interpreted especially among the working classes as being synonymous with scrounging. It would appease popular discontent at the behaviour of some senior managers of privatized utilities who had rewarded themselves with salaries far in excess of their deserts. A party that was trying to distance itself from the accusation of excessive devotion to taxing and spending could nevertheless afford the introduction of one such tax. The programme might even help with reducing unemployment, though that was more likely to depend on the success of New Labour's economic management than on its New Deal.

PRUDENCE

Labour's Achilles heel had always been its questionable competence as an economic manager. It was a reputation difficult to repair out of office. At least New Labour could attempt to win a character for prudence. That was now the priority. There was great concern not to repeat the error of John Smith's shadow budget before the 1992 election. On 20 January 1997, Gordon Brown, the shadow Chancellor, promised not to raise income tax rates for the five years of the next Parliament. It would appear that Brown had wished to keep open the possibility of a higher rate on high incomes. But Blair had been warned by his adviser Philip Gould, who had taken the opinion of focus groups, that 'Large numbers think that a higher-rate band, even when set at £100,000, is a tax on success. And there is a deep-seated unease with such a tax; to many it seems punitive rather than fair.'[19] Given the sensitivity of the issue, and his wish to win the franchise of 'middle England', Blair vetoed increases in income tax and Brown accepted the veto. Brown further promised that a Labour government would live within the Major government's public expenditure plans for the first two years of the Parliament. By these two promises Blair and Brown blocked in advance the pressure that, in the immediate aftermath of a Labour victory, would undoubtedly arise from the trade unions and backbench MPs for additional expenditures to meet social requirements. By the same token, they had demolished a further barrier to a Labour victory, their Party's notoriety as too keen on taxation and too ready to spend. Thereby Blair and Brown were equally demolishing one of the residual elements of socialist policy, its eagerness to increase spending on welfare or, to employ the pejorative words employed by the opponents of socialism, to throw money at social problems. Brown's Golden Rule would also prove a deterrent to Cabinet spendthrifts. It would dissuade his Cabinet colleagues from demanding that old Labour recipe for progress toward socialism, borrowing. Public borrowing would be limited by the size of public investment, not expanded to meet the appetites of departmental Ministers for current spending. It was not foolproof, but it showed good intentions.

Only hinted at before the General Election, but clearly planned well in advance, was Brown's first step as Chancellor of the Exchequer. Within days, operational independence was given to the Bank of England in setting interest rates to meet a government-indicated inflation target.[20] This partial transfer of monetary policy to the Bank was clearly intended to win the confidence of the market. The markets would grant greater credibility to a monetary policy conducted by the Bank of England than by the Treasury – by the Bank rather than a Labour government. Among other advantages, it would act as yet a further constraint on a Cabinet anxious to spend, even if necessary by excessive borrowing. It would give the Chancellor a new and powerful weapon in the control of public expenditure. He could now threaten his colleagues not just with the wrath of the market but with the reaction of the Monetary Policy Committee at the Bank. The Prime Minister and Chancellor would warn them of what would happen to interest rates if they were fiscally irresponsible. Independence for the Bank was a profoundly unsocialist action. It showed respect for the markets but none for socialist ideology. Socialists had always insisted on controlling all the levers of economic management. It was one thing that socialists had in common with Mrs Thatcher, who also believed that all the instruments of economic policy must be in her hands. It would have been impossible to conceive of a socialist conceding that monetary policy should be managed, outside political control, by a nominated monetary committee at the Bank of England. Where would central planning be if monetary policy was controlled by the Bank? What would Dalton and Gaitskell have thought of it, they who had refused to raise interest rates even when sterling was threatened? Yet Blair and Brown had not merely placed monetary policy beyond political control. They boasted of having done so. Implicitly Blair and Brown had also decided that they would not rely on the TUC for support in the battle against inflation. For that battle the Bank of England was better equipped, even though it meant that there would be no return to a level of unemployment that rendered the country hostage to trade union demands. The irony is that trade unionists were as much victims as perpetrators of post-war inflation.

Partly because of earlier follies, and the suspicions of Labour competence that they had aroused, less could now be done by way of redistribution and help to the poor than might otherwise have been possible. The middle and upper classes might now well conclude that their privileges and property would be better defended by a Labour party that had rejected drastic redistribution than by a Conservative party that provoked the hostility of the working classes.

CONSTITUTIONAL REFORM

In one area the intentions of a Blair government were clearly radical. It was prepared to concede devolution, particularly to Scotland. It was radical in the sense that the roots of an old constitutional settlement were being torn up. It was a great deal more doubtful whether any new roots were being put down. It cannot at this writing be claimed that the abolition of the rights of hereditary peers in the House of Lords is radical because it remains unknown what will be the final form and powers of the second chamber. John Smith had been in charge of devolution under Michael Foot during the Callaghan government and was said to regard the failure at that time to secure the necessary referendum consents as 'unfinished business'. To this extent the devolution plans of the Blair government were an inheritance from John Smith, not one necessarily welcomed with enthusiasm by Blair himself. But there was more to it than that. There is undoubted disaffection in Scotland with the English connection. There was disillusion with the UK's economic performance with, for most of the post-war period, Scotland lagging even further behind. The end of empire deprived Britons of a source of employment and adventure. The discovery of oil in the North Sea appeared to promise the people of Scotland a bonanza, at least if the OPEC cartel survived and could enforce its will. It was, in any case, nonsense to suppose that an independent Scotland could not prosper and the existence of the European Union offered the psychological comfort of an embrace alternative to that of England, of which many Scots have grown tired.

The Labour party proposed to lubricate the discontent in Scotland by creating a devolved Scottish Parliament with certain legislative and tax-raising powers. A referendum was to be held to confirm Scottish support for the idea, but, in a striking demonstration of lack of self-confidence in English and Scottish Labour, it would not offer the alternative of independence. Nor would it offer the people of England any say in the matter. Whether the treatment will meet the sickness is another question. Major constitutional changes were being planned without any consideration of their implications for the remainder of the UK. The devolution of power from Westminster was to be forced through in a way that was bound to create dissension in England and might thus exacerbate relations between England and Scotland rather than improve them. Scotland was to be rewarded with an advantageous financial settlement, and with an inequitable representation in the Westminster parliament where Scottish MPs would be able to vote on English questions of a kind which in Scotland, would be reserved to the Scottish Parliament. Taking account of devolution intended for Wales and Northern Ireland, approximately one-sixth of the members of the Westminster Parliament would be entitled to vote on matters that would not concern their constituents. The expected beneficiary of these inequitable arrangements was the Labour party, which feared that, without Scotland and Wales, it would seldom be able to govern England. It may be to no avail. It may be found that devolution is both offensive to the English and comes nowhere near meeting Scottish ambitions. In the far distance, perhaps, there is a federal solution, with English regions gaining powers comparable to those devolved in Scotland. It would be optimistic to imagine that the federal option answers the dilemma. Scotland is a nation with its own legal system and traditions. Regarding itself as such, it is at least questionable whether it would accept a final settlement as merely the equivalent of an English region. But at least a federal solution would have had some logic as compared with the ill-considered and ill-prepared dash to preserve Labour's position in Scotland at any cost by means of the constitutional outrage of devolution.

FAREWELL TO CROSLAND

The new Labour leaders thought of themselves as engaged in the modernization of Labour. They were not engaged in a revision of socialism. Modernization was not revisionism. Modernization was concerned with the problem of making the Labour party electable once more and also with finding whether its residual socialism, egalitarianism and the relief of poverty, was acceptable to the electorate and capable of being accommodated in a world characterized by the free movement of capital. If it could, well and good. The leaders would feel more comfortable with their own past. But if it could not, then everything from the past must give way to the quest for victory and the alternative comfort of Ministerial chairs. For the modernizers to claim to be socialists would have required a far more dramatic redefinition than that which Crosland had attempted to impose on the Labour party.

An essential element in Crosland's revisionism was the belief that one could, by socialist methods, combine greater equality with faster growth. This idea is to be found in both Durbin and Crosland, the foremost British philosophers of democratic socialism. In Crosland, faster growth is an essential condition of greater equality. When, however, it is found that socialist methods do not produce faster growth, may in fact inhibit faster growth, does the logic require the dropping of equality? The modernizers could excuse their abandonment of equality by insisting that socialism had not yielded the expected dividend of higher growth, that there had been no evidence that it ever would yield such a dividend, that therefore they had been compelled to become managers of capitalism and hence to abandon equality. The best answer a modernizer could provide to the accusation that he had abandoned equality is that his way – the free market way – *would* lead to faster growth and hence probably to a higher standard of living for the great majority of the population than would be achieved under a programme which gave priority to equality. That may be true, but it might still do very little for all those disadvantaged to whom, in the past, Labour has held out a promise of help. Thus, while it may be true, it is not socialism. Moreover it cannot be proved.

Despite Blair's refashioning of the Labour party, its claim to election still lay primarily in disgust with the Tories. They had been in office too long, were behaving arrogantly and in some cases dishonestly. Provided Labour could persuade the electorate that it would govern prudently, would avoid socialist ideology and would make as few concessions as possible to its trade union partners, there could be hope that the electorate might be prepared to gamble with a bunch of fresh faces in government. Such moderation was sensible if not precisely exciting or replete with hope for any major improvement in the performance of the economy. In one respect, however, modernization became populism and showed a readiness to make compromises against the weight of the evidence. Crosland had regarded it as a not unimportant reason for being a member of the Labour party that its attitudes were liberal on penal issues. New Labour's policy on crime and punishment attempted to strengthen its claims on the confidence of the electorate by pandering to popular prejudice. Blair's slogan as shadow Home Secretary had been 'Tough on crime, tough on the causes of crime'. Tough on crime meant following in the footsteps of the lamentable Conservative Home Secretary Michael Howard, whose principal achievement was to fill the prisons to bursting point. Tough on the causes of crime suggested that there were special Labour insights into the causes of crime, just as once there had been thought to be special socialist insights into economic growth. The policy encapsulated in the slogan ignored much research which it was politically convenient to discount, but in electoral terms it was riskless. Crime statistics, in any case unreliable, may go up or down. If they went down, there would be credit to claim, however unjustifiably. If they went up, a Labour government would no doubt find the political answer in even further increases in the use of imprisonment. Either way, the electorate would feel content that it had a government tough on crime even if ineffective. Because of contamination in prison, an earlier, and more attractive, Conservative Home Secretary, Douglas Hurd, had described the excessive use of imprisonment as an expensive way of making bad people worse. But New Labour was not to be diverted by such liberal conceits. Crosland's liberalism was being forgotten together with his socialism.

MODERNIZERS AND REVISIONISTS

Gradually there emerged a distinction between modernizers and revisionists. The distinction was not black and white. There was often something of a modernizer in a revisionist and often something of a revisionist in a modernizer. Hattersley, spokesman for a diminishing band within the higher ranks of the Labour party, was not essentially a modernizer. He was a revisionist. Revisionism acknowledged the need to make changes in policy in order to win an election. But revisionists were determined to hang on to something they could call socialism. They had by this time abandoned much that was in Crosland, for example nationalization as a way to efficiency, but they clung to as much of his legacy as their view of practical politics permitted. Essentially this meant some movement towards greater equality, however small, and therefore some readiness to raise direct taxes in order to redistribute income and to fund policies of benefit to the poorer sections of the community. It was little enough but sufficient, in his view, to entitle Hattersley to adopt a high moral tone in his relations with the modernizers.

The battle between revisionists and modernizers had been settled by the death of John Smith and the election of Tony Blair. There were two principal modernizers in the Labour party, Tony Blair and Gordon Brown. These two overshadowed the rest, Blair by personality and Brown by intellect. Brown was a modernizer because he saw the need to adapt policy. Blair was a modernizer because he was ambitious for victory. Brown sought some thread linking his thought to that of Crosland. He was for equality, even if not exactly equality in the sense that Crosland would have understood it.[21] Blair carried no ideological baggage, unless it be the importance of discipline. A Blair state could not permit unconditional rights. There would be rights but there would also be obligations. He had replaced socialism by a cool Christian benevolence, and only as much of that as Brown, as shadow Chancellor, would allow him to dispense. He spoke of Labour as the party of the 'new radical centre'.[22] It was one of those phrases, lacking distinct meaning, that a politician of the right might use if he wished to broaden his appeal. Blair seemed to feel no debts to Labour's past. There was, however, much in it from which he wished to learn. For example, he wished to be sure that he could never be smeared with the accusation levelled against Wilson and Callaghan. There must never be any justification to accuse him of betrayal. It was said of Blair that he wished to get his betrayal in first. He had written, 'With the ideology and organisational change, there has to come the attitude of mind of a party to govern. Part of this means that activists should not rise to every bait held out by the press or revive the old "betrayal" psychology that has dogged the party before.'[23]

The modernizers attracted to their cause some old Labour stalwarts whose priority was office, a priority which they could adopt with a good conscience because, to them, it had become obvious that socialism was politically dead. There is a limit to the amount of time one can sensibly devote to praying round a corpse. The modernizers even drew to their support many from the far left of the Labour party. They too had concluded that it was desirable that Labour should, once again, form a government and they were prepared to make what they saw as the inevitable compromises. They no longer believed that socialism was a good electoral cry. Those sucked in from a far-left position by the vacuum left by the death of socialism included Margaret Beckett, once a devoted supporter of Tony Benn and of the plans to nationalize twenty-five major companies under the aegis of an NEB. Benn found himself increasingly isolated. He retained his eloquence and his charm. He was still a great entertainer. He would still be listened to in the House of Commons on constitutional issues, on which he had originally made his name. But as to managing the economy, or regenerating British industry, he was seen as a relic from a remote past, studied intently by Labour archaeologists, and other students of a mythological age, but not suitable any longer for exposure on Labour's front bench. At last he was harmless, the final indignity. Another old warrior not attracted to the modernization project was Arthur Scargill, President of the NUM, a man of the far left who never knew when he was beaten and who, as a result, was beaten time and again. It was entirely logical, in the circumstances, that Scargill should leave the Labour party and form a Socialist Labour party. It attracted negligible support. But it was difficult to know whether this was due more to popular distaste for socialism, to disbelief among Labour voters that their Party had actually abandoned socialism, or simply to the perception that to be led by Scargill was not a recipe for survival.

The division between the modernizers and the revisionists sprang to public notice within a few weeks of Blair's victory in the 1997 General Election. The argument between the two centred on the question whether equality of opportunity was an adequate objective for a Labour government or whether it should have more regard to outcomes. Crosland in *The Future of Socialism* had insisted that equality of opportunity was not enough to create a just, and hence socialist, society.

> equal opportunity, if still combined ... with a marked stratification between an élite and the rest of the population, will not remove all the discontents which extreme inequality creates, and in particular cases may even intensify them ... an aristocracy of talent is an obvious improvement on a hereditary aristocracy, since no one is in fact denied an equal chance. Yet I do not believe, as a personal value judgement, that it can be described as a 'just' society.[24]

557

Eighteen years later, in *Socialism Now*, Crosland repeated this message.

> By equality, we meant more than a meritocratic society of equal opportu-
> nities in which the greatest rewards would go to those with the most
> fortunate genetic endowment and family background ... We also meant
> more than a simple ... redistribution of income. We wanted a wider
> social equality embracing also the redistribution of property, the edu-
> cational system, social-class relationships, power and privilege in industry
> – indeed all that was enshrined in the age-old socialist dream of a more
> 'classless society'.[25]

Hattersley had asserted in *Choose Freedom* that 'The equality we seek
is equality of outcome.'[26] He elaborates,

> All that 'equality of outcome' demands is that society should attempt to
> replace ... 'imposed' and ever-increasing inequalities with a conscious
> effort to remove or to reduce them. Equality of outcome is, in reality, a
> just distribution of the nation's resources – not the chance to grab some-
> thing extra (which is equality of opportunity) but the real prospect of
> receiving a fair share of wealth and power.[27]

Bringing down upon his old friends the ultimate penalty of excommuni-
cation, Hattersley proclaimed that 'it is hard to describe New Labour
as a democratic socialist party'. He expressed surprise and distress that,
unlike Attlee after 1945 and Wilson after 1964 and 1974, the New
Labour government appeared unwilling to follow the traditional
inflationary policies of incoming Labour governments justified by their
intended effect in relieving poverty and inequality. He attacked David
Blunkett, now Secretary of State for Education and Employment, for
saying in February 1997: 'The truth is that any government entering
the 21st century cannot hope to create a more equal or egalitarian
society simply by taking from one set of people and redistributing it to
others, as envisaged when the rich were very rich and the poor made
up the rest.' Hattersley accused the new Labour government of abandoning the belief that 'the good society is the equal society'. It was not
'a force for a more equal society. That ideological apostasy has freed
egalitarians from the obligation to support all it does. Loyalty to the
idea ... not only justifies dissent. It demands it.'[28]

The new government clearly considered that this attack on its socialist
credentials from a former deputy leader required a response from its
highest levels. Blunkett replied in a letter in the *Guardian*. 'You can
give the poor some money for a period of time but they still remain
poor.' What was necessary was to help them to escape from poverty by
providing, for example, education and training. He accepted that there

would still be those, the 'vulnerable,' who would need support of the old kind.[29] But, bearing in mind how slow acting is improvement in the system of education, even if it is known how to bring such an improvement about, it is no wonder that an old-fashioned revisionist like Hattersley should remain unpersuaded. Gordon Brown provided a response of wider scope in another article in the *Guardian*. It was a straight rebuttal of the Hattersley ideology. Brown began by genuflecting in the direction of old Labour and all other men and women of goodwill. He reassured the world that Labour, in the course of its modernization, had not yet reneged on its 'fundamental belief in the equal worth of every human being'.[30] He then got down to the real argument. He rejected 'old solutions that fail to address the problems of the 1990s'. Equality of outcome was 'unattainable'. It was 'neither desirable nor feasible'. He accepted that what he called 'narrow equality of opportunity' was also not enough. But the right policy was equality of opportunity bolstered by all the other steps the government was taking. He listed the steps that would place equality of opportunity in the right context. The new government was encouraging movement from welfare to work; it would reduce unemployment, a major source of poverty; it would ensure that work 'pays'; it would improve the quality of education and training; it would introduce a minimum wage at a 'sensible' level. 'Merely to pursue a strategy to raise benefits by a few pounds – as Roy Hattersley suggests – would do nothing more than compensate people for their poverty, without tackling the causes.' Of course there were the sick, the elderly and the disabled, who would need support.[31] There would also, unsaid, be a long gap in time before the Brown remedies could yield their benefits. In a separate essay Brown attempted to secure his link to Crosland, even though that might have the appearance of reverting to old solutions that failed to address the problems of the 1990s. He writes, 'we reject – as Anthony Crosland did – both an unrealisable equality of outcome and a narrow view of equality of opportunity'.[32]

In this battle of the mini-titans, what was mainly evident was that a breach had opened up. The breach probably existed also within the government because it was not to be assumed that everyone in the government was comfortable with the views of Blunkett and Brown, or indeed that Blunkett was happy with the views of Brown. Hattersley was fighting for all that was left of the socialism of his youth. Brown was fighting for the only way he saw of regenerating the British economy and hence for the future. What he wrote could have been written by any member of the previous government, give or take the politically necessary side-kicks at the new right. Polemics do not always do justice to the enemy, especially perhaps when the enemy is within one's own ranks. Hattersley did not want simply to compensate people for poverty. He wanted a policy that would raise people from poverty and understood that would need the regeneration of the economy. That certainly did not, in his view, limit the upper income tax rate to only 40 per cent. Moreover, for the old and sick, a few pounds now would be more valuable than promises of a brighter future. Hattersley realized that equality of outcome was unattainable. That did not rule out a fairer outcome than he saw emerging from Brown's policies. He could also argue, as Crosland had done, that equality of opportunity was itself 'unattainable' within so unequal a society.

Brown, on the other hand, while attempting unavailingly to defend the government's socialist values, could claim that, if Britain was to prosper within the global economy, his was the only road the government could choose. He might well be right in that judgement. But it left him with a variety of problems. To describe his policies as socialist would have been to stretch the meaning of that word far beyond its possible elasticity. His main problem though was that he could not guarantee success. He was beset by all the uncertainties of economic management. He had given hostages to fortune, as all Chancellors do who make great claims. His words might well come back to mock him. But how could a Chancellor in a Labour government confess that he had taken the capitalist road, inequality but prosperity? Socialism might be dead, but the time for such confessions was not yet.

VICTORY

It had proved exceedingly difficult to prise the Party free from the drug of socialism. At least the Party had now modernized itself to some extent. It had modernized itself rather more slowly than British capitalism normally responds to foreign competition. But at last something had been done. Blair had forced his Party into a new mould which he called New Labour. It had to be Labour even if it was New Labour. That tribute to Labour's past had to be paid so that he could collect the dividend of Labour's traditional vote. By 1997 almost all socialists had realized that they were condemned to live in a capitalist society and world. Capitalism was no longer necessarily evil nor even a necessary evil. On the contrary it was positively good – provided only that it was pulled and pushed a bit in the interests of equality of some kind and by some definition, and even that now seemed dispensable to some. Caution, however, continued to require that approving references should be to the market rather than to capitalism.

By the time of the General Election there were five discernible aspects to New Labour. First came the abandonment of socialism in any traditional sense of the word; secondly, an insistence on economic prudence in order to recapture the confidence of the electorate but also in the hope that stability would encourage growth; thirdly, in domestic policy, a moralistic attitude to the reform of social welfare, emphasizing work rather than dependence; fourthly, an inclination to a more pro-European stance than that of most of its predecessor British governments, though heavily modified by threats of the use of the 'veto' if British interests were threatened;[33] fifthly, a distancing, though probably not a break, from the trade unions. In addition, priority was to be given to education and health, but that hardly distinguished New Labour from other varieties of Labour. The programme had the attraction that it eschewed the exaggerated ambitions of the Attlee and Wilson governments. It had the appearance of modesty appropriate to modern governments. It was not designed, almost deliberately, to disappoint. Whether it was, even so, still too ambitious, its supporters would have to wait patiently to discover.

On 1 May 1997, New Labour won an overwhelming majority of 179 in the House of Commons, a majority exceeding even that of Attlee in July 1945. It was a result flattered by the grossly disproportionate electoral system. The Major government had become totally discredited and, at about 31 per cent, the Conservative party attracted its lowest share of the vote since 1832. Yet Labour and its new leader had still to be satisfied with less than a 44 per cent share. As a share, this was 4 per cent less than old Labour had won in 1945 and 1966. Despite everything Blair had done to conciliate the electorate, there still seemed to be many doubts. Blair declared encouragingly that, having been elected as New Labour, he would govern as New Labour. It was not a declaration designed to bring comfort to socialists. But, once in office, Labour's poll ratings rose spectacularly. The absence of any crisis following the election appears to have removed, for the time being, any anxiety about the risks taken in electing an inexperienced Labour government.

On 2 May 1997, Blair became Prime Minister of a much diminished

United Kingdom. In one sense it was diminished in the way that all national governments had been diminished. Globalization had not eliminated the discretion of national governments though it had tightly constrained it. But there were other senses in which the UK was diminished that were all its own. It was no longer the centre of an empire or of a sterling area. It was hardly even the centre of a Commonwealth. True, it still had its nuclear bomb and its permanent membership of the UN Security Council. It had armed forces which were respectable as compared with those of its European partners. But its military capability was as nothing compared with that of the USA. At the same time Europe, in which it had a voice if not a major influence, had never succeeded in organizing its foreign policy or military resources in a way which would give it an international credibility comparable with that of the USA. In these respects the diminution of the UK's status in the world had been inevitable. However there were other aspects of its diminution which were fundamentally the result of post-war British policy. Its international economic influence had been eroded by failures in economic performance and the weakness of its currency. It was part of the European Union but, despite all its efforts, it had never succeeded in extracting any share of leadership from the Franco-German alliance or even in joining it. It was isolated by its scepticism on monetary union, which had become the prime project of its continental neighbours. Blair wanted Britain to become a beacon to the world. But other countries would clearly take much convincing before they saw much value in following a light flickering offshore. Rather their policies would be guided by their own experience and their own judgement.

To all appearances, Britain had left itself with no choice or been left with no choice but, in the words with which Adam Smith completed *The Wealth of Nations*, 'to accommodate her future views and designs to the real mediocrity of her circumstances'. British governments of all persuasions want for their country something more than mediocrity. Blair wants Britain to be 'the creative powerhouse of the world'.[34] He wants to regenerate the economy, to punch in international affairs above Britain's weight, to exercise influence in Europe. He may even want his country to shine in the creative arts. Yet, outside the area of defence, and there questionably, there is no sign that the Blair government has policies directed to such ends. However prudent the Chancellor, however warm the love affair with business, however close the relationship with the newly triumphant social democrats in Europe, the necessary policies are still lacking. Nor is it at all clear where they will be found.

THE PREACHING TENDENCY

Despite the lack of policies commensurate with its ambitions, in one respect at least New Labour has been infected with the same disease as old Labour and, indeed, old Conservative. The preaching tendency is strong within it. New Labour's Europeanism moved on from the social market to labour flexibility and competitiveness. As unemployment rose on the mainland of Europe, and fell in Britain, Labour's leaders began to preach the lessons they had learnt from Mrs Thatcher. Thus New Labour, with the ardour of the convert, preaches labour-market flexibility in Europe. It is right that a British government should defend British interests as it sees them. This is, however, a requirement short of telling others how to manage their affairs. The preaching started before the Blair government had any record in government to justify it. The post-war British economic record is not so splendiferous as to constitute a pulpit from which to preach to others. Equally it might have been advisable if the Blair government had waited for its economic policies to achieve success before advocating them broadcast, and, even then, hesitated. But such modesty is outwith the capacity of British governments. Alternatively, they are so persuaded of their various economic panaceas, each one in turn, that, new light having dawned, generosity to the world forbids their keeping the message to themselves even for a moment. Britain may have lost one global role but its leaders cherish another, that of missionary (though not for socialism). British Prime Ministers are preachers or they are nothing. In this, at least, there is no learning from history.

The third way

THE THIRD WAY

A few months after its election, the Blair government launched a search for a political philosophy with the provisional title of the 'third way'. The pragmatists of the Blair government had evidently decided that they needed not just policies, if they could find any equal to their self-imposed tasks, but a marching tune, some theme that would give coherence to their pragmatism and make presentation simpler. Having accepted so much from Mrs Thatcher and the preceding Conservative governments, it was ungrateful of Labour Ministers, once in office, to abuse their inheritance. Ingratitude did not, however, blind them to the possibility that the successes of Thatcherism, such as they were, were attributable to the power of the neo-liberal idea. They were encouraged thereby to seek an idea of their own as powerful as Thatcherism had been supposed to be. If they could discover one, it might help with the regeneration of the British economy and reputation to which they felt themselves pledged. Those dispirited by vacuous ejaculations like the 'third way' should not attribute the barren search that has since followed simply to the stupidity of Britain's new political leaders. Rather it is attributable to the political imperatives that led apparently sensible men to spend time on this folly.

First, members of the Labour government, in an era when ideology is at a discount, are searching desperately for an 'idea' which separates them from their Conservative opponents but which yet will appeal to voters, especially among the middle classes on whom their hope of re-election is thought to depend. So arises all the waffle about the importance New Labour attributes to 'community' as contrasted with the alleged *laissez-faire* attitudes of the displaced Tories. The second imperative is stronger and yet far more difficult to satisfy. Blair had earned leadership of the Labour party by promising it victory. That promise he has kept. But how should he preserve the discipline he had enforced in the days of opposition and aspiration, how avoid accusations of betrayal, once victory had been won? There are still numerous social-ists scattered under the arches of Labour's broad church awaiting the opportunity to bellow forth their dissent. There were two ways of fight-ing their antediluvian views. The first was the imposition within the Labour party of autocratic central control, even to the extent of denying dissidents the democratic privilege for which the right had fought in its battle against Benn, OMOV. That might be necessary, though equally it might offend not just socialists but a wider public that might think that freedom of speech was permissible even within political parties, and that the OMOV policy was no less appropriate with Labour in government than when it was on its best behaviour seeking the responsi-bilities of government. It would be a defeat if Blair actually had to turn to the trade union block vote to bolster his control of his Party. The alternative way was to find an idea, an idea as vibrant as socialism, with the assistance of which Blair could persuade his dissident troops that he could offer them something at least as attractive as the vision from which they had been asked to turn their eyes. It seemed worth the attempt even though, in that task, the prospects of success were always slim. To the dissident wing of the Labour party, socialism dead remains more seductive than the third way living.

The problem continues to be the lack of powerful ideas on the left of the new centre. Presumably the new idea must find some way of reconciling the market with all its faults with socialist values with all their opacity. The left has provided no help in the search for a new idea. This is not surprising because the sterility of the left predates Aneurin Bevan. Certainly recession has led to the advocacy of more restrictions on the 'free market'. This advocacy comes from a variety of sources but, oddly and perhaps encouragingly, that includes Marxists. One cannot blame socialists for deriving whatever pleasure they can from the failings of capitalism. But even some Marxists seem now to understand that no answer is be found in socialism to the congenital recessions and depressions of capitalism. The most the left can now offer as a policy is the better regulation of the capitalist economy – not a prescription likely to inspire the masses. This bankruptcy of the left is the best evidence that capitalism has won the ideological battle not merely over Soviet socialism but equally over democratic socialism and its twin sister social democracy. Thus the Marxist historian Eric Hobsbawm can find no relief from his ideological humiliation other than to tell his readers that the operation and progress of the global economy 'are not identical to the policy of extreme *laissez-faire*', which, of course, they never have been, and that the actors in the global market 'require the equivalent of a system of law with sanctions to guarantee the performance of contracts', which, of course, they always have done. Hobsbawm adds that the basic problem is now twofold. 'It is how we control and regulate the operations of a capitalist market economy.' Secondly, 'it is how to distribute the enormous wealth generated and accumulated by our society to its inhabitants'.[1] These banalities speak for themselves. There is no way of providing absolute security against the re-emergence of failed doctrines. Dead trees and dead doctrines have an uncanny habit of putting down live roots. But, when Marxists such as Hobsbawm acknowledge the enormous productivity of the capitalist economy and look for their response to capitalist crisis in the better regulation of capitalism rather than to socialism, it certainly signals the final intellectual triumph of the market economy. Others, apart from Marxists, look for better regulation of the 'free market' in order to preserve standards of living in countries threatened by recession. But that the discussion should be of this nature demonstrates once more that the époque during which capitalism was receiving premature last rites from the purveyors of socialism is over and that the time has come, or even is past, for celebrating the obsequies of socialism.

Nor will there be much in the way of ideological refurbishment to be derived from the business community, with which Blair is conducting a love affair. Blair feels more comfortable with businessmen than with union leaders. The preference is venial, but to expect too much from it would be an error. The unions watch bemused as businessmen rather than trade unionists arrive as welcome guests at No. 10 Downing Street, exercising influence and accepting Ministerial appointments and peerages from a Labour Prime Minister. The objection to the love affair lies not in the attempt to establish good relations with industrial and financial management but rather in the danger that government policy will be unduly swayed by quite narrow perspectives coming from the selection of businessmen who gain favour or who seek influence. Closer acquaintance will not necessarily make the hearts on either side of the love affair grow fonder. The imperatives of government are as likely to distance it from business as to draw it closer. The love affair parallels that between Wilson and the industrial leaders of his time. It did not then last long. By 1969, Wilson had fallen out with the business community as well as with the trade unions. The business community has its own criteria by which it judges governments. They do not include the number of peerages and knighthoods awarded or even the number of Ministerial appointments. Gratitude for these benefactions is of short duration, and patronage once granted cannot be withdrawn. It merely gives critics a higher profile. Business will judge by how far the policies of the government ease its tasks or, alternatively, make them more difficult. It will not accept criticism from a government, short of industrial experience, which accuses it of failures to improve competitiveness. It may even be so heterodox as to suggest that an oil magnate from BP or a retailer from Sainsbury have little to teach a mechanical or electrical engineer, let alone a purveyor of financial services. The dilemmas of government policy will not reconcile the business community to high interest rates or a high exchange rate. It will always believe that there is a way of reconciling contrary objectives provided only that the government listens to it rather than to the Treasury or the Bank. The opportunities for dissension between a Labour government and the business community are manifold. They also include the unreliability of the business community as a source of support. Business leaders are influenced by current intellectual fashions. But they tend to turn aside when the going gets difficult. A study of the changing attitudes of the business community on the question of British participation in the ERM, from enthusiastic support to bitter hostility, will demonstrate that there is no comfort to be derived from the companionship of business leaders in a jungle inhabited by market forces.

There being no other source of third-way ideas external to government, the flower of academia has been recruited to fill the ideological gap. Recruitment has not presented any problems. Nature abhors a vacuum and strong forces and strong intellects have crowded in to fill this particular vacuum. Friendly social and political scientists treasure the opportunity to influence the thinking of government. They are offering their own stuffing with which to fill out the empty carcass of the third way. An ally in the search for the third way has been the Clinton administration in the USA. Seminars have been held in New York and Washington with the most distinguished attendance, including heads of government. Continental European leaders have been invited. But there is no sign yet of an approximation between the social-market tradition of continental Europe and the free-market philosophy of the USA. On the contrary, with the increasing dominance on the European continent of left-wing governments which cherish the social market and find the American example socially unappealing, a third way that united

Britain and America would alienate Britain further from Europe. It may also alienate the Blair government from the British trade union movement, which discovered in the social-market tradition of continental Europe one of the allurements of European integration.

Meanwhile, even at this early stage in the elaboration of the new philosophy, a few observations on the emerging content of the third way are possible. In the simplest terms the third way may be intended to sustain socialist values after the collapse of socialism by insisting that market forces must operate fairly, not a constraint that they will easily accept. It may be a way of saving capitalism from itself by humanizing it, but capitalism is no longer under threat for want of any alternative. It therefore does not need to be saved. It may be a way of disguising the fact that differences between political parties on economic and social issues have diminished towards vanishing point. Professor Anthony Giddens, prominent in the search for a third way, offers as the prime motto of what he calls the new politics 'no rights without responsibilities', probably the most right-wing cry to emerge from anyone regarding themselves, as he does, as a social democrat.[2] There is much talk of citizenship, democracy, decentralization, community, participation, social justice, not to mention other admirable objectives. All these can be incorporated in the third way without provoking much excitement or controversy, but equally without providing much enlightenment. There was some suggestion that the third way is economic efficiency plus social cohesion. None of this is likely to propel partisan blood to the head. Ministers examined their departmental operations and selected items suitable for registration under the heading of the third way. By the time of Tony Blair's 1998 Fabian pamphlet entitled *The Third Way*, the public was being invited to admire a political philosophy fully fledged with the help of departmental briefs. Interspersed with Blair's own text were the supposedly relevant programmes of the different departments of his government. They extend from the welfare-to-work programmes, through public–private partnerships, to incentives for excellence. Herbert Morrison is supposed to have said, and may well have said, that socialism is what a Labour government does. We have already discussed this *obiter dictum* and interpreted it as what a Labour government is *prepared* to do. The third way may turn out to be what a New Labour government is prepared to do, anything that it is prepared to do.

Is the third way a compass or a policy? By definition, a third way rejects two other ways, presumably the way to the right and the way to the left. In this sense it seems to be a compass. However, after some hesitation it turned out to be a policy, not one rigorously defined but characterized as some form of social democracy. Blair writes, 'The Third Way stands for a modernised social democracy, passionate in its commitment to social justice and the goals of the centre-left, but flexible, innovative and forward-looking in the means to achieve them.'[3] Passion would seem to be the least likely characteristic of the third way. Giddens regards the third way as the renewal of social democracy. He then constructs a wish-list of desirable policies in both the domestic and international fields to most of which Crosland would have given assent, though he would probably have found it inadequate on the score of equality. It remains unclear why a wish-list should attract the description of the third way. The probability must be that when the third-way travellers set out on their journey they did not know where they would arrive and that it is has been a surprise to them as well as to others that, having circled the world of political thought, they have arrived back at social democracy. This evocation of social democracy should not be too constricting. After all, the term 'social democracy' has been defined and redefined over the decades, almost always moving to the right. The third way is on the left of the new centre but only just. The question that arises is why, if it is a revised form of social democracy, it is necessary to persist with the confusing designation of the third way. The term the 'third way' will always carry the undesirable implication that policies are chosen not on merit, nor on the basis of political principle, but because they are different from someone else's policies.

The middle way was an attempt, certainly misguided, to combine what were perceived as the best features of capitalism with the best features of socialism. The best features of capitalism were entrepreneurial vigour and private property. The best features of socialism were regarded as being protection, planning, some public ownership, security in employment and concern for the disadvantaged in society. The mixture that emerged, though described most fully in Macmillan's book of that name, came, with the addition of some redistribution, to represent the actual policy of Labour governments in the post-war years. The third way, presumably, is very different. Presumably, it excludes both *laissez-faire* capitalism and socialism. It does not incorporate them. It provides assurance that the Blair government is not socialist. It believes in market forces, flexible labour markets, prudent budgets and privatization, but it does not believe in *laissez-faire* capitalism. It seeks to regulate capitalism domestically and to influence its regulation transnationally.

By denying *laissez-faire* capitalism, it attempts to limit its apostasy from socialism, even the recently confirmed democratic socialism of the new Clause Four. But, in rejecting *laissez-faire* capitalism, it is rejecting a figment. It does not exist outside textbooks. Its rejection will not console those fearing that in voting Labour they have not elected a caring government.

The advocates of the third way will be tempted to proceed by caricaturing the views of those to the right and the left. The views of the right-wing 'neo-liberals' will be particular victims of such distortions, perhaps because the Blair government wishes to approach as near as possible to neo-liberalism while still differentiating itself from it for domestic political reasons. Comfort for the third way is found in the need for regulation if the market is to operate successfully and in harmony with social needs. There is nothing more certain than that the market requires regulation, that this is no discovery of third-way theorists, and that the need is accepted by most neo-liberals. The neo-liberalism of governments is not so pure as third-way theorists would have it. It has been moulded by experience. The problem with domestic regulation is to find ways that on balance improve the operations of the market rather than distort them in undesirable ways. The problem with transnational regulation, as advocated for example by Giddens, is to find a basis of agreement between the participants that is both effective and able to survive occasional, and probably inevitable, capitalist crises.[4] But the idea that this would be something new and attributable to third-way insights is anachronistic to say the least. The IMF and the World Bank have not been cruising a world in economic recession in search of victims to rescue in the application of some neo-liberal philosophy. Finance Ministers of the Groups of Seven, Eight, Twenty-two and Twenty-four do not meet in attempts to co-ordinate policy to avoid or mitigate economic recession because they are captivated by neo-liberal obsessions. These activities are blighted not by ideology but by ignorance. After 300 years of economics, economic processes are still not well understood, largely because of their complexity and because decisions are being taken by governments, corporations and individual human beings with a variety of motivations.

There is another problem for those stuffing the carcass of the third way. Giddens inserts in it one element which the neo-liberals have never been foolish enough to supply. That is the flattening out of market fluctuations on the macro or micro level. This would be a real achievement. It has, unfortunately, yet to be shown that it is within the capacity of governments, whatever way they seek to follow.[5] Global capitalism is on the attack. The British economy will always be under pressure, and the pressure may well increase. This will create opportunities as well as dangers, but the opportunities will have to be seized. The third way seems too much like an attempt to mask acceptance of the constraints imposed by market forces. This is dangerous because it represents a refusal to educate the public in the existence of those constraints. The right way round is to accept the constraints publicly, and then seek what within them can be done to fulfil the purposes of government in protecting the interests of its own people. Content inserted into the third way which may seem viable today may have become unviable tomorrow under the headlong assault of global capitalism.

Democratic governments will seek to preserve social gains but, from time to time, they may find it necessary to retreat to new lines of defence. Thus the Blair government will defend the welfare state but not the welfare state as we have known it. It will go in for some redistribution, but by stealth and at the margin. It will present the world with an extreme case of moderation subject only to the flexibility necessary to prosper in a world of global capitalism. It will try not to allow the philosophy of the third way to inhibit that necessary flexibility. Or, at any rate, it will not intend to. It must avoid the impression that the third way is the way not of hard choices but of complacency – the complacency that has characterized Labour governments, though not of Labour governments alone, throughout the post-war period. Whatever criticisms New Labour may make of Mrs Thatcher, and of her various failures, she was not a complacent Prime Minister. It will need to be on its guard lest the third way constitutes a new intellectual straitjacket of the kind that has, in the past, delayed the adaptation of the Labour party to the pressure of events. Commitment to a third way, filled by now with content of all kinds, may well be inconsistent with flexibility. The government should wait to see, not burden itself in advance with optimistic scenarios. That mistake has been made before. The best way of reconciling competitiveness with humanity will appear as events unfold. Finally, therefore, the third way, if it is to be a success, must be a philosophy without commitment. It must be a philosophy which, like stockings, can be kept ever spotless and both worn and discarded at a moment's notice.[6] But that is not much of a philosophy and it is unlikely to inspire a marching tune. New Labour will not fully have entered the modern world until it learns to love capitalism with all its warts. Meanwhile, the greatest achievement of the third way may prove to be that it will protect Labour Ministers from the necessity of using the word 'capitalism' in a spirit of approval, or at least of having to use it too often.

NOTES

PREFACE

1 Wilson (1971) 713.

PROLOGUE – *A short history of British socialism*

1 The word 'socialism' dates from 1827. Magee (1962) 79n.
2 Blair 4.

CHAPTER 1: *A new Jerusalem*

1 Tawney 37–8.
2 Campbell (1997) 19.
3 Fienburgh 17.
4 Attlee (1937) 168.
5 HC Debs, 22 Nov. 1932.
6 Anthony Crosland (1964) 286.
7 Strachey (1933) 89.
8 Attlee (1937) 15.
9 Attlee (1937) 155–6, 161.
10 Strachey (1933) 67.
11 Strachey (1933) 54.
12 Snowden, *Labour and the New World*, Waverley, London, 1921, 111, quoted Thompson 63.
13 Tawney 224.
14 Jay (1947) 3.
15 Crosland confirms this as a pre-war socialist view. Anthony Crosland (1964) 285.
16 Philip Williams 68.
17 Laski 102.
18 Naturally socialist economists saw the need for reserves, accumulated somehow, out of which investment could be funded. They differed on how this should be done. Elizabeth Durbin 122–5.
19 Attlee (1937) 28.

20 Attlee (1937) 281.
21 Attlee (1937) 148.
22 Tawney 227.
23 Tawney 39.
24 Tawney 42.
25 Shaw 94; see also 49 and 384–5.
26 Shaw 78.
27 Tawney 221.
28 Tawney 167–8.
29 The Marxists believed they had a particularly subtle understanding of human nature and that it was a factor necessitating a stage of socialism on the way to communism. See Strachey (1936) Chapters XI and XII.
30 Thompson 40. See also Michael Freeden, 'J. A. Hobson and Welfare Liberalism', *PQ*, vol. 69, no. 4, Oct.–Dec. 1998.
31 Thompson 9.

CHAPTER 2: *The Labour party goes socialist*

1 Francis Williams 101.
2 G. D. H. Cole (1948) 3.
3 G. D. H. Cole (1948) 71.
4 The wording was later amended to add the words 'distribution and exchange' after 'the means of production'.
5 G. D. H. Cole (1948) 56.
6 Attlee (1937) 48–9.
7 G. D. H. Cole (1948) 65.
8 Tawney 119.
9 Magee (1962) 96–100 discusses the nonsensical results of this left–right axis.
10 Quoted Attlee (1937) 16.
11 Hattersley 12.
12 Attlee (1937) 162.

13 For example sympathetic strikes were outlawed.
14 Donoughue and Jones 80.
15 Taylor 11.
16 Attlee (1937) 65.
17 Attlee (1937) 65–6.
18 Attlee (1937) 64–5.
19 Sir Alfred Mond was Chairman of ICI. Ben Turner was Chairman of the General Council of the TUC.
20 Beatrice Webb diary, 2 Feb. 1936, quoted Donoughue and Jones 247.
21 Dangerfield 207.
22 For example F. W. Pethick Lawrence and Arthur Ponsonby.
23 *New Fabian Essays* 182.
24 Quoted Pimlott (1985) 30.
25 Shaw 94–5.
26 Donoughue and Jones 336.
27 Anthony Crosland (1964) 135n.
28 Pimlott (1985) 144.
29 Magee (1962) 120–4.
30 Jay (1980) 32.
31 Attlee (1937) 55–6; Dalton (1935) 19–22.
32 Dalton (1935) 23.
33 Philip Williams 40, 67.
34 Bryant 109.
35 Bryant 111–12.
36 Elizabeth Durbin 74.
37 Quoted Elizabeth Durbin 88–9. See also Kramnick and Sheerman 311.
38 Philip Williams 66.
39 Dalton (1935) 237–8.
40 Pimlott (1985) 209–10 and 237.
41 From Dalton, *The Fateful Years: Memoirs 1931–1945*, London, Frederick Muller, 1957, vol. 2, 59–60, quoted Elizabeth Durbin 86 and Kramnick and Sheerman 314–15.
42 Dalton (1935) 140.
43 Pimlott (1985) 212–13.
44 Taylor 33.
45 Bullock (1967) 308.
46 Bullock (1960) 512.

CHAPTER 3: *The unmapped road*

1 Marquand (1992) 45.
2 Strachey (1933) 262.
3 Strachey (1936) 152.
4 Strachey (1936) 152.

5 Dalton (1935) 70.
6 Philip Williams 57–8.
7 HC Debs, 27 Apr. 1933, cols 309–23, quoted Campbell (1997) 56.
8 Strachey (1936) 210.
9 Strachey (1936) 368.
10 *New Fabian Essays* 33.
11 See Figes.
12 Strachey (1933) 327.
13 Donoughue and Jones 98–103.
14 Philip Williams 85.
15 Laski 274–5.
16 Laski 318.
17 Laski 188.
18 Laski 138–9.
19 Strachey (1933) 194n.
20 Laski 287.
21 Laski 213.
22 Laski 283.
23 Laski 321–2.
24 Laski 150.
25 Attlee (1937) 123.
26 Labour Party Conference 1923, quoted Foote 30.
27 See Blair interview on Radio 4, 13 Sept. 1994, quoted Philip Gould 218.
28 Economists within the Labour party did discuss how to manage capitalism on the way to the ultimate destination of socialism. But such learned disquisitions had little popular exposure or appeal. For a thorough exposition of this work, see Elizabeth Durbin and Noel Thompson.
29 Magee (1962) 43.
30 Dalton (1935) 7.
31 Dalton (1935) 77n.
32 Elizabeth Durbin 270.
33 Jay (1947) 193, 223.
34 Jay (1947) 195.
35 Campbell (1997) 140.
36 Hayek 47n. Harold Laski, in an article in the *New Statesman*, 10 Sept. 1932, and in his book *Democracy in Crisis*, published in 1933.
37 Laski 266.
38 Laski 280.
39 Pimlott (1985) 222.
40 Philip Williams 388.
41 Philip Williams 412.
42 Jay (1947) 51.
43 Laski 184.

44 E. F. M. Durbin (1940) 86.
45 Dalton (1935) 223.
46 E. F. M. Durbin (1940) 103.
47 E. F. M. Durbin (1940) 135.
48 Beveridge Report 166–7.
49 E. F. M. Durbin (1940) 147.
50 E. F. M. Durbin (1940) 91.
51 Macmillan (1978) 317–18.
52 Strachey (1933) 144.
53 E. F. M. Durbin (1940) 138.
54 E. F. M. Durbin (1940) 357–8.
55 E. F. M. Durbin (1940) 359.
56 E. F. M. Durbin (1940) 360.
57 E. F. M. Durbin (1940) 96.
58 E. F. M. Durbin (1940) 87 – Durbin's emphasis.
59 E. F. M. Durbin (1940) 271.
60 *New Fabian Essays* 35.
61 E. F. M. Durbin (1940) 261.
62 E. F. M. Durbin (1940) 275, 278.
63 E. F. M. Durbin (1940) 259.
64 Dangerfield 90.
65 Dangerfield 67.
66 E. F. M. Durbin (1940) 287, 311–12.
67 E. F. M. Durbin (1940) 287.
68 E. F. M. Durbin (1940) 288.
69 Dalton (1935) 32, 75–6.
70 E. F. M. Durbin (1940) 252.
71 Bevan 100.
72 Bevan 100.
73 E. F. M. Durbin (1940) 295–7.
74 E. F. M. Durbin (1940) 298–301.
75 E. F. M. Durbin (1940) 298.
76 E. F. M. Durbin (1940) 299–300.
77 Attlee (1937) 192.
78 E. F. M. Durbin (1940) 305–6.
79 Attlee (1937) 181–2.
80 Attlee (1937) 195–6.
81 Attlee (1937) 235–6.

CHAPTER 4: *We are all socialists now*

1 Attlee (1937) 132.
2 Dalton (1935) 26–7.
3 Quoted Donoughue and Jones 184.
4 Elizabeth Durbin 133.
5 Bevan 149.
6 *New Fabian Essays* 161.
7 Morgan (1998) 227.
8 Attlee (1937) 51.
9 Macmillan (1978) 66.
10 Addison 33.

11 Jay (1947) 40.
12 Macmillan (1978) 367.
13 Donoghue and Jones 247.
14 During a Ministerial visit to Poland in the 1970s, I met the Polish Prime Minister. The Prime Minister told me that it was necessary to combine the best features of socialism with the best features of capitalism. He explained, 'The trouble in Poland is that we do not have any unemployment.'
15 Macmillan (1978) 109.
16 Macmillan (1978) 119.
17 Macmillan (1978) 374.
18 *New Fabian Essays* 36.
19 Taylor 24.
20 Elizabeth Durbin 252.
21 Mervyn Jones 31.
22 HC Debs, 27 Feb. 1930, col. 2462, quoted Campbell (1997) 37. Almost forty years later, a similar attitude to the coal industry was to be taken by the Wilberforce Court of Inquiry into the miners' dispute of 1971–2. In recommending a substantial increase in pay, the Court commented that 'if it cannot be paid out of the NCB's revenue account ... we think that the public, through the Government, should accept the charge'. Quoted Taylor 199.
23 Attlee (1937) 186.
24 Attlee (1937) 186.
25 Jay (1947) 271 – Jay's emphasis.
26 Dalton (1935) 304.
27 Dalton (1935) 305, 308.
28 Macmillan (1978) 271–2.
29 Macmillan (1978) 182.
30 Macmillan (1978) 182.
31 1936.
32 Dalton (1935) 246–7.
33 Jay (1947) 278–9.
34 Dalton (1935) 243.
35 Dalton (1935) 259.
36 Quoted Pimlott (1985) 211.
37 Dalton (1935) 254–5.
38 Dalton (1935) 114–15.
39 Pimlott (1985) 213–16.
40 Attlee (1937) 10.
41 Harris 126.
42 On 11 January 1932, quoted Strachey (1933) 239.

43 Harris 129.
44 Macmillan (1978) 176.
45 Dalton (1935) 312–15.
46 E. F. M. Durbin (1940) 302.
47 Donoughue and Jones 183.
48 Campbell (1997) 131.
49 Quoted Addison 72.
50 Dalton (1935) 250.
51 Strachey (1933) 138. See also Strachey (1936) 37–8.
52 Macmillan (1978) 273.
53 Dalton (1935) 249.
54 Attlee (1937) 49.
55 Macmillan (1978) 295.
56 Macmillan (1978) 285–6.
57 Macmillan (1978) 279–80.
58 Macmillan (1978) 281.
59 Macmillan (1978) 198–9.
60 E. F. M. Durbin (1940) 136.
61 Quoted Macmillan (1978) 206.
62 Morgan (1984) 95.
63 Hennessy (1992) 206.
64 Fforde 7.
65 Elizabeth Durbin 120.
66 Attlee (1937) 180–1.
67 Thompson 40.
68 Foote 167.
69 Macmillan (1978) 95–7.
70 Macmillan (1978) 102.
71 *Daily Herald*, 16 October 1934.
72 Attlee (1937) 224.
73 Bullock (1960) 592.
74 Laski 95.
75 Quoted Pimlott (1985) 219.

CHAPTER 5: *The third way of John Maynard Keynes*

1 See *General Theory* 364–71 and Lenin's *Imperialism*, passim, largely based on Hobson's *Imperialism*, still in print after nearly 100 years.
2 Quoted Foote 129.
3 Cmd 6527.
4 Quoted Addison 245.
5 Chapter IV, Cmd 6527.
6 Chapter VI, Cmd 6527.
7 Cairncross and Watts 79.
8 Cairncross and Watts 80.
9 Cairncross and Watts 81.
10 Harris 253–4.
11 Strachey (1933) 205.

12 The Economic section of the Cabinet Office was formed late in 1939 to give advice to the War Cabinet. It recruited from outside government service and was headed by leading economists such as James Meade and Robert Hall. It survived the war and, in 1953, was transferred from the Cabinet Office to the Treasury.
13 Elizabeth Durbin 136, 152.
14 Quoted Elizabeth Durbin 152–3.
15 Quoted Taylor 20.
16 Cairncross and Watts 150. Debate on the right level of unemployment.
17 Skidelsky (1992) 120.
18 Beveridge Report 164. Beveridge later accepted the practicability of reducing unemployment below 3 per cent. See ed. Crafts and Woodward 232 and Peter Clarke in Marquand and Seldon 71.
19 *Collected Works*, vol. xxvii, no. 3, 16 Dec. 1944, quoted Skidelsky (1992) 120.
20 Quoted Cairncross and Watts 73, 'The prevention of general unemployment' EC (S) (41) 22 in T 230/13.
21 Cairncross and Watts 99–100.
22 Cairncross and Watts 78, Economic Section paper PR (43) 26, 'The maintenance of employment', 18 May 1943 in CAB 87/13.
23 Cairncross and Watts 98–9.
24 HC Debs, 23 June 1944, cols 526–7.
25 Bevan 154.
26 Bevan 154–6.
27 Jay (1980) 62.
28 *New Statesman*, 20 Nov. 1937, quoted Elizabeth Durbin 150.
29 Jay (1980) 124.
30 Jay (1947) 267. ICI at its best was never as good as it should have been. So this was less of a compliment than Jay intended.
31 Jay (1947) 195.
32 Jay (1947) 116.
33 Jay (1947) 29 – Jay's emphasis.
34 Jay (1947) 29.
35 Jay (1947) 279.
36 Jay (1947) 273 – Jay's emphasis.
37 Jay (1980) 62–3.
38 Jay (1947) 197.

CHAPTER 6: *In the foothills of socialism*

1 ed. Butler and Jones 2.23.
2 In Addison.
3 Pimlott (1985) 365.
4 Addison 263, Donoughue and Jones 330–1, 333, Morgan (1984) 32–3, Paul Foot 128 and for exchange with Mikardo – see Morgan (1997) 52–3 and Campbell (1997) 136.
5 Dangerfield 6.
6 Cairncross and Watts 164.
7 Dalton (1962) 239.
8 Attlee (undated) 178, Paul Foot 32, Campbell (1997) 151.
9 FO 371/45699.
10 Bevan 121.
11 Attlee (1937) 175.
12 To get a rough idea of a current equivalence, multiply by twenty. But that still underestimates the significance of this figure for an economy much smaller in 1945 than in 2000. It was of the order of 20 per cent of GDP.
13 CAB 129/1, CP (45) 112, Note by Chancellor of the Exchequer on Our Overseas Financial Prospects, dated 14 August 1945.
14 Dalton (1962) 73.
15 CAB 129/1, CP (45) 112, 14 August 1945, Note by Chancellor of the Exchequer, Our Overseas Financial Prospects, Annex by Lord Keynes.
16 Meade (1990) 153.
17 T 236/3241, 11/3/52.
18 Dalton would have liked a binding interpretation of the Article of the Bretton Woods Agreement which would have permitted any country to depreciate its exchange rate if it was suffering from persistent and chronic unemployment. Meade (1990) 172.
19 MS Attlee dep. 25. Halifax was the British Ambassador to Washington.
20 *Guardian*, 26 July 1997. Hattersley's statement needs qualification. The National Insurance Act made provision for the whole of society and not just the poor.
21 ed. Crafts and Woodward 47.
22 Attlee (undated) 190.
23 Campbell (1997) 206–7.
24 Beveridge Report 8.
25 The Attlee government was not entirely lacking in prudence. The pension rate was below subsistence. Therefore the means test came back through the necessity of making additional provision.
26 Addison 222.
27 Addison 225.
28 Dalton (1962) 183.
29 The Treasury could give its assent to a Bank initiative.
30 Figes 766.
31 Elizabeth Durbin 276.
32 Taylor 47.
33 Shaw 383.
34 Donoughue and Jones 330.
35 Attlee (1937) 74.
36 Dalton (1935) 100–1.
37 E. F. M. Durbin (1940) 315.
38 E. F. M. Durbin (1940) 303.
39 *New Fabian Essays* 125.
40 A speech at Bristol on 20 October 1946, quoted Bryant 372.
41 *New Fabian Essays* 2.
42 *New Fabian Essays* 126 and Donoughue and Jones 446.
43 Jay (1947) 265.
44 Attlee (undated) 190.
45 Dalton (1935) 312–15.
46 Marris.
47 Wilson (1957).
48 Marris.
49 Marris.
50 Marris.
51 Marris.
52 'Trotsky argued that the ability of socialism to conscript forced labour was its main advantage over capitalism.' Figes 723.
53 Cairncross and Watts 170.
54 Cairncross and Watts 240.
55 Quoted Taylor 61.
56 Dell (1973) passim.
57 Dell (1973) 30.
58 Bryant 186.
59 Donoughue and Jones 414. See also Harris 350.
60 Cmd 7572.
61 Pimlott (1985) 486
62 See Howard (1990) 141–2 regarding

R. H. S. Crossman's surprise at Marshall Aid.
63 Plowden 39.
64 Plowden 27.
65 Bullock (1985) 415.
66 Harris 343. For a discussion of the nationalization of steel, see R. Ranieri in ed. R. Millward and J. Singleton, *Industrial Organisation and the Road to Nationalisation in Britain, 1920–50*, Cambridge University Press, Cambridge, 1995.
67 Campbell (1997) 206–7.
68 Campbell (1997) 205.

CHAPTER 7: *Full employment in two worlds*

1 Morgan (1984) 184.
2 HC Debs. Written answer, 22 March 1951 T 230/305.
3 Philip Williams 314.
4 *New Fabian Essays* 39–40.
5 Dow xv.
6 Cairncross and Watts 251–2.
7 Cairncross and Watts 150.
8 Marris.
9 PREM 8/489.
10 Attlee (undated) 210.
11 T273/375.
12 20 July 1949, T 273/375.
13 20 July 1949, T 273/375.
14 T 273/375. The OEEC was the Organization for European Economic Co-operation set up as the European pillar of Marshall Aid. The ITO was the International Trade Organization, which never came into being because of the US failure to ratify the Havana Charter.
15 Wilson (1957).
16 T 273/375.
17 T 273/375.
18 Philip Williams 197.
19 Gaitskell (1983) 130.
20 Philip Williams 198.
21 Hall (1991), 11 July 1949.
22 MS Attlee dep. 87.
23 Philip Williams 198.
24 Wilson (1957).
25 Attlee (undated) 128; cf. 206, 221.
26 Quoted Foote 166.

27 April 1949, quoted Foote 199.
28 Fieldhouse 95–6.
29 Fieldhouse 97–8.
30 Fieldhouse 98.
31 Fieldhouse 98–102.
32 Newton 171–2.
33 Newton 177.
34 MS Attlee dep. 59/2.
35 MS Attlee dep. 59/2.
36 Canadian Institute of Foreign Affairs, Toronto, January 1950.
37 T 232/183.
38 30 June 1950, F. C. Everson of the Foreign Office, FO 371/87161.
39 Memo from E. A. Cohen, Board of Trade, 18 November 1949, FO 371/87161.
40 See, for example, Sir Hugh Ellis-Rees, Historical Memorandum on the 1947 convertibility crisis, T 267/3.
41 Dell (1995) 108.
42 For the full story see Dell (1995) passim.
43 HC Debs, 22 Jan. 1948, col. 395.
44 *New Fabian Essays* 72.
45 *Manchester Guardian*, 9 June 1950.
46 Cmd 7970/13.
47 Hall (1992), 2 Apr. 1961.
48 Quoted Campbell (1997) 212.

CHAPTER 8: *The climb interrupted*

1 Pelling 103.
2 T 230/334, Butt to Hall, 21 May 1951.
3 Philip Williams 248.
4 Philip Williams 248.
5 For example Philip Williams 657.
6 Philip Williams 167–8.
7 Philip Williams 176–7.
8 Campbell (1997) 191–2.
9 Campbell (1997) 195.
10 MS Attlee dep. 102.
11 Gaitskell (1983) 266.
12 To Robert Hall, 11 June 1948, T 230/145, Cairncross and Watts 183; see also 184.
13 Addison 280.
14 Dalton (1962) 239.
15 Howard (1990) 153.
16 Donoughue and Jones 455–6.
17 ed. Butler and Jones 3–23.
18 Donoughue and Jones 465.

19 ed. Butler and Jones 3–23.
20 Dangerfield 8.

CHAPTER 9: *Pathfinders in defeat*

1 HC Debs, 23 Apr. 1951, cols 34–43, quoted Campbell (1997) 242.
2 *New Fabian Essays* 214.
3 *New Fabian Essays* 215.
4 Strachey (1933) 241.
5 Pelling 116.
6 Philip Williams 315–16.
7 Philip Williams 354.
8 Butler (1971) 146.
9 *New Fabian Essays* 188.
10 *New Fabian Essays* 196.
11 *New Fabian Essays* 31.
12 Butler (1971) 160.
13 For a discussion of Robot, see Dell (1996) Chapter 5.
14 Quoted Thompson 161.
15 *Fabian Essays in Socialism*, 1889, 1948 edition, 94.
16 *New Fabian Essays* 15.
17 *New Fabian Essays* 46.
18 *New Fabian Essays* 60.
19 21 May 1952.
20 25 May 1952.
21 24 May 1952.
22 July 1952.
23 *New Fabian Essays* 1.
24 *New Fabian Essays* 25.
25 *New Fabian Essays* 3.
26 *New Fabian Essays* 197–8.
27 *New Fabian Essays* 68.
28 *New Fabian Essays* 68, 74.
29 *New Fabian Essays* 114.
30 *New Fabian Essays* 26–7.
31 *New Fabian Essays* 196–7.
32 *New Fabian Essays* 197.
33 *New Fabian Essays* 144.
34 *New Fabian Essays* 42.
35 Jay (1947) xiii.
36 *New Fabian Essays* 38.
37 *New Fabian Essays* 36.
38 *New Fabian Essays* 63–4.
39 *New Fabian Essays* 66–7.
40 *New Fabian Essays* 29.
41 *New Fabian Essays* 27.
42 *New Fabian Essays* 27.
43 *New Fabian Essays* 28.
44 *New Fabian Essays* 83–4.

45 Pimlott (1993) 129–31.
46 *New Fabian Essays* 88–9.
47 See for example Albu and Hewett.
48 He was considered ten years later.
49 *New Fabian Essays* 83.
50 *New Fabian Essays* 80.
51 Strachey (1936) 128.
52 *New Fabian Essays* 74.
53 Jay (1947) ix.
54 *New Fabian Essays* 122.
55 *New Fabian Essays* 139.
56 Bevan 138.
57 Bevan 17.
58 Bevan 19.
59 Bevan 39.
60 Bevan 29.
61 Bevan 114.
62 Bevan 37.
63 Bevan 37.
64 Bevan 36.
65 Bevan 47.
66 Bevan 31.
67 Bevan 164.
68 Bevan 50.
69 Campbell (1997) 362.
70 Bevan 109.
71 Bevan 152–3.
72 Bevan 14.
73 Bevan 130.
74 Bevan 123.
75 *New Fabian Essays* 204, 207. Strachey's emphasis.
76 Bevan 118.
77 Bevan 60–1.
78 Bevan 164.
79 Bevan 32.
80 Campbell (1997) 256.
81 *New Fabian Essays* 214.
82 *New Fabian Essays* 214.
83 Bevan 117.
84 Bevan 114–15.
85 Bevan 98–9.
86 Anthony Crosland (1953) 75–6.
87 Anthony Crosland (1953) 76.
88 Anthony Crosland (1953) 62 ff.
89 Anthony Crosland (1953) 75.
90 Anthony Crosland (1953) 129.
91 Anthony Crosland (1953) 131.
92 Anthony Crosland (1953) 136.
93 Anthony Crosland (1953) 189–92.
94 Anthony Crosland (1953) 194–9.
95 Anthony Crosland (1953) 195–6.

96 Anthony Crosland (1953) 198-9.
97 Peter Clarke 176.
98 *Resources for Freedom*, A Report to the President by the President's Materials Policy Commission, Washington DC, June 1952, quoted Anthony Crosland (1953) 80-1.
99 Anthony Crosland (1953) 81.
100 Anthony Crosland (1953) 77.
101 Anthony Crosland (1953) 82.
102 Anthony Crosland (1953) 45.
103 Anthony Crosland (1953) 87.
104 Anthony Crosland (1953) 39.
105 Anthony Crosland (1953) 98.
106 Anthony Crosland (1953) 40.
107 Anthony Crosland (1953) 98-9. But when the terms of trade turned in the UK's favour after 1952, the Economic Section concluded that agricultural expansion had been overdone and sought some way of abating the level of guaranteed prices for home-grown foodstuffs. Cairncross and Watts 294.
108 Anthony Crosland (1953) 101 ff.
109 Anthony Crosland (1953) 108-13.
110 Anthony Crosland (1953) 107.
111 Anthony Crosland (1953) 119-20.
112 Anthony Crosland (1953) 119.
113 Anthony Crosland (1953) 146.
114 Anthony Crosland (1953) 156. The dollar pool was at the core of the sterling area. Member countries paid into the pool the dollars they earned from exports to the dollar area and drew from it the dollars they needed for purchases from the dollar area.
115 Anthony Crosland (1953) 163-4.
116 Anthony Crosland (1953) 164.
117 Anthony Crosland (1953) 165.
118 Anthony Crosland (1953) 134.

CHAPTER 10: *The Future of Socialism*

1 Anthony Crosland (1964) 216.
2 Anthony Crosland (1964) 223.
3 Anthony Crosland (1964) 60.
4 A contrary view is expressed by David Lipsey in ed. Leonard 14. But he provides no evidence.
5 Anthony Crosland (1964) 342.
6 Anthony Crosland (1964) 343.
7 Anthony Crosland (1964) 7-8.
8 Anthony Crosland notes the possibility of full employment being undermined by 'severe crises . . . abroad. But these would present a problem different in character and magnitude from the pre-war unemployment problem.' Anthony Crosland (1964) 59 n2.
9 Anthony Crosland (1964) 242.
10 Anthony Crosland (1964) 294.
11 Anthony Crosland (1964) 8.
12 Anthony Crosland (1964) 32.
13 Tawney, Chapter V.
14 Tawney discusses the question of risk in his Chapter VII.
15 Anthony Crosland (1964) 38.
16 Anthony Crosland (1964) 42.
17 Anthony Crosland (1964) 15.
18 Anthony Crosland (1964) 7.
19 Anthony Crosland (1964) 145.
20 'Nepotic' is the word used by Durbin in discussing this issue. E. F. M. Durbin (1940) 126, 128-33.
21 Anthony Crosland (1964) 15.
22 Anthony Crosland (1964) 28.
23 *New Fabian Essays* 72.
24 Gaitskell (1956) and Philip Williams 167.
25 Anthony Crosland (1964) 272-6.
26 Gaitskell (1956).
27 G. D. H. Cole (1957).
28 Anthony Crosland (1964) 9.
29 Anthony Crosland (1964) 26.
30 Anthony Crosland (1964) 15.
31 Anthony Crosland (1964) 42.
32 Anthony Crosland (1964) 34.
33 Anthony Crosland (1964) 61.
34 Anthony Crosland (1964) 33.
35 G. D. H. Cole (1957).
36 Anthony Crosland (1964) 218.
37 Anthony Crosland (1964) 70.
38 Gaitskell (1956).
39 Anthony Crosland (1964) 71.
40 Anthony Crosland (1964) 311.
41 Anthony Crosland (1964) 293-4.
42 Anthony Crosland (1964) 287-8.
43 Anthony Crosland (1964) 68.
44 Anthony Crosland (1964) 213.
45 Anthony Crosland (1964) 174.
46 Anthony Crosland (1964) 227.

47 Anthony Crosland (1964) 225.
48 Anthony Crosland (1964) 168.
49 Anthony Crosland (1964) 168.
50 Anthony Crosland (1964) 168.
51 There is much learned discussion about what Crosland really meant by equality. For example Raymond Plant argues (ed. Leonard 26 ff.) that Crosland favoured neither equality of opportunity (because of different opportunities) nor equality of outcome but something which John Rawls later (1971) called 'democratic equality'. Crosland adopts John Rawls's democratic equality in *Socialism Now* 15. But it would be an exaggeration to claim that this clarifies Crosland's views.
52 Anthony Crosland (1964) 135–6.
53 Anthony Crosland (1964) 123.
54 Anthony Crosland (1964) 125.
55 Anthony Crosland (1964) 101.
56 Anthony Crosland (1964) 207.
57 Anthony Crosland (1964) 147–9.
58 Anthony Crosland (1964) 204.
59 Anthony Crosland (1964) 204–5.
60 Anthony Crosland (1964) 205–6.
61 Anthony Crosland (1964) 207.
62 Anthony Crosland (1964) 186.
63 Anthony Crosland (1964) 76.
64 Anthony Crosland (1964) 94.
65 Anthony Crosland (1964) 341.
66 Anthony Crosland (1964) 341.
67 Anthony Crosland (1964) 343–4.
68 Anthony Crosland (1964) 346.
69 Anthony Crosland (1964) 346.
70 Anthony Crosland (1964) 347.
71 Anthony Crosland (1964) 342.
72 Anthony Crosland (1964) 344.
73 Anthony Crosland (1964) 345.
74 Anthony Crosland (1964) 350.
75 Anthony Crosland (1964) 350–1.
76 Anthony Crosland (1964) 352.
77 Quoted Anthony Crosland (1964) 328.
78 So does Gaitskell – see Gaitskell (1956).
79 Anthony Crosland (1964) 328–9.
80 Anthony Crosland (1964) 329–30.
81 Anthony Crosland (1964) 330.
82 Anthony Crosland (1964) 332–3.
83 Anthony Crosland (1964) 333.
84 Anthony Crosland (1964) 323.
85 Anthony Crosland (1964) 323.
86 Anthony Crosland (1964) 41.
87 Anthony Crosland (1964) 320.
88 Anthony Crosland (1964) 40.
89 Anthony Crosland (1964) 316.
90 Anthony Crosland (1964) 318.
91 Anthony Crosland (1964) 318.
92 Anthony Crosland (1964) 320–2.
93 Anthony Crosland (1964) 322.
94 Anthony Crosland (1964) 319.
95 Anthony Crosland (1964) 228, 318.
96 Anthony Crosland (1964) 327.
97 Anthony Crosland (1964) 336–9.
98 Anthony Crosland (1964) 334.
99 Anthony Crosland (1964) 334.
100 Anthony Crosland (1964) 327.
101 Anthony Crosland (1964) 334.
102 Anthony Crosland (1964) 336.
103 Anthony Crosland (1964) 336.
104 Hatfield 208.
105 See, for example, Anthony Crosland (1964) 334, 336.
106 Anthony Crosland (1964) 340.
107 Philip Williams 357.
108 Anthony Crosland (1964) 96.
109 In this book I have used the 1964 edition of *The Future of Socialism*, which eliminates the material that Crosland failed to cut in the 1956 edition.
110 Attlee (undated) 189.
111 Quoted Martin Francis, 'Mr Gaitskell's Ganymede? Reassessing Crosland's *The Future of Socialism*', *CBH*, vol. 11, no. 2, Summer 1997, 62.
112 Quoted Tudor Jones (1996) 31, Thompson 157.
113 G. D. H. Cole (1957).
114 G. D. H. Cole (1957).
115 *Twentieth Century Socialism* 16–17.
116 *Twentieth Century Socialism* 152.
117 *Twentieth Century Socialism* 70n.
118 *Twentieth Century Socialism* 149.
119 *Twentieth Century Socialism* 125.
120 *Twentieth Century Socialism* 148.
121 *Twentieth Century Socialism* 125.
122 Philip Williams 392–3.
123 Philip Williams 387.
124 *Twentieth Century Socialism* 125.
125 *Twentieth Century Socialism* 151.
126 Anthony Crosland (1964) 360–1.

127 Anthony Crosland (1964) 357.
128 Anthony Crosland (1964) 361.

CHAPTER 11: *Two leaders*

1 Dangerfield 265.
2 Benn (1994) 251, 21-28 Oct. 1957.
3 Howard (1990) 162-3.
4 Philip Williams 464.
5 Anderson and Mann 307.
6 Quoted Taylor 101.
7 Philip Williams 387.
8 Quoted Taylor 128.
9 Philip Williams 523.
10 Philip Williams 449.
11 Philip Williams 565.
12 Gaitskell (1956).
13 *Tribune*, 26 July and 23 Sept. 1957, quoted Campbell (1997) 329.
14 Campbell (1997) 329.
15 Philip Williams 613, 633, Brivati 373.
16 Quoted Magee (1962) 165.
17 Philip Williams 491.
18 Quoted Campbell (1997) 363 and Pimlott (1993) 230.
19 Philip Williams 570.
20 Philip Williams 548.
21 Philip Williams 672.
22 Philip Williams 613, 633, Brivati 373.
23 And the French.
24 Brivati 406.
25 Wilson (1979) 17.
26 Paul Foot 118.
27 Crossman (1975) 118, 3 Jan. 1965.
28 Morgan (1997) 49.
29 Pimlott (1993) 248.
30 Pimlott (1993) 248. The claim was often repeated. See Paul Foot 326.
31 The transferable rate was the rate at which sterling could be converted into foreign currencies outside official transactions. Supporting the transferable rate meant that unofficial transactions would now take place at or near the official rate of exchange. This in practice made sterling freely convertible.
32 Philip Williams 464.
33 Wilson (1957).
34 Wilson (1957).
35 Ziegler 112.

36 Quoted Thompson 184.
37 Ziegler 386.
38 Wilson (1971) 90.
39 Wilson (1971) 90.
40 Wilson spoke of 'the white heat of this revolution', but as 'this' referred to a revolution in the use of technology, the popular representation of his speech is entirely justified.
41 Quoted Pimlott (1993) 307 from Wilson, *The New Britain: Labour's Plan*, Penguin, Harmondsworth, 1964, 9-15.
42 *Daily Mirror*, 18 Jan. 1956, quoted Pimlott (1993) 198.
43 Pimlott (1993) 199.
44 Quoted Magee (1962) 102n.
45 ICBH seminar on the DEA, and Callaghan 164.
46 *Twelve Wasted Years* 1. OECD was the Organization for Economic Co-operation and Development which succeeded OEEC. OECD was different from OEEC in that it incorporated a number of non-European countries such as the USA, Australia, Canada and New Zealand.
47 *Twelve Wasted Years* 16; see also 20.
48 *Twelve Wasted Years* 12.
49 *Twelve Wasted Years* 31.
50 *Twelve Wasted Years* 31.
51 *Twelve Wasted Years* 22.
52 *Twelve Wasted Years* 22.
53 *Twelve Wasted Years* 23-4.
54 *Twelve Wasted Years* 45. The estimate was by Peter Townsend – see *Twelve Wasted Years* 50.
55 *Twelve Wasted Years* 50.
56 *Twelve Wasted Years* 67.

CHAPTER 12: *Harold Wilson's hundred days*

1 Paul Foot 273.
2 Attlee (1937) 167. Attlee's emphasis.
3 Wilson (1971) xvii.
4 Wilson (1971) xvii.
5 Taylor 131.
6 Brown 92.
7 Crossman (1975) 11.
8 Paul Foot 118.
9 The author also entered the Com-

mons in 1964 and was the second, after Peter Shore, to be elevated to the status of Privy Counsellor.

10 Castle (1984) ix.
11 Castle (1984) xi.
12 He had lost his Devonport seat in 1955.
13 Wilson (1971) 4.
14 Wilson (1971) 4.
15 Wilson (1971) 6.
16 Wilson (1971) 6.
17 Crossman (1975) 26, 22 Oct. 1964.
18 Crossman (1975) 71, 24 Nov. 1964.
19 Castle (1984) xiii.
20 Crossman (1975) 80, 3 Dec. 1964.
21 HC Debs, 4 Nov. 1964, col. 239.
22 Quoted Taylor 130.
23 Quoted Taylor 131.
24 Mervyn Jones 285.
25 Wilson (1971) 9 refers to this department as the Ministry of Land and Planning but it soon lost much of its planning functions in a battle with the Ministry of Housing.
26 Crossman (1975) 117, 3 Jan. 1965.
27 Wilson (1971) 5.
28 Brivati 418.
29 Crossman (1975) 130–1, 14 Jan. 1965.
30 Brown 95–6.
31 Brown 114.
32 Castle (1984) 9, 5 Feb. 1965.
33 Brown 97.
34 Brown 98–9.
35 Brown 100.
36 Brown 119.
37 Quoted Ziegler 271.
38 Quoted Paul Foot 196.
39 Quoted Pimlott (1993) 555.
40 Crossman (1975) 102, 15 Dec. 1964.
41 Crossman (1975) 51, 10 Nov. 1964.
42 Castle (1984) xvi.
43 Castle (1984) 14–15, 21 Feb. 1965.
44 Castle (1984) 10, 10 Feb. 1965.
45 Crossman (1975) 118, 3 Jan. 1965.
46 Castle (1984) 26–7, 30 Mar. 1965.
47 PREM 13/103.
48 Crossman (1975) 93–5, 11 Dec. 1964.
49 Ziegler 204–5.
50 See also Ziegler 221.
51 Wilson (1971) 80.
52 Morgan (1997) 225–6.
53 Ziegler 222–3.

54 Pimlott (1993) 375.
55 Crossman (1975) 96, 12 Dec. 1964.
56 Crossman (1975) 96–7, 13 Dec. 1964.
57 Benn (1987) 206, 216.
58 Castle (1984) 3–4, 26 Jan. 1965.
59 Castle (1984) 3–4, 26 Jan. 1965.
60 Crossman (1975) 139, 26 Jan. 1965.
61 Crossman (1975) 144, 31 Jan. 1965.

CHAPTER 13: *The crusade aborted*

1 Crossman (1975) 189, 30 Mar. 1965.
2 Under Agreements made in 1954 and 1962, the UK and the USSR were co-chairmen of a Geneva Conference dedicated to finding a way to peace in Vietnam.
3 Ziegler 226.
4 Wilson (1971) 373.
5 Wilson (1971) 381–6.
6 Wilson (1971) 126.
7 Wilson (1971) 131–3, Taylor 136.
8 Crossman (1975) 27, 22 Oct. 1964.
9 Castle (1984) 20–1, 18 Mar. 1965.
10 Crossman (1975) 212, 6 and 10 May 1965.
11 Jay (1980) 325.
12 Pimlott (1993) 430.
13 Morgan (1997) 236.
14 Paul Foot 172.
15 HC Debs, 27 July 1966, col. 1726.
16 HC Debs, 27 July 1966, col. 1848.
17 Cousins told this author that he had recommended him for promotion to Minister of Technology. It was not advice that Wilson was likely then to take.
18 Ziegler 214.
19 Benn (1987) 211.
20 The author.
21 Macmillan (1978) 184, 196.
22 Macmillan (1978) 215–16.
23 Thompson 40.
24 Dalton (1935) 143.
25 Taylor 12, 29, 46, 62, 84, 217.
26 Taylor 129, 136.
27 Peter Jenkins (1970) 14.
28 Peter Jenkins (1970) 26.
29 Wilson (1971) 419.
30 HC Debs, 10 Jul. 1967, col. 264.
31 HC Debs, 7 Nov. 1967, col. 875.

32 Morgan (1997) 254.
33 For a fuller account, see Dell (1973) 105–21.
34 Brandt, *My Life in Politics*, Hamish Hamilton, London, 1992, 420.
35 Quoted Paul Foot 224.
36 Jay (1980) 349.
37 Wilson (1971) 468.
38 Crossman (1976) 626, 31 Dec. 1967.
39 Morgan (1997) 246.
40 Cockett 168–72.
41 Cockett 186.
42 Quoted Cockett 179.
43 Taylor 146.

CHAPTER 14: *Interpretations of defeat*

1 Benn (1970) 6, 27.
2 Quoted Hatfield 79–80.
3 Benn (1989) 18; see also 37.
4 Shaw 389.
5 Benn (1970) 23–5.
6 Benn (1988) 346.
7 Benn (1988) 361.
8 Ziegler 393.
9 Benn (1988) 318.
10 Benn (1989) 12.
11 Benn (1988) 457.
12 Benn (1970) 22.
13 Benn (1988) 428, 438–9, 441.
14 Benn (1988) 441.
15 Benn (1988) 427.
16 Benn (1989) 61, 26 Sept. 1973.
17 Benn (1989) 6.
18 Quoted Wilson (1979) 43.
19 Pimlott (1992) 614.
20 Anthony Crosland (1970) 1.
21 At Crosland's request I rewrote the opening chapter of *Socialism Now*, though without in any way changing the argument. But the opening chapter is simply an extended version of Anthony Crosland (1970).
22 Anthony Crosland (1974) 18–22.
23 Michael Stewart in ed. Beckerman 110–11.
24 Anthony Crosland (1974) 26. The same argument appears in Anthony Crosland (1970).
25 Anthony Crosland (1974) 18–19.
26 Anthony Crosland (1970) 2.

27 Anthony Crosland (1974) 43. See also Benn (1989) 38.
28 Lipsey in ed. Leonard 15.
29 Anthony Crosland (1974) 107.
30 Anthony Crosland (1974) 36–7.
31 Anthony Crosland (1974) 48.
32 Anthony Crosland (1974) 37. Crosland's emphasis.
33 By a flexible exchange rate policy Crosland did not mean floating but 'timely adjustments whenever the alternative would be serious deflation'. Anthony Crosland (1970) 8.
34 Anthony Crosland (1974) 83.
35 Benn (1989) 4.
36 Hatfield 88.
37 Quoted Hatfield 86.
38 Addressed to the Trade Union Public Services International in Copenhagen, Anthony Crosland (1974) 247.
39 Susan Crosland 218, 219.
40 Susan Crosland 224.
41 Ziegler 386.
42 I was among the sixty-nine. The following day I resigned from the front bench, the first to do so. I was already 'semi-detached'. About this time I seriously considered an approach from the Heath government as to whether I would be interested in appointment as the first Director General of Fair Trade. Crosland dissuaded me over a bottle of whisky.
43 Susan Crosland 252.
44 Benn (1988) 318, 325–6.
45 Morgan (1997) 394.
46 Pimlott (1993) 585.
47 Pelling 156.
48 Quoted Benn (1988) 455.
49 Wilson (1979) 53–4.
50 Wilson (1979) 51.
51 Benn (1988) 316.
52 For example from this author.
53 Wilson (1979) 29.
54 Hatfield 40.
55 According to the NIESR, in 1958 the top 100 firms accounted for 31 per cent of UK manufacturing production, and in 1970 for 45 per cent. Moreover 20 per cent of UK manufacturing assets were foreign owned

and, in the electronic-components business, it was 49 per cent. Hatfield 41.

56 I was an advocate of a state holding company, though not on anything like the scale proposed by the NEC. At no stage in my Parliamentary career was I opposed to public ownership as a matter of principle. I continued to think that there was a role for it, but a limited role.

57 Quoted Hatfield 80–1.

58 Hatfield 111. See also Roy Jenkins (1991) 353–4, which seems a somewhat offhand reference to this important speech. A similar message emerged in Jenkins's *What Matters Now*, Fontana, London, 1972, of which Noel Thompson writes, 'Seldom has the case for a substantial extension of public ownership been better put . . .' Thompson 221.

59 See, for example, Thompson 215, 221.

60 The author.

61 Benn (1989) 11.

62 *Labour's Programme 1973*, 7.

63 Hatfield 197 cf. Healey 370. Healey's quip might seem rather less devastating after the turbulence at Marks and Spencer in 1998.

64 According to Benn, it was Wilson who made this remark disrespectful of one wing of the Labour Movement. Benn seems to have misheard. But then he was probably taking notes for his diary. Benn (1989) 38. According to Hatfield 197, the comparison between M & S and the Co-op was made by Healey on 31 May 1973.

65 Benn (1989) 49.

66 Benn (1989) 37.

67 Quoted Hatfield 129.

68 *Labour's Programme 1973*, 19. See also Benn (1989) 42.

69 Quoted Mervyn Jones 336 from Jack Jones 262, 259.

70 Pimlott (1993) 610.

71 Ziegler 350.

CHAPTER 15: *The age of reluctant enlightenment*

1 Dell (1991) 12.

2 This was not true in my own case. The meagre assistance by ASTMS (now MSF) for the Birkenhead Labour party was withdrawn due to my support for the government of which I was a member.

3 Taylor 231–2, 242.

4 Dell (1991) 153.

5 Mervyn Jones 401–7.

6 Wilson (1979) 13

7 HC Debs, 26 Mar. 1974, col. 278.

8 Dell (1991) 52.

9 Morgan (1997) 482.

10 Benn (1989) 222–3.

11 Attlee (1937) 167.

12 Benn (1989) 66, 2 Oct. 1973.

13 Wilson (1979) 26.

14 Wilson (1979) 33.

15 Wilson (1979) 125.

16 For a fuller account, see Dell (1992).

17 The Central Policy Review Staff had been created under Heath as a source of advice to the Cabinet independent of government departments. It was abolished by Mrs Thatcher.

18 Over £1 billion.

19 Donoughue 53.

20 Quoted Taylor 233.

21 Wilson (1979) 44. Dell (1991) 145–6 tells the story of how Wilson attempted to prevent my stating the truth about real national income.

22 HC Debs, 15 Apr. 1975, cols 281–2.

23 Jack Jones 299–300.

24 To get an approximate equivalent to £8500 in present-day terms (2000), multiply by four.

25 Wilson (1976) 118.

26 *Daily Telegraph*, 8 Mar. 1976. See also HC Debs, 9 Mar. 1976, col. 227 and Brian Sedgemore, HC Debs, 9 Mar. 1976, cols 305–6.

27 Attlee (1937) 167.

28 Mervyn Jones 390–1.

29 Morgan (1997) 515.

30 Benn archive, quoted Burk and Cairncross 47.

31 Callaghan 426–7.

32 Dell (1991) 251.
33 Susan Crosland 377.
34 Susan Crosland 355.
35 Susan Crosland 377.
36 Benn (1989) 654, 23 Nov. 1976.
37 Crosland did have advisers but did his own thinking.
38 Susan Crosland 342.
39 Morgan (1997) 583.
40 Iain Mikardo added the name of Dell.
41 As Secretary of State for Trade, I was in the lead on industrial democracy within the government and rejected the conclusions of the Bullock Report for the reasons here stated.
42 Panitch and Leys 150.
43 In my last conversation with him as Prime Minister, days before my resignation from the government, Callaghan asked me how long he should stay on as Prime Minister after the election. I replied that he should stay on as long as he felt fit enough to serve.
44 Taylor 260.
45 Donoughue 191.
46 Wilson (1979) 128.
47 As a Treasury Minister, I negotiated the pension reform with Barbara Castle. Her diaries show that she was not, invariably, pleased with me.
48 Pelling 173.

CHAPTER 16:   *The holy anger of the left*

1 Benn (1989) xii.
2 Quoted Mervyn Jones 438.
3 Panitch and Leys 4.
4 Crewe and King 197.
5 Panitch and Leys 163.
6 Philip Gould 240.
7 Healey 477.
8 Benn (1990) 498, 503–4.
9 Panitch and Leys 169.
10 According to Panitch and Leys 207 the Falklands war was worth to Mrs Thatcher a 7 per cent swing against Labour.
11 Jay (1980) 355.

CHAPTER 17:   *The flexibility of the soft left*

1 Quoted Tudor Jones (1994) 568–9.
2 Eileen Jones 45.
3 Susan Crosland 356–7.
4 Kinnock 535.
5 Pimlott (1993) 227.
6 Kinnock 537.
7 Eileen Jones 70.
8 Quoted Pelling 191.
9 Eileen Jones 127.
10 Quoted Eileen Jones 73.
11 Eileen Jones 73.
12 Morgan (1997) 162–3.
13 Quoted Magee (1962) 141.
14 *Guardian* article of 26 July 1997.
15 Bryan Gould 79.
16 Donoughue 106–9.
17 Kinnock 541, Eileen Jones 78.
18 Philip Gould 96, 158.
19 Bryan Gould, Chapter 6.
20 Blair 5.
21 Eileen Jones 78–9.
22 Bryan Gould 90.
23 Martin J. Smith 557.
24 Quoted Eileen Jones 84.
25 Riddell (1997) 27 quoting Colin Hughes and Patrick Wintour, *Labour Rebuilt: The New Model Party*, Fourth Estate, London, 1990, 69–70.
26 Bryan Gould 121.
27 Quoted Tudor Jones (1994) 581, Eileen Jones 120 and Tudor Jones (1996) 123.
28 Quoted Tudor Jones (1994) 579.
29 Tudor Jones (1994) 578.
30 Kellner, *Independent*, 8 May 1989, quoted Tudor Jones (1996) 127.
31 Eileen Jones 70.
32 *Guardian*, 1 May 1998.
33 Fielding 595.
34 Quoted Eileen Jones 174.

CHAPTER 18:   *Alternative medicine for the market economy*

1 Panitch and Leys 15.
2 Bryan Gould 83.
3 Hattersley 46.
4 Hattersley 65.
5 I was a member too.

6 Hattersley 119.
7 See, for example, Andrew Adonis and Stephen Pollard in their 1997 book *A Class Act: The Myth of Britain's Classless Society*. (Hamish Hamilton, London, 1997)
8 Hattersley 25.
9 Hattersley 114.
10 Hattersley 241.
11 Hattersley 179.
12 Hattersley 190.
13 Hattersley 185 – Hattersley's emphasis.
14 Hattersley 23.
15 Hattersley 21–2.
16 Hattersley 62.
17 Hattersley 54.
18 Hattersley 141.
19 Tudor Jones (1994) 576.
20 Blair 7.
21 Marquand pays tribute to Ronald Dore, who in his work uses the phrase 'developmental state'.
22 Marquand (1988) 160.
23 Marquand (1997) 184.
24 Marquand (1988) 152.
25 Marquand (1988) 175.
26 Hutton 53.
27 Marquand (1988) 143.
28 Marquand (1988) 166.
29 Marquand (1997) 67.
30 Marquand (1997) 6.
31 Marquand (1997) 33.
32 Hutton 112.
33 Hutton 300.
34 Hutton 17.
35 Hutton 281.
36 Hutton 19.
37 Hutton 245–6.
38 Hutton 247.
39 Hutton 256.
40 Hutton 26.
41 Hutton 313 ff.
42 Hutton 30.
43 Hutton 256.
44 Routledge (1999) 169 ff. gives an account of an early synopsis that would have been even more unpopular in suspect quarters of the Labour party than was the published book.
45 Mandelson and Liddle 169.
46 Mandelson and Liddle 7.
47 Mandelson and Liddle 108.
48 Mandelson and Liddle 16.
49 Mandelson and Liddle 87.
50 *New Fabian Essays* xiii.
51 Mandelson and Liddle 150.
52 Quoted the *Economist*, 15 Nov. 1997.

CHAPTER 19: *Obsequies for socialism*

1 Quoted Philip Gould 161.
2 Mandelson and Liddle 51.
3 Philip Gould 272.
4 Riddell (1997) 31.
5 Quoted Kenny and Smith.
6 Quoted Peter Riddell, *The Times*, 28 Apr. 1998.
7 Riddell (1997) 32.
8 Riddell (1997) 37.
9 Riddell (1997) 40.
10 Routledge (1998) 221.
11 *Economist*, 27 Sept. 1997.
12 Riddell (1997) 44.
13 Quoted Kenny and Smith.
14 Interview with Martin Kettle in the *Guardian*, quoted Panitch and Leys 229.
15 HC Debs, 14 May 1997, col. 65.
16 Macmillan (1978) 33–4. Macmillan's emphasis.
17 ed. Leonard 201.
18 Desmond King and Mark Wickham-Jones in *PQ*, vol. 70, no. 1, Jan.–Mar. 1999, 69.
19 Philip Gould 287, 289–90.
20 Brown was evidently unwilling to give the Bank of England the degree of independence enjoyed by the United States Federal Reserve and, until monetary union, by the Bundesbank, where decisions on monetary policy are not constrained by an inflation target imposed by the national government. That, according to some of Brown's advisers, was undemocratic, British democracy being more clamorous, evidently, than American and German democracy. This was surprising given Brown's enthusiasm for EMU.
21 Routledge (1998) 320 ff.
22 *Guardian*, 12 Apr. 1996.
23 In an article in the *Guardian*, July

1995. Labour leaders had, understandably, become sensitive to accusations of betrayal. For example, Kinnock, in deserting his previous convictions on nuclear disarmament and public ownership, had reportedly told Peter Mandelson that he would prefer to get his betrayal in before the coming general election rather than afterwards. Routledge (1999) 132.

24 Anthony Crosland (1964) 167.
25 Anthony Crosland (1974) 15–16.
26 Hattersley 44.
27 Hattersley 37.
28 *Guardian*, 26 July 1997.
29 *Guardian*, 29 July 1997.
30 The equal worth of every human being is a favourite Brown theme. See, for example, Brown in ed. Leonard 40.

31 *Guardian*, 2 Aug. 1997.
32 Brown in ed. Leonard 42.
33 Philip Gould assures his readers that Blair in insisting on a referendum before British membership of EMU 'was slowly reappropriating Labour's patriotic heritage'. Philip Gould 270.
34 Quoted *Economist*, 27 Sept. 1997.

EPILOGUE: *The third way*

1 *Marxism Today*, special issue, October 1998.
2 Giddens 65. Gidden's emphasis.
3 Blair 1.
4 See, for example, Giddens, Chapter 5.
5 *New Statesman*, 1 May 1998.
6 With apologies to Wilkie Collins.

SELECT BIBLIOGRAPHY

Public Record Office files, Parliamentary debates and private collections

As indicated in Notes

Books and articles

Contemporary British History, cited in Notes as *CBH*.
Contemporary Record, cited in Notes as *CR*.
Political Quarterly, cited in Notes as *PQ*.

Addison, Paul, *The Road to 1945: British Politics and the Second World War*, Jonathan Cape, London, 1975.

Albu, Austen, and Hewett, Norman, *The Anatomy of Private Industry: A Socialist Policy for the Future of the Joint Stock Company*, Fabian Research Series No. 145, March 1951.

Anderson, Paul, and Mann, Nyta, *Safety First: The Making of New Labour*, Granta Books, London, 1997.

Attlee, C. R., *The Labour Party in Perspective*, Victor Gollancz, London, 1937.

Attlee, C. R., *As It Happened*, Odhams, London, undated.

Balfour, Corinna, *The Anglo-American Loan Negotiations – The US viewpoint*, Appendix C to John Fforde, *The Bank of England and Public Policy, 1941–58*, Cambridge University Press, Cambridge, 1992.

Barnett, Correlli, *The Audit of War: The Illusion and Reality of Britain as a Great Nation*, Papermac, London, 1991.

Barnett, Correlli, *The Lost Victory: British Dreams, British Realities, 1945–1950*, Macmillan, London, 1995.

Barnett, Joel, *Inside the Treasury*, André Deutsch, London, 1982.

ed. Beckerman, Wilfred, *The Labour Government's Economic Record, 1964–1970*, Gerald Duckworth, London, 1972.

Beer, M., *A History of British Socialism*, with an Introduction by R. H. Tawney, George Allen & Unwin, London, 1948.

Belloc, Hilaire, *The Servile State*, with an Introduction by Robert Nisbet, Liberty Fund, Indianapolis, 1977.

Benn, Anthony Wedgwood, *The New Politics: A Socialist Reconnaissance*, Fabian Tract 402, September 1970.

Benn, Tony, *Out of the Wilderness: Diaries, 1963–67*, Hutchinson, London, 1987.

Benn, Tony, *Office without Power: Diaries, 1968–72*, Hutchinson, London, 1988.

Benn, Tony, *Against the Tide: Diaries, 1973–76*, Hutchinson, London, 1989.

Benn, Tony, *Conflicts of Interest: Diaries, 1977–80*, Hutchinson, London, 1990.

Benn, Tony, *Years of Hope: Diaries, Papers and Letters, 1940–62*, Hutchinson, London, 1994.

Bevan, Aneurin, *In Place of Fear*, William Heinemann, 1952.

Beveridge, William, *Social Insurance and Allied Services* (Beveridge Report), Cmd 6404, HMSO, London, November 1942.

Beveridge, William, *Power and Influence: An Autobiography*, Hodder & Stoughton, London, 1953.

Blair, Tony, *The Third Way: New Politics for the New Century*, Fabian Pamphlet 588, 1998.

Bridges, Lord [Edward], *The Treasury*, 2nd edition, George Allen & Unwin, London, 1966.

Brittan, Samuel, *Steering the Economy*, Penguin Books, London, 1971.

Brittan, Samuel, *The Role and Limits of Government: Essays in Political Economy*, Temple Smith, London, 1983.

Britton, Andrew, *Macroeconomic Policy in Britain, 1974–87*, Cambridge University Press, Cambridge, 1991.

Brivati, Brian, *Hugh Gaitskell*, Richard Cohen Books, London, 1996.

Brown, George, *In my Way. The Political Memoirs of Lord George-Brown*, Victor Gollancz, London, 1971.

Bryant, Chris, *Stafford Cripps: The First Modern Chancellor*, Hodder & Stoughton, London, 1997.

Budge, Ian, 'Relative Decline as a Political Issue: Ideological Motivations of the Politico-Economic Debate in Post-War Britain', in *Contemporary Record*, vol. 7, no. 1, Summer 1993.

Bullock, Alan, *Ernest Bevin: Trade Union Leader, 1881–1940*, William Heinemann, London, 1960.

Bullock, Alan, *Ernest Bevin: Minister of Labour, 1940–1945*, William Heinemann, London, 1967.

Bullock, Alan, *Ernest Bevin: Foreign Secretary, 1945–51*, Oxford University Press, Oxford, 1985.

Burk, Kathleen, and Cairncross, Alec, *'Goodbye, Great Britain': The 1976 IMF Crisis*, Yale University Press, London and New Haven, 1992.

Butler, David, and Freeman, Jennie, *British Political Facts, 1900–1960*, Macmillan, London, 1964.

ed. Butler, Lawrence, and Jones, Harriet, *Britain in the Twentieth Century*, vol. II: *1939–70*, Institute of Contemporary British History and William Heinemann, London and Oxford, 1995.

Butler, R. A., *The Art of the Possible: The Memoirs of Lord Butler*, Hamish Hamilton, London, 1971.

Butler, R. A. *The Art of Memory: Friends in Perspective*, Hodder & Stoughton, London, 1982.

Cairncross, Alec, *Years of Recovery: British Economic Policy, 1945–51*, Methuen, London, 1985.

Cairncross, Alec, *The British Economy since 1945: Economic Policy and Performance, 1945–1990*, Basil Blackwell for the Institute of Contemporary British History, Oxford and London, 1992.

Cairncross, Alec, *The Wilson Years: A Treasury Diary, 1964–69*, The Historians' Press, London, 1997.

Cairncross, Alec, and Watts, N., *The Economic Section, 1939–61: A Study in Economic Advising*, Routledge, London, 1989.

Callaghan, James, *Time and Chance*, William Collins, London, 1987.

Campbell, John, *Edward Heath*, Jonathan Cape, London, 1993.

Campbell, John, *Nye Bevan*, Richard Cohen Books, London, 1997.

Castle, Barbara, *The Castle Diaries, 1974–76*, Weidenfeld & Nicolson, London, 1980.

Castle, Barbara, *The Castle Diaries, 1964–70*, Weidenfeld & Nicolson, London, 1984.

Clarke, Peter, *Hope and Glory: Britain, 1900–1990*, Allen Lane, The Penguin Press, London, 1996.

Clarke, Sir Richard, *Anglo-American Economic Collaboration in War and Peace, 1942–49*, ed. Alec Cairncross, Clarendon Press, Oxford, 1982.

Cockett, Richard, *Thinking the Unthinkable: Think-Tanks and the Economic Counter-Revolution, 1931–1983*, Fontana Press, London, 1995.

Cole, G. D. H., *A History of the Labour Party from 1914*, Routledge & Kegan Paul, London, 1948.

Cole, G. D. H., *Capitalism in the Modern World*, Fabian Tract 310, October 1957.

Cole, John, *As It Seemed to Me: Political Memoirs*, Weidenfeld & Nicolson, London, 1995.

Cooke, Colin, *The Life of Richard Stafford Cripps*, Hodder & Stoughton, London, 1957.

Coopey, Richard, 'The Ministry of Technology 1974–76 (Witness Seminar Transcript)', *Contemporary Record*, vol. 5, no. 1, Summer 1991.

Coopey, Richard, 'The White Heat of Scientific Revolution',
   Contemporary Record, vol. 5, no. 1, Summer 1991.

Cosgrave, Patrick, *The Strange Death of Socialist Britain: Post War British
   Politics*, Constable, London, 1992.

ed. Crafts, N. F. R., and Woodward, Nicholas, *The British Economy since
   1945*, Clarendon Press, Oxford, 1991.

Crewe, Ivor, and King, Anthony, *SDP: The Birth, Life and Death of the
   Social Democratic Party*, Oxford University Press, Oxford, 1995.

Crosland, Anthony, *Britain's Economic Problem*, Jonathan Cape, London,
   1953.

Crosland, Anthony, *The Future of Socialism*, Jonathan Cape, London,
   1964 (abridged and revised).

Crosland, Anthony, *A Social Democratic Britain*, Fabian Tract 404,
   November 1970.

Crosland, Anthony, *Socialism Now and Other Essays*, Jonathan Cape,
   London, 1974.

Crosland, Susan, *Tony Crosland*, Jonathan Cape, London, 1982.

ed. Crossman, Richard, *New Fabian Essays*, Turnstile Press, London,
   1952.

Crossman, Richard, *The Diaries of a Cabinet Minister*, vol. 1: *Minister of
   Housing, 1964–66*, ed. Janet Morgan, Hamish Hamilton and Jonathan
   Cape, London, 1975.

Crossman, Richard, *The Diaries of a Cabinet Minister*, vol. 2: *Lord
   President of the Council and Leader of the House of Commons, 1966–68*,
   ed. Janet Morgan, Hamish Hamilton and Jonathan Cape, London,
   1976.

Crossman, Richard, *The Diaries of a Cabinet Minister*, vol. 3: *Secretary of
   State for Social Services, 1968–70*, ed. Janet Morgan, Hamish
   Hamilton and Jonathan Cape, London, 1977.

Crossman, Richard, *The Backbench Diaries*, ed. Janet Morgan, Hamish
   Hamilton and Jonathan Cape, London, 1981.

Dalton, Hugh, High *Tide and After: Memoirs, 1945–1960*, Frederick
   Muller, London, 1962.

Dalton, Hugh, *Practical Socialism for Britain*, George Routledge, London,
   1935.

Dalton, Hugh, *The Political Diary of Hugh Dalton, 1918–40, 1945–60*, ed.
   Ben Pimlott, Jonathan Cape in association with the London School
   of Economics and Political Science, London, 1986.

Damchev, Alex, *Oliver Franks: Founding Father*, Clarendon Press, Oxford,
   1993.

Dangerfield, George, *The Strange Death of Liberal England*, Constable,
   London, 1938.

Dell, Edmund, *Political Responsibility and Industry*, George Allen & Unwin, London, 1973.

Dell, Edmund, 'The Politics of Economic Interdependence', Fifth Rita Hinden Memorial Lecture, February 1977.

Dell, Edmund, *The Politics of Economic Interdependence*, Macmillan, London, and St Martin's Press, New York, 1987.

Dell, Edmund, *A Hard Pounding: Politics and Economic Crisis*, Oxford University Press, Oxford, 1991.

Dell, Edmund, 'The Chrysler UK Rescue', *Contemporary Record*, vol. 6, no. 1, Summer 1992.

Dell, Edmund, 'The Origins of Petroleum Revenue Tax', *Contemporary Record*, vol. 7, no. 2, Autumn, 1993.

Dell, Edmund, 'Britain and the Origins of the European Monetary System', *Contemporary European History*, vol. 3, part 1, March 1994.

Dell, Edmund, *The Schuman Plan and the British Abdication of Leadership in Europe*, Clarendon Press, Oxford, 1995.

Dell, Edmund, *The Chancellors: A History of the Chancellors of the Exchequer, 1945–90*, HarperCollins, London, 1996.

Dell, Sidney, *International Development Studies*, Duke University Press, London 1991.

Delors Report, see *Report on Economic and Monetary Union in the European Community*.

Dobson, Alan P., *The Politics of the Anglo-American Economic Special Relationship*, Wheatsheaf Books, Brighton, 1988.

Donoughue, Bernard, *Prime Minister: The Conduct of Policy under Harold Wilson and James Callaghan*, Jonathan Cape, London, 1987.

Donoughue, Bernard, and Jones, George, *Herbert Morrison: Portrait of a Politician*, Weidenfeld & Nicolson, London, 1973.

Dow, J. C. R., *The Management of the British Economy, 1945–60*, Cambridge University Press, Cambridge, 1964.

Dow, J. C. R., and Saville, I. D., *A Critique of Monetary Policy*, Oxford University Press, Oxford, 1990.

Durbin, E. F. M., *The Politics of Democratic Socialism: An Essay in Social Policy*, with a foreword by the Rt Hon. Hugh Gaitskell CBE MP, Routledge & Kegan Paul, London, first published 1940, sixth impression 1965.

Durbin, E. F. M., *Problems of Economic Planning*, Papers on planning, economics, etc. Routledge & Kegan Paul, London, 1949.

Durbin, Elizabeth, *New Jerusalems: The Labour Party and the Economics of Democratic Socialism*, with a foreword by Roy Hattersley, Routledge & Kegan Paul, London, 1985.

Economic Survey, 1947, Cmd 7046, HMSO, London.

Economic Trends, published for the Central Statistical Office by Her Majesty's Stationery Office, various dates.

Elliott, John, *Conflict or Cooperation: The Growth of Industrial Democracy*, Kogan Page, London, 1978.

Employment Policy White Paper, 26 May 1944, Cmd 6527, HMSO, London.

Estorick, Eric, *Stafford Cripps*, William Heinemann, London, 1949.

Fay, Stephen, and Young, Hugo, 'The Day the £ Nearly Died', *Sunday Times*, 14, 21 and 28 May 1978.

Fforde, John, *The Bank of England and Public Policy, 1941–58*, Cambridge University Press, Cambridge, 1992.

Fieldhouse, D. K., *The Labour Governments and the Empire–Commonwealth, 1945–51 in* ed. Ritchie Ovendale, *The Foreign Policy of the British Labour Governments, 1945–51*, Leicester University Press, Leicester, 1984.

Fielding, Steven, 'Neil Kinnock: An Overview of the Labour Party', *Contemporary Record*, vol. 8, no. 3, Winter 1994.

Fienburgh, Wilfred, *25 Momentous Years: A 25th Anniversary in the History of the Daily Herald*, Odhams Press, London, 1955.

Figes, Orlando, *A People's Tragedy: The Russian Revolution, 1891–1924*, Jonathan Cape, London, 1996.

Foot, Michael, *Aneurin Bevan, 1945–1960*, Davis Poynter, London, 1973.

Foot, Paul, *The Politics of Harold Wilson*, Penguin Books, Harmondsworth, 1968.

Foote, Geoffrey, *The Labour Party's Political Thought: A History*, Macmillan, London, 1997.

Gaitskell, Hugh, *Socialism and Nationalisation*, Fabian Tract 300, July 1956.

Gaitskell, Hugh, *The Diary of Hugh Gaitskell, 1945–1956*, ed. Philip Williams, Jonathan Cape, London, 1983.

Gardner, Nick, *Decade of Discontent: The Changing British Economy since 1973*, Basil Blackwell, Oxford, 1987.

Gardner, R., *Sterling–Dollar Diplomacy*, Oxford University Press, Oxford, 1956.

Giddens, Anthony, *The Third Way: The Renewal of Social Democracy*, Polity Press, Cambridge, 1998.

Gilmour, Ian (Lord Gilmour), *Dancing with Dogma: Britain under Thatcherism*, Simon & Schuster, London, 1992.

Gould, Bryan, *A Future for Socialism*, Jonathan Cape, London, 1989.

Gould, Philip, *The Unfinished Revolution: How the Modernisers Saved the Labour Party*, Little Brown, London, 1998.

Haines, Joe, *The Politics of Power*, Jonathan Cape, London, 1977.

Hall, Robert, *The Robert Hall Diaries, 1947–53*, ed. Alec Cairncross, Unwin Hyman, London, 1991.

Hall, Robert, *The Robert Hall Diaries, 1954–61*, ed. Alec Cairncross, Unwin Hyman, London, 1992.

Harmon, Mark D., *The British Labour Government and the 1976 IMF Crisis*, Macmillan, London, and St Martin's Press, New York, 1997.

Harris, Kenneth, *Attlee*, Weidenfeld & Nicolson, London, 1982.

Harrod, Roy, *The Life of John Maynard Keynes*, Macmillan, London, 1951.

Hatfield, Michael, *The House the Left Built: Inside Labour Policy-Making, 1970–75*, Victor Gollancz, 1978.

Hattersley, Roy, *Choose Freedom: The Future for Democratic Socialism*, Penguin Books, London, 1987.

Hayek, F. A., *The Road to Serfdom*, Routledge & Kegan Paul, London, 1944.

Healey, Denis, *The Time of my Life*, Michael Joseph, London, 1989.

Heath, Edward, *The Course of my Life*, Hodder & Stoughton, London, 1998.

Heclo, Hugh, and Wildavsky, Aaron, *The Private Government of Public Money*, Macmillan, London, 1974.

ed. Helm, Dieter, *The Economic Borders of the State*, Oxford University Press, Oxford, 1989.

Hennessy, Peter, '1949 Devaluation (Transcription of a Witness Seminar on 4 October 1989)', *Contemporary Record*, vol. 5, no. 3, Winter 1991.

Hennessy, Peter, *Never Again: Britain, 1945–1951*, Jonathan Cape, London, 1992.

Hennessy, Peter, and Arends, Andrew, *Mr Attlee's Engine Room: Cabinet Committee Structure and the Labour Government, 1945–51*, Strathclyde Papers on Government and Politics, 1983.

ed. Hennessy, Peter, and Seldon, Anthony, *Ruling Performance: British Governments from Attlee to Thatcher*, Basil Blackwell, Oxford, 1987.

Hogan, Michael J., *The Marshall Plan: America, Britain, and the Reconstruction of Western Europe, 1947–1952*, Cambridge University Press, Cambridge, 1987.

Horne, Alistair, *Macmillan*, vol. 1: *1891–1956*, Macmillan, London, 1990.

Horne, Alistair, *Macmillan*, vol. 2: *1957–1986*, Macmillan, London, 1989.

House of Commons, *Official Report*.

Howard, Anthony, *RAB: The Life of R. A. Butler*, Jonathan Cape, London, 1987

Howard, Anthony, *Crossman: The Pursuit of Power*, Jonathan Cape, London, 1990.

Hunter, Leslie, *The Road to Brighton Pier*, Arthur Barker, London, 1959.

Hutton, Will, *The State We're In*, Jonathan Cape, London, 1995.

Jay, Douglas, *The Socialist Case*, with a foreword by C. R. Attlee, Faber & Faber, London, 1947, first published 1938.

Jay, Douglas, *Change and Fortune: A Political Record*, Hutchinson, London, 1980.

Jay, Douglas, *Sterling*, Oxford University Press, Oxford, 1986.

Jefferys, Kevin, *Anthony Crosland*, Richard Cohen Books, London, 1999.

Jenkins, Peter, *The Battle of Downing Street*, Charles Knight, London, 1970.

Jenkins, Peter, *Mrs Thatcher's Revolution: The Ending of the Socialist Era*, Jonathan Cape, London, 1987.

Jenkins, Roy, *Essays and Speeches*, William Collins, London, 1967.

Jenkins, Roy, *European Diary, 1977–1981*, William Collins, London, 1989.

Jenkins, Roy, *A Life at the Centre*, Macmillan, London, 1991.

Jones, Eileen, *Neil Kinnock*, Robert Hale, London, 1994.

Jones, Jack, *Union Man: An Autobiography of Jack Jones*, William Collins, London, 1986.

Jones, Mervyn, *Michael Foot*, Victor Gollancz, London, 1994.

Jones, Tudor, 'Labour Revisionism and Public Ownership', *Contemporary Record*, vol. 5, no. 3, Winter 1991.

Jones, Tudor, 'Neil Kinnock's Socialist Journey: From Clause Four to the Policy Review', *Contemporary Record*, vol. 8, no. 3, Winter 1994.

Jones, Tudor, *Remaking the Labour Party: From Gaitskell to Blair*, Routledge, London, 1996.

Kavanagh, Denis, *Thatcherism and British Politics: The End of Consensus?*, Oxford University Press, Oxford, 1990.

Keegan, William, and Pennant-Rea, Rupert, *Who Runs the Economy: Control and Influence in British Economic Policy*, Maurice Temple Smith, 1979.

Kenny, Michael, and Smith, Martin J., '(Mis)understanding Blair', *Political Quarterly*, vol. 68, no. 3, July–September 1997.

Keynes, John Maynard (Lord Keynes), *The General Theory of Employment, Interest and Money*, Macmillan, London, 1947.

King, Cecil, *The Cecil King Diary, 1965–1970*, Jonathan Cape, London, 1972.

Kinnock, Neil, 'Reforming the Labour Party', *Contemporary Record*, vol. 8, no. 3, Winter 1994.

Kramnick, Isaac, and Sheerman, Barry, *Harold Laski: A Life on the Left*, Hamish Hamilton, London, 1993.

Kyle, Keith, *Suez*, Weidenfeld & Nicolson, London, 1992.

Kynaston, David, *The Financial Times: A Centenary History*, Viking, London, 1988.

Labour in Action, The Labour Party, London, 1970.

Lamb, Richard, *The Macmillan Years, 1957–1963: The Emerging Truth*, John Murray, London, 1995.

Laski, Harold J. *The State in Theory and Practice*, George Allen & Unwin, London, 1935.

Nigel Lawson, *The View from No. 11: Memoirs of a Tory Radical*, Corgi Books, London, 1993.

ed. Leonard, Dick, *Crosland and New Labour*, Macmillan in association with the Fabian Society, London, 1999.

Andrew Likierman, *Public Expenditure: The Public Spending Process*, Penguin Books, London, 1988.

MacDougall, Donald, *Don and Mandarin: Memoirs of an Economist*, John Murray, London, 1987.

ed. McKie, David, and Cook, Chris, *The Decade of Disillusion: British Politics in the Sixties*, Macmillan and St Martin's Press, London, 1972.

Macmillan, Harold, *Tides of Fortune, 1945–55*, Macmillan, London, 1969.

Macmillan, Harold, *Riding the Storm, 1956–59*, Macmillan, London, 1971.

Macmillan, Harold, *Pointing the Way, 1959–61*, Macmillan, London, 1972.

Macmillan, Harold, *At the End of the Day, 1961–63*, Macmillan, London, 1973.

Macmillan, Harold, *The Middle Way: A Study of the Problem of Economic and Social Progress in a Free and Democratic Society*, EP Publishing, Wakefield, 1978.

Magee, Bryan, *The New Radicalism*, Secker & Warburg, London, 1962.

Magee, Bryan, *The Democratic Revolution*, The Bodley Head, London, 1964.

Mandelson, Peter, and Liddle, Roger, *The Blair Revolution: Can New Labour Deliver?*, Faber & Faber, London, 1996.

Marquand, David, 'Sir Stafford Cripps', in Michael Sissons and Philip French, eds, *The Age of Austerity*, Hodder & Stoughton, London, 1963.

Marquand, David, *Ramsay MacDonald*, Jonathan Cape, London, 1977.

Marquand, David, *The Unprincipled Society: New Demands and Old Politics*, Jonathan Cape, London, 1988.

Marquand, David, *The Progressive Dilemma: From Lloyd George to Kinnock*, William Heinemann, London, 1992.

Marquand, David, *The New Reckoning: Capitalism, States and Citizens*, Polity Press, Cambridge, 1997.

ed. Marquand, David, and Seldon, Anthony, *The Ideas That Shaped Post-War Britain*, Fontana Press, London, 1996.

Marris, Robin, *The Machinery of Economic Policy*, Fabian Research Series No. 168, November 1954.

Marx, Karl, *Capital: A Critique of Political Economy*, vols 2 and 3, trans. Ernest Unterman, ed. Frederick Engels, Charles Kerr, Chicago, 1933.

Marx, Karl, *Capital: A Critical Analysis of Capitalist Production*, vol. 1, trans. Samuel Moore and Edward Aveling, ed. Frederick Engels, George Allen & Unwin, London, 1938.

Meade, James E., *The Intelligent Radical's Guide to Economic Policy*, George Allen & Unwin, London, 1975.

Meade, James E., *The Cabinet Office Diary, 1944–46: The Collected Papers*, vol. IV, ed. Susan Howson and Donald Moggridge, Unwin Hyman, London, 1990.

Milward, Alan S., *The Reconstruction of Western Europe, 1945–51*, Methuen, London, 1984.

Milward, Alan S., *The European Rescue of the Nation-State*, Routledge, London, 1992.

Mitchell, Joan, *Crisis in Britain, 1951*, Secker & Warburg, London, in association with the University of Nottingham, 1963.

Mises, Ludwig von, *Socialism: An Economic and Sociological Analysis*, trans. J. Kahane, Liberty Fund, Indianapolis, 1981.

Morgan, Kenneth O., *Labour in Power, 1945–1951*, Clarendon Press, Oxford, 1984.

Morgan, Kenneth O., *The People's Peace: British History, 1945–1989*, Oxford University Press, Oxford, 1990.

Morgan, Kenneth O., *Callaghan: A Life*, Oxford University Press, Oxford, 1997.

Morgan, Kenneth O., *Rebirth of a Nation: A History of Modern Wales*, Oxford University Press, Oxford, and University of Wales Press, 1998.

Mullard, Maurice, 'The Politics of Public Expenditure Control: A Problem of Politics or Language Games?' *Political Quarterly*, vol. 68, no. 3, July–September 1997.

Newton, Scott, *Britain, the Sterling Area and European Integration, 1945–50*, Journal of Imperial and Commonwealth History, vol. XIII, no. 3, May 1985, Cass.

Oakeshott, Michael, *Rationalism in Politics and Other Essays*, Liberty Fund, Indianapolis, 1991.

Panitch, Leo, and Leys, Colin, *The End of Parliamentary Socialism: From New Left to New Labour*, Verso, London, 1997.

Pelling, Henry, *A Short History of the Labour Party*, St Martin's Press, New York, 1994.

Pimlott, Ben, *Hugh Dalton*, Jonathan Cape, London, 1985.

ed. Pimlott, Ben, *The Political Diary of Hugh Dalton*, Jonathan Cape in association with the London School of Economics and Political Science, London, 1986.

Pimlott, Ben, *Harold Wilson*, HarperCollins, London, 1993.

Pliatzky, Leo, *Getting and Spending: Public Expenditure, Employment and Inflation*, Basil Blackwell, Oxford, 1982.

Pliatzky, Leo, *Paying and Choosing: The Intelligent Person's Guide to the Mixed Economy*, Basil Blackwell, Oxford, 1985.

Pliatzky, Leo, *The Treasury under Mrs Thatcher*, Basil Blackwell, Oxford, 1989.

Plowden, Edwin (Lord Plowden), *An Industrialist in the Treasury: The Postwar Years*, André Deutsch, London, 1989.

Popper, Karl, *The Open Society and Its Enemies*, Routledge & Kegan Paul, London, 1966.

Procter, Stephen J., 'Floating Convertibility: The Emergence of the Robot Plan, 1951–52', *Contemporary Record*, vol. 7, no. 1, Summer 1993.

Pryke, Richard, *Public Enterprise in Practice: The British Experience of Nationalization over Two Decades*, MacGibbon & Kee, London, 1971.

Public Expenditure White Papers, London, HMSO, various dates.

Report of the Committee on Industrial Democracy (Chairman, Lord Bullock), Cmnd 6706, HMSO, London, 1977.

Report on Economic and Monetary Union in the European Community (Delors Report), Office for Official Publications of the European Communities, Luxembourg, 1989.

Rhodes James, Robert, *Ambitions and Realities: British Politics, 1964–1970*, Weidenfeld & Nicolson, London, 1972.

Riddell, Peter, 'The End of Clause IV, 1994–95', *CBH*, vol. 11, no. 2, summer 1997.

Riddell, Peter, *The Thatcher Government*, Martin Robertson, Oxford, 1983.

Rodgers, William, *The Politics of Change*, Secker & Warburg, London, 1982.

Roll, Eric, *Crowded Hours*, Faber & Faber, London, 1985.

Roll, Eric, *Where Did We Go Wrong? From the Gold Standard to Europe*, Faber & Faber, London, 1995.

Roseveare, Henry, *The Treasury: The Evolution of a British Institution*, Allen Lane, The Penguin Press, Harmondsworth, 1969.

Routledge, Paul, *Gordon Brown*, Simon & Schuster, London, 1998.

Routledge, Paul, *Mandy: The Unauthorised Biography of Peter Mandelson*, Simon & Schuster, London, 1999.

Royal Commission on Trade Unions and Employers' Associations 1965–68, Chairman Lord Donovan, Cmnd 3623, HMSO, London, 1968.

Sassoon, Donald, *One Hundred Years of Socialism: The West European Left in the Twentieth Century*, I. B. Tauris Publishers, London, 1996.

Schenk, Catherine R., 'The Sterling Area and British Policy Alternatives in the 1950s', *Contemporary Record*, vol. 6, no. 2, Autumn 1992.

Shaw, George Bernard, *The Intelligent Woman's Guide to Socialism and Capitalism*, Constable, London, 1929.

Shonfield, Andrew, *Modern Capitalism: The Changing Balance of Public and Private Power*, Royal Institute of International Affairs and Oxford University Press, London, 1965.

ed. Sissons, Michael, and French, Philip, *Age of Austerity*, Hodder & Stoughton, London, 1963.

Skidelsky, Robert, *Oswald Mosley*, Macmillan, London, 1975.

Skidelsky, Robert, *John Maynard Keynes*, vol. 2: *The Economist as Saviour, 1920–1937*, Macmillan, London, 1992.

Smith, Adam, *The Wealth of Nations*, Dent 'Everyman', London, 1947.

Smith, David, *The Rise and Fall of Monetarism: The Theory and Politics of an Economic Experiment*, Penguin Books, Harmondsworth, 1987.

Smith, Martin J., 'Neil Kinnock and the Modernisation of the Labour Party', *Contemporary Record*, vol. 8, no. 3, Winter 1994.

Snowdon, Brian, 'Politics and the Business Cycle', *Political Quarterly*, vol. 68, no. 3, July–September 1997.

Stewart, Michael (Lord Stewart), *Life and Labour: An Autobiography*, Sidgwick & Jackson, London, 1980.

Strachey, John, *The Coming Struggle for Power*, Victor Gollancz, London, 1933.

Strachey, John, *The Theory and Practice of Socialism*, Victor Gollancz, London, 1936.

Tawney, R. H., *The Acquisitive Society*, G. Bell & Sons, London, 1948 (first published 1921).

Taylor, Robert, *The Trade Union Question in British Politics: Government and Unions since 1945*, Institute of Contemporary British History and Basil Blackwell, Oxford, 1993.

Thatcher, Margaret, *The Downing Street Years*, HarperCollins, London, 1993.

Thirlwall, Anthony P., *Nicholas Kaldor*, Wheatsheaf Books, Brighton, 1987.

Thompson, Noel, *Political Economy and the Labour Party*, UCL Press, London, 1996.

Tomlinson, James, *Marshall Aid and the 'Shortage Economy' in Britain in the 1940s*, Discussion Paper Series, Department of Government, Brunel University, Uxbridge, 1997.

Twelve Wasted Years, Labour Party Research Department, London, September 1963.

Twentieth Century Socialism, The Economy of Tomorrow, Socialist Union and Penguin Books, London, 1956.

Utiger, R. E., *Never Trust an Expert: Nuclear Power, Government and the Tragedy of the Invergordon Aluminium Smelter*, Business History Unit, Occasional Paper 1995 No. 1.

Watkins, Alan, *The Road to Number 10: From Bonar Law to Tony Blair*, Duckworth, London, 1998.

Williams, Francis, *Fifty Years' March: The Rise of the Labour Party*, with a foreword by C. R. Attlee, Odhams Press, London, 1949.

Williams, Geoffrey, and Reed, Bruce, *Denis Healey and the Policies of Power*, Sidgwick & Jackson, London, 1971.

Williams, Philip, *Hugh Gaitskell: A Political Biography*, Jonathan Cape, London, 1979.

Williams, Shirley, *Politics Is for People*, Penguin Books, London, 1981.

Wilson, Harold, *Post-War Economic Policies in Britain*, Fabian Tract 309, September 1957.

Wilson, Harold, *The Labour Government, 1964–1970: A Personal Record*, Weidenfeld & Nicolson and Michael Joseph, London, 1971.

Wilson, Harold, *The Governance of Britain*, Weidenfeld & Nicolson and Michael Joseph, London, 1976.

Wilson, Harold, *Final Term: The Labour Government, 1974–76*, Weidenfeld & Nicolson and Michael Joseph, London, 1979.

Wright, John F., *Britain in the Age of Economic Management*, Oxford University Press, Oxford, 1979.

Young, Hugo, *This Blessed Plot: Britain and Europe from Churchill to Blair*, Macmillan, London, 1998.

Ziegler, Philip, *Harold Wilson: The Authorised Life*, Weidenfeld & Nicolson, London, 1993.

INDEX

of 499, 526, 530, 542, 554–60; New Labour 537–8, 543–4, 554–5, 558, 560–1; one member one vote (OMOV) 481–2, 485, 540, 544, 565; Policy Review (1989) 278, 507–8; pragmatism vs ideology 277; Research Department (LPRD) 313–14, 418; right-wing of 236–9, 246, 277, 303, 412, *see also* Gaitskellites; splits 98, 196, 200, 205, 208, 210, 247–8, 285, 316, 412, 416, 472–3, 483, 559; *see also* National Executive Committee; Parliamentary Labour Party

Labour Party Conference: 1918 22, 23; 1932 40; 1935 37; 1944 122; 1949 138, 145; 1950 207; 1952 213; 1955 272, 284; 1959 235, 293–4, 497; 1960 295, 298; 1962 304, 338, 377; 1963 308–10; 1964 351; 1967 373; 1968 363; 1970/1971 421; 1972 399, 416–17; 1973 438; 1974 440; 1975 451; 1976 455–6; 1978 467; 1979 476, 480; 1981 486; 1984 499; 1985 496; 1986 495; 1988 506; 1989 507; 1990 495; 1993 540, 544, 547; 1994 543; special conferences 485, 546; trade unions and 21, 43, 286, 287

Labour Party in Perspective, The (Attlee) 91
Labour Representation Committee 20
Labour's Immediate Programme (1937) 41, 73
Labour's Programme for Britain 426
Labour's Programme 1973 423, 426
Lafontaine, Oskar 104, 510, 536
laissez-faire 14, 62–6, 115, 224, 566; in Board of Trade 364; economists 61; end of 78–82, 83, 89, 93, 103, 226–7, 254, 569–70; Macmillan and 87; stakeholding as enemy of 530, 531; Tory instinct for 218, 564; and unemployment 241
Land and Natural Resources, Ministry of 336
Lansbury, George 37, 126
Laski, Harold 69, 101, 106, 259, 324; advocate of democracy 46, 53–5, 67; Bevin and 43; on capitalism 61, 62, 81, 104; and irreversibility 60; on knowledge 14; Marxist influence on 52; on scepticism 98; socialism of 113
Lawson, Nigel 514
Lawther, Sir William 188, 286
Lee, Fred 357
Lee, Jennie 437
Left Book Club 52
Lend-Lease 124–5, 128–9, 131, 146, 158, 237
Lenin, V.I. 11, 51, 89, 101, 141, 477, 479

Let Us Face the Future 25, 73, 114, 122–3, 125, 129, 140, 147
Let Us Go with Labour 327
Leyton by-election (1965) 351, 352
Liaison Committee 401, 452
Liberal Democrats 513
Liberal party xv; break up of 33; and capitalism 31; election results 317, 433; Fabians and 21; governments 8, 57; and Ireland 68; relations with Labour 20, 30–1, 35, 466; trade unions and 20
Liberal-SDP Alliance 479–80, 483, 484, 486, 488–9, 513
liberal socialism 115
liberalism: abandonment of 555; in Conservative policy 219; socialism as 277
liberty 262, 276, 523; and economic priority 359; free market and 529, 534; and incomes policy 152; and planning 89–90, 96, 112–13, 115, 149, 228; and private property 229, 234, 279
Lincoln by-election 399
Lipsey, David 404
Liverpool 496
Lloyd George, David 68, 90, 282; government of 8, 57, 85
London Passenger Transport Board 143
Long-Term Programme 157–8
Lord President's Committee 147

Maastricht Treaty (1992) 499; Social Chapter of 511, 547
MacDonald, Ramsay 126, 300, 473, 490; attitude to World War I 22; elelctoral defeat of 209; forms National Government 36; oratory of 195; and trade unions 42; on unemployment 9
MacDonald government 35–8; Cabinet 32, 83; and electoral reform 70; failure of 1, 38, 40, 45, 78, 98, 112; relations with TUC 42; *see also* National government
McGowan, Lord 94
machine tools 271, 289
Macleod, Iain 392
Macmillan, Harold 64; advocate of alternative economic strategy 460; advocate of planning 90, 91, 93, 297; on economic management 149; *The Middle Way* 81–3, 86–7, 96, 297, 323, 460, 549, 569; opposes appeasement 97; promotes industrial reorganization 366; as protectionist 86–7, 92–3; as social reformer 81; on socialist totalitarianism 96; and trades unions 366